MUSIC
ANALYSES

An Annotated Guide
to the Literature

MUSIC

ANALYSES

An Annotated Guide

to the Literature

HAROLD J. DIAMOND

SCHIRMER BOOKS
A Division of Macmillan, Inc.
NEW YORK

Collier Macmillan Canada
TORONTO

Maxwell Macmillan International
NEW YORK   OXFORD   SINGAPORE   SYDNEY

Schirmer Books
A Division of Macmillan, Inc.
866 Third Avenue, New York, N. Y. 10022

Collier Macmillan Canada, Inc.
1200 Eglinton Avenue East, Suite 200
Don Mills, Ontario M3C 3N1
Library of Congress Catalog Card Number: 90–13432

Printed in the United States of America

printing number
1   2   3   4   5   6   7   8   9   10

Library of Congress Cataloging-in-Publication Data

Diamond, Harold J.
    Music analyses : an annotated guide to the literature / Harold J.
Diamond.
        p.   cm.
    Includes bibliographical references and index.
    ISBN 0-02-870110-0
    1. Musical analysis—Bibliography. I. Title.
ML128.A7D5 1991
016.781—dc20   90-13432
                                                                    CIP
                                                                    MN

To my daughter
Lolly

CONTENTS

PREFACE

~~~~

Music's power to affect emotions, to appeal to the intellect, and to delight the spirit is not fully understood. How may we better understand this puzzling gift? One approach is to take music apart, study its components, and examine what holds it together, in other words, analyze it. Analysis identifies the musical elements that unify a composition and seeks to explain, on objective grounds, why a work has artistic validity. Since only the well-trained may attempt their own analyses, others, such as students, concertgoers and non-professionals must turn to the literature about music. But which literature?

Biographies, concertgoers' "companions" and record-jacket notes are insufficient for serious students. Books primarily about the music of a composer may not be at the right level for the reader or may be outdated. Therefore, the public must sift through a vast literature to find the analyses that truly probe a particular composition's working parts. Both the library patron and the music librarian will find it difficult or impossible to devote the required amount of time to locating just the right level of analysis.

Music Analyses addresses the problem by citing and describing selected analytic literature on Western art music. It encompasses and goes beyond the 2,000 entries of my previous book, *Music Criticism*. The 4,600 citations in the present work were gleaned from more than 750 books, 100 periodicals, and 400 dissertations. Except for listings with self explanatory titles, each entry is annotated to inform the reader of the nature and level of the analysis cited. Analyses containing musical examples are so indicated to help the user decide if a score is necessary to follow the analysis. Some analyses are meant for the beginner or undergraduate student, while others are highly technical and of little use to the uninitiated. Occasionally, the cited material is not analytic at all. For example, the reason why there are four overtures to *Fidelio* is a question commonly asked of undergraduates and is of interest to the musical amateur.

I have included many doctoral dissertations and masters' theses because they are frequently the only sources of information on obscure topics. This is especially true for works by less known composers. One may obtain these materials through the interlibrary loan services of university or public libraries or by direct purchase. *Dissertation Abstracts International* contains full information for ordering by telephone or mail.

A problem familiar to music librarians is whether to use titles of musical works in the original foreign language or in English. I have chosen the title most likely to be used by English-speaking readers. Oddly enough, in many cases this is the original, foreign-language title; for example, *Winterreise, Götterdämmerung, Davidsbündlertänze, Années de Pèlerinage, Das Lied von der Erde.*

Because the principal use of *Music Analyses* will be to find analyses of one, or perhaps a few, compositions at a time, citations are given in their complete form for all entries for the convenience of the user. This has meant repeating complete citations and annotations rather than substituting abbreviations, codes, and cross-references to other entries.

Music Analyses confines itself to English-language listings to ensure availability in most college, university, and large public libraries in the United States and Great Britain. Scholars requiring total bibliographic coverage in all languages will find this volume a useful part of their search.

Special thanks are due Susan T. Sommer, Head of the Music Library of the New York Public Library and President of the Music Library Association. It was Ms. Sommer who persuaded me that a book of this kind needed to be done in depth, offering me invaluable guidance and support.

I am also grateful to Ms. Sommer for recommending Stephen Davison to me. Mr. Davison's assistance, under a PSC-CUNY Research Award, was on two levels: first, with many of the citations themselves and later by devising a computer program within dBase III + with which this manuscript was prepared. His calm responses to my hysterical software emergency calls-in-the-night were both effective and soothing. But even more remarkable was his clarity of thought, erudition, and imagination. It seems unreasonable to enjoy the services of a doctoral candidate in music and a computer expert, all in one person, who also has an exceptional command of the language. I am indeed privileged to have worked with Mr. Davison.

Authors remain unknown without publishers. Special thanks to Schirmer Books' Maribeth Anderson Payne, Editor-in-Chief, Robert Axelrod, Associate Editor, and Bob Wilson, Editorial Production Supervisor, for their patience and hard work. I am grateful for their guidance in seeing this project through to its conclusion.

Boundless gratitude is due Dr. Larry E. Sullivan, who was, during the research and writing of this book, Chief Librarian at Lehman College, where I am Music Librarian. His advice and encouragement provided the nourishing atmosphere vital to the life and health of this project. I am also indebted to Lehman College for its award to me of the George N. Shuster Fellowship Grant.

Thanks, too, to Dr. Edward F. Kravitt, Professor of Music at Lehman College of the City University of New York and stalwart friend. His professional advice and personal encouragement made it possible for me to face this task with confidence.

And thanks to my wife, Ellen, for her editorial gift, calming influence, patience, and understanding.

Harold J. Diamond

Hastings-on-Hudson
New York

MUSIC
ANALYSES

An Annotated Guide
to the Literature

ANALYSES

~

ALBÉNIZ, ISAAC, 1860–1909

DISSERTATIONS AND THESES

Iberia

1. **Mast, Paul Buck.** "Style and Structure in *Iberia* by Isaac Albéniz." Ph.D., University of Rochester, Eastman School of Music, 1974,
419 pp., DA 35-2322A.

ALBINONI, TOMASO, 1671–1750

General

2. **Solie, John E.** "Aria Structure and Ritornello Form in the Music
of Albinoni." *Musical Quarterly,* 63 (January 1977): 31–47.
    Advanced discussion on recurring structural patterns. Compari-
sons with Vivaldi, Torelli. Musical examples.

3. **Talbot, Michael.** "Albinoni: The Professional Dilettante." *Musical Times,* 112 (June 1971): 538–541.
    Biographical background, stylistic characteristics, and influence
on others.

Cantatas

4. **Talbot, Michael.** "Albinoni's Solo Cantatas." *Soundings,* 5 (1975):
9–28.
    A wide-ranging discussion that covers historical position; chrono-
logical problems; the manuscript and printed sources; the texts;
recitatives; arias. Stylistic and formal elements in recitatives and
arias are identified.

1

Concertos

5.   Talbot, Michael. "The Concerto Allegro in the Early Eighteenth Century." *Music and Letters*, 52, no. 2 (1971): 163–165.
   The development of the concerto form in nonfugal allegros by Italian composers up to 1720, including Albinoni. Discusses analytic procedure. Advanced discussion.

Concertos for Oboe

6.   Talbot, Michael. "Albinoni's Oboe Concertos." *Consort*, 29 (1973): 14–22.
   Thorough discussion of background, style, and development of the oboe concertos. Musical examples.

ANONYMOUS

Sumer is icumen in

7.   Reese, Gustave. *Music in the Middle Ages.* New York: W. W. Norton, 1940, 396–397.
   Brief remarks on background, with analytic descriptions of the Canon.

8.   Sanders, Ernest H. "Sumer is icumen in." In *The New Grove Dictionary of Music and Musicians.* Vol. 18. Edited by Stanley Sadie, 366–368. London: Macmillan, 1980.
   Article on the background, structure, and characteristics of the *Sumer* Canon, with bibliography for further reference.

Veni Creator Spiritus

9.   Cogan, Robert, and Pozzi Escot. *Sonic Design: The Nature of Sound and Music,* 105–113, 243–248. Englewood Cliffs, NJ: Prentice-Hall, 1976.
   A discussion of mode of this chant as well as that of *Kyrie Dens Sempiterne.* Includes linear reductions of the melodies. Focus is on rhythm and structure.

ANTHEIL, GEORGE, 1900–1959

General

10.   Whitesitt, Linda. *The Life and Music of George Antheil, 1900–1959.* Ann Arbor, MI: UMI Research Press, 1983, 351 pp.

2

a composer of more conventional music and of film scores. Many analytic comments and musical examples.

ARGENTO, DOMINICK, 1927–

From the Diary of Virginia Woolf

11.   Gebuhr, Ann K. "Structure and Coherence in the *Diary*: From Dominick Argento's Cycle." *Indiana Theory Review*, 1, no. 3 (1978): 12–21.

DISSERTATIONS AND THESES

The Boor

12.   Brewer, Tracey Adams. "Characterization in Dominick Argento's Opera, *The Boor*." D.M.A., University of Texas at Austin, 1981, 138 pp., DA 42-2921A.

BABBITT, MILTON, 1916–

General

13.   Gamer, Carlton, and Paul Lansky. "Fanfares for the Common Tone." *Perspectives of New Music*, 14, no. 2; 15, no. 1 (1976): 228–235.
Babbitt's theory of pitch-class invariance in transposition explored.

Composition for Twelve Instruments

14.   Westergaard, Peter. "Some Problems Raised by the Rhythmic Procedures in Milton Babbitt's Composition for Twelve Instruments." *Perspectives of New Music*, 5, no. 1 (1966): 170.

Compositions for Piano, Op. 11

15.   Griffiths, Paul. *Modern Music: The Avant-Garde Since 1945*, 38–41. New York: George Braziller, 1981.
Identifies and illustrates rhythmic serial method, combinatorality, and derived sets. Musical examples.

Compositions for Piano, Op. 11, No. 1

16.   Perle, George. *Serial Composition and Atonality: An Introduction to the Music of Schoenberg, Berg, and Webern.* 5th ed., rev., 99–102, 128–134. Berkeley: University of California Press, 1981.
  Illustrates the principle of combinatorality used in this piece. Also discusses the serial manipulation of rhythm and dynamics. Musical examples.

Du

17.   Rahn, John. "How Do You *Du.*" *Perspectives of New Music,* 14, no. 2; 15, no. 1 (1976): 61–80.
  Extensive analysis for the advanced student. Musical examples.

Ensemble for Synthesizer

18.   Brunner, Lance W. "Bowling Green State University Second Annual New Music Festival: A Review." *Perspectives of New Music,* 19, nos. 1–2 (1981–1982): 484 + .
  Brief comments on the RCA Mark II electronic sound synthesizer and the impressions created by the compositions realized on it.

Images for Saxophonist and Synthesized Tape

19.   Brunner, Lance W. "Bowling Green State University Second Annual New Music Festival: A Review." *Perspectives of New Music,* 19, nos. 1–2 (1981–1982): 484 + .
  Brief comments on the RCA Mark II electronic sound synthesizer and the impressions created by the compositions realized on it.

Minute Waltz (1977)

20.   Blaustein, Susan, and Martin Brody. "Criteria for Grouping in Milton Babbitt's *Minute* Waltz (or) + ⅛." *Perspectives of New Music,* 24, no. 2 (1986): 30–79.
  Advanced theoretical analysis with musical examples and charts.

Occasional Variations for Tape

21.   Brunner, Lance W. "Bowling Green State University Second Annual New Music Festival: A Review." *Perspectives of New Music,* 19, nos. 1–2 (1981–1982): 484 + .
  Brief comments on the RCA Mark II electronic sound synthesizer and the impressions created by it.

Quartet for Strings No. 2

22.   Strauss, Joseph. "Listening to Babbitt." *Perspectives of New Music*, 24, no. 2 (1986): 10–24.
An analytic look at how a single passage (the first eighteen measures) might be heard by the listener, rather than how the composer conceived it. Musical examples.

23.   Zuckerman, Mark. "On Milton Babbitt's String Quartet No. 2." *Perspectives of New Music*, 14, no. 2; 15, no. 1 (1976): 85–110.
Analysis. Musical examples.

Quartet for Strings No. 3

24.   Arnold, Stephen, and Graham Hair. "An Introduction and a Study—String Quartet No. 3." *Perspectives of New Music*, 14, no. 2; 15, no. 1 (1976): 155–186.
Analysis. Musical examples.

Quartet for Strings No. 5

25.   Lake, William E. "The Architecture of a Superarray Composition: Milton Babbitt's String Quartet No. 5." *Perspectives of New Music*, 24, no. 2 (1986): 88–111.
Advanced theoretical analysis with musical examples and charts.

Semi-Simple Variations

26.   Barkin, Elaine. "A Simple Approach to Milton Babbitt's *Semi-Simple* Variations." *Music Review*, 28, no. 4 (1967): 316–322.
Analysis. Musical examples.

27.   Wintle, Christopher. "Milton Babbitt's *Semi-Simple* Variations." *Perspectives of New Music*, 14. no. 2; 15, no. 1 (1976): 111–154.
Detailed analysis. Musical examples.

Sextets

28.   Capalbo, Marc. "Charts." *Perspectives of New Music*, 19, nos. 1–2 (1981–1982): 317 + .
An analysis of pitch-class relationships by means of pitch-syntactical charts.

DISSERTATIONS AND THESES

General

29.   Borders, Barbara Ann. "Formal Aspects in Selected Instrumental Works of Milton Babbitt." Ph.D., University of Michigan, 1987, 232 pp., DA 40-4290A.

5

Post Partitions

30. Lieberson, Peter Goddard. "Milton Babbitt's *Post-Partitions.*" Ph.D., Brandeis University, 1985, 67 pp., DA 46-1550A.

BACH, CARL PHILIPP EMANUEL, 1714–1788

General

31. Barford, Philip. *The Keyboard Music of C. P. E. Bach.* New York: October House, 1966, 186 pp.

Thorough treatment of Bach's total output for keyboard. Historical perspective and relationship to the sonata principle emphasized. Musical examples.

32. Schulenberg, David. *The Instrumental Music of Carl Philipp Emanuel Bach.* Ann Arbor, MI: UMI Research Press, 1984, 192 pp.

A general study that includes historical background as well as an analysis and critical appraisal of Bach's instrumental music. Analytic commentary of texture, structures, rhythm, and other unifying elements, with musical examples drawn from numerous works. Two works are analyzed in detail: Rondo in G, H. 268 (pp. 148–153) and Fantasie in C, H. 284 (pp. 153–159)—both from works for *Kenner und Liebhaber.* Musical examples.

33. Stevens, Jane R. "The Keyboard Concertos of Carl Philipp Emanuel Bach." *Current Musicology,* 9 (1969): 197–200.

Two reviews of doctoral dissertations on the subject. The reviews cover many of the formal, stylistic, and harmonic traits of the concertos under discussion.

Concertos for Harpsichord

34. Crickmore, Leon. "C. P. E. Bach's Harpsichord Concertos." *Music and Letters,* 39 (July 1958): 227–241.

Overview of C. P. E. Bach's achievement in this genre. Context, stylistic traits, and common formal patterns identified. Some discussion of individual works. Musical examples.

Free Fantasy in C Minor

35. Helm, Ernest. "The *Hamlet* Fantasy and the Literary Element in C. P. E. Bach's Music." *Musical Quarterly,* 58, no. 2 (1972): 277–296.

Bach's well-known composition for clavichord served, during his lifetime, as material for an unusual experiment by poet and playwright Heinrich Wilhelm von Gerstenberg. Two texts were set to the piece, transforming it into a kind of *Lied*. Background and description.

Quartet for Clavier in A Minor, W. 93

36.   Corrao, Timothy. "C. P. E. Bach's Clavier Quartet in A Minor, Wotquenne 93." *Bach*, 13, no. 2 (1982): 23–27.
Analysis. Bibliography.

Rondos for Piano

37.   Cole, Malcolm Stanley. "Rondos, Proper and Improper." *Music and Letters*, 51, no. 4 (1970): 388–399.
Shows how Bach departed from normal rondo structure. Musical examples.

Rondo Espresivo for Piano

38.   Agay, Denes. "The Search for Authenticity." *Clavier*, 14, no. 8 (1975): 29–31.
Speculations on the compositional history of Bach's Rondo. Musical examples.

Solfegietto

39.   Dumm, Robert. "Piano Footnotes: An Analytic-Interpretive Lesson on C. P. E. Bach's *Solfegietto*." *Clavier*, 2, no. 3 (1963): 21–23.
Brief analytic remarks with a view towards performance. Music for entire piece is included.

Sonatas for Piano

40.   Rosen, Charles. *Sonata Forms*, 171–173. New York: W. W. Norton, 1980.
Discussion of the structure of the exposition of the Sonata in A Major of the *Sechs Clavier Sonaten für Kenner und Liebhaber*. Musical examples.

DISSERTATIONS AND THESES

General

41.   Chamblee, James Monroe. "The Cantatas and Oratorios of Carl Philipp Emanuel Bach. Vol. 1, A Style Analysis. Vol. 2, Musical Supplement." Ph.D., University of North Carolina at Chapel Hill, 1973, 543 pp., DA 34-2676A.

7

42.   Rose, Juanelva M. "The Harmonic Idiom of the Keyboard Works of Carl Philipp Emanuel Bach." Ph.D., University of California at Santa Barbara, 1970, 293 ppl, DA 31-6102A.

Concertos

43.   Wade, Rachel W. "The Keyboard Concertos of Carl Philipp Emanuel Bach: Sources and Style." Ph.D., New York University, 1980, 511 pp. DA 40-5645A.

BACH, JOHANN CHRISTIAN, 1735–1782

General

44.   Warburton, Ernest. "J. C. Bach's Church Music." *Musical Times,* 123 (November 1982): 781 + .
   A review of stylistic elements in J. C. Bach's church music.

Concertos

45.   Simon, Eric J. "The Double Exposition in the Classic Concerto." *Journal of the American Musicological Society,* 10 (Summer 1957): 111–118.
   Commentary on origins of the double exposition in the classic concerto as well as an in-depth analysis of the first movement of an early Bach concerto in B-flat. Diagrams of form.

46.   Wellesz, Egon, and F. W. Sternfeld. "The Concerto." In *The New Oxford History of Music.* Vol. 7, *The Age of Enlightenment, 1745–1790.* Edited by Egon Wellesz and F. W. Sternfeld, 483–485. London: Oxford University Press, 1973.
   Brief critical and descriptive remarks with musical examples. Bach's style and output in this form mentioned. This article is part of a larger article on the history of the concerto form.

Concerto for Piano No. 4, Op. 13 in B-Flat Major

47.   Rosen, Charles. *Sonata Forms,* 88–95. New York: W. W. Norton, 1980.
   Description of the structure of the first movement. Identifies themes, formal divisions, tonalities, and other unifying elements. Musical examples.

"Gloria" in D Major

48.   Vos, Marie Ann. "Johann Christian Bach as a Choral Composer." *American Choral Review*, 17, no. 3 (1975): 21–25.
   Historical background and brief analysis.

Symphony No. 4, Op. 18 in D Major

49.   Rosen, Charles. *Sonata Forms*, 251–255. New York: W. W. Norton, 1980.
   Discussion of the structure of the development section. Musical examples.

BACH, JOHANN SEBASTIAN, 1685–1750

General

50.   Boyd, Malcolm. *Bach.* London: J. M. Dent and Sons, 1983, 290 pp.
   Typical "life and works" volume in the Dent "Master Musician" series. Numerous analytical comments on works from all genres— on form, style, and texture. No extended analyses of any individual works. Includes list of works.

51.   Bukofzer, Manfred. *Music in the Baroque Era.* New York: W. W. Norton, 1947, 489 pp.
   Historical background, influences, stylistic development, and critical assessment of Bach's place in music history. Musical examples.

52.   Chafe, Eric. "Key Structure and Tonal Allegory in the Passions of J. S. Bach: An Introduction." *Current Musicology*, 31 (1981): 39–54.
   Discussion of the allegorical use of tonality in the Passions. Demonstrates how Bach, in the manner of his predecessor, Kuhnau, uses keys as symbols. For instance, sharp keys (*Kreuztonarte*) for the section of the *Saint John* Passion dealing with the cross. Highly detailed discussion and analysis. Musical examples.

53.   Dickinson, A. E. F. *Bach's Fugal Works: With an Account of Fugue Before and After Bach.* London: Sir Isaac Pitman and Sons, 1956, 280 pp.
   Thorough analytic survey of Bach's fugal works, dealing with the organ works, *Well-Tempered Clavier*, *Art of the Fugue*, and the chorale fugues of the cantatas, Magnificat and Mass in B Minor. A

9

separate chapter on Bach's fugal craftsmanship divides the discussion according to the individual components of the fugue. Musical examples.

54.   Eickhoff, Henry J. "Bach's Chorale-Ritornello Forms." *Music Review*, 28, no. 4 (1967): 257–276.
A discussion and analysis with historic commentary on Bach's new structural approach to chorale ritornello forms. Musical examples.

55.   Gehring, Philip. "Rhythmic Character in Bach's Organ Music." *American Music Teacher*, 19, no. 1 (1969): 33–35 +.
The sources of Bach's rhythmic ideas as seen in his vocal, keyboard, violin, and dance styles.

56.   Geiringer, Karl. "Bach's Oratorios." *American Choral Review*, 9, no. 3 (1967): 22–25.
A broad overview of the oratorios with comparisons between the parodies upon which they are based. Brief and descriptive. Musical examples.

57.   Grace, Harvey. *The Organ Works of Bach.* London: Novello, n.d., 319.
Thorough overview with critical and analytic comments. Musical examples.

58.   Grew, Eva, and Sydney Grew. *Bach.* London: J. M. Dent and Sons, 1947, 239 pp.
A "Master Musician" series treatment of the life and works of Bach. The discussion of the works is descriptive, with analytic observations intended for the undergraduate student. Musical examples.

59.   Keller, Hermann. *The Organ Works of Bach.* Translated by Helen Hewitt. New York: C. F. Peters, 1967, 312 pp.
Detailed annotated catalog of all Bach's organ works. Descriptive commentary with performance suggestions. Useful for occasional remarks on structure and important musical features. Musical examples.

60.   Little, Meredith E. "The Contribution of Dance Steps to Musical Analysis and Performance.: 'La Bourgogne.' " *Journal of the American Musicological Society*, 28, no. 1 (1975): 112–123.
In-depth discussion of Bach's use of French dance forms. Advanced level.

61.   Mann, Alfred. "Bach Studies: Approaches to the B Minor Mass." *American Choral Review*, 27, no. 1 (1985).
Entire issue devoted to a survey of Bach's choral music. Background, style, structure, and performance discussed.

62.   Marshall, Robert L. "Bach the Progressive: Observations on His Later Works." *Musical Quarterly*, 62, no. 3 (1976): 313–357.
The evolution of Bach's style as influenced by the musical activity in Dresden from the 1730s to early 1740s. Musical examples.

63.   Marshall, Robert L. *The Music of Johann Sebastian Bach.* New York: Schirmer Books, 1989, 375 pp.
In examining Bach's historical significance, his compositional process, authenticity questions, and performance practice, many analytic observations made on a variety of compositions. Special treatment of the *Magnificat* and the *Mass in B Minor.* Musical examples.

64.   Matthews, Denis, ed. *Keyboard Music,* 68–101. New York: Praeger, 1972.
Summary by Charles Rosen of Bach's keyboard achievement. Historical perspective, stylistic traits, and analytic remarks on individual pieces. Musical examples.

65.   Mellers, Wilfrid. *Bach and the Dance of God.* London: Faber and Faber, 1980, 324 pp.
Extended analyses of the *Saint John Passion, Mass in B Minor,* as well as consideration of the cello suites, a selection of the Forty-eight Preludes and Fugues, the *Goldberg Variations,* and other works. Analyses go beyond the merely objective and consider religious, philosophical, and psychological aspects. Musical examples.

66.   Pirro, Andre. *J. S. Bach.* Translated by Mervyn Savill. New York: Orion Press, 1957, 269 pp.
Descriptive commentary with background. Some critical remarks. Musical examples.

67.   Rueb, Phyllis K. "Handel's Keyboard Suites: A Comparison with Those of J. S. Bach." *American Music Teacher*, 20, no. 5 (1971): 33–36
A comparison of stylistic characteristics in the Handel suites with those of Bach's keyboard suites.

68.   Schweitzer, Albert. *J. S. Bach.* Translated by Ernest Newman. 2 vols. London: Breitkopf and Härtel, 1911.
Still useful to undergraduates for basic concepts on word painting and imagery. Musical examples.

11

69. Spitta, Philipp. *Johann Sebastian Bach.* Translated by Clara Bell and J. J. Fuller-Maitland. 3 vols. London: Novello, 1899.
   Nineteenth-century descriptive and critical commentary highlighting stylistic traits. Not analytic.

70. Steinitz, Paul. *Bach's Passions.* London: Paul Elek, 1979, 137 pp.
   Thorough treatment of Bach's Passions, including the German Passion tradition, performance practice, the Passion texts, and commentaries describing each movement of each Passion in a short paragraph mentioning word painting, form, style, thematic content. Musical examples.

71. Steinitz, Paul. "German Church Music." In *The New Oxford History of Music.* Vol. 5, *Opera and Church Music,* 653–658. Edited by Anthony Lewis and Nigel Fortune. Oxford University Press, 1975.
   Good capsule overview of Bach's achievement in this genre. Stylistic high points are illustrated with musical examples.

72. Terry, Charles Sanford. Bach: An Introduction. 1933. Reprint. New York: Dover Publications, 1963, 104 pp.
   Background and critical commentary, with some analytic insights for the undergraduate. Musical examples.

73. Williams, C. F. Abdy. *Bach.* London: J. M. Dent and Sons, 1934, 240 pp.
   Descriptive and critical commentary intended for student or musical amateur. Musical examples.

74. Williams, Peter. *Bach Organ Music.* Seattle: University of Washington Press, 1972, 71 pp.
   A "BBC Music Guide" for the concertgoer and undergraduate student. Surveys all of Bach's organ music. Many musical examples and analytic comments on individual pieces.

75. Williams, Peter. "*Figurae* in the Keyboard Works of Scarlatti, Handel, and Bach: An Introduction." In *Bach, Handel, Scarlatti: Tercentenary Essays.* Edited by Peter Williams, 327–346. London: Cambridge University Press, 1985.
   Defines "figurae" (motifs, figures, *Figuren*), gives a brief background, and then discusses their use in the keyboard works of the above composers. Musical examples.

76. Williams, Peter. *The Organ Music of J. S. Bach.* 2 vols. Cambridge Studies in Music. Cambridge: Cambridge University Press, 1980.
   Thorough overview containing analyses of all the organ works. Discussed autograph sources and traces derived materials back to their origins.

77.   **Wolff, Konrad.** *Masters of the Keyboard: Individual Style Elements in the Piano Music of Bach, Haydn, Mozart, Beethoven, and Schubert,* 1–62. Bloomington: Indiana University Press, 1983.
Although this is written primarily for performers rather than those seeking analyses, the discussion of the composer's keyboard style contains many analytic comments on individual works. Musical examples.

78.   **Young, Percy M.** *The Choral Tradition.* Rev. ed., 130–136. New York: W. W. Norton, 1981.
Both the *Saint John* Passion and *Saint Matthew* Passion discussed briefly. Musical examples.

Art of the Fugue

79.   **Bertalot, John.** "Number Symbolism in Bach." *Musical Opinion,* 104 (August 1981): 414.
Brief discussion for the undergraduate.

80.   **David, Hans T.** *"The Art of the Fugue." Bach,* 1, no. 3 (1970): 5–21.
Historical background, analysis, performance practice.

81.   **Heinrich, Adel.** *Bach's "Die Kunst der Fuge": A Living Compendium of Fugal Procedures with a Motivic Analysis of All the Fugues.* Landam, MD: University Press of America, 1983, 351 pp.
An extensive analysis of the motives and fugal techniques in the *Art of the Fugue.* Contains many tables, charts, and musical examples. Chapter headings: (1) Purpose, History and Extant Editions; (2) Fugue Types and Overall Structures; (3) Subjects, Expositions and Countersubjects; (4) Episodes, Free Material, and Codas; (5) Conclusions.

82.   **Heinrich, Adel.** "A Collation of the Expositions in *Die Kunst der Fuge* of J. S. Bach." *Bach,* 12, no. 2 (1981): 28–40.
Charts comparing entry of voices, rhythmic characteristics, contrasts, augmentation, diminution, and stretto. Shows how Bach crafted distinct fugues based on the same subject. Bibliography.

83.   **Heinrich, Adel.** "Significance of the Original Subject and Its Variants in Bach's *Die Kunst der Fuge.*" *Bach,* 15, no. 3 (1984): 24–32.
Demonstrates that though no two subjects are exactly the same for all the fugues, Bach's seemingly simple original subject embodied the concept for the work as a whole. Each new idea presented adds to previous concepts cumulatively. Musical examples. Bibliography.

13

84. Rivera, Benito V. "Bach's Use of Hitherto Unrecognized Types of Countersubjects in the *Art of the Fugue." Journal of the American Musicological Society*, 31, no. 2 (1978): 344–362.
> Speculation that Bach reversed the order of the second and third fugues, based on a reexamination of the fugue subjects. Useful analytic insights build a case for the author's theory.

85. Stauffer, George, et al. "Bach's *Art of the Fugue*: An Examination of the Sources." *Current Musicology*, 19 (1975): 47–80.
> A seminar report dealing with the sources, dissemination of the work, the simple fugues, Bach's revisions in the *Augmentation* Canon, and the unfinished last Fugue. For the advanced student.

86. Tovey, Donald Francis. *A Companion to "The Art of the Fugue."* London: Oxford University Press, 1931, 79 pp.
> Exhaustive, seventy-nine-page analysis. Musical examples.

87. Tovey, Donald Francis. *Essays in Musical Analysis: Chamber Music*, 75–89. London: Oxford University Press, 1944.
> Background and full analysis for the student. Shorter than the exhaustive treatment by Tovey cited above. Musical examples.

88. Ulrich, Homer. *Music: A Design for Listening*, 125–126. New York: Harcourt, Brace, 1957.
> Chart displaying structure of the fugue in the first movement.

Brandenburg Concertos (*See* Concertos)

Canonic Variations on "Vom Himmel hoch da komm ich her."

89. Adams, Gwen E. "Bach's Canonic Variations on 'Vom Himmel hoch': Text and Context." *Diapason*, 76 (July 1985): 9–11.
> Historical background, theoretical framework, and the cantus firmus discussed. Musical examples.

90. Kasling, Kim R. "Canonic Variations on 'Vom Himmel hoch da komm ich her.' " *Diapason*, 62 (May 1971): 16–17.
> Thorough treatment focusing on background, analysis, and numerology. Musical examples.

91. Keller, Hermann. *The Organ Works of Bach*, 286–291. Translated by Helen Hewitt. New York: C. F. Peters, 1967.
> Background, descriptive and analytic commentary. Formal plan and canonic techniques outlined. Musical examples.

92. **Williams, Peter.** *The Organ Music of J. S. Bach*, Vol. II, 315–327. New York: Cambridge University Press, 1980.
   Thorough treatment of origins and history, with analysis. Musical examples.

Cantatas

93. **Hirsch, Arthur.** "Number Symbolism in Bach's First Cantata Cycle: 1723–1724." *Bach*, 6, no. 3 (1975): 11–19; 6, no. 4 (1975): 14–19; 7 no. 1 (1976): 27–32.

94. **Hudson, Frederick.** "Bach's Wedding Music." *Current Musicology*, 7 (1968): 111–120.
   Background and descriptive commentary. Musical examples.

95. **Marshall, Robert L.** "Bach the Progressive: Observations on His Later Years." *Musical Quarterly*, 62, no. 3 (1976): 313–357.
   Background, stylistic traits, and musical influences examined.

96. **Palisca, Claude.** *Baroque Music*, 202–215. Englewood Cliffs, NJ: Prentice-Hall, 1968.
   Concise summation, with remarks on specific musical features. Musical examples.

97. **Robertson, Alec.** *The Church Cantatas.* New York: Praeger, 1972, 356 pp.
   A guide to all the church cantatas. Descriptive commentary, with information on instrumentation, composition date, and other relevant facts.

98. **Robertson, Alec.** *Requiem: Music of Mourning and Consolation*, 183–201. New York: Praeger, 1968.
   Six cantatas (nos. 32, 106, 262, 82, 95, and 27) described and commented upon. Analytic insights, with musical examples.

99. **Schenbeck, Lawrence.** "Tempo and Rhythm in Bach's Cantata Ouvertures." *Bach*, 17, no. 1 (1986): 3–17.
   An investigation of French overtures and "ouverture"-influenced movements in the cantatas. The discussion is limited to rhythmic notation, the performance of these rhythms, and to tempo considerations. No complete analyses. Musical examples.

100. **Steinitz, Paul.** "German Church Music." In *The New Oxford History of Music.* Vol. 5, *Opera and Church Music, 1630–1750.* Edited by Anthony Lewis and Nigel Fortune, 741–764. London: Oxford University Press, 1975.

Excellent overview of the high points, with closer examination of specific stylistic traits and formal principles common to the cantatas. Musical examples.

101.   Westrup, Jack. *Bach Cantatas.* London: British Broadcasting Corporation, 1966, 60 pp.
A general discussion of Bach's technique and style in the cantatas. Many specific works used as examples. Influences, symbolism, use of chorale melodies are some aspects mentioned. Musical examples.

Cantata No. 4 ("Christ lag in Todesbanden")

102.   Thoburn, Crawford R. "Pachelbel's *Christ lag in Todesbanden*: A Possible Influence on Bach's Work." *American Choral Review,* 19, no. 1 (1977): 3–16.
Melody, structure, instrumental forces, setting, and treatment of voice considered in comparing Bach's setting of this text with Pachelbel's. Musical examples.

Cantata No. 11 ("Lobet Gott in seinem Reichen")

103.   Cole, William. *The Form of Music: An Outline of Musical Designs Used by the Great Composers,* 64–67. London: Associated Board of the Royal Schools of Music, n.d.
Brief outline of the structure in table form. Example of ritornello form.

Cantata No. 79 ("Gott, der Herr, ist Sonn' und Schild")

104.   Leaver, Robin A. "The Libretto of Bach's Cantata No. 79." *Bach,* 6, no. 1 (1975): 3–11.
Not a discussion of the music, but some thoughts on the possible librettist for this cantata.

Cantata No. 131 ("Aus der Tiefe rufe ich, Herr, zu dir")

105.   Herz, Gerhard. "BWV 131: Bach's First Cantata." In *Studies in Eighteenth-Century Music.* Edited by H. C. Robbins Landon, 272–291. London: George Allen and Unwin, 1970.
Thorough discussion for the advanced student including background and analysis of this cantata. Musical examples.

106.   Herz, Gerhard. *Essays on J. S. Bach,* 127–145. Ann Arbor: UMI Research Press, 1985.
Background and thorough analysis of this cantata, *Aus der Tiefe rufe ich, Herr, zu dir.* Musical examples.

Cantata No. 140 ("Wachet auf, ruft uns die Stimme")

107.   Herz, Gerhard, ed. *Cantata No. 140, "Wachet auf, ruft uns die Stimme."* Norton Critical Scores. New York: W. W. Norton, 1972, 175 pp.

Historical background, the complete score, and analytical essays on each movement (written by Herz). Includes comments on the chorale melody and Bach's adaptation; structure; forms; orchestration and tonality. Tables and musical examples. Analysis is on pp. 109–150.

Chorale Preludes

108.   Tusler, Robert L. *The Style of Bach's Chorale Preludes.* 1956. Reprint. New York: Da Capo Press, 1968, 75 pp.

Thorough treatment including background, organs, style, and ornamentation. Musical examples.

Chorale Preludes ("Schübler"), BWV 645-650

109.   Currie, Randolph N. "Cyclic Unity in Bach's 'Sechs Chorale': A New Look at the *Schüblers.*" *Bach*, 4, no. 1 (1973): 26–38.

Analysis. Musical examples and bibliography.

Chorale Preludes, BWV 651-668

110.   Cantrell, Scott. "J. S. Bach's Eighteen Leipzig Chorales." *American Organist*, 13, no. 5 (1979): 39–41.

Capsule description of each chorale. Some analytic commentary. Musical examples.

Chorales (Four-Part)

111.   Marshall, Robert L. "How Bach Composed Four-Part Chorales." *Musical Quarterly*, 56, no. 2 (1970): 198–220.

Bach's techniques of composition. Musical examples.

Christmas Oratorio

112.   Grinde, Nils. "Problems in Interpreting Symbols in Baroque Music." *Studia Musicologica Norvegica*, 12 (1986): 75–87.

Discusses problem of inappropriate musical symbolism in some cases of parody. For instance, the aria from the secular cantata "Lasst uns sorgen, lasst uns wachen" (BWV 213) becomes Mary's aria "Schlafe, mein Liebster, geniesse der Ruh" in the *Christmas* Oratorio. Compares arias from the point of view of the music and the symbols.

113.   Young, Percy M. *The Choral Tradition*, 112–116. New York: W. W. Norton, 1971.

Brief descriptive and critical remarks. Musical examples.

Chromatic Fantasy and Fugue in D Minor

114.   Lambert, J. Philip. "Eighteenth-Century Harmonic Theory in Concept and Practice: Kollmann's Analysis of J. S. Bach's *Chromatic Fantasy.*" *In Theory Only,* 8, no. 3 (1984): 11–29.
  Commentary on an eighteenth-century analysis of the *Chromatic Fantasy and Fugue.*

115.   Schenker, Heinrich. *J. S. Bach's "Chromatic" Fantasy and Fugue: Critical Edition with Commentary.* Translated and edited by Hedi Siegel. New York: Longman, 1984, 101 pp.
  Exhaustive analysis of the entire work according to the Schenker method. Full scores of the standard version, variant version, and Schenker's edition provided.

Clavierübung III

116.   David, Hans T. "Bach Form—A Letter and Ground Plan." *Bach,* 1, no. 2 (1970): 14–17.
  Demonstrates that Bach chose the organ chorales in the order of their religious significance, but they were published in alphabetical order, thereby disrupting the intended symmetry and coherence of the work. Article written in 1942 and its findings are accepted now.

117.   Humphreys, David. *The Esoteric Structure of Bach's "Clavierübung III."* Cardiff: University College, 1983, 99 pp.
  Uncovers the plan behind the ordering of the pieces in the set. The analysis of the overall design necessarily includes analytical comments on many individual pieces and comments on tonal organization, number symbolism, and theological symbolism.

Concertos

118.   Hill, Ralph, ed. *The Concerto,* 18–37. London: Penguin Books, 1952.
  Critical and analytic commentary for the undergraduate student. Musical examples.

119.   Veinus, Abraham. *The Concerto,* 53–62. Rev. Ed. New York: Dover Publications, 1964.
  General observations on the origins of Bach's concertos and the balance between soloist and orchestra. Less of a discussion on individual works than an overview of Bach's achievement in the concerto form.

Brandenburg Concertos

120. Carrel, Norman. *Bach's "Brandenburg" Concertos.* London: George Allen and Unwin, 1963, 130 pp.
Full treatment of all the *Brandenburg* Concertos, including the characteristics of the instruments used and extensive analyses. Musical examples.

121. Hutchings, Arthur. *The Baroque Concerto,* 226–237. New York: W. W. Norton, 1961.
Observations on style, form, instruments, and historical context. Musical examples.

122. Leichtentritt, Hugo. *Musical Form,* 361–373. Cambridge, MA: Harvard University Press, 1959.
Bar-by-bar analyses of all the *Brandenburg* Concertos. Best used with a score.

123. Veinus, Abraham. *The Concerto,* 27–33. Rev. ed. New York: Dover Publications, 1964.
Descriptive remarks highlighting form and instrumentation. Shows place of Bach in the development of the concerto form.

Brandenburg Concerto No. 1 in F Major

124. Warburton, A. O. "Set Works for 'O' Level, GCE." *Music Teacher,* 48 (June 1969): 10+.
Thorough descriptive and analytic commentary with background. For the undergraduate student.

Brandenburg Concerto No. 2 in F Major

125. Davie, Cedric Thorpe. *Musical Structure and Design,* 100–101. New York: Dover Publications, 1966.
Compact measure-by-measure analysis. Musical examples. First movement only.

126. George, Graham. *Tonality and Musical Structure,* 122–127. New York: Praeger, 1970.
Analysis focusing on tonality. Musical examples. Chart.

127. Nelson, Wendell. *The Concerto,* 10–11. Dubuque, IA: William C. Brown, 1969.
Brief remarks with musical examples.

128. Ulrich, Homer. *Music: A Design for Listening,* 236–237. New York: Harcourt, Brace, 1957.
Descriptive breakdown by measures. Musical examples.

129.   Warburton, A. O. *Analyses of Musical Classics.* Book 4, 36–42. London: Longman, 1974.
> Full measure-by-measure analysis. Score needed to follow analysis.

130.   Warburton, A. O. "Set Works for 'O' Level, GCE." *Music Teacher,* 49 (July 1970): 10 + .
> Brief description and analysis for the undergraduate student.

Brandenburg Concerto No. 4 in G Major

131.   Cole, William. *The Form of Music: An Outline of Musical Designs Used by the Great Composers,* 63–64. London: Associated Board of the Royal Schools of Music, n.d.
> Brief outline of the ritornello structure in table form.

Brandenburg Concerto No. 5 in D Major

132.   Kerman, Joseph. *Listen,* 101–103. 2d ed. New York: Worth Publishers, 1976.
> Analysis with musical examples. For the undergraduate student.

133.   Morehen, John. "Bach's *Brandenburg* Concerto No. 5 (set by Oxford)." *Music Teacher,* 56 (July 1977): 17–18.
> Background, descriptive, and analytic commentary for the undergraduate student. Brief bibliography.

Concerto for Harpsichord No. 1 in D Minor

134.   David, Cedric Thorpe. *Musical Structure and Design,* 104–106. New York: Dover Publications, 1966.
> Compact bar-by-bar analysis. Musical examples. First movement only.

135.   Leichtentritt, Hugo. *Musical Form,* 314, 359–361. Cambridge, MA: Harvard University Press, 1959.
> Brief but compact analysis with no musical examples. Best used with a score.

Concerto for Two Harpsichords in C Minor

136.   Pazur, Robert. "Bach, 2 Clavier Concerto in C minor (S. 1060), Mvt. 1: A Case for Synthesis." *In Theory Only,* 1 (December 1976): 9–16.
> Analysis. For the advanced student. Musical examples.

English Suites, BWV 806-811

137.   Cameron, Rosaline. "Bach's Six *English* Suites." *Music Journal*, 32 (July 1974): 6–7.
> Background and brief descriptive remarks. No discussion of individual works in detail.

138.   De Gastyne, Serge. "Bach's *English* Suites: A New Approach." *Piano Quarterly*, 30, no. 1 (1981–1982): 45–47.
> The *English* Suites revealed as variations on the twenty-fifth entry in the *Little Notebook of Anna Magdalena Bach* of 1725, "Bist du bei mir." Musical examples.

Fantasia in C Minor, BWV 906

139.   Bryant, Celia M. "Eighteenth Century Showcase." *Clavier*, 6, no. 8 (1967): 51–54.
> Analytic observations with musical examples. For performers rather than analysts. Score is on pp. 29–32.

Fantasy and Fugue in G Minor, BWV 542

140.   Tischler, Hans. *The Perceptive Music Listener*, 101–103. Englewood Cliffs, NJ: Prentice-Hall, 1955.
> Condensed analyses to be used with score in hand.

141.   Warburton, A. O. "Set Works for 'O' Level, GCE." *Music Teacher*, 51 (March 1972): 13–14.
> Descriptive and analytic commentary for the undergraduate student.

French Suite No. 4 in E-Flat, BWV 815

142.   Cogan, Robert, and Pozzi Escot. *Sonic Design: The Nature of Sound and Music*, 25–34. Englewood Cliffs, NJ: Prentice-Hall, 1976.
> Deals only with the "Allemande" movement. An analysis of spatial aspects. Discusses individual lines and the relationships between them. Also a discussion of rhythm. Includes musical examples and graphs.

French Suite No. 6 in E Major, BWV 817

143.   Warburton, A. O. "Set Works for 'O' Level, GCE." *Music Teacher*, 51 (May 1972): 16–17.
> Description and analysis for the undergraduate student.

21

Fugue for Organ in E Minor, BWV 548

144.   Jander, Owen. "The *Wedge* Fugue: Bach's Concerto for Display of the Four-Manual Organ." *Diapason*, 70 (November 1979): 10–13.
   Analysis, with discussion of how Bach exploited resources of the four-manual organ.

Fugue on a Theme by Legrenzi in C Minor, BWV 574

145.   Swale, David. "Bach's Fugue After Legrenzi." *Musical Times*, 126 (November 1985): 687 +.
   The true link to Legrenzi uncovered in this analytic description. Musical examples.

Goldberg Variations

146.   Cogan, Robert, and Pozzi Escot. *Sonic Design: The Nature of Sound and Music*, 264–276. Englewood Cliffs, NJ: Prentice-Hall, 1976.
   Discussion of rhythm and variation techniques. Includes a table of variation techniques to show their grouping into categories.

147.   David, Hans T. "Bach Form—Ground Plans (*Goldberg* Variations)." *Bach*, 1, no. 1 (1970): 15–16.
   Illustrates key, thematic, textural, and formal relationships.

148.   Ehle, Robert. "Comments on the *Goldberg* Variations." *American Music Teacher*, 19, no. 2 (1969): 20–22.
   Brief analytic comments, with musical examples.

149.   Green, Douglass M. *Form in Tonal Music*, 102–104, 107–108. New York: Holt, Rinehart, and Winston, 1965.
   Discussion of types of counterpoint employed and a chart of the schematic order of the variations. Musical examples.

150.   Jander, Owen. "Rhythmic Symmetry in the *Goldberg* Variations." *Musical Quarterly*, 52, no. 2 (1966): 204–208.
   Reveals mathematical symmetry Bach imposed on the music as a numerological game. Musical examples.

151.   Street, Alan. "The Rhetorico-Musical Structure of the *Goldberg* Variations: Bach's *Clavierübung IV* and the *Institutio Oratoria* of Quintilian." *Music Analysis*, 6, nos. 1–2 (July 1987): 89–131.
   Not a traditional analysis. Rather, it is an analysis of the extramusical structure of the work. It analyzes the work as a musical reply to criticisms of Bach by Johannes Scheibe, conceived according to the rules of oratory. Discusses rhetorical functions of the Variations in detail. Musical examples and tables. For the advanced student.

152.   Sutton, Wadham. "J. S. Bach: The *Goldberg* Variations." *Music Teacher*, 54 (July 1975): 18; (August 1975): 11.
Brief analytic overview for the undergraduate student.

153.   Tovey, Donald Francis. *Essays in Musical Analysis: Chamber Music*, 28–73. London: Oxford University Press, 1944.
Background and full analysis for the student. Musical examples.

Goldberg Variations (Canons), BWV 1087

154.   Currie, Randolph N. "Bach's Newly Discovered Canons in a First Edition: Some Observations." *Bach*, 8, no. 2 (1977): 15–22; no. 3 (1977): 3–12; no. 4 (1977): 3–9.
Background and analytic observations. Bibliography.

155.   Kenyon, Nicholas. "A Newly Discovered Group of Canons by Bach." *Musical Times*, 117 (May 1976): 391–393.
Historical background, description, analysis, and speculation on the numerology of the work. Musical examples.

156.   Marshall, Robert L. "Bach the Progressive: Observations on His Later Works." *Musical Quarterly*, 62, no. 3 (1976): 342–353.
Background, speculation on stylistic traits derived from Scarlatti, and analytic observations on the progressive aspects of the work.

157.   Tulan, Frederick. "Bach's New Canons." *Music (AGO)*, 10 (October 1976): 36–38.
Historical background and analysis. Musical examples.

158.   Wolff, Christoph. "Bach's Handexemplar of the *Goldberg* Variations: A New Source." *Journal of the American Musicological Society*, 29, no. 2 (1976): 224–241.
Discussion includes analytic description of each of the Canons.

Inventions

159.   Adams, Courtney S. "Organization in the Two-Part Inventions of Johann Sebastian Bach." *Bach*, 13, no. 2 (1982): 6–16.
Complete structural analysis for each of the inventions. Bibliography.

160.   Boyd, Malcolm. *Bach's Instrumental Counterpoint*. London: Barrie and Rockliff, 1967, 36 pp.
A study of the harmony and counterpoint in Bach's two- and three-part inventions. Separate chapters on: Melodic Characteristics;

Harmony; Rhythm and Texture; Musical Forms. This is actually a short textbook. It concludes with practical exercises. Musical examples.

161.   Derr, Ellwood S. "The Two-Part Inventions: Bach's Composers' Vademecum." *Music Theory Spectrum*, 3 (1981): 26–48.
A detailed study of the inventions. Compares them with their earlier versions in *Clavier-Büchlein vor Wilhelm Friedemann Bach*. The order in the *Clavier-Büchlein* makes more sense tonally. For the advanced student. No complete analyses.

162.   Herford, Julius. "Bach's Model of 'Good' Inventions." *Bach*, 2, no. 4 (1971): 10–14.
A stylistic analysis focusing on Bach's method of shaping themes through stepwise, zigzag movements and rhythmic stresses. Phrasing also discussed. Musical examples.

163.   Satterfield, John. "The Emotional Content of the Bach Two-Part Inventions." *Music Review*, 19 (August 1958): 173–179.
How melodic and durational accents affect the emotional content. Advanced analysis. Tables. No musical examples.

164.   Vassar, James B. "The Bach Two-Part Inventions: A Question of Authorship." *Music Review*, 33, no. 1 (1972): 14–21.
Analytic examination focusing on Bach's collaboration with his son, Wilhelm Friedemann. Musical examples.

Invention No. 1 in C Major

165.   Larson, Steve. "On Analysis and Performance: The Contribution of Durational Reduction to the Performance of J. S. Bach's Two-Part Invention in C Major." *In Theory Only*, 7 (May 1983): 31–45.
Analysis exposing important musical events by a systematic reduction of the durational values of notes. This system makes it possible to sing or play the analysis rather than just be able to refer to it. More significant as a demonstration of an analytic technique than an analysis of the work itself. Musical examples.

166.   Travis, Roy. "Invention No. 1 in C Major: Reduction and Graph." *In Theory Only*, 2 (October 1976): 3–7.
Advanced analysis. Musical examples.

167.   Walton, Charles W. *Basic Forms in Music*, 148–150. Port Washington, NY: Alfred Publishing Co., 1974.
Condensed analysis, with complete score included.

168.   Zabrack, Harold. "The Inventions Were Meant to Be Teaching Pieces." *Clavier*, 13, no. 8 (1974): 28–30.
>   Brief observations on melodic contour, texture, harmonic structure, and rhythm to aid interpretation. Musical examples.

Invention No. 4 in D Minor

169.   Kresky, Jeffrey. *Tonal Music: Twelve Analytic Studies*, 56–67. Bloomington: Indiana University Press, 1977.
>   In-depth analysis dealing with form and tonality. Advanced. Musical examples and diagrams.

Invention No. 6 in E Major

170.   Schroder, Charles F. "Piano Lesson: Two-Part Invention No. 6 in E Major by Johann Sebastian Bach." *Clavier*, 3, no. 4 (1964): 27–30.
>   Remarks for performance, with analytic observations. Complete score.

Invention No. 8 in F Major

171.   Beard, Katherine. "Exploring the Two-Part Inventions." *Clavier*, 24, no. 3 (1985): 18–21.
>   Analysis, with performance suggestions. Score included.

Invention No. 13 in A Minor

172.   Adrian, Jack S. "J. S. Bach's Invention in A Minor: A Re-View." *In Theory Only*, 8, no. 7 (1985): 15–27.
>   An analysis using Schenkerian terminology, methodology, and notation. For the advanced student. Musical examples.

173.   Travis, Roy. "Invention No. 13 in A Minor: Reduction and Graph." *In Theory Only*, 2 (November 1976): 29–33.
>   Graphic analysis for the advanced student. Musical examples.

Invention No. 14 in B-Flat Major

174.   Beard, Katherine. "Exploring the Two-Part Inventions." *Clavier*, 24, no. 3 (1985): 18–21.
>   Analysis, with performance suggestions. Score included.

25

"Jesu, meine Freude" (Motet)

175. Engel, James. "J.S. Bach's Motets, Especially 'Jesu, meine Freude.' " *American Organist,* 14 (March 1980): 34–41.
   Historical background and detailed analysis. Musical examples and bibliography.

176. Tovey, Donald Francis. *Essays in Musical Analysis.* Vol. 5, 73–82. London: Oxford University Press, 1937.
   Descriptive, critical and analytic commentary for the informed student. Musical examples.

Magnificat

177. Tovey, Donald Francis. *Essays in Musical Analysis.* Vol. 5, 50–60. London: Oxford University Press, 1937.
   Thorough analysis and critical commentary for the informed student. Musical examples.

178. Warburton, A. O. "Set Works for 'O' Level, GCE." *Music Teacher,* 50 (April 1971): 13–14 + .
   Thorough background, descriptive, and analytic commentary for the undergraduate student.

179. Young, Percy M. *The Choral Tradition,* 149–151. New York: W. W. Norton, 1971.
   Brief descriptive remarks, with musical examples.

Magnificat: "Deposuit Potentes."

180. Cole, William. *The Form of Music: An Outline of Musical Designs Used by the Great Composers,* 62. London: Associated Board of the Royal Schools of Music, n.d.
   Brief outline of the structure in table form. Example of ritornello form.

Mass in B Minor

181. Cowart, Georgia. "Symbolic Correspondence in the Duets of Bach's Mass in B Minor." *Bach,* 15, no. 1 (1984): 17–24; no. 2 (1984): 19–25.
   The duets compared for symbolic use of instrumentation, style, key, form, and contrapuntal devices. The effect of symbolism viewed in the stylistic unity of the *Mass* as a whole. Bibliography.

182.   **David, Hans T.** "Johann Sebastian Bach's Great Mass." *Bach,* 2, no. 1 (1971): 29–32.
   Brief explanatory remarks on plan of work. Detailed chart showing plan and tonality appended.

183.   **Janower, David M.** "Aria Form in the Bach B Minor Mass." *Choral Journal,* 22, no. 4 (1981): 17–19 +.
   A study of Bach's aria form in the *Mass,* showing its conformity and nonconformity to the typical aria form.

184.   **Leaver, Robin A.** "Number Associations in the Structure of Bach's Credo, BWV 232." *Bach,* 7, no. 3 (1976): 17–24.
   Number symbolism in the Credo, traced in detail.

185.   **Tovey, Donald Francis.** *Essays in Musical Analysis.* Vol. 5, 20–40. London: Oxford University Press, 1937.
   Thorough analysis and critical commentary for the informed student. Musical examples.

186.   **Warburton, A. O.** "Set Works for 'O' Level, GCE." *Music Teacher,* 52 (April 1973): 16–17 +.
   Thorough descriptive and analytic commentary on the *Sanctus* and *Agnus Dei* movements for the undergraduate student.

187.   **Young, Percy M.** *The Choral Tradition,* 140–149. New York: W. W. Norton, 1971.
   Discussion with concise analysis. Musical examples.

Motets

188.   **Pisano, Richard C.** "On Bach's Motets." *Choral Journal,* 9, no. 1 (1968): 21–22; no. 2 (1968): 19–21.
   Brief analytic commentary focusing on the influence of text on structure, choice of tonality, symbolism, and pictorial devices. Musical examples. Brief bibliography.

Musical Offering

189.   **David, Hans T.** *J. S. Bach's "Musical Offering": A History, Interpretation, and Analysis.* New York: G. Schirmer, 1945, 190 pp.
   Written to accompany the Schirmer edition of the music, this book discusses the forms, overall structure, instrumentation, interpretation, sources, and editions. The "Analysis" section is descriptive, with some analytic comments. Musical examples.

190.   Radice, Mark A. "An Inventory of Bach's *Musical Offering.*" *Bach,* 6, no. 1 (1975): 12–16.
  Analytic discussion dealing with the "correct" order of the pieces. Bibliography.

191.   Wolff, Christoph. "New Research on Bach's *Musical Offering.*" *Musical Quarterly,* 57, no. 3 (1971): 379–408.
  Scholarly research to shed light on long-standing mysteries on the order of the pieces, instrumentation, and conception. Musical examples.

Orgelbüchlein

192.   Benitez, Vincent P. "Musical-Rhetorical Figures in the *Orgelbüchlein* of J. S. Bach." *Bach,* 18, no. 1 (1987): 3–22.
  Essentially a brief catalog of musical-rhetorical figures selected from chorales in the *Orgelbüchlein* (BWV 606, 614, 625, 637, 644). Suggests reason for the use of certain musical-rhetorical figures with specific texts. Musical examples.

Partita for Harpsichord No. 1 in B-Flat Major, BWV 825

193.   Lambert, Arthur. "A Dance Suite—The Bach Partita in B♭." *Clavier,* 8, no. 1 (1969): 13–22.
  Analysis with complete score.

194.   Todd, Dennis. "Bach's Partita No. 1 in B-Flat Major (Set Works for 'O' Level)." *Music Teacher,* 60 (February 1981): 13.
  Background, brief descriptive and analytic commentary for the undergraduate student.

Partitas for Violin

195.   Ulrich, Homer. "The Nationality of Bach's Solo Violin Partitas." In *Paul A. Pisk: Essays in His Honor,* edited by John Glowacki, 96–102. Austin: University of Texas Press, 1966.
  Examination of the formal structure and speculation on Bach's use of French and English forms.

Partita for Violin Unaccompanied No. 2 in D Minor (Chaconne), BWV 1004

196.   Cantrell, Byron. "Three B's—Three Chaconnes." *Current Musicology,* 12 (1971): 63–66 + .
  Analysis with musical examples.

197.   Cogan, Robert, and Pozzi Escot. *Sonic Design: The Nature of Sound and Music*, 261–264. Englewood Cliffs, NJ: Prentice-Hall, 1976.
Briefly discusses overall rhythmic shape.

198.   Leichtentritt, Hugo. *Musical Form*, 312–314. Cambridge, MA: Harvard University Press, 1959.
Condensed breakdown of variation structure. Musical examples.

199.   Walton, Charles W. *Basic Forms in Music*, 105–109. Port Washington, NY: Alfred Publishing Co., 1974.
Condensed analysis with musical examples.

Passacaglia for Organ in C Minor, BWV 582

200.   Kee, Piet. "The Secrets of Bach's Passacaglia." *Diapason*, 74 (June 1983): 10–12; (July 1983): 4–6; (August 1983): 11–13.
Highly detailed demonstration of the allegorical and theological relationship between Bach's Passacaglia and Werckmeister's *Musicalische Paradoxal-Discourse*. Musical examples.

201.   Leichtentritt, Hugo. *Musical Form*, 311–312. Cambridge, MA: Harvard University Press, 1959.
Brief, but condensed analytic remarks. Musical examples.

202.   Mulbury, David. "Bach's Passacaglia in C Minor." *Bach*, 3, no. 2 (1972): 14–27; no. 3 (1972): 12–20; no. 4 (1972): 17–21.
Historical background, structure, numerology, performance practice. Musical examples. Bibliography.

203.   Tischler, Hans. *The Perceptive Music Listener*, 211–214. Englewood Cliffs, NJ: Prentice-Hall, 1955,
Descriptive and analytical, with musical examples.

204.   Walton, Charles W. *Basic Forms in Music*, 101–105. Port Washington, NY: Alfred Publishing Co., 1974.
Condensed analytic outline, with musical examples.

Prelude and Fugue for Organ in F Minor, BWV 534

205.   Humphreys, David. "Did J. S. Bach Compose the F Minor Prelude and Fugue, BWV 534?" In *Bach, Handel, Scarlatti: Tercentenary Essays*. Edited by Peter Williams, 175–181. London: Cambridge University Press, 1985.
Analytic comments with a view to establish its authenticity. The article suggests that the work may be by Johann Christian Kittel.

29

Prelude and Fugue for Organ in B Minor, BWV 544

206. Stephens, Howard. "Prelude and Fugue in B Minor by J. S. Bach (Set by Cambridge)." *Music Teacher*, 56 (May 1977): 21.
   Descriptive and analytic commentary for the undergraduate student.

Prelude and Fugue for Organ in C Major, BWV 547

207. Newman, Anthony. " 'Strong' and 'Weak' Measures in Bach's Prelude in C Major, BWV 547." *Music (AGO)*, 11 (April 1977): 46–49.
   Though written from the performer's point of view, this discussion includes many analytic insights. Full score included.

Prelude and Fugue for Organ in E-Flat Major ("Saint Anne"), BWV 552

208. Bertalot, John. "Number Symbolism in Bach." *Musical Opinion*, 104 (August 1981): 413 + .

209. O'Donnell, John. "And Yet They Are Not Three Fugues: But One Fugue in E-Flat." *Diapason*, 68 (December 1976): 10–12.
   Detailed discussion of the numerology in this work. Musical examples.

210. Peterson, John D. "Symbolism in J. S. Bach's Prelude and Fugue in E-Flat and Its Effect on Performances." *Diapason*, 67 (February 1976): 1 + .
   Detailed discussion of numerology and symbolism. Musical examples.

211. Warburton, A. O. "Set Works for 'O' Level, GCE." *Music Teacher*, 51 (April 1972): 27 + .
   Brief but solid description and analysis for the undergraduate student.

Saint John Passion

212. Cone, Edward T. "On the Structure of *Ich Folge Dir*." *College Music Symposium*, 5 (1965): 77–87.
   A Schenkerian approach. For the advanced student.

213. Lippman, Edward A. "An Interpretation of Bach's *Ich Folge Dir Gleichfalls*." *College Music Symposium*, 5 (1965): 88–96.
   Scattered analytic observations, with special focus on the application of rhetoric. For the advanced student.

Saint Matthew Passion

214.   Brainard, Paul. "Bach's Parody Procedure and the *St. Matthew Passion.*" *Journal of the American Musicological Society*, 22, no. 2 (1969): 241–260.
Bach's use of preexisting material in this work examined.

215.   Chafe, Eric. "J. S. Bach's *St. Matthew* Passion: Aspects of Planning, Structure and Chronology." *Journal of the American Musicological Society*, 35, no. 1 (1982): 49–114.
In-depth study, including information on editions of text, composition as related to theology, musical structure, and chronology. Some discussion of symbolism. Musical examples and tables.

216.   Konecni, Vladimir J. "Bach's *St. Matthew* Passion: A Rudimentary Psychological Analysis. Part 2." *Bach*, 17, no. 4 (1986): 3–16.
Examines the psychological effects of the use of tonality, volume, ornamentation, counterpoint. Topics covered include "arousal-raising devices"; "ecological variables" (refers to associations learned by contiguity, using the well-known chorales as an example); "expectations"; "symbols"; "arousal moderating devices." Part 1 of this article is in the previous issue, but it has no analysis. Musical examples.

217.   Lerdahl, Fred, and Ray Jackendorff. *A Generative Theory of Tonal Music*, 142–145. Cambridge, MA: M.I.T. Press, 1983.
A time-span reduction of the chorale "O Haupt voll Blut und Wunden." Musical examples and diagrammatic representation/ reduction.

218.   Schellhous, Rosalie A. "Form and Spirituality in Bach's *St. Matthew* Passion." *Musical Quarterly*, 71, no. 3 (1985): 295 + .
Analytic commentary focusing on parallels between music and text. Reprinting of text discussed and charts displaying relationship of text to symbols.

219.   Schenker, Heinrich. *Five Graphic Music Analyses*, 32–33. New York: Dover Publications, 1969.
Purely graphic analysis of the chorale "Ich bin's sollte büssen." There is no accompanying analytic commentary. Score necessary.

220.   Smith, Timothy A. "More Evidence of Numerical-Logical Design of Bach's *St. Matthew* Passion." *Bach*, 17, no. 2 (1986): 24–30.
Not an analysis. A discussion of the number symbolism that underlies this work.

31

Sonata for Viola da Gamba and Harpsichord in G Minor, BWV 1029

221. **Dreyfus, Laurence.** "J. S. Bach and the Status of Genre: Problems of Style in the G Minor Sonata, BWV 1029." *Journal of Musicology*, 5, no. 1 (1987): 55–78.

  Discusses Bach's notion of genre, using this work as an example. Examines the reasons for its problematic generic identification. Commentary on the combination of French and Italian styles. Musical examples.

Sonata for Violin Unaccompanied No. 3 in F Major, BWV 1005

222. **Schenker, Heinrich.** "The Largo of J. S. Bach's Sonata No. 3 for Unaccompanied Violin (BWV 1005)." In *The Music Forum*, Vol. 4. Edited by Felix Salzer and Carl Schachter, 141–159. New York: Columbia University Press, 1976.

  Detailed analysis, with Schenker's discussion of Schumann's piano accompaniment to the *largo* of this Sonata. Advanced.

Sonata for Violin and Harpsichord in B Minor, BWV 1014

223. **Cole, William.** *The Form of Music: An Outline of Musical Designs Used by the Great Composers*, 102–105. London: Associated Board of the Royal Schools of Music, n.d.

  Brief analytic comments.

Suite for Orchestra No. 1 in C Major

224. **Morehen, John.** "J. S. Bach: Overture (Orchestral Suite) No. 1 in C Major." *Music Teacher*, 54 (August 1975): 13.

  Brief discussion of background, with analytic commentary. Brief bibliography.

225. **Schmidt, Henry.** "Bach's C Major Orchestral Suite: A New Look at Possible Origins." *Music and Letters*, 57, no. 2 (1976): 152–163.

  Some themes of this suite traced to earlier works. Musical examples.

226. **Tovey, Donald Francis.** *Essays in Musical Analysis.* Vol. 6, 1–7. London: Oxford University Press, 1969.

  Critical and analytic with musical examples. For the undergraduate student.

Suite for Orchestra No. 2 in B Minor

227.   Green, Douglass M. *Form in Tonal Music*, 284–286. New York: Holt, Rinehart, and Winston, 1965.
Opening fugal movement analyzed, with chart of fugue.

Suite for Orchestra No. 3 in D Major

228.   Pilgrim, Jack. "Set Works for 'O' Level, GCE: J. S. Bach: Overture (Orchestral Suite) No. 3 in D Major." *Music Teacher*, 53 (July 1974): 18–19.
Background, descriptive, and analytic commentary for the undergraduate student.

229.   Stedman, Preston. *The Symphony*, 10–11. Englewood Cliffs, NJ: Prentice-Hall, 1979.
Very brief description of the form of the gavotte. Musical examples and diagram.

230.   Warburton, A. O. "Set Works for 'O' Level, GCE." *Music Teacher*, 48 (May 1969): 16 + .
Background, descriptive, and analytic commentary for the undergraduate student.

Suite for Violoncello Unaccompanied No. 1, BWV 1007

231.   Laming, Frank M. "Set Works for 'O' Level, GCE." *Music Teacher*, 53 (July 1974): 19–20.
Background, descriptive, and analytic commentary for the undergraduate student.

232.   Pratt, George. "Bach's First Cello Suite—A Question in the Gigue." *Strad*, 89 (January 1979): 811 + .
Analysis of several bars based on conflicting evidence seen in three different manuscript versions.

Suite for Violoncello Unaccompannied No. 3, BWV 1009

233.   Schenker, Heinrich. "The Sarabande of J. S. Bach's Suite No. 3 for Unaccompanied Violoncello, BWV 1009." In *The Music Forum*, Vol. 3. Edited by William J. Mitchell and Felix Salzer, 274–282. New York: Columbia University Press, 1973.
In-depth Schenkerian analysis for the advanced student. Musical examples.

Suite for Violoncello Unaccompanied No. 6, BWV 1012

234.   Tischler, Hans. *The Perceptive Music Listener,* 108–110. Englewood Cliffs, NJ: Prentice-Hall, 1955.
Brief analysis. Musical examples.

Toccata for Organ in F Major, BWV 540

235.   Cole, William. *The Form of Music: An Outline of Musical Designs Used by the Great Composers,* 117–118. London: Associated Board of the Royal Schools of Music, n.d.
Brief outline of the structure in table form.

Toccata, Adagio, and Fugue in C Major, BWV 564

236.   Stephens, Howard. "Toccata, Adagio, and Fugue in C, BWV 564 (Set by the Cambridge Board)." *Music Teacher,* 56 (January 1977): 10–11.
Background, descriptive, and analytic commentary for the undergraduate student. Brief bibliography.

Well-Tempered Clavier

237.   Elder, Dean. "Jorg Demus." *Clavier,* 6, no. 1 (1967): 20–27.
Demus's general remarks for performance. Stylistic and analytic remarks. Musical examples.

238.   Fuller-Maitland, John A. *The "48": Bach's "Wohltemperirtes Clavier."* 1925. Reprint. 2 vols. New York: Books for Libraries Press, 1970.
Lightweight discussion on all forty-eight preludes and fugues. Musical examples.

239.   Gray, Cecil. *The Forty-Eight Preludes and Fugues of J. S. Bach.* London: Oxford University Press, 1952, 148 pp.
Overview with analytic insights. Musical examples.

240.   Iliffe, Frederick. *Bach's Forty-Eight Preludes and Fugues: Analyzed for Students by Frederick Iliffe.* 2 vols. Kent: Novello, n.d.
Formal and tonal analyses of all forty-eight preludes and fugues. Full musical examples provided.

241.   Keller, Hermann. *The Well-Tempered Clavier by Johann Sebastian Bach.* Translated by L. Gerdine. New York: W. W. Norton, 1976, 207 pp.

Analyzes briefly each prelude and fugue of books 1 and 2. The writing is clear and suitable for the undergraduate student. Musical examples.

242. Leichtentritt, Hugo. *Musical Form,* 302–308. Cambridge, MA: Harvard University Press, 1959.
Overview, highlighting different types of preludes, with analytic remarks. Musical examples.

243. Schat, Peter. "The Dream of Reason." *Key Notes,* 4 (1976): 39–45.
Analysis for the advanced student.

244. Williams, Peter. "J. S. Bach's *Well-Tempered Clavier*: A New Approach." *Early Music,* 11 no. 1 (1983): 46–52; no. 3 (1983): 332–339.
Stylistic and historical observations reveal Bach's intentions in writing the "forty-eight." Helpful insights on important musical features. Musical examples.

Well-Tempered Clavier. Book 1: Fugue No. 1 in C Major

245. George, Graham. *Tonality and Musical Structure,* 96–97. New York: Praeger, 1970.
Brief analysis concentrating on tonality alone. Musical examples and chart.

246. Greenberg, Beth. "Bach's C Major Fugue (WTC I): A Subjective View." *In Theory Only,* 2 (June–July 1976): 13–17.
Advanced analysis. Musical examples.

Well-Tempered Clavier. Book 1: Fugue No. 2 in C Minor

247. Bryant, Celia M. "Can He Understand a Fugue?" *Clavier,* 4, no. 3 (1965): 26–31.
Very brief analysis to aid the performer.

248. Cole, William. *The Form of Music: An Outline of Musical Designs Used by the Great Composers,* 133–134. London: Associated Board of the Royal Schools of Music, n.d.
Brief outline of the structure in table form.

249. George, Graham. *Tonality and Musical Structure,* 98–101. New York: Praeger, 1970.
Brief analysis with chart and musical examples.

250.   Herford, Julius. *"The Well-Tempered Clavier,* Book 1: An Analysis." *Bach,* 4, no. 3 (1973): 36–40.
Analysis with musical examples.

Well-Tempered Clavier. Book 1: Fugue No. 8 in D-Sharp Minor

251.   Berry, Wallace. "J. S. Bach's Fugue in D-Sharp Minor (WTC 1, no. 8): A Naive Approach to Linear Analysis." *In Theory Only,* 2 (January 1977): 4–7.
Advanced analysis. Musical examples.

252.   Davie, Cedric Thorpe. *Musical Structure and Design,* 164–165. New York: Dover Publications, 1966.
Bar-by-bar analysis to be used with score in hand.

253.   DeYoung, Lyndon. "Fugue: The Treatment of Thematic Materials." *Clavier,* 7, no. 7 (1968): 37–40.
Explanation of a fugue, with complete analysis of Fugue no. 8. Full score included.

254.   Tischler, Hans. *The Perceptive Music Listener,* 103–105. Englewood Cliffs, NJ: Prentice-Hall, 1955.
Condensed analysis to be used with score in hand.

Well-Tempered Clavier. Book 1: Fugue No. 10 in E Minor

255.   David, Hans T. "J. S. Bach's Fugue in E Minor From *The Well-Tempered Clavier,* Book 1." *Bach,* 2, no. 3 (1971): 15–16.
Analysis.

Well-Tempered Clavier. Book 1: Fugue No. 21 in B-Flat Major

256.   Schachter, Carl. "Bach's Fugue in B$^\flat$ Major, *Well-Tempered Clavier,* Book 1, No. 21." In *The Music Forum,* Vol. 3. Edited by William J. Mitchell and Felix Salzer, 239–267. New York: Columbia University Press, 1970.
Extensive Schenkerian analysis for the advanced student. Musical examples.

Well-Tempered Clavier. Book 1: Preludes 1 and 2

257.   Herford, Julius. "The C Major and C Minor Preludes of the *Well-Tempered Clavier,* Book 1." *Bach,* 4, no. 2 (1973): 17–24.
Analysis and comparison for the advanced student.

Well-Tempered Clavier. Book 1: Prelude No. 1 in C Major

258. Drabkin, William. "A Lesson in Analysis from Heinrich Schenker: The C Major Prelude from Bach's *Well-Tempered Clavier*, Book 1." *Music Analysis*, 4 no. 3 (1985): 241–258.
A discussion of Schenker's analysis in *Five Graphic Music Analyses* (*see* item no. 260). Includes translations of two letters from Schenker. For the advanced student. Musical examples.

259. Lerdahl, Fred, and Ray Jackendorff. *A Generative Theory of Tonal Music*, 260–264. Cambridge, MA: M.I.T. Press, 1983.
Time-span and prolongational reductions, with analytic comments. Diagrams and musical examples. Advanced.

260. Schenker, Heinrich. *Five Graphic Music Analyses*, 36–37. New York: Dover Publications, 1969.
Purely graphic analysis for the advanced student. There is no accompanying commentary. Score necessary.

Well-Tempered Clavier. Book 1: Prelude No. 2 in C Minor

261. Wagner, Edyth. "Analyzing a Bach Prelude." *Clavier*, 8, no. 7 (1969): 35–38.
Performer's analysis, with complete musical score.

Well-Tempered Clavier. Book 1: Prelude No. 10 in E Minor

262. David, Hans T. "Bach Analyses." *Bach*, 2, no. 2 (1971): 18–19.
Analysis.

Well-Tempered Clavier. Book 1: Prelude No. 16 in G Minor

263. Ricci, Robert. "The Division of the Pulse: Progressive and Retrogressive Rhythmic Forces." *In Theory Only*, 1 (November 1975): 13–19.
Advanced analysis focusing on rhythm. Musical examples.

Well-Tempered Clavier. Book 1: Prelude No. 21 in B-Flat Major

264. Bryant, Celia M. "Becoming a Well-Tempered Musician." *Clavier*, 11, no. 8 (1972): 27–30.
Performer's notes, with analytic observations. Complete score.

Well-Tempered Clavier. Book 1: Prelude and Fugue No. 2 in C Minor

265. Wiles, Edward. "Set Works for 'O' Level." *Music Teacher*, 53 (August 1974): 18–19.
   Background, descriptive, and analytic commentary for the undergraduate student.

Well-Tempered Clavier. Book 1: Prelude and Fugue No. 16 in G Minor

266. Schering, Arnold. "Bach's Prelude and Fugue in G Minor (*Well-Tempered Clavier*, Vol. 1)." *Piano Teacher*, 8, no. 1 (1965): 6–10.
   An analytical essay.

Well-Tempered Clavier. Book 2: Fugue No. 3 in C Minor

267. Walton, Charles W. *Basic Forms in Music*, 156–159. Port Washington, NY: Alfred Publishing Co., 1974.
   Compact analysis with complete score.

Well-Tempered Clavier. Book 2: Fugue No. 5 in D Major

268. Walton, Charles W. *Basic Forms in Music*, 151–154. Port Washington, NY: Alfred Publishing Co., 1974.
   Compact analysis with complete score.

Well-Tempered Clavier. Book 2: Fugue No. 6 in D Minor

269. Walton, Charles W. *Basic Forms in Music*, 154–156. Port Washington, NY: Alfred Publishing Co., 1974.
   Compact analysis with complete score.

Well-Tempered Clavier. Book 2: Fugue No. 9 in E Major

270. Davie, Cedric Thorpe. *Musical Structure and Design*, 162–164. New York: Dover Publications, 1966.
   Bar-by-bar analysis to be used with score in hand.

Well-Tempered Clavier. Book 2: Prelude No. 2 in C Minor

271. Wintle, Christopher. " 'Skin and Bones': The C Minor Prelude from J. S. Bach's *Well-Tempered Clavier*, Book 2." *Music Analysis*, 5, no. 1 (1986): 85–96.

An analysis using Schenkerian techniques. Illustrates connections between foreground motives and the background structure. Musical examples.

DISSERTATIONS AND THESES

General

272.   Schultz, John A. "The Soli-Tutti Concept in the Choral Works of Johann Sebastian Bach." D.M.A., University of Illinois at Urbana, 1980, 161 pp., DA 41-456A.

Cantatas

273.   Morrongiello, Lydia A. "Music Symbolism in Selected Cantatas and Chorale Preludes." Ed.D., Columbia University, 1975, 184 pp., DA 36-1158A.

Cantata No. 5 ("Wo soll ich fliehen hin")

274.   Augenblick, John Walter. "J. S. Bach's Cantata No. 5: A Conductor's Analysis." D.M.A., University of Miami, 1978, 79 pp., DA 39-6385A.

Inventions

275.   Leckie, Thomas Conley. "A Comparison of Thematic and Episodic Analysis of the Bach Two-Part Invention." Ph.D., University of Oklahoma, 1980, 212 pp., DA 41-845A.

Inventions and Sinfonias

276.   Hawthorne, Walter William. "Inventions and Sinfonias: An Analysis." Ph.D., University of Cincinnati, 1980, 197 pp., DA 41-2821A-2A.

277.   Ide, Yumiko. "A Structural and Stylistic Analysis of Selected Inventions and Sinfonias of Johann Sebastian Bach." Ed.D., Columbia University, Teachers College, 1980, 271 pp., DA 41-1463A.

Orgelbüchlein

278.   Benitez, Vincent Perez, Jr. "Musical-Rhetorical Figures in the *Orgelbüchlein* of J.S. Bach." D.M.A., Arizona State University, 143 pp., DA 46-2118A.

Preludes for Organ

279.   Stauffer, George Boyer. "The Free Organ Preludes of Johann Sebastian Bach." Ph.D., Columbia University, 1978, 322 pp., DA 39-1921A-2A.

Well-Tempered Clavier. Book 1

280.   Oberacker, Betty. "The Preludes of the *Well-Tempered Clavier,* Vol. 1, of Johann Sebastian Bach: A Commentary and Analysis." D.M.A., Ohio State University, 1972, 63 pp., DA 33-1771A.

BALAKIREV, MILY, 1837–1910

General

281.   Garden, Edward. *Balakirev.* New York: St. Martin's Press, 1967, 352 pp.
    Analyses and overview of Balakirev's output. Musical examples.

Concerto for Piano in E-Flat Major

282.   Garden, Edward. "Three Russian Piano Concertos." *Music and Letters,* 60, no. 2 (1979): 166–179.
    Background, analyses and comparisons made between Balakirev's Piano Concerto in C-Sharp Minor and Tchaikovsky's Piano Concerto No. 1 in B-flat Minor. Musical examples.

BARBER, SAMUEL, 1910–1981

General

283.   Broder, Nathan. *Samuel Barber.* New York: G. Schirmer, 1954, 111 pp.
    Descriptive and critical discussion highlighting salient musical features. Musical examples.

284.   Fairleigh, James P. "Serialism in Barber's Solo Piano Works." *Piano Quarterly,* 18, no. 72 (1970): 13–17.
    Shows fusion of serial and tonal elements as a compositional device. Musical examples.

Concerto for Piano

285.   Broder, Nathan. "Current Chronicle: New York." *Musical Quarterly,* 49, no. 1 (1963): 93–97.
    Brief analytic/descriptive commentary of concerto, with emphasis on coloristic effects. Musical examples.

286.   Nelson, Wendell. *The Concerto,* 101–104. Dubuque, IA: William C. Brown, 1969.
Analysis with critical observations. Musical examples.

Sonata for Piano

287.   Chittum, Donald. "The Synthesis of Materials and Devices in Nonserial Counterpoint." *Music Review,* 31, no. 2 (1970): 123–135.
Analytic insights. Advanced. Musical examples.

288.   Tischler, Hans. *The Perceptive Music Listener,* 276–281. Englewood Cliffs, NJ: Prentice-Hall, 1955.
Analysis with musical examples.

Vanessa

289.   Freeman, John. "To Weep and Remember." *Opera News,* 29 (April 3, 1965): 24–25.
Brief descriptive overview of the opera, with occasional analytic observations. Musical examples.

DISSERTATIONS AND THESES

General

290.   Kreiling, Jean Louis. "The Songs of Samuel Barber: A Study in Literary Taste and Text-Setting." Ph.D., University of North Carolina at Chapel Hill, 1986, 379 pp., DA 47-1526A.

291.   Sifferman, James Philip. "Samuel Barber's Works for Solo Piano." D.M.A., University of Texas at Austin, 1982, 140 pp., DA 43-2151A.

Hermit Songs

292.   Davis, Alycia Kathleann. "Samuel Barber's *Hermit Songs,* Op. 19: An Analytic Study." M.M., Webster University, 1983, 101 pp., DA 22-63A.

Sonata for Piano

293.   Mathes, James Robert. "Texture and Musical Structure: An Analysis of First Movements of Select Twentieth-Century Piano Sonatas." Ph.D., Florida State University, 1986, 271 pp., DA 47-2363A.

BARTÓK, BÉLA, 1881–1945

General

294.   Antokoletz, Elliott. *The Music of Béla Bartók: A Study of Tonality and Progression in Twentieth-Century Music.* Berkeley: University of California Press, 1984, 342 pp.

Thorough analytic survey dwelling on harmonization of folk tunes, principles of symmetrical pitch construction, tonal centricity, and interaction of diatonic, octatonic, and whole-tone formations. Musical examples.

295.   Carner, Mosco. "Music in the Mainland of Europe: 1918–1939." In *The New Oxford History of Music.* Vol. 10. *The Modern Age: 1890–1960.* Edited by Martin Cooper, 274–299. London: Oxford University Press, 1974.

Stylistic overview discussing folk-song types, as established by Bartók, and influence of folk song in his compositions. Bartók's techniques further explored by analytic comments on the third and fourth string quartets. Musical examples.

296.   Ferguson, Donald N. *Image and Structure in Chamber Music,* 273–292. Minneapolis: University of Minnesota Press, 1964.

Solid critical and analytic discussion of the chamber music. Musical examples.

297.   Griffiths, Paul. *Bartók,* 115–127. London: J. M. Dent and Sons, 1984.

Analytic remarks and descriptive commentary on the concertos, *Out of Doors* and *Mikrokosmos.* Musical examples.

298.   Kroó, György. "A Guide to Bartók. Translated by R. Pataki and M. Steiner. London: Clematis Press, 1974, 249 pp.

Overview of Bartók's principal compositions. Some useful descriptive, critical, and analytic observations.

299.   Lendvai, Erno. *Béla Bartók: An Analysis of His Music.* London: Kahn and Averill, 1971, 115 pp.

Lendvai's monograph on the "Golden Section" and its use by Bartók as a basis for constructing scales, harmonies, and formal structures. Musical examples and diagrams.

300.   Lesznai, Lajos. *Bartók.* Translated by P. M. Young. London: J. M. Dent and Sons, 1973, 219 pp.

Mainly descriptive and critical commentary on Bartók's output, with some analytic observations intended for the undergraduate student. Musical examples.

301.   **McCabe, John.** *Bartók Orchestral Music.* London: British Broadcasting Corporation, 1975, 64 pp.
Descriptive, critical, and analytic overview of Bartók's principal works for orchestra. Intended for the undergraduate student. Musical examples.

302.   **Nordwall, Ova.** "Béla Bartók and Modern Music." *Studia Musicologica,* 9, nos. 3–4 (1967): 265–280.
Comprehensive analysis of many Bartók compositions, including the concertos.

303.   **Schmid, Angeline.** "Bartók's Rumanian Christmas Carols." *Clavier,* 20, no. 8 (1981): 30–31.
Stylistic overview, with performance suggestions. Musical examples.

304.   **Seiber, Mátyás.** "Béla Bartók's Chamber Music." In *Béla Bartók: A Memorial Review,* 23–35. New York: Boosey and Hawkes, 1950.
Solid analyses of the quartets and sonatas. Musical examples.

305.   **Stevens, Halsey.** *The Life and Music of Béla Bartók.* New York: Oxford University Press, 1953, 364 pp.
Thorough treatment of style, with scattered analytic insights. Musical examples.

306.   **Weismann, John.** "Bartók's Piano Music." In *Béla Bartók: A Memorial Review,* 60–71. New York: Boosey and Hawkes, 1950.
Descriptive commentary on all the piano works. No musical examples.

307.   **Whittall, Arnold.** *Music Since the First World War,* 31–50. London: J. M. Dent and Sons, 1977.
Analytic comments on Bartók's principal works. Musical examples.

Allegro Barbaro

308.   **Austin, William W.** *Music in the Twentieth Century.* N.Y.: W. W. Norton and Co., 1966, 230–235.
Analysis, comparing *Allegro Barbaro* with Bartók's Dirge No. 2 for Piano. Musical examples.

Bagatelles for Piano, Op. 6

309.   **Antokoletz, Elliott.** "The Musical Language of Bartók's Fourteen Bagatelles for Piano." *Tempo,* 137 (June 1981): 8–16.

43

Detailed analytic commentary demonstrating the evolution of Bartók's musical language from the folk modes to abstract pitch formations found in his compositions. Musical examples.

310.   **Purswell, Joan.** "Bartók's Early Music: Forecasting the Future." *Clavier,* 20, no. 8 (1981): 23–27.
Analytic observations with performance suggestions. Musical examples for Bagatelle No. 5 only.

Bagatelles for Piano, Op. 6, No. 8

311.   **Forte, Allen.** *Contemporary Tone-Structures,* 74–89. New York: Columbia University Press, 1955.
Thorough analysis dealing with formal structure, tonality, internal relationships, and general stylistic characteristics. Musical examples and analytic sketches.

Bagatelles for Piano, Op. 6, No. 9

312.   **Woodward, James E.** "Understanding Bartók's Bagatelle, Op. 6/9." *Indiana Theory Review,* 4, no. 2 (1981): 11–32.
Advanced analysis. Musical examples.

Bluebeard's Castle

313.   **Freeman, John W.** "Bartók's *Castle.*" *Opera News,* 35 (October 31, 1970): 6–7.
Brief description and critical commentary. Musical examples.

314.   **Griffiths, Paul.** *Bartók,* 59–65. London: J. M. Dent and Sons, 1984.
Analytic remarks, including a summary of the plot and discussion of its background. Musical examples.

315.   **Jellinek, George.** "First and Only—There Is a Significance in *Bluebeard's Castle* Being Bartók's Solitary Opera." *Opera News,* 39 (February 22, 1975): 11–13.
Brief discussion of background, style, harmonic idiom, musical and dramatic structure, and essential message of the opera.

316.   **Stevens, Halsey.** *The Life and Music of Béla Bartók.* 285–294. New York: Oxford University Press, 1953.
Well-rounded discussion of linguistics, plot, and musical features. Mentions some affective devices. Musical examples.

317. **Veress, Sandor.** *"Bluebeard's Castle."* In *Béla Bartók: A Memorial Review*, 36–53. New York: Boosey and Hawkes, 1950.
Thorough analysis. Treats plot, form, motives, tonalities, and style. Musical examples.

Cantata Profana

318. **Griffiths, Paul.** *Bartók*, 140–144. London: J. M. Dent and Sons, 1984.
Analytic remarks. Musical examples.

319. **Stevens, Halsey.** *The Life and Music of Béla Bartók.* 164–169. New York: Oxford University Press, 1964.
Analytic and critical commentary with musical examples.

Concertos

320. **Hill, Ralph, ed.** *The Concerto*, 327–356. London: Penguin Books 1952.
Critical and analytic commentary for the undergraduate student. Musical examples.

Concerto for Orchestra

321. **French, Gilbert G.** "Continuity and Discontinuity in Bartók's Concerto for Orchestra." *Music Review*, 28, no. 2 (1967): 122–134.
Thorough analysis focusing on psychological cohesion of the work.

322. **Griffiths, Paul.** *Bartók*, 175–178. London: J. M. Dent and Sons, 1984.
Analytic remarks. Musical examples.

323. **Hopkins, Antony.** *Talking About Concertos*, 135–144. London: Heinemann, 1964.
Extended analytic essay describing tonal, thematic, and formal events.

324. **Machlis, Joseph.** *Introduction to Contemporary Music*, 191–194. New York: W. W. Norton and Co., 1961.
Brief descriptive commentary with musical examples. For the beginning student.

325. **Suchoff, Benjamin, ed.** *Béla Bartók Essays*, 431. New York: St. Martin's Press, 1976.
Bartók's own brief analysis.

45

Concertos for Piano

326. **Meyer, John A.** "Beethoven and Bartók—A Structural Parallel." *Music Review,* 31, no. 4 (1970): 315–321.
Traces, in detail, Bartók's use of the scheme of Beethoven's Piano Concerto No. 4 as a model for his own piano concertos. Musical examples.

Concerto for Piano No. 2

327. **Bartók, Béla.** "The Second Piano Concerto." *Tempo,* 65 (Summer 1963): 4–7.
Bartók's own analysis (*see* item no. 329). Musical examples.

328. **Somfai, Laszlo.** "The Rondo-Like Sonata Form Exposition in the First Movement of the Piano Concerto No. 2." *New Hungarian Quarterly,* 22, no. 84 (1981): 86–92.
Traces and identifies editing errors in Bartók's analysis of his Piano Concerto No. 2. Should be read with the uncorrected editions of the analysis.

329. **Suchoff, Benjamin, ed.** *Béla Bartók Essays,* 419–423. New York: St. Martin's Press, 1976.
Bartók's own analysis with musical examples (*see* item no. 327).

330. **Watkins, Glenn.** *Soundings: Music in the Twentieth Century,* 438–441. New York: Schirmer Books, 1987.
Structural outline.

Concerto for Piano No. 3

331. **Meyer, John A.** "Beethoven and Bartók—A Structural Parallel." *Music Review,* 31, no. 4 (1970): 315–321.
Traces, in detail, Bartók's use of the scheme of Beethoven's Piano Concerto No. 4 as a model. Musical examples.

332. **Suchoff, Benjamin.** "Some Observations on Bartók's Third Piano Concerto." *Tempo,* 65 (Summer 1963): 8–10.
Brief observations of an analytic nature. Traces possible hints of Bartók's foreknowledge of his death during composition of this concerto.

333. **Ulrich, Homer.** *Music: A Design for Listening,* 430–432. New York: Harcourt, Brace, 1957.
Analytic/descriptive breakdown by measures. Musical examples.

Concerto for Viola

334. Dalton, David. "The Genesis of Bartók's Viola Concerto." *Music and Letters*, 57, no. 2 (1976): 117–129.

An interview with Tibor Serly and William Primrose, who were closely associated with this unfinished work at the time of the composer's death. Helps clarify the extent of outside influences in the concerto's composition.

335. Serly, Tibor. "A Belated Account of the Reconstruction of a Masterpiece." *College Music Symposium*, 15 (1975): 7–25.

The full account of the reconstruction of this uncompleted concerto, published posthumously. Musical examples.

Concerto for Violin No. 1

336. Mason, Colin. "Bartók's Early Violin Concerto." *Tempo*, 49 (Autumn 1958): 11–16.

Background with critical and analytic commentary. Musical examples.

Concerto for Violin No. 2

337. Bachmann, Peter J. "An Analysis of Béla Bartók's Music Through Fibonaccian Numbers and the Golden Mean." *Musical Quarterly*, 65, no. 1 (1979): 72–82.

A theory that the same mathematical model that underlies the structure of sunflowers, beehives, and other forms of nature is to be found in Bartók's music. An analysis of mathematical relationships found in this work supports the author's theory. Musical examples.

338. Griffiths, Paul. *Bartók*, 163–166. London: J. M. Dent and Sons, 1984.

Analytic remarks. Musical examples.

339. Kerman, Joseph. *Listen*, 341–346. 2d ed. New York: Worth Publishers, 1976,

Analysis with musical examples. For the undergraduate student.

340. Nelson, Wendell. *The Concerto*, 92–95. Dubuque, IA: William C. Brown, 1969.

Descriptive and critical commentary with musical examples.

47

341.   Payne, Elsie. "The Theme and Variation in Modern Music." *Music Review,* 19 (May 1958): 119–124.
    Analysis showing that the variations become more complex as the work progresses and then return to the simplicity of the introductory germinal material. Musical examples.

Contrasts

342.   Kárpáti, János. "Alternative Structures in Bartók's Contrasts." *Studia Musicologica,* 23, nos. 1–4 (1981): 201–207.
    Analysis demonstrating the compatibility of two different modes (polymodality), despite the coexistence of major and minor intervals.

Divertimento for String Orchestra

343.   Fenton, John. "Bartók's Divertimento (Set by London University)." *Music Teacher,* 59 (April 1980): 14–18.
    Thorough analysis with background and brief bibliography. Musical examples.

Duos (44). Book 2, No. 19 ("Fairy Tale")

344.   Dobszay, Laszló. "The Absorption of Folksong in Bartók's Composition." *Studia Musicologica,* 24, nos. 3–4 (1982): 303–313.
    A discussion of the techniques used in arranging a Transylvanian folksong into a piano piece. Also, a detailed analysis of this duet, and of the song on which it is based. Melodic structure of each; comments on form, tonality and rhythm. Complete score included.

Duos for Two Violins

345.   Warburton, A. O. "Set Works for 'O' Level, GCE." *Music Teacher,* 49 (December 1970): 12–14.
    Description and analysis for the undergraduate student.

Hungarian Peasant Songs

346.   Dumm, Robert. "A Bartók Ballad from Fifteen Hungarian Peasant Songs." *Clavier,* 15, no. 3 (1976): 33–37.
    Performer's analysis of Fifteen Hungarian Peasant Songs for Piano. Score of Ballad included.

Improvisations on Hungarian Peasant Songs, Op. 20

347. Wilson, Paul. "Concepts of Prolongation and Bartók's Opus 20." *Music Theory Spectrum,* 6 (1984): 79–89.
Discusses the evidence for long-range structure in these pieces and in Bartók's music generally. Uses Schenkerian terminology and diagrams. For the advanced. Musical examples.

Kossuth

348. Griffiths, Paul. *Bartók,* 11–13. London: J. M. Dent and Sons, 1984.
Analytic remarks. Musical examples.

Mikrokosmos

349. Elkin, Robert. "*Mikrokosmos*: An Analysis of Three Pieces by Bartók." *Music in Education,* 28, no. 308 (1964): 167.
"Free Variations," "From the Diary of a Fly," and the second of Six Dances in Bulgarian Rhythm analyzed briefly.

350. Franklin, Adele. "Comments on Béla Bartók's *Mikrokosmos.*" *Music Teacher,* 50 (June 1971): 9+.
Background and analytic commentary.

351. Starr, Lawrence. "Melody-Accompaniment Textures in the Music of Bartók, as Seen in His *Mikrokosmos.*" *Journal of Musicology,* 4, no. 1 (1985–1986): 91–104.
An exploration of Bartók's "unusual, often richly complex" textures in his accompaniments in *Mikrokosmos.* Musical examples.

352. Suchoff, Benjamin. "Bartók's Musical Microcosm." *Clavier,* 16, no. 5 (1977): 18–25.
Comments on background, style, and folk elements.

353. Suchoff, Benjamin. "Béla Bartók Contributions to Music Education." *Tempo,* 60 (Winter 1961–1962): 37–43.
Analytic and critical remarks. Musical examples.

354. Suchoff, Benjamin. "History of Béla Bartók's *Mikrokosmos.*" *Journal of Research in Music Education,* 7, no. 2 (1959): 185–196.
Historical background. Not a discussion of the music.

355. Warburton, A. O. "Set Works for 'O' Level, GCE." *Music Teacher and Piano Student,* 46 (May 1967): 17.
Analytic summary of Nos. 102, 103, 105, and 109.

49

Mikrokosmos. Book 3

356. Franklin, Adele. "Bartók: *Mikrokosmos*, Book 3." *Music Teacher*, 55 (December 1976): 12–13.
Analytic sketches of Nos. 69–92 for the undergraduate student. Musical examples.

Mikrokosmos. Book 4

357. Franklin, Adele. "Bartók: *Mikrokosmos*, Book 4." *Music Teacher*, 56 (January 1977): 17–18; (February 1977): 15–16.
Analytic discussion of Nos. 97–121. Musical examples.

358. Warburton, A. O. "Set Works for 'O' Level, GCE." *Music Teacher*, 49 (March 1970): 13–14+.
Analytic sketches of Nos. 97–111 for the undergraduate student.

359. Warburton, A. O. "Set Works for 'O' Level, GCE." *Music Teacher and Piano Student*, 46 (May 1967): 17.
Analyses of Nos. 102, 103, 105, and 109.

Mikrokosmos. Book 4: No. 99 ("Crossed Hands")

360. Cogan, Robert, and Pozzi Escot. *Sonic Design: The Nature of Sound and Music*, 176–181. Englewood Cliffs, NJ: Prentice-Hall, 1976.
Discusses note collections and cell distribution.

Mikrokosmos. Book 5

361. Travis, Roy. "Towards a New Concept of Tonality?" *Journal of Music Theory*, 3 (November 1959): 257–284.
Examines tonal coherence in modern music. Analyses of "Syncopation" and "Staccato" (pp. 273–281) are offered to support the thesis that "music is tonal when its motion unfolds through time a particular tone, interval, or chord." For the advanced student.

Mikrokosmos. Book 5: No. 131

362. Parks, Richard S. "Harmonic Resources in Bartók's 'Fourths.'" *Journal of Music Theory*, 25, no. 2 (1981): 245–247.
Set-theoretic discourse, with charts and musical examples for theoreticians. Advanced.

Mikrokosmos. Book 6

363. Bryant, Celia M. "The Music Lesson." *Clavier*, 5, no. 4 (1966): 33–36.
Analytic remarks, with a view toward performance. Complete score provided.

364. Warburton, A. O. "Set Works for 'O' Level, GCE." *Music Teacher*, 51 (November 1972): 16–17.
Descriptive and analytic commentary on Nos. 148–153.

Mikrokosmos. Book 6: No. 143 ("Divided Arpeggios")

365. Waldbauer, Ivan F. "Intellectual Construct and Tonal Direction in Bartók's 'Divided Arpeggios.'" *Studia Musicologica*, 24, nos. 3–4 (1982): 527–536.
The piece is viewed as a mechanical construct, which is symmetrical, and in a traditional tonal context, applying the theories of Schenker. Musical examples.

Miraculous Mandarin

366. Crow, Todd, ed. and comp. *Bartók Studies*, 22–38. Detroit: Information Coordinators, 1976.
Background, with analytic observations. Musical examples.

367. Griffiths, Paul. *Bartók*, 90–94. London: J. M. Dent and Sons, 1984.
Analytic remarks. Musical examples.

368. Vinton, John. "The Case of *The Miraculous Mandarin*." *Musical Quarterly*, 50, no. 1 (1964): 1–17.
Historical commentary and background information, with discussion of revisions of the score that were made in 1924. Musical examples.

Music for Strings, Percussion, and Celesta

369. Bachmann, Peter J. "An Analysis of Béla Bartók's Music Through Fibonaccian Numbers and the Golden Mean." *Musical Quarterly*, 65, no. 1 (1979): 72–82.
A theory that the same mathematical model that underlies the structure of sunflowers, beehives, and other nature forms is to be found in Bartók's music. An analysis of mathematical relationships found in this work supports the author's theory. Musical examples.

51

370. Chittum, Donald. "The Synthesis of Materials and Devices in Non-Serial Counterpoint." *Music Review,* 31, no. 2 (1970): 130–135.
Analysis. Musical examples.

371. Crow, Todd, ed. and comp. *Bartók Studies,* 43–44. Detroit: Information Coordinators, 1976.
Brief "golden mean" analysis showing underlying structure. Musical examples.

372. Deri, Otto. *Exploring Twentieth-Century Music,* 251–256. New York: Holt, Rinehart, and Winston, 1968.
Analysis with musical examples. For the intermediate student.

373. Griffiths, Paul. *Bartók,* 154–157. London: J. M. Dent and Sons, 1984.
Analytic remarks. Musical examples.

374. Hansen, Peter. *An Introduction to Twentieth-Century Music.* 2d ed, 242–245. Boston: Allyn and Bacon, 1967.
Descriptive commentary with analytic insights. For the beginning student. Musical examples.

375. Hartog, Howard, ed. *European Music in the Twentieth Century,* 33–39. London: Routledge and Kegan Paul, 1957.
Analysis for the undergraduate student.

376. Lendvai, Erno. "The Quadraphonic Stage of Bartók's Music for Strings, Percussion, and Celesta." *New Hungarian Quarterly,* 22, no. 84 (1981): 70–85.
A discussion of the inherent spatial quality of this composition. Explains how Bartók incorporated laws of natural growth into the structure of the composition by using the Fibonacci sequence.

377. Machlis, Joseph. *Introduction to Contemporary Music,* 194–196. New York: W. W. Norton, 1961.
Brief descriptive commentary with musical examples. For the beginning student.

378. Reti, Rudolph. *Tonality, Atonality, Pantonality: A Study of Some Trends in Twentieth Century Music,* 73–74, 77–78, 142–143. London: Rockliff, 1958.
Brief analytic comments on tonality. Third movement only. Musical examples.

379. Salzman, Eric. *Twentieth Century Music: An Introduction.* 2d ed., 217–219. Englewood Cliffs, NJ: Prentice-Hall, 1974.
Illustrates the accommodation of an intervallic chromaticism to modal/tonal music. Musical examples.

380.   Smith, Robert. "Béla Bartók's Music for Strings, Percussion, and Celesta." *Music Review*, 20 (August–November 1959): 264–276.
An in-depth formal and structural analysis. Musical examples.

381.   Warburton, A. O. "Set Works for 'O' Level, GCE." *Music Teacher and Piano Student*, 46 (May 1967): 17–18 + .
Brief descriptive commentary, with analytic observations.

Quartets for Strings

382.   Abraham, Gerald. *Slavonic and Romantic Music*, 339–349. New York: St. Martin's Press, 1968.
Traces Bartók's style in the quartets. Analytic, with musical examples.

383.   Carner, Mosco. *Major and Minor*, 92–121. New York: Holmes and Meier, 1980.
Background, remarks on style and artistic development seen in the quartets as a whole. Extended, individual analyses of each of the six quartets as well. Musical examples.

384.   Ferguson, Donald N. *Image and Structure in Chamber Music*, 273–292. Minneapolis: University of Minnesota Press, 1964.
Analyses of the six Quartets. Musical examples.

385.   Gow, David. "Tonality and Structure in Bartók's First Two String Quartets." *Music Review*, 34, nos. 3–4 (1973): 259–271.
Detailed analysis focusing on tonality as a structural device. Musical examples.

386.   Griffiths, Paul. *Bartók*, 128–135. London: J. M. Dent and Sons, 1984.
Analytic remarks on Quartets 3 and 4. Musical examples.

387.   Hartog, Howard, ed. *European Music in the Twentieth Century*, 14–25. London: Routledge and Kegan Paul, 1957.
Brief analyses of all six Quartets. For the undergraduate student.

388.   Kárpáti, János. *Bartók's String Quartets*. Translated by F. Macnicol. London: Barrie and Jenkins, 1975, 280 pp.
Thorough discussion of the six Quartets, including influences, musical characteristics, and analyses. Musical examples.

389.   Locke, Derek. "Numerical Aspects of Bartók's String Quartets." *Musical Times*, 128 (June 1987): 322–325.
Author applies the theory of the "Golden Section" to the string quartets. Arithmetical proportions related to the Fibonacci num-

bers observed in nature are revealed in the quartets (Golden Section). Examines the proportions of Quartets 4, 5, and 6 to demonstrate Bartók's use of the "Golden Section." Includes tables of numbers of beats, ratios, and other numerical symmetries.

390. Perle, George. "The String Quartets of Béla Bartók." In *A Musical Offering: Essays in Honor of Martin Bernstein*. Edited by Edward H. Clinkscale and Claire Brook, 193–210. New York: Pendragon Press, 1977.
  Background and brief but concentrated analyses of all six quartets. Musical examples.

391. Robertson, Alec, ed. *Chamber Music*, 220–252. Baltimore: Penguin Books, 1957.
  Thorough critical and analytic overview. Musical examples.

392. Suchoff, Benjamin, ed. *Béla Bartók Essays*, 412–415. New York: St. Martin's Press, 1976.
  Brief, highly condensed formal analyses with charts. Score needed.

393. Ulrich, Homer. *Chamber Music*. 2d ed., 355–357. New York: Columbia University Press, 1966.
  Brief summary of the characteristics of the quartets.

394. Watkins, Glenn. *Soundings: Music in the Twentieth Century*, 407–408. New York: Schirmer Books, 1987.
  Brief analytic comments on some important musical features of the Third, Fourth, and Fifth Quartets.

Quartet for Strings No. 1

395. Griffiths, Paul. *Bartók*, 49–51. London: J. M. Dent and Sons, 1984.
  Analytic remarks with musical examples.

Quartet for Strings No. 2

396. Griffiths, Paul. *Bartók*, 84–87. London: J. M. Dent and Sons, 1984.
  Analytic remarks with musical examples.

397. Suchoff, Benjamin. "Bartók Second String Quartet: Stylistic Landmark." *American Music Teacher*, 15, no. 2 (1965): 30–32.
  A brief analysis showing the major themes. Relates the composition to Eastern folk music. Musical examples.

398.   Whittall, Arnold. "Bartók's Second String Quartet." *Music Review*, 32, no. 3 (1971): 265–270.
    Analysis, with musical examples. Advanced discussion.

Quartet for Strings No. 3

399.   Berry, Wallace. "Symmetrical Interval Sets and Derivative Pitch Materials in Bartók's String Quartet No. 3." *Perspectives of New Music*, 18, nos. 1–2 (1980–1981): 287 + .
    Dense theoretical analysis demonstrating the function of tonality, interval sets, and pitch as structural devices in this quartet. Musical examples.

400.   Whittall, Arnold. *Music Since the First World War*, 33–42. London: J. M. Dent and Sons, 1977.
    Analytic discussion. Musical examples.

Quartet for Strings No. 4

401.   Antokoletz, Elliott. "Principles of Pitch Organization in Bartók's Fourth String Quartet." *In Theory Only*, 3 (September 1977): 3–22.

402.   Forte, Allen. "Bartók's 'Serial' Composition." *Musical Quarterly*, 46, no. 2 (1960): 233–245.
    An extensive and detailed analytical study with a discussion of serial aspects of this work. Musical examples.

403.   Forte, Allen. *Contemporary Tone-Structures*, 139–143. New York: Columbia University Press, 1955.
    Analysis dealing with formal structure, tonality, and technique. Musical examples and analytic sketches.

404.   Hansen, Peter. *An Introduction to Twentieth Century Music.* 2d ed., 237–242. Boston: Allyn and Bacon, 1967.
    Analysis for the undergraduate student. Musical examples.

405.   Monelle, Raymond. "Notes on Bartók's Fourth Quartet." *Music Review*, 29, no. 2 (1968): 123–129.
    Analysis focusing on form and structure. Musical examples.

406.   Perle, George. "Berg's Master Array of the Interval Cycles." *Musical Quarterly*, 63, no. 1 (1977): 13–17.
    Three symmetrical tetrachords are identified as basic cells of the Fourth Quartet. The permutations of these cells are traced mathematically. Advanced.

407. Salzman, Eric. *Twentieth Century Music: An Introduction.* 2d ed., 216–217. Englewood Cliffs, NJ: Prentice-Hall, 1974.
Identifies the intervallic content providing unity in the first movement. Musical examples.

408. Travis, Roy. "Tonal Coherence in the First Movement of Bartók's Fourth String Quartet." In *The Music Forum.* Edited by William J. Mitchell and Felix Salzer, 298–371. New York: Columbia University Press, 1970.
Advanced analysis of the first movement using Schenkerian concepts. Musical examples.

409. Treitler, Leo. "Harmonic Procedure in the Fourth Quartet of Béla Bartók." *Journal of Music Theory,* 3 (November 1959): 292–298.
Analysis of "specific pitch areas" important to the harmonic structure. Musical examples.

Quartet for Strings No. 5

410. Griffiths, Paul. *Bartók,* 146–151. London: J. M. Dent and Sons, 1984.
Analytic remarks. Musical examples.

411. Rosen, Charles. *Sonata Forms,* 330–335. W. W. Norton, 1980.
Discussion of the atonal analogue to sonata form in this work. Musical examples.

412. Winrow, Barbara. "Allegretto Con Differencia: A Study of the 'Barrel Organ' Episode in Bartók's Fifth Quartet." *Music Review,* 32, no. 2 (1971): 102–106.
Shows organic relationship of "barrel organ" episode to the whole. Musical examples.

Quartet for Strings No. 6

413. Austin, William W. *Music in the Twentieth Century,* 325–328. New York: W. W. Norton, 1966.
Descriptive and analytic commentary. Musical examples.

414. Griffiths, Paul. *Bartók,* 167–171. London: J. M. Dent and Sons, 1984.
Analytic remarks. Musical examples.

415. Suchoff, Benjamin. "Structure and Concept in Bartók's Sixth Quartet." *Tempo,* 83 (Winter 1967–1968): 2–11.
Evidence presented showing that the abrupt breaking off of the dance movement to lead into the "parlando rubato" section was a late revision in reaction to the invasion of Poland. Facsimiles.

416.   Vinton, John. "New Light on Bartók's Sixth Quartet." *Music Review*, 25, no. 3 (1964): 224–238.

An analysis of structure and form, with reference to the original draft of the quartet. Historical commentary as well. Musical examples.

417.   Whittall, Arnold. *Music Since the First World War*, 45–47. London: J. M. Dent and Sons, 1977.

Brief analytic comments. Musical examples.

Rumanian Christmas Carols

418.   Warburton, A. O. "Set Works for 'O' Level, GCE." *Music Teacher*, 49 (December 1970): 12–14.

Background, descriptive and analytic commentary for the undergraduate student. Musical examples.

Scherzo ("Burlesque")

419.   Mason, Colin. "Bartók's Scherzo for Piano and Orchestra." *Tempo*, 65 (Summer 1963): 10–13.

Analytical observations. Musical examples.

Sonata for Piano

420.   Burge, David. "Bartók's Piano Sonata." *Contemporary Keyboard*, 4 (September 1978): 56.

Analytic observations about the motivic material of the first movement, primarily to aid the performer. Score included.

Sonata for Two Pianos and Percussion

421.   Crow, Todd, ed. and comp. *Bartók Studies*, 40–43, 51 + . Detroit: Information Coordinators, 1976.

"Golden mean" analysis showing underlying structure and acoustic (overtone) system. Chart.

422.   Griffiths, Paul. *Bartók*, 158–161. London: J. M. Dent and Sons, 1984.

Analytic remarks. Musical examples.

Sonatas for Solo Violin Nos. 1 and 2

423.   Griffiths, Paul. *Bartók*, 101–105. London: J. M. Dent and Sons, 1984.

Analytic remarks. Musical examples.

Sonata for Solo Violin (1944)

424.   Griffiths, Paul. *Bartók,* 179–181. London: J. M. Dent and Sons, 1984.
Analytic remarks. Musical examples.

Sonata for Violin and Piano No. 1

425.   Kárpáti, János. "Tonal Divergences of Melody and Harmony: A Characteristic Device in Bartók's Musical Language." *Studia Musicologica,* 24, nos. 3–4 (1982): 373–380.
Author examines the use of the chain of thirds as an organizing feature of this work. Musical examples.

Sonata for Violin and Piano No. 2

426.   Samson, Jim. *Music in Transition: A Study of Tonal Expansion and Atonality, 1900–1920,* 51–55. New York: W. W. Norton, 1977.
Concise, advanced analysis. Musical examples.

Suite for Orchestra No. 2, Op. 4

427.   Waldbauer, Ivan F. "Bartók's Four Pieces for Two Pianos." *Tempo,* 53–54 (Spring–Summer 1960): 17–22.
Biographical background and stylistic observations on the orchestral Suite, with a description of the transcription for two pianos.

Suite for Piano, Op. 14

428.   Griffiths, Paul. *Bartók,* 80–82. London: J. M. Dent and Sons, 1984.
Analytic remarks. Musical examples.

Wooden Prince

429.   Griffiths, Paul. *Bartók,* 71–76. London: J. M. Dent and Sons, 1984.
Analytic remarks. Musical examples.

DISSERTATIONS AND THESES

General

430.   Campfield, Donald John. "A Study of Interval Configuration and Related Parameters in Selected Chromatic Melodies of Béla Bartók." D.M.A., Cornell University, 1985, 74 pp., DA 46-830A.

431.   **Knapp, Calvin Horace.** "A Study, Analysis and Performance of Representative Piano Works of Various Periods of Béla Bartók." Ed.D., Columbia University, 1973, 209 pp., DA 34-4825A.

Etudes, Op. 18

432.   **Kessler, Richard Carner.** "Béla Bartók's Etudes Op. 18: An Analysis for Performers." Mus.A.D., Boston University, 1984, 177 pp., DA 45-982A.

Improvisations on Hungarian Peasant Songs, Op. 20

433.   **Ng-Quinn, David.** "Improvisations on Hungarian Peasant Songs, Op. 20 for Solo Piano by Béla Bartók." D.M.A., Stanford University, 1984, 161 pp., DA 45-3023A.

Mikrokosmos

434.   **Hodges, Janice Kay.** "The Teaching Aspects of Bartók's *Mikrokosmos.*" D.M.A., University of Texas at Austin, 1974, 97 pp., DA 35-5444A-5A.

435.   **Skoog, James Alfred.** "Set Syntax in Béla Bartók's *Mikrokosmos.*" Ph.D., Indiana University, 1985, 225 pp., DA 47-342A.

Quartet for Strings No. 5

436.   **Bates, Karen Anne.** "The Fifth String Quartet of Béla Bartók: An Analysis Based on the Theories of Erno Lendvai." Ph.D., University of Arizona, 1986, 261 pp., DA 47-1103A.

Sonata for Piano (1926)

437.   **Waxman, Sheila.** "Béla Bartók's Sonata for Piano: An Analytical Study." D.M.A., Boston University, 1985, 186 pp., DA 47-17A.

Sonatas for Violin

438.   **Sidoti, Raymond Benjamin.** "The Violin Sonatas of Béla Bartók: An Epitome of the Composer's Development." D.M.A., Ohio State University, 1972, 55 pp., DA 33-17773A.

BAX, ARNOLD, 1883–1953

General

439. Aprahamian, Felix. *Bax: A Composer and His Times.* London: Scolar Press, 1983, 534 pp.

> Biography, with analytic discussion of the music. Musical examples.

440. Scott-Sutherland, Colin. *Arnold Bax.* London: J. M. Dent and Sons, 1973, 214 pp.

> Discussions of all the major works—particularly of the symphonies. Style, main themes, and form treated. More descriptive than analytic.

Symphonies

441. Simpson, Robert, ed. *The Symphony.* Vol. 2, 153–165. New York: Drake Publishers, 1972.

> Brief overview with descriptive and analytic comments. Musical examples.

BEACH, AMY, 1867–1944

DISSERTATIONS AND THESES

General

442. Miles, Marmaduke Sidney. "The Solo Piano Works of Mrs. H. H. A. Beach." D.M.A., Peabody Conservatory of Music, 1985, 175 pp., DA 46-1775A.

443. Piscitelli, Felicia Ann. "The Chamber Music of Mrs. H. H. A. Beach (1867–1944)." M.M., University of New Mexico, 1983, 85 pp., DA 22-384A.

BEETHOVEN, LUDWIG VAN, 1770–1827

General

444. Abraham, Gerald, ed. *The New Oxford History of Music,* Vol. 8. *The Age of Beethoven, 1790–1830.* London: Oxford University Press, 1982, 747 pp.

> Thorough discourse on Beethoven's compositions in all genres. Structure, harmony, form, tonality, and other musical elements are discussed in context. Strong coverage of historical back-

ground, influences, and Beethoven's place in history. Musical examples and bibliography.

445.   Arnold, Denis, and Nigel Fortune, eds. *The Beethoven Companion.* London: Faber and Faber, 1971, 542 pp.
Thorough discussion in symposium format of all genres of Beethoven's music, focusing on influences, style, idiomatic writing, structure, and harmony. Mention is also made of Beethoven's pianos. Musical examples.

446.   Bekker, Paul. *Beethoven.* Translated by M. M. Bozman. London: J. M. Dent and Sons, 1925, 391 pp.
Descriptive overview. Not analytic.

447.   Burk, John N. *The Life and Works of Beethoven.* New York: Random House, 1943, 469 pp.
Descriptive, program note–type treatment of Beethoven's output. Clear discussion of significant musical elements. Musical examples.

448.   Ferguson, Donald N. *Image and Structure in Chamber Music,* 75–133. Minneapolis: University of Minnesota Press, 1964.
Overview of the chamber music, with brief analyses. Musical examples.

449.   Ferguson, Donald N. *Piano Music of Six Great Composers,* 39–123. New York: Books for Libraries Press, 1947.
Descriptive, critical, and analytic commentary, showing stylistic growth of the composer. Many useful general remarks on sonata form as well. Musical examples.

450.   Fiske, Roger. *Beethoven Concertos and Overtures.* Seattle: University of Washington Press, 1970, 64 pp.
Compact analyses of all Beethoven's concertos and overtures. Musical examples.

451.   Johnson, Douglas. "1794–1795: Decisive Years in Beethoven's Early Development." In *Beethoven Studies 3.* Edited by Alan Tyson, 1–28. Cambridge: Cambridge University Press, 1982.
Beethoven's growing mastery in the distribution of thematic material throughout the musical texture and his facile use of polyphony anywhere in the movement; remote key relationships; organic relationships among the parts of a movement or work; use of instability within thematic statements as a way of sustaining momentum, as seen in the Piano Trios Op. 1; the Sonatas Op. 2, the C Major Piano Concerto, and other works of this period.

61

452. Matthews, Denis, ed. *Keyboard Music,* 168–185. New York: Praeger, 1972,
Background, historical perspective, stylistic traits, and critical observations on specific works. Musical examples.

453. Mellers, Wilfrid. *Beethoven and the Voice of God.* London: Faber and Faber, 1983, 453 pp.
Analyses of piano sonatas from all three periods of Beethoven's development, as well as the *Missa Solemnis.* In addition to the formal elements of music, Mellers attempts to penetrate the meaning of the music. Musical examples.

454. Riezler, Walter. *Beethoven.* Translated by G. D. Pitcock. 1936. Reprint. New York: Vienna House, 1972, 300 pp.
Basic analytic overview of Beethoven's principal works. In-depth analysis for the undergraduate of the *Eroica* Symphony (first movement). Musical examples.

455. Ringer, Alexander L. "Beethoven and the London Pianoforte School." In *The Creative World of Beethoven.* Edited by Paul Henry Lang, 240–256. New York: W. W. Norton, 1971.
Clear demonstration of the influence of London pianoforte school composers on Beethoven in his piano compositions. Musical examples.

456. Rosen, Charles. "The Piano as the Key to 'Late Beethoven.'" *Stereo Review,* 24 (June 1970): 69–71.
Beethoven's approach to keyboard writing and how he viewed the piano as a medium for his compositions.

457. Scherman, Thomas K., and Louis Biancolli, eds. *The Beethoven Companion.* New York: Doubleday, 1972, 1230 pp.
Comprehensive but light coverage of all genres of Beethoven's compositions. Program note–style commentaries highlighting significant musical features. Background and biographical information included.

458. Scott, Marion M. *Beethoven.* Revised by Sir Jack Westrup. London: J. M. Dent and Sons, 1974, 339 pp.
A typical "life and works" volume in the "Master Musician" series. There are brief discussions of all the major works, with some analytic comments. Musical examples.

459. Ulrich, Homer. *Chamber Music.* 2d ed., 217–262. New York: Columbia University Press, 1966.
Thorough survey of the chamber works, their background, influences, and style.

460. Wolff, Konrad. *Masters of the Keyboard: Individual Style Elements in the Piano Music of Bach, Haydn, Mozart, Beethoven, and Schubert,* 110–159. Bloomington: Indiana University Press, 1983.
Though mainly a discussion of keyboard style of interest to performers, there are occasional analytic comments of interest to undergraduate students. Musical examples.

An die ferne Geliebte

461. Bouman, Michael. "Some Notes on Beethoven's *An die ferne Geliebte.*" *NATS Bulletin,* 27, no. 2 (1970): 13 + .
Structural organization, role of the piano part, and strophic procedures discussed.

Andante con Variazioni, Op. 26

462. Cole, William. *The Form of Music: An Outline of Musical Designs Used by the Great Composers,* 146–147. London: Associated Board of the Royal Schools of Music, n.d.
Brief outline of the structure in table form.

Bagatelles

463. Cone, Edward T. "Beethoven's Experiments in Composition: The Late Bagatelles." In *Beethoven's Studies 2.* Edited by Alan Tyson, 84–105. London: Oxford University Press, 1977.
Close examination of formal, tonal, rhythmic, and structural experiments the author theorizes Beethoven was conducting in these compositions. Musical examples.

464. Lorince, Margaret. "The Beethoven Bagatelles." *American Music Teacher,* 32, no. 1 (1982): 8–11.
Overview of the bagatelles for the pianist. Analytic remarks are interspersed with performance suggestions. Musical examples.

Bagatelles, Op. 119, Nos. 7–11

465. Marston, Nicholas. "Trifles or a Multi-Trifle? Beethoven's Bagatelles, Op. 119, Nos. 7–11." *Music Analysis,* 5, nos. 2–3 (July–October 1985): 193–206.
An analytic discussion drawing distinctions between pieces in collections featuring closed forms and "multi-pieces," or pieces belonging to a larger group displaying unifying factors related to the group. A close examination of the motivic unity and overall tonal structure supports author's thesis. Musical examples.

Bagatelles, Op. 126

466. Schmalfeldt, Janet. "On the Relation of Analysis to Performance: Beethoven's Bagatelles Op. 126, Nos. 2 and 5." *Journal of Music Theory*, 29, no. 1 (1985): 1–31.
Analytic discussion of these two bagatelles. Uses Schenkerian methods and diagrams. Discussion is written from the differing viewpoints of the analyst and performer. Musical examples.

Bagatelle, Op. 126, No. 2 in G Minor

467. Dumm, Robert. "The Inner Meaning: An Analytic-Interpretive Lesson." *Clavier*, 2, no. 1 (1963): 22–25.
Analytic remarks with a view towards performance. Score included.

Bagatelle, WoO 60 in B-Flat Major

468. Dunsby, Jonathan. "A Bagatelle on Beethoven's WoO 60." *Music Analysis*, 3, no. 1 (1984): 57–68.
Theoretical analysis. For the advanced student. Musical examples.

The Battle of Victoria

469. Misch, Ludwig. *Beethoven Studies*, 153–166. Norman, OK: University of Oklahoma Press, 1953.
A traditionally discredited work placed in proper perspective. Critical commentary with musical examples.

Christ on the Mount of Olives

470. Tyson, Alan. "Beethoven's Oratorio." *Musical Times*, 111 (April 1970): 373–375.
Descriptive and critical commentary, with Beethoven's deafness and stylistic development considered. Musical examples.

471. Tyson, Alan. "The 1803 Version of Beethoven's *Christus am Ölberge*." *Musical Quarterly*, 56, no. 4 (1970): 551–584.
A discussion of versions. Musical examples.

Concertos

472. Fiske, Roger. *Beethoven Concertos and Overtures*. London: British Broadcasting Corp., n.d., 64 pp.
Brief analyses for the undergraduate student. Musical examples.

473.   Hill, Ralph, ed. *The Concerto*, 119–142. London: Penguin Books, 1952.

Critical and analytic commentary for the undergraduate student. Musical examples.

474.   Veinus, Abraham. *The Concerto.* Rev. ed., 127–153. New York: Dover Publications, 1964.

General discussion of social and historical factors affecting the concerto during Beethoven's time. Also, Beethoven's models and stylistic development are highlighted in individual works.

Concertos for Piano

475.   Robert, Walter. "The Piano Concertos." *Clavier*, 19, no. 9 (1980): 44–46.

Brief remarks on structure, cadenzas, and stylistic growth.

Concerto for Piano (1815, Unfinished)

476.   Lockwood, Lewis. "Beethoven's Unfinished Piano Concerto of 1815." *Musical Quarterly*, 56, no. 4 (1970): 624–646.

An investigation of the sketches for what would have been Beethoven's sixth piano concerto. Musical examples.

Concerto for Piano No. 1, Op. 15 in C Major

477.   Warburton, A. O. "Beethoven's Orchestral Works." *Music Teacher and Piano Student*, 38 (October 1959): 462 + .

Brief background and analysis for the undergraduate student.

Concerto for Piano No. 2, Op. 19 in B-Flat Major

478.   Hopkins, Antony. *Talking About Concertos*, 35–36. London: Heinemann, 1964.

Extended analytic essay describing tonal, thematic, and formal events.

Concerto for Piano No. 3, Op. 37 in C Minor

479.   Machlis, Joseph. *The Enjoyment of Music*, 291–294. New York: W. W. Norton, 1970.

Analytic overview for the undergraduate student. Musical examples.

480.   Nelson, Wendell. *The Concerto,* 36–40. Dubuque, IA: William C. Brown, 1969.

Background information, with a brief analysis and critical remarks. Musical examples.

481.   Warburton, A. O. "Set Works for 'O' Level, GCE." *Music Teacher,* 51 (July 1972): 24–25.

Descriptive and analytic commentary for the undergraduate student.

Concerto for Piano No. 4, Op. 58 in G Major

482.   Cone, Edward T. "Viewpoint: Beethoven's Orpheus—or Jander's." *Nineteenth Century Music,* 8, no. 3 (1985): 283–286.

A response to Jander's article cited below. Offers another interpretation of the second movement.

483.   Jander, Owen. "Beethoven's 'Orpheus in Hades': The Andante Con Moto of the Fourth Piano Concerto." *Nineteenth Century Music,* 8, no. 3 (1985): 195–212.

Suggests that this movement was composed with an "Orpheus and Euridice" program. Examines the evidence for this and describes the relationship between the speculative program and the musical structure. Musical examples.

484.   Meyer, John A. "Beethoven and Bartók—A Structural Parallel." *Music Review,* 31, no. 4 (1970): 315–321.

Traces, in detail, Bartók's use of the scheme of Beethoven's Fourth Piano Concerto as a model for his own piano concertos. Musical examples.

485.   Rosen, Charles. *The Classical Style: Haydn, Mozart, Beethoven.* Rev. ed., 387–392. London: Faber and Faber, 1976.

Analytic comments on specific passages and comparisons with works by Haydn and Mozart. Musical examples.

486.   Truscott, Harold. "Beethoven's Fourth Piano Concerto." *Music and Dance,* 50 (January 1960): 8–11.

Descriptive and critical remarks, with observations on the innovative aspects of this concerto. This article also found in *Monthly Musical Record* 88 (May–June 1958): 91–96.

487.   Warburton, A. O. "Set Works for 'O' Level, GCE." *Music Teacher,* 49 (August 1970): 13–14.

Background, descriptive, and analytic commentary for the undergraduate student.

Concerto for Piano No. 5, Op. 73 in E-Flat Major ("Emperor")

488. George, Graham. *Tonality and Musical Structure*, 141–144. New York: Praeger Publishers, 1970.
  Brief tonal analysis. Musical examples. Chart.

489. Green, Douglass M. *Form in Tonal Music*, 240–242. New York: Holt, Rinehart, and Winston, 1965.
  Compact analysis, with charts, symbols, and musical examples. First movement only.

490. Hopkins, Antony. *Talking About Concertos*, 61–73. London: Heinemann, 1964.
  Extended analytic essay describing tonal, thematic, and formal events.

491. Nelson, Wendell. *The Concerto*, 40–44. Dubuque, IA: William C. Brown, 1969.
  Brief analysis with critical remarks. Musical examples.

492. Rosen, Charles. *Sonata Forms*, 237–244. New York: W. W. Norton, 1980.
  Discussion of tonality and instrumentation in the exposition of the first movement. Musical examples.

Concerto for Violin, Op. 61 in D Major

493. Asher, De Witt. "The Beethoven Violin Concerto, Opus 61— History and Analysis." *American String Teacher*, 16, no. 4 (1966): 24–26.
  Background and descriptive commentary for the beginning student.

494. Cole, William. *The Form of Music: An Outline of Musical Designs Used by the Great Composers*, 74–79. London: Associated Board of the Royal Schools of Music, n.d.
  Brief outline of the structure in table form.

495. Hopkins, Antony. *Talking About Concertos*, 47–60. London: Heinemann, 1964.
  Extended analytic essay describing tonal, thematic, and formal events.

496. Nelson, Wendell. *The Concerto*, 44–48. Dubuque, IA: William C. Brown, 1969.
  Brief analysis, with critical remarks. Musical examples.

497.   Tyson, Alan. "The Textual Problems of Beethoven's Violin Concerto." *Musical Quarterly*, 53, no. 4 (1967): 482–502.
Examines the four available sources for the score of Op. 61 and some textually dubious passages. Compares Beethoven's Violin Concerto with his later arrangement of the work as a piano concerto. Not an analysis.

Coriolan Overture, Op. 62

498.   Tovey, Donald Francis. *Essays in Musical Analysis.* Vol. 4, 43–45. London: Oxford University Press, 1969.
Critical and analytic study with musical examples. For the undergraduate student.

Diabelli Variations, Op. 120

499.   Blom, Eric. *Classics Major and Minor: With Some Other Musical Ruminations*, 48–78. London: J. M. Dent and Sons, 1958.
Background and descriptive commentary, with analytic observations on each variation. Musical examples.

500.   Geiringer, Karl. "The Structure of Beethoven's *Diabelli* Variations." *Musical Quarterly*, 50, no. 4 (1964): 496–503.
Thorough structural analysis with diagram.

501.   Kinderman, William. "The Evolution and Structure of Beethoven's *Diabelli* Variations." *Journal of the American Musicological Society*, 35, no. 2 (1982): 306–328.
Analytic and historical, this article concentrates on the variations that were added late in composition (1822–1823). Musical examples.

502.   Leichtentritt, Hugo. *Musical Form*, 98–103. Cambridge, MA: Harvard University Press, 1959.
Analytic discussion displaying Beethoven's variation technique. Musical examples.

503.   Plantinga, Leon. *Romantic Music*, 57–60. New York: W. W. Norton, 1984.
Analytic comments. Musical examples.

504.   Porter, David H. "The Structure of Beethoven's *Diabelli* Variations, Op. 120." *Music Review*, 31, no. 4 (1970): 295–301.

A response to Geiringer's analysis (*see* item no. 500), in which the audible effects of the composition are taken into account along with the visual structural relationships perceived by the eye.

505. Tovey, Donald Francis. *Essays in Musical Analysis: Chamber Music*, 124–136. London: Oxford University Press, 1956.
Critical observations and analysis with musical examples.

506. Truscott, Harold. "The *Diabelli* Variations." *Musical Times*, 100 (March 1959): 139–140.
Brief survey of compositions using Diabelli's theme as a basis for variations.

Egmont Overture

507. Kerman, Joseph. *Listen.* 2d ed., 198–199. New York: Worth Publishers, 1976.
Brief analysis, with musical examples. For the undergraduate student.

508. Misch, Ludwig. *Beethoven Studies*, 76–105. Norman, OK: University of Oklahoma Press, 1953.
Survey of some analytic views, with emphasis on the thematic treatment. Advanced. Musical examples.

509. Tovey, Donald Francis. *Essays in Musical Analysis.* Vol. 4, 45–47. London: Oxford University Press, 1936.
Critical and analytic commentary with musical examples. For the undergraduate student.

Fidelio

510. Ashbrook, William. "Hero in Chains." *Opera News*, 24 (February 13, 1960): 4+.
Brief critical overview of the opera, with commentary on individual sections. Explores some reasons for the opera's neglect.

511. Berges, Ruth. "The Ideal Beloved." *Opera News*, 24 (February 13, 1960): 8–9.
Beethoven's views on women and the influence of those views on *Fidelio*.

512. Burk, John N. *The Life and Works of Beethoven*, 313–319. New York: Modern Library, 1953.
Short, descriptive commentary, with no musical examples.

513. Carner, Mosco. *Major and Minor,* 186–252. New York: Holmes and Meier, 1980.

Thorough discussion dealing with the genesis of the opera, influences and models, musical style, word setting, formal plan, tonality, motifs, and a musical comparison of the 1805, 1806, and 1814 versions. The three *Leonore* overtures and the overture to *Fidelio* are discussed as well. Musical examples.

514. Carner, Mosco. "Simone Mayr and His *L'Amor Coniugale.*" *Music and Letters,* 52, no. 3 (1971): 239–258.

A study in detail of Mayr's work as one of the three forerunners of Beethoven's *Fidelio.* Advanced.

515. Dean, Winton. "Beethoven and Opera." In *The Beethoven Companion.* Edited by Denis Arnold and Nigel Fortune, 331–381. London: Faber and Faber, 1971.

Complete background, with discussion of the many sketches and versions leading to the completed *Fidelio.* Also, influences found in *Fidelio* are traced. Not an analysis.

516. Dent, Edward J. *The Rise of Romantic Opera,* 125–134. Cambridge: Cambridge University Press, 1976.

Examination of romantic traits and tendencies. Critical remarks on music and observations on style.

517. Dickinson, A. E. F. *Beethoven,* 140–151. London: Thomas Nelson and Sons, 1941.

Background and critical remarks.

518. Donington, Robert. *The Opera,* 106–109. New York: Harcourt Brace Jovanovich, 1978.

Brief discussion of the dramatic and musical action. Includes a thumbnail analysis of the overture. Musical examples.

519. Harrison, John. "A Perilous Quest." *Opera News,* 36 (March 11, 1972): 24–25.

The three-part structure of *Fidelio* is viewed as a mythical undercurrent representing the heroine's journey from the world of domesticity to the world of danger and then back to the everyday world bearing the gift of liberty.

520. Kolodin, Irving. *The Interior Beethoven,* 188–199. New York: Alfred A. Knopf, 1975.

Traces the many changes leading to the finished *Fidelio.* Not an analysis, but a detailed commentary on Beethoven's creative process.

521.   **Lee, M. O.** "More Than an Opera: Beethoven's Fidelio Reaches Beyond Its Flaws to Exalt the Resilience of Man." *Opera News*, 44 (February 2, 1980): 14 + .

Brief evaluative commentary focusing on significant events in the opera. Useful for opinions on characterization and plot.

522.   **Mann, William.** "The Opera with Four Overtures." *About the House*, 4, no. 3 (1973): 54–55.

Brief background on how Beethoven came to compose four overtures to *Fidelio*.

523.   **Marek, George.** "Where Were You the Night of November 20, 1805?" *Opera News*, 35 (January 2, 1971): 24–26.

Historical setting in which *Fidelio* was composed. Comments on its premier reception.

524.   **Misch, Ludwig.** *Beethoven Studies*, 139–152. Norman, OK: University of Oklahoma Press, 1953.

The background of the four overtures to *Fidelio*. Not an analytic discussion of the music.

525.   **Nettl, Paul.** "On the Barricades." *Opera News*, 24 (February 13, 1960): 6–7.

Brief remarks on compositional background and Beethoven's sources for *Fidelio*.

526.   **Porter, Andrew.** "Paths of Glory." *Opera News*, 40 (February 7, 1976): 26–28.

Fidelio's roots in the French Revolution examined and speculation on why Beethoven wrote only one opera.

527.   **Sadie, Stanley.** *Beethoven*, 38–43. London: Faber and Faber, 1967.

Basic remarks on plot and music. Musical examples.

528.   **Scherman, Thomas K., and Louis Biancolli, eds.** *The Beethoven Companion*, 654–669. New York: Doubleday, 1972.

Background, plot summary, and analytic remarks by various writers on music.

529.   **Selden, Margery Stomne.** "The First Romantic?" *Opera News*, 24 (February 13, 1960): 12 + .

Cherubini's *Les Deux Journeés* may have been the model for *Fidelio*. The two operas are compared.

71

Fidelio Overture

530.   Tovey, Donald Francis. *Essays in Musical Analysis.* Vol. 4. London: Oxford University Press, 1936, 41–43.
   Brief critical and analytic remarks for the undergraduate student. Musical examples.

Für Elise

531.   Horton, John. "The Girl Who Never Was? Beethoven's 'Für Elise.' " *Music Teacher,* 60 (April 1981): 21.
   Brief analysis and speculation on Elise's identity. For the undergraduate student.

Grosse Fuge, Op. 133 in B-Flat Major

532.   Kirkendale, Warren. "The Great Fugue, Op. 133: Beethoven's 'Art of Fugue.' " *Acta Musicologica,* 35, no. 1 (1963): 14–24.
   Advanced analytic discussion.

533.   Laprade, Paul A. "Beethoven's Op. 133, the Grosse Fuge: An Examination of Thematic Material." *Triangle,* 79, no. 4 (1985): 17.
   Brief Schenkerian analysis of some thematic material. Musical examples.

534.   Misch, Ludwig. *Beethoven Studies,* 3–13. Norman, OK: University of Oklahoma Press, 1953.
   Analysis with musical examples.

535.   Ratner, Leonard. *Classic Music: Expression, Form, and Style,* 269–270. New York: Schirmer Books, 1980.
   Brief analytic comments.

Leonore Overtures

536.   Misch, Ludwig. *Beethoven Studies,* 139–152. Norman, OK: University of Oklahoma Press, 1953.
   Overview of reasons for revisions and the consequent four *Leonore* overtures.

Leonore Overture No. 1

537.   Tovey, Donald Francis. *Essays in Musical Analysis.* Vol. 4, 40–41. London: Oxford University Press, 1936.
   Brief critical and analytic remarks for the student. Musical examples.

538.   Tyson, Alan. "The Problem of Beethoven's 'First' *Leonore* Overture." *Journal of the American Musicological Society*, 28, no. 2 (1975): 292–334.

> A discussion of the reasons motivating Beethoven to write four overtures to *Fidelio*. Remarks on the place of *Leonore* No. 1 among the four overtures.

Leonore Overture No. 2

539.   Tovey, Donald Francis. *Essays in Musical Analysis.* Vol. 4, 28–40. London: Oxford University Press, 1936.
> Critical and analytic study, with musical examples. For the undergraduate student.

Leonore Overture No. 3

540.   Tovey, Donald Francis. *Essays in Musical Analysis.* Vol. 4, 28–40. London: Oxford University Press, 1936.
> Critical and analytic study, with musical examples. For the undergraduate student.

541.   Warburton, A. O. "Beethoven's Orchestral Works." *Music Teacher and Piano Student*, 38 (October 1959): 462.
> Brief background and analysis for the undergraduate student.

Masses

542.   Robertson, Alec. "Beethoven and the Liturgy." *Musical Times,* 111 (December 1970): 1260–1262.
> Beethoven's view of the liturgy as an explanation for some musical ideas. Musical examples.

Mass in C Major, Op. 86

543.   Knapp, J. Merrill. "Beethoven's Mass in C Major, Op. 86." In *Beethoven Essays: Studies in Honor of Elliot Forbes.* Edited by Lewis Lockwood and Phyllis Benjamin, 199–216. Cambridge, MA: Harvard University Press, 1984.
> Discusses background, text, structure, tonality, harmony, and the relationship between text and music. Musical examples.

544.   Stoltzfus, Fred. "Beethoven's Mass in C: Notes on History, Structure, and Performance Practice." *Choral Journal*, 23, no. 3 (1982): 26–30.

545.   Young, Percy M. *The Choral Tradition,* 205–213. New York: W. W. Norton, 1971.
Descriptive and critical remarks. Musical examples.

Missa Solemnis

546.   Cooper, Martin. *Beethoven: The Last Decade, 1817–1827,* 221–275. London: Oxford University Press, 1970.
Thorough discussion with analytic insights. Musical examples.

547.   Fiske, Roger. *Beethoven's "Missa Solemnis."* London: Paul Elek, 1979, 123 pp.
Thorough discussion focusing on background, composition history, analysis, and orchestration. Musical examples.

548.   Hutchings, Arthur. "Beethoven: Mass in D." *Music and Musicians,* 19 (December 1970): 30–36.
Thorough background and analysis. Musical examples.

549.   Kinderman, William. "Beethoven's Symbol for the Deity in the *Missa Solemnis* and the Ninth Symphony." *Nineteenth Century Music,* 9, no. 2 (1985): 102–118.
Discusses specific tonal sonorities in the Credo of the Mass; their genesis, interpretation (i.e., symbolism), structural importance, and the corresponding use of these sonorities in the "Benedictus" and the Ninth Symphony. Table showing structure of the Credo. Musical examples.

550.   Kirkendale, Warren. "New Roads to Old Ideas in Beethoven's *Missa Solemnis.*" *Musical Quarterly,* 56, no. 4 (1970): 665–701.
A discussion of both the traditional musical devices in liturgical settings as Beethoven used them and those he created. Provides insights into how Beethoven composed musical effects. Musical examples.

551.   Tovey, Donald Francis. *Essays in Musical Analysis.* Vol. 5, 161–184. London: Oxford University Press, 1937.
Thorough analytic and critical commentary for the informed student. Musical examples.

Namensfeier Overture

552.   Tovey, Donald Francis. *Essays in Musical Analysis.* Vol. 4, 47–50. London: Oxford University Press, 1936.
Critical and analytic study with musical examples. For the undergraduate student. Beware of an error in Tovey, giving the wrong opus number to this work. The correct number is Op. 115.

Quartets for Strings

553.   Cooke, Deryck. "The Unity of Beethoven's Late Quartets." *Music Review*, 24, no. 1 (1963): 30–49.
Analysis based on the premise that the set of five quartets constitutes a self-contained unity and that Beethoven viewed them as a single creative process. Musical examples.

554.   Cooper, Martin. *Beethoven: The Last Decade, 1817–1827*, 349–414. London: Oxford University Press, 1970.
Thorough critical and analytic overview of Opp. 127, 130, 131, 135. Musical examples.

555.   Drabkin, William. "Beethoven and the Open String." *Music Analysis*, 4, nos. 1–2 (1985): 15–28.
Discusses the open-string sonority in classical chamber music, especially that of Beethoven.

556.   Kerman, Joseph. *The Beethoven Quartets*. New York: Alfred A. Knopf, 1967, 386 pp.
Thorough discussion of all the quartets, including background, descriptive, and analytic commentary to demonstrate Beethoven's stylistic growth. Musical examples and diagrams.

557.   Lam, Basil. *Beethoven String Quartets*. 2 vols. London: British Broadcasting Corp., 1976.
Descriptive/analytic overview of all the string quartets. For the undergraduate student. Musical examples.

558.   Mann, Robert. "1770–1970—Beethoven's 200th year. 'Es muss sein.' " *Music Journal*, 28 (October 1970): 36 + .
Critical overview of entire string quartet output.

559.   Marliave, Joseph de. *Beethoven's Quartets*. New York: Dover Publications, 1961, 379 pp.
Full descriptions written for the undergraduate student highlighting significant musical features of each quartet. Musical examples.

560.   Radcliffe,   Philip. *Beethoven's   String   Quartets.* London: Hutchinson Publishing Group, 1965, 192 pp.
A survey of the quartets. An introductory chapter places the quartets in the context of the work of Beethoven's predecessors and contemporaries. Subsequent chapters discuss the quartets in chronological order and in analytic terms. Discusses structure, thematic content, style, tonality, and other unifying factors. Musical examples.

561. Rieseling, Robert A. "Motivic Structures in Beethoven's Late Quartets." In *Paul A. Pisk: Essays in His Honor.* Edited by John Glowacki, 141–162. Austin: University of Texas Press, 1966.

Analytic discourse for the advanced student. Musical examples.

562. Truscott, Harold. *Beethoven's Late String Quartets.* London: Dennis Dobson, 1968, 148 pp.

These essays are aimed at the informed general reader/listener. Descriptive commentary interspersed with analytic observations. Musical examples.

Quartet for Strings, Op. 18, No. 1 in F Major

563. Green, Michael D. "Beethoven's Path Toward Large-Scale Rhythmic Development: The Exposition of the First Movement of Opus 18, No. 1." *Indiana Theory Review,* 7, no. 1 (1986): 3–22.

564. Warburton, A. O. "Set Works for 'O' Level, GCE." *Music Teacher,* 52 (August 1973): 18–19.

Analysis for the student. To be used with score.

Quartet for Strings, Op. 18, No. 2 in G Major

565. Warburton, A. O. "Set Works for 'O' Level, GCE." *Music Teacher,* 48 (October 1969): 19–20 + .

Analysis for the student. To be used with score.

Quartet for Strings, Op. 59, No. 1 in F Major ("Razumovsky")

566. Greene, David B. *Temporal Processes in Beethoven's Music,* 72–97. New York: Gordon and Breach Science Publishers, 1982.

In-depth analysis focusing on temporal progression. Musical examples and chart. Discusses first movement only.

567. Ratner, Leonard. *Classic Music: Expression, Form, and Style,* 422–435. New York: Schirmer Books, 1980.

Treats first movement only. Analytic discussion of the texture, harmony, melodic characteristics, structure, plan of keys, phrase structure. Portrays this movement as one of Beethoven's most characteristic, impressive and worthy to be considered the high point of the classic style. Musical examples.

Quartet for Strings, Op. 59, No. 3 in C Major ("Razumovsky")

568.   Bruce, Robert. "The Lyrical Element in Schubert's Instrumental Forms." *Music Review*, 30, no. 2 (1969): 131–137.
A comparison of this work to Schubert's Quartet for Strings in C Minor, D.703, to show Schubert's lyrical emphasis as opposed to Beethoven's dramatic character.

569.   Hatten, I. Robert S. "An Approach to Ambiguity in the Opening of Beethoven's String Quartet, Op. 59, No. 3." *Indiana Theory Review*, 3, no. 3 (1980): 28–35.
A refutation of Schenker's analysis. For the advanced student. First movement only.

Quartet for Strings, Op. 127 in E-Flat Major

570.   George, Graham. *Tonality and Musical Structure*, 152–160. New York: Praeger, 1970.
Analysis focusing on tonality. Musical examples. Advanced.

Quartet for Strings, Op. 130 in B-Flat Major

571.   Brodbeck, David L., and J. Platoff. "Dissociation and Integration: The First Movement of Beethoven's Opus 130." *Nineteenth Century Music*, 7, no. 2 (1983): 149–162.
Detailed exploration of how Beethoven used traditional forms in an unconventional manner, leaving some expectations unfulfilled and, conversely, causing the unexpected to occur. The essay discusses how these introduced discontinuities are resolved. Musical examples.

572.   Dahlhaus, Carl. *Nineteenth-Century Music*. Translated by J. Bradford Robinson, 85–86. Berkeley: University of California Press, 1989.
Demonstrates that the vocal models underlying the Cavatina are adapted to the instrumental idiom through motivic connections. Remarks on form in the Cavatina. Advanced.

573.   George, Graham. *Tonality and Musical Structure*, 160–171. New York: Praeger, 1970.
Analysis focusing on tonality. Musical examples. Advanced.

574.   Ratner, Leonard. *Classic Music: Expression, Form, and Style*, 234–236. New York: Schirmer Books, 1980.
Brief analysis of the form in the first movement.

Quartet for Strings, Op. 131 in C-Sharp Minor

575. George, Graham. *Tonality and Musical Structure,* 101–106. New York: Praeger, 1970.
  Analysis concentrating on tonal structure only. The Grosse Fuge Op. 133 analyzed briefly for comparison. Musical examples and chart.

576. Glauert, Amanda. "The Double Perspective in Beethoven's Opus 131." *Nineteenth Century Music,* 4, no. 2 (1980): 113–120.
  Detailed examination of how Beethoven transcends established classical norms in this quartet by superimposing a more powerful order of his own over the traditional classical designs.

577. Plantinga, Leon. *Romantic Music,* 71–76. New York: W. W. Norton, 1984.
  Analytic discussion. Musical examples.

578. Ratner, Leonard. *Classic Music: Expression, Form, and Style,* 267–269. New York: Schirmer Books, 1980.
  Analytic comments on Beethoven's treatment of fugue. Musical examples.

Quartet for Strings, Op. 132 in A Minor

579. Greene, David B. *Temporal Processes in Beethoven's Music,* 142–180. New York: Gordon and Breach Science Publishers, 1982.
  In-depth analysis focusing on structure and temporal organization. Musical examples and charts.

Quartet for Strings, Op. 135 in F Major

580. Kramer, Jonathan D. "Multiple and Non-Linear Time in Beethoven's Opus 135." *Perspectives of New Music,* 11, no. 3 (1973): 122–145.
  Demonstrates that the musical events in Beethoven's work must be seen in terms of their musical relationship to one another, rather than in their physical linear placement (clock-time). In the work under discussion, a later event may infuse new significance on an earlier one, or an earlier event may skip across intervening events to complete a musical gesture. Author sees similarity in Beethoven's use of time to that of contemporary music. Musical examples.

581.   Lochhead, Judith. "The Temporal in Beethoven's Opus 135: When Are the Ends Beginnings?" *In Theory Only,* 4 (January 1979): 3–30.

The first ten measures examined for the temporal function. Advanced. Musical examples.

Quintet for Strings, Op. 29 in C Major

582.   Hatch, Christopher. "Thematic Interdependence in Two Finales by Beethoven." *Music Review,* 45, nos. 3–4 (1984): 194–207.

Thorough discussion of thematic kinships in the formal shaping of the movements. Musical examples.

Sonatas for Piano

583.   Blom, Eric. *Beethoven's Pianoforte Sonatas Discussed.* 1938. Reprint. New York: Da Capo Press, 1968, 251 pp.

Discusses all thirty-two sonatas in order. All movements are analyzed in turn: form, thematic ideas, important motives, tonal relationships, and other unifying factors. Musical examples.

584.   Brendel, Alfred. "Beethoven: Form and Psychology." *Music and Musicians,* 19 (June 1971): 20–24.

General remarks on style and composition procedure, with analytic observations.

585.   Cooper, Martin. *Beethoven: The Last Decade, 1817–1827,* 145–220. London: Oxford University Press, 1970.

Thorough descriptive commentary, with background information on the later sonatas. Interspersed with analytic observations. Musical examples.

586.   Dale, Kathleen. *Nineteenth-Century Piano Music: A Handbook for Pianists.* London: Oxford University Press, 1954, 320 pp.

Highlights stylistic traits and unique contributions to the literature of the piano. Form, harmony, and other musical aspects discussed in relation to style.

587.   Elder, Dean. "Alfred Brendel Talks About Beethoven." *Clavier,* 12, no. 9 (1973): 10–20.

Stylistic characteristics shared by all Beethoven's piano sonatas. Use of foreshortening, treatment of harmony, and inner psychological processes are discussed. Special attention given to Sonatas No. 22, Op. 54, and No. 32, Op. 111. Musical examples.

588.   Fischer, Edwin. *Beethoven's Pianoforte Sonatas.* London: Faber and Faber, 1959, 118 pp.
    Brief analytical comments on each sonata. Musical examples.

589.   Matthews, Denis. *Beethoven Piano Sonatas.* Seattle: University of Washington Press, 1969, 56 pp.
    Discussion of all the sonatas, showing Beethoven's development as a composer.

590.   McIntyre, Paul. "A Pathway Through the Beethoven Sonatas." *Piano Teacher*, 8, no. 2 (1965): 12–15.
    General description and characterization of the sonatas, with occasional analytic remarks.

591.   Reti, Rudolph. *Thematic Patterns in Sonatas of Beethoven.* New York: Macmillan, 1967, 204 pp.
    Advanced analyses demonstrating that in each work Beethoven established a thematic pattern. This pattern is seen as the keystone governing the entire architectural plan of the composition.

592.   Robertson, Alec, ed. *Chamber Music*, 262–267. Baltimore: Penguin Books, 1957.
    Critical remarks, with musical examples.

593.   Thompson, Harold. "An Evolutionary View of Neapolitan Formations in Beethoven's Pianoforte Sonatas." *College Music Symposium*, 20, no. 2 (1980): 144–162.
    Detailed examination of Beethoven's increasing mastery of Neapolitan chords in the sonatas. Musical examples.

594.   Tovey, Donald Francis. *A Companion to Beethoven's Pianoforte Sonatas.* London: Associated Board of the Royal Schools of Music, 1931, 284 pp.
    Bar-by-bar analyses of all the sonatas. Musical examples.

Sonata for Piano No. 1, Op. 2, No. 1 in F Minor

595.   Walton, Charles W. *Basic Forms in Music*, 52–56. Port Washington, NY: Alfred Publishing Co., 1974.
    Condensed analysis, with full musical quotation. No score needed. Second movement only.

Sonata for Piano No. 3, Op. 2, No. 3 in C Major

596.   Walton, Charles W. *Basic Forms in Music*, 65–76. Port Washington, NY: Alfred Publishing Co., 1974.
    Condensed analysis with complete score of the movement provided. Last movement only.

Sonata for Piano No. 4, Op. 7 in E-Flat Major

597.   Kamien, Roger. "Chromatic Details in Beethoven's Piano Sonata in E-Flat Major, Op. 7." *Music Review,* 35, no. 2 (1974): 149–156.
  Detailed discussion of the various functions that Beethoven makes the same chromatic tone perform. For instance, a passing tone at one point becomes the dominant of a new key at another; a chromatic tone in the tonic area is later heard as a progression to a remote key area. Other instances, supported by musical examples are treated.

Sonata for Piano No. 5, Op. 10, No. 1 in C Minor

598.   Cole, William. *The Form of Music: An Outline of Musical Designs Used by the Great Composers,* 45. London: Associated Board of the Royal Schools of Music, n.d.
  Brief outline of the structure in table form. Example of modified sonata form. Second movement only.

599.   Ricci, Robert. "The Division of the Pulse: Progressive and Retrogressive Rhythmic Forces." *In Theory Only,* 1 (November 1975): 13–19.

Sonata for Piano No. 7, Op. 10, No. 3 in D Major

600.   Imbrie, Andrew. " 'Extra' Measures and Metrical Ambiguity in Beethoven." In *Beethoven Studies.* Edited by Alan Tyson, 45–54. New York: W. W. Norton, 1973.
  Advanced analysis focusing on rhythmic characteristics. Musical examples.

601.   Reti, Rudolph. *Thematic Patterns in Sonatas of Beethoven,* 190–192. New York: Macmillan, 1967.
  Brief analytic comments on the prime thematic cells. Musical examples.

602.   Wintle, Christopher. "Kontra-Schenker: Largo e Mesto from Beethoven's Op. 10, No. 3." *Music Analysis,* 4, nos. 1–2 (1985): 145 + .
  Differing theoretical viewpoints explored in detail. Musical examples and bibliography.

Sonata for Piano No. 8, Op. 13 in C Minor ("Pathétique")

603.   Davie, Cedric Thorpe. *Musical Structure and Design,* 50–51. New York: Dover Publications, 1966.
  Measure-by-measure analysis of the slow movement as an example of rondo form. To be used with score.

81

604.   Kresky, Jeffrey. *Tonal Music: Twelve Analytic Studies,* 92–107. Bloomington: Indiana University Press, 1977.
  In-depth analysis of the second movement, dealing with small and large formal divisions and tonality. Advanced. Musical examples and diagrams.

605.   Newman, William S. "K. 457 and Op. 13—Two Related Masterpieces in C Minor." *Music Review,* 28, no. 1 (1967): 38–44.
  Demonstrates influence of Mozart's Piano Sonata in C Minor, K. 457, on Beethoven's *Pathétique* Sonata. Musical examples.

606.   Reti, Rudolph. *Thematic Patterns in Sonatas of Beethoven,* 15–94. New York: Macmillan, 1967.
  A very detailed analysis using principles expounded in Reti's *Thematic Process in Music.* Musical examples.

Sonata for Piano No. 9, Op. 14, No. 1 in E Major

607.   Cole, William. *The Form of Music: An Outline of Musical Designs Used by the Great Composers,* 42–43, 49–50. London: Associated Board of the Royal Schools of Music, n.d.
  Brief outline of the structure in table form.

608.   Reti, Rudolph. *Thematic Patterns in Sonatas of Beethoven,* 192–195. New York: Macmillan, 1967.
  Comments on how motifs can change their character depending on context. Musical examples.

Sonata for Piano No. 10, Op. 14, No. 2 in G Major

609.   Reti, Rudolph. *Thematic Patterns in Sonatas of Beethoven,* 195–198. New York: Macmillan, 1967.
  Analytic comments on thematic consistency and transformation. Musical examples.

Sonata for Piano No. 11, Op. 22 in B-Flat Major

610.   Williams, Edgar W. "Rehearings: Beethoven. In and About a Few Measures of Beethoven." *Nineteenth Century Music,* 7, no. 2 (1983): 143–148.
  A demonstration of an analytic technique emphasizing context and musical intent. Helps view nonchordal tones and other apparently anomalous musical gestures accurately. Musical examples.

Sonata for Piano No. 12, Op. 26 in A-Flat Major

611.   Davie, Cedric Thorpe. *Musical Structure and Design*, 133–135. New York: Dover Publications, 1966.

Measure-by-measure analysis to be used with score in hand.

Sonata for Piano No. 14, Op. 27, No. 2 in C-Sharp Minor ("Moonlight")

612.   Rogers, Michael R. "Rehearings: Chopin Prelude in A Minor, Op. 28, No. 2." *Nineteenth Century Music*, 4, no. 3 (1981): 248–250.

Evidence that harmonic and melodic events conform exactly to the overall rhythmic design of the first movement of this sonata. A "golden mean" analysis. Musical examples.

Sonata for Piano No. 15, Op. 28 in D Major

613.   Coren, Daniel. "Structural Relations Between Op. 28 and Op. 36." In *Beethoven Studies 2*. Edited by Alan Tyson, 66–83. London: Oxford University Press, 1977.

Detailed analysis of structure, tonality and formal scheme. Comparison made to Beethoven's Symphony No. 2, composed at about the same time in the same key. Musical examples.

Sonata for Piano No. 17, Op. 31, No. 2 in D Minor ("Tempest")

614.   Lerdahl, Fred, and Ray Jackendorff. *A Generative Theory of Tonal Music*, 255–257. Cambridge, MA: M.I.T. Press, 1983.

An analysis of motivic relationships using time-span reduction techniques. Diagrams and musical examples. Advanced.

615.   Misch, Ludwig. *Beethoven Studies*, 39–53. Norman, OK: University of Oklahoma Press, 1953.

Analytic considerations on a sonata that deviates from traditional form. Musical examples.

616.   Plantinga, Leon. *Romantic Music*, 32–37. New York: W. W. Norton, 1984.

Analytic comments. Musical examples.

617.   Reti, Rudolph. *Thematic Patterns in Sonatas of Beethoven*, 176–186. New York: Macmillan, 1967.

Examines the concept of "architectural resolution through motive dissolution" (i.e., how a basic thematic shape is reflected in the overall structure).

618. Warburton, A. O. "Set Works for 'O' Level, GCE." *Music Teacher*, 50 (July 1971): 13–14.
Descriptive and analytic commentary for the undergraduate student.

Sonata for Piano No. 18, Op. 31, No. 3 in E-Flat Major

619. Cogan, Robert, and Pozzi Escot. *Sonic Design: The Nature of Sound and Music*, 41–49. Englewood Cliffs, NJ: Prentice-Hall, 1976.
Analyzes "musical space." Graphs and musical examples. Only the opening of the piece is analyzed.

Sonata for Piano No. 19, Op. 49, No. 1 in G Minor

620. Walton, Charles W. *Basic Forms in Music*, 168–174. Port Washington, NY: Alfred Publishing Co., 1974.
Condensed analysis outline with score of movement provided. First movement only.

Sonata for Piano No. 21, Op. 53 in C Major ("Waldstein")

621. Chávez, Carlos. "Anatomic Analysis: Beethoven's *Waldstein* Op. 53." *Piano Quarterly*, 21, no. 82 (1973): 17–18.
Full diagrammatic analysis. Musical examples. First movement only.

622. Crain, Anthony J. "Problems in the Beethoven Literature." *Clavier*, 9, no. 1 (1970): 30–36.
Performer's analysis, with musical examples.

623. Davie, Cedric Thorpe. *Musical Structure and Design*, 51–52. New York: Dover Publications, 1966.
Measure-by-measure analysis to be used with score in hand. Rondo movement only.

624. Leichtentritt, Hugo. *Musical Form*, 118. Cambridge, MA: Harvard University Press, 1959.
Condensed analysis. Finale only.

625. Reti, Rudolph. *Thematic Patterns in Sonatas of Beethoven*, 166–175. New York: Macmillan, 1967.
An examination of thematic relationships. Shows that all the themes can be derived from one model. Musical examples.

626. Rosen, Charles. *The Classical Style: Haydn, Mozart, Beethoven.* Rev. ed., 396–399. London: Faber and Faber, 1976.

Analytic comments on thematic and harmonic characteristics in the first movement, with historical commentary. For the intermediate student. Musical examples.

627.   Schramm, Harold. "Beethoven's *Waldstein* and *Appassionata* Sonatas." *Piano Quarterly*, 19 no. 73 (1970): 18–19.
Descriptive and historical commentary on the two works. Focuses on the "new" romantic traits. Not analytic.

Sonata for Piano No. 22, Op. 54 in F Major

628.   Elder, Dean. "Alfred Brendel Talks About Beethoven." *Clavier*, 12, no. 9 (1973): 10–20.
General remarks on Beethoven's style in the sonatas and specific analytic remarks on Op. 54. Musical examples.

Sonata for Piano No. 23, Op. 57 in F Minor ("Appassionata")

629.   Carpenter, Patricia. "*Grundgestalt* as Tonal Function." *Music Theory Spectrum*, 5 (1983): 15–38.
Examines Schoenberg's *Grundgestalt* theory (i.e., "basic shape"). Theory is elaborated through application to the *Appassionata*. Discusses relationships and how the use of *Grundgestalt* functions "to make manifest that tonality." Musical examples. For the advanced student.

630.   Reti, Rudolph. *Thematic Patterns in Sonatas of Beethoven*, 95–126. New York: Macmillan, 1967.
A detailed analytic discussion of the thematic structure and form. Based on principles expounded in Reti's *Thematic Process in Music*. Musical examples.

631.   Rosen, Charles. *Sonata Forms*, 190–194. New York: W. W. Norton, 1980.
Discusses transformations of the principal motive in the first movement. Musical examples.

632.   Schramm, Harold. "Beethoven's *Waldstein* and *Appassionata* Sonatas." *Piano Quarterly*, 19, no. 73 (1970): 18–19.
Analytic remarks focusing on the "new" romantic traits.

633.   Tischler, Hans. *The Perceptive Music Listener*, 268–272. Englewood Cliffs, NJ: Prentice-Hall, 1955.
Analysis with musical examples.

Sonata for Piano No. 26, Op. 81a in E-Flat Major ("Les Adieux")

634. Rosen, Charles. *Sonata Forms*, 183–186. New York: W. W. Norton, 1980.
   Discussion of fragmentation in the first movement. Musical examples.

Sonata for Piano No. 27, Op. 90 in E Minor

635. Greene, David B. *Temporal Processes in Beethoven's Music*, 125–142. New York: Gordon and Breach Science Publishers, 1982.
   In-depth analysis focusing on temporality; that is, how the music organizes time to convey a sense of past, present, and future. First movement only. Musical examples. Chart.

Sonata for Piano No. 29, Op. 106 in B-Flat Major ("Hammerklavier")

636. Friedmann, Michael L. "Hexachordal Sources of Structure in Beethoven's *Hammerklavier* Sonata, Op. 106." *In Theory Only*, 4 (November–December 1978): 3–16.

637. Greene, David B. *Temporal Processes in Beethoven's Music*, 110–123. New York: Gordon and Breach Science Publishers, 1982.
   In-depth analysis focusing on how the musical ideas are organized to create a sense of past, present, and future. Musical examples.

638. Leichtentritt, Hugo. *Musical Form*, 326–339. Cambridge, MA: Harvard University Press, 1959.
   Exhaustive, intense analysis with musical examples.

639. Newman, William S. "Some Nineteenth-Century Consequences of Beethoven's *Hammerklavier* Sonata, Op. 106." *Piano Quarterly*, 17, no. 67 (1969): 12–18.
   An historical essay dwelling on performances of the work during Beethoven's lifetime, tracing influence of *Hammerklavier* on certain composers, especially Mendelssohn and Brahms. Musical examples.

640. Newman, William S. *"Hammerklavier* Sonata, Op. 106." *Piano Quarterly*, 17 no. 68 (1969): 12–17.
   A continuation of the above article (*see* item no. 639).

641. Rosen, Charles. *The Classical Style: Haydn, Mozart, Beethoven.* Rev. ed., 409–434. London: Faber and Faber, 1976.

A detailed analytic discussion of thematic content, tonal relationships, and structure. For the advanced student. Musical examples.

Sonata for Piano No. 30, Op. 109 in E Major

642. Bliss, Russell. "Late Beethoven: Playing Sonata Op. 109." *Clavier*, 15, no. 1 (1976): 19–22.
For the performer, but useful here for its analytic view. Musical examples.

643. Davie, Cedric Thorpe. *Musical Structure and Design*, 135–137. New York: Dover Publications, 1966.
Bar-by-bar analysis to be used with score in hand. Last movement only.

644. Forte, Allen. *The Compositional Matrix.* New York: Music Teachers National Association, 1961, 95 pp.
Book-length analysis of the first three movements and examination of the sketches. Not for the beginner. Musical examples.

645. Kerman, Joseph. *Listen.* 2d ed., 200–205. New York: Worth Publishers, 1976.
Analysis, with musical examples. For the undergraduate student.

646. Mulder, Michael. "An Unpublished Letter Treating the Piano Sonata, Op. 109 by Ludwig Van Beethoven." *In Theory Only*, 5 (May 1981): 16–20.
Analysis in the form of a mock letter from Beethoven. Formal proportions, tonal design, arpeggiation, and texture are explained. Musical examples.

Sonata for Piano No. 31, Op. 110 in A-Flat Major

647. Ashforth, Alden. "The Relationship of the Sixth in Beethoven's Piano Sonata, Opus 110." *Music Review*, 32, no. 2 (1971): 93–101.
Demonstrates that structural elements normally part of conventional analysis do not explain the "rightness" of sound of some baffling modulations in this sonata. The interval of the sixth is revealed to be the subtle, larger force behind these modulations. Musical examples.

648. Misch, Ludwig. *Beethoven Studies*, 54–75. Norman, OK: University of Oklahoma Press, 1953.
Analytic insights on an advanced level. Musical examples.

Sonata for Piano No. 32, Op. 111 in C Minor

649.   Hackman, Willis H. "Rhythmic Analysis as a Clue to Articulation in the Arietta of Beethoven's Op. 111." *Piano Quarterly*, 24, no. 93 (1976): 26–28.

650.   Rosen, Charles. *The Classical Style: Haydn, Mozart, Beethoven.* Rev. ed., 441–444, 446–448. London: Faber and Faber, 1976.
Analytic comments on the opening harmonies of the work. Also comments on the slow movement with respect to tempo and the passage of time. Musical examples.

Sonatas for Violin and Piano

651.   Robertson, Alec, ed. *Chamber Music*, 262–267. Baltimore: Penguin Books, 1957.
Critical remarks with musical examples.

Sonata for Violin and Piano, Op. 23 in A Minor

652.   Hatch, Christopher. "Thematic Interdependence in Two Finales by Beethoven." *Music Review*, 45, nos. 3–4 (1984): 194 + .
Thorough discussion of thematic kinships in the formal opening of the movements (Finales of Violin Sonatas Op. 29 in C Major and Op. 23 in A Minor). Musical examples.

Sonata for Violin and Piano, Op. 29 in C Major

653.   Hatch, Christopher. "Thematic Interdependence in Two Finales by Beethoven." *Music Review*, 45, nos. 3–4 (1984): 194 + .
Thorough discussion of thematic kinships in the formal opening of the movements (Finales of Violin Sonatas Op. 29 in C Major and Op. 23 in A Minor). Musical examples.

Sonata for Violin and Piano, Op. 47, in A Major ("Kreutzer")

654.   Reti, Rudolph. *Thematic Patterns in Sonatas of Beethoven*, 145–165. New York: Macmillan, 1967.
Examination of the relationship between a basic thematic idea and the form. Musical examples.

Sonata for Violin and Piano, Op. 96 in G Major

655. Obelkevich, Mary R. "The Growth of a Musical Idea—Beethoven's Opus 96." *Current Musicology,* 11 (1971): 91–114.
An examination of the creative process from the first rough draft to the polished work at completion. Musical examples.

Symphonies

656. Cuyler, Louise. *The Symphony,* 49–83. New York: Harcourt Brace Jovanovich, 1973.
All the symphonies. Good, analytic treatment with musical examples. Shows formal structure clearly.

657. Grove, George. *Beethoven and His Nine Symphonies.* 3d ed., 1898. Reprint. New York: Dover Publications, 1962, 407 pp.
Full treatment of the formal plan of all the symphonies. Some mention of the sketches and the creative process. Musical examples.

658. Hill, Ralph, ed. *The Symphony,* 92–125. Harmondsworth: Penguin Books, 1950.
All the symphonies. Light, brief treatment.

659. Hopkins, Antony. *The Nine Symphonies of Beethoven.* London: Heinemann, 1981, 290 pp.
All the symphonies analyzed to show structure, sonata form, thematic relationships, tonal unity, texture, and rhythmic patterns. For the undergraduate. Musical examples.

660. LaRue, Jan. "Harmonic Rhythm in the Beethoven Symphonies." *Music Review,* 18 (February 1957): 8–20.
A detailed look at the relationships between harmony and rhythm, revealing an enormously close integration of the two. Author feels that the unity so achieved partly explains the music's sense of inevitability. Musical examples.

661. Simpson, Robert. *Beethoven Symphonies.* Seattle: University of Washington Press, 1971, 62 pp.
Critical and analytic guide to all the symphonies. For the undergraduate student. Musical examples.

662. Simpson, Robert, ed. *The Symphony.* Vol. 1, 104–174. New York: Drake Publishers, 1972.
Thorough stylistic and analytic overview for the student. Musical examples.

663.   Stedman, Preston. *The Symphony*, 65–78. Englewood Cliffs, NJ: Prentice-Hall, 1979.

Brief description for the undergraduate of form, thematic unity, style, and tonality. Symphonies 1 through 6 and Symphony No. 9 discussed.

664.   Tovey, Donald Francis. *Essays in Musical Analysis.* Vol 1, 21–83. London: Oxford University Press, 1935.

Elevated, intelligent treatment meant for informed amateur. Objective, analytic approach to all the symphonies, including a bar-by-bar analysis of the Ninth Symphony.

Symphony No. 1, Op. 21 in C Major

665.   Haggin, B. H. *A Book of the Symphony*, 121–131. London: Oxford University Press, 1937.

Straightforward description dealing with formal plan only. Brief background remarks, with no discussion of tonality, rhythm, or texture. For the musical amateur or undergraduate student concerned with form. Musical examples.

666.   Hantz, Edwin. "A Pitch for Rhythm: Rhythmic Patterns in Beethoven's First Symphony: III (*Minuetto*)." *In Theory Only*, 1 (July 1975): 17–21.

Advanced analysis focusing on rhythmic patterns. Musical examples.

667.   Levarie, Sigmund. "Once More: The Slow Introduction to Beethoven's First Symphony." *Music Review*, 40, no. 3 (1979): 168–175.

Background and historical accuracy of the reports of its public reception examined, followed by an analysis and discussion of the organic relationship of the twelve-measure introduction to the rest of the movement. Musical examples.

668.   Pike, Lionel. *Beethoven, Sibelius, and the "Profound Logic": Studies in Symphonic Analysis*, 31–35. London: Athlone Press, 1978.

Brief tonal analysis demonstrating how enlarged structure caused the expansion of classical tonality. Musical examples.

Symphony No. 2, Op. 36 in D Major

669.   Haggin, B. H. *A Book of the Symphony*, 132–139. London: Oxford University Press, 1937.

Straightforward description dealing with formal plan only. Brief background remarks, with no discussion of tonality, rhythm, or texture. For the musical amateur or undergraduate student concerned with form. Musical examples.

670.   **Pazur, Robert.** "The Development of the Fourth Movement of Beethoven's Second Symphony Considered As a Variation of the Development of the First Movement." *In Theory Only*, 2 (April–May 1976): 3–4.
Advanced analysis with musical examples.

671.   **Pike, Lionel.** *Beethoven, Sibelius, and the "Profound Logic":* *Studies in Symphonic Analysis*, 35–38. London: Athlone Press, 1978.
Tonal analysis demonstrating how structural enlargement caused the expansion of classical tonality. Musical examples.

Symphony No. 3, Op. 55 in E-Flat Major ("Eroica")

672.   **Bernstein, Leonard.** *The Infinite Variety of Music*, 195–227. New York: Simon and Schuster, 1966.
Analysis, similar to Bernstein's television talks. Full discussion with many analytic insights for the undergraduate student and musical amateur. Musical examples.

673.   **Downs, Philip G.** "Beethoven's 'New Way' and the *Eroica*." *Musical Quarterly*, 56 (October 1970): 585–604.
Advanced analytic discussion focusing on Beethoven's techniques for formal expansion. Musical examples.

674.   **Eiseman, David.** "A Structural Model for the *Eroica* Finale?" *College Music Symposium*, 22, no. 2 (1982): 138–147.
Evidence presented that the unique structure of the Finale may have been inspired by Beethoven's studies of Bach. Musical examples.

675.   **George, Graham.** *Tonality and Musical Structure*, 89–93. New York: Praeger, 1970.
Tonality viewed as a principal unifying factor. Detailed, with musical examples.

676.   **Green, Douglass M.** *Form in Tonal Music*, 112–117. New York: Holt, Rinehart, and Winston, 1965.
Analysis focusing on variations. Musical examples. Chart.

677.   **Haggin, B. H.** *A Book of the Symphony*, 140–153. London: Oxford University Press, 1937.
Straightforward description dealing with formal plan only. Brief background remarks, with no discussion of tonality, rhythm, or texture. For the musical amateur or undergraduate student concerned with form. Musical examples.

91

678.   Lang, Paul Henry, ed. *The Creative World of Beethoven*, 83–102. New York: W. W. Norton, 1970.

Extensive treatment, emphasizing significance of structure and place of this symphony in Beethoven's style. Musical examples.

679.   Lockwood, Lewis. *"Eroica* Perspectives: Strategy and Design in the First Movement." In *Beethoven Studies 3*. Edited by Alan Tyson, 85–106. Cambridge: Cambridge University Press, 1982.

A summation of current views, with special focus on certain well-known and long-established analytic perspectives on the *Eroica*. Lockwood introduces new analytic insights on aspects that have been neglected. Musical examples.

680.   Meikle, Robert B. "Thematic Transformation in the First Movement of Beethoven's *Eroica* Symphony." *Music Review*, 32 (August 1971): 205–218.

The role of the "new" theme introduced in the development section and its relationship to the whole. Musical examples.

681.   Nadeau, Roland. *The Symphony: Structure and Style*, 88–100. Boston: Crescendo, 1973.

Measure-by-measure analysis of the entire symphony. Musical examples.

682.   Pike, Lionel. *Beethoven, Sibelius, and the "Profound Logic": Studies in Symphonic Analysis*, 39–47. London: Athlone Press, 1978.

Tonal analysis focusing on expansion of classical principles to accommodate unprecedented length of symphonic form. Musical examples.

683.   Plantinga, Leon. *Romantic Music*, 38–45. New York: W. W. Norton, 1984.

Analytic discussion. Musical examples.

684.   Ratner, Leonard. *Classic Music: Expression, Form, and Style*, 236–237, 258–259. New York: Schirmer Books, 1980.

Brief analytic comments on the form.

685.   Ringer, Alexander L. "Clementi and the *Eroica*." *Musical Quarterly*, 47, no. 4 (1961): 454–468.

Exploration of Beethoven's debt to Clementi for many of the ideas (particularly the main theme) found in the *Eroica*. Musical examples.

686.   Rosen, Charles. *The Classical Style: Haydn, Mozart, Beethoven,* 392–395. New York: Viking Press, 1971.
Discussion of the structural implications, unifying elements and expansion of classical sonata form as found in this symphony. Musical examples.

687.   Tischler, Hans. *The Perceptive Music Listener,* 347–352. Englewood Cliffs, NJ: Prentice-Hall, 1955.
Compact analysis, with musical examples.

688.   Ulrich, Homer. *Music: A Design for Listening,* 282–286. New York: Harcourt, Brace, 1957.
Descriptive/analytic breakdown by measures with analytic commentary. Musical examples.

Symphony No. 4, Op. 60 in B-Flat Major

689.   Haggin, B. H. *A Book of the Symphony,* 154–163. London: Oxford University Press, 1937.
Straightforward description dealing with formal plan only. Brief background remarks, with no discussion of tonality, rhythm, or texture. For the musical amateur or undergraduate student concerned with form. Musical examples.

690.   Pike, Lionel. *Beethoven, Sibelius, and the "Profound Logic": Studies in Symphonic Analysis,* 117–123. London: Athlone Press, 1978.
Analysis focusing on the importance of rhythm as a unifying device in this symphony. Mention also made of tonal and thematic elements. Musical examples.

Symphony No. 5, Op. 67 in C Minor

691.   Bernstein, Leonard. *The Joy of Music,* 73–93. New York: Simon and Schuster, 1959.
The script of Bernstein's television shows. Displays creative process in arriving at the final version. Discussion of sketches. Musical examples.

692.   Chusid, Martin. "Schubert's Cyclic Compositions of 1824." *Acta Musicologica,* 36, no. 1 (1964): 34–35.
Brief remarks on cyclic unity of this work in a comparison to Schubert's use of cyclic form.

693.   Forbes, Elliott, ed. *Ludwig Van Beethoven: Symphony No. 5 in C Minor.* Norton Critical Scores. New York: W. W. Norton, 1971. 202 pp.

Historical background, analysis, views of Beethoven's contemporaries. Full score and bibliography.

694.   Haggin, B. H. *A Book of the Symphony,* 164–172. London: Oxford University Press, 1937.

Straightforward description dealing with formal plan only. Brief background remarks, with no discussion of tonality, rhythm, or texture. For the musical amateur or undergraduate student concerned with form. Musical examples.

695.   Kerman, Joseph. *Listen,* 191–195. New York: Worth Publishers, 1972.

Analysis with musical examples. Intended for the undergraduate student.

696.   Machlis, Joseph. *The Enjoyment of Music.* 3d ed., 279–285. New York: W. W. Norton, 1970.

Analytic overview for the undergraduate music student. Musical examples.

697.   Pike, Lionel. *Beethoven, Sibelius, and the "Profound Logic": Studies in Symphonic Analysis,* 47–53, 146–155. London: Athlone Press, 1978.

Analysis focusing on interaction of rhythm, macrorhythm, and tonality. Also examines the tonal struggle to reach C major and the expansion of classical tonality. Musical examples.

Symphony No. 6, Op. 68 in F Major ("Pastoral")

698.   Haggin, B. H. *A Book of the Symphony,* 173–181. London: Oxford University Press, 1937.

Straightforward description dealing with formal plan only. Brief background remarks, with no discussion of tonality, rhythm, or texture. For the musical amateur or undergraduate student concerned with form. Musical examples.

699.   Kirby, Frank E. "Beethoven's *Pastoral* Symphony as a 'Sinfonia Caracteristica.' " *Musical Quarterly,* 56, no. 4 (1970): 605–623.

Demonstrates how Beethoven remained within the traditional framework of symphonic form, while superimposing musical devices such as bird calls, drones, and thunderstorm effects to convey a poetic, unifying idea. Musical examples.

700. Nadeau, Roland. *The Symphony: Structure and Style,* 193–215. Boston: Crescendo, 1973.

Score of first movement analytically marked to show structure and thematic treatment.

701. Pike, Lionel. *Beethoven, Sibelius, and the "Profound Logic": Studies in Symphonic Analysis,* 178–188. London: Athlone Press, 1978.

Analysis focusing on thematic, rhythmic, tonal, and harmonic features as they relate to the *Pastoral* programmatic idea.

702. Warburton, A. O. "Set Works for 'O' Level, GCE." *Music Teacher,* 47 (November 1968): 13–14+.

Measure-by-measure analysis for the intermediate student.

Symphony No. 7, Op. 92 in A Major

703. Below, Robert. "Some Aspects of Tonal Relationships in Beethoven's Seventh Symphony." *Music Review,* 37, no. 1 (1976): 1–4.

Concise, analytic commentary focusing on extraordinary importance of the dominant key. Score needed to follow argument.

704. Cooke, Deryck. "In Defence of Functional Analysis." *Musical Times,* 100 (September 1959): 456–460.

To demonstrate analytic technique, Cooke analyzes Beethoven's Symphony No. 7 in detail. Musical examples.

705. Haggin, B. H. *A Book of the Symphony,* 182–191. London: Oxford University Press, 1937.

Straightforward description dealing with formal plan only. Brief background remarks, with no discussion of tonality, rhythm, or texture. For the musical amateur or undergraduate student concerned with form. Musical examples.

706. Machlis, Joseph. *The Enjoyment of Music.* 3d ed., 287–291. New York: W. W. Norton, 1970.

Compact analysis for the student. Musical examples.

707. Pike, Lionel. *Beethoven, Sibelius, and the "Profound Logic": Studies in Symphonic Analysis,* 53–58, 164–169. London: Athlone Press, 1978.

Brief but concentrated analytic focus on the importance of rhythm, motion, and cessation of motion as a crucial structural device in this symphony. Also shows through a tonal analysis the tension between home and foreign keys and the expansion of classical tonality. Musical examples.

708.   Stedman, Preston. *The Symphony*, 78–85. Englewood Cliffs, NJ: Prentice-Hall, 1979.

Extended description of form, tonality, rhythmic structure, and thematic activity. Some commentary on instrumentation. Musical examples and diagrams.

709.   Temperley, Nicholas. "Schubert and Beethoven's Eight-Six Chord." *Nineteenth Century Music*, 5, no. 2 (1981): 142–154.

In showing how Schubert was influenced by Beethoven, a harmonic analysis of the trio movement of this symphony is included for comparison to Schubert. Musical examples.

Symphony No. 8, Op. 93 in F Major

710.   Anderson, William R. "A GCE Symphony." *Music Teacher and Piano Student*, 32 (April 1953): 192 + .

Descriptive commentary, with some analytic observations.

711.   Broyles, Michael. "Beethoven, Symphony No. 8." *Nineteenth Century Music*, 6, no. 1 (1982): 39–46.

In-depth analysis to explain a controversial movement (recapitulation of the first movement). Musical examples.

712.   Gauldin, Robert. "A Labyrinth of Fifths: The Last Movement of Beethoven's Eighth Symphony." *Indiana Theory Review*, 1, no. 3 (1978): 4–11.

Advanced analysis of the last movement refuting theory that it comprises a "coda" to a sonata-allegro. Musical examples.

713.   Haggin, B. H. *A Book of the Symphony*, 192–198. London: Oxford University Press, 1937.

Straightforward description dealing with formal plan only. Brief background remarks, with no discussion of tonality, rhythm, or texture. For the musical amateur or undergraduate student concerned with form. Musical examples.

714.   Pike, Lionel. *Beethoven, Sibelius, and the "Profound Logic": Studies in Symphonic Analysis*, 123–130. London: Athlone Press, 1978.

Tonal and rhythmic analysis emphasizing the importance of the number three in unifying this work. Musical examples.

715.   Ratner, Leonard. *Classic Music: Expression, Form, and Style*, 254–255. New York: Schirmer Books, 1980.

Brief analysis of form in the Finale.

716. Stedman, Preston. *The Symphony*, 85–91. Englewood Cliffs, NJ: Prentice-Hall, 1979.

Discussion of form, tonality, scoring, and thematic activity. Musical examples and diagram.

Symphony No. 9, Op. 125 in D Minor ("Choral")

717. Chittum, Donald. "Symphony of Psalms: Compositional Similarities in Beethoven and Stravinsky." *Music Review*, 30, no. 4 (1969): 285–290.

Discussion of similarity of motion and harmonic plan of Beethoven's Ninth Symphony and Stravinsky's *Symphony of Psalms*.

718. Cooper, Martin. *Beethoven: The Last Decade, 1817–1827*, 277–348. London: Oxford University Press, 1970.

Exhaustive treatment of entire symphony. Discussion on high level, with musical examples. Also treats Beethoven's creative process in the work, including some of his sketches for the symphony.

719. Friedheim, Philip. "On the Structural Integrity of Beethoven's Ninth Symphony." *Music Review*, 46, no. 2 (1985): 93–117.

An analytical study of the structure of the symphony. Shows the form of each movement "growing" from the preceding one and that this progression promotes the breakdown of traditional structural patterns in the last movement. Tables, musical examples.

720. Haggin, B. H. *A Book of the Symphony*, 199–217. London: Oxford University Press, 1937.

Straightforward description dealing with formal plan only. Brief background remarks, with no discussion of tonality, rhythm, or texture. For the musical amateur or undergraduate student concerned with form. Musical examples.

721. Hoyt, Reed J. "In Defence of Music Analysis." *Musical Quarterly*, 71, no. 1 (1985): 46–49.

In defending music analysis and refuting Treitler's analysis (*see* item no. 727) of this work, Hoyt includes many useful analytic insights.

722. Kirby, Frank E. "Beethoven and the 'geselliges Lied.' " *Music and Letters*, 47, no. 2 (1966): 116–125.

Advanced discussion of the choral portion of the Ninth Symphony. Specific remarks on Beethoven's intention in adding a choral movement to an instrumental work and the forms he drew upon.

723.   Pike, Lionel. *Beethoven, Sibelius, and the "Profound Logic":* *Studies in Symphonic Analysis,* 59–78, 155–169. London: Athlone Press, 1978.

An extensive examination of the pace and tension generated by rhythm, pauses, and tonality as well as a close look at the expansion of classical tonality and the consequent weakening of the dominant key. Demonstrates the crucial role that tonality plays in structural organization. Musical examples.

724.   Plantinga, Leon. *Romantic Music,* 63–69. New York: W. W. Norton, 1984.

Analytic comments. Musical examples.

725.   Sanders, Ernest H. "Form and Content in the Finale of Beethoven's Ninth Symphony." *Musical Quarterly,* 50, no. 1 (1964): 59–76.

Extensive analysis emphasizing tonality as the major binding force of this movement. Contains summary table of the structure. Musical examples.

726.   Tovey, Donald Francis. *Essays in Musical Analysis.* Vol. 2, 1–45. London: Oxford University Press, 1935.

Intelligent, clear treatment, including a thorough analysis. Vol. 1 has a shorter version of the analysis found here. Musical examples.

727.   Treitler, Leo. "History, Criticism, and Beethoven's Ninth Symphony." *Nineteenth Century Music,* 3, no. 3 (1980): 193–210.

Discourse on the function of analysis and criticism and how they explain Beethoven's Ninth Symphony. An attempt to probe the Symphony's underlying meaning, its musical effects, and the problem of the last movement. Advanced.

728.   Truscott, Harold. "The Ninth in Perspective." *Monthly Musical Record,* 88 (November–December 1958): 223–228.

An essay that attempts to show that Beethoven's Ninth Symphony is best seen as a product of the eighteenth century and not principally a nineteenth-century work. Contains some analytical observations in support of the thesis.

729.   Ulrich, Homer. *Music: A Design for Listening,* 290–292. New York: Harcourt, Brace, 1957.

Descriptive/analytic breakdown by measures. Musical examples.

730.   Vaughan Williams, Ralph. *Some Thoughts on Beethoven's "Choral" Symphony,* 1–52. London: Oxford University Press, 1959.

Observations by a famous composer on this work. Subjective musings with analytic observations on the entire Ninth Symphony.

Trio for Piano, Op. 1, No. 2 in G Major

731. Greene, David B. *Temporal Processes in Beethoven's Music*, 61–72. New York: Gordon and Breach Science Publishers, 1982.
  In-depth analysis focusing on proportions. Musical examples and chart. First Movement only.

Trio for Piano, Op. 97 in B-Flat Major ("Archduke")

732. Greene, David B. *Temporal Processes in Beethoven's Music*, 99–110. New York: Gordon and Breach Science Publishers, 1982.
  In-depth analysis focusing on temporal organization. Musical examples.

Variations (32) on an Original Theme in C Minor

733. Cantrell, Byron. "Three B's—Three Chaconnes." *Current Musicology*, 12 (1971): 67–69+.
  A brief look at the formal scheme, contrapuntal devices, rhythmic movement, and harmonic progression. Musical examples.

734. Davie, Cedric Thorpe. *Musical Structure and Design*, 123–126. New York: Dover Publications, 1966.
  Measure-by-measure analysis, to be used with score in hand.

735. Kochevitsky, George. "Beethoven's Thirty-two Variations in C Minor." *Clavier*, 6, no. 6 (1967): 37–43+.
  Performance notes, with descriptive and analytic commentary. Musical examples.

736. Leichtentritt, Hugo. *Musical Form*, 104–106. Cambridge, MA: Harvard University Press, 1959.
  Analysis, displaying Beethoven's variation techniques.

Variations on an Original Theme, Op. 34 in F Major

737. Tischler, Hans. *The Perceptive Music Listener*, 215–217. Englewood Cliffs, NJ: Prentice-Hall, 1955.
  Descriptive and analytic, with musical examples. Focuses on variation form.

Variations for Piano, Op. 35 in E-Flat Major ("Eroica Variations")

738. Derr, Ellwood S. "Beethoven's Long-Term Memory of C. P. E. Bach's Rondo in E Flat, W.61/1 (1787), Manifest in the Variations in

99

E-Flat for Piano Opus 35." *Musical Quarterly*, 70, no. 1 (1984): 45–76.
Point-by-point comparison showing that the variations have their
origins in Bach's Rondo. Musical examples.

739.   Tovey, Donald Francis. *Essays in Musical Analysis.* Vol. 6, 31–
35. London: Oxford University Press, 1969.
Analysis intended for the undergraduate student. Musical examples.

Wellington's Victory

740.   Donaldson, Byrna. "The Battle of Beethoven." *Instrumentalist*,
25 (December 1970): 30–31.
Brief historical background. Not an analysis. Bibliography.

DISSERTATIONS AND THESES

Diabelli Variations

741.   Kinderman, William Andrew. "Beethoven's 'Variations on a
Waltz by Diabelli': Genesis and Structure." Ph.D., University of California at Berkeley, 1980, 281 pp., DA 42-908A.

Quartets for Strings

742.   DeKenessey, Stefania Maria. "The Quartet, the Finale, and the
Fugue: A Study of Beethoven's Opus 130/133." Ph.D., Princeton University, 1984, 341 pp., DA 44-3198A.

Quartets for Strings, Op. 59

743.   Campbell, Bruce Benedict. "Beethoven's Quartets Op. 59: An
Investigation into Compositional Process." Ph.D., Yale University,
1982, 359 pp., DA 47-1917A.

Quartet for Strings, Op. 131 in C-Sharp Minor

744.   Crotty, John Edward. "Design and Harmonic Organization in
Beethoven's String Quartet, Op. 131." Ph.D., University of Rochester,
Eastman School of Music, 1986, 215 pp., DA 47-1104A.

745.   Dougherty, William Patrick. "An Examination of Semiotics in
Musical Analysis: The Neapolitan Complex in Beethoven's Op. 131."
Ph.D., Ohio State University, 1985, 258 pp, DA 46-2479A.

100

Sonatas for Piano

746.   Carr, Cassandra Irene. "Wit and Humor as a Dramatic Force in the Beethoven Sonatas." Ph.D., University of Washington, 1985, 309 pp., DA 47-1104A.

747.   Ralph, Bobbie Jeffers. "A Study of the Use of Contrapuntal Techniques in Selected Piano Sonatas of Ludwig Van Beethoven." Ph.D., University of Oklahoma, 1970, 205 pp., DA 31-2960A-61A.

Sonata for Piano No. 23, Op. 57 in F Minor ("Appassionata")

748.   Moore, William Howard. "The Cyclical Principle as Used in the Construction of Piano Sonatas." Ed.D., Columbia University, 1975, 189 pp, DA 36-1365A.

Sonatas for Violoncello and Piano

749.   Szabo, Edward Joseph. "The Violoncello-Piano Sonatas of Ludwig Van Beethoven." Ed.D., Columbia University, 1966, 149 pp., DA 31-418.

Trios for Piano

750.   Hiebert, Elfrieda Franz. "The Piano Trios of Beethoven: An Historical and Analytical Study." Ph.D., University of Wisconsin, 1970, 407 pp., DA 31-5447A.

BELLINI, VINCENZO, 1801–1835

General

751.   Dent, Edward J. *The Rise of Romantic Opera*, 162–175. Cambridge: Cambridge University Press, 1976.
Examination of Romantic traits and tendencies. Critical remarks on music and observations on style.

752.   Oliver, A. Richard. "Romanticism and Opera." *Symposium*, 23, nos. 3–4 (1969): 325–332.
Shows relationship of French melodrama at the beginning of the nineteenth century to the beginning of Romantic opera in western Europe, with special reference to Bellini.

753. Orrey, Leslie. *Bellini.* New York: Farrar, Straus, and Giroux, 1969, 176 pp.

Bellini's works from a musical point of view rather than a historical one. Discusses melodic style, influences, method of composition, and compares the melodic writing of Bellini and Chopin.

754. Weinstock, Herbert. *Vincenzo Bellini: His Life and His Operas.* New York: Alfred A. Knopf, 1971, 554 pp.

Background and descriptive commentary, with some musical examples. Not analytic.

Beatrice di Tenda

755. Borome, Joseph A. "Bellini and *Beatrice di Tenda.*" *Music and Letters*, 42, no. 4 (1961): 319–335.

Background, story synopsis, and act-by-act commentary, with musical examples.

Norma

756. Freeman, John W. "The Long Line." *Opera News*, 34 (April 4, 1970): 24–25.

Musical forms and melodic line are explained. Musical examples.

Pirata

757. Commons, Jeremy. "Bellini and the *Pirates.*" *Music and Musicians*, 14 (May 1966): 18–19.

Background, composition history, and critical remarks.

Puritani

758. Faria, Carlo. "A Cry of the Spirit." *Opera News*, 40 (February 28, 1976): 36–39.

The art of Bel Canto as seen in *I Puritani*. Musical examples.

759. Porter, Andrew. "Bellini's Last Opera." *Opera*, 11 (May 1960): 315–321.

Circumstances surrounding the composition of *I Puritani*. Little discussion of the music itself.

Sonnambula, La

760. Dahlhaus, Carl. *Nineteenth-Century Music.* Translated by J. Bradford Robinson, 117–120. Berkeley: University of California Press, 1989.

Brief but concentrated examination of the Andante Cantabile, "Ah! non credea mirarti." Form, meter, harmonic structure, motivic relationships uncover the basis for Bellini's long melodies. Musical examples. Advanced.

BERG, ALBAN, 1885–1935

General

761. **Carner, Mosco.** *Alban Berg: The Man and the Work.* New York: Holmes and Meier Publishers, 1975, 255 pp.
Analytic overview of all Berg's output. Musical examples.

762. **Carner, Mosco.** "Music in the Mainland of Europe: 1918–1939." In *The New Oxford History of Music.* Vol. 10, *The Modern Age: 1890–1960.* Edited by Martin Cooper, 362–372. London: Oxford University Press, 1974.
Stylistic overview with analytic descriptions of technique used in *Wozzeck, Lulu,* Chamber Concerto, Lyric Suite, and the Violin Concerto, which receives a brief analysis of its own. Musical examples.

763. **Jarman, Douglas.** *The Music of Alban Berg.* Berkeley: University of California Press, 1979, 266 pp.
Substantial analytic overview of Berg's output. Musical examples.

764. **Redlich, Hans.** *Alban Berg: The Man and His Music.* London: John Calder, 1957, 316 pp.
A "life and works" study, with detailed analytic studies on all Berg's major works. Musical examples.

765. **Reich, Willi.** *Alban Berg.* Translated by Cornelius Cardew. New York: Harcourt, Brace, and World, 1965.
General analytic essays on the major works. The works treated in most depth are *Wozzeck, Lulu,* Lyric Suite, Chamber Concerto, Violin Concerto. Also includes translations of three articles written by Berg. Musical examples and diagrams.

766. **Whittall, Arnold.** *Music Since the First World War,* 143–156. London: J. M. Dent, 1977.
Analytic comments on all his major works. Musical examples.

Chamber Concerto

767. **Carner, Mosco.** *Alban Berg: The Man and the Work,* 129–136. New York: Holmes and Meier, 1975.
Full discussion and analysis. Musical examples.

768.   Congdon, David. "Composition in Berg's 'Kammerkonzert.' " *Perspectives of New Music,* 24, no. 1 (1985): 234–269.
A detailed analysis. Concentrates on the Rondo. For the very advanced student. Musical examples, charts, tables.

769.   Leibowitz, René. *Schoenberg and His School.* Translated by Dika Newlin. 1949. Reprint, 154–156. New York: Da Capo Press, 1970.
Brief analysis. Musical examples.

770.   Nygren, Dennis Quentin. "The Chamber Music of Berg." *Clarinet,* 13, no. 3 (1986): 26–31.
Brief analyses of Four Pieces for Clarinet and Piano, Op. 5; the *Adagio* for Chamber Concerto arranged for violin, clarinet, and piano. Includes "suggestions for performers." Musical examples.

771.   Reich, Willi. *Alban Berg.* Translated by Cornelius Cardew, 143–148. New York: Harcourt, Brace, and World, 1965.
Thorough analysis by Berg.

Concerto for Violin

772.   Carner, Mosco. *Alban Berg: The Man and the Work,* 136–144. New York: Holmes and Meier, 1975.
Full discussion and analysis, with musical examples.

773.   Hansen, Peter. *An Introduction to Twentieth Century Music.* 2d ed., 124–216. Boston: Allyn and Bacon, 1967.
Brief remarks on important musical features. Musical examples.

774.   Hill, Ralph, ed. *The Concerto,* 362–379. London: Penguin Books, 1952.
Critical and analytic commentary for the undergraduate student. Musical examples.

775.   Hurd, Michael. "Berg: Violin Concerto." *Music in Education,* 38, no. 370 (1974): 270–273.
Detailed analysis with musical examples.

776.   Leibowitz, René. *Schoenberg and His School.* Translated by Dika Newlin. 1949. Reprint, 163–165. New York: Da Capo Press, 1970.
Brief outline of formal scheme. Musical examples.

777.   Machlis, Joseph. *Introduction to Contemporary Music,* 379–382. New York: W. W. Norton, 1961.
Brief, but compact analysis with musical examples. Easy-to-read style on a complex musical work. Meant for undergraduate student.

778. Redlich, Hans. *Alban Berg: The Man and His Music*, 203–214. London: John Calder, 1957.
Thorough analysis with musical examples. Advanced.

779. Reich, Willi. *Alban Berg*. Translated by Cornelius Cardew, 178–185. New York: Harcourt, Brace, and World, 1965.
Thorough analysis with musical examples.

780. Reti, Rudolph. *Tonality, Atonality, Pantonality: A Study of Some Trends in Twentieth Century Music*, 138–141. London: Rockliff, 1958.
A brief summary of Berg's twelve-tone technique. Musical examples.

781. Salzman, Eric. *Twentieth Century Music: An Introduction*. 2d ed., 225–226. Englewood Cliffs, NJ: Prentice-Hall, 1974.
Brief analysis of the synthesis of row techniques and tonality. Musical examples.

782. Taylor, Clifford. "The Contemporaneity of Music in History." *Music Review*, 24, no. 3 (1963): 205–217.
Music viewed in the context of its period. Comparison of Berg's methods (in Violin Concerto) and Mozart's (in Symphony No. 39) to illustrate how the period affected the music. Largely a philosophic discussion on style.

783. Warburton, A. O. *Analyses of Musical Classics*. Book 4, 247–260. London: Longman, 1974.
Full measure-by-measure analysis. Because there are no musical examples, it is necessary to have a score in hand for proper use of this analysis.

784. Watkins, Glenn. *Soundings: Music in the Twentieth Century*, 372–379. New York: Schirmer Books, 1987.
Chart of formal plan, prime set (tone row), and use of folk and chorale elements identified. Berg's secret program discussed. Musical examples.

Lulu

785. Carner, Mosco. *Alban Berg: The Man and the Work*, 195–242. New York: Holmes and Meier, 1975.
Thorough discussion and analysis with musical examples.

786. Hall, Patricia. "The Progress of a Method: Berg's Tone Rows for *Lulu*." *Musical Quarterly*, 71, no. 4 (1985): 500+.

787. Headlam, David. "The Derivation of Rows in *Lulu.*" *Perspectives of New Music*, 24, no. 1 (1985): 198–233.
Explains the derivations of the rows associated with different characters. Tables, musical examples. For the very advanced student.

788. Holloway, Robin. "The Complete *Lulu.*" *Tempo*, 129 (June 1979): 36–39.
Critical commentary on the newly revealed Act 3.

789. Jarman, Douglas. "Berg's Surrealistic Opera." *Music Review*, 31, no. 3 (1970): 232–240.
Background, analytic remarks with musical examples, and comparison of Berg's sources with the libretto.

790. Jarman, Douglas. "Dr. Schön's Five-Strophe Aria: Some Notes on Tonality and Pitch Association in Berg's *Lulu.*" *Perspectives of New Music*, 8, no. 2 (1970): 23–48.

791. Jarman, Douglas. "Rhythmic and Metric Technique in Alban Berg's *Lulu.*" *Musical Quarterly*, 56, no. 3 (1970): 349–366.
Advanced analytic commentary. Berg's use of rhythm as a structural element.

792. Krenek, Ernst. *Exploring Music.* Translated by Margaret Sheffield and Geoffrey Skelton, 113–122. New York: October House, 1966.
General discussion, mentioning Berg's treatment of Wedekind's original text, his tonal language and orchestration. Some comparison with *Wozzeck*. Not an analysis.

793. Leibowitz, René. *Schoenberg and His School.* Translated by Dika Newlin. 1949. Reprint, 160–162, 177–182. New York: Da Capo Press, 1970.
Capsule analysis of formal scheme is given on pp. 160–162. Extended discussion of relationship of musical form to plot, how musical devices portray characters, and overall unity of the work on pp. 177–182.

794. Perle, George. "The Character of *Lulu*: A Sequel." *Music Review*, 25, no. 4 (1964): 311–319.
A discussion of the character of Lulu as presented in the libretto and Berg's musical realization of that character in his work. Also, compares Berg's own final version with the usually performed earlier version.

795.   Perle, George. "A Note on Act 3 of *Lulu.*" *Perspectives of New Music*, 2, no. 2 (1964): 8–13.

A report on the manuscript material in Vienna. Contains some comments on form.

796.   Perle, George. "*Lulu*: The Formal Design." *Journal of the American Musicological Society*, 17, no. 2 (1964): 179–192.

Formal and structural analysis of the work. Score necessary.

797.   Perle, George. "*Lulu*: Thematic Material and Pitch Organization." *Music Review*, 26, no. 4 (1965): 269–302.

Extensive analysis for the advanced student. Musical examples.

798.   Perle, George. "Martyr to His Profession." *Opera News*, 49 (January 19, 1985): 10–13.

Structural aspects of *Lulu* and its place within the context of Berg's life.

799.   Perle, George. *The Operas of Alban Berg.* Vol. 2, *"Lulu"*. Berkeley: University of California Press, 1984, 313 pp.

Thorough book-length discussion of the opera. Traces its origins, examines text and formal design, symbolism in the music, and the musical language of the opera. Musical examples.

800.   Perle, George. *Serial Composition and Atonality: An Introduction to the Music of Schoenberg, Berg, and Webern.* 5th ed., rev., 135–145. Berkeley: University of California Press, 1981.

A discussion of the various series used in *Lulu*, relationships between them, and their structural functions. Musical examples.

801.   Redlich, Hans. *Alban Berg: The Man and His Music*, 163–202. London: John Calder, 1957.

Exhaustive analysis. Musical examples.

802.   Reich, Willi. *Alban Berg.* Translated by Cornelius Cardew, 156–177. New York: Harcourt, Brace, and World, 1965.

Exhaustive analysis, scene by scene.

803.   Steinberg, Michael. "An Essay in Virtuosity." *Opera News*, 41 (April 2, 1977): 33–35.

Analytic commentary focusing on structural features, text-articulation devices, and orchestration. Musical examples.

804.   Steiner, Eva. "Why *Lulu* Stayed Unfinished." *Music and Musicians*, 26 (April 1978): 28–29.

A letter by Schoenberg exploring reasons for the delay in the completion of *Lulu*.

805. Tortolano, William. "An Appreciation of Alban Berg and *Lulu.*" *NATS Bulletin,* 36, no. 1 (1979): 10–15.
   Critical and analytic commentary.

Lyric Suite

806. Bauer-Mengelberg, Stephen, and Melvin Ferentz. "On Eleven-Interval Twelve-Tone Rows." *Perspectives of New Music,* 3, no. 2 (1965): 93–103.

807. Ferguson, Donald N. *Image and Structure in Chamber Music,* 296–301. Minneapolis: University of Minnesota Press, 1964.
   Analysis. Musical examples.

808. Green, Douglass M. "The Allegro Misterioso of Berg's *Lyric* Suite." *Journal of the American Musicological Society,* 30, no. 3 (1977): 507–516.
   Analytic commentary for the advanced reader on structural uses of rhythm. Includes a table that breaks down the movement into its sections. Musical examples.

809. Green, Douglass M. "The Allegro Misterioso of Berg's *Lyric* Suite: Comments and Issues." *Journal of the American Musicological Society,* 33, no. 1 (1980): 211–212.
   More on Berg's use of rhythm (*see* item no. 808).

810. Hansen, Peter. *An Introduction to Twentieth Century Music.* 2d ed., 210–213. Boston: Allyn and Bacon, 1967.
   Descriptive commentary. For the beginning student. Musical examples.

811. Leibowitz, René. *Schoenberg and His School.* Translated by Dika Newlin. 1949. Reprint, 156–160. New York: Da Capo Press, 1970.
   Brief but solid analysis. Musical examples.

812. Perle, George. "The Secret Programme of the *Lyric* Suite." *Musical Times,* 118 (August 1977): 629–631; (September 1977): 709–713; (October 1977): 809 +.
   Microscopic examination of Berg's annotated manuscript to decipher clues. Cryptograms and number symbolism reveal the secret program of the *Lyric* Suite. Musical examples.

813. Redlich, Hans. *Alban Berg: The Man and His Music,* 137–154. London: John Calder, 1957.
   Thorough analysis, with musical examples.

814.   Reich, Willi. *Alban Berg.* Translated by Cornelius Cardew, 149–152. New York: Harcourt, Brace, and World, 1965.
Analysis.

815.   Straus, Joseph N. "Tristan and Berg's *Lyric* Suite." *In Theory Only,* 8, no. 3 (1984): 33–41.
Examines the influence of *Tristan und Isolde* on the *Lyric* Suite and the quotations from *Tristan* in the *Lyric* Suite. Musical examples.

Orchestral Songs (Five), Op. 4 ("Altenberg")

816.   Chadwick, Nicholas. "Thematic Integration in Berg's *Altenberg* Songs." *Music Review,* 29, no. 4 (1968): 300–304.
The theme as a unifying device. Musical examples.

817.   DeVoto, Mark. "Some Notes on the Unknown *Altenberg Lieder.*" *Perspectives of New Music,* 5, no. 1 (1966): 37–74.
Exhaustive analyses of songs No. 1 and 5. Musical examples.

818.   Watkins, Glenn. *Soundings: Music in the Twentieth Century,* 52–55, New York: Schirmer Books, 1987.
Compositional influences on Berg identified, followed by a description with analytic commentary. Musical examples and English and German words to the songs provided.

Pieces (Four) for Clarinet and Piano, Op. 5

819.   DeFotis, William. "Berg's Op. 5: Rehearsal Instructions." *Perspectives of New Music,* 17, no. 1 (1978): 131–137.
Analytic observations for the performer. Advanced. Musical examples.

820.   Nygren, Dennis Quentin. "The Chamber Music of Berg." *Clarinet,* 13, no. 3 (1986): 26–31.
Brief analyses of all four pieces. The *Adagio* from Berg's Chamber Concerto also analyzed briefly. Includes "suggestions for performers." Musical examples.

Pieces (Four) for Clarinet and Piano, Op. 5, No. 2

821.   Perone, James. "Tonal Implications and the Role of the Symmetrical Hexachord in Alban Berg's Four Pieces for Clarinet and Piano Opus 5, No. 2." *Interface,* 16, no. 1–2 (1987): 49–53.
Demonstrates that this is a veiled tonal piece. Uses a combination of Schenkerian and Forte-style set-theory techniques. For the advanced student. Musical examples.

Pieces (Four) for Clarinet and Piano, Op. 5, No. 3

822.   Lewis, C. "Tonal Focus in Atonal Music: Berg's Op. 5/3." *Music Theory Spectrum*, 3 (1981): 84–97.
   Berg's piece is analyzed in order to demonstrate the operation of a tonal focus in an atonal work. Forte's set theory notation is utilized. For the advanced student.

Pieces (Three) for Orchestra, Op. 6

823.   Carner, Mosco. *Alban Berg: The Man and the Work*, 124–127. New York: Holmes and Meier, 1975.
   Background, description, and analytic remarks.

824.   DeVoto, Mark. "Alban Berg's Marche Macabre." *Perspectives of New Music*, 22, nos. 1–2 (1984): 386 + .
   Thorough analytic dissection. Musical examples.

825.   Watkins, Glenn. *Soundings: Music in the Twentieth Century*, 55–60. New York: Schirmer Books, 1987.
   Compositional influences on Berg identified followed by description with analytic commentary. Musical examples.

Pieces (Three) for Orchestra, Op. 6, No. 1

826.   Micznic, Vera. "Gesture as Sign: A Semiotic Interpretation of Berg's Op. 6, No. 1." *In Theory Only*, 9, no. 4 (1986): 19–35.
   Intensive analysis seeking to identify and decode connotative signs. Musical examples.

Quartets for Strings

827.   Murray, Robert. "A Closer Look at the Berg Quartets." *American String Teacher*, 33, no. 2 (1983): 16–20.
   Analyses with musical examples.

828.   Redlich, Hans. *Alban Berg: The Man and His Music*, 49–55. London: John Calder, 1957.
   Concise analytic commentary. Musical examples.

Quartet for Strings, Op. 3

829.   Leibowitz, René. *Schoenberg and His School.* Translated by Dika Newlin. 1949. Reprint, 145–148. New York: Da Capo Press, 1970.
   Brief analysis. Musical examples

Sonata for Piano, Op. 1

830.   Leibowitz, René. *Schoenberg and His School.* Translated by Dika Newlin. 1949. Reprint, 140–144. New York: Da Capo Press, 1970.
Brief analysis and comparison to Schoenberg. Musical examples.

831.   Matthews, Denis, ed. *Keyboard Music,* 327–328. New York: Praeger Publishers, 1972.
Brief critical and analytic discussion. Musical examples.

832.   Redlich, Hans. *Alban Berg: The Man and His Music,* 47–49. London: John Calder, 1957.
Brief analysis. Musical examples.

833.   Samson, Jim. *Music in Transition: A Study of Tonal Expansion and Atonality, 1900–1920,* 117–121. New York: W. W. Norton, 1977.
Concise, advanced analysis of the first eleven measures establishes the stylistic premises for the work as a whole. Musical examples.

Songs (Four), Op. 2

834.   Samson, Jim. *Music in Transition: A Study of Tonal Expansion and Atonality, 1900–1920,* 121–126. New York: W. W. Norton, 1977.
Analytic description of harmonic features conveying a sense of unity. Musical examples.

835.   Wennerstrom, M. H. "Pitch Relationships in Berg's Songs, Op. 2." *Indiana Theory Review,* 1, no. 1 (1977): 12–22.

Songs (Four), Op. 2, No. 2

836.   Ayrery, Craig. "Berg's *Scheideweg*: Analytical Issues in Op. 2/2." *Music Analysis,* 1, no. 2 (1982): 189–202.
Tonal links examined for their impact on the structure of the piece. Musical examples.

Songs (Four), Op. 2, No. 4

837.   Stuckenschmidt, H. H. "Debussy or Berg?: The Mystery of Chord Progression." *Musical Quarterly,* 51, no. 3 (1965): 453–459.
Analytic discussion on influence of Debussy on Berg. Musical examples.

Wozzeck

838.   Carner, Mosco. *Alban Berg: The Man and the Work,* 145–194. New York: Holmes and Meier, 1975.
Thorough discussion and analysis, with musical examples.

839. Chittum, Donald. "The Triple Fugue in Berg's *Wozzeck.*" *Music Review,* 28, no. 1 (1970): 52–62.
Detailed musical analysis with musical examples of Act II, Scene II.

840. Davies, Laurence. *Paths to Modern Music: Aspects of Music from Wagner to the Present Day,* 87–99. London: Barrie and Jenkins, 1971.
Discussion centers on the literary aspects and musical devices used to enhance drama.

841. Deri, Otto. *Exploring Twentieth-Century Music,* 331–343. New York: Holt, Rinehart, and Winston, 1968.
Analysis with musical examples. For the intermediate student.

842. Donington, Robert. *The Opera,* 201–204. New York: Harcourt Brace Jovanovich, 1978.
Observations on the dramatic and musical action. Structure, tonality, and form discussed briefly. Musical examples.

843. Forte, Allen. "Pitch-Class Set Analysis Today." *Music Analysis,* 4, nos. 1–2 (1985): 29–58.

844. Forte, Allen. "Tonality, Symbol, and Structural Levels in Berg's *Wozzeck.*" *Musical Quarterly,* 71, no. 4 (1985): 474–499.

845. Freeman, John W. "The Man Who Feels." *Opera News,* 33 (April 12, 1969): 24–25.
Background, musical structure, musical devices, and characterization briefly treated. Musical examples.

846. Hansen, Peter. *An Introduction to Twentieth Century Music.* 2d ed., 207–210. Boston: Allyn and Bacon, 1967.
Plot description accompanied by condensed musical analysis. Mentions Berg's use of instruments and musical devices to achieve drama and unity.

847. Holmberg, Arthur. "Core of Loneliness." *Opera News,* 44 (March 8, 1980): 20–23.
Background and essential message of the play *Woyzeck* and how Berg adapted it to his needs.

848. Klein, John W. "*Wozzeck*—A Summing Up." *Music and Letters,* 44, no. 2 (1963): 132–139.
Background, plot strengths and weaknesses, Berg's musical relationship to Schoenberg.

849. **Leibowitz, René.** *Schoenberg and His School.* Translated by Dika Newlin. 1949. Reprint, 171–177. New York: Da Capo Press, 1970.
Analysis. Musical examples.

850. **Machlis, Joseph.** *Introduction to Contemporary Music,* 371–382, New York: W. W. Norton, 1961.
Descriptive commentary with analytic insights. For the undergraduate student and musical amateur.

851. **Perle, George.** "Martyr to His Profession." *Opera News,* 49 (January 19, 1985): 10–13.
Structural aspects of *Wozzeck* and its place within the context of Berg's life.

852. **Perle, George.** "The Musical Language of *Wozzeck.*" In *The Music Forum.* Vol. 1. Edited by William J. Mitchell and Felix Salzer, 204–259. New York: Columbia University Press, 1967.
Technical discussion on organizational elements used in place of tonality and how a tonal center may be achieved by atonal means. Shows that whole tone patterns and scale segments are other units of Berg's musical vocabulary.

853. **Perle, George.** *The Operas of Alban Berg.* Vol. 1, *"Wozzeck."* Berkeley: University of California Press, 1980, 231 pp.
A comprehensive study of the opera. Discusses the compositional background, the development of the libretto from Büchner's play *Woyzeck,* the formal structure of the opera, leitmotives, and other musical symbolism. The musical analysis includes discussion of pitch organization, rhythm and tempo. Musical examples and diagrams.

854. **Perle, George.** "Representation and Symbol in the Music of *Wozzeck.*" *Music Review,* 32, no. 4 (1971): 281–308.
Thorough analysis, examining the leitmotives and their role. Quite detailed. Musical examples.

855. **Perle, George.** *Serial Composition and Atonality: An Introduction to the Music of Schoenberg, Berg, and Webern.* 5th ed., rev., 34–39. Berkeley: University of California Press, 1981.
Brief discussion of "centricity" (the stabilization of a pitch, or a collection of pitches, as a focal element) in *Wozzeck.* Musical examples.

856. **Perle, George.** "*Woyzeck* and *Wozzeck.*" *Musical Quarterly,* 53, no. 2 (1967): 206–216.
Detailed recounting of Berg's adaptation of Büchner's original text *Woyzeck* for his libretto *Wozzeck.* Not a discussion of the music.

113

857. **Radice, Mark A.** "The Anatomy of a Libretto: The Music Inherent in Büchner's *Woyzeck.*" *Music Review*, 41, no. 3 (1980): 223–233.
Detailed discussion of the music embodied in the libretto, such as texts of folk songs, comments by characters relating to music, and stage directions involving music. Musical examples.

858. **Rawlins, Joseph T.** "*Moses und Aron* and *Wozzeck*: Monumental Music." *Opera Journal*, 18, no. 1 (1985): 11–18.
The serial writing of Berg and Schoenberg compared. Berg's music is serial, but retains many traditional "tonal" relationships. Schoenberg is dodecaphonic-serial, systematically avoiding tonal relationships. Bibliography.

859. **Redlich, Hans.** *Alban Berg: The Man and His Music*, 74–111. London: John Calder, 1957.
Full treatment. Influences, form, characterization, tonality, and place *Wozzeck* occupies in Berg's stylistic development. Musical examples. Berg's own lecture on *Wozzeck* is on pp. 261–285.

860. **Reich, Willi.** *Alban Berg.* Translated by Cornelius Cardew, 117–142. New York: Harcourt, Brace, and World, 1965.
Exhaustive analysis, taken scene by scene.

861. **Reich, Willi.** "*Wozzeck*, A Guide to the Words and Music." *Musical Quarterly*, 38, no. 1 (1952): 1–21.
Step-by-step analysis, with musical examples.

862. **Schmalfeldt, Janet.** *Berg's "Wozzeck": Harmonic Language and Dramatic Design.* New Haven: Yale University Press, 1983, 281 pp.
A detailed study of the opera. The analytic technique used is that of Allen Forte (his pitch class–set theory). The theoretical approach is illustrated by a thorough analysis of Act I, Scene I. Two chapters are devoted to the way in which Berg characterizes Wozzeck and Marie respectively—again through pitch-class analysis. The discussion of the opera is limited to pitch structure. Musical examples and tables.

863. **Simon, John.** "Meeting of Minds." *Opera News*, 49 (January 19, 1985): 14+.
Backgruond on Büchner's *Woyzeck*, its story and Berg's adaptation.

864. **Watkins, Glenn.** *Soundings: Music in the Twentieth Century*, 357–372. New York: Schirmer Books, 1987.
Literary background, descriptive and analytic commentary. Formal plan, use of sonata principle, leitmotives, and chord patterns discussed. Musical examples.

DISSERTATIONS AND THESES

Chamber Concerto

865.   **Crawford, Robert Sheldon.** "Dynamic Form and the Adagio of Alban Berg's Chamber Concerto, An Essay." Ph.D., Washington University, 1982, 121 pp., DA 44-316A.

Concerto for Violin

866.   **McCandless, William Edgar.** "Cantus Firmus Techniques in Selected Instrumental Compositions, 1910–1960." Ph.D., Indiana University, 1974, 329 pp., DA 35-4593A.

867.   **Shreffler, Theodore Wilson.** "An Analysis of the Violin Concerto (1935) by Alban Berg." Ph.D., University of California at Los Angeles, 1979, 161 pp., DA 40-3622A.

Lyric Suite

868.   **Parish, George David.** "Motivic and Cellular Structure in Alban Berg's *Lyric* Suite." Ph.D., University of Michigan, 1970, 328 pp., DA 31-6650A.

Schliesse mir die Augen beide

869.   **Ray, Karen.** "Alban Berg As *Liedkomponist*: An Analytical Study of His Two Settings of *Schliesse mir die Augen beide*, 1907 and 1925." M.M., North Texas State University, 1986, 178 pp., DA 24-320A.

BERIO, LUCIANO, 1925–

General

870.   **Whittall, Arnold.** *Music Since the First World War*, 246–250. London: J. M. Dent and Sons, 1977.
   Brief analytic comments on a variety of works. One musical example from *Circles.*

Circles

871.   **Donat, Misha.** "Berio and His *Circles.*" *Musical Times*, 105 (February 1964): 105–107.
   A brief descriptive analysis.

115

872.   Griffiths, Paul. *Modern Music: The Avant-Garde Since 1945,* 130–131. New York: George Braziller, 1981.
Analytic remarks. Musical examples.

Sinfonia

873.   Griffiths, Paul. *Modern Music: The Avant-Garde Since 1945,* 207–208. New York: George Braziller, 1981.
Brief analytic remarks.

874.   Hicks, Michael. "Text, Music, and Meaning in the Third Movement of Luciano Berio's *Sinfonia.*" *Perspectives of New Music,* 20, nos. 1–2 (1982–1983): 199+.
Demonstrates how Berio's use of the Mahler Second Symphony Scherzo as the immense Cantus Firmus forms the basis of this movement. Musical examples.

875.   Osmond-Smith, David. *Playing on Words: A Guide to Luciano Berio's "Sinfonia."* London: Royal Musical Association, 1985, 104 pp.
A very detailed study of *Sinfonia.* Includes consideration of the sources and structure of the text, the pitch set, the rhythmic set, quotations (musical and textual), semantic associations, the relationship between text and music. For the advanced student. Musical examples. Diagrams.

Tempi Concertati

876.   Jarvlepp, Jan. "Compositional Aspects of *Tempi Concertati* by Luciano Berio." *Interface,* 11, no. 4 (1982): 179–193.
Berio's compositional approach, his instrumentation and some of his remarks on the music discussed. An analysis and bibliography follows discussion.

Thema ("Omaggio a Joyce")

877.   Schrader, Barry. *Introduction to Electro-Acoustic Music,* 49–50. Englewood Cliffs, NJ: Prentice-Hall, 1982.
Analytic comments.

DISSERTATIONS AND THESES

Sequenza V

878.   Pellman, Samuel Frank. "An Examination of the Role of Timbre in a Musical Composition, As Exemplified by an Analysis of *Sequenza V by Luciano Berio.*" D.M.A., *Cornell University, 1979, 160 pp., DA 40-4794A.*

Wasserklavier

879.   Mann, Richard Ensor. "Pitch Structure and Poetic Imagery in Luciano Berio's *Wasserklavier* and *Erdenklavier.*" Ph.D., University of Rochester, Eastman School of Music, 1986, 68 pp., DA 47-15A.

BERLIOZ, HECTOR, 1803–1869

General

880.   Barzun, Jacques. *Berlioz and the Romantic School.* 2 vols. Boston: Little, Brown and Co., 1950.
Background and critical remarks on Berlioz's output.

881.   Dickinson, A. E. F. "Berlioz's Songs." *Musical Quarterly,* 55, no. 3 (1969): 329–343.
Thorough descriptive and critical overview. Musical examples.

882.   Dickinson, A. E. F. "Berlioz's Stage Works." *Music Review,* 31, no. 2 (1970): 136–157.
An overview of Berlioz's stage works, with musical examples. Particularly useful for discussion of Berlioz's lesser-known works.

883.   Dickinson, A. E. F. *The Music of Berlioz,* 305–307. New York: St. Martin's Press, 1972.
Substantial discussion focusing on background, influences, and creative impulse behind the music. Includes analyses with musical examples.

884.   Elliot, John H. *Berlioz.* London: J. M. Dent and Sons, 1967, 234 pp.
Critical remarks with musical examples. Intended for the undergraduate student.

885.   MacDonald, Hugh. *Berlioz.* London: J. M. Dent and Sons, 1982, 261 pp.
Mainly descriptive overview of Berlioz's output. Some analytic observations and a chapter on Berlioz's style. For the undergraduate student. Musical examples.

886.   MacDonald, Hugh. *Berlioz Orchestral Music.* London: British Broadcasting Corporation, 1969, 64 pp.
Analytic guide for the student. Musical examples.

887.   Orr, N. Lee. "Liszt, Christus, and the Transformations of the Oratorio." *Journal of the American Liszt Society,* 9 (1981): 11 + .

117

An overview of the French oratorio during the nineteenth century, with a brief description of stylistic elements in *L'Enfance du Christ*.

888.   Primmer, Brian. *The Berlioz Style.* London: Oxford University Press, 1973, 202 pp.
A detailed technical study of the music of Berlioz. There are chapters devoted to melody and harmony as well as Berlioz's place in French music. Musical examples.

Béatrice and Bénédict Overture

889.   Tovey, Donald Francis. *Essays in Musical Analysis.* Vol. 6, 53–54. London: Oxford University Press, 1969.
Critical and analytic with musical examples. For the undergraduate student.

Benvenuto Cellini

890.   Cairns, David. *"Benvenuto Cellini." Music and Musicians,* 15 (January 1967): 18–20.
Background, performance history, and critical remarks.

891.   MacDonald, Hugh. "The Original *Benvenuto Cellini." Musical Times,* 107 (December 1966): 1042–1045.
Traces the many versions and reasons for variant versions. Musical examples.

Corsair Overture

892.   Tovey, Donald Francis. *Essays in Musical Analysis.* Vol. 6, 50–52. London: Oxford University Press, 1969.
Critical and analytic discussion with musical examples. For the undergraduate student.

Damnation of Faust

893.   Bass, Edward C. "Thematic Unification of Scenes in Multimovement Works of Berlioz." *Music Review,* 28, no. 1 (1967): 45–51.

894.   Plantinga, Leon. *Romantic Music,* 215–219. New York: W. W. Norton, 1984.
Analytic comments. Musical examples.

895. Rushton, Julian. "The Genesis of Berlioz's *La Damnation de Faust.*" *Music and Letters,* 56, no. 2 (1975): 129–146.
Compositional history, with critical remarks on Berlioz's alterations of the original material from which this work is drawn. Musical examples.

Grande Messe des Morts

896. Cone, Edward T. "Berlioz's Divine Comedy: The *Grande Messe des Morts.*" *Nineteenth Century Music,* 4, no. 1 (1980): 3–16.
A detailed examination of how the dramatic and musical aspects of this work are fused to reinforce each other. Musical examples.

Harold in Italy

897. Cone, Edward T. "Inside the Saint's Head: The Music of Berlioz." *Musical Newsletter,* 4 (October 1971): 16–20.
Author postulates that Berlioz added a new "spatial" dimension and "multiple perspective" to music, and discusses these ideas in conjunction with passages from the *Requiem* and *Harold in Italy.* Musical examples.

898. Langford, Jeffrey. "The Dramatic Symphonies of Berlioz as an Outgrowth of the French Operatic Tradition." *Musical Quarterly,* 69, no. 1 (1983): 97–101.
An examination of operatic technique used in the symphony.

Herminie

899. Dickinson, A. E. F. "Berlioz' Rome Prize works." *Music Review,* 25, no. 3 (1964): 163–185.
Descriptive commentary, background, and analytic observations. Musical examples.

King Lear Overture

900. Adelson, Deborah M. "Interpreting Berlioz's Overture to *King Lear,* Opus 4: Problems and Solutions," *Current Musicology,* 35 (1983): 46–56.
An examination of the programmatic basis of this work.

901. Tovey, Donald Francis. *Essays in Musical Analysis,* Vol. 4, 82–86. London: Oxford University Press, 1969.
Critical and analytic study with musical examples. For the undergraduate student.

Mort de Cléopâtre

902. Dickinson, A. E. F. "Berlioz' Rome Prize Works." *Music Review*, 25, no. 3 (1964): 163–185.
Cleopatre is mentioned on p. 172. The article is mainly a discussion of Berlioz' Rome Prize works with background, commentary, and some analytic remarks. Musical examples.

Mort d'Orphée

903. Dickinson, A. E. F. "Berlioz' Rome Prize works." *Music Review*, 25, no. 3 (1964): 163–185.
Descriptive commentary with background and analytic observations (pp. 166–169). Musical examples.

Mort de Sardanapale

904. Dickinson, A. E. F. "Berlioz' Rome Prize works." *Music Review*, 25, no. 3 (1964): 163–185.
Descriptive commentary and analytic remarks (pp. 173–178). Musical examples.

Requiem

905. Cone, Edward T. "Inside the Saint's Head: The Music of Berlioz." *Musical Newsletter*, 4 (October 1971): 16–20.
Author postulates that Berlioz added a new "spatial" dimension and "multiple perspective" to music and discusses these ideas in conjunction with passages from the *Requiem* and *Harold in Italy*. Musical examples.

906. Janower, David M. "Tonal Unity in Berlioz's *Requiem*." *Choral Journal*, 26, no. 8 (1986): 31 +.
Discusses the tonal relationships among movements, as well as some related harmonic progressions within the movement. Musical examples and tables.

907. Robertson, Alec. *"Requiem": Music of Mourning and Consolation*, 85–95. New York: Praeger Publishers, 1968.
Background, influences, and extensive discussion of the music. Musical examples.

Romeo and Juliet

908. Bass, Edward C. "Thematic Unification of Scenes in Multi-movement Works of Berlioz." *Music Review*, 28, no. 1 (1967): 45–51.
Structural analysis to support author's theory. Musical examples.

909.   Friedheim, Philipp. "Berlioz' *Romeo* Symphony and the Romantic Temperament." *Current Musicology*, 36 (1983): 101–111.
Author demonstrates how this symphony is characteristic of the Romantic period in its sustained emotionality, loose adherence to original script, emphasis on the supernatural, and the intrusion of biographical elements.

910.   Silverman, Richard S. "Synthesis in the Music of Hector Berlioz." *Music Review*, 34, nos. 3–4 (1973): 348–350.
Berlioz's technique of combining themes examined. Musical examples.

Symphonie Fantastique

911.   Banks, Paul. "Coherence and Diversity in the *Symphonie Fantastique*." *Nineteenth Century Music*, 8, no. 1 (1984): 37–43.
Compositional history, showing how alterations strengthened unity.

912.   Cone, Edward T., ed. *Hector Berlioz: "Fantastic Symphony."* Norton Critical Scores. New York: W. W. Norton, 1971, 305 pp.
Orchestral score accompanied by critical commentary, historical background, contemporary criticism, analysis by Edward Cone, and views by other composers on this symphony.

913.   Cuyler, Louise. *The Symphony*, 139–143. New York: Harcourt Brace Jovanovich, 1973.
Brief analysis of entire symphony, with musical examples.

914.   Dahlhaus, Carl. *Nineteenth-Century Music.* Translated by J. Bradford Robinson, 154–156. Berkeley: University of California Press, 1989.
Close examination of the theme (*idée fixe*) adapting to its differing formal functions throughout the symphony. Compares Berlioz's melody type with Beethoven's concise theme types in their formal applications. Advanced.

915.   Dickinson, A. E. F. *The Music of Berlioz*, 125–138. London: Faber and Faber, 1972.
Substantial discussion focusing on background and creative impulse. Includes analysis with musical examples.

916.   Elliot, John H. *Berlioz*, 136–140. New York: Farrar, Straus, and Giroux, 1967.
Brief treatment, mainly critical rather than analytic.

121

917.   Kerman, Joseph. *Listen.* 3d ed., 345–350. New York: Worth Publishers, 1980.
Descriptive commentary for the student. Musical examples.

918.   Langford, Jeffrey. "The Dramatic Symphonies of Berlioz as an Outgrowth of the French Operatic Tradition." *Musical Quarterly,* 69, no. 1 (1983): 85–103.
An examination of operatic technique used in the symphony.

919.   Leichtentritt, Hugo. *Musical Form,* 315. Cambridge, MA: Harvard University Press, 1959.
Brief, but compact statement analyzing the variations. Fourth movement only.

920.   Machlis, Joseph. *The Enjoyment of Music.* 3d ed., 111–114. New York: W. W. Norton, 1970.
Analytic overview for the student. Musical examples.

921.   Nadeau, Roland. *The Symphony: Structure and Style.* Shorter ed., rev., 115–133. Boston: Crescendo, 1974.
Measure-by-measure analysis. Detailed and objective.

922.   Plantinga, Leon. *Romantic Music,* 207–214. New York: W. W. Norton, 1984.
Analytic discussion. Musical examples.

923.   Silverman, Richard S. "Synthesis in the Music of Hector Berlioz." *Music Review,* 34, nos. 3–4 (1973): 346–348.
Berlioz's technique of combining themes examined. Musical examples.

924.   Stedman, Prestony. *The Symphony,* 127–135. Englewood Cliffs, NJ: Prentice-Hall, 1979.
Program synopsis, section-by-section description of formal scheme, and use of *idée fixe.* Musical examples and diagram.

925.   Temperley, Nicholas. "The *Symphonie Fantastique* and Its Program." *Musical Quarterly,* 57, no. 4 (1971): 593–608.
The function of Berlioz's program in this symphony and his reasons for supplying a program are discussed.

926.   Ulrich, Homer. *Music: A Design for Listening,* 312–316. New York: Harcourt, Brace, 1957.
Descriptive/analytic breakdown by measures, with analytic observations. Musical examples.

Symphonie Funebre et triomphale

927. Wilson, Cecil B. "Some Remarks on Berlioz' Symphony for Band." *Instrumentalist,* 29 (November 1974): 48–52; (December 1974): 44–46.
Background, analysis, and performance practice. Musical examples.

Les Troyens (The Trojans)

928. Cairns, David. "Berlioz and Virgil: A Consideration of *Les Troyens* as a Virgilian Opera." *Proceedings of the Royal Musical Association,* 95 (1968–1969): 97–110.
Derivation of Berlioz's opera from the *Aeneid* and consideration of debt to Virgil.

929. Fogel, Susa Lee. "An Unusual Sound." *Opera News,* 34 (September 20, 1969): 14–16.
Berlioz's unique treatment of the orchestra in relation to voice. Musical characterization illustrated.

930. Heyworth, Peter, ed. *Berlioz, Romantic and Classic: Writings by Ernest Newman,* 197–233. London: Victor Gollancz, 1972.
Critical commentary. Not analytic.

931. Klein, John W. "Berlioz's Sublime Epic." *Opera,* 20 (September 1969): 753–758.
Descriptive and critical commentary.

932. Langford, Jeffrey. "Berlioz, Cassandra, and the French Operatic Tradition." *Music and Letters,* 62, nos. 3–4 (1981): 310+.
Author argues that even as Berlioz broke away from traditional opera forms, he chose not to free himself from some of the most common operatic traditions. The character of Cassandra is seen as just such an example. Also suggests that Berlioz borrowed material from the Finale of Rossini's *Siege of Corinth* to complete *Les Troyens.*

Les Troyens (The Trojans) Overture

933. Rushton, Julian. "The Overture to *Les Troyens.*" *Music Analysis,* 4, nos. 1–2 (1985): 119+.
Complex analysis. Advanced. Musical examples and bibliography.

BERNSTEIN, LEONARD, 1918–1990

Chichester Psalms

934.   Winnick, William. "Pivot Analysis in Bernstein's *Chichester* Psalms: A Guide for Singers." *Choral Journal*, 24, no. 7 (1984): 17–19+.

DISSERTATIONS AND THESES

General

935.   Snyder, Linda June. "Leonard Bernstein's Work for the Musical Theatre: How the Music Functions Dramatically." D.M.A., University of Illinois at Urbana, 1982, 290 pp., DA 43-3751A.

Dybbuk

936.   Pearlmutter, Alan Jay. "Leonard Bernstein's *Dybbuk*: An Analysis Including Historical, Religious, and Literary Perspectives of Hasidic Life and Lore." D.M.A., Peabody Conservatory of Music, 1985, 376 pp., DA 46-1776A.

Mass

937.   Andre, Don Alan. "Leonard Bernstein's Mass As Social and Political Commentary on the Sixties." D.M.A., University of Washington, 1979, 186 pp., DA 41-841A.

BILLINGS, WILLIAM, 1746–1800

General

938.   Barbour, James M. *The Church Music of William Billings.* East Lansing, MI: Michigan State University Press, 1960, 167 pp.
    A discussion of the stylistic characteristics of the music with extensive treatment of rhythm, melody, counterpoint, harmony, tonality, texture, and form. Musical examples.

Continental Harmony

939.   Nathan, Hans. "William Billings: *The Continental Harmony* (1794)." *American Choral Review*, 18, no. 4 (1976): 27–36.
    Background, analysis, critical commentary. Musical examples.

Jargon

940. Gryc, Stephen M. "Explicating William Billings's *Jargon.*" *In Theory Only*, 3 (April 1977): 22–28.
Background and analysis. Advanced. Musical examples.

BINCHOIS, GILLES, C. 1400–1460

De Plus en Plus

941. Williams, J. Kent. "Rhythmic Structure in Selected Works of Binchois and Dufay." *Indiana Theory Review*, 1, no. 3 (1978): 31–48.

BIZET, GEORGES, 1838–1875

General

942. Cooper, Martin. *Georges Bizet.* London: Oxford University Press, 1938, 136 pp.
Descriptive and critical remarks with mention of background and influences in Bizet's music. Musical examples.

943. Dean, Winton. *Georges Bizet: His Life and Work.* Rev. ed. London: J. M. Dent and Sons, 1965, 304 pp.
Brief descriptive commentary with analytic observations on all of Bizet's operas. Musical examples.

L'Arlésienne

944. Klein, John W. "The Centenary of Bizet's *L'Arlésienne.*" *Music and Letters*, 53, no. 4 (1972): 363–368.
Background and critical remarks.

L'Arlésienne: Suite No. 1

945. Laming, Frank M. "Set Works for 'O' Level, GCE." *Music Teacher*, 53 (November 1974): 11–12.
Background and analysis for the undergraduate student. Musical examples.

Carmen

946. Donington, Robert. *The Opera,* 172–175. New York: Harcourt Brace Jovanovich, 1978.
Brief summary of dramatic action, remarks on structural, melodic, and orchestral features. Musical examples.

947. Machlis, Joseph. *The Enjoyment of Music.* 3d ed., 195–201. New York: W. W. Norton, 1970.
Analytic overview with musical examples.

Djamileh

948. Klein, John W. "Reflections on Bizet's *Djamileh.*" *Music Review,* 35, nos. 3–4 (1974): 293–300.
Background and critical remarks on this little-known opera.

Pearl Fishers

949. Klein, John W. "The Centenary of Bizet's *The Pearl Fishers.*" *Music Review,* 25, no. 4 (1964): 302–310.
Performance history, place in Bizet's output, and critical commentary.

BLOCH, ERNEST, 1880–1959

General

950. Robertson, Alec, ed. *Chamber Music,* 215–219. Baltimore: Penguin Books, 1957.
Critical remarks, with musical examples.

951. Wheeler, Charles L. "Ernest Bloch's Solo Piano Music." *American Music Teacher,* 30, no. 2 (1980): 22–24.
A survey of Bloch's piano music, with critical and analytic observations. Musical examples.

Macbeth

952. Franck, Georges. "Artistic Truth and Honesty: Ernest Bloch's *Macbeth.*" *Opera Journal,* 15, no. 2 (1982): 15–23.
Background and critical commentary.

Quartet for Strings No. 2

953. Rimmer, Frederick. "Ernest Bloch's Second String Quartet." *Tempo*, 52 (Autumn 1959): 11–16.
> A formal and harmonic analysis of the whole work. Musical examples.

954. Tischler, Hans. *The Perceptive Music Listener*, 306–311. Englewood Cliffs, NJ: Prentice-Hall, 1955.
> Analysis, with musical examples.

Sonata for Piano

955. Melvin, Sophia. "Recollections of Ernest Bloch." *Clavier*, 19, no. 9 (1980): 32–35.
> Brief analysis. Musical excerpt included.

BLOW, JOHN, 1649–1708

General

956. Spink, Ian. *English Songs: Dowland to Purcell*, 241–252. London: B. T. Batsford, 1974.
> An analytic discussion of the songs. Places the composer in historical context, identifies stylistic traits, and discusses relationships between text and music. Musical examples.

BORODIN, ALEXANDER, 1833–1887

General

957. Abraham, Gerald. "Arab Melodies in Rimsky-Korsakov and Borodin." *Music and Letters*, 56, nos. 3–4 (1975): 313–318.
> Historic and analytic survey of Rimsky-Korsakov's borrowing of Arab melodies from various sources and his treatment of those melodies. Musical examples.

958. Abraham, Gerald. *Borodin: The Composer and His Music*, 64–118. London: William Reeves, n.d.
> Descriptive commentary, with musical examples.

959. Dianin, Serge. *Borodin*. Translated by Robert Lord. London: Oxford University Press, 1963, 356 pp.
> Descriptive and analytic commentary. Musical examples.

127

960. Ferguson, Donald N. *Image and Structure in Chamber Music,* 220–222. Minneapolis: University of Minnesota Press, 1964.
Brief analytic remarks.

On the Steppes of Central Asia

961. Abraham, Gerald. *Borodin: The Composer and His Music,* 56–62. London: William Reeves, n.d.
Descriptive commentary with musical examples.

Prince Igor

962. Dianin, Serge. *Borodin.* Translated by Robert Lord, 271–326. London: Oxford University Press, 1963.
Full description of background leading to completed version. Analytic discussion with motifs traced thoroughly. Musical examples.

963. Warburton, A. O. "Set Works for 'O' Level, GCE." *Music Teacher,* 48 (February 1969): 17.
Brief background, descriptive, and analytic remarks for the undergraduate student.

Quartet for Strings No. 2 in D Major

964. Garden, Edward. "The 'Programme' of Borodin's Second Quartet." *Musical Times,* 128 (February 1987): 76–78.
General analytic comments on thematic material, style, and evidence of programmatic content.

Symphony No. 1

965. Ballantine, Christopher. *Twentieth Century Symphony,* 147–149. London: Dennis Dobson, 1984.
Brief analytic comments. First movement only.

BOULEZ, PIERRE, 1925–

General

966. Evans, Peter. "Music of the European Mainstream: 1940–1960." In *The New Oxford History of Music* Vol. 10, *The Modern Age: 1890–1960.* Edited by Martin Cooper, 441–454. London: Oxford University Press, 1974.
Overview of Boulez's stylistic development, with analytic observations on *Psalmodies* for piano, *Structures* and *Le Marteau sans maître.* Musical examples.

967. Matthews, Denis, ed. *Keyboard Music,* 340–345. New York: Praeger, 1972.
Critical and analytic discussion, with musical examples.

968. Whittall, Arnold. *Music Since the First World War,* 250–255. London: J. M. Dent and Sons, 1977.
Brief analytic overview.

Constellation-Miroir

969. Trenkamp, Wilma-Anne. "The Concept of 'Alea'; in Boulez's *Constellation-Miroir."* *Music and Letters,* 57, no. 1 (1976): 1–10.
A detailed discussion of Boulez's use of chance elements in this work. Musical examples.

Eclat

970. Kohn, Karl. "Current Chronicle: Los Angeles." *Musical Quarterly,* 51, no. 4 (1965): 702–707.
Description and analysis of this work, which was later expanded by Boulez into *Eclat/Multiples.* Musical examples.

Eclat/Multiples

971. Chanan, Michael. "Boulez's *Eclat/Multiples."* *Tempo,* 95 (Winter 1970–1971): 30–33.
Critical and analytic commentary.

972. Griffiths, Paul. "Boulez Reflects: *Eclat/Multiples."* *Musical Times,* 112 (August 1971): 753–754.
Analytic commentary.

973. Griffiths, Paul. *Modern Music: The Avant-Garde Since 1945,* 276–281. New York: George Braziller, 1981.
Analytic discussion. Musical examples.

Marteau sans maître

974. Griffiths, Paul. *Modern Music: The Avant-Garde Since 1945,* 97–101. New York: George Braziller, 1981.
Analytic observations. Musical examples.

975. Machlis, Joseph. *The Enjoyment of Music.* 5th ed., 587–589. New York: W. W. Norton, 1984.
Background and descriptive commentary for the undergraduate student. Each section treated separately.

129

976.   Stockhausen, Karlheinz. "Music and Speech." *Reihe*, 6 (1964): 40–64.

An examination of text/music relationships, including discussion of poetry, phonetics, rhythm, instrumentation, and other unifying factors. Musical examples, graphs, tables. For the advanced student.

977.   Winick, Steven D. "Symmetry and Pitch-Duration Associations in Boulez's *Le Marteau sans Maître*." *Perspectives of New Music*, 24, no. 2 (1986): 280–321.

Pli Selon Pli

978.   Griffiths, Paul. *Modern Music: The Avant-Garde Since 1945*, 121–124. New York: George Braziller, 1981.

Analytic observations.

Soleil des Eaux

979.   Hopkins, G. W. "Boulez's *Le Soleil des Eaux*." *Tempo*, 68 (Spring 1964): 35–37.

An analytical introduction to this work.

Sonata for Piano No. 1

980.   Peyser, Joan. *Boulez*, 39–42. New York: Schirmer Books, 1976.

Brief descriptive, background, and analytic remarks. Musical examples.

981.   Reti, Rudolph. *Tonality, Atonality, Pantonality: A Study of Some Trends in Twentieth Century Music*, 96, 152. London: Rockliff, 1958.

Brief analysis of the pitch structure of the opening measures. Musical examples.

Sonata for Piano No. 2

982.   Griffiths, Paul. *Modern Music: The Avant-Garde Since 1945*, 25–29. New York: George Braziller, 1981.

Extended discussion of compositional techniques. Musical examples.

983.   Heiles, William. "The Second Piano Sonata of Pierre Boulez." *American Music Teacher*, 22, no. 3 (1973): 34–37.

Analysis, with musical examples.

984. Peyser, Joan. *Boulez*, 47–49. New York: Schirmer Books, 1976.
Brief analytic comments.

Sonata for Piano No. 3

985. Black, Robert. "Boulez's Third Piano Sonata: Surface and Sensibility." *Perspectives of New Music*, 20, nos. 1–2 (1982–1983): 182 + .
Thorough discussion of the inspirational sources for this work, with analytic observations to aid the performer in interpretation.

986. Griffiths, Paul. *Modern Music: The Avant-Garde Since 1945*, 119–121. New York: George Braziller, 1981.
Analytic observations. Musical examples.

987. Ligeti, György. "Some Remarks on Boulez's Third Piano Sonata." *Reihe*, 5 (1961): 56–58.
Analytic observations.

988. Maw, Nicholas. "Boulez and Tradition." *Musical Times*, 103 (March 1962): 162–164.
Brief descriptive and analytic commentary.

989. Peyser, Joan. *Boulez*, 126–128, 150–152. New York: Schirmer Books, 1976.
Boulez discusses the pitch structure and serial procedure of the "Tropes" movement of this sonata as well as the overall structure of the entire work. Musical examples.

990. Wait, Mark. "Liszt, Scriabin, and Boulez." *Journal of the American Liszt Society*, 1 (June 1977): 9–16.
Analysis. Musical examples and bibliography.

Sonatina for Flute and Piano

991. Baron, Carol K. "An Analysis of the Pitch Organization in Boulez's 'Sonatine for Flute and Piano.'" *Current Musicology*, 20 (1975): 87–95.

992. Griffiths, Paul. *Modern Music: The Avant-Garde Since 1945*, 22–24. New York: George Braziller, 1981.
Brief analytic remarks. Musical examples.

Structures I

993. Griffiths, Paul. *Modern Music: The Avant-Garde Since 1945*, 56–61. New York: George Braziller, 1981.
Analytic remarks. Musical examples.

131

Structures II for Two Pianos

994.   Kohn, Karl. "Current Chronicle: Los Angeles." *Musical Quarterly*, 49, no. 3 (1963): 365–369.
  Descriptive passages on performance of the work, with some analytic observations. Musical examples.

Structures Ia, Ib, and Ic

995.   Peyser, Joan. *Boulez*, 68–69. New York: Schirmer Books, 1976.
  Brief analytic comments.

DISSERTATIONS AND THESES

Pli Selon Pli

996.   Miller, Roger L. "*Pli Selon Pli*: Pierre Boulez and the 'New Lyricism.' " Ph.D., Case Western Reserve, 1978, 456 pp., DA 39-5794A.

Sonata for Piano No. 3

997.   Trenkamp, Wilma Anne. "A Throw of the Dice: An Analysis of Selected Works by Pierre Boulez." Ph.D., Case Western Reserve, 1973, 254 pp., DA 34-5237A.

Structures for Two Pianos

998.   Trenkamp, Wilma Anne. "A Throw of the Dice: An Analysis of Selected Works by Pierre Boulez." Ph.D., Case Western Reserve, 1973, 254 pp., DA 34-5237A.Boyce, William, 1711–1779

BOYCE, WILLIAM, 1711–1779

DISSERTATIONS AND THESES

General

999.   McIntosh, Robert Dale. "The Dramatic Music of William Boyce." Ph.D., University of Washington, 1979, 357 pp., DA 40-530.

BRAHMS, JOHANNES, 1833–1897

General

1000.   Beechey, Gwilyn. "The Organ Music of Brahms." *American Organist*, 17 (May 1983): 43–46.

Critical and analytic overview of Brahms's entire output for organ. Musical examples and bibliography.

1001. Colles, Henry C. *The Chamber Music of Brahms.* London: Oxford University Press, 1933, 64 pp.
Descriptive and analytic commentary for the undergraduate student. Musical examples.

1002. Dale, Kathleen. *Nineteenth-Century Piano Music: A Handbook for Pianists.* London: Oxford University Press, 1954, 320 pp.
Highlights the stylistic traits and unique contribution to the literature of the piano. Form, harmony, and other musical aspects discussed in relation to style.

1003. Dunsby, Jonathan. *Structural Ambiguity in Brahms.* Ann Arbor: UMI Research Press, 1981, 120 pp.
Analyzes Variations on a Theme by Handel, Piano Quartet in C Minor, Op. 60 (first movement), and Intermezzo Op. 119, No. 1, with focus on structure. Advanced. Musical examples.

1004. Evans, Edwin. *Historical, Descriptive, and Analytic Account of the Entire Works of Johannes Brahms.* 4 vols. London: William Reeves, 1912.
Analytic and descriptive remarks on the orchestral, chamber, and piano works. Charts on form. Musical examples. Useful to the undergraduate despite its age.

1005. Fairleigh, James P. "Neo-Classicism in the Later Piano Works." *Piano Quarterly,* 15 no. 58 (1966–1967): 24–26.
General analytic remarks about Opp. 76, 79, 117, 118, 119. Brief comments on Neoclassic elements: key relationships, formal structures. Diagrams.

1006. Ferguson, Donald N. *Image and Structure in Chamber Music,* 175–218. Minneapolis: University of Minnesota Press, 1964.
Overview of the chamber music with brief analyses. Musical examples.

1007. Ferguson, Donald N. *Piano Music of Six Great Composers,* 251–318. New York: Books for Libraries Press, 1947.
Descriptive and critical commentary on the piano music, showing stylistic development. Musical examples.

1008. Friedlaender, Max. *Brahms's Lieder.* Translated by C. Leonard Leese. London: Oxford University Press, 1928, 263 pp.
Brief remarks on all the songs. Musical examples.

1009. Frisch, Walter. *Brahms and the Principle of Developing Variation.* Berkeley: University of California Press, 1984, 217 pp.

Overview of Brahm's output through Schoenberg's concept of the "developing variation," which is a way of viewing the logical flow of the music as a kind of variation on the basic musical idea of the work. Advanced analytic discussion. Musical examples.

1010. Geiringer, Karl. *Brahms: His Life and Work.* 2d ed. New York: Oxford University Press, 1947, 383 pp.

Background, descriptive, and critical commentary.

1011. Gotwals, Vernon. "Brahms and the Organ." *Music (AGO),* 4 (April 1970): 38–55.

Thorough survey of Brahms's organ works. Descriptive and analytic commentary, with musical examples.

1012. Harrison, Max. *The Lieder of Brahms.* London: Cassell, 1972, 152 pp.

Discussion of the influences, style, and formal design of all Brahms's *Lieder.* Musical examples.

1013. Horton, John. *Brahms Orchestral Music.* London: British Broadcasting Corporation, 1968, 64 pp.

Analytic guide for the undergraduate student. Musical examples.

1014. Keys, Ivor. *Brahms Chamber Music.* London: British Broadcasting Corporation, 1974, 68 pp.

Mainly descriptive overview intended for the undergraduate student. Some analytic remarks. Musical examples.

1015. Kross, Siegfried. "The Choral Music of Johannes Brahms." *American Choral Review,* 25, no. 4 (1983): Entire issue.

Overview with background and analytic commentary. The *German Requiem, Lieder und Romanzen* Op. 44, *Gesang der Parzen* Op. 89, *Regina Coeli,* Five Songs for Men's Chorus Op. 41, and the Alto Rhapsody are some of the works discussed in detail. Musical examples.

1016. Latham, Peter. *Brahms.* London: J. M. Dent and Sons, 1975, 230 pp.

A "life and works" approach, with emphasis on the music. Mainly descriptive commentary with analytic observations for the undergraduate student. Musical examples.

1017. Mason, Daniel Gregory. *The Chamber Music of Brahms.* New York: Macmillan, 1933, 276 pp.

Background, with descriptive and analytic commentary. Musical examples.

1018.   Matthews, Denis. *Brahms Piano Music.* Seattle: University of Washington Press, 1978, 76 pp.

Mainly a descriptive survey for the undergraduate student, with scattered analytic observations. Musical examples

1019.   Musgrave, Michael. *The Music of Brahms.* London: Routledge and Kegan Paul, 1985, 329 pp.

Thorough survey of Brahms's output. Discussions include background, stylistic traits, form, overall structure, tonality, rhythm, and text settings. Musical examples.

1020.   Niemann, Walter. *Brahms.* Translated by Catherine Alison Phillips. New York: Cooper Square, 1969, 492 pp.

Background and descriptive commentary on Brahms's output in program-note style.

1021.   Pascall, Robert. "Ruminations on Brahms's Chamber Music." *Musical Times,* 116 (August 1975): 697–699.

Descriptive overview, with analytic insights.

1022.   Plantinga, Leon. *Romantic Music,* 411–434. New York: W. W. Norton, 1984.

Analytic comments. Musical examples.

1023.   Robertson, Alec, ed. *Chamber Music,* 191–201. Baltimore: Penguin Books, 1957.

Critical and analytic remarks. Musical examples.

1024.   Sams, Eric. *Brahms's Songs.* Seattle: University of Washington Press, 1972, 68 pp.

A BBC Guide. An introduction places the Brahms songs in historical context and makes some general analytic and stylistic observations. The remaining chapters survey the songs chronologically. Musical examples drawn from individual songs are used to make many analytic observations.

1025.   Specht, Richard. *Johannes Brahms.* Translated by Eric Blom, 201–215. London: J. M. Dent and Sons, 1930.

Descriptive and critical comments. Antiquated style, but still useful for its objective observations.

1026.   Tovey, Donald Francis. *The Main Stream of Music and Other Essays,* 220–270. New York: Meridian, 1959.

Thorough overview of Brahms's chamber music, with mention of many specific works. Descriptive, critical and analytic. For the undergraduate student. Musical examples.

1027.   Ulrich, Homer. "Brahms and Chamber Music." *American Music Teacher,* 32, no. 5 (1983): 10–11.
 Overview, with general observations on Brahms's early and late musical characteristics. Musical examples.

Alto Rhapsody

1028.   Berry, Wallace. "Text and Music in the *Alto* Rhapsody." *Journal of Music Theory,* 27, no. 2 (1983): 239–253.
 Examines relation of text to music, showing how the music supports or accents the text. Analyzes structure as well. Advanced. Musical examples.

1029.   Forte, Allen. "Motive and Rhythmic Contour in the *Alto* Rhapsody." *Journal of Music Theory,* 27, no. 2 (1983): 255–271.

1030.   Garlington, Aubrey S., Jr. "Harzreise als Herzreise: Brahms *Alto* Rhapsody." *Musical Quarterly,* 69, no. 4 (1983): 527–542.
 A discussion of how the Alto Rhapsody reflects the emotional struggle that Brahms was experiencing at the time of its composition.

Ballade, Op. 10, No. 1 in D Major

1031.   Fiske, Roger. "Brahms and Scotland." *Musical Times,* 109 (December 1968): 1106–1110.
 Discusses Brahms's settings of Herder's translations of Scottish ballads in his simple "folk song" style. Musical examples.

Capriccio, Op. 76, No. 8 in C Major

1032.   Lewin, David. "On Harmony and Meter in Brahms's Op. 76, No. 8." *Nineteenth Century Music,* 4, no. 3 (1981): 261–265.

Capriccio, Op. 116, No. 3 in G Minor

1033.   Dalhaus, Carl. *Nineteenth-Century Music.* Translated by J. Bradford Robinson, 258–260. Berkeley: University of California Press, 1989.
 Concentrated analytic remarks dwelling on form, use of counterpoint, and "developing variation." Musical examples. Advanced.

Capriccio, Op. 116, No. 7 in D Minor

1034. Bryant, Celia M. "Catching the Temperament of a Brahms 'Caprice.' " *Clavier*, 8, no. 4 (1969): 29–33.
Performer's analysis, with complete musical example.

Chorale Preludes for Organ, Op. 122

1035. Bond, Ann. "Brahms Chorale Preludes, Op. 122." *Musical Times*, 112 (September 1971): 898–890.
Background, overview of stylistic traits, and critical commentary on specific pieces. Musical examples.

1036. Heusinkveld, Francis. "Brahms Chorale Preludes." *American Music Teacher*, 21, no. 6 (1972): 26–27.
Elementary overview and general description. No analyses.

1037. Miller, Max B. "The Brahms Chorale Preludes Master Lesson." *American Organist*, 13, no. 4 (1979): 43–47.
Critical and analytic remarks on all eleven Chorale Preludes. Musical examples and bibliography.

Concertos

1038. Hill, Ralph, ed. *The Concerto*, 187–205. London: Penguin Books, 1952.
Critical and analytic commentary for the undergraduate student. Musical examples.

1039. Veinus, Abraham. *The Concerto*. Rev. ed., 227–234. New York: Dover Publications, 1964.
General remarks of an evaluative nature. Places Brahms's contribution in historical perspective.

Concerto for Piano No. 1, Op. 15 in D Minor

1040. Hopkins, Antony. *Talking About Concertos*, 85–97. London: Heinemann, 1964.
Extended analytic essay describing tonal, thematic, and formal events.

1041. James, Burnett. *Brahms: A Critical Study*, 73–77. New York: Praeger, 1972.
Descriptive commentary, with background. Musical examples.

1042.   Nelson, Wendell. *The Concerto*, 66–70. Dubuque, IA: William C. Brown, 1969.
Background and analysis, with musical examples.

1043.   Reynold, Christopher. "A Choral Symphony by Brahms." *Nineteenth Century Music*, 9, no. 1 (1985): 3–25.
A study of extramusical allusions to be found in the sketches for a two-piano sonata, which later was reworked to become plans for a symphony, and later reworked again to become parts of the Piano Concerto No. 1 and the Requiem. Identifies and comments upon motives from these two works. No complete analysis of either work. Much discussion on references between the works of Schumann and Brahms. Musical examples and tables.

Concerto for Violin, Op. 77 in D Major

1044.   Hopkins, Antony. *Talking About Concertos*, 98–111. London: Heinemann, 1964.
Extended analytic essay describing tonal, thematic, and formal events.

1045.   Nelson, Wendell. *The Concerto*, 71–76. Dubuque, IA: William C. Brown, 1969.
Descriptive, critical, and analytic commentary with musical examples.

1046.   Plantinga, Leon. *Romantic Music*, 423–429. New York: W. W. Norton, 1984.
Analytic discussion. Musical examples.

1047.   Swalin, Benjamin F. *The Violin Concerto: A Study in German Romanticism*, 125–140. Chapel Hill: University of North Carolina Press, 1941.
Thorough treatment, providing background and analysis with critical observations. Musical examples.

Fantasies, Op. 116

1048.   Dunsby, Jonathan. "The Multi-Piece in Brahms's Fantasien, Op. 116." In *Brahms: Biographical, Documentary, and Analytic Studies.* Edited by Robert Pascall, 167–189. Cambridge: Cambridge University Press, 1983.
An analytic study of the ways in which the seven separate pieces of Op. 116 are related to one another. Includes discussions of var-

ious possible analytic approaches, the work of other Brahms scholars, and an examination of thematic and harmonic links between the pieces. Musical examples.

Four Serious Songs

1049. Boyd, Malcolm. "Brahms and the *Four Serious Songs*." *Musical Times*, 108 (July 1967): 593–595.
Background and analytic commentary demonstrating motivic similarities between the first three songs. Musical examples.

1050. Frisch, Walter. *Brahms and the Principle of Developing Variation*, 151–156. Berkeley: University of California Press, 1984.
Analysis of "O Tod, O Tod wie bitter bist du" of this set, using Schoenberg's principle of "developing variation," which is a way of viewing the logical flow of the music as a variation on the basic musical idea of the work. For the advanced student. Musical examples.

1051. Kielian, Marianne, et al. "Analysis Symposium." *In Theory Only*, 2 (September 1976): 16–29+.
Advanced analysis of "Der Tod, dast ist die kühle Nacht" of this set. Musical examples.

1052. Schoenberg, Arnold. *Style and Idea: Selected Writings of Arnold Schoenberg*. Translated by L. Black. Edited by Leo Stein, 431–435. New York: St. Martin's Press, 1975.
Analysis of the motivic structure of "O Tod, O Tod, wie bitter bist du."

1053. Whittal, Arnold. "The Vier ernste Gesänge, Op. 121: Enrichment and Uniformity." In *Brahms: Biographical, Documentary, and Analytical Studies*. Edited by Robert Pascall, 191–207. Cambridge: Cambridge University Press, 1983.
An analytical discussion of these songs. Schenkerian principles are adapted and the emphasis is on questions of voice leading and harmony. For the advanced student. Musical examples.

German Folk Songs

1054. Cogan, Robert, and Pozzi Escot. *Sonic Design: The Nature of Sound and Music*, 148–157. Englewood Cliffs, NJ: Prentice-Hall, 1976.
Discusses harmony, harmonic progression, and voice leading of "Wach' auf, mein Hort" of this set.

German Requiem

1055. Boyd, Malcolm. "Brahms's Requiem: A Note on Thematic Integration." *Musical Times,* 113 (February 1972): 140–141.
Brief discussion of subtle thematic relationships as a structural element. Musical examples.

1056. Musgrave, Michael. "Historical Influences in the Growth of Brahms's Requiem." *Music and Letters,* 53, no. 1 (1972): 3–17.
An examination of the influence of Bach's chorales on the shape and unity of the Requiem.

1057. Newman, William S. "A 'Basic Motive' in Brahms's German Requiem." *Music Review,* 24, no. 3 (1963): 190–194.
Analytic commentary on unifying melodic concepts in the Requiem. Musical examples.

1058. Reynold, Christopher. "A Choral Symphony by Brahms." *Nineteenth Century Music,* 9, no. 1 (1985): 3–25.
A study of extramusical allusions to be found in the sketches for a two-piano sonata, which later was reworked to become plans for a symphony, and later reworked again to become parts of the Piano Concerto No. 1 and the Requiem. Identifies and comments upon motives from these two works. No complete analysis of either work. The focus is on cross-references between works of Schumann and Brahms. Musical examples and tables.

1059. Robertson, Alec. *Requiem: Music of Mourning and Consolation,* 175–182. New York: Praeger, 1968.
Background, descriptive, and critical commentary. Musical examples.

1060. Tovey, Donald Francis. *Essays in Musical Analysis.* Vol. 5, 211–225. London: Oxford University Press, 1937.
Thorough analytic and critical commentary for the informed student. Musical examples.

1061. Warburton, A. O. "Set Works for 'O' Level, GCE." *Music Teacher and Piano Student,* 46 (February 1967): 13; (November 1967): 23.
Overview of the Requiem, with descriptive and analytic commentary.

1062. Warburton, A. O. "Set Works for 'O' Level, GCE." *Music Teacher,* 48 (January 1969): 16.

Brief descriptive and analytic commentary of "Selig sind, die da Leid tragen" and "Wie lieblich" for the undergraduate student.

1063.   Young, Percy M. *The Choral Tradition,* 243–246. New York: W. W. Norton, 1971.
Brief remarks, with analysis.

Intermezzo, Op. 76, No. 1 in A Minor

1064.   Horton, Charles T. "Chopin and Brahms: On A Common Meeting (Middle) Ground." *In Theory Only,* 6 (December 1982): 19–22.
A comparison of Brahms's treatment of this Intermezzo's melody with Chopin's treatment of the same melody in his Nocturne Op. 55, No. 1 in F Minor. Musical examples.

Intermezzo, Op. 76, No. 7 in A Minor

1065.   Kresky, Jeffrey. *Tonal Music: Twelve Analytic Studies,* 120–134. Bloomington: Indiana University Press, 1977.
In-depth analysis dealing with form, melody, tonality, and rhythm. Advanced. Musical examples and diagrams.

Intermezzo, Op. 117, No. 1 in E-Flat Major

1066.   Fiske, Roger. "Brahms and Scotland." *Musical Times,* 109 (December 1968): 1106–1110.
Discusses Brahms's settings of Herder's translations of Scottish ballads in his simple "folk song" style. Musical examples.

1067.   Zabrack, Harold. "Musical Timing: A View of Implicit Musical Reality as It Affects Musical Flow in Brahms's Intermezzo Op. 117, No. 1 in E-Flat Major." *Journal of the American Liszt Society,* 16 (1984): 89–97.
Analytic discussion focusing on compositional devices such as hemiola, contrapuntal imitation, and deceptive cadences. Musical examples.

Intermezzo, Op. 117, No. 2 in B-Flat Minor

1068.   Cadwallader, Allen. "Schenker's Unpublished Graphic Analysis of Brahms's Intermezzo Op. 117, No. 2: Tonal Structure and Concealed Motivic Repetition." *Music Theory Spectrum,* 6 (1984): 1–13.

1069. Zabrack, Harold. "Projecting Emotions: A Lesson on a Brahms Intermezzo." *Clavier*, 14, no. 6 (1975): 26–34.

Brief analysis, focusing on structure, texture, dynamics, and phrasing. Score included.

Intermezzo, Op. 117, No. 3 in C-Sharp Minor

1070. Davie, Cedric Thorpe. *Musical Structure and Design*, 46–48. New York: Dover Publications, 1966.

Measure-by-measure analysis to be used with score in hand.

Intermezzo, Op. 118, No. 1 in A Minor

1071. Citron, Ronald P. "Exempli Gratia: A Middleground Anticipation." *In Theory Only*, 2 (October 1976): 44–45.

Brief but advanced analysis of the first ten measures of the Intermezzo. Musical examples.

Intermezzo, Op. 119, No. 1 in B Minor

1072. Cadwallader, Allen. "Motivic Unity and Integration of Structural Levels in Brahms's B Minor Intermezzo Op. 119, No. 1." *Theory and Practice*, 8, no. 2 (1983): 5–24.

Demonstrates how disguised repetitions of an initial foreground motive are reflected in the work's formal and harmonic structure and how the expansion of this motive acts as a unifying factor integrating structural levels. Musical examples.

1073. Dunsby, Jonathan. *Structural Ambiguity in Brahms*, 85–105. Ann Arbor: UMI Research Press, 1981.

Advanced analytic essay. Musical examples and tables.

1074. Newbould, Brian. "A New Analysis of Brahms's Intermezzo in B Minor." *Music Review*, 38 (February 1977): 33–34.

Thorough, intense analysis for the advanced student. Musical examples.

1075. Warburton, A. O. "Set Works for 'O' Level, GCE." *Music Teacher*, 48 (January 1969): 16.

Brief analysis for the undergraduate student.

Intermezzo, Op. 119, No. 2 in E Minor

1076. Dumm, Robert. "Playing One of the Intermezzos: A Performer's Analysis." *Clavier*, 13, no. 2 (1974): 29–32.

Analysis, with complete score of the Intermezzo.

Motet, Op. 29, No. 2

1077.   Locke, Benjamin. "Melodic Unity in Brahms's *Schaffe in mir, Gott, ein rein Herz.*" *Choral Journal,* 27, no. 9 (1987): 5–7.
Identifies melodic similarities between movements and makes other analytic observations. Musical examples.

Quartet for Piano and Strings, Op. 25, No. 1 in G Minor

1078.   Dahlhaus, Carl. *Nineteenth-Century Music.* Translated by J. Bradford Robinson, 256–257. Berkeley: University of California Press, 1989.
Brief but concentrated analytic remarks on phrase structure and the "developing variation," a technique for "drawing far-reaching conclusions from a limited base of material." Advanced.

1079.   Frisch, Walter. *Brahms and the Principle of Developing Variation,* 66–74. Berkeley: University of California Press, 1984.
Analysis using Schoenberg's principle of "developing variation," which is a way of viewing the logical flow of the music as a variation on the basic musical idea of the work. For the advanced student. Musical examples.

1080.   Tischler, Hans. *The Perceptive Music Listener,* 301–306. Englewood Cliffs, NJ: Prentice-Hall, 1955.
Analysis with musical examples.

1081.   Tovey, Donald Francis. *Essays in Musical Analysis: Chamber Music,* 185–193. London: Oxford University Press, 1944.
Analysis with musical examples.

Quartet for Piano and Strings, Op. 26, No. 2 in A Major

1082.   Frisch, Walter. *Brahms and the Principle of Developing Variation,* 77–83. Berkeley: University of California Press, 1984.
Analysis using Schoenberg's principle of "developing variation," which is a way of viewing the logical flow of the music as a variation on the basic musical idea of the work. For the advanced student. Musical examples.

1083.   Tovey, Donald Francis. *Essays in Musical Analysis: Chamber Music,* 194–202. London: Oxford University Press, 1944.
Analysis with musical examples.

Quartet for Piano and Strings, Op. 60, No. 3 in C Minor

1084.   Dunsby, Jonathan. *Structural Ambiguity in Brahms,* 19–39. Ann Arbor: UMI Research Press, 1981.
  Advanced analytic essay. Musical examples and tables.

1085.   Tovey, Donald Francis. *Essays in Musical Analysis: Chamber Music,* 203–214. London: Oxford University Press, 1944.
  Analysis with musical examples.

Quartet for Strings, Op. 51, No. 1 in C Minor

1086.   Forte, Allen. "Motivic Design and Structural Levels in the First Movement of Brahms's String Quartet in C Minor." *Musical Quarterly,* 69, no. 4 (1983): 471 +.

1087.   Frisch, Walter. *Brahms and the Principle of Developing Variation,* 109–116. Berkeley: University of California Press, 1984.
  Analysis using Schoenberg's principle of "developing variation," which is a way of viewing the logical flow of the music as a variation on the basic musical idea of the work. For the advanced student. Musical examples.

Quartet for Strings, Op. 51, No. 2 in A Minor

1088.   Frisch, Walter. *Brahms and the Principle of Developing Variation,* 109–116. Berkeley: University of California Press, 1984.
  Analysis using Schoenberg's principle of "developing variation," which is a way of viewing the logical flow of the music as a variation on the basic musical idea of the work. For the advanced student. Musical examples.

1089.   Schoenberg, Arnold. *Style and Idea: Selected Writings of Arnold Schoenberg.* Translated by L. Black. Edited by Leo Stein, 430–435. New York: St. Martin's Press, 1975.
  Discussion of motivic elaboration and organization of the main theme of the *andante* movement.

Quintet for Piano and Strings, Op. 34 in F Minor

1090.   Frisch, Walter. *Brahms and the Principle of Developing Variation,* 83–88. Berkeley: University of California Press, 1984.
  Analysis using Schoenberg's principle of "developing variation," which is a way of viewing the logical flow of the music as a vari-

ation on the basic musical idea of the work. For the advanced student. Musical examples.

1091.   Newbould, Brian. "Analysis in the Sixth Form. 5." *Music Teacher*, 54 (July 1975): 16–17.
Background and analytic commentary.

Rhapsodies for Piano, Op. 79

1092.   Smith, Edwin. "Brahms: Two Rhapsodies for Piano Op. 79." *Music Teacher*, 55 (May 1976): 13–14.
Brief analytic remarks.

Rhapsody for Piano, Op. 79, No. 2 in G Minor

1093.   Greenberg, Beth. "Brahms's 'Rhapsody in G Minor Op. 79, No. 2: A Study of Analyses by Schenker, Schoenberg, and Jonas." *In Theory Only*, 1 (December–January 1976–1977): 21–29.
Compares analyses of the harmonic organization of the tonally ambiguous opening (mm. 1–8). Includes analytic comments by Charles J. Smith on pp. 31–32. Musical examples.

1094.   Smith, Charles J. "Comment on Greenberg." *In Theory Only*, 1 (December–January 1976–1977): 31–32.
Commentary on B. Greenberg's article (*see* item no.1093) on a study of analyses by Schenker, Schoenberg, and Jonas on this work.

Rhapsody for Piano, Op. 119, No. 4 in E-Flat Major

1095.   Warburton, A. O. "Set Works for 'O' Level, GCE." *Music Teacher*, 48 (January 1969): 37.
Brief analysis for the undergraduate student.

Scherzo for Piano, Op. 4 in E-Flat Major

1096.   Joseph, Charles M. "Origins of Brahms's Structural Control." *College Music Symposium*, 21, no. 1 (1981): 7–23.
Discussion of formal coherence as a high compositional priority in Brahms's compositions; historical-analytic study of the Scherzo Op. 4; examination of later works displaying similar structural controls. The Scherzo is discussed on pp. 13–18. Musical examples. Further brief comments on this article in "Let-

ters to the Editor" by Eric Nisula and a reply to Nisula's letter by Charles Joseph in *College Music Symposium*, 22, no. 1 (1982): 194–196.

Serenades

1097. Niemann, Walter. *Brahms.* Translated by Catherine Alison Phillips, 302–306. New York: Alfred A. Knopf, n.d.
   Brief descriptive and critical commentary.

Sextet for Strings, Op. 18 in B-Flat Major

1098. Truscott, Harold. "Brahms and Sonata Style." *Music Review,* 25, no. 3 (1964): 186–201.
   Deals with the first movement only. Use of sonata form examined.

Sonata for Clarinet, Op. 120, No. 1 in F Minor

1099. Frisch, Walter. *Brahms and the Principle of Developing Variation,* 147–151. Berkeley: University of California Press, 1984.
   Analysis using Schoenberg's principle of "developing variation," which is a way of viewing the logical flow of the music as a variation on the basic musical idea of the work. For the advanced student. Musical examples.

Sonatas for Piano

1100. Kirby, Frank E. "Brahms and the Piano Sonata." In *Paul A. Pisk: Essays in His Honor.* Edited by John Glowacki, 163–180. Austin: University of Texas Press, 1966.
   Thorough analyses and historical perspective on all three of Brahms's piano sonatas. Musical examples.

Sonata for Piano No. 1, Op. 1 in C Major

1101. Fiske, Roger. "Brahms and Scotland." *Musical Times,* 109 (December 1968): 1106–1110.
   Discusses Brahms's settings of Herder's translations of Scottish ballads in his "folk song" style, which Brahms converted for use in this sonata. Musical examples.

1102. Newman, William S. "Some Nineteenth Century Consequences of Beethoven's Hammerklavier Sonata Op. 106." *Piano Quarterly,* 17, no. 68 (1969): 14–15.

Traces influences of the Hammerklavier Sonata on other composers, especially Mendelssohn and Brahms. Musical examples.

Sonata for Piano No. 3, Op. 5 in F Minor

1103. **Frisch, Walter.** *Brahms and the Principle of Developing Variation,* 35–40. Berkeley: University of California Press, 1984.
Analysis using Schoenberg's principle of "developing variation," which is a way of viewing the logical flow of the music as a variation on the basic musical idea of the work. For the advanced student. Musical examples.

1104. **Sutton, Wadham.** "Brahms: Sonata in F Minor." *Music Teacher,* 52 (August 1973): 12–13.
Brief analytic remarks.

Sonata for Violin No. 1, Op. 78 in G Major

1105. **Frisch, Walter.** *Brahms and the Principle of Developing Variation,* 116–120. Berkeley: University of California Press, 1984.
Analysis using Schoenberg's principle of "developing variation," which is a way of viewing the logical flow of the music as a variation on the basic musical idea of the work. For the advanced student. Musical examples.

Sonata for Violoncello No. 1, Op. 38 in E Minor

1106. **Klenz, William.** "Brahms, Op. 38: Piracy, Pillage, Plagiarism, or Parody?." *Music Review,* 34, no. 1 (1973): 39–50.
A detailed comparison of Brahms's Sonata for Violoncello Op. 38 with its predecessor, Bernhard Romberg's Op. 38, to show how heavily Brahms was indebted to Romberg.

1107. **Pascall, Robert.** "Set Works for 'O' Level, GCE." *Music Teacher,* 60 (May 1981): 18.
Brief background and analytic commentary for the undergraduate student. Brief bibliography.

Songs, Op. 3, No. 3 ("Liebe und Fruehling")

1108. **Braus, Ira.** "Brahms's 'Liebe und Fruehling' II, Op. 3, No. 3: A New Path to the Artwork of the Future?" *Nineteenth Century Music,* 10, no. 2 (1986): 135–156.

This article demonstrates the influence of Wagner's writings on Brahms's early *Lied* composition—and that Op. 3, No. 3 in turn influenced Wagner's composition of *Tristan*. Includes detailed discussion of parallels between poetic and musical rhetoric, with musical analysis of the song. Musical examples. The analysis is on pp. 138–146. For the advanced student.

Songs, Op. 105, No. 1

1109. Clarkson, Austin and Edward Laufer. "Analysis Symposium: Brahms, Op. 105, no. 1." *Journal of Music Theory*, 15, nos. 1–2 (1971): 2–57.

Exhaustive analysis of "Wie Melodien zieht es mir" of this set. Score included. Advanced.

Song of Destiny

1110. Luhring, Alan A. "Dialectical Thought in Nineteenth-Century Music and Exhibited in Brahms's Setting of Hoelderin's 'Schicksalslied.' " *Choral Journal*, 25, no. 8 (1985): 5–13.

Symphonies

1111. Cuyler, Louise. *The Symphony*, 104–125. New York: Harcourt Brace Jovanovich, 1973.

Analytic commentary on all the symphonies. Background and general characteristics of the symphonies as well as a detailed musical analysis.

1112. Harrison, Julius. *Brahms and His Four Symphonies.* 1939. Reprint. New York: Da Capo Press, 1971, 312 pp.

Background, stylistic characteristics, and orchestration, as well as formal analysis. Quite thorough.

1113. Horton, John. *Brahms Orchestral Music*, 32–38. Seattle: University of Washington Press, 1968.

Critical and analytic commentary intended for the undergraduate student.

1114. Kross, Siegfried. "Brahms the Symphonist." In *Brahms: Biographical, Documentary and Analytical Studies.* Edited by Robert Pascall, 125–145. Cambridge: Cambridge University Press, 1988.

Brahms's technical and artistic development traced through the symphonies. Analytic commentary on texture, tonality, harmony, and themes. Musical examples.

1115.   Musgrave, Michael. *The Music of Brahms,* 130–141, 213–217, 219–230. London: Routledge and Kegan Paul, 1985.
Thorough analytic commentary dealing with form, tonality, structural principles, motives, and the place of each of the symphonies in Brahms's artistic development. Musical examples.

1116.   Niemann, Walter. *Brahms.* Translated by Catherine Alison Phillips, 323–348. New York: Cooper Square, 1969.
Background, critical and analytic commentary.

1117.   Smith, Raymond R. "Motivic Procedure in Opening Movements of the Symphonies of Schumann, Bruckner, and Brahms." *Music Review,* 36, no. 2 (1975): 130–134.
Advanced discussion on motivic treatment as an important element of sonata form.

1118.   Specht, Richard. *Johannes Brahms.* Translated by Eric Blom, 265–285. London: J. M. Dent and Sons, 1930.
Critical commentary with analytic remarks.

1119.   Tovey, Donald Francis. *Essays in Musical Analysis.* Vol. 1, 84–115. London: Oxford University Press, 1935.
Descriptive and analytic commentary intended for the undergraduate student. Musical examples.

1120.   Wiseman, Herbert. "Johannes Brahms (1833–1897)." In *The Symphony.* Edited by Ralph Hill, 224–246. Harmondsworth: Penguin Books, 1949.
Brief descriptive commentary on each symphony. For the undergraduate student or musical amateur. Musical examples.

Symphony No. 1, Op. 68 in C Minor

1121.   George, Graham. *Tonality and Musical Structure,* 174–178. London: Oxford University Press, 1970.
Tonal analysis. Musical examples.

1122.   Haggin, B. H. *A Book of the Symphony,* 238–251. London: Oxford University Press, 1937.
Straightforward description dealing with formal plan only. Brief background remarks, with no discussion of tonality, rhythm, or texture. For the musical amateur or undergraduate student concerned with form. Musical examples.

149

1123. Musgrave, Michael. "Brahms's First Symphony: Thematic Coherence and Its Secret Origin." *Music Analysis*, 2, no. 2 (1983): 117–133.
   Advanced analysis.

1124. Stedman, Preston. *The Symphony*, 158–165. Englewood Cliffs, NJ: Prentice-Hall, 1979.
   Extensive description of formal plan, tonality, thematic and motivic activity, scoring, and texture. For the undergraduate student. Musical examples and diagram.

Symphony No. 2, Op. 73 in D Major

1125. Frisch, Walter. *Brahms and the Principle of Developing Variation*, 121–142. Berkeley: University of California Press, 1984.
   Analysis using Schoenberg's principle of "developing variation," which is a way of viewing the logical flow of the music as a variation on the basic musical idea of the work. For the advanced student. Musical examples.

1126. Haggin, B. H. *A Book of the Symphony*, 252–261. London: Oxford University Press, 1937.
   Straightforward description dealing with formal plan only. Brief background remarks, with no discussion of tonality, rhythm, or texture. For the musical amateur or undergraduate student concerned with form. Musical examples.

1127. Schachter, Carl. "The First Movement of Brahms's Second Symphony: The Opening Theme and Its Consequences." *Music Analysis*, 2, no. 1 (1983): 55–68.
   Advanced analysis.

1128. Stedman, Preston. *The Symphony*, 150–153. Englewood Cliffs, NJ: Prentice-Hall, 1979.
   Extended description of thematic and motivic activity, formal structure, instrumentation, meter, and tonality.

1129. Ulrich, Homer. *Music: A Design for Listening*, 384–389. New York: Harcourt, Brace, 1957.
   Analytic observations accompanied by a descriptive/analytic breakdown by measures. Musical examples.

Symphony No. 3, Op. 90 in F Major

1130. Brown, A. Peter. "Brahms's Third Symphony and the New German School." *Journal of Musicology*, 2, no. 4 (1983): 434–452.

A demonstration of extramusical aspects of the Third Symphony, placing Brahms closer to the Wagner-Liszt school of program music than is customarily done. Musical examples.

1131. Dahlhaus, Carl. *Nineteenth-Century Music.* Translated by J. Bradford Robinson, 269–271. Berkeley: University of California Press, 1989.

Brief but concentrated analytic remarks dwelling on motives, form, and tonality. Advanced.

1132. Frisch, Walter. *Brahms and the Principle of Developing Variation,* 121–142. Berkeley: University of California Press, 1984.

Analysis using Schoenberg's principle of "developing variation," which is a way of viewing the logical flow of the music as a variation on the basic musical idea of the work. For the advanced student. Musical examples.

1133. George, Graham. *Tonality and Musical Structure,* 179–182. London: Oxford University Press, 1970.

Tonal analysis. Musical examples.

1134. Haggin, B. H. *A Book of the Symphony,* 262–270. London: Oxford University Press, 1937.

Straightforward description dealing with formal plan only. Brief background remarks, with no discussion of tonality, rhythm, or texture. For the musical amateur or undergraduate student concerned with form. Musical examples.

1135. Machlis, Joseph. *The Enjoyment of Music.* 3d ed, 154–156. New York: W. W. Norton, 1970.

Analytic overview for the undergraduate student. Musical examples.

1136. Stedman, Preston. *The Symphony,* 153–154. Englewood Cliffs, NJ: Prentice-Hall, 1979.

Brief description for the undergraduate student of thematic and motivic activity, formal structure, and tonality.

Symphony No. 4, Op. 98 in E Minor

1137. Bernstein, Leonard. *The Infinite Variety of Music,* 229–262. New York: Simon and Schuster, 1966.

Thorough critical review with many analytic insights. For the undergraduate student or musical amateur. Musical examples. First movement only.

151

1138.   Boretz, Benjamin. "Meta-Variations, Part IV: Analytic Fallout." *Perspectives of New Music,* 11, no. 2 (1973): 160–166.
  Highly technical analysis of the first eighteen measures focusing on how the "time-structure" of the passage analyzed is defined by its third cycles. Musical examples.

1139.   Cantrell, Byron. "Three B's—Three Chaconnes." *Current Musicology,* 12 (September 1971): 69–73.
  Advanced discussion of Brahms's use of chaconne in this work. Compares with the chaconnes of Bach and Beethoven.

1140.   Dunsby, Jonathan. *Structural Ambiguity in Brahms,* 41–83. Ann Arbor: UMI Research Press, 1981.
  Advanced analytic essays. Musical examples and tables.

1141.   George, Graham. *Tonality and Musical Structure,* 182–187. London: Oxford University Press, 1970.
  Tonal analysis. Musical examples.

1142.   Haggin, B. H. *A Book of the Symphony,* 271–282. London: Oxford University Press, 1937.
  Straightforward description dealing with formal plan only. Brief background remarks, with no discussion of tonality, rhythm, or texture. For the musical amateur or undergraduate student concerned with form. Musical examples.

1143.   Hendrickson, Hugh. "Rhythmic Activity in the Symphonies of Brahms." *In Theory Only,* 2 (September 1976): 5–12 + .
  Advanced analysis of rhythmic structure excluding the factors of pitch, register, timbre, intensity, and position in texture. Musical examples.

1144.   Kerman, Joseph. *Listen,* 278–283. New York: Worth Publishers, 1972.
  Analysis with musical examples.

1145.   Knapp, Raymond. "The Finale of Brahms's Fourth Symphony: The Tale of the Subject." *Nineteenth Century Music,* 13, no. 1 (1989): 3–17.
  An examination of the ostinato subject of the last movement. Its origins in Bach's Cantata No. 150 and Buxtehude's E Minor Chaconne mentioned and reasons why Brahms chose it explored. The ostinato's role in the shape of the movement examined as well. Advanced. Musical examples.

1146.   Leichtentritt, Hugo. *Musical Form,* 315. Cambridge, MA: Harvard University Press. 1959.
> Brief but compact statement analyzing the variations. Must be used with score. Fourth movement only.

1147.   Osmond-Smith, David. "The Retreat from Dynamism: A Study of Brahms's Fourth Symphony." In *Brahms: Biographical, Documentary, and Analytical Studies.* Edited by Robert Pascall, 147–165. Cambridge: Cambridge University Press, 1983.
> An analytic essay including discussion of form, thematic content, tonal relationships, and the position the work occupies in Brahms's artistic development. Musical examples and diagrams.

1148.   Stedman, Preston. *The Symphony,* 154–158. Englewood Cliffs, NJ: Prentice-Hall, 1979.
> Descriptive, commentary for the undergraduate student. Deals with thematic and motivic activity, tonality, and formal plan.

Tragic Overture

1149.   Tovey, Donald Francis. *Essays in Musical Analysis.* Vol. 6, 55–57. London: Oxford University Press, 1969.
> Critical and analytic with musical examples. For the undergraduate student.

1150.   Webster, James. "Brahms's *Tragic* Overture: The Form of Tragedy." In *Brahms: Biographical, Documentary and Analytical Studies.* Edited by Robert Pascall, 99–124. Cambridge: Cambridge University Press, 1983.
> Exhaustive analysis concentrating on the first musical group and opening motto; the form of the whole and an assessment of those musical aspects that can be labeled "tragic." Finally, the work is placed in the context of Brahms's other orchestral pieces and other comparable nineteenth-century overtures. Musical examples.

Trio for Piano No. 1, Op. 8 in B Major

1151.   Frisch, Walter. *Brahms and the Principle of Developing Variation,* 56–63. Berkeley: University of California Press, 1984.
> Analysis using Schoenberg's principle of "developing variation," which is a way of viewing the logical flow of the music as a variation on the basic musical idea of the work.

153

Variations on a Theme by Handel, Op. 24

1152.   Dunsby, Jonathan. *Structural Ambiguity in Brahms*, 3–18. Ann Arbor: UMI Research Press, 1981.
  Advanced analytic essay. Musical examples and tables.

1153.   Tovey, Donald Francis. *Essays in Musical Analysis: Chamber Music*, 167–172. London: Oxford University Press, 1944.
  Critical observations and analytic insights. Musical examples.

Variations on a Theme by Paganini, Op. 35

1154.   Tovey, Donald Francis. *Essays in Musical Analysis: Chamber Music*, 172–185. London: Oxford University Press, 1944.
  Critical observations and analytic insights. Musical examples.

Variations on a Theme by Schumann, Op. 23

1155.   Crowder, Louis. "Brahms's Early Tribute to the Schumanns." *Clavier*, 5, no. 7 (1966): 18–25.
  Descriptive and analytic overview, with background remarks. Musical examples.

"Vorüber," Op. 58

1156.   Bozart, George S. "Synthesizing Work and Tone: Brahms's Setting of Hebbel's *Vorüber*." In *Brahms: Biographical, Documentary, and Analytical Studies*. Edited by Robert Pascall, 77–98. Cambridge: Cambridge University Press, 1983.
  Discussion compositional history and the word-tone synthesis achieved by Brahms in this song. Sources, variant versions, and sketches discussed in detail. Musical examples.

Waltzes

1157.   Gruber, Albion. "Some Viewpoints on Brahms: Understanding Rhythm in the Piano Music." *Clavier*, 13, no. 2 (1974): 9–13.
  Analytic insights on rhythm. Musical examples.

DISSERTATIONS AND THESES

General

1158.   Breslauer, Peter Seth. "Motivic and Rhythmic Contrapuntal Structure in the Chamber Music of Johannes Brahms." Ph.D., Yale University, 1984, 188 pp., DA 46-548A.

1159.   Cai, Camilla. "Brahms's Short, Late Piano Pieces—Opus Numbers 116–119: A Source Study, An Analysis, and Performance Practice." Ph.D., Boston University, 1986, 563 pp., DA 47-340A.

1160.   Rose, Michael Paul. "Structural Integration in Selected Mixed A Cappella Choral Works of Brahms." Ph.D., University of Michigan, 1971, 280 pp., DA 32-4051A.

Capriccios

1161.   Feinstein, Bernice. "The Seven Capriccios of Johannes Brahms: Op. 76, Nos. 1, 2, 5, 8, and Op. 116, Nos. 1, 3, 7." Ed.D., Columbia University, 1972, 245 pp., DA 33-891A-2A.

Concerto for Piano No. 1, Op. 15 in D Minor

1162.   James, Roberta Aileen. "Johannes Brahms: Concerto No. 1 in D Minor, Op. 15." D.M.A., Stanford University, 1981, 60 pp., DA 42-2924A.

German Requiem

1163.   Westafer, Walter. "Over-All Unity and Contrast in Brahms's *German* Requiem." Ph.D., University of North Carolina at Chapel Hill, 1973, 330 pp., DA 35-507A.

Intermezzos

1164.   Cadwallader, Allen Clayton. "Multileveled Motivic Repetition in Selected Intermezzi for Piano of Johannes Brahms." Ph.D., University of Rochester, Eastman School of Music, 1983, 238 pp., DA 43-3450A.

Intermezzo, Op. 118, No. 6 in E-Flat Minor

1165.   Miller, Lynus Patrick. "From Analysis to Performance: The Musical Landscape of Johannes Brahms's Op. 118, No. 6." Ph.D., University of Michigan, 1979, 161 pp., DA 40-530A-31A.

"O Heiland, Reiss die Himmel Auf"

1166.   Locke, Benjamin Ross. "Performance and Structural Levels: A Conductor's Analysis of Brahms's Op. 74, No. 2, 'O Heiland, Reiss Die Himmel Auf.' " D.M.A., University of Wisconsin at Madison, 1985, 240 pp., DA 47-15A.

Pieces (Six) for Piano, Op. 118

1167.   **Lamb, James Boyd.** "A Graphic Analysis of Brahms, Op. 118, with an Introduction to Schenkerian Theory and the Reduction Process." Ph.D., Texas Technical University, 1979, 162 pp., DA 41-454A.

Romanzen (Fifteen) aus Tieck's Magalone, Op. 33

1168.   **Jack, Dwight Christian.** "Two Romantic Song Cycles: An Analytical Description of the Schumann-Eichendorff *Liederkreis II,* Op. 39 and the Brahms-Tieck *Romanzen aus Magalone.*" D.M.A., University of Miami, 1973, 131 pp., DA 35-500A.

Song of Destiny

1169.   **Bellamy, Kathrine Elizabeth.** "Motivic Development in Two Larger Choral Works of Johannes Brahms." Ph.D., University of Wisconsin, 1973, 370 pp., DA 34-6680A.

Variations on a Theme of Haydn, Op. 56a

1170.   **Magrill, Samuel Morse.** "The Principle of Variation: A Study in the Selection of Differences with Examples from Dallapiccola, J. S. Bach, and Brahms." D.M.A., University of Illinois at Urbana, 1983, 253 pp., DA 43-3749A.

BRIAN, HAVERGAL, 1876–1972

General

1171.   **Nettel, Reginald.** *Havergal Brian and His Music.* London: Dennis Dobson, 1976, 223 pp.
   Descriptive and analytic overview of Brian's output. Musical examples.

Symphonies

1172.   **MacDonald, Malcolm.** *The Symphonies of Havergal Brian.* 3 vols. London: Kahn and Averill, 1973–1983.
   Analytic essays on the music of Brian. Vol. 1 contains essays on Symphonies 1–12; vol. 2 covers Symphonies 13–29; vol. 3 contains essays on Symphonies 30–32, and a further eleven chapters on various aspects of Brian and his music: harmony, tonality,

form, orchestration. The essays are best described as "descriptive analysis." The reader is walked through each work with commentary and music examples. Appendices contain lists of works, manuscripts, editions, recordings, and performances.

1173.   Simpson, Robert, ed. *The Symphony.* Vol. 2, 140–152. New York: Drake Publishers, 1972.
Overview of the first ten of Brian's thirty-two symphonies. Mainly descriptive commentary, with analytic insights on tonality and form. Musical examples.

BRIDGE, FRANK, 1879–1941

General

1174.   Payne, Anthony. *Frank Bridge: Radical and Conservative.* London: Thames Publishing, 1984, 111 pp.
Thorough analytic review, including catalogue of works, bibliography, and discography. Musical examples.

1175.   Payne, Anthony. "The Music of Frank Bridge." *Tempo,* 106 (1973): 18–25; 107 (1973): 11–18.
In-depth critical and analytic assessment of Bridge's music. Musical examples.

1176.   Webber, Julian Lloyd. *The Cello Music of Frank Bridge."* Strad, 86 (April 1976): 905 + .
Descriptive and critical commentary.

Idylls

1177.   Bray, Trevor. "Bridge's Novelletten and *Idylls.*" *Musical Times,* 11 (November 1976): 905–906.
Brief analytic commentary. Musical examples.

Sonata for Piano

1178.   Pirie, Peter J. "Frank Bridge's Piano Sonata." *Music and Musicians,* 24 (January 1976): 28–30 + .
Critical, descriptive, and analytic commentary.

DISSERTATIONS AND THESES

General

1179.   Keating, Roderic Maurice. "The Songs of Frank Bridge." D.M.A., University of Texas at Austin, 115 pp., DA 31-3583A.

BRITTEN, BENJAMIN, 1913–1976
General

1180.   Brown, David. "Stimulus and Form in Britten's Work." *Music and Letters*, 39 (July 1958): 218–226.
Mainly a discussion of form used in *The Holy Sonnets of John Donne* and the Second String Quartet. Includes background information and analytic commentary.

1181.   Churchill, John. "The Sacred World of Benjamin Britten." *Music (AGO)*, 11 (November 1977): 40–43.
Descriptive commentary, with a view towards performance. Bibliography.

1182.   Elliott, Graham. "The Operas of Benjamin Britten: A Spiritual View." *Opera Quarterly*, 4, no. 3 (1986): 28–44.
A discussion of the spiritual aspects of Britten's operas, such as the "messages" they convey, or parables they demonstrate. Analytical comments on keys representing good and evil as well as on other symbolic musical devices. Musical examples.

1183.   Elson, James. "The Songs of Benjamin Britten." *NATS Bulletin*, 35, no. 4 (1979): 14–16.
Descriptive survey, with a view towards performance. Bibliography.

1184.   Evans, Peter. "The Music of Benjamin Britten. Minneapolis: University of Minnesota Press, 1979, 564 pp.
A survey of all Britten's music. Descriptive commentary, with analytic observations useful to the general reader and undergraduate student. Musical examples.

1185.   Hines, Robert S. "Benjamin Britten (1913–): A Review of His Choral Compositions." *Choral Journal*, 11, no. 6 (1971): 17–19 + .
Overview with descriptive thumbnail sketches meant to aid the performer in choosing repertoire. Useful here for occasional analytic comments.

1186.   Howard, Patricia. *The Operas of Benjamin Britten: An Introduction.* 1969. Reprint. Westport, CT: Greenwood, 1976, 236 pp.
Discusses the operas up to and including *The Burning Fiery Furnace*, omitting *Prodigal Son; Owen Wingrave; Death in Venice.* The first opera, *Paul Bunyan*, is also omitted. There is a synopsis of the plot of each opera and a discussion of the drama and the music. Discussions include analytic comments and musical examples. For the general reader and undergraduate student.

1187. Hutchings, Arthur. "Music in Britain 1916–1960." In *The New Oxford History of Music* Vol. 10, *The Modern Age: 1890–1960.* Edited by Martin Cooper, 543–556. London: Oxford University Press, 1974.
Overview of Britten's style, with analytic comments on *Sinfonia da Requiem, Peter Grimes,* the *Holy Sonnets of John Donne* and the three Canticles.

1188. Kennedy, Michael. *Britten.* London: J. M. Dent and Sons, 1981.
Brief commentary on each work, with analytic comments, and music examples for the more important works.

1189. Martin, George. "Benjamin Britten: Twenty-Five Years of Opera." *Yale Review,* 60, no. 1 (1970): 24–44.
General discussion of Britten's operas and reason for successes and failures. Mentions recurrent themes in his work.

1190. McCray, James. "Britten's Music for Voices and Organ." *Diapason,* 68 (May 1977): 1 + .
Critical and analytic commentary.

1191. Mitchell, Donald, and Hans Keller, eds. *Benjamin Britten: A Commentary on His Works from a Group of Specialists.* London: Rockliff, 1952, 410 pp.
A collection of essays, analytical in orientation, covering Britten's music up to publication (1952). Individual chapters on different genres—with three chapters on *Peter Grimes,* the most important work to that date. The depth of the discussions vary from detailed analytic observations to general discussions of style. Musical examples.

1192. Palmer, Christopher, ed. *The Britten Companion.* London: Faber and Faber, 1984, 485 pp.
Probably the most extensive collection of analytic writing on Britten's music. The articles, by numerous authors, are mostly reprints from a variety of sources. They range from reminiscences of associates to analytic discussions of major works.

1193. Snyder, Robert E. "Britten's Short Choral Works Without Organ Accompaniments." *Diapason,* 68 (May 1977): 1 + .
Descriptive and critical commentary with analytic observations.

1194. Warburton, A. O. "Set Works for 'O' Level, GCE." *Music Teacher,* 49 (April 1970): 19–20.
Brief background and descriptive commentary for the undergraduate student.

1195. Webber, Julian Lloyd. "The Cello Music of Benjamin Britten." *Strad*, 86 (September 1975): 387 + .
Descriptive and critical commentary.

1196. White, Eric Walter. *Benjamin Britten: His Life and Operas.* Edited by J. Evans. London: Faber and Faber, 1983, 322 pp.
Mainly a descriptive and critical overview, accompanied by analytic observations. Includes synopsis and background.

1197. Whittall, Arnold. *The Music of Britten and Tippett: Studies in Themes and Techniques.* Cambridge: Cambridge University Press, 1982, 314 pp.
A collection of essays on the music of these two composers. The essays are all detailed analytic studies of a single work or of a number of works. Musical examples.

1198. Whittall, Arnold. *Music Since the First World War*, 109–115. London: J. M. Dent and Sons, 1977.
Analytic observations on the operas.

1199. Whittall, Arnold. "Tonality in Britten's Song Cycles With Piano." *Tempo*, 96 (Spring 1971): 2–11.
Detailed, analytic discussion of the various types of expanded tonality used in Britten's song cycles. Musical examples.

A Ceremony of Carols

1200. Anderson, Julia S. "Britten's *A Ceremony of Carols*." *American Harp Journal*, 7, no. 4 (1980): 24–31.
Critical and analytic commentary. Bibliography.

Billy Budd

1201. Mitchell, Donald. "Britten's Revisionary Practice: Practical and Creative." *Tempo*, 66–67 (Autumn–Winter 1963): 15–22.
Describes differences between the original and revised versions of the opera. Musical examples.

1202. Sutcliffe, James H. "The Infinite Sea." *Opera News*, 48 (April 1984): 16–18 + .
Discussion of revisions and cuts made to form the two-act 1960 version. Symbolism, word painting, motives, and characters also reviewed.

1203. Whittall, Arnold. "A War and a Wedding: Two Modern British Operas." *Music and Letters*, 55, no. 3 (1974): 299–306.

A critical evaluation, mainly concerned with dramatic action. A few outstanding musical devices are mentioned in relation to the action they help portray.

Canticles

1204.   Egbert, Lovard E. "Britten's Five Canticles." *Diapason*, 68 (May 1977): 1 + .
Analyses with observations on stylistic characteristics. Musical examples.

Curlew River

1205.   Evans, Peter. "Current Chronicle: England." *Musical Quarterly*, 52, no. 4 (1966): 503–507.
Descriptive remarks supported with musical examples. Highlights of outstanding musical features.

1206.   Flynn, William T. "Britten the Progressive." *Music Review*, 44, no. 1 (1983): 44–52.
Britten's juxtaposition of stable and unstable chord types and of tonally centered and uncentered areas are shown to account for the dramatic unity and organization of the opera. Musical examples.

1207.   Warrack, John. "Britten's *Curlew River*." *Tempo*, 70 (Autumn 1964): 19–22.
Description of the work, with musical examples.

Death in Venice

1208.   Dickinson, A. E. F. "Britten's New Opera." *Musical Quarterly*, 60, no. 3 (1974): 470–478.
Analytic commentary, with musical examples.

1209.   White, Eric Walter. "The Voyage to Venice." *Opera News*, 39 (December 14, 1974): 15–19.
Overview of Britten's output, with descriptive remarks on *Death in Venice*. Musical examples.

Hymn to Saint Cecilia

1210.   Unger, Mel. "Britten's Hymn to St. Cecilia: An Exegesis." *Choral Journal*, 22, no. 8 (1982): 17–21.
Descriptive and analytic commentary. Bibliography.

Midsummer Night's Dream

1211.   Evans, Peter. "Britten's New Opera: A Preview." *Tempo*, 53–54 (Spring–Summer 1960): 34–48.
A description of the whole opera, with analytical observations and musical examples.

1212.   Redlich, Hans. "Britten's Idiom." *Music Review*, 22, no. 3 (1961): 262–263.
Analysis to shed light on the proper way to perform Britten's opera. Musical examples.

1213.   Roseberry, Eric. "A Note on the Four Chords in Act II of *A Midsummer Night's Dream*." *Tempo*, 66–67 (Autumn–Winter 1963): 36–37.
A very brief "note" on these serially derived chords, which are found in both *A Midsummer Night's Dream* and Serenade.

Missa Brevis in D Major, Op. 63

1214.   Roseberry, Eric. "A Note on Britten's *Missa Brevis*." *Tempo*, 53–54 (Spring–Summer 1960): 11–16.
A brief description of the work. Musical examples.

Night Piece (Notturno), Op. 70

1215.   Miller, Carl. "Meditation on Benjamin Britten's Nocturnal." *Guitar Review*, 42 (Fall 1977): 15–16.
Critical and analytic discussion.

1216.   Waterman, Fanny. "Britten's New Piano Pieces." *Tempo*, 66–67 (Autumn–Winter 1963): 34–36.
A brief introduction and description, with musical examples.

Noye's Flood

1217.   Mellers, Wilfrid. "Music for Twentieth-Century Children: From Magic to Drama." *Musical Times*, 105 (June 1964): 422–427.
A descriptive overview of the opera. Musical examples.

1218.   Roseberry, Eric. "The Music of *Noye's fludde*." *Tempo*, 49 (Autumn 1958): 2–11.
Analytical overview of the whole opera. Musical examples.

1219. Warburton, A. O. "Set Works for 'O' level, GCE." *Music Teacher*, 47 (March 1968): 14 +.

Thorough background, descriptive, and analytic commentary for the undergraduate student.

Owen Wingrave

1220. Evans, Peter. "Britten's Television Opera." *Musical Times*, 112 (May 1971): 425–428.

Synopsis, analytical comments, and story sources.

1221. Raynor, Henry. "Opera: *Owen Wingrave.*" *Music Review*, 32, no. 3 (1971): 271–273.

An assessment of *Owen Wingrave* as a television opera, with critical commentary on selected highlights.

Peter Grimes

1222. Brett, Philip, ed. *Benjamin Britten: "Peter Grimes."* Cambridge: Cambridge University Press, 1983, 217 pp.

A volume in the Cambridge Opera Handbooks series. Includes analytic essays by Hans Keller and David Matthews. Relationship between text and music, the building of music structures out of short motifs, use of tonality to heighten dramatic action, as well as discussions of background, text, interpretation, and other related factors. Musical examples.

1223. Donington, Robert. *The Opera*, 215–216. New York: Harcourt Brace Jovanovich, 1978.

Brief remarks on dramatic and musical features. Musical examples.

1224. Garbutt, John W. "Music and Motive in *Peter Grimes.*" *Music and Letters*, 44, no. 4 (1963): 334–342.

A critical assessment of the dramatic integrity of *Peter Grimes*. Some mention made of the music, but not an analysis.

1225. John, Nicholas, ed. *Peter Grimes.* London: John Calder, 1984, 128 pp.

An introduction to the opera for the general public. Analytic comments with background information. Musical examples.

1226. Lackey, Lionel. "Gnats, Wasps, and Horseflies." *Opera News*, 37 (March 24, 1973): 24–25.

Brief remarks on characterization. Musical examples.

1227. McDonald, Katherine. "At Home with the Sea." *Opera News,* 31 (February 11, 1967): 24–25.
Analytic and critical commentary, with musical examples.

1228. Payne, Anthony. "Dramatic Use of Tonality in *Peter Grimes.*" *Tempo,* 66–67 (Autumn–Winter 1963): 22–26.

1229. Schmidgall, Gary. "Out of the Borough." *Opera News,* 42 (December 10, 1977): 11–15.
A comparison of the play *The Borough* by George Crabbe, on which *Peter Grimes* is based, with the opera.

Peter Grimes: Four Sea Interludes

1230. Machlis, Joseph. *The Enjoyment of Music.* 5th ed., 523–525. New York: W. W. Norton, 1984.
Descriptive commentary for the undergraduate student. Salient musical features highlighted. Musical examples.

Prodigal Son

1231. Matthews, David. "Britten's *The Prodigal Son.*" *Tempo,* 85 (Summer 1968): 28–30.
Descriptive and critical commentary.

Psalm 150

1232. Warburton, A. O. "Set Works for 'O' Level, GCE." *Music Teacher,* 49 (April 1970): 19–20.
Background, descriptive, and analytic commentary for the undergraduate student.

Quartet for Strings No. 3

1233. Matthews, David. "Britten's Third Quartet." *Tempo,* 125 (June 1978): 21–24.
Criticism and analysis. Musical examples.

Rejoice in the Lamb

1234. LePage, Peter V. "Benjamin Britten's *Rejoice in the Lamb.*" *Music Review,* 33, no. 2 (1972): 122–137.
Descriptive commentary and formal analysis of the work. Musical examples.

1235. Warburton, A. O. "Set Works for 'O' Level, GCE." *Music Teacher*, 49 (April 1970): 19–20.

Background, descriptive, and analytic commentary for the undergraduate student.

Saint Nicolas

1236. Warburton, A. O. "Set Works for 'O' Level, GCE." *Music Teacher*, 47 (April 1968): 13–14.

Thorough background, descriptive, and analytic commentary for the undergraduate student.

Serenade for Tenor, Horn, and Strings, Op. 31

1237. Roseberry, Eric. "A Note on the Four Chords in Act II of *A Midsummer Night's Dream.*" *Tempo*, 66–67 (Autumn–Winter 1963): 36–37.

Very brief note on these serially derived chords, which also appear in this work.

1238. Warburton, A. O. "Set Works for 'O' Level, GCE." *Music Teacher*, 53 (February 1974): 12–13 +.

Thorough descriptive and analytic commentary for the undergraduate student.

Sonata for Violoncello and Piano, Op. 65

1239. Evans, Peter. "Britten's Cello Sonata." *Tempo*, 58 (Summer 1961): 8–16.

An analysis of the structure of all five movements. Musical examples.

Songs from the Chinese, Op. 58

1240. Noble, Jeremy. "Britten's Songs from the Chinese." *Tempo*, 52 (Autumn 1959): 25–29.

Description and analysis of each of the six songs. Musical examples.

Suite for Violoncello, No. 3, Op. 87

1241. Webber, Julian Lloyd. "Britten's Third Cello Suite." *Strad*, 91 (March 1981): 796–797.

Brief descriptive commentary.

Symphony for Cello and Orchestra, Op. 68

1242. Evans, Peter. "Britten's Cello Symphony." *Tempo*, 66–67 (Autumn–Winter 1963): 2–15.
  Formal analysis of the complete work. Musical examples.

1243. Warrack, John. "Britten's Cello Symphony." *Musical Times*, 105 (June 1964): 418–419.
  A brief descriptive introduction to the work.

Turn of the Screw

1244. Howard, Patricia, ed. *The Turn of the Screw*. Cambridge: Cambridge University Press, 1985, 164 pp.
  Volume in the Cambridge Opera Handbooks series. Sketches, relationships between dramatic and musical structures, the twelve-tone theme and tonality, variation structures, orchestral technique, sources, background, and stage history discussed. Included is a detailed analysis of Act II, Scene VIII. Musical examples.

1245. Mitchell, Donald. "Britten's Revisionary Practice: Practical and Creative." *Tempo*, 66–67 (Autumn–Winter 1963): 15–22.
  Describes the revision of the Finale of Act II. Musical examples.

War Requiem

1246. Lang, Paul Henry. "Choral Music in the Twentieth Century." *American Choral Review*, 19, no. 2 (1977): 15–16.
  Brief remarks on formal construction and critical commentary.

1247. Robertson, Alec. *Requiem: Music of Mourning and Consolation*, 265–285. New York: Praeger, 1968.
  Extensive commentary with background and critical assessment. Musical examples.

1248. Whittall, Arnold. "Tonal Instability in Britten's *War* Requiem." *Music Review*, 24, no. 3 (1963): 201–204.
  Formal analysis. Score needed to follow argument.

Winter Words

1249. Bartlett, Ian. *"Winter Words."* *Music Teacher*, 58 (September 1979): 19–21 + .

Thorough background, descriptive, and analytic commentary for the undergraduate student. Musical examples and brief bibliography.

DISSERTATIONS AND THESES

General

1250.   Dundore, Mary Margaret. "The Choral Music of Benjamin Britten." D.M.A., University of Washington, 1969, 166 pp., DA 30-5012A-13A.

1251.   Tibbetts, George Richard. "An Analysis of the Text-Music Relationship in Selected Songs of Benjamin Britten." Ed.D., Columbia University Teachers College, 1984, 166 pp., DA 46-17A.

Billy Budd

1252.   Boubel, Karen Brandser. "The Conflict of Good and Evil: A Musical and Dramatic Study of Britten's *Billy Budd*." Ph.D., University of Wisconsin at Madison, 1985, 236 pp., DA 46-2119A.

Curlew River

1253.   Mayer, Mark. "A Structural and Stylistic Analysis of the Benjamin Britten *Curlew River*." Ed.D., Columbia University Teachers College, 1983, 89 pp., DA 44-1370A.

Midsummer Night's Dream

1254.   Bach, jan Morris. "An Analysis of Britten's *A Midsummer Night's Dream*." D.M.A., University of Illinois at Urbana, 1971, 424 pp., DA 32-4647A.

Peter Grimes

1255.   Deavel, R. Gary. "A Study of Two Operas of Benjamin Britten: *Peter Grimes* and *Turn of the Screw*." Ph.D., University of Rochester, Eastman School of Music, 1970, 344 pp., DA 31-1831A.

1256.   Packales, Joseph. "Benjamin Britten's *Peter Grimes*: An Analysis." Ph.D., Kent State University, 1984, 118 pp., DA 45-983A.

Phaedra

1257. Shelton, Margaret Meier. "The ABC of *Phaedra*: Word Painting As Structure in Britten's *Phaedra*." Ph.D., University of California, 1983, 113 pp., DA 44-2289A.

Serenade for Tenor, Horn, and Strings

1258. Oosting, Stephen. "Text-Music Relationships in Benjamin Britten's Serenade for Tenor, Horn and Strings." D.M.A., University of Rochester, Eastman School of Music, 1985, 203 pp., DA 46-1124A.

Suites for Solo Cello

1259. Taggart, Mark Alan. "An Analysis of Suite for Cello, Op. 72 and Second Suite for Cello, Op. 80, by Benjamin Britten." D.M.A., Cornell University, 1983, 84 pp., DA 44-320A.

Turn of the Screw

1260. Deavel, R. Gary. "A Study of Two Operas of Benjamin Britten: *Peter Grimes* and *The Turn of the Screw*." Ph.D., University of Rochester, Eastman School of Music, 1970, 344 pp., DA 31-1831A.

Winter Words

1261. Litten, Jack Dane. "Three Song Cycles of Benjamin Britten." Ed.D., Columbia University, 1969, 293 pp., DA 31-788A.

BRUCH, MAX, 1838–1920

Concerto for Two Pianos, Op. 88

1262. Berkofsky, Martin. "Bruch Duo-Piano Concerto Rediscovered." *Music Journal*, 32 (October 1974): 8–9.
Background information on this little-known work.

1263. Mancinelli, Aldo. "From Our Readers." *Music Journal*, 33 (March 1975): 56–58.
Remarks on the controversial publication history of this work.

Concertos for Violin

1264.   Swalin, Benjamin F. *The Violin Concerto: A Study in German Romanticism,* 94–104. Chapel Hill: University of North Carolina Press, 1941.
Critical and analytic remarks on Violin Concertos Nos. 1 and 2. Musical examples.

Concerto for Violin No. 1, Op. 26 in G Minor

1265.   Tovey, Donald Francis. *Essays in Musical Analysis.* Vol. 3, 194–197. London: Oxford University Press, 1936.
Background, style, and form discussed. Musical examples.

BRUCKNER, ANTON, 1824–1896

General

1266.   Grant, Parks. "Bruckner and Mahler—The Fundamental Dissimilarity of Their Styles." *Music Review,* 32 (February 1971): 36–55.
Refutes the alleged similarity of Bruckner and Mahler by close examination of stylistic traits. Musical examples.

1267.   Liebergen, Patrick M. "The Cecilian Movement in the Nineteenth Century—Summary of the Movement." *Choral Journal,* 21, no. 9 (1981): 13–16.
Discussion of Bruckner's Mass in E Minor and the motets *Os Juste* and *Pange Lingua* to show how they conform to Cecilian concepts. Musical examples.

1268.   Watson, Derek. *Bruckner.* London: J. M. Dent and Sons, 1975, 174 pp.
Critical and analytic remarks for student or musical amateur. Musical examples.

1269.   Wolff, Werner. *Anton Bruckner: Rustic Genius.* New York: Cooper Square, 1973, 283 pp.
Descriptive and analytic commentary for the undergraduate student. Musical examples.

Symphonies

1270.   Barford, Philip. *Bruckner Symphonies.* Seattle: University of Washington Press, 1978, 68 pp.
Critical and analytic remarks. Musical examples.

1271.   Cooke, Deryck. "The Bruckner Problem Simplified." *Musical Times*, 110 (1969): 20–22, 142–144, 362–365, 479–482.
   Full discussion of the many versions. Not analytic.

1272.   Moravcsik, Michael J. "The Coda in the Symphonies of Anton Bruckner." *Music Review*, 34, nos. 3–4 (1973): 241–258.
   Detailed discussion of the structural elements in Bruckner's symphonies as seen in the codas.

1273.   Smith, Raymond R. "Motivic Procedure in Opening Movements of the Symphonies of Schumann, Bruckner, and Brahms." *Music Review*, 36, no. 2 (1975): 130–134.
   Advanced discussion on motivic treatment as an important element of sonata form.

Symphony No. 4 in E-Flat Major ("Romantic")

1274.   Pike, Lionel. *Beethoven, Sibelius, and the "Profound Logic": Studies in Symphonic Analysis*, 79–86. London: Athlone Press, 1978.
   Tonal analysis demonstrating that the principles of tonal expansion Bruckner learned from Beethoven were not matched by the rhythmic invention necessary to fill so large a conception.

1275.   Stedman, Preston. *The Symphony*, 186–190. Englewood Cliffs, NJ: Prentice-Hall, 1979.
   Descriptive commentary dealing with formal plan, tonality, and stylistic mannerisms. For the undergraduate student. Musical examples and diagrams.

1276.   Tovey, Donald Francis. *Essays in Musical Analysis.* Vol. 2, 69–79. London: Oxford University Press, 1935.
   Analytic discourse, placing Bruckner in perspective. Musical examples.

Symphony No. 5 in B-Flat Major

1277.   Pope, Stanley. "A Performer's Rights." *Chord and Discord*, 2, no. 10 (1963): 109–123.
   Guide for the conductor, but many analytic insights for the student. Musical examples.

Symphony No. 6 in A Major

1278.   Dahlhaus, Carl. *Nineteenth-Century Music.* Translated by J. Bradford Robinson, 272–274. Berkeley: University of California Press, 1989.

Brief but concentrated analytic remarks on the exposition of the first movement to demonstrate rhythmic coherence. Advanced.

1279. Pope, Stanley. "A Performer's Rights." *Chord and Discord*, 2, no. 9 (1960): 78–86.
Guide for the conductor, but many analytic insights for the student. Musical examples.

Symphony No. 7 in E Major

1280. Simpson, Robert. "The Seventh Symphony of Bruckner: An Analysis." *Chord and Discord*, 2, no. 10 (1963): 57–67.
Very thorough measure-by-measure analysis, with musical examples.

Symphony No. 8 in C Minor

1281. Dawson-Bowling, Paul. "Theme and Tonal Unity in Bruckner's Eighth Symphony." *Music Review*, 30, no. 3 (1969): 225–236.
Advanced analytic discussion. Musical examples.

1282. Leichtentritt, Hugo. *Musical Form*, 379–424. Cambridge, MA: Harvard University Press, 1959.
Exhaustive, intense analysis with musical examples.

Te Deum

1283. Dahlhaus, Carl. *Nineteenth-Century Music.* Translated by J. Bradford Robinson, 188–190. Berkeley: University of California Press, 1989.
Symphonic techniques, motivic transformation, and rhythmic unity examined. Musical example. Advanced.

DISSERTATIONS AND THESES

Masses

1284. Mathews, Theodore Kenneth. "The Masses of Anton Bruckner." Ph.D., University of Michigan, 1974, 397 pp., DA 5449A.

BULL, JOHN, c. 1562–1628

General

1285. Cunningham, Walker. *The Keyboard Music of John Bull.* Ann Arbor: UMI Research Press, 1984, 274 pp.

An extended and comprehensive study. Includes discussion of authenticity, critical assessment, and stylistic development. Musical examples.

BUSONI, FERRUCCIO, 1866–1924
General

1286.   Beaumont, Antony. *Busoni the Composer.* London: Faber and Faber, 1985, 408 pp.
Background and analytic overview of Busoni's output. Musical examples.

Doktor Faust

1287.   Arias, Enrique. "Pre-Existent Material in Busoni's *Doktor Faust.*" *Opera Journal,* 17, no. 3 (1984): 5–15.
Critical and analytic commentary tracing earlier works of Busoni in *Doktor Faust.* Musical examples and bibliography.

DISSERTATIONS AND THESES
General

1288.   Winfield, George Alexander. "Ferruccio Busoni's Compositional Art: A Study of Selected Works for Piano Solo Composed Between 1907 and 1923." Ph.D., Indiana University, 1981, 218 pp., DA 42-4972A.

BUXTEHUDE, DIETRICH, c. 1637–1707
General

1289.   Snyder, Kerala J. *Dieterich Buxtehude.* New York: Schirmer Books, 1987.
Extensive "life and works" treatment providing detailed descriptive and analytic commentary on Buxtehude's output. Historical perspective, Buxtehude's style, and performance practices of the music discussed as well. The most thorough treatment on Buxtehude to date. For the advanced undergraduate and graduate student as well as musicologist.

Passacaglia in D Minor

1290.   Kee, Piet. "Astronomy in Buxtehude's Passacaglia." *Diapason,* 75 (December 1984): 19–21.
Detailed demonstration that Buxtehude's Passacaglia is a perfect numerological parallel of the lunar month. Musical examples.

BYRD, WILLIAM, 1543–1623

General

1291. Andres, Herbert K. *The Technique of Byrd's Vocal Polyphony.* London: Oxford University Press, 1966, 306 pp.
Thorough analytic discussion of Byrd's style. Advanced. Musical examples.

1292. Brett, Philip. "Word-Setting in the Songs of Byrd." *Proceedings of the Royal Musical Association*, 98 (1971–1972): 47–64.

1293. Brown, Alan. "Keyboard Music by Byrd 'Upon a Plainsong.' " *Organ Yearbook*, 5 (1974): 30–39.
Survey of Byrd's small output of keyboard music based on Gregorian melodies. Musical examples.

1294. Fellowes, Edmund H. *William Byrd.* 2d ed. London: Oxford University Press, 1948, 271 pp.
Thorough study of all Byrd's works, focusing on historical significance. Musical examples.

1295. Gray, Walter. "Motivic Structure in the Polyphony of William Byrd." *Music Review*, 29, no. 3 (1968): 223–233.

1296. Kerman, Joseph. "Byrd, Tallis, and the Art of Imitation." In *Aspects of Medieval and Renaissance Music: A Birthday Offering to Gustave Reese.* Edited by Jan La Rue, 519–537. New York: W. W. Norton, 1966.
Graduate- and faculty-level discussion of the use of imitation as compared to Tallis's use of the technique. Musical examples.

1297. Kerman, Joseph. *The Masses and Motets of William Byrd.* Berkeley: University of California Press, 1981, 360 pp.
Stylistic and analytic overview. Musical examples.

1298. Monson, Craig. "The Preces, Psalms, and Litanies of Byrd and Tallis: Another 'Virtuous Contention in Love.' " *Music Review*, 40, no. 4 (1979): 257–271.
Critical observations on the compositions, with remarks on Byrd's debt to Tallis and others. Musical examples.

1299. Neighbour, Oliver. *The Consort and Keyboard Music of William Byrd.* Berkeley: University of California Press, 1978, 272 pp.
Stylistic and analytic overview of the consort and keyboard music. Musical examples.

1300.   Neighbour, Oliver. "New Keyboard Music by Byrd." *Musical Times*, 112 (July 1971): 657–659.

Critical commentary on specific works and an assessment of Byrd's keyboard writing.

"Bow Thine Ear"

1301.   Sargent, Brian. "Set Works for 'O' Level: Two Byrd Anthems." *Music Teacher*, 60 (March 1981): 13 + .

Background, descriptive, and analytic commentary for the undergraduate student.

Canon (Six in One)

1302.   Roberts, Anthony. "Byrd's Other Conceite." *Musical Times*, 116 (May 1975): 423–427.

Detailed exploration of the Canon to solve the riddle found at the bottom of the folio. Musical examples.

Cantiones Sacrae

1303.   Monson, Craig. "Byrd and the 1575 Cantiones Sacrae." *Musical Times*, 116 (December 1975): 1089 + .

Background and analytic remarks on Byrd's contributions to the *Cantiones Sacrae* and his use of imitation. Musical examples.

1304.   Sternfeld, Frederick W., et al., eds. *Essays on Opera and English Music in Honour of Sir Jack Westrup*, 25–43. Oxford: Blackwell, 1975.

An examination of stylistic traits and use of old and new musical techniques. Close analytic look at "Tribue, Domine" of this set. Musical examples.

Laudate Dominum

1305.   Hynson, Richard. "The Two Choral Styles of William Byrd." *Choral Journal*, 19, no. 4 (1978): 20–22.

Commentary on style, structure and tonality.

Masses

1306.   Brett, Philip. "Homage to Taverner in Byrd's Masses." *Early Music*, 9, no. 2 (1981): 169–176.

Byrd's debt to Taverner in his Masses is examined in detail. Musical examples.

Praise Our Lord

1307. Hynson, Richard. "The Two Choral Styles of William Byrd." *Choral Journal,* 19, no. 4 (1978): 20–22.
Commentary on style, structure, and tonality.

Sing Joyfully

1308. Sargent, Brian. "Set Works for 'O' Level: Two Byrd Anthems." *Music Teacher,* 60 (March 1981): 13 + .
Background, descriptive, and analytic commentary for the undergraduate student.

CABEZÓN, ANTONIO DE, 1510–1566

Tiento XVIII

1309. Howell, Almont C. "Cabezón: Essay in Structural Analysis." *Musical Quarterly,* 50, no. 1 (1964): 18–30.
Offers a "methodology for analyses" of Cabezón's works by presenting a detailed structural analysis of *Tiento* XVIII. Complete score included.

CACCINI, GIULIO, c. 1548–1618

Nuove Musiche

1310. Baron, John H. "Monody: A Study in Terminology." *Musical Quarterly,* 54, no. 4 (1968): 462–474.
An examination of monodic style and the *Nuove Musiche.* Musical examples.

1311. Fortune, Nigel. "Solo Song and Cantata." In *The New Oxford History of Music.* Vol. 4, *The Age of Humanism, 1540–1630.* Edited by Gerald Abraham, 154–159. London: Oxford University Press, 1968.
The significance of the *Nuove Musiche* as well as a discussion of the music itself. Musical examples.

CAGE, JOHN, 1912–

General

1312. Griffiths, Paul. *Cage.* London: Oxford University Press, 1981, 50 pp.
Analytic remarks, with observations on Cage's rhythmic systems, chromatic studies, and views on silence. Musical examples.

1313. O'Grady, Terence J. "Aesthetic Value in Indeterminate Music." *Musical Quarterly*, 67, no. 3 (1981): 366–381.

The effect of the level of the indeterminacy on the potential "value" of a piece. Cage's *Cartridge Music, HPSCHD*, Reich's *Pendulum Music*, and Terry Riley's *In C* are discussed.

1314. Whittall, Arnold. *Music Since the First World War*, 206–210. London: J. M. Dent and Sons, 1977.

Brief analytic discussion.

Amores

1315. Minor, Martha D. "Preparing a Piano." *Clavier*, 16, no. 8 (1977): 41–43.

Brief commentary focusing on the technical aspects of preparing the piano for this piece, an analysis and bibliography.

Chance Music

1316. Griffiths, Paul. *Modern Music: The Avant-Garde Since 1945*, 66–70. New York: George Braziller, 1981.

Describes compositional method that uses chance operations.

Concerto for Prepared Piano

1317. Nyman, Michael. "Cage/Cardew." *Tempo*, 107 (December 1973): 33–34.

Brief descriptive and critical commentary focusing on Cage's purpose and artistic development.

HPSCHD

1318. Austin, Larry. "HPSCHD." *Source*, 2, no. 2 (1968): 10–19.
Interviews with John Cage and Lejaren Hiller concerning *HPSCHD* (Hiller did programming for the composition). Describes the use of the computer in this composition and includes examples of flowcharts used for computer decision-making.

Imaginary Landscape No. 4

1319. Welsh, John. "Music in the Air: Here and There—A Radio Landscape." *Interface*, 13, no. 4 (1984): 199+.

Discussion of the composer's intentions followed by analytic observations. Musical examples, bibliography, and selected list of works follows.

Quartet for Strings in Four Parts

1320.   Dickinson, Peter. "Case of Neglect: Cage String Quartet." *Music and Musicians*, 20 (January 1972): 28–29.
Brief analysis and critical commentary.

Sonatas and Interludes

1321.   Griffiths, Paul. *Modern Music: The Avant-Garde Since 1945*, 34–37. New York: George Braziller, 1981.
Discussion of durational proportions and rhythmic structure. Musical examples.

Variations II

1322.   De Lio, Thomas. "John Cage's Variations II, the Morphology of a Global Structure." *Perspectives of New Music*, 19, nos. 1–2 (1980–1981): 351 +.
Extensive analysis, with charts, diagrams, and equations.

Williams Mix

1323.   Schrader, Barry. *Introduction to Electro-Acoustic Music*, 25–28. Englewood Cliffs, NJ: Prentice-Hall, 1982.
Analytic comments.

DISSERTATIONS AND THESES

General

1324.   Beeler, Charles Alan. "*Winter Music, Cartridge Music, Atlas Eclipticalis*: A Study of Three Seminal Works of John Cage." Ph.D., Washington University, 1973, 78 pp., DA 34-6016A.

1325.   Campana, Deborah Ann. "Form and Structure in the Music of John Cage." Ph.D., Northwestern University, 1985, 197 pp., DA 46-2119A.

1326.   Francis, John Richard. "Structure in the Solo Piano Works of John Cage." Ph.D., Florida State University, 1976, 111 pp., DA 37-3255A.

1327.   Petkus, Janetta. "The Songs of John Cage (1932–1970)." Ph.D., University of Connecticut, 1986, 266 pp., DA 47-2365A.

CAMPION, THOMAS, 1567–1620

General

1328.   Eldridge, Muriel T. *Thomas Campion: His Poetry and Music.* New York: Vantage Press, 1971, 165 pp.
  Background, with thorough discussion of the music. Musical examples.

CARISSIMI, GIACOMO, 1605–1674

General

1329.   Dixon, Graham. *Carissimi.* Oxford: Oxford University Press, 1986, 84 pp.
  An analytic study of the works of Carissimi, with a brief introductory biographical chapter and a concluding overall assessment. The analytic chapters discuss musical style, liturgical music, music for oratorios, and the cantata. Musical examples.

CARTER, ELLIOTT, 1908–

General

1330.   Schiff, David. *The Music of Elliott Carter.* New York: Da Capo Press, 1983, 371 pp.
  A comprehensive study of the music of Carter. Detailed analytic commentary on each work, placing each in the context of the composer's development. The commentaries cover all technical aspects of the music, formal structure, and nonmusical elements such as text and dance. Musical examples, diagrams, and charts.

1331.   Whittall, Arnold. *Music Since the First World War,* 219–234. London: J. M. Dent and Sons, 1977.
  Brief analytic discussion. Musical examples.

Canon for Three

1332.   De Lio, Thomas. "Spatial Design in Elliott Carter's Canon for Three." *Indiana Theory Review*, 4, no. 1 (1980): 1–12.

Concerto for Brass

1333.   Bernard, Jonathan W. "Spatial Sets in Recent Music of Elliott Carter." *Music Analysis*, 2, no. 1 (1983): 5–34.

Concerto for Harpsichord and Piano with Two Chamber Orchestras

1334.   Salzman, Eric. "Report from New York: The New Virtuosity." *Perspectives of New Music*, 1, no. 2 (1963): 174–175 + .
General analytic observations with a musical example.

Concerto for Orchestra

1335.   Bernard, Jonathan W. "Spatial Sets in Recent Music of Elliott Carter." *Music Analysis*, 2, no. 1 (1983): 5–34.

1336.   Griffiths, Paul, and Richard Evidon. "Proms." *Musical Times*, 116 (October 1975): 894–895.
Review of a performance. Includes brief descriptive and critical remarks.

1337.   Kenyon, Nicholas. "Elliott Carter." *Music and Musicians*, 24 (October 1975): 50 + .
Brief critical and analytic remarks.

Concerto for Piano

1338.   Bernard, Jonathan W. "Spatial Sets in Recent Music of Elliott Carter." *Music Analysis*, 2, no. 1 (1983): 5–34.

1339.   Bowen, Meiron. "Carter's Piano Concerto." *Music and Musicians*, 18 (May 1970): 60–61.
Brief critical review, with some analytic remarks.

Double Concerto for Harpsichord, Piano, and Two Chamber Orchestras

1340.   Whittall, Arnold. "Post-Twelve-Note Analysis." *Proceedings of the Royal Musical Association*, 94 (1967–1968): 12–16.

Analytic comments on relationships between the performing groups, rhythm, intervallic structure, and other musical elements. Musical examples.

Duo for Violin and Piano

1341. Derby, Richard. "Carter's Duo for Violin and Piano." *Perspectives of New Music*, 20, nos. 1–2 (1982–1983): 149 + .
Thorough analysis, with musical examples.

Eight Pieces for Four Timpani

1342. Larrick, Geary H. "Eight Pieces for Four Timpani by Elliott Carter—Analysis." *Percussionist*, 12, no. 1 (1974): 12–15.

1343. McCormick, Robert M. "Eight Pieces for Four Timpani, by Elliott Carter—Analysis." *Percussionist*, 12, no. 1 (1974): 7–11.

Quartets for Strings

1344. Morgan, Robert P. "Elliott Carter's String Quartets (Analysis)." *Musical Newsletter*, 4, no. 3 (1974): 3–11.

Quartet for Strings No. 1

1345. Tingley, George P. "Metric Modulation and Elliott Carter's First String Quartet." *Indiana Theory Review*, 4, no. 3 (1981): 3–11.
Metric modulation is a "precise and controlled method of proceeding from one metronomic speed to another," which can involve two or more lines. In addition to shaping the microstructural levels of a work, it also influences the macrostructural levels. The article discusses the use of these procedures in this quartet. Musical examples.

Quartet for Strings No. 2

1346. Cogan, Robert, and Pozzi Escot. *Sonic Design: The Nature of Sound and Music*, 59–71. Englewood Cliffs, NJ: Prentice-Hall, 1976.
An analysis of the first thirty-four measures of the introduction. Includes musical examples and graphs.

1347. Gass, Glenn. "Elliott Carter's Second String Quartet: Aspects of Time and Rhythm." *Indiana Theory Review*, 4, no. 3 (1981): 12–23.

1348.   Goldman, Richard Franko. "Current Chronicle: New York." *Musical Quarterly*, 46, no. 3 (1960): 361–364.

Discussion of formal features of the work with an interesting perspective on instruments as "characters."

1349.   Steinberg, Michael. "Elliott Carter's Second String Quartet." *Score*, 27 (July 1960): 22–26.

An introduction and brief analysis of the complete work.

Quartet for Strings No. 3

1350.   Kenyon, Nicholas. "Elliott Carter." *Music and Musicians*, 24 (October 1975): 50+.

Brief descriptive and analytic remarks.

Sonata for Piano

1351.   Below, Robert. "Elliott Carter's Piano Sonata: An Important Contribution to Piano Literature." *Music Review*, 34, nos. 3–4 (1973): 282–293.

Critical evaluation of the Sonata's place in piano literature and a full analysis. Musical examples.

A Symphony of Three Orchestras

1352.   Clements, Andrew. "Carter's Triple Symphony." *Music and Musicians*, 27 (March 1979): 19–20.

A short review of the work, including comments by Carter.

Variations for Orchestra

1353.   Machlis, Joseph. *Introduction to Contemporary Music*, 592–594. New York: W. W. Norton, 1961.

Brief descriptive and analytic commentary, with musical examples. For the undergraduate student.

1354.   Stewart, Robert. "Serial Aspects of Elliott Carter's Variations for Orchestra." *Music Review*, 34, no. 1 (1973): 62–65.

Analysis with musical examples.

DISSERTATIONS AND THESES

Quartets for Strings

1355.   Harris, Jane Duff. "Compositional Process in the String Quartets of Elliott Carter." Ph.D., Case Western Reserve, 1983, 320 pp., DA 44-3200A.

Sonata for Flute, Oboe, Cello, and Harpsichord

1356. Shinn, Randall Alan. "An Analysis of Elliott Carter's Sonata for Flute, Oboe, Cello, and Harpsichord (1952)." D.M.A., University of Illinois at Urbana, 1975, 183 pp., DA 36-5631A.

Sonata for Violoncello and Piano

1357. Kies, Christopher R. "A Discussion of the Harmonic Organization in the First Movement of Elliott Carter's Sonata for Violoncello and Piano." Ph.D., Brandeis University, 1984, 131 pp., DA 47-342A.

Variations for Orchestra

1358. Beckstrom, Robert Allen. "Analysis of Elliott Carter's Variations for Orchestra (1955)." Ph.D., University of California at Los Angeles, 1983, 170 pp., DA 45-1233A.

1359. Wyatt, Lucius Reynolds. "The Mid-Twentieth-Century Orchestral Variation, 1953–1963." Ph.D., University of Rochester, Eastman School of Music, 1974, 504 pp., DA 34-723A.

CAVALLI, FRANCESCO, 1602–1676

General

1360. Glover, Jane. *Cavalli.* London: B. T. Batsford, 1978, 192 pp. A "life and works" treatment, including discussion of analysis of forms, methods of composition, characterization, orchestration, performance practice. Appendices contain information on sources, documentary evidence, editions, and lists of works. Musical examples.

CHABRIER, EMMANUEL, 1841–1894

General

1361. Cortot, Alfred. *French Piano Music.* Translated by Hilda Andrews, 140–177. London: Oxford University Press, 1932.
Descriptive overview, with observations on Chabrier's style.

1362. Myers, Rollo. *Emmanuel Chabrier and His Circle.* London: J. M. Dent and Sons, 1969, 178 pp.
  Background, descriptive, and critical commentary for the under-graduate student.

DISSERTATIONS AND THESES

1363. Telesco, Paula Jean. "A Harmonic Analysis of Selected Piano Music of Emmanuel Chabrier." M.M., University of Arizona, 1985, 170 pp., DA 23-415A.

CHARPENTIER, MARC ANTOINE, c. 1636–1704

General

1364. Anthony, James R. *French Baroque Music from Beaujoyeulx to Rameau.* New York: W. W. Norton, 1974, 429 pp.
  A study of French Baroque style elements seen in historical con-text. Specific works in different genres discussed, with musical examples.

CHAUSSON, ERNEST, 1855–1899

Symphony in B-Flat Major, Op. 20

1365. Barricelli, Jean-Pierre, and Leo Weinstein, 164–176. *Ernest Chausson.* Norman: University of Oklahoma Press, 1955.
  Descriptive commentary with musical examples.

CHÁVEZ, CARLOS, 1899–1978

General

1366. Béhague, Gerard. *Music in Latin America: An Introduction,* 135–140, 246–252. Englewood Cliffs, NJ: Prentice-Hall, 1979.
  Analyses of the Piano Concerto, Violin Concerto, *Sinfonía India,* and *Sinfonía de Antígona.* Musical examples.

1367. Parker, Robert L. *Carlos Chávez, Mexico's Modern-Day Or-pheus.* Boston: Twayne, 1983, 166 pp.
  Thorough analytic review of Chávez's output. Musical examples.

183

Symphony No. 3

1368. Parker, Robert L. "Clare Booth Luce, Carlos Chávez, and Sinfonía No. 3." *Latin American Music Review*, 5, no. 1 (1984): 48–65.
Background and analysis, with musical examples.

DISSERTATIONS AND THESES

Toccata for Percussion Instruments

1369. Peterman, Timothy James. "An Examination of Two Sextets of Carlos Chávez: Toccata for Percussion Instruments and Tambuco for Six Percussion Players." D.M.A., North Texas State University, 1986, 85 pp., DA 47-2793A.

CHERUBINI, LUIGI, 1760–1842

General

1370. Deane, Basil. *Cherubini*. London: Oxford University Press, 1965, 53 pp.
Descriptive overview with analytic observations for the undergraduate student. Musical examples.

Quartets for Strings

1371. Freed, Richard. "Formal Integrity and Astonishing Substance in Luigi Cherubini's Six String Quartets." *Stereo Review*, 38 (January 1977): 84–85.
Brief remarks for the musical amateur.

Quartet for Strings No. 6 in A Minor

1372. Arias, Enrique. "The Application of General System Theory to Musical Analysis." *Music Review*, 43, nos. 3–4 (1982): 236+.
Detailed analysis of the scherzo movement of this work. Musical examples.

Requiem

1373. Robertson, Alec. *Requiem: Music of Mourning and Consolation*, 75–85. New York: Praeger, 1968.
Solid discussion of the music. Musical examples.

CHOPIN, FRÉDÉRIC, 1810–1849

General

1374. Abraham, Gerald. *Chopin's Musical Style.* London: Oxford University Press, 1960, 128 pp.
Detailed discussion of stylistic traits, with many analytic insights. Musical examples.

1375. Bidou, Henri. *Chopin.* Translated by Catherine Alison Phillips. New York: Alfred A. Knopf, 1927, 267 pp.
Mainly a life of Chopin. Some analytic observations along the way. Lack of index to compositions makes the book difficult to use.

1376. Dale, Kathleen. *Nineteenth-Century Piano Music: A Handbook for Pianists.* London: Oxford University Press, 1954, 320 pp.
Highlights stylistic traits and unique contribution to the literature of the piano. Form, harmony, and other musical aspects discussed in relation to style. Musical examples.

1377. Einstein, Alfred. *Music in the Romantic Era,* 213–220. New York: W. W. Norton, 1947.
Some specific works mentioned, but mainly a portrait of Chopin with comparisons to Schumann.

1378. Elder, Dean. "A Conversation with Arthur Rubinstein." *Clavier,* 8, no. 6 (1969): 14–20.
Stylistic and interpretive insights. Musical examples.

1379. Ferguson, Donald N. *Piano Music of Six Great Composers,* 213–249. New York: Books for Libraries Press, 1947.
Descriptive and critical commentary with analytic insights. Musical examples.

1380. Hedley, Arthur. *Chopin.* London: J. M. Dent and Sons, 1974. 214 pp.
Descriptive, critical, and analytic commentary aimed at informed amateur or undergraduate student. Musical examples.

1381. Higgins, Thomas. "Tempo and Character in Chopin." *Musical Quarterly,* 59, no. 1 (1973): 106–120.
Chopin's use of metronome indications. Some discussion of individual character of works. Musical examples.

1382. Kelley, Edgar Stillman. *Chopin the Composer.* New York: G. Schirmer, 1913, 190 pp.
Copious analytic observations for the undergraduate student. Excellent index to works. Musical examples.

1383.   Longyear, Rey M. *Nineteenth-Century Romanticism in Music,*
88–94. Englewood Cliffs, NJ: Prentice-Hall, 1969.
    Overview with descriptive and critical remarks intended for the
undergraduate student. Musical examples.

1384.   Matthews, Denis, ed. *Keyboard Music,* 213–230. New York:
Praeger, 1972.
    Background, historical perspective, innovations, stylistic traits
with discussion of specific pieces. Musical examples.

1385.   Niecks, Frederick. *Frederick Chopin As a Man and Musician.* 2
vols. London: Novello, 1902.
    Mainly background and descriptive commentary, with brief men-
tion of themes, structure, and tonality. For the musical amateur or
undergraduate student.

1386.   Plantinga, Leon. *Romantic Music,* 190–203. New York: W. W.
Norton, 1984.
    Analytic comments on the piano music. Musical examples.

1387.   Riedel, Johannes. *Music of the Romantic Period,* 116–122.
Dubuque, IA: William C. Brown, 1969.
    Brief descriptive remarks on Chopin's stylistic traits for the un-
dergraduate student. Musical examples.

1388.   Samson, Jim. *The Music of Chopin.* London: Routledge and
Kegan Paul, 1985, 243 pp.
    Analytically oriented discussion of style and structure, melody,
tonality, rhythm, and other unifying factors. Schenkerian terminology and level of treatment make this book suitable for the
moderately advanced student. Musical examples.

1389.   Walker, Alan, ed. *The Chopin Companion.* New York: W. W.
Norton, 1966, 312 pp.
    Good overview, with analyses of individual works. Thorough, with
musical examples and index.

1390.   Walker, Alan, ed. *Frederic Chopin: Profiles of the Man and the
Musician.* New York: Taplinger, 1967, 334 pp.
    Background and critical commentary, with emphasis on Chopin's
tonality. Musical examples.

1391.   Weinstock, Herbert. *Chopin: The Man and His Music.* New
York: Alfred A. Knopf, 1959, 336 pp.
    Brief program-note remarks on background and description of the
music.

Ballades

1392.   Griffel, L. Michael. "The Sonata Design in Chopin's Ballades." *Current Musicology*, 36 (1983): 125–136.
   Each of the four Ballades is examined for its individual use of the sonata-allegro form.

1393.   Witten, David. "Chopin Ballades: The Question of Form." *College Music Symposium*, 20, no. 2 (1980): 188–189.
   An examination of the four Ballades with respect to harmonic ingenuity and form. The author contends that an underlying linear structure of the melodies derived from the scale steps 6-5 is adopted on the harmonic level, with step 6 acting to delay the arrival on the structural dominant. "Schenkerian" analysis for the advanced student.

Ballade No. 1 in G Minor

1394.   Kerman, Joseph. *Listen*. 2d ed., 232–233. New York: Worth Publishers, 1976.
   Brief analysis, with musical examples. For the undergraduate student.

1395.   Warburton, A. O. "Set Works for 'O' Level, GCE." *Music Teacher*, 49 (September 1970): 19+.
   Descriptive and analytic commentary.

Barcarolle, Op. 60

1396.   Montparker, Carol. "Chopin's Barcarolle." *Clavier*, 22, no. 4 (1983): 16–22.
   A symposium of pianists on performance of the Barcarolle. Some analytic insights into rhythm, tone painting and structure. Musical examples.

Concertos

1397.   Abraham, Gerald. *Slavonic and Romantic Music*, 23–27. New York: St. Martin's Press, 1968.
   Concentrates on the orchestral writing. Scoring, use of instruments, and structural role of the orchestral part mentioned. Musical examples.

1398.   Hill, Ralph, ed. *The Concerto*, 162–169. London: Penguin Books, 1952.
   Critical and analytic commentary for the undergraduate student. Musical examples.

1399. Veinus, Abraham. *The Concerto.* Rev. ed. 219–226. New York: Dover Publications, 1964.
> Critical remarks and historical perspective. Not analytic.

Concerto for Piano No. 1 in E Minor

1400. Nelson, Wendell. *The Concerto,* 60–62, Dubuque, IA: William C. Brown, 1969.
> Brief analysis, with critical observations. Musical examples.

Concerto for Piano No. 2 in F Minor

1401. Tovey, Donald Francis. *Essays in Musical Analysis.* Vol. 3, 103–106. London: Oxford University Press, 1936.
> Critical and analytic remarks, with musical examples.

Etudes

1402. Tovey, Donald Francis. *Essays in Musical Analysis: Chamber Music,* 155–163. London: Oxford University Press, 1944.
> Critical observation on *Etudes* Op. 25, nos. 7 and 12 and *Méthode des Méthodes,* nos. 1 and 3.

Etude, Op. 10, No. 3 in E Major

1403. Hantz, Edwin. "Exempli Gratia: A Study in Meter." *In Theory Only,* 1 (November 1975): 28–30.
> Citing the irrational barring of three passages, the author notes that performance-as-written is impossible. Musical examples.

Etude, Op. 10, No. 8 in F Major

1404. Schenker, Heinrich. *Five Graphic Music Analyses,* 47–51. New York: Dover Publications, 1969.
> Purely graphic analysis for the advanced student. There is no accompanying analytic commentary. Score necessary.

Etude, Op. 10, No. 12 in C Minor ("Revolutionary")

1405. Phipps, Graham H. "A Response to Schenker's Analysis of Chopin's Etude Op. 10, No. 12, Using Schoenberg's *Grundgestalt* Concept." *Musical Quarterly,* 69, no. 4 (1983): 543–569.
> A comparison of Schenker's view of this work with Schoenberg's. Advanced. (*See* item no. 1406 below.) Musical examples.

1406.   Schenker, Heinrich. *Five Graphic Music Analyses*, 54–61. New York: Dover Publications, 1969.
Purely graphic analysis for the advanced student. There is no accompanying analytic commentary. Score necessary.

1407.   Smith, Charles J. "(Supra-) Durational Patterns in Chopin's *Revolutionary* Etude." *In Theory Only*, 2 (August 1976): 3–12.

Etude, Op. 25, No. 3 in F Major

1408.   Salzer, Felix. "Chopin's Etude in F Major, Opus 25, No. 3: The Scope of Tonality." In *The Music Forum*. Vol. 3. Edited by William J. Mitchell and Felix Salzer, 281–290. New York: Columbia University Press, 1973.
In-depth analysis, according to the Schenker method. For the advanced student. Musical examples.

Etude, Op. 25, No. 9 in G-Flat Major ("Butterfly")

1409.   Smith, Charles J. "Registering Distinctions: Octave Non-Equivalence in Chopin's *Butterfly* Etude." *In Theory Only*, 3 (August 1977): 32–40.

Fantaisie Impromptu, Op. 66 in C-Sharp Minor

1410.   Davie, Cedric Thorpe. *Musical Structure and Design*, 45–46. New York: Dover Publications, 1966.
Measure-by-measure analysis, to be used with score in hand.

Impromptu, Op. 36 in F-Sharp Major

1411.   Tovey, Donald Francis. *Essays in Musical Analysis: Chamber Music*, 163–166. London: Oxford University Press, 1944.
Critical observations and analytic insights for the informed undergraduate student. Musical examples.

Mazurka, Op. 6, No. 2 in C-Sharp Minor

1412.   Viljoen, Nicol. "The Drone Bass and Its Implications for the Tonal Voice-Leading Structure in Two Selected Mazurkas by Chopin." *Indiana Theory Review*, 6, nos. 1–2 (1983–1984): 17–35.

Mazurka, Op. 7, No. 1 in B-Flat Major

1413.   Dumm, Robert. "Piano Footnotes on Chopin's Mazurka Op. 7, No. 1." *Clavier,* 4, no. 1 (1965): 33–35.

Notes to aid the performer, but close descriptive commentary helpful to nonperformers studying this work. Complete musical example.

Mazurka, Op. 17, No. 4 in A Minor

1414.   Thomson, William. "Functional Ambiguity in Musical Structures." *Music Perception,* 1, no. 1 (1983): 17–21.

Advanced analytic discussion. Score included.

Mazurka, Op. 41, No. 4 in A-Flat Major

1415.   Lester, Joel. "Quaestionis Gratia: Curious Curtailment or Cliff-hanger?" *In Theory Only,* 3 (April 1977): 31.

Refutes the notion that this Mazurka should have a more definitive ending. (*See* item no. 1416 below.)

1416.   Riseling, Robert, and Wallace Berry. "Quaestionis Gratia: Curious Curtailment or Cliffhanger?" *In Theory Only,* 2 (January 1977): 35–39.

Proposes possible alternative endings for this Mazurka. Musical examples.

Mazurka, Op. 63, No. 2 in F Minor

1417.   Zabrack, Harold. "The Difficulty Is in the Subtlety: A Lesson on the Chopin Mazurka." *Clavier,* 6, no. 2 (1967): 31–32.

Brief observations on form, rhythm, and harmony. Score included.

Mazurka, Op. 67, No. 2 in G Minor

1418.   Kielian, Marianne. "Exempli Gratia: When Repetition Is Not Repetition." *In Theory Only,* 2 (November 1976): 20–24.

A Schenkerian analysis. Illustrates that a literal repetition in a piece can have a different structural interpretation. Musical examples.

Mazurka, Op. 68, No. 3 in F Major (Op. Posthumous)

1419.   Kresky, Jeffrey. *Tonal Music: Twelve Analytic Studies,* 80–81. Bloomington: Indiana University Press, 1977.

In-depth analysis dealing with formal structure and tonality. Advanced. Musical examples and diagrams.

Nocturne, Op. 9, No. 2 in E-Flat Major

1420. Warburton, A. O. "Set Works for 'O' Level, GCE." *Music Teacher*, 48 (November 1969): 15–16.
   Analysis for the undergraduate student.

Nocturne, Op. 15, No. 2 in F Major

1421. Warburton, A. O. "Set Works for 'O' Level, GCE." *Music Teacher*, 48 (November 1969): 15–16.
   Analysis for the undergraduate student.

Nocturne, Op. 27, No. 1 in C-Sharp Minor

1422. Dumm, Robert. "Piano Footnotes: An Analytic Interpretive Lesson on Chopin's Nocturne in C-Sharp Minor." *Clavier*, 3, no. 1 (1964): 27–30.
   Remarks for performance. Some analytic observations. Score included.

1423. Salzer, Felix. "Chopin's Nocturne in C-Sharp Minor Opus 27, No. 1." In *The Music Forum*. Vol. 3. Edited by William J. Mitchell and Felix Salzer, 283–297. New York: Columbia University Press, 1973.
   In-depth analysis, according to the Schenker method. For the advanced student. Musical examples.

Nocturne, Op. 32, No. 1 in B Major

1424. Warburton, A. O. "Set Works for 'O' Level, GCE." *Music Teacher*, 48 (November 1969): 15–16.
   Analysis for the undergraduate student.

Nocturne, Op. 37, No. 1 in G Minor

1425. David, Cedric Thorpe. *Musical Structure and Design*, 44. New York: Dover Publications, 1966.
   Condensed measure-by-measure analysis to be used with score in hand.

Nocturne, Op. 55, No. 1 in F Minor

1426. Horton, Charles T. "Chopin and Brahms: On a Common Meeting (Middle) Ground." *In Theory Only*, 6 (December 1982): 19–22.

A comparison of Chopin's treatment of this Nocturne's melody with Brahms's treatment of the same melody in his Intermezzo Op. 76, No. 1. Musical examples.

Nouvelles Etudes, No. 3 in A-Flat Major

1427. Smith, Charles J. "Toward the Construction of Intersecting Divergent Models for Chopin's 'Three Against Two' Etude." *In Theory Only*, 1 (June 1975): 19–25.

Advanced "Schenker"-style analysis tracing the interval of the major third and augmented triad. Includes analytic graph.

Polonaise Fantaisie, Op. 61

1428. Payne, Donald. "Achieving the Effect of Freedom in Musical Composition." *Piano Quarterly*, 20, no. 78 (1971–1972): 12–14 + .

Analytic remarks with musical examples.

Preludes, Op. 28

1429. Higgins, Thomas, ed. *Frédéric Chopin: "Preludes, Opus 28."* Norton Critical Scores. New York: W. W. Norton, 1973, 101 pp.

Historical background, analyses, comments by Chopin's contemporaries as well as modern critical views. Full score and bibliography. Special emphasis on Preludes 2 and 6.

1430. Smith, Charles J. "On Hearing the Chopin Preludes As a Coherent Set: A Survey of Some Possible Structural Models for Op. 28." *In Theory Only*, 1 (July 1975): 5–10 + .

Offers a summary of ideas as to how the Preludes could be related to each other and therefore be seen as a whole. Explores "linking-relations, unresolved pitches or voice-leading, motives, and common pitches." Advanced.

1431. Warburton, A. O. "Set Works for 'O' Level, GCE." *Music Teacher*, 51 (August 1972): 17–18.

Preludes No. 6, 15, and 20 analyzed briefly.

1432. Warburton, A. O. "Set Works for 'O' Level, GCE." *Music Teacher*, 52 (September 1973): 20–21.

Brief comments on Nos. 1–5, 7, 8, 17–20.

Prelude No. 1, Op. 28 in C Major

1433. Smith, Charles J. "Exempli Gratia: A Motive of Chords in Chopin's C Major Prelude." *In Theory Only*, 4 (July 1978): 33–35.

A discussion of three different successions of sonorities functioning both as harmonic progressions and motivic chord-successions. Advanced.

1434.   Talley, Howard. "Take It Apart—Put It Together: A Key to the Study and Mastery of Music, Demonstrated Through Analysis of a Chopin Prelude." *Clavier*, 3, no. 4 (1964): 31–33.
A simple harmonic reduction and chordal analysis. Score included.

Prelude No. 2, Op. 28 in A Minor

1435.   Hoyt, Reed J. "Chopin's Prelude in A Minor Revisited: The Issue of Tonality." *In Theory Only*, 8, no. 6 (1985): 7–16.

1436.   Kielian-Gilbert, Marianne. "Motive Transfer in Chopin's A minor Prelude." *In Theory Only*, 9, no. 1 (1986): 21–32.

1437.   Kramer, Lawrence. "Romantic Meaning in Chopin's Prelude in A Minor." *Nineteenth Century Music*, 9, no. 2 (1985): 145–155.
An analytical essay. Includes discussion of previous analytic points of view of other authors; the place of this piece in the cycle of Preludes Op. 28; and seeks parallels with Romantic literature. Musical examples.

1438.   Meyer, Leonard B. *Emotion and Meaning in Music*, 93–97. Chicago: University of Chicago Press, 1956.
Analysis with musical examples. This analysis may also be found in Thomas Higgins, ed. *Chopin Preludes Op. 28*, 76–79. Norton Critical Scores. New York: W. W. Norton, 1973.

1439.   Rogers, Michael R. "Chopin, Prelude in A Minor Op. 28, No. 2." *Nineteenth Century Music*, 4, no. 3 (1981): 244–250.
An explanation of the harmonic and melodic ambiguity in this Prelude may lie in its macrorhythmic proportions. According to the "golden mean," the Prelude's temporal proportions provide clues to melodic and harmonic events that have puzzled theorists and performers for decades. Musical examples.

Prelude No. 3, Op. 28 in G Major

1440.   Schachter, Carl. "Rhythm and Linear Analysis, Durational Reduction." In *The Music Forum*. Vol. 5. Edited by Felix Salzer and Carl Schachter, 202–211 +. New York: Columbia University Press, 1980.
Advanced, Schenkerian analysis. Musical examples.

Prelude No. 4, Op. 28 in E Minor

1441.   Clark, Francis, and David Kraehenbuehl. "An Interpretive Analysis of Chopin's Prelude in E Minor." *American Music Teacher,* 12, no. 5 (1963): 16–17 + .
Analytic remarks for the performer. Musical examples.

1442.   Kresky, Jeffrey. *Tonal Music: Twelve Analytic Studies,* 41–45. Bloomington: Indiana University Press, 1977.
In-depth analysis dealing with harmony and melodic line. Advanced. Musical examples and diagrams.

Prelude No. 6, Op. 28 in B Minor

1443.   Guck, Marion, and Charles J. Smith. "Exempli Gratia: The Case of the Chimerical Cadence, m. 15–16." *In Theory Only,* 2 (August 1976): 30–34.
An attempt to clarify the significance of these two measures, which appear cadential but are modified by events of the preceding phrase. Musical examples.

Prelude No. 20, Op. 28 in C Minor

1444.   Cogan, Robert, and Pozzi Escot. *Sonic Design: The Nature of Sound and Music,* 4–14. Englewood Cliffs, NJ: Prentice-Hall, 1976.
Discusses melody, musical space, color, rhythm, "musical language."

Prelude No. 22, Op. 28 in G Minor

1445.   Hoyt, Reed J. "Harmonic Process, Melodic Process, and Interpretive Aspects of Chopin's Prelude in G Minor." *Indiana Theory Review,* 5, no. 3 (1982): 22–42.

Sonata for Piano, Op. 58 in B Minor

1446.   Sutton, Wadham. "Sonata in B Minor Op. 58." *Music Teacher,* 52 (July 1973): 13 + .
For the pianist, but interspersed with analytic remarks.

Waltz, Op. 64, No. 2 in C-Sharp Minor

1447.   Warburton, A. O. "Set Works for 'O' Level, GCE." *Music Teacher,* 47 (December 1968): 31.
Brief analysis for the undergraduate student.

DISSERTATIONS AND THESES

Concerto for Piano No. 1, Op. 11 in E Minor

1448. Ai, Chia-Huei. "Chopin's Concerto in E Minor, Op. 11: An Analysis for Performance." D.M.A., Ohio State University, 1986, 83 pp., DA 47-1523A.

Mazurkas

1449. Marks, Frank William. "Form and the Mazurkas of Chopin." D.M.A., University of Washington, 1970, 168 pp., DA 31-5449A.

Preludes, Op. 28

1450. Dorfman, Allen Arthur. "A Theory of Form and Proportion in Music." Ph.D., University of California at Los Angeles, 1986, 472 pp., DA 47-1105A.

Scherzos for Piano

1451. Lam (Fang), Julia Tiev-Luong. "Chopin's Approach to Form in His Four Piano Scherzos." Ph.D., Michigan State University, 1979, 121 pp. DA 40-3617A.

CILEA, FRANCESCO, 1866–1950

Adriana Lecouvreur

1452. Daniels, Robert D. *"Adriana* From Five to Four." *Opera News,* 33 (April 19, 1969): 24–25.
A look at the original drama to shed light on the libretto. No discussion of the music.

CLEMENTI, MUZIO, 1752–1832

General

1453. Dale, Kathleen. *Nineteenth-Century Piano Music: A Handbook for Pianists.* London: Oxford University Press, 1954, 320 pp.

195

Highlights stylistic traits and unique contribution to the literature of the piano. Form, harmony, and other musical aspects discussed in relation to style.

1454. Ehle, Robert. "The Writer of Sonatas." *Clavier*, 9, no. 8 (1970): 17+.
Background, influences, and critical comments on specific works. Musical examples.

1455. Plantinga, Leon. *Clementi: His Life and Music.* London: Oxford University Press, 1977, 346 pp.
Thorough treatment, with analytic insights on all his works. Clementi's influences on other composers discussed. Musical examples.

1456. Plantinga, Leon. "Clementi, Virtuosity, and the 'German Manner.'" *Journal of the American Musicological Society*, 25, no. 3 (1972): 303–330.
Clementi's contributions to idiomatic keyboard writing. Influences on Clementi discussed. Musical examples.

Etudes

1457. Ganz, Peter F. "Clementi: A Ladder to Parnassus." *Clavier*, 9, no. 8 (1970): 16.
Brief critical and descriptive commentary. Musical examples.

Preludes and Cadences, Op. 19

1458. Badura-Skoda, Eva. "Clementi's 'Musical Characteristics,' Op. 19." In *Studies in Eighteenth Century Music.* Edited by H. C. Robbins Landon, 53–67. New York: Oxford University Press, 1970.
Examination of Clementi's deliberate parodies of musical styles. Musical examples.

Sonatas for Piano

1459. Pauly, Reinhard. *Music in the Classic Period.* 2d ed., 121–123. Englewood Cliffs, NJ: Prentice-Hall, 1973.
Brief remarks on stylistic traits, with mention of a few specific sonatas. Musical examples.

Sonata for Piano, Op. 8, No. 1 in G Minor

1460. Bloch, Joseph. "A Forgotten Clementi Sonata." *Piano Quarterly*, 21, no. 79 (1972): 24–31.

Brief overview of Clementi's piano sonata output. Special reference is made to Op. 8, no. 1, which has not, as of this article, been reprinted since the original Breitkopf and Härtel edition. Complete score included.

Sonatina for Piano, Op. 36, No. 5 in C Major

1461.   Walton, Charles W. *Basic Forms in Music*, 175–177. Port Washington, NY: Alfred Publishing Co., 1974.
Condensed analysis outline with complete score.

COMPÈRE, LOYSET, c. 1445–1518

Missa Alles Regretz

1462.   Novack, Saul. "Fusion of Design and Tonal Order in Mass and Motet: Josquin Desprez and Heinrich Isaac." In *The Music Forum*. Vol. 2. Edited by William J. Mitchell and Felix Salzer, 187–195. New York: Columbia University Press, 1970.
A close examination of the relationship of design to tonality. Musical examples.

COPLAND, AARON, 1900–1990

General

1463.   Berger, Arthur. *Aaron Copland*, 72–82. New York: Oxford University Press, 1963.
Analytic commentary on Copland's output. Musical examples.

1464.   Butterworth, Neil. *The Music of Aaron Copland*. London: Toccata Press, 1985, 262 pp.
Copland's development, with commentaries on each piece and biographical details where appropriate. Analytic comments on style, technique and form are included in the discussions. Musical examples.

1465.   Newlin, Dika. "The Piano Music of Aaron Copland." *Piano Quarterly*, 28, no. 111 (1980): 6–8 +.
The Piano Concerto, Four Piano Blues: No. 1, *The Young Pioneers*, Piano Variations, Piano Sonata, Piano Fantasy discussed. Musical examples.

1466.   Smith, Julia. *Aaron Copland.* New York: E. P. Dutton, 1955, 336 pp.
Background, descriptive, critical, and analytic commentary, with musical examples.

1467.   Starr, Lawrence. "Copland's Style." *Perspectives of New Music,* 19, nos. 1–2 (1981–1982): 68 + .
A general survey of Copland's style. Brief analytic comments on a wide range of works. Musical examples.

1468.   Young, Douglas. "The Piano Music." *Tempo,* 95 (Winter 1970–1971): 15–22.
Describes the Variations, Piano Sonata, and Fantasy, showing sharp stylistic differences.

Appalachian Spring

1469.   Burns, Mary T. "An Analysis of Selected Folk-Style Themes in the Music of Bedrich Smetana and Aaron Copland." *American Music Teacher,* 25, no. 2 (1975): 8–10.
Comparison of type and use of folk melody used in the *Moldau* and *Appalachian Spring.* Musical examples.

Concerto for Clarinet

1470.   Maxey, Larry. "The Copland Clarinet Concerto." *Clarinet,* 12, no. 4 (1985): 28–32.
Analytic comments are interspersed with performance suggestions for the clarinet. Musical examples.

Connotations

1471.   Evans, Peter. "Copland on the Serial Road: An Analysis of *Connotations.*" *Perspectives of New Music,* 2, no. 2 (1964): 141–149.
Analysis, with musical examples. For the advanced student. This is the same analysis cited here in *Perspectives on American Composers,* pp. 147–155 (*see* item no. 1472).

1472.   Evans, Peter. "Copland on the Serial Road: An Analysis of *Connotations.*" In *Perspectives on American Composers.* Edited by Benjamin Boretz and E. T. Cone, 147–155. New York: W. W. Norton, 1971.

Analysis, with musical examples for the advanced student. This is the same analysis cited here in *Perspectives of New Music*, 2, no. 2 (1964): 141–149 (*see* item no. 1471).

1473. Evans, Peter. "Copland's *Connotations* for Orchestra." *Tempo*, 64 (Spring 1963): 30–33.
Less complex and shorter analysis by same author cited above. Musical examples.

Inscape

1474. Henderson, Robert. "Copland's *Inscape*." *Tempo*, 87 (Winter 1968–1969): 29–30.
Brief but solid analysis.

Passacaglia for Piano

1475. Coolidge, Richard. "Aaron Copland's Passacaglia: An Analysis." *Musical Analysis*, 2, no. 2 (1974): 33–36.
For the advanced student.

Piano Blues No. 3

1476. Forte, Allen. *Contemporary Tone-Structures*, 63–72. New York: Columbia University Press, 1955.
Thorough analysis dealing with formal structure, tonality, internal relationships, and general stylistic characteristics. Musical examples and analytic sketches.

Piano Fantasy

1477. Berger, Arthur. "Aaron Copland's Piano Fantasy." *Juilliard Review*, 5, no. 1 (Winter 1957–1958): 13–27.
An analysis and assessment, with a discussion of Copland's use of the twelve-tone method of composition.

1478. Copland, Aaron. "Piano Fantasy." *Tempo*, 46 (Winter 1958): 13–14.
A brief analytical overview by the composer.

1479. Fisher, Fred. "Contemporary American Style: How Three Representative Composers Use the 'Row.'" *Clavier*, 14, no. 4 (1975): 34–37.
Copland's use of the tone row in this piece.

199

Piano Variations

1480.   Berger, Arthur. *Aaron Copland*, 42–48. New York: Oxford University Press, 1953.
Brief background and analytic remarks. Musical examples.

Rodeo

1481.   Alexander, Michael. "Copland and the Dance Episodes From *Rodeo*." *Music Teacher*, 59 (September 1980): 17–18.
Analytical notes on the four episodes extracted from the ballet. Brief discussion of the melodic, harmonic, and rhythmic content of each.

Salón México

1482.   Brown, Alan. "Copland: *El salón México*." *Music Teacher*, 55 (June 1976): 17–18.
Analysis.

1483.   Cole, Hugo. "Popular Elements in Copland's Music." *Tempo*, 95 (Winter 1970–1971): 6–10.
Copland's sophisticated handling of popular music elements discussed. Musical examples.

Symphony No. 3

1484.   Berger, Arthur. *Aaron Copland*, 72–82. New York: Oxford University Press, 1953.
Analytic commentary, touching on Copland's orchestration, chord spacing, and folk idiom.

1485.   Berger, Arthur. "The Third Symphony of Aaron Copland." *Tempo* (Autumn 1948): 20–27.
Critical and analytic discussion.

1486.   Hansen, Peter. *An Introduction to Twentieth Century Music*. 2d ed., 325–328. Boston: Allyn and Bacon, 1967.
Short summary of analytic highlights. Musical examples.

1487.   Machlis, Joseph. *Introduction to Contemporary Music*, 487–491. New York: W. W. Norton, 1961.
Light, analytical treatment of entire symphony. For the undergraduate student. Musical examples.

1488.   Smith, Julia. *Aaron Copland*, 241–245. New York: E. P. Dutton, 1955.
Thorough, descriptive commentary on the entire symphony. Musical examples.

1489.   Stedman, Preston. *The Symphony*, 370–377. Englewood Cliffs, NJ: Prentice-Hall, 1979.
Description and analytic breakdown of all the sections, with commentary on Copland's style. Musical examples and diagram.

The Tender Land

1490.   Hilliard, Quincy. *"The Tender Land* Revisited." *Opera Journal*, 20, no. 1 (1987): 27–35.
Introduction to the libretto and the music. Includes analytic comments on harmony and tonality. Musical examples.

Twelve Poems of Emily Dickinson

1491.   Smith, Julia. *Aaron Copland*, 253–257. New York: E. P. Dutton, 1955.
Critical discussion with musical examples.

1492.   Young, Douglas. "Copland's *Dickinson* Songs." *Tempo*, 103 (1972): 33–37.
Critical and analytic remarks. Musical examples.

DISSERTATIONS AND THESES

General

1493.   Case, Nelly Maude. "Stylistic Coherency in the Piano Works of Aaron Copland." Ph.D., Boston University, 1984, 1127 pp., DA 45-980A.

1494.   Spicknall, Joan Singer. "The Piano Music of Aaron Copland: A Performance-Tape and Study of His Original Work for Piano Solo." D.M.A., University of Maryland, 1974, 33 pp., DA 36-595A.

Orchestral Variations

1495.   Wyatt, Lucius Reynolds. "The Mid-Twentieth-Century Orchestral Variation, 1953–1963." Ph.D., University of Rochester, Eastman School of Music, 1974, 504 pp., DA 34-7273A.

Symphonies

1496. Hilliard, Quincy Charles. "A Theoretical Analysis of the Symphonies of Aaron Copland." Ph.D., University of Florida, 1984, 230 pp., DA 45-1910A.

Twelve Poems of Emily Dickinson

1497. Daugherty, Robert Michael. "An Analysis of Aaron Copland's *Twelve Poems of Emily Dickinson.*" D.M.A., Ohio State University, 1980, 224 pp., DA 41-2819A.

1498. Mabry, Sharon Cody. *"Twelve Poems of Emily Dickinson* by Aaron Copland: A Stylistic Analysis." D.M.A., George Peabody College for Teachers, 1977, 234 pp., DA 38-2403A-4A.

CORELLI, ARCANGELO, 1653–1713

General

1499. Harris, Simon. "Lully, Corelli, Muffat, and the Eighteenth-Century Orchestral String Body." *Music and Letters,* 54, no. 2 (1973): 197–202.
   Not an analysis, but a discussion of the kind of orchestra Corelli had in mind and the influence of his work on others.

1500. Libbey, Dennis. "Interrelationships in Corelli." *Journal of the American Musicological Society,* 26, no. 2 (1973): 263–287.
   Thorough analytic discussion of Corelli's stylistic traits and his methods of unification. Tonal and formal patterns are examined for interrelationships. Musical examples.

1501. Pincherle, Marc. *Corelli: His Life, His Work.* Translated by Hubert E. M. Russell. New York: W. W. Norton, 1956, 236 pp.
   A "life and works" study. The musical discussion is restricted to the six published collections of instrumental music. The general analytic discussion is illustrated with musical examples from specific works. Remarks on background, musical structure, orchestration, and stylistic characteristics.

Concertos

1502. Bukofzer, Manfred. *Music in the Baroque Era,* 222–227. New York: W. W. Norton and Co., 1947.
   Corelli's contribution to the evolving concerto form. Some mention of Corelli's' unique stylistic traits. Musical examples.

1503. Hutchings, Arthur. *The Baroque Concerto,* 106–113. New York: W. W. Norton, 1961.

Examines the influences on Corelli as well as his impact on the concerto form. Musical examples.

1504. Jander, Owen. "Concerto Grosso Instrumentation in Rome in the 1660's and 1670's." *Journal of the American Musicological Society,* 21, no. 2 (1968): 168–180.

Demonstrates that many features of instrumentation associated with Corelli were anticipated by Stradella. Not an analytic discussion.

1505. Talbot, Michael. "The Concerto Allegro in the Early Eighteenth Century." *Music and Letters,* 52 (1971): 8–18, 159–172.

The development of the concerto form by Italian composers up to 1720, including Vivaldi. Advanced discussion.

1506. Veinus, Abraham. *The Concerto.* Rev. ed., 13–17. New York: Dover Publications, 1964.

Mainly descriptive commentary, with remarks on Corelli's life and place in the development of the concerto form.

Sonatas for Violin, Op. 5

1507. Cole, William. *The Form of Music: An Outline of Musical Designs Used by the Great Composers,* 96–98. London: Associated Board of the Royal Schools of Music, n.d.

Brief analytic comments.

Trio Sonatas

1508. Reeve, Robert. "Corelli: Trio Sonatas." *Music Teacher,* 58 (July 1979): 21–22.

Analytic comments on Op. 1, No. 3 and Op. 2, No. 10. Mainly a discussion of performance practice, but some analytic comments and mention of stylistic features. Musical examples.

Trio Sonata, Op. 2, No. 5 in B-Flat Major

1509. Warburton, A. O. "Set Works for 'O' Level, GCE." *Music Teacher,* 53 (April 1974): 16–17.

Brief analytic remarks with commentary on the flute writing in this work.

Trio Sonata, Op. 3, No. 9 in F Minor

1510. Stedman, Preston. *The Symphony,* 8–9. Englewood Cliffs, NJ: Prentice-Hall, 1979.
  Brief descriptive commentary focusing on fugal style, form, and harmony. Musical examples.

CORIGLIANO, JOHN, 1938–

DISSERTATIONS AND THESES

General

1511. Bobetsky, Victor V. "An Analysis of Selected Works for Piano (1959–1978) and the Sonata for Violin and Piano (1964)." D.M.A., University of Miami, 1982, 109 pp., DA 44-10A.

Concerto for Clarinet

1512. Polley, Jo Ann Marie. "An Analysis of John Corigliano's Concerto for Clarinet and Orchestra." Ph.D., Michigan State University, 1983, 124 pp., DA 44-2619A.

A Dylan Thomas Trilogy

1513. Townsend, Alfred S. "Unity and Variety in *A Dylan Thomas Trilogy* by John Corigliano." Ph.D., New York University, 1986, 341 pp., DA 47-2941A.

COUPERIN, FRANÇOIS, 1668–1733

General

1514. Mellers, Wilfrid. *François Couperin and the French Classical Tradition.* 1950. Reprint. New York: Dover Publications, 1968, 408 pp.
  Stylistic and critical, with a few scattered analytic observations. Shows Couperin in historical context. Musical examples.

1515. Tunley, David. *Couperin.* London: British Broadcasting Corporation, 1983.

Brief overview of Couperin's output with discussion of style, forms, and ornamentation. For the undergraduate student. Musical examples.

COWELL, HENRY, 1897–1965

Ostinato Pianissimo

1516.   Hitchcock, H. Wiley. "Henry Cowell's *Ostinato Pianissimo.*" *Musical Quarterly*, 70, no. 1 (1984): 23–44.
Background, analysis, and general discussion of the piece. Musical examples.

CRAMER, JOHANN BAPTIST, 1771–1858

General

1517.   Dale, Kathleen. *Nineteenth-Century Piano Music: A Handbook for Pianists.* London: Oxford University Press, 1954, 320 pp.
Highlights stylistic traits and unique contribution to the literature of the piano. Form, harmony, and other musical aspects discussed in relation to style.

CRUMB, GEORGE, 1929–

Ancient Voices of Children

1518.   De Dobay, Thomas R. "The Evolution of Harmonic Style in the Lorca Works of Crumb." *Journal of Music Theory*, 27, no. 2 (1984): 89–111.
Advanced analytic essay.

1519.   Machlis, Joseph. *The Enjoyment of Music.* 5th ed., 584–587. New York: W. W. Norton, 1984.
Background and descriptive commentary for the undergraduate student. Each section treated separately.

Echoes (Eleven) of Autumn (Echoes I)

1520.   Henahan, Donal. "Reviews of Records." *Musical Quarterly*, 55, no. 2 (1969): 280–284.
Brief analytic remarks with musical examples.

1521.   Thomas, Janet. "The Use of Color in Three Chamber Works of the Twentieth Century." *Indiana Theory Review*, 4, no. 3 (1981): 24–40.

Crumb developed a new sonorous vocabulary for twentieth-century music by exploiting some unusual possibilities of an instrument. Each of the *Echoes* is analyzed for its sonorous qualities.

Echoes of Time and the River (Echoes II)

1522.   Borwick, Doug. "The Instrumental Theater Piece—An Introduction to Form and Analysis." *Woodwind World—Brass and Percussion*, 15, no. 4 (1976): 35–36.

1523.   Henahan, Donal. "Current Chronicle: Chicago." *Musical Quarterly*, 54, no. 1 (1968): 83–87.

A review of a performance, but interspersed with analytic observations. Musical examples.

Madrigals

1524.   De Dobay, Thomas R. "Madrigals, Books I–IV." *Journal of Music Theory*, 27, no. 2 (1984): 92–100, 104–107.

Night Music I

1525.   De Dobay, Thomas R. "The Evolution of Harmonic Style in the Lorca Works of Crumb." *Journal of Music Theory*, 27, no. 2 (1984): 90–94.

1526.   Lewis, Robert H. "George Crumb: *Night Music* I." *Perspectives of New Music*, 3, no. 2 (1965): 143–151.

An analytic essay including discussion of form, style, rhythm, vocal style, and instrumentation. Musical examples and table.

1527.   Stone, Kurt. "Current Chronicle: Lenox, Mass." *Musical Quarterly*, 51, no. 4 (1965): 692–694.

Review of a performance. Mainly descriptive. Musical examples.

Night of the Four Moons

1528.   De Dobay, Thomas R. "The Evolution of Harmonic Style in the Lorca Works of Crumb." *Journal of Music Theory*, 27, no. 2 (1984): 104.

Pieces (Five) for Piano

1529.   Reuter, Rocky J. "Symmetrical Structures in George Crumb's Five Pieces for Piano." *Journal of the Graduate Music Students at the Ohio State University*, 9 (Spring 1985): 41–52.

Songs, Drones, and Refrains of Death

1530.   De Dobay, Thomas R. "The Evolution of Harmonic Style in the Lorca Works of Crumb." *Journal of Music Theory*, 27, no. 2 (1984): 98–111.

DISSERTATIONS AND THESES

General

1531.   De Dobay, Thomas R. "Harmonic Materials and Usages in the Lorca Cycle of George Crumb." Ph.D., University of Southern California, 1982, DA 43-1739A.

1532.   Ott, David Lee. "The Role of Texture and Timbre in the Music of George Crumb." D.M.A., University of Kentucky, 1982, 277 pp., DA 44-2704A.

1533.   Shuffett, Robert Vernon. "The Music, 1971–1975, of George Crumb: A Style Analysis." D.M.A., Peabody Conservatory of Music, 1979, 576 pp., DA 40-1744A-5A.

Makrokosmos

1534.   Matthews, Nell Wright. "George Crumb's *Makrokosmos*, Vols. 1 and 2: Considerations for Performance, Including Observations by David Burge, Robert Miller, and Lambert Orkis." D.M.A., University of Oklahoma, 1981, 178 pp., DA 42-4641A.

Music for a Summer Evening

1535.   DeBaise, Joseph Ralph. "George Crumb's *Music for a Summer Evening*: A Comprehensive Analysis." Ph.D., University of Rochester, Eastman School of Music, 1983, 546 pp., DA 43-3748A.

Night of the Four Moons

1536.   McGee, William James. "An Expanded Concept of Timbre and Its Structural Significance, with a Timbral Analysis of George Crumb's *Night of the Four Moons*." Ph.D., University of Arizona, 1982, 251 pp., DA 43-1741A.

DALLAPICCOLA, LUIGI, 1904–1975

General

1537.   Evans, Peter. "Music of the European Mainstream: 1940–1960." In *The New Oxford History of Music.* Vol. 10, *The Modern Age: 1890–1960.* Edited by Martin Cooper, 420–424. London: Oxford University Press, 1974.

Brief stylistic overview, with analytic observations on *Job, Quaderno Musicale di Annalibera, Cinque Canti,* and *Concerto per la Notte de Natale.* Musical examples.

1538.   Mancini, David. "Twelve-Tone Polarity in Late Works of Luigi Dallapiccola." *Journal of Music Theory,* 30, no. 2 (1986): 203–224.

Demonstrates that Dallapiccola's use of the twelve-tone system gives priority to an interval or a pitch-class set. Includes analytic comments on *Sicut Umbra* ... (1970), *Commiato* (1972), and *Preghiere* (1962). Uses set-theory terminology. For the advanced student. Musical examples and diagrams.

1539.   Nathan, Hans. "The Twelve-Tone Compositions of Luigi Dallapiccola." *Musical Quarterly,* 44 (July 1958): 289–310.

Detailed analysis of Dallapiccola's unique twelve-tone style, showing how he differs from the Viennese school of Berg and Schoenberg. Includes list of completely dodecaphonic compositions. Musical examples.

Canti di Prigionia

1540.   Boyd, Malcolm. " 'Dies Irae': Some Recent Manifestations." *Music and Letters,* 49, no. 4 (1968): 351–352.

Dallapiccola's use of the "Dies Irae" plainsong in this work. Musical examples.

Goethe-Lieder

1541.   Eckert, Michael. "Text and Form in Dallapiccola's *Goethe-Lieder.*" *Perspectives of New Music,* 17, no. 2 (1979): 98–111.

Goethe-Lieder No. 2

1542.   De Lio, Thomas. "A Proliferation of Canons: Luigi Dallapiccola's *Goethe Lieder* No. 2." *Perspectives of New Music,* 23, no. 2 (1985): 186–195.

A detailed analysis. Musical examples, diagrams.

Quaderno musicale di Annalibera

1543. Shackleford, Rudy. "Dallapiccola and the Organ." *Tempo*, 111 (Winter 1974–1975): 15–22.
Brief descriptive analysis and discussion of the problems in making a transcription for organ from the version for piano and orchestra (*Variazione per Orchestra*).

Three Questions with Two Answers

1544. Petrobelli, Pierluigi. "Dallapiccola's Last Orchestral Piece." *Tempo*, 123 (December 1977): 2–6.
This orchestral piece was integrated into his opera *Ulisse*. The article explores this integration through analysis of the row utilized by the composer. Musical examples.

DISSERTATIONS AND THESES

General

1545. Mancini, David Lee. "Form and Polarity in Late Works of Luigi Dallapiccola." Ph.D., Yale University, 1984, 278 pp., DA 46-1123A.

Piccola Musica Notturna

1546. Dwelley, Robert R. "An Analysis of Luigi Dallapiccola's *Piccola Musica Notturna*." Ph.D., University of Rochester, Eastman School of Music, 1985, 110 pp., DA 46-831A.

DEBUSSY, CLAUDE, 1862–1918

General

1547. Abraham, Gerald. "The Reaction Against Romanticism: 1890–1914." In *The New Oxford History of Music*. Vol. 10, *The Modern Age: 1890–1960*. Edited by Martin Cooper, 90–100. London: Oxford University Press, 1974.
Brief overview of the origins and development of Debussy's unique idiom. Debussy's technique of theme transformation, use of pentatonic scale, unresolved chords, "weightless" harmony, and chord colorization. Musical examples.

1548.   Adams, John K. "Debussy: Part 1—The Early Piano Works." *Piano Quarterly*, 35, no. 137 (1987): 36–40.

An introduction to the early piano works. Descriptive rather than analytic. Identifies stylistic features to be found in later, more mature works. Musical examples.

1549.   Adams, John K. "Debussy: Part 2—The Later Piano Works." *Piano Quarterly*, 35, no. 138 (1987): 48–53.

Part 2 of a three-part series. A descriptive survey of Debussy's piano music from *Estampes* on. Musical examples.

1550.   Adams, John K. "Debussy: Part 3—The Later Works." *Piano Quarterly*, 35, no. 139 (1987): 40–43.

Descriptive survey beginning with the Preludes and ending with the Etudes. Musical examples.

1551.   Cortot, Alfred. *French Piano Music.* Translated by Hilda Andrews, 1–36. London: Oxford University Press, 1932.

Descriptive overview with observations on Debussy's style.

1552.   Dawes, Frank. *Debussy's Piano Music.* London: British Broadcasting Corporation, 1969, 63 pp.

A "BBC Music Guide." General introduction covering all the works for one and two pianos. Considers the composer's harmonic innovations and influences that shaped his music. Musical examples.

1553.   Ferguson, Donald N. *Piano Music of Six Great Composers*, 319–344. New York: Books for Libraries Press, 1947.

Descriptive and critical overview. Musical examples.

1554.   Howat, Roy. *Debussy in Proportion: A Musical Analysis.* Cambridge: Cambridge University Press, 1983, 239 pp.

Analysis from the point of view of temporal proportion and how it underlies the music's dramatic and expressive quality.

1555.   Jarocinski, Stephen. *Debussy: Impressionism and Symbolism.* Translated by R. Myers. London: Eulenberg Books, 1976, 175 pp.

A discussion of impressionism and symbolism and how they are manifested in Debussy's music. Analytic overview of Debussy's output in the last chapter of the book. Musical examples.

1556.   Lockspeiser, Edward. *Debussy.* London: J. M. Dent and Sons, 1972, 304 pp.

Descriptive and critical commentary with occasional analytic remarks. A "Master Musician" series for the undergraduate student. Musical examples.

1557.   Lockspeiser, Edward. *Debussy: His Life and Mind.* 2 vols. New York: Macmillan, 1962.
Mainly Debussy's life and background information on his compositions. However, the chapter titled "Debussy's Musical Language" (pp. 229–245) deals with stylistic aspects of the music. Musical examples.

1558.   Long, Marguerite. *At the Piano with Debussy.* Translated by Olive Senior-Ellis. London: J. M. Dent and Sons, n.d., 112 pp.
A pianist's observations on Debussy's piano music. Descriptive and critical commentary with a view toward performance. Musical examples.

1559.   Matthews, Denis, ed. *Keyboard Music,* 272–280. New York: Praeger, 1972.
Overview with observations on style and influences. Musical examples.

1560.   Nichols, Roger. *Debussy.* London: Oxford University Press, 1973, 86 pp.
Detailed technical study of Debussy's music. Though the book is short, the discussion is quite technical. Analytic comments on a wide variety of works. Musical examples.

1561.   Orledge, Robert. *Debussy and the Theatre.* Cambridge: Cambridge University Press, 1983, 383 pp.
Descriptive and analytic commentary concentrating on *Pelléas, Khamma, La boîte à joujoux, Le Martyre de Saint Sebastien, Prelude to the Afternoon of a Faun,* and other works for theater. Musical examples.

1562.   Palmer, Christopher. *Impressionism in Music.* London: Hutchinson, 1973, 248 pp.
Analytic comments (in the introduction) as part of a discussion of musical impressionism. Musical examples.

1563.   Raad, Virginia. "Debussy and the Magic of Spain." *Clavier,* 18, no. 3 (1979): 13–21.
Brief comments on style, rhythm, and structure in some of the "Spanish" piano works. Musical examples.

1564.   Rayner, Josephine. "The Piano Music of Claude Debussy." *Music in Education,* 34, no. 341 (1970): 26–27; no. 342 (1970): 80–82; no. 343 (1970): 154–155.
Brief analytic remarks on some representative pieces. Musical examples.

1565. Schmitz, E. Robert. *The Piano Works of Claude Debussy.* New York: Duell, Sloan, and Pearce, 1950, 236 pp.

Debussy's piano works are discussed individually in chronological order. The discussions focus on style and structure, as well as noting points of interpretation for the performer. Though the "analyses" tend to be somewhat more descriptive than analytic, there are some valuable analytic comments.

1566. Thompson, Oscar. *Debussy: Man and Artist.* New York: Dover Publications, 1967, 393 pp.

Purely descriptive commentary, except for the chapter "Debussy's Musical Processes," which offers a brief discussion of musical techniques.

1567. Wenk, Arthur. *Claude Debussy and the Poets.* Berkeley: University of California Press, 1976, 345 pp.

Detailed discussions of Debussy's musical treatment of text. Works examined closely are *Prelude to the Afternoon of a Faun* and most of the songs. Musical examples and diagrams.

1568. Wenk, Arthur. *Claude Debussy and Twentieth Century Music.* Boston: Twayne, 1983, 165 pp.

Analytic overview of Debussy's output, focusing on *Pelléas et Mélisande, String Quartet,* and *Prelude to the Afternoon of a Faun.* Musical examples.

1569. Wenk, Arthur. "Parsing Debussy: Proposal for a Grammar of His Melodic Practice." *In Theory Only,* 9, no. 8 (May 1987): 5–19.

A theory of Debussy's melodic structure based on theories of Baroni and Jacobini. Melodic fragments from several works analyzed using this theory to show their generations, structure and "Debussian" style. Musical examples.

1570. Whittall, Arnold. "Tonality and the Whole-Tone Scale in the Music of Debussy." *Music Review,* 36, no. 4 (1975): 261–271.

Compact analysis on an advanced level. Musical examples.

Balcon

1571. Wenk, Arthur. *Claude Debussy and Twentieth Century Music,* 32–33. Boston: Twayne, 1983.

A detailed study of Debussy's musical language, describing its revolutionary aspects and its implications for twentieth-century music as a whole. Discusses Wagnerian influences in this work. From *Cinq Poèmes de Baudelaire.* Musical examples.

Boîte à joujoux

1572.   Orledge, Robert. "Another Look Inside Debussy's *Toybox*." *Musical Times*, 117 (December 1976): 987–989.
Background, story, choreography, and score discussed briefly. Analytic remarks on the music. Musical examples.

Chansons (Three) de France (1904)

1573.   Shearin, Arthur. "The Choral Music of Debussy and Ravel." *Choral Journal*, 19, no. 6 (1979): 7–9.
A comparison of the setting of these medieval poems. Discusses texture, use of modality, phrase structure, vocal ranges.

Children's Corner Suite

1574.   Warburton, A. O. "Set Works for 'O' Level, GCE." *Music Teacher*, 49 (February 1970): 17–18.
Brief analytic commentary on each piece of the suite.

"Clair de Lune" (Suite Bergamasque)

1575.   Lockspeiser, Edward. "Debussy's Two Settings of *Clair de Lune*." *Music and Letters*, 49, no. 1 (1968): 100–101.
Response to Nichols' article (*see* item no. 1576).

1576.   Nichols, Roger. "Debussy's Two Settings of *Clair de Lune*." *Music and Letters*, 48, no. 3 (1967): 229–235.
Compares the two settings of the work (1882–1884 and 1892). Detailed analysis with musical examples. Score recommended since measure numbers are used throughout.

Damoiselle élue

1577.   Wenk, Arthur. *Claude Debussy and Twentieth Century Music*, 26–32. Boston: Twayne, 1983.
A detailed study of Debussy's musical language, describing its revolutionary aspects and its implications for twentieth-century music as a whole. Describes harmony, Renaissance influences, form, recurring themes in this work. Musical examples.

L'Enfant prodigue

1578.   Wenk, Arthur. *Claude Debussy and Twentieth Century Music*, 21–26. Boston: Twayne, 1983.

A detailed study of Debussy's musical language, describing its revolutionary aspects and its implications for twentieth-century music as a whole. Discusses Debussy's early style; describes form, harmony and elaboration procedures in this work. Musical examples.

Epigraphes antiques

1579. Escher, Rudolf. "Debussy and the Musical Epigram." *Key Notes*, 10, no. 2 (1979): 59–63.

Analytic comments on the six pieces of this set, each of which arises from an "arabesque."

Estampes: "La soirée dans grenade"

1580. Raad, Virginia. "Debussy and the Magic of Spain." *Clavier*, 18, no. 3 (1979): 13–21.

A discussion of Spanish elements in Debussy's piano music, focusing on the melodic influences in this work, as well as in *Lindaraja*, *La Sérénade interrompue*, and *La Puerto del Vino*.

Etude No. 4: "Pour les sixtes"

1581. Gaudlin, Robert, et al. "Debussy Etude *Pour les sixtes*." *Journal of Music Theory*, 22, no. 2 (1978): 237 + .

Full score provided, with extensive analyses by three theorists.

Etude No. 7: "Pour les degrés chromatiques"

1582. Parks, Richard S. "Tonal Analogues as Atonal Resources and Their Relation to Form in Debussy's *Chromatic* Etude." *Journal of Music Theory*, 29, no. 1 (1985): 33–60.

A detailed analytic study of this Etude. Uses set-theoretic terminology. For the very advanced student. Musical examples and diagrams.

Etude No. 10: "Pour les sonorités opposées"

1583. Wenk, Arthur. *Claude Debussy and Twentieth Century Music*, 86–91. Boston: Twayne, 1983.

A detailed study of Debussy's musical language, describing its revolutionary aspects and its implications for twentieth-century music as a whole. Discusses pitch relations, dynamics, disposition, and attack in this work. Musical examples.

Fall of the House of Usher

1584. Orledge, Robert. "Debussy's *House of Usher* Revisited." *Musical Quarterly*, 62, no. 4 (1976): 536–553.
Traces development of Debussy's unfinished score and relates the work to the three known versions of the libretto. Some brief remarks on the music. Musical examples.

Fantaisie for Piano and Orchestra

1585. Mueller, Richard. "Javanese Influence on Debussy's *Fantaisie* and Beyond." *Nineteenth Century Music*, 10, no. 2 (1986): 157–186.
Analyzes the influence of Javanese melody on the cyclic theme of the *Fantaisie*. Includes many musical examples of Javanese melodies and examples from the *Fantaisie* and other Debussy works.

Images for Orchestra

1586. Cox, David V. *Debussy Orchestral Music*, 34–45. Seattle: University of Washington Press, 1975.
A "BBC Music Guide." Descriptive and analytic commentary for the undergraduate student. Musical examples.

Images for Orchestra: "Ibéria"

1587. Machlis, Joseph. *Introduction to Contemporary Music*, 129–130. New York: W. W. Norton, 1961.
Brief descriptive commentary with musical examples. For the undergraduate student.

Images for Piano: "Reflets dans l'eau"

1588. Burge, David. "Private Lesson: Striking Harmonic Juxtapositions in Debussy's *Reflets dans l'eau*." *Keyboard Magazine*, 12 (February 1986): 34–35.
Brief comments on the harmony of this piece. Musical examples.

1589. Reti, Rudolph. *Tonality, Atonality, Pantonality: A Study of Some Trends in Twentieth Century Music*, 23–26, 134–135. London: Rockliff, 1958.
Brief comments on Debussy's new uses of traditional harmony. Musical examples.

Jeux

1590.   Berman, Laurence D. *"Prelude to the Afternoon of a Faun* and *Jeux*: Debussy's Summer Rites." *Nineteenth Century Music*, 3, no. 3 (1980): 225–238.

A comparison of *Jeux, Faun,* and Mallarmé's poem to examine their relationship to one another.

1591.   Cox, David V. *Debussy Orchestral Music,* 50–54. Seattle: University of Washington Press, 1975.

A "BBC Music Guide." Descriptive and analytic commentary for the undergraduate student. Musical examples.

1592.   Orledge, Robert. "The Genesis of Debussy's *Jeux."* *Musical Times,* 128 (February 1987): 68–73.

Concerned mainly with manuscripts, chronology, and variants, but does contain some analytic comments. Musical examples.

1593.   Pasler, Jann. "Debussy, *Jeux*: Playing With Time and Form." *Nineteenth Century Music,* 6, no. 1 (1982): 60–75.

Detailed analysis focusing on rhythmic organization. Musical examples.

1594.   Wenk, Arthur. *Claude Debussy and Twentieth Century Music,* 73–82. Boston: Twayne, 1983.

A detailed study of Debussy's musical language, describing its revolutionary aspects and its implications for twentieth-century music as a whole. Discusses tonal framework and chromatic procedures. Compares *Jeux* with Stravinsky's *Rite of Spring.* Musical examples.

Khamma

1595.   Orledge, Robert. "Debussy's Orchestral Collaborations." *Musical Times,* 116 (January 1975): 30–31 + .

Debussy's collaboration with Charles Koechlin on this tone poem. Musical examples.

Martyre de Saint-Sebastien

1596.   Orledge, Robert. "Debussy's Orchestral Collaborations, 1911–13 *Le Martyre de Saint-Sebastien."* *Musical Times,* 115 (December 1974): 1030–1033.

Detailed account of Debussy's collaboration with Andre Caplet on *Le Martyre.* Musical examples.

La Mer

1597.   Cox, David V. *Debussy Orchestral Music*, 24–31. Seattle: University of Washington Press, 1975.
A "BBC Music Guide." Descriptive and analytic commentary for the undergraduate student. Musical examples.

La Mer: Jeux de Vagues

1598.   Wenk, Arthur. *Claude Debussy and Twentieth Century Music*, 67–73. Boston: Twayne, 1983.
A detailed study of Debussy's musical language, describing its revolutionary aspects and its implications for twentieth-century music as a whole. Discussion of the harmonic structure, form (including comparison of analyses by other authors), and motivic transformations in this work. Musical examples.

Nocturnes

1599.   Cox, David V. *Debussy Orchestral Music*, 18–23. Seattle: University of Washington Press, 1975.
A "BBC Music Guide." Brief descriptive and analytic remarks for the undergraduate student. Musical examples.

1600.   Kerman, Joseph. *Listen.* 2d ed., 308–311. New York: Worth Publishers, 1976.
Background and analysis with musical examples. For the undergraduate student.

Nocturnes: "Fêtes"

1601.   Warburton, A. O. "Set Works for 'O' Level, GCE." *Music Teacher*, 52 (December 1973): 13–14.
A brief look at the correlation between instrumental colors and thematic events.

Nocturnes: "Nuages"

1602.   Cogan, Robert, and Pozzi Escot. *Sonic Design: The Nature of Sound and Music*, 385–397. Englewood Cliffs, NJ: Prentice-Hall, 1976.
An analysis of register and timbre. Included are graphs, tables, and musical examples.

217

Nocturnes: "Sirènes"

1603. Wenk, Arthur. *Claude Debussy and Twentieth Century Music,* 62–64. Boston: Twayne, 1983.

A detailed study of Debussy's musical language, describing its revolutionary aspects and its implications for twentieth-century music as a whole. Discusses the nonfunctional nature of Debussy's harmony, stratification techniques, and symmetrical relations in this work. Musical examples.

Pelléas et Mélisande

1604. Abbate, Carolyn. *"Tristan* in the Composition of *Pelléas."* *Nineteenth Century Music,* 5, no. 2 (1981): 117–141.

Detailed exploration of the relationships of *Pelléas* to Wagner's *Tristan and Isolde.*

1605. Cooper, Martin. *French Music: From the Death of Berlioz to the Death of Fauré,* 114–118. London: Oxford University Press, 1951.

Compact treatment dealing with influences leading to Pelléas; the relationship of text and music, harmony, orchestral color, and characterization.

1606. Gilman, Lawrence. *Debussy's "Pelléas et Mélisande."* New York: G. Schirmer, 1907, 84 pp.

Written during Debussy's lifetime, but still useful for its tracing of leitmotivs and story synopsis.

1607. Grayson, David A. *The Genesis of Debussy's "Pelléas et Mélisande."* Ann Arbor: UMI Research Press, 1986, 342 pp.

A documentary narrative of the opera's genesis followed by a study of its sources and comments on the compositional process. A detailed study of the revisions to this work results in many analytic observations. Includes a discussion of Debussy's leitmotiv technique in this opera.

1608. Liebich, Louise. *Claude Achille Debussy,* 64–80. London: John Lane, 1918.

Description with analytic remarks written during Debussy's lifetime. Musical examples.

1609. Lockspeiser, Edward. *Debussy,* 209–228. London: J. M. Dent and Sons, 1951.

Concise summary of outstanding features. Recitative, leitmotivs and musical influences are discussed.

1610. Lockspeiser, Edward. *Debussy: His Life and Mind.* Vol. 1, 189–202. New York: Macmillan, 1962.

Influences, both literary and musical, that helped shape *Pelléas.* Some analytic commentary on the music.

1611. Luten, C. J. "Emerging from a Shadow." *Opera News,* 36 (January 29, 1972): 24–25.

Brief critical remarks focusing on the atmosphere generated by the orchestral part and drama of the vocal line. Musical examples.

1612. Nichols, Roger. *Debussy,* 33–45. London: Oxford University Press, 1973.

Clear discussion of Debussy's aims and method. Specific musical effects are analyzed. Musical examples.

1613. Osborne, Charles. " 'Out of Darkness': Maeterlinck's Symbolism in *Pelléas et Mélisande."* *Opera News,* 42 (March 4, 1978): 26–28.

Maeterlinck's symbolism in *Pelléas* discussed, with some observations on how well Debussy's music evokes the atmosphere of the script.

1614. Simon, John. "Behind a Veil of Tears." *Opera News,* 47 (January 15, 1983): 8–10+.

Discussion of Maeterlinck's drama, which was used by Debussy in his only opera.

1615. Thompson, Oscar. *Debussy: Man and Artist,* 343–352. New York: Dover Publications, 1967.

Background, plot, and discussion of the music.

1616. Watkins, Glenn. *Soundings: Music in the Twentieth Century,* 75–94. New York: Schirmer Books, 1987.

General description of musical devices, such as association of certain characters with particular keys and text-determined harmonic design, gliding parallel sonorities, and other stylistic features. Libretto in French and English included. Musical examples.

1617. Wenk, Arthur. *Claude Debussy and Twentieth Century Music,* 35–50. Boston: Twayne, 1983.

A detailed study of Debussy's musical language, describing its revolutionary aspects and its implications for twentieth-century music as a whole. Discusses symbolism and atonality, melodic motives, rhythmic patterns, harmonic symbolism, symbolism of sonority, and tonal symbolism in the opera. Musical examples.

Petite Suite

1618. Warburton, A. O. "Set Works for 'O' Level, GCE." *Music Teacher*, 50 (November 1971): 18–20.
Brief analytic overview of each movement.

Pour le Piano: "Sarabande"

1619. Raad, Virginia. "Claude Debussy's *Sarabande*." *American Music Teacher*, 30, no. 6 (1981): 22–23.
Brief background and analytic remarks. Musical examples.

Prelude to the Afternoon of a Faun

1620. Austin, William W. *Music in the Twentieth Century*, 15–23. New York: W. W. Norton, 1966.
Brief analysis. Comparison with *Syrinx*. Musical examples.,

1621. Austin, William W., ed. *Debussy: "Prelude to the Afternoon of a Faun."* Norton Critical Scores. New York: W. W. Norton, 1971, 167 pp.
Background, criticism, and analysis with complete score included.

1622. Berman, Laurence D. "*Prelude to the Afternoon of a Faun* and *Jeux*: Debussy's Summer Rites." *Nineteenth Century Music*, 3, no. 3 (1980): 225–238.
A comparison of *Jeux*, *Faun*, and Mallarmé's poem to examine their relationship to one another.

1623. Cox, David V. *Debussy Orchestral Music*, 9–18. Seattle: University of Washington Press, 1975.
Thorough analytic discussion. Musical examples.

1624. Crotty, John E. "Symbolist Influences in Debussy's *Prelude to the Afternoon of a Faun*." *In Theory Only*, 6 (May 1982): 9–11.

1625. Warburton, A. O. "Set Works for 'O' Level, GCE." *Music Teacher*, 52 (November 1973): 15.
Brief analytic overview of the piece.

Preludes for Piano

1626. Beechey, Gwilyn. "The Originality of Debussy: Some Notes on Selected Preludes for Piano." *Musical Opinion*, 104 (October 1980): 10–12.

Analytic comments on *La Cathédrale Engloutie* (Book 1, No. 10) with musical examples. Also brief comments on *Minstrels* (Book 1, No. 12) and *Canope* (Book 2, No. 10).

1627. Freundlich, Irwin. "Random Thoughts on the Preludes of Claude Debussy." *Piano Quarterly*, 22, no. 87 (1974): 17–18+.
Analytic discussion of all the preludes, with mention of their literary allusions. Musical examples. This article also appears in *Current Musicology*, edited by L. Michael Griffel and Margaret Ross Griffel, vol. 13, pp. 48–57. New York: Columbia University, 1972.

1628. Haimo, Ethan. "Generated Collections and Interval Control in Debussy's Preludes." *In Theory Only*, 4 (February–March 1979): 3–15.

1629. Haimo, Ethan. "Reply." *In Theory Only*, 5 (July 1979): 25–27.
Haimo's reply to J. Rahn's comments (*see* item no. 1630) on Haimo's original article (*see* item no. 1628). Advanced.

1630. Rahn, John. "Comment." *In Theory Only*, 5 (May–June 1979): 19–22.
Response to E. Haimo's article "Generated Collections and Interval Control in Debussy's Preludes" (*see* item no. 1628).

Preludes for Piano, Book I

1631. Todd, Dennis. "Three Preludes by Debussy (Set by Oxford 1978)." *Music Teacher*, 56 (April 1977): 13–14.
Descriptive and analytic commentary on *Voiles; La Fille aux Cheveux de Lin; La Cathédrale Engloutie.*

Preludes for Piano, Book I: "La Cathédrale engloutie"

1632. Dumm, Robert. "Lesson on a Debussy Prelude." *Clavier*, 6, no. 9 (1967): 18–25.
Performance notes, with descriptive and analytic observations. Complete score of Prelude provided.

1633. Hache, Reginald. "The Legendary Cathedral of Brittany." *Journal of the American Liszt Society*, 19 (June 1986): 67–76.
Contains remarks on the church modes used by Debussy in this work. Musical examples.

1634. Warburton, A. O. "Set Works for 'O' Level, GCE." *Music Teacher*, 49 (February 1970): 17–18.
Brief analytic overview for the undergraduate student.

Preludes for Piano, Book I: "Des pas sur la neige"

1635. Guck, Marion A. "One Path Through Debussy's *Des pas sur la neige*: Insights into the Methodology of Sketch-Rejection." *In Theory Only*, 1 (August 1975): 4–8.

By examining the composer's sketch of the Prelude, the author isolates several features, including relationships of motive to the entire piece and the relationship of two distinct diatonic collections. Musical examples.

Preludes for Piano, Book I. "La fille aux cheveux de lin"

1636. Kresky, Jeffrey. *Tonal Music: Twelve Analytic Studies,* 151–163. Bloomington: Indiana University Press, 1977.

In-depth analysis focusing on the triad that underlies the music and tonality. Advanced. Musical examples and diagrams.

1637. Warburton, A. O. "Set Works for 'O' Level, GCE." *Music Teacher,* 49 (February 1970): 17–18.

Brief analytic commentary for the undergraduate student.

Preludes for Piano, Book I: "Minstrels"

1638. Bryant, Celia M. "Surprise Adds Humor to a Piano Piece." *Clavier,* 6, no. 1 (1967): 42–45.

Performance notes with descriptive and analytic observations. Musical examples.

1639. Warburton, A. O. "Set Works for 'O' Level, GCE." *Music Teacher,* 53 (January 1974): 14–15.

Brief analytic commentary for the undergraduate student.

Preludes for Piano, Book I: "Voiles"

1640. Persky, Stanley. "Debussy the Progressive." *In Theory Only,* 1 (October 1975): 3–7.

Discussion of the integration of the whole-tone and pentatonic scales in this work.

1641. Warburton, A. O. "Set Works for 'O' Level, GCE." *Music Teacher,* 49 (February 1970): 17–18.

Brief analytic overview for the undergraduate student.

Preludes for Piano, Book II: "Brouillards"

1642. Parks, Richard S. "Pitch Organization in Debussy: Unordered Sets in *Brouillards.*" *Music Theory Spectrum,* 2 (1980): 119–134.

1643. Schnebel, Dieter. *"Brouillards*—Tendencies in Debussy." *Reihe,* 6 (1964): 33–39.
Analytic discussion. Musical examples.

Promenoir des deux amants

1644. Youens, Susan. "Debussy's *Le Promenoir des deux amants* of 1911." *NATS Journal,* 43, no. 2 (1986): 22–25.
A commentary on the song cycle, with analytic observations on both the text and the music. Musical examples.

Quartet for Strings

1645. Ferguson, Donald N. *Image and Structure in Chamber Music,* 257–258. Minneapolis: University of Minnesota Press, 1964.
Brief analysis. Musical examples.

1646. Nichols, Roger. *Debussy,* 24–30. London: Oxford University Press, 1973.
Analytic and critical observations. Musical examples.

Sonata for Violoncello and Piano

1647. Moevs, Robert. "Intervallic Procedures in Debussy: *Serenade* from the Sonata for Cello and Piano, 1915." *Perspectives of New Music,* 8, no. 1 (1969): 82–101.

Syrinx

1648. Austin, William W. *Music in the Twentieth Century,* 7–14. New York: W.W. Norton and Co., 1966.
Analysis. Comparison with *Prelude to the Afternoon of a Faun.* Musical examples.

1649. Cogan, Robert, and Pozzi Escot. *Sonic Design: The Nature of Sound and Music,* 92–101. Englewood Cliffs, NJ: Prentice-Hall, 1976.
An analysis of "linguistic elements," such as cells, scale, interval content. Includes voice-leading diagrams and musical examples.

Trio Sonata for Flute, Viola, and Harp

1650. Wenk, Arthur. *Claude Debussy and Twentieth Century Music,* 82–85. Boston: Twayne, 1983.

A detailed study of Debussy's musical language, describing its revolutionary aspects and its implications for twentieth-century music as a whole. Discussion of tonal organization in this work. Musical examples.

DISSERTATIONS AND THESES

General

1651. Alfred, Everett Maurice. "A Study of Selected Choral Works of Claude Debussy." Ph.D., Texas Technical University, 1980, 415 pp., DA 41-4878A.

1652. Hsu, Samuel. "Imagery and Diction in the Songs of Claude Debussy." Ph.D., University of California at Santa Barbara, 1972, 218 pp., DA 33-2413A.

Etudes

1653. Peterson, William John. "Debussy's *Douze Etudes*." Ph.D., University of California at Berkeley, 1981, 271 pp., DA 42-2927A.

Images for Orchestra

1654. Bein, Joseph H. "Debussy's Orchestral *Images*: Harmonic Analysis and Other Features of the Style." Ph.D., University of Rochester, 1970, 240 pp., DA 30-3965A-6A.

La Mer

1655. Rolf, Marie. "Debussy's *La Mer*: A Critical Analysis in the Light of Early Sketches and Editions." Ph.D., University of Rochester, Eastman School of Music, 1976, 367 pp., DA 37-6833A-4A.

Preludes

1656. Ráfols, Alberto Pedro. "Debussy and the Symbolist Movement: The Preludes." D.M.A., University of Washington, 1975, 195 pp., DA 37-683A.

Première Rhapsodie for Clarinet

1657. Nygren, Dennis Quentin. "The Music for Accompanied Clarinet Solo of Claude Debussy: An Historical and Analytical Study of the *Première Rhapsodie* and *Petite Piece*." D.M., Northwestern University, 1982, 183 pp., DA 44-2922A.

Trois poèmes de Mallarmé

1658.   Andreacchi, Peter. "Part 1: An Examination of the Relation of Text to Music in Claude Debussy's *Trois poèmes de Mallarmé.*" Ph.D., City University of New York, 1986, 360 pp., DA 47-703A.

DEL TREDICI, DAVID, 1937–

I Hear an Army

1659.   Knussen, Oliver. "David Del Tredici and *Syzygy.*" *Tempo*, 118 (September 1976): 8–15.
Overview of stylistic features of this work.

Syzygy

1660.   Knussen, Oliver. "David Del Tredici and *Syzygy.*" *Tempo*, 118 (September 1976): 8–15.
The composition is based on the use of the palindrome, which is differentiated by dynamics, meter, and pitch level. Musical examples.

DELIUS, FREDERICK, 1862–1934

General

1661.   Beecham, Sir Thomas. *Frederick Delius.* New York: Alfred A. Knopf, 1960, 228 pp.
Mainly about Delius's life, but included here for those influences that affected his music. Not analytic.

1662.   Hutchings, Arthur. *Delius.* London: Macmillan, 1949, 193 pp.
Descriptive and critical commentary, with occasional analytic observations. Musical examples.

1663.   Jefferson, Alan. *Delius.* London: J. M. Dent and Sons, 1972, 179 pp.
Critical assessment and descriptive overview of Delius's output. Analytic observations on *Brigg Fair* on pp. 113–120. Musical examples.

1664.   Klein, John W. "Delius As a Musical Dramatist." *Music Review*, 22, no. 4 (1961): 294–301.
Mainly a discussion of Delius as a dramatist in his operas with comparisons to other composers.

1665. Palmer, Christopher. *Delius: Portrait of a Cosmopoliltan.* New York: Holmes and Meier, 1976, 199 pp.

Thorough critical review showing influences that helped shape Delius's style. Musical examples.

1666. Redwood, Christopher, ed. *A Delius Companion,* 217–238. London: John Calder, 1976.

Extensive critical and descriptive overview of the operas.

1667. Warlock, Peter. *Frederick Delius.* New York: Oxford University Press, 1952, 224 pp.

Written by a friend and admirer of Delius, the discussion is critical and descriptive, with remarks on tone color, harmony, and style. Musical examples.

American Rhapsody

1668. Jones, Philip. "Delius' *American* Rhapsody." *Musical Times,* 127 (December 1986): 677–679.

Studies the relationship between *American* Rhapsody for orchestra and *Appalachia* for orchestra and chorus. Includes analytic observations and musical examples.

Brigg Fair

1669. Barber, Nicola J. "*Brigg Fair*: A Melody, Its Use and Abuse." *Grainger Journal,* 6, no. 2 (1984): 3–20.

Full background on origins of *Brigg Fair* melody, its setting by Percy Grainger and, later, Delius. Structural plan of Delius's setting outlined. Musical examples.

Concertos

1670. Hill, Ralph, ed. *The Concerto,* 261–275. London: Penguin Books, 1952.

Critical and analytic commentary for the undergraduate student. Musical examples.

Concerto for Violin

1671. Cooke, Deryck. "Delius and Form: A Vindication." In *A Delius Companion.* Edited by Christopher Redwood, 253–262. London: John Calder, 1976.

An analysis of the thematic and rhythmic elements of the work, designed to demonstrate its formal coherence. Musical examples. The same article also appears in *The Musical Times*, 103 (June–July 1962): 460–465.

1672. Tovey, Donald Francis. *Essays in Musical Analysis.* Vol. 3, 203–205. London: Oxford University Press, 1936.
Brief critique and analysis with musical examples.

Fennimore and Gerda

1673. Redwood, Christopher. "Delius's Danish 'Pictures.' " *Opera*, 21 (May 1970): 403–404.
Not an analysis, but Delius's words about his new theories that form the basis of this opera.

Koanga

1674. Palmer, Christopher. "Delius's Negro Opera." *Opera*, 23 (May 1972): 403–407.
Comments on the Negro folk-element and the assimilation of the Negro dialect. Musical examples.

Margot la rouge

1675. Eccott, David. *"Margot la rouge*: Background and Libretto." *Delius Society Journal*, 69 (October 1980): 9–14.
Background on plot and brief synopsis.

1676. Eccott, David. *"Margot la rouge*: The Music." *Delius Society Journal*, 70 (January 1981): 8–17.
Examination of the thematic construction of the opera, with a concordance between the vocal score and the full score of the *Prelude and Idyll*. Musical examples.

Mass of Life

1677. Boyle, Andrew J. "A Mass of Life and Its 'Bell-Motif.' " *Music Review*, 43, no. 1 (1982): 44–50.
The bell-motif, in its various guises seen as a unifying device. Musical examples.

1678. Payne, Anthony. "Also sprach Delius." *Music and Musicians*, 13 (November 1964): 20–21.
Brief program note–style commentary.

Requiem

1679. Payne, Anthony. "Delius's *Requiem*." *Tempo*, 76 (Spring 1966): 12–17.
Description with analytical observations. Musical examples.

1680. Rippin, John. "Delius' *Requiem*." *Musical Opinion*, 89 (May 1966): 465–467.
Background and descriptive commentary.

1681. Robertson, Alec. *Requiem: Music of Mourning and Consolation*, 262–264. New York: Praeger, 1968.
Critical assessment. Not analytic. Musical examples.

Sonatas for Violin

1682. Beechey, Gwilyn. "Delius's Violin Sonatas." *Musical Opinion*, 107 (June 1984): 259–261.
Overview of the violin sonatas, with occasional analytic comments.

Song of the High Hills

1683. Boyle, Andrew J. *"The Song of the High Hills."* *Studia Musicologica Norvegica*, 8 (1982): 143–148.
General discussion of Delius's use of horn calls to evoke moods of mountain landscapes. Musical examples.

Village Romeo and Juliet

1684. Cooke, Deryck. "Delius' Operatic Masterpiece." *Opera*, 13 (April 1962): 226–232.
Describes genesis of the opera. Contains an account of the plot and a very general assessment of the music. Not analytic.

1685. Jefferson, Alan. *Delius*, 47–49. New York: Octagon Books, 1972.
Brief remarks on influences and characters in opera.

Zum Carnival

1686. Hinson, Maurice. "Frederick Delius: Individualist and Student of Nature." *Clavier*, 20, no. 7 (1981): 26–31.
Analysis with performance suggestions on this early piano piece. Score included.

DISSERTATIONS AND THESES

General

1687.   Caldwell, Donald Graham. "The Choral Music of Frederick Delius." D.M.A., University of Illinois at Urbana, 1975, 311 pp., DA 36-5622A.

1688.   Hutchings, Edward Gilmore. "The Published Songs of Frederick Delius." D.M.A., University of Miami, 1980, 109 pp., DA 41-4881A.

Songs

1689.   Allman, Anne Williams. "The Songs of Frederick Delius: An Interpretive and Stylistic Analysis and Performance of Representative Compositions." Ed.D., Columbia University Teachers College, 1983, 265 pp., DA 44-3314A.

DELLO JOIO, NORMAN, 1913–

General

1690.   Hinson, Maurice. "The Solo Piano Music of Norman Dello Joio." *American Music Teacher*, 19, no. 3 (1970): 34, 48.
   A brief descriptive summary of the published piano music by Dello Joio. Not really analytic, but a summary of style of each piece.

DISSERTATIONS AND THESES

General

1691.   Whang, Un-Yong. "An Analysis of Dello Joio's Chamber Music for Piano and Strings with Performance Suggestions." Ed.D., Columbia University Teachers College, 1986, 261 pp., DA 47-2072A.

DESPREZ (*SEE* JOSQUIN DESPREZ)

DIAMOND, DAVID, 1915–

DISSERTATIONS AND THESES

Songs

1692.   Friday, Raymond. "Analyses and Interpretations of Selected Songs of David Diamond." Ph.D., New York University, 1984, 200 pp., DA 45-2295A.

DITTERSDORF, KARL DITTERS VON, 1739–1799

Quartets for Strings

1693. Beechey, Gwilyn. "Dittersdorf's String Quartets." *Musical Opinion*, 104 (March 1981): 232 + .
Brief commentary on each movement of his G-Major and E-Flat-Major quartets.

DONIZETTI, GAETANO, 1797–1848

General

1694. Ashbrook, William. *Donizetti.* London: Cassell, 1965, 561 pp.
Part 1 of this volume deals with Donizetti's life; Part 2, the music. Form in the operas and style are treated in separate chapters. Musical examples.

1695. Dean, Winton. "Donizetti's Serious Operas." *Proceedings of the Royal Musical Association*, 100 (1973–1974): 123–141.
Full discussion of style and influence with comparisons to Verdi. Musical examples.

1696. Gossett, Philip. *"Anna Bolena" and the Artistic Maturity of Gaetano Donizetti.* London: Oxford University Press, 1985, 183 pp.
This is essentially a study of the composition of the opera, rather than a straightforward analysis. However, there is some analytic discussion, especially on the sections of the score that Donizetti revised. Many diagrams, musical examples. For the advanced student.

Don Pasquale

1697. Ashbrook, William. "Eleven-Day Wonder." *Opera News*, 35 (December 5, 1970): 24–25.
Discusses speed of composition, Donizetti's self-borrowings, with anecdotes on *Don Pasquale's* compositional history. Musical examples.

1698. Lelash, Marjorie. "Triumph of Incongruity." *Opera News*, 29 (January 9, 1965): 24–25.
Element of surprise in music is examined. Musical examples.

Emilia di Liverpool

1699. Commons, Jeremy. *"Emilia di Liverpool." Music and Letters,* 40 (July 1959): 207–228.
Full discussion of stage history, sources, libretto, and music.

Fille du Regiment

1700. Ashbrook, William. "Reenter Marie." *Opera News,* 36 (March 25, 1972): 24–25.
Refutes story that *La Fille* was intended for Naples and was a pastiche of previously written music. Historical evidence and analytic observations support thesis that this opera is original and composed for the French audience of the Opéra Comique. Musical examples.

Lucia di Lammermoor

1701. Dahlhaus, Carl. *Nineteenth-Century Music.* Translated by J. Bradford Robinson, 122–124. Berkeley: University of California Press, 1989.
Form and overall design of the concluding arias, Lucia's mad scene, and the death of Edgardo examined. Advanced.

1702. McDonald, Katherine. "Fatal Meeting." *Opera News,* 30 (February 16, 1966): 24–25.
Critical commentary, with observations on musical characterization. Musical examples.

DOWLAND, JOHN, 1562–1626

General

1703. Poulton, Diana. *John Dowland.* 2d ed. Berkeley: University of California Press, 1982, 528 pp.
Thorough treatment of the solo lute music and songbooks. Also brief chapters on psalms, spiritual songs, and consort music. The discussions of the music include descriptions of the manuscript sources, early printed sources, and analytic commentaries on the music. Musical examples.

1704. Spink, Ian. *English Songs: Dowland to Purcell.* London: B. T. Batsford, 1974, 312 pp.

An analytic discussion of the songs. Places the composer in historical context, identifies influences on him and his influence on others; identifies stylistic traits, discusses musical techniques, and relationships between text and music. Includes a critical assessment. Musical examples.

1705.   Warburton, A. O. "Set Works for 'O' Level, GCE." *Music Teacher,* 48 (May 1969): 16.
Brief descriptive commentary with analytic observations on "Burst forth, my tears," "Come again," "Sweet love. . . ," "Come, heavy sleep."

DUFAY, GUILLAUME, c. 1400–1474

General

1706.   Fallows, David. *Dufay.* London: J. M. Dent and Sons, 1982, 321 pp.
Thorough analytic discussion of Dufay's output and place in music history. Musical examples.

1707.   Reese, Gustave. *Music in the Renaissance.* Rev. ed., 48–86. New York: W. W. Norton, 1959.
Detailed descriptive overview with musical examples.

1708.   Van den Borren, Charles. "Dufay and His School." In *The New Oxford History of Music.* Vol. 3, *Ars Nova and the Renaissance, 1300–1540.* Edited by Dom Anselm Hughes and Gerald Abraham, 214–231. London: Oxford University Press, 1960.
Thorough overview of Dufay's place and style. The motets, masses, songs, and dance forms discussed. Musical examples.

Serviteur hault guerdonne

1709.   Kottick, Edward L. "Flats, Modality, and Musica Ficta in Some Early Renaissance Chansons." *Journal of Music Theory,* 12, no. 2 (1968): 271–273.

DISSERTATIONS AND THESES

Chansons

1710.   Bashour, Frederick Joseph. "A Model for the Analysis of Structural Levels and Tonal Movement in Compositions of the Fifteenth Century." Ph.D., Yale University, 1975, 295 pp., DA 36-2473A.

DUKAS, PAUL, 1865–1935

General

1711. Cortot, Alfred. *French Piano Music.* Translated by Hilda Andrews, 178–208. London: Oxford University Press, 1932.
Descriptive overview with observations on Dukas's style.

DUNSTABLE, JOHN, c. 1380–1453

General

1712. Bent, Margaret. *Dunstaple.* London: Oxford University Press, 1981, 92 pp.
Analytic overview of Dunstable's output, focusing on style, settings of liturgical texts, the isorhythmic motets, and compositions for the *Mass Ordinary.* Musical examples.

1713. Trowell, Brian. "Proportion in the Music of Dunstable." *Journal of the Royal Musical Association,* 105 (1978–1979): 100–141.
A study of the structural principles underlying the music, focusing on proportional analyses of isorhythmic and nonisorhythmic works. Musical examples.

DUSSEK, JAN, 1760–1812

Sonatas for Piano

1714. Schwarting, Heino. "The Piano Sonatas of Johann Ladislaus Dussek." *Piano Quarterly,* 23, no. 91 (1975): 41–45.
Brief overview of stylistic traits. Musical examples.

DISSERTATIONS AND THESES

Concertos for Piano

1715. Richter, Leonard. "An Analytic Study of Selected Piano Concertos of Jan Ladislav Dussek." Ph.D., New York University, 1985, 179 pp., DA 46-642A.

Sonatas for Piano

1716. Grossman, Orin Louis. "The Piano Sonatas of Jan Ludislaw Dussek (1760–1812)." Ph.D., Yale University, 1975, 258 pp., DA 36-2479.

233

1717. Sandlin, Julkian Dan. "Romantic Elements in the Piano Sonatas of Jan Ladislav Dussek (1760–1812)." D.M.A., University of Miami, 1974, 53 pp., DA 35-3798A.

DVOŘÁK, ANTONÍN, 1841–1904

General

1718. Abraham, Gerald. *Slavonic and Romantic Music*, 52–63. New York: St. Martin's Press, 1968.
    Analytic discussion of Dvořák's musical style. Musical examples.

1719. Clapham, John. *Antonín Dvořák: Musician and Craftsman.* New York: St. Martin's Press, 1966, 341 pp.
    Analytic study of all Dvořák's output. Musical examples.

1720. Clapham, John. "The Operas of Antonín Dvořák." *Proceedings of the Royal Musical Association*, 84 (1957–1958): 55–69.
    A survey of the operas. Describes the genesis of the operas and includes remarks on style and characterization.

1721. Colles, Henry C. "The Operas." In *Antonín Dvořák: His Achievement.* Edited by Viktor Fischl, 134–165. Westport, CT: Greenwood Press, 1970.
    Summarizes Dvořák's operatic achievement. Critical commentary, with remarks on harmony and form. Musical examples.

1722. Dale, Kathleen. *Nineteenth-Century Piano Music: A Handbook for Pianists.* London: Oxford University Press, 1954, 320 pp.
    Highlights stylistic traits. Form, harmony, and other musical aspects discussed in relation to style.

1723. Ferguson, Donald N. *Image and Structure in Chamber Music*, 227–238. Minneapolis: University of Minnesota Press, 1964.
    Overview of the chamber music, with brief analyses. Musical examples.

1724. Fischl, Viktor, ed. *Antonín Dvořák: His Achievement.* 1933. Reprint. Westport: Greenwood Press, 1970, 297 pp.
    Critical discussion of specific works, with remarks on harmony and form. Musical examples.

1725. Hughes, Gervase. *Dvořák: His Life and Music.* New York: Dodd, Mead, 1967, 247 pp.
    A chronological account of Dvořák's life and works. Contains only general analytic remarks on pieces.

1726.   Plantinga, Leon. *Romantic Music*, 351–358. New York: W. W. Norton, 1984.
Brief analytic comments. Musical examples.

1727.   Robertson, Alec. *Dvořák*. Rev. ed. London: J. M. Dent and Sons, 1964, 234 pp.
Mainly descriptive commentary, with analytic observations on style, themes, and motives and a critical assessment. Musical examples.

Concertos

1728.   Layton, Robert. *Dvořák Symphonies and Concertos*. Seattle: University of Washington Press, 1978, 68 pp.
Brief critical, descriptive, and analytic overview for the undergraduate student. Musical examples.

1729.   Veinus, Abraham. *The Concerto*. Rev. ed., 237–241. New York: Dover Publications, 1964.
General remarks of a historical and critical nature. Not analytic.

Concerto for Violoncello, Op. 104 in B Minor

1730.   Clapham, John. "Dvořák's Cello Concerto in B Minor: A Masterpiece in the Making." *Music Review*, 40, no. 2 (1979): 123 + .
Discussed in terms of form, structure, harmony, rhythm, and other musical characteristics, this examination of Dvořák's sketches offers many analytic insights, while reconstructing the composer's creative process. Musical examples.

1731.   Hopkins, Antony. *Talking About Concertos*, 112–122. London: Heinemann, 1964.
Extended analytic essay describing tonal, thematic, and formal events.

1732.   Nelson, Wendell. *The Concerto*, 80–84. Dubuque, IA: William C. Brown, 1969.
Analysis with critical commentary. Musical examples.

1733.   Tischler, Hans. *The Perceptive Music Listener*, 331–334. Englewood Cliffs, NJ: Prentice-Hall, 1955.
Analysis with musical examples.

1734.   Tovey, Donald Francis. *Essays in Musical Analysis*. Vol. 3, 148–152. London: Oxford University Press, 1936.
Analysis with critical commentary and musical examples.

Jakobin

1735. Brewer, Michael. "The *Jakobin.*" *Music Teacher,* 59 (June 1980): 15–16.
A review of a performance, but included here for its brief but analytic comments.

Mass in D Major

1736. Hilse, Walter. "Reviews of Records." *Musical Quarterly,* 62, no. 1 (1976): 149–152.
A record review, but included here for its descriptive commentary highlighting tonal plan, themes, motives, and harmony.

Quartet for Strings, Op. 96 in F Major ("American")

1737. Beveridge, David. "Sophisticated Primitivism: The Significance of Pentatonicism in Dvořák's *American* Quartet." *Current Musicology,* 24 (1977): 25–36.

Requiem

1738. Robertson, Alec. *Requiem: Music of Mourning and Consolation,* 110–116. New York: Praeger, 1968.
Critical evaluation, with musical examples.

Serenade in D Minor, Op. 44

1739. Warburton, A. O. "Set Works for 'O' Level, GCE." *Music Teacher,* 51 (September 1972): 16–18.
Background and analysis.

Sonatina for Violin and Piano, Op. 100 in G Major

1740. Warburton, A. O. "Set Works for 'O' Level, GCE." *Music Teacher and Piano Student,* 46 (February 1967): 31 + .
Brief analytic overview for the undergraduate student.

Symphonies

1741. Layton, Robert. *Dvořák Symphonies and Concertos.* Seattle: University of Washington Press, 1978, 68 pp.
Brief critical, descriptive, and analytic overview for the undergraduate student. Musical examples.

1742. Simpson, Robert, ed. *The Symphony.* Vol. 1, 374–378. New York: Drake Publishers, 1972.
Thorough critical and analytic overview for the undergraduate student. Musical examples.

Symphony No. 7, Op. 70 in D Minor

1743. Clapham, John. "Dvořák's Symphony in D Minor—The Creative Process." *Music and Letters,* 42, no. 2 (1961): 103–116.
Detailed comparison of sketches leading to final version. Historic commentary and analytic remarks. Musical examples.

1744. Stedman, Preston. *The Symphony,* 197–204. Englewood Cliffs, NJ: Prentice-Hall, 1979.
Extended description and analysis dealing with formal plan, structure, motives, tonality, and style. Musical examples and diagram.

Symphony No. 9, Op. 95 in E Minor ("New World")

1745. Bernstein, Leonard. *The Infinite Variety of Music,* 149–169. New York: Simon and Schuster, 1966.
Analysis, similar to Bernstein's television talks, on influences, "Americanisms," and stylistic traits. Musical examples.

1746. Clapham, John. "The Evolution of Dvořák's Symphony *From the New World.*" *Musical Quarterly,* 44, no. 2 (1958): 167–183.
Describes the *New World* Symphony as it emerged in Dvořák's mind. Compares sketches with completed score, discusses choice of instruments and use of folk elements. Musical examples.

1747. Cuyler, Louise. *The Symphony,* 159–161. New York: Harcourt Brace Jovanovich, 1973.
Concentrated analysis of the entire symphony.

1748. Fischl, Viktor, ed. *Antonín Dvořák: His Achievement.* 1933. Reprint, 84–89. Westport, CT: Greenwood Press, 1970.
Descriptive commentary, mentioning some of the folk tunes used.

1749. Machlis, Joseph. *The Enjoyment of Music.* 3d ed., 144–150. New York: W. W. Norton, 1970.
Analysis with musical examples.

1750. Stedman, Preston. *The Symphony,* 195–197. Englewood Cliffs, NJ: Prentice-Hall, 1979.
Brief description of form, thematic activity, style, and texture.

1751. Tovey, Donald Francis. *Essays in Musical Analysis.* Vol. 2, 106–110. London: Oxford University Press, 1935.
Analysis of the entire symphony. Musical examples.

ELGAR, EDWARD, 1857–1934

General

1752. Kennedy, Michael. *Elgar Orchestral Music.* London: British Broadcasting Corporation, 1970, 30 pp.
Critical/analytic overview of Elgar's output. For the undergraduate student. Musical examples.

1753. Kennedy, Michael. *Portrait of Elgar.* London: Oxford University Press, 1968, 324 pp.
Background and descriptive commentary. Some analytic observations. Musical examples.

1754. Moore, Jerrold N. *Edward Elgar: A Creative Life.* London: Oxford University Press, 1984, 841 pp.
Thorough descriptive and analytic review of Elgar's output viewed in the context of his creative development. Musical examples.

1755. Parrott, Ian. *Elgar.* London: J. M. Dent and Sons, 1971, 143 pp.
Analytic comments on all his major works, though brief. Musical examples.

1756. Young, Percy M. *Elgar, O. M.: A Study of a Musician.* London: Collins, 1955, 447 pp.
Descriptive and critical commentary, with occasional analytic observations. Musical examples.

Cockaigne Overture

1757. Tovey, Donald Francis. *Essays in Musical Analysis.* Vol. 4, 152–154. London: Oxford University Press, 1969.
Critical and analytic study, with musical examples. For the undergraduate student.

Concertos

1758. Hill, Ralph, ed. *The Concerto,* 252–260. London: Penguin Books, 1952.
Critical and analytic commentary for the undergraduate student. Musical examples.

Concerto for Violin, Op. 61 in B Minor

1759.   Tovey, Donald Francis. *Essays in Musical Analysis.* Vol. 3, 152–158. London: Oxford University Press, 1936.
Substantial commentary, with analytic remarks. Musical examples.

Concerto for Violoncello, Op. 85 in E Minor

1760.   Elkin, Robert. "Elgar's Cello Concerto: An Analysis." *Music in Education,* 27, no. 304 (1963): 185–187.
Not an analysis, as stated, but useful for its description of the main themes. Musical examples.

1761.   Tovey, Donald Francis. *Essays in Musical Analysis.* Vol. 3, 200–203. London: Oxford University Press, 1936.
Descriptive, critical, and analytic remarks. Musical examples.

Dream of Gerontius

1762.   Fenton, John. "Elgar's Use of the 'Leitmotiv' in the *Dream of Gerontius.*" *Music Teacher,* 54 (January 1975): 11–12; (February 1975): 12–13.

1763.   Robertson, Alex. *Requiem: Music of Mourning and Consolation,* 239–251. New York: Praeger, 1968.
Background and descriptive commentary. Musical examples.

1764.   Young, Percy M. *The Choral Tradition.* Rev. ed., 256–260. New York: W. W. Norton, 1981.
Brief analytic comments.

Enigma Variations

1765.   Burley, Rosa, and Frank C. Carruthers. *Edward Elgar: The Record of a Friendship,* 116–129. London: Barrie and Jenkins, 1972.
The circumstances of the composition of the Variations, with commentary on each variation and the people represented.

1766.   Fiske, Roger. "The *Enigma:* A Solution." *Musical Times,* 110 (November 1969): 1124–1126.
"Proof" that the theme that is never heard is *Auld Lang Syne.* Musical examples.

1767.   Hogan, Eugene E. "A Musical Detective Story—After Seventy-five Years: The Solution of Elgar's *Enigma.*" *Musical Opinion,* 99 (November 1975): 75–77.

Elgar's own words examined for clues to his *Enigma.*

1768.   Kennedy, Michael. *Portrait of Elgar,* 55–75. London: Oxford University Press, 1968.

Thorough discussion tracing the "friends" depicted in the Variations. Some remarks on the music.

1769.   Moore, Jerrold N. "An Approach to Elgar's *Enigma.*" *Music Review,* 20 (February 1959): 38–44.

A discussion of the musical structure as well as the aesthetic of the music. Analytic remarks and discussion of clues to the *Enigma.* Musical examples.

1770.   Parrott, Ian. "Elgar's Two-Fold *Enigma:* A Religious Sequel." *Music and Letters,* 54, no. 1 (1973): 57–60.

Speculation that Bach is the key to the mystery of the theme that "goes" but is not played in these variations. Specifically, sixteen notes of the Bach unfinished pedal *Exercitium* form the basis of the mystery theme. Musical examples.

1771.   Poole, Geoffrey. "Questioning the *Enigma.*" *Music and Musicians,* 19 (August 1971): 26–29.

Theory advanced that the *Enigma* is based on an alphabet code that yields the names of Elgar's wife and daughter.

1772.   Portnoy, Marshall A. "The Answer to Elgar's *Enigma.*" *Musical Quarterly,* 71, no. 2 (1985): 205–210.

Focuses on *Enigma* main motive and its origins. Suggests Bach as Elgar's inspiration, and cites examples to prove his point. Musical examples.

1773.   Sams, Eric. "Variations on an Original Theme (*Enigma*)." *Musical Times,* 111 (March 1970): 258–262.

More controversy over the key to Elgar's *Enigma.* Possible clues to mysterious overall theme. Musical examples.

1774.   Skouenborg, Ulrik. "Elgar *Enigma*: The Solution." *Music Review,* 43, nos. 3–4 (1982): 161+.

Speculation that Brahms's *Vier ernste Gesänge* are the larger theme that "goes" through and over the whole set but is not played. Musical examples.

1775. Tovey, Donald Francis. *Essays in Musical Analysis.* Vol. 4, 149–152. London: Oxford University Press, 1969.
Critical and analytic study with musical examples. For the under-graduate student.

1776. Van Houten, Theodore. " 'You of All People': Elgar's *Enigma.*" *Music Review,* 37, no. 2 (1976): 130–142.
Speculation that *Rule, Britannia* is the key to Elgar's puzzle. Musical examples.

Falstaff

1777. Tovey, Donald Francis. *Essays in Musical Analysis.* Vol. 4, 3–16. London: Oxford University Press, 1969.
Thorough critical and analytic study with musical examples.

Introduction and Allegro for Strings

1778. Tovey, Donald Francis. *Essays in Musical Analysis.* Vol. 6, 87–89. London: Oxford University Press, 1969.
Critical and analytic discussion with musical examples. For the undergraduate student.

Symphonies

1779. Simpson, Robert, ed. *The Symphony.* Vol. 2, 15–28. New York: Drake Publishers, 1972.
Descriptive commentary focusing on style, orchestration, form, and tonality. Musical examples.

FALLA, MANUEL DE, 1876–1946

General

1780. Crichton, Ronald. *Falla.* Seattle: University of Washington Press, 1983, 104 pp.
A "BBC Music Guide." A short "life and works" treatment, with music emphasized in the discussion. Many musical examples, with analytical observations on the major works.

1781. Demarquez, Suzanne. *Manuel de Falla.* Translated by Salvator Attanasio. Philadelphia: Chilton Book Co., 1968, 253 pp.
Background, critical, and analytic remarks on Falla's output. Musical examples.

1782. Todd, Dennis. "Falla Reconsidered—Some Centenary Thoughts." *Music Teacher*, 55 (October 1976): 11–12.
A brief assessment of Falla's achievement, with some analytical comments concerning style.

Concerto for Harpsichord

1783. Demarquez, Suzanne. *Manuel de Falla*. Translated by Salvator Attanasio, 157–169. Philadelphia: Chilton Book Co., 1968.
Thorough analysis. Musical examples.

Fantasia Bética

1784. Demarquez, Suzanne. *Manuel de Falla*. Translated by Salvator Attanasio, 109–118. Philadelphia: Chilton Book Co., 1968.
Background and analysis.

Spanish Dances

1785. Esteban, Julio. "De Falla's *Andaluza:*" A Master Lesson." *Clavier*, 15, no. 7 (1976): 19–27.
Analytic and interpretive comments. Score included.

FAURÉ, GABRIEL, 1845–1924

General

1786. Beechey, Gwilyn. "Gabriel Fauré—His Piano Music and Songs." *Musical Opinion*, 98 (November 1974): 61–63 +.
L'Absent (No. 11 of *Twenty Melodies*) and Nocturne Op. 33 analyzed. Other works in both genres analyzed briefly in this overview. Musical examples.

1787. Bowman, Robin. "Eight Late Songs of Fauré: An Approach to Analysis." *Musical Analysis*, 1, no. 1 (1972): 3–5.
Statistical analysis of interval size and direction in the voice parts. *Mirages* Op. 113 (1919) and *L'Horizon Chimérique* Op. 118 (1922) discussed. Tables.

1788. Cortot, Alfred. *French Piano Music*. Translated by Hilda Andrews, 109–139. London: Oxford University Press, 1932.
Descriptive overview, with observations on Fauré's style.

1789. Ferguson, Donald N. *Image and Structure in Chamber Music,* 250–257. Minneapolis: University of Minnesota Press, 1964.
Overview of the chamber music, with brief analyses. Musical examples.

1790. Matthews, Denis, ed. *Keyboard Music,* 265–268. New York: Praeger, 1972.
Stylistic traits, influences, and mention of specific pieces. Musical examples.

1791. Orledge, Robert. *Gabriel Fauré.* New York: Da Capo Press, 1982, 367 pp.
Thorough overview of Fauré's output. Descriptive and analytic remarks. Musical examples.

1792. Suckling, Norma. *Fauré.* London: J. M. Dent and Sons, 1946, 229 pp.
Handy "Master Musician" guide for the undergraduate student. Critical and analytic, with musical examples.

1793. Vuillermoz, Emile. *Gabriel Fauré.* Translated by Kenneth Schapiro. Philadelphia: Chilton Book Co., 1969, 265 pp.
Descriptive and critical commentary.

Chanson, Op. 94 in E Minor (1907)

1794. Austin, William W. *Music in the Twentieth Century,* 150–153. New York: W. W. Norton, 1966.
Brief analysis. Musical examples.

Improvisations for Piano, Op. 84, No. 5

1795. Dumm, Robert. "A Fauré Improvisation." *Clavier,* 15, no. 4 (1976): 20–23.
Performer's analysis. Score included.

Requiem

1796. Boyd, Malcolm. "Fauré's Requiem: A Reappraisal." *Musical Times,* 104 (June 1963): 408–409.
Brief critical and analytic remarks. Musical examples.

1797. Primmer, Brian. "Fauré's Requiem." *Music Teacher,* 57 (January 1978): 15–18.
An introductory analytical essay. Includes a discussion of instrumentation, style, and harmony. Not a complete analysis.

1798. Robertson, Alec. *Requiem: Music of Mourning and Consolation*, 117–122. New York: Praeger, 1968.
    Critical discussion of the music. Musical examples.

Sonatas for Violin and Piano

1799. Beechey, Gwilyn. "The Violin Sonatas of Gabriel Fauré." *Strad*, 86 (December 1975): 559 + .
    Mainly descriptive, with remarks on style. Not analytic. Musical examples.

Sonata for Violin and Piano, Op. 13 in A Major

1800. Rorick, William C. "The A Major Sonatas of Fauré and Franck: A Stylistic Comparison." *Music Review*, 42, no. 1 (1981): 46–55.
    Analytic observations, focusing on stylistic traits of both composers. Musical examples.

Sonatas for Violoncello

1801. Beechey, Gwilyn. "The Cello Sonatas of Gabriel Fauré." *Strad*, 8 (June 1977): 151 + .
    Brief look at thematic ideas found in the sonatas.

DISSERTATIONS AND THESES

General

1802. Bland, Stephen F. "Form in the Songs of Gabriel Fauré." Ph.D., Florida State University, 1976, 108 pp., DA 37-3251A–2A.

1803. Rinsinger, Dan Howard. "The Seven Song Collection of Gabriel Fauré." D.M.A., University of Illinois at Urbana, 1971, 211 pp., DA 32-5827A.

1804. Sommers, Paul Bartholin. "Fauré and His Songs: The Relationship of Text, Melody, and Accompaniment." D.M.A., University of Illinois, 1969, 175 pp., DA 31-791A.

1805. Wegren, Thomas Joseph. "The Solo Piano Music of Gabriel Fauré." Ph.D., Ohio State University, 1973, 301 pp., DA 34-7272A.

Nocturnes

1806. Valicenti, Joseph Anthony. "The Thirteen Nocturnes of Gabriel Fauré." D.M.A., University of Miami, 1980, 108 pp., DA 41-1833A.

FELDMAN, MORTON, 1926–1987

Durations 3, III

1807. De Lio, Thomas. "Toward an Art of Imminence: Morton Feldman's *Durations* 3, III." *Interface*, 12, no. 3 (1983): 465–480.
An analytic examination of four "gestures" that occur throughout this work. Musical examples.

FERRABOSCO, ALFONSO, THE YOUNGER, 1575–1628

General

1808. Duffy, John. *The Songs and Motets of Alfonso Ferrabosco, the Younger (1575–1628).* Ann Arbor: UMI Research Press, 1980, 479 pp.
An extensive study that was originally a doctoral dissertation. Brief biographical introduction, with full commentary on text setting. For the advanced student. Musical examples.

FIELD, JOHN, 1782–1837

General

1809. Branson, David. *John Field and Chopin.* New York: St. Martin's Press, 1972, 216 pp.
An analytical commentary on the works of John Field, focusing on the relationship between his music and that of Chopin. Major chapter on the Nocturnes and the Piano Concertos. Musical examples.

1810. Dale, Kathleen. *Nineteenth-Century Piano Music: A Handbook for Pianists.* London: Oxford University Press, 1954, 320 pp.
Highlights stylistic traits and unique contribution to the literature of the piano. Form, harmony, and other musical aspects discussed in relation to style.

1811. Piggot, Patrick. *The Life and Music of John Field: 1782–1837.* Berkeley: University of California Press, 1973, 287 pp.

Thorough critical and analytic treatment, with background information. Shows Field's influence on other composers, notably Chopin. Musical examples.

FINNEY, ROSS LEE, 1906–

General

1812.   Onderdonk, Henry. "Aspects of Tonality in the Music of Ross Lee Finney." In *Perspectives on American Composers*. Edited by Benjamin Boretz and E. T. Cone, 248–268. New York: W. W. Norton, 1971.
The Sixth String Quartet, Six Spherical Madrigals, Variations for Orchestra, and the Second and Third Symphonies discussed.

FOSS, LUKAS, 1922–

A Parable of Death

1813.   McCray, James. "*A Parable of Death:* Comments on Structure and Performance." *American Choral Review*, 18, no. 3 (1976): 12–13.

DISSERTATIONS AND THESES

General

1814.   Browne, Bruce Sparrow. "The Choral Music of Lukas Foss." D.M.A., University of Washington, 1976, 184 pp., DA 37-1287A.

FRANCK, CÉSAR, 1822–1890

General

1815.   Cortot, Alfred. *French Piano Music.* Translated by Hilda Andrews, 37–107. London: Oxford University Press, 1932.
Descriptive overview, with observations on Franck's style.

1816.   Davies, Laurence. *Franck.* London: J. M. Dent and Sons, 1973, 141 pp.
Brief overview of Franck's output, with critical and analytic remarks. Musical examples.

1817. Demuth, Norman. *César Franck.* London: Dennis Dobson, 1949, 228 pp.
Background, descriptive, critical, and analytic commentary. Musical examples.

1818. Dufourcq, Norbert. "The Milieu, Work, and Art of César Franck." *Diapason*, 63 (May 1972): 4–5.
Descriptive commentary on salient details of each of the following chorales: No. 1 in E Major; No. 2 in B Minor; No. 3 in A Minor.

1819. Ferguson, Donald N. *Image and Structure in Chamber Music*, 242–249. Minneapolis: University of Minnesota Press, 1964.
Overview of the chamber music, with brief analyses. Musical examples.

1820. Horton, John. *César Franck.* London: Oxford University Press, 1946, 66 pp.
Descriptive, critical, and analytic commentary. Musical examples.

1821. Nordgren, Quentin R. "A Study in Chromatic Harmony." *American Music Teacher*, 15, no. 4 (1966): 20–21.
Advanced discussion of Franck's harmonic idiom in the organ music. Musical examples.

1822. Peeters, Flor. "César Franck's Organ Music." *Musical Times*, 113 (April 1972): 395 + ; (May 1972): 499–500.
Discussion of registration used on Franck's organ, with mention of many of the organ works.

1823. Peeters, Flor. "The Organ Works of César Franck." *Music (AGO)*, 5 (August 1971): 22–27 + ; (September 1971): 40–42.
Overview, with descriptive and analytic comments on specific works. Musical examples.

1824. Vallas, Léon. *César Franck.* Translated by Hubert Foss. London: Oxford University Press, 1951, 283 pp.
Background, descriptive, and critical summary of Franck's output.

Sonata for Violin and Piano in A Major

1825. Rorick, William C. "The A Major Violin Sonatas of Fauré and Franck: A Stylistic Comparison." *Music Review*, 42, no. 1 (1981): 46–55.
Analytic observations focusing on stylistic traits of both composers. Musical examples.

Symphony in D Minor

1826.   Benjamin, William E. "Interlocking Diatonic Collections as a Source of Chromaticism in Late Nineteenth Century Music." *In Theory Only*, 1 (February–March 1976): 35–39+.

1827.   Cuyler, Louise. *The Symphony*, 148–150. New York: Harcourt Brace Jovanovich, 1973.
  Brief but compact analysis.

1828.   Dahlhaus, Carl. *Nineteenth-Century Music.* Translated by J. Bradford Robinson, 274–276. Berkeley: University of California Press, 1989.
  Brief but concentrated analytic remarks on the unifying principles of this work. Advanced.

1829.   Davies, Laurence. *César Franck and His Circle*, 237–240. London: Barrie and Jenkins, 1970.
  Criticism and analysis, with musical examples.

1830.   Davies, Laurence. *Franck*, 102–104. London: J. M. Dent and Sons, 1973.
  Brief analysis, with musical examples.

1831.   Demuth, Norman. *César Franck*, 80–87. London: Dennis Dobson, 1949.
  Analytic and critical commentary, with musical examples.

1832.   Haggin, B. H. *A Book of the Symphony*, 311–319. London: Oxford University Press, 1937.
  Straightforward description dealing with formal plan only. Brief background remarks, with no discussion of tonality, rhythm, or texture. For the musical amateur or undergraduate student concerned with form. Musical examples.

1833.   Martin, Henry J. "Comment: The Linear Analysis of Chromaticism." *In Theory Only*, 2 (April–May 1976): 47–50.
  Advanced analytic discussion in reply to the W. E. Benjamin work cited here (*see* item no. 1826). Musical examples.

1834.   Stedman, Preston. *The Symphony*, 206–212. New Jersey: Prentice-Hall, 1979.
  Description and analytic breakdown of formal structure. Discussion on orchestral technique. Musical examples and diagram.

1835.   Tovey, Donald Francis. *Essays in Musical Analysis.* Vol. 2, 62–69. London: Oxford University Press, 1935.
Thorough analysis, with musical examples.

1836.   Vallas, Léon. *César Franck.* Translated by Hubert Foss, 209–216. London: Oxford University Press, 1951.
Mainly background and evaluative commentary.

DISSERTATIONS AND THESES

1837.   Wilkins, Judith Ann. "Harmony and Tonality in Franck's Symphony in D Minor." M.Mus., University of Arizona, 1985, 194 pp., DA 23-421A.

FRESCOBALDI, GIROLAMO, 1583–1643

General

1838.   Hammond, Frederick. *Girolamo Frescobaldi: His Life and Music.* Cambridge, MA: Harvard University Press, 1983, 408 pp.
The most detailed book on Frescobaldi to date. Analytic discussion of style, tonality (modes), structure, texture, rhythm, and other unifying factors. Performance practice also covered. Musical examples.

DISSERTATIONS AND THESES

Fiore Musicali (1635)

1839.   Owens, Samuel Battie. "The Organ Mass and Girolamo Frescobaldi's *Fiore Musicali* of 1635." D.M.A., George Peabody College for Teachers, 1974, 295 pp., DA 35-4597A–8A.

FROBERGER, JOHANN, 1616–1667

DISSERTATIONS AND THESES

Toccatas

1840.   Kosnik, James Walter. "The Toccatas of Johann Jakob Froberger: A Study of Style and Aspects of Organ Performance." D.M.A., University of Rochester, Eastman School of Music, 1979, 168 pp., DA 40-1143A.

1841.   Kolbuck, Edith Henry. "An Analytical Study of Selected Toccatas of Johann Jakob Froberger: Some Possible Insights into Problems of Performance Practice." D.M.A., University of Oregon, 1976, 144 pp., DA 37-7394A–5A.

GABRIELI, GIOVANNI, c. 1544–1612

General

1842.   Arnold, Denis. *Giovanni Gabrieli.* London: Oxford University Press, 1974, 70 pp.
   An overview for the undergraduate student. Descriptive, critical, and analytic commentary on a selection of Gabrieli's total output focusing on influences, style, and texture. Musical examples.

1843.   Arnold, Denis. *Giovanni Gabrieli and the Music of the Venetian High Renaissance.* London: Oxford University Press, 1979, 322 pp.
   Solid overview of Gabrieli's output, with discussion of background, influences, and pupils. Mainly a descriptive survey of the music, with analytic observations placed in historical perspective. Musical examples.

1844.   Bradshaw, Murray C. "Tonal Design in the Ventian Intonation and Toccata." *Music Review*, 35, no. 2 (1974): 101–108+.

1845.   Kenton, Egon. *Life and Works of Giovanni Gabrieli.* N.P.: American Institute of Musicology, 1967, 557 pp.
   Survey focusing on style and analysis of Gabrieli's output. Musical examples.

GEMINIANI, FRANCESCO, 1687–1762

Concertos

1846.   Veinus, Abraham. *The Concerto.* Rev. ed., 18–19. New York: Dover Publications, 1964.
   Brief descriptive and critical remarks on the music, with a comparison to Corelli.

GERHARD, ROBERTO, 1896–1970

General

1847.   Donat, Misha. "Thoughts on the Late Works." *Tempo*, 139 (December 1981): 39–43.
   General overview, with occasional descriptive and analytic comments. Musical examples.

L'Alta Naixenca del Rei en Jaume

1848. Drew, David. "Gerhard's Cantata: A Note on the Music."
Tempo, 139 (December 1981): 17–18.
Brief analytic overview.

Plague

1849. Payne, Anthony. "First Performance: Roberto Gerhard's *The
Plague*." *Tempo*, 69 (Summer 1964): 26–28.
A brief introduction to the serial procedure used in the composi-
tion.

Quintet for Wind Instruments

1850. Nash, P. P. "The Wind Quintet." *Tempo*, 139 (December 1981):
5–11.
Analysis focusing mainly on the tone row and influences upon this
work, principally by the composer's teacher, Schoenberg. Musical
examples.

Symphony No. 1

1851. Ballantine, Christopher. *Twentieth Century Symphony*, 202–
206. London: Dennis Dobson, 1984.
Brief analytic comments.

1852. Whittall, Arnold. *Music Since the First World War*, 185–188.
London: J. M. Dent and Sons, 1977.
Brief analytic discussion. Musical examples.

Symphony No. 2 ("Metamorphoses")

1853. Bradshaw, Susan. "Symphony No. 2/*Metamorphoses*; The
Compositional Background." *Tempo*, 139 (December 1981): 28–32.
A discussion of Gerhard's row and how it affects both the rhythmic properties and the harmonic curve of the work. Musical examples.

GERSHWIN, GEORGE, 1898–1937

General

1854. Ewen, David. *A Journey to Greatness*. Englewood Cliffs, NJ:
Prentice-Hall, 1970, 354 pp.

Descriptive commentary for the lay reader and undergraduate student. Background and program to *American in Paris*, descriptive commentary on Concerto in F, *Porgy and Bess*, *Rhapsody in Blue*, and other works.

1855.   Gilbert, Stephen E. "Gershwin's Art of Counterpoint." *Musical Quarterly*, 70, no. 4 (1984): 423–456.

Extended analytic discussion of Concerto in F, *American in Paris*, and Variations on *I Got Rhythm* to demonstrate Gershwin's contrapuntal style and skill. Musical examples.

1856.   Goldberg, Isaac. *George Gershwin: A Study in American Music.* New York: Frederick Ungar, 1958, 387 pp.

Background and descriptive commentary on Gershwin's output for the lay reader and undergraduate student. Musical examples.

1857.   Goodfriend, James. "Is Gershwin Classical or Popular?" *Stereo Review*, 31 (September 1973): 79–80.

Some opinions on a continuing controversy. Not analytic.

1858.   Schwartz, Charles M. *Gershwin: His Life and Music.* Indianapolis: Bobbs-Merrill, 1973, 428 pp.

Background, compositional history, and analytic remarks on Gershwin's output. Gershwin's stylistic traits examined closely in a separate chapter.

Porgy and Bess

1859.   Grunfeld, Frederic V. "The Great American Opera." *Opera News*, 24 (March 19, 1960): 6–9.

Brief remarks on background, with a critical assessment.

1860.   Mellers, Wilfrid. *Music in a New Found Land*, 392–413. New York: Alfred A. Knopf, 1965.

Background, descriptive, and analytic commentary with musical examples. Shows relationship of Gershwin's opera to jazz and pop.

1861.   Rorem, Ned. "Living With Gershwin." *Opera News*, 49 (March 16, 1985): 10–14.

Another composer's views on the place of *Porgy* in the repertoire. Reminiscences, observations on influences, style, and plot.

1862.   Starr, Lawrence. " 'Bess, You Is My Woman Now': The Sophistication and Subtlety of a Great Time." *Musical Quarterly*, 72, no. 4 (1986): 429–448.

Thorough analysis, dissecting the song to examine its rhythmic, harmonic, formal, and cultural components. Musical examples.

Rhapsody in Blue

1863. Levine, Henry. "Gershwin, Handy, and the 'Blues.' " *Clavier,* 9, no. 7 (1970): 10–20.
Specific examples of Handy's influence on Gershwin in the *Rhapsody in Blue.* Musical examples.

1864. Machlis, Joseph. *The Enjoyment of Music.* 5th ed., 544–548. New York: W. W. Norton, 1984.
Background and descriptive commentary for the undergraduate student. Salient musical features identified. Musical examples.

DISSERTATIONS AND THESES

General

1865. Conrad, Jon Alan. "Style and Structure in Songs by George Gershwin, Published 1924–1938." Ph.D., Indiana University, 1985, 302 pp., DA 46-3528A.

GESUALDO, DON CARLO, c. 1560–1613

General

1866. Dent, Edward J. "The Sixteenth Century Madrigal." In *The New Oxford History of Music, Vol. 4, The Age of Humanism, 1540– 1630.* Edited by Gerald Abraham, 67–69. London: Oxford University Press, 1968.
Brief examination of Gesualdo's unique style. Musical examples.

1867. Einstein, Alfred. *The Italian Madrigal.* Vol. 2, Translated by Alexander H. Krappe, Robert H. Sessions and Oliver Strunk, 688– 717. Princeton: Princeton University Press, 1949.
Excellent discourse for the more advanced student. Musical examples.

1868. Heseltine, Philip, and Cecil Gray. *Carlo Gesualdo, Prince of Venosa.* 1926. Reprint. Westport, CT: Greenwood Press, 1971, 145 pp.
Extended discussion of the music, though not as substantial as the Watkins book listed below (*see* item no. 1869). Musical examples.

1869. Watkins, Glenn. *Gesualdo: The Man and His Music.* Chapel Hill: University of North Carolina Press, 1973, 334 pp.
Thorough analytic discussion of the music, with background information. Musical examples.

GIBBONS, ORLANDO, 1583–1625

General

1870.   Salter, Lionel. "Gibbons: Keyboard Pieces." *Music Teacher,* 58 (June 1979): 17–18.
Analysis of *Pavan and Galliard* written on the death of Robert Cecil in 1612.

Song 34 ("Angel's Song")

1871.   Matthews, P. H. "A Further Note on Song 34." *Music Teacher and Piano Student,* 102 (October 1961): 652–653.
A continuation of the article below (*see* item no. 1872).

1872.   Matthews, P. H. "Gibbons' Song 34: A Suggestion." *Music Teacher and Piano Student,* 102 (August 1961): 515–516.
A discussion of the problem of rhythm in this hymn.

What Is Our Life?

1873.   Aston, Peter. "Orlando Gibbons and the English Musical Tradition." *Music Teacher,* 59 (June 1980): 17–18.
An analysis of thematic content and style.

GINASTERA, ALBERTO, 1916–1983

General

1874.   Hanely, Sister Mary Ann. "The Solo Piano Music of Alberto Ginastera." *American Music Teacher,* 24, no. 6 (1975): 17–20; 25, no. 1 (1975): 6–9.
Overview of Ginastera's piano output. Descriptive with analytic observations. Musical examples.

Bomarzo

1875.   Margrave, Wendell. "Current Chronicle: Washington, D.C." *Musical Quarterly,* 51, no. 2 (1965): 411–413.
Brief review of a performance of *Bomarzo,* with descriptive and analytic observations. No musical examples.

1876. Salter, Lionel. "Dark Deeds in *Bomarzo*." *Opera*, 27 (November 1976): 997–1001.
Comments on the compositional techniques in the opera.

Cantáta par América Mágica

1877. Béhague, Gerard. *Music in Latin America: An Introduction*, 330–331. Englewood Cliffs, NJ: Prentice-Hall, 1979.
Brief analysis. Musical examples.

Concerto for Piano

1878. Béhague, Gerard. *Music in Latin America: An Introduction*, 331–332. Englewood Cliffs, NJ: Prentice-Hall, 1979.
Brief analysis. Musical examples.

Don Rodrigo

1879. Béhague, Gerald. *Music in Latin America: An Introduction*, 333–335. Englewood Cliffs, NJ: Prentice-Hall, 1979.
Brief analysis with chart of scene relationships.

1880. Suarez Urtubery, P. "Alberto Ginastera's *Don Rodrigo*." *Tempo*, 74 (Autumn 1965): 11–18.
Scene-by-scene analysis of the opera's structure, with other analytical observations. Musical examples.

Duo for Flute and Oboe

1881. Smith, Carleton Sprague. "Alberto Ginastera's Duo for Flute and Oboe." *Latin American Music Review*, 6, no. 1 (1985): 85–93.
Background and brief critical remarks.

Sonata for Violoncello and Piano

1882. Kuss, Maria Elena. "First Performances: Ginastera's Cello Sonata." *Tempo*, 132 (March 1980): 41–42.
Brief description of form and composer's technique of framing different movements with a repetition of a single chord.

DISSERTATIONS AND THESES

Don Rodrigo

1883. Richards, James Edward, Jr. "Pitch Structure in the Opera *Don Rodrigo* of Alberto Ginastera." Ph.D., University of Rochester, Eastman School of Music, 1983, 156 pp., DA 46-3530A.

GIORDANO, UMBERTO, 1867–1948

Andrea Chenier

1884. Ashbrook, William. "Love and Revolution." *Opera News,* 41 (March 26, 1977): 14–15.
   Brief background, with analytic comments on highlights. Musical examples.

GLASS, PHILIP, 1937–

Glassworks: "Floe"

1885. Machlis, Joseph. *The Enjoyment of Music.* 5th ed., 600–603. New York: W. W. Norton, 1984.
   Background and description of Glass's style. Descriptive commentary on *Floe.* Musical examples.

GLAZUNOV, ALEXANDER, 1865–1936

Quartets for Strings

1886. Abraham, Gerald. "Glazunov and the String Quartet." *Tempo,* 73 (Summer 1965): 16–21.
   Brief analytic observations on each of the seven quartets.

1887. Abraham, Gerald. *Slavonic and Romantic Music,* 218–224. New York: St. Martin's Press, 1968.
   Analytic comments. Musical examples.

GLIÉRE, REINHOLD, 1875–1956

Concerto for Violoncello, Op. 87

1888. Dale, S. S. "Contemporary Cello Concerti: Myaskovsky and Glière." *Strad,* 86 (July 1975): 193 + .
   Brief analytic remarks.

GLINKA, MIKHAIL, 1804–1857

General

1889. Brown, David. *Mikhail Glinka: A Biographical and Critical Study.* London: Oxford University Press, 1974, 340 pp.
   Thorough treatment. Includes background, brief plot summary, creative process, and many analytic remarks. Musical examples.

GLUCK, CHRISTOPH WILLIBALD, 1714–1787

General

1890. Cooper, Martin. "Opera in France." In *The New Oxford History of Music. Vol. 7; The Age of Enlightenment, 1745–1790.* Edited by Egon Wellesz and F. W. Sternfeld, 226–239. London: Oxford University Press, 1973.
  Traces Gluck's operas, mentioning stylistic characteristics and Gluck's place in music history.

1891. Einstein, Alfred. *Gluck.* Translated by Eric Blom. London: J. M. Dent and Sons, 1936, 238 pp.
  Good summary of Gluck's achievement. Critical remarks on individual works.

1892. Garlington, Aubrey S., Jr. " 'Le Merveilleux' and Operatic Reform in Eighteenth Century French Opera." *Musical Quarterly,* 49, no. 4 (1963): 484–497.
  Gluck's treatment of "the marvelous," or scenes depicting heaven, hell, magic, and other extrahuman phenomena.

1893. Howard, Patricia. *Gluck and the Birth of Modern Opera.* London: Barrie and Rockliff, 1963, 118 pp.
  Gluck's innovations in the development of the aria, recitative, overture, and other crucial aspects of opera. Musical examples.

1894. Newman, Ernest. *Gluck and the Opera: A Study in Musical History.* London: Victor Gollancz, 1964, 300 pp.
  Summary of Gluck's achievement.

Iphigénie en Aulide Overture

1895. Tovey, Donald Francis. *Essays in Musical Analysis.* Vol. 6, 12–19. London: Oxford University Press, 1969.
  Critical and analytic remarks, with musical examples. For the undergraduate student.

Iphigénie en Tauride

1896. Rushton, Julian. "*Iphigénie en Tauride:* The Operas of Gluck and Piccini." *Music and Letters,* 53, no. 4 (1972): 411–430.
  A comparison of the settings of *Iphigénie* by Gluck and Piccini. Background and critical remarks on the drama and music. Musical examples.

Orfeo ed Euridice

1897. Howard, Patricia, ed. *C. W. von Gluck: "Orfeo."* Cambridge: Cambridge University Press, 1981, 143 pp.
  Thorough treatment, including discussion of the libretto and its sources, a synopsis, analytic commentary, performance history, and historical context. Bibliography, discography, and musical examples.

1898. Warburton, A. O. "Set Works for 'O' Level, GCE. *Music Teacher and Piano Student*, 44 (August 1965): 314, 326.
  Description of the opera, with analytic observations.

Orfeo ed Euridice Overture

1899. Tovey, Donald Francis. *Essays in Musical Analysis.* Vol. 6, 12–19. London: Oxford University Press, 1969.
  Critical and analytic remarks, with musical examples. For the undergraduate student.

GODOWSKY, LEOPOLD, 1870–1938

Studies on the Chopin Etudes

1900. McKeever, James. "Godowsky Studies on the Chopin Etudes." *Clavier*, 19, no. 3 (1980): 21–28.
  Descriptive and analytic overview, with musical examples and brief bibliography.

GOLDMARK, KARL, 1830–1915

Concerto for Violin in A Minor

1901. Swalin, Benjamin F. *The Violin Concerto: A Study in German Romanticism*, 108–113. Chapel Hill: University of North Carolina Press, 1941.
  Critical and analytic commentary, with musical examples.

GOTTSCHALK, LOUIS MOREAU, 1829–1869

DISSERTATIONS AND THESES

General

1902. Korf, William E. "The Orchestral Music of Louis Moreau Gottschalk." Ph.D., University of Iowa, 1974, 264 pp., DA 35-4589.

GOUNOD, CHARLES, 1818–1893

General

1903. Harding, James. *Gounod.* New York: Stein and Day, 1973, 251 pp.
Critical commentary. No analyses or musical examples.

Faust

1904. Fogel, Susan Lee. "The Uses of Simplicity." *Opera News,* 36 (February 26, 1972): 24–25.
Musical devices used to strengthen characterization. Musical examples.

Romeo and Juliet

1905. McDonald, Katherine Griffith. "The Variety of the Heart." *Opera News,* 32 (April 13, 1968): 24–25.
Remarks on musical style and musical depiction. Comparison of the three love scenes. Musical examples.

GRAINGER, PERCY, 1882–1961

General

1906. Foreman, Lewis, ed. *The Percy Grainger Companion.* London: Thames Publishing, 1981, 268 pp.
Background, critical discussion, and analytic observations on Grainger's output. Musical examples.

1907. Fred, Herbert W. "Percy Grainger's Music for Wind Band." *Journal of Band Research,* 1, no. 1 (1964): 10–16.
A survey with analytic comments on form, harmony, instrumentation, and rhythm.

Country Gardens

1908. Fennell, Frederick. "Basic Band Repertory: *Country Gardens,* by Percy Grainger." *Instrumentalist,* 37 (January 1983): 20–21.
Discusses form of the entire piece, detailing the a-b-a form of the opening section.

Hill Song No. 1

1909. Balough, Teresa, ed. *A Musical Genius From Australia*, 82–91. Nedlands: University of Western Australia Press, 1982.
   Grainger's own analysis of this work. Musical examples.

1910. Grainger, Percy. "Percy Aldridge Grainger's Remarks About His *Hill Song* No. 1." *Grainger Journal*, 1, no 2 (1978): 14–23.
   Grainger's philosophy behind the music and his own analysis. Musical examples.

Hill Song No. 2

1911. Fennell, Frederick. "Basic Band Repertory: *Hill Song* No. 2, by Percy Aldridge Grainger." *Instrumentalist*, 38 (February 1984): 22–29.
   Mainly a discussion of performance problems, with occasional remarks on important musical features. Musical examples.

Irish Tune from County Derry

1912. Fennell, Frederick. "Percy Grainger's *Irish Tune from County Derry* and *Shepherd's Hey*." *Instrumentalist*, 33 (September 1978): 18–25.
   Structural analysis of both folk songs on which the orchestral compositions are based. Includes compressed score for band.

Lincolnshire Posy

1913. Slattery, Thomas. "The Life and Work of Percy Grainger." *Instrumentalist*, 22 (December 1967): 47–49.
   Brief commentary on each of the six variations of this work. Musical examples.

Marching Song of Democracy

1914. Kreines, Joseph. "*Marching Song of Democracy:* A Neglected Masterpeice." *Grainger Journal*, 5, no. 1 (1982): 21–25.
   Background, composer's intentions, and structural plan outlined.

The Power of Rome and the Christian Heart

1915. Josephson, David S. "Percy Grainger—Some Problems and Approaches." *Current Musicology*, 18 (1974): 62–66.

By examining the autograph sketches, Josephson reveals Grainger's compositional process and consequent organization of the work. Musical examples.

GRÉTRY, ANDRÉ, 1741–1813
General

1916. Charlton David. *Grétry and the Growth of Opéra-Comique.* Cambridge: Cambridge University Press, 1986, 371 pp.
A study of Grétry's contribution to the opéra comique. Reviews twenty-four works in detail. Includes biographical details, performance statistics, analytic comments on individual works, traces the growth of the genre, and assesses Grétry's contribution. Musical examples.

GRIEG, EDVARD, 1843–1907
General

1917. Abraham, Gerald, ed. *Grieg: A Symposium.* Norman: University of Oklahoma Press, 1950, 144 pp.
Critical and descriptive overview for the student. Some analytic remarks and commentary on Grieg's style. Musical examples.

1918. Dale, Kathleen. *Nineteenth-Century Piano Music: A Handbook for Pianists.* London: Oxford University Press, 1954, 320 pp.
Highlights stylistic traits and unique contributions to the literature of the piano. Form, harmony, and other musical aspects discussed in relation to style.

1919. Horton, John. *Grieg.* London: J. M. Dent and Sons, 1974, 255 pp.
Critical overview for the student. Part of the "Master Musician" series. Musical examples.

1920. Matthews, Denis, ed. *Keyboard Music,* 297–300. New York: Praeger, 1972.
Brief critical summation, with musical examples.

1921. Schjelderup-Ebbe, Dag. *Edvard Grieg 1858–1867, With Special Reference to the Evolution of His Harmonic Style.* London: Allen and Unwin, 1964, 363 pp.
A chronological study, with emphasis on music and particularly on Grieg's harmony and its development. Musical examples and tables.

1922. Skyllstad, Kjell. "Thematic Structure in Relation to Form in Edvard Grieg's Cyclic Works." *Studia Musicologica Norvegica,* 3 (1977): 75–94.

Concerto for Piano in A Minor

1923. Abraham, Gerald. "The Piano Concerto." In *Grieg: A Symposium.* Edited by Gerald Abraham, 26–31. Norman: University of Oklahoma Press, 1950.
Background and critical remarks. Focuses on Grieg's orchestration of the concerto and compares versions.

1924. Machlis, Joseph. *The Enjoyment of Music.* 3d ed., 162–164. New York: W. W. Norton, 1970.
Mini-analysis for the undergraduate student. Concise treatment with critical remarks and musical examples.

In Autumn Overture

1925. Skyllstad, Kjell. "Thematic Structure in Relation to Form in Edvard Grieg's Works: The Nordic Tradition—Op. 8 and 11." *Studia Musicologica Norvegica,* 6 (1980): 102–109.

Lyric Pieces, Op. 12, No. 2 ("Waltz")

1926. Tilkens, Neil A., George Kelver, and Vila Hartman. "Teacher's Roundtable." *American Music Teacher,* 19, no. 5 (1970): 34–35.
Three very short analyses for the performer. A few comments on form, tonality, and harmony followed by performance advice.

Sonata for Piano, Op. 7 in E Minor

1927. Sutton, Wadham. "Grieg: Sonata in E minor, Op. 7." *Music Teacher,* 52 (May 1973): 13–14.
Overview for the performer, with interspersed analytic comments.

DISSERTATIONS AND THESES

Sonatas for Violin and Piano

1928. Yarrow, Anne. "An Analysis and Comparison of the Three Sonatas for Violin and Piano by Edvard Grieg." Ph.D., New York University, 1985, 404 pp., DA 46-1777A.

GRIFFES, CHARLES TOMLINSON, 1884–1920

General

1929. Moore, John, and David Reeves. "The Published German Songs of Charles T. Griffes." *NATS Bulletin,* 41, no. 2 (1984): 7–12.
Discussion of the songs, with analytic comments and musical examples. Includes brief discussion of texts and background.

1930. Sanders, George P. "The Piano Compositions of Charles Tomlinson Griffes." *American Music Teacher,* 35, no. 1 (1985): 28–29.
Brief critical evaluation highlighting stylistic traits and the importance of these compositions to American music.

Sonata for Piano

1931. Maisel, Edward. *Charles T. Griffes.* Rev. ed. New York: Alfred A. Knopf, 1984, 399 pp.
Mainly a life of Griffes, but contains an analysis of the sonata. Musical examples.

DISSERTATIONS AND THESES

General

1932. Johnson, Richard Oscar. "The Songs of Charles Tomlinson Griffes." D.M.A., University of Iowa, 1977, 192 pp., DA 38-1727A-8A.

HANDEL, GEORGE FRIDERIC, 1685–1759

General

1933. Abraham, Gerald, ed. *Handel: A Symposium.* London: Oxford University Press, 1954, 328 pp.
Thorough overview, including the oratorios, cantatas, and church music. Descriptive and analytic commentary. Musical examples.

1934. Best, Terence. "Handel's Keyboard Works." *Musical Times,* 112 (September 1971): 845–848.
An annotated listing of Handel's keyboard works, with some critical commentary. Musical examples.

1935. Bukofzer, Manfred. *Music in the Baroque Era,* 333–341. New York: W. W. Norton, 1947.

Descriptive overview of Handel's output, including the operas, with comments on musical style. Mentions characteristic forms, aria types, and dance rhythms used. Not analytic.

1936. Dean, Winton. *Handel and the Opera Seria.* London: Oxford University Press, 1970, 220 pp.

Focus is on Handel's theatrical craftsmanship and highlighting the differences between the several types of opera employed by Handel. Mention of aria and recitative style. Musical examples.

1937. Dean, Winton. *Handel's Dramatic Oratorios and Masques.* London: Oxford University Press, 1959, 694 pp.

Thorough, scholarly treatment. Discussion includes plot summary, general criticism, analysis and orchestration, history and text, editions, and autograph. Musical examples.

1938. Dean, Winton, and John Merrill Knapp. *Handel's Operas: 1704-1726.* Oxford: Clarendon Press, 1987, 751 pp.

Exhaustive treatment of the operas, providing full background, composition history, performance history, sources for librettos, and analytic observations. Musical examples.

1939. Dent, Edward J. "The Operas." In *Handel: A Symposium.* Edited by Gerald Abraham, 12-65. New York: Oxford University Press, 1954.

Thorough musical discussion of Handel's operas. Many analytic comments and observations.

1940. Fiske, Roger. "Handel's Organ Concertos—Do They Belong to Particular Oratorios?" *Organ Yearbook,* 3 (1972): 14-22.

Scholarly examination of the evidence of the relationship between the oratorios and the organ concerti. Musical examples.

1941. Harris, Ellen. *Handel and the Pastoral Tradition.* London: Oxford University Press, 1980, 292 pp.

Historical overview of those operas based on the pastoral drama. Analytic commentary included in general discussion of the operas. Musical examples.

1942. Lam, Basil. "The Orchestral Music." In *Handel: A Symposium.* Edited by Gerald Abraham, 200-232. London: Oxford University Press, 1954.

Very thorough treatment—descriptive, critical, and analytic comments on Handel's orchestral output, including the concertos. Style and influence mentioned as well. Musical examples.

1943. Lang, Paul Henry. *George Frideric Handel.* New York: W. W. Norton, 1966, 731 pp.

Overview of Handel's works, commenting on formal and stylistic musical characteristics.

1944. Matthews, Denis, ed. *Keyboard Music,* 101–107. New York: Praeger, 1972.

Brief overview of Handel's keyboard output by Charles Rosen. Handel's place in the art of keyboard writing, stylistic traits, and critical observations on selected pieces. Musical examples.

1945. Rolland, Romain. *Handel.* 1916. Reprint, 134–143. New York: Johnson Reprint, 1969.

Very brief overview.

1946. Rueb, Phyllis K. "Handel's Keyboard Suites: A Comparison with Those of J. S. Bach." *American Music Teacher,* 20, no. 5 (1971): 33–36.

A comparison of stylistic characteristics in the Handel suites with those of Bach's keyboard suites.

1947. Williams, Peter. " 'Figurae' in the Keyboard Works of Scarlatti, Handel, and Bach: An Introduction." In *Bach, Handel, Scarlatti: Tercentenary Essays.* Edited by Peter Williams, 327–346. London: Cambridge University Press, 1985.

Defines the term "figurae" (motifs, figures, *Figuren*), gives a brief background, and then discusses their use in the keyboard works of the above composers. Musical examples.

1948. Wolff, Hellmuth Christian. "Italian Opera." In *The New Oxford History of Music.* Vol. 5; *Opera and Church Music, 1630–1750.* Edited by Anthony Lewis and Nigel Fortune, 138–151. London: Oxford University Press, 1975.

Discusses librettos, musical characteristics, performance practice, and prior influences. A survey.

1949. Young, Percy M. *Handel.* Rev. ed. London: J. M. Dent and Sons, 1975, 254 pp.

Analytic comments on Handel's output. For the undergraduate student. Musical examples.

1950. Young, Percy M. *The Oratorios of Handel.* London: Dennis Dobson, 1949, 244 pp.

Thorough treatment, including background of the oratorio as a genre and a discussion of the music itself. Musical examples.

Acis and Galatea

1951. Warburton, A. O. "Set Works for 'O' Level, GCE." *Music Teacher*, 49 (June 1970): 17–18.
Brief analytic comments occur within a short description of each number of Part 2 of this work.

Capriccio in G Minor

1952. Dumm, Robert. "Performer's Analysis of a Handel Capriccio." *Clavier*, 14, no. 8 (1975): 24–28.
Phrase-by-phrase descriptive commentary for the performer. Score included.

Chandos Anthems

1953. Lock, William. "Handel's *Chandos* Anthems." *Choral Journal*, 25, no. 8 (1985): 28–33 + .
Commentary on form, free counterpoint, and tone painting.

Chandos Anthems, No. 6

1954. Warburton, A. O. "Set Works for 'O' Level, GCE." *Music Teacher and Piano Student*, 45 (August 1966): 304 + .
Brief analyses of all eight movements. Concerned primarily with form and tonality.

Concertos

1955. Hutchings, Arthur. *The Baroque Concerto*, 292–303. New York: W. W. Norton, 1961.
An overview of Handel's concerto achievement, mentioning stylistic traits, influences on Handel, as well as his influence on others.

1956. Sadie, Stanley. *Handel Concertos.* London: British Broadcasting Corporation, 1973, 72 pp.
An analytic survey of the Concerti Grossi, Oboe Concertos, Organ Concertos, Double Concertos, *Water Music*, and *Fireworks* music. Though written for the musical amateur, the approach is analytical. Includes discussion of background, orchestration, forms, and style. Musical examples.

Concerti Grossi, Op. 6

1957. Morehen, John. "Concerti Grossi, Op. 6, Nos. 1 and 6." *Music Teacher*, 55 (April 1976): 15–16.
Analytical notes emphasizing formal aspects of Nos. 1 and 6 of the *Concerti Grossi*.

1958. Rolland, Romain. *Handel.* Translated by A. Eaglefield Hull, 166–181. New York: Henry Holt, 1916.
Descriptive commentary on nos. 2, 4, 6 of the *Concerti Grossi*. Musical examples.

Concerto Grosso, Op. 6, No. 9 in F Major

1959. Redlich, Hans. "The Oboes in Handel's Op. 6." *Musical Times*, 109 (June 1968): 530–531.
A discussion of sources for this work. Not an analysis.

1960. Tischler, Hans. *The Perceptive Music Listener*, 317–319. Englewood Cliffs, NJ: Prentice-Hall, 1955.
Analysis, with musical examples.

Concerto for Organ, Op. 4, No. 2 in B-Flat Major

1961. Warburton, A. O. "Set Works for 'O' Level, GCE." *Music Teacher*, 50 (May 1971): 16+.
Brief analysis of the first movement.

Concerto for Organ, Op. 7, No. 2 in A Major

1962. Wollenberg, Susan. "Handel and Gottlieb Muffat: A Newly Discovered Borrowing." *Musical Times*, 113 (May 1972): 448–449.
Brief but detailed account of Handel's borrowing of a melody from Muffat. Musical examples.

Fantasia for Harpsichord in C Major

1963. Warburton, A. O. "Set Works for 'O' Level, GCE." *Music Teacher*, 50 (May 1971): 16+.
Brief analytic overview intended for the undergraduate student.

Flavio

1964. Dean, Winton. "A Handel Tragicomedy." *Musical Times*, 110 (August 1969): 819–822.
Background, plot, and critical commentary on the music.

Israel in Egypt

1965.   Tovey, Donald Francis. *Essays in Musical Analysis,* 82–113. London: Oxford University Press, 1937.
Thorough analysis and critical commentary for the informed undergraduate student. Musical examples.

Messiah

1966.   Cole, William. *The Form of Music: An Outline of Musical Designs Used by the Great Composers,* 62. London: Associated Board of the Royal Schools of Music, n.d.
Brief outline of the ritornello form of the aria "Thou shalt break them." Table.

1967.   Gelles, George. "Mozart's Version of *Messiah.*" *American Choral Review,* 10, no. 2 (1968): 55–65.
A close examination of Mozart's orchestration of the *Messiah.* Musical examples.

1968.   Hogwood, Christopher. "In Search of the True Messiah with Christopher Hogwood." *Ovation,* 5 (January 1985): 26–31.
An overview of the performance history of this work with remarks on its different editions. Not an analysis.

1969.   Larsen, Jens Peter. *Handel's "Messiah": Origins, Composition, Sources.* 2nd ed. New York: W.W. Norton, 1972, 337 pp.
Book-length treatment of the *Messiah,* including background, thorough descriptive/analytic survey of the entire work, versions, sources, and bibliography. Musical examples.

1970.   Redlich, Hans *"Messiah:* The Struggle for Definite Text." *Music Review,* 27, no. 4 (1966): 287–293.
A discussion of the difficulties involved in finding a definitive text, focusing mainly on the variations in editions by John Tobin and Watkins Shaw. Musical examples.

1971.   Tobin, John. *Handel's "Messiah."* London: Cassel, 1969, 279 pp.
Scholarly, in-depth treatment of many aspects of *Messiah.* Editions, sources, orchestra, performance style, harmonic structure, and a critical evaluation. Musical examples.

1972.   Wolff, Christoph. "Mozart's *Messiah:* 'The Spirit of Handel' from van Swieten's Hands." In *Music and Civilization: Essays in*

Honor of Paul Henry Lang. Edited by Edmond Strainchamps and Maria Rika Maniates, 1–14. New York: W. W. Norton, 1984.

The changes Mozart made to Handel's score for a performance. Handel's original score compared with Mozart's and some of the reasons why the changes were made. Musical examples.

1973.   Young, Percy M. *The Choral Tradition.* Rev. ed., 116–124. New York: W. W. Norton, 1981.

Brief descriptive, critical, and analytic comments for the undergraduate student.

Ode for the Birthday of Queen Anne

1974.   Lincoln, Stoddard. "Handel's Music for Queen Anne." *Musical Quarterly,* 45, no. 2 (1959): 191–207.

Background on Handel's admission into England as an accepted composer. Formal analysis of ode form, followed by a detailed account of the *Birthday Ode* and problematic compositional aspects involved. Analysis of *Utrecht Te Deum* included. Musical examples.

Ottone

1975.   Dean, Winton. "Handel's *Ottone.*" *Musical Times,* 112 (October 1971): 955–958.

Background, performance history, and critical commentary.

Saul

1976.   Webb, Ralph T. "Views and Viewpoints: Handel's Oratorios as Drama." *College Music Symposium,* 23, no. 2 (1983): 129–144.

Instead of the usual alternation of recitative and aria, Handel unified this oratorio by periodic returns to C major and through his use of the chorus. Tables.

Solomon

1977.   Webb, Ralph T. "Views and Viewpoints: Handel's Oratorios as Drama." *College Music Symposium,* 23, no. 2 (1983): 126–129.

A discussion of Act II, relating musical features to the dramatic events. Deals with tonal structure and melody. Tables.

Sonata for Two Violins and Continuo, Op. 2, No. 6 in G Minor

1978.   Cole, William. *The Form of Music: An Outline of Musical Designs Used by the Great Composers,* 98–100. London: Associated Board of the Royal Schools of Music, n.d.
  Brief analytic comments.

Suite for Harpsichord No. 5 in E Major

1979.   Warburton, A. O. "Set Works for 'O' Level, GCE." *Music Teacher and Piano Student,* 46 (June 1967): 10+.
  Brief analytic comments.

Tamerlano

1980.   Knapp, J. Merrill. "Handel's . . .Tamerlano: The Creation of an Opera." *Musical Quarterly,* 56, no. 3 (1970): 405–430.
  Examines sources for libretto and how Handel adapted them. Also looks at Handel's compositional process.

Teseo

1981.   Kimbell, David. "The Libretto of Handel's *Teseo.*" *Music and Letters,* 44, no. 4 (1963): 371–379.
  Story synopsis and comparison of libretto to source, Quinault's *Thésée.*

Utrecht Te Deum

1982.   Lincoln, Stoddard. "Handel's Music for Queen Anne." *Musical Quarterly,* 45, no. 2 (1959): 191–207.
  Analysis. Musical examples.

Water Music

1983.   Morehen, John. "Handel: *Water Music.*" *Music Teacher,* 55 (April 1976): 16–17.
  Brief analytical observations on form. For the undergraduate student.

Zadok the Priest

1984.   Warburton, A. O. "Set Works for 'O' Level. GCE." *Music Teacher,* 51 (May 1972): 16–17.
  Brief analysis for the undergraduate student.

DISSERTATIONS AND THESES

Psalms

1985.   Parker-Hale, Mary Ann Elizabeth. "Handel's Latin Psalm Settings." Ph.D., University of Rochester, Eastman School of Music, 1981, 174 pp., DA 42-4036A.

Te Deum

1986.   Beeks, Graydon Fisher. "The *Chandos* Anthems and *Te Deum* of Georg Frideric Handel (1685–1759)." Ph.D., University of California at Berkeley, 1981, 969 pp., DA 42-2921A.

HANSON, HOWARD, 1896–1981

Symphony No. 2 ("Romantic")

1987.   Hansen, Peter. *An Introduction to Twentieth Century Music,* 344–346. 2d ed. Boston: Allyn and Bacon, 1967.
  Brief analytic synopsis.

HARRIS, ROY, 1898–1979

General

1988.   Stehman, Dan. *Roy Harris: An American Musical Pioneer.* Boston: Twayne, 1984, 296 pp.
  A discussion of the composer's life and music. The emphasis is on the music, with brief analytic commentaries on all his major works. Although the division of the chapter is by genre, discussion of his life and his symphonies are integrated. Musical examples and tables.

Symphony No. 3

1989.   Ballantine, Christopher. *Twentieth Century Symphony,* 121–123, 173–176. London: Dennis Dobson, 1984.
  Brief analytic comments, with the composer's own formal plan. Musical examples.

1990.   Hansen, Peter. *An Introduction to Twentieth Century Music.* 2d ed., 330–333. Boston: Allyn and Bacon, 1967.
  Short analysis of the symphony, with discussion of compositional style.

1991.   Machlis, Joseph. *Introduction to Contemporary Music,* 474–475. New York: W. W. Norton, 1961.
Brief remarks for the undergraduate student. Musical examples.

Symphony No. 7 (1952)

1992.   Stedman, Preston. *The Symphony,* 347–353. Englewood Cliffs, NJ: Prentice-Hall, 1979.
Description and analytic breakdown of each variation and commentary on Harris's style. Musical examples and diagram.

DISSERTATIONS AND THESES

General

1993.   Bargmann, Theodore John. "The Solo and Instrumental Chamber Works for Piano by Roy Harris." D.M.A., American Conservatory of Music, 1986, 158 pp., DA 47-1524A.

Symphonies

1994.   Stehman, Dan. "The Symphonies of Roy Harris: An Analytical Study of the Linear Materials and of Related Works." Ph.D., University of Southern California, 1973, 1598 pp., DA 34-7272A.

HAYDN, FRANZ JOSEPH, 1732–1809

General

1995.   Brenet, Michael. *Haydn.* Translated by C. Leonard Leese, 61–69. London: Oxford University Press, 1926.
Light descriptive overview. Some critical remarks.

1996.   Brown, A. Peter. *Joseph Haydn's Keyboard Music: Sources and Style.* Bloomington: Indiana University Press, 1986, 450 pp.
Background, sources, authenticity, keyboard idiom, structure, and style discussed in full. Musical examples.

1997.   Ferguson, Donald N. *Image and Structure in Chamber Music,* 30–45. Minneapolis: University of Minnesota Press, 1964.
Overview of the chamber music, with brief analyses. Musical examples.

1998. Geiringer, Karl. *Haydn: A Creative Life in Music.* Berkeley: University of California Press, 1968, 434 pp.
Background with descriptive, critical, and analytic overview. Stylistic traits highlighted. Musical examples.

1999. Hughes, Rosemary. *Haydn.* London: J. M. Dent and Sons, 1962, 271 pp.
A standard "life and works" book in the Dent "Master Musician" series. The works are treated genre by genre—analytic remarks, with musical examples.

2000. Hunter, M. "Haydn's Sonata-Form Arias." *Current Musicology,* 37–38 (1984): 19–32.
Primarily concerned with the eleven Italian operas that Haydn wrote at Eszterhaza between 1766 and 1783. Analyses with musical examples.

2001. Landon, H. C. Robbins. *Haydn: Chronicle and Works.* 5 vols. Bloomington: Indiana University Press, 1976.
Systematic examination of Haydn's entire output. Discussion includes background, style, influences, sources, patronage, critical appraisal, and analysis. Musical examples.

2002. Landon, H. C. Robbins, and David Wyn Jones. *Haydn: His Life and Music.* Bloomington: Indiana University Press, 1988, 383 pp.
An easier to use condensation of the author's *Haydn: Chronicle and Works* (5 vols.) Largely rewritten, with additional material and with newly discovered Haydn letters in mind. Includes analytic commentary on Haydn's output. For the advanced undergraduate and graduate student. Musical examples.

2003. Olleson, Edward. "Church Music and Oratorio." In *The New Oxford History of Music.* Vol. 7, *The Age of Enlightenment, 1745–1790.* Edited by Egon Wellesz and F. W. Sternfeld, 332–335. London: Oxford University Press, 1973.
Brief descriptive commentary.

2004. Rosen, Charles. *The Classical Style: Haydn, Mozart, Beethoven.* Rev. ed., 366–375. London: Faber and Faber, 1976.
Analytic comments on some of the church works. Brief analysis of the opening of the *Creation.* Musical examples.

2005. Wellesz, Egon, and F. W. Sternfeld. "The Concerto." In *The New Oxford History of Music.* Vol. 7; *The Age of Enlightenment, 1745–1790.* Edited by Egon Wellesz and F. W. Sternfeld, 472–477. London: Oxford University Press, 1973.

Brief overview of Haydn's concerto achievement. Focus on characteristic musical traits and reason why Haydn's concertos are less popular than his other forms. The article on Haydn's concertos falls within an article on the history of the concerto form. Musical examples.

2006. Wolff, Konrad. *Masters of the Keyboard: Individual Style Elements in the Piano Music of Bach, Haydn, Mozart, Beethoven, and Schubert*, 63–75. Bloomington: Indiana University Press, 1983.
A discussion of keyboard style for performers containing some useful analytic comments. Musical examples.

Chorale Saint Antoni

2007. Lerdahl, Fred, and Ray Jackendorff. *A Generative Theory of Tonal Music*, 203–210. Cambridge, MA: M.I.T. Press, 1983.
A prolongational reduction in detail of this chorale (attr. to Haydn) as arranged by Brahms in his *Haydn* Variations. The music is reproduced with diagrams and explanations of the authors' theory. Musical examples.

Concertos

2008. Hill, Ralph, ed. *The Concerto*, 38–48. London: Penguin Books, 1952.
Critical and analytic commentary for the undergraduate student. Musical examples.

Concertos for Organ

2009. Haselboeck, Martin. "The Organ Concertos of Joseph Haydn." *American Organist*, 16 (December 1982): 38–41.
Background, brief descriptive and analytic remarks, commentary on the organs Haydn used, and his use of the orchestra. Bibliography.

Concerto for Trumpet in E-Flat Major

2010. Landon, H. C. Robbins. *Haydn: Chronicle and Works*. Vol. 4, 225–240. Bloomington: Indiana University Press, 1977.
Thorough critical and analytic discourse. Musical examples.

Concerto for Violoncello in D Major

2011.   Tovey, Donald Francis. *Essays in Musical Analysis.* Vol. 3, 62–63. London: Oxford University Press, 1936.
Brief remarks on style. Musical examples.

Creation

2012.   Brown, A. Peter. "Haydn's 'Chaos': Genesis and Genre." *Musical Quarterly*, 73, no. 1 (1989): 18–59.
Extended discussion of the "Representation of Chaos," movement placing it in historical context and comparing it to Rameau's and Rebel's depictions of chaos. Sketches examined and music analyzed. Advanced. Musical examples.

2013.   Hadden, J. Cuthbert. *Haydn,* 116–127. London: J. M. Dent and Sons, 1934.
Brief summary and critical discussion of the *Creation* and *Seasons*. For the undergraduate student.

2014.   Levarie, Siegmund. "The Closing Numbers of *Die Schöpfung.*" In *Studies in Eighteenth-Century Music.* Edited by H. C. Robbins Landon, 315–322. London: Allen and Unwin, 1970.
Advanced discussion of structural balance of this work. Musical examples.

2015.   Olleson, Edward. "The Origin and Libretto of Haydn's *Creation.*" In *Haydn Yearbook.* Vol. 4, 148–168. Bryn Mawr, PA: Theodore Presser, n.d.
Background only. No discussion of the music itself.

2016.   Rosen, Charles. *Sonata Forms,* 160–169. New York: W. W. Norton, 1980.
Analysis identifying the form of the Kyrie movement as sonata with central trio. Musical examples.

2017.   Smith, Edwin. "Set Works for 'O' Level, GCE." *Music Teacher,* 54 (October 1975): 14–15.
An overview correlating musical events with the text.

2018.   Stephens, Howard. "Set Works for 'O' Level, GCE." *Music Teacher,* 58 (January 1979): 16–17.
Brief remarks on the relationship of music to text. For the undergraduate student.

2019. Tovey, Donald Francis. *Essays in Musical Analysis.* Vol. 5, 114–146. London: Oxford University Press, 1937.

Thorough analysis and critical commentary for the informed student. Musical examples.

2020. Young, Percy M. *The Choral Tradition.* Rev. ed, 182–190. New York: W. W. Norton, 1981.

Background and descriptive remarks on the *Creation* and the *Seasons.* Musical examples.

Divertimenti

2021. Meyer, Eve R. "The Viennese Divertimento." *Music Review,* 29, no. 3 (1968): 166–170.

Places Haydn's divertimenti in the context of the Viennese divertimenti upon which they are based. Highlights Haydn's original use of the form.

Masses

2022. Olleson, Edward. "Church Music and Oratorio." In *The New Oxford History of Music.* Vol. 7; *The Age of Enlightenment, 1745–1790.* Edited by Egon Wellesz and F. W. Sternfeld, 319–327. London: Oxford University Press, 1973.

Overview of Haydn's masses, highlighting musical style and period influences. Musical examples.

Missa Brevis in F Major

2023. McCaldin, Denis. "Haydn's First and Last Work—The Missa Brevis in F Major." *Music Review,* 28, no. 3 (1967): 165–172.

Discussion of the two versions of this work: the first, composed in 1749, and the revision of the work when Haydn rediscovered it in 1805. Mostly a comparison of the two versions, with analytic remarks and some historic commentary. Musical examples.

Quartets for Strings

2024. Barret-Ayres, Reginald. *Joseph Haydn and the String Quartet.* New York: Schirmer Books, 1974, 417 pp.

Exhaustive study of style, influences, and innovations, with analytic comments on specific works. Musical examples.

2025. Cuyler, Louise. "Tonal Exploitation in the Later Quartets of Haydn." In *Studies in Eighteenth-Century Music*. Edited by H. C. Robbins Landon, 136–150. London: Allen and Unwin, 1970.
Advanced discussion on Haydn's daring use of tonality. Musical examples.

2026. Drabkin, William. "Beethoven and the Open String." *Music Analysis*, 4, no. 1–2 (1985): 15–28.
Discusses the open string sonority in Classical chamber music.

2027. Geiringer, Karl. "The Rise of Chamber Music." In *The New Oxford History of Music*. Vol. 7, *The Age of Enlightenment, 1745–1790*. Edited by Egon Wellesz and F. W. Sternfeld, 553–563, 565–566. London: Oxford University Press, 1973.
Brief overview focusing on Haydn's contribution to the medium. Stylistic traits mentioned. Musical examples.

2028. Hickman, Roger. "Haydn and the 'Symphony in Miniature.' " *Music Review*, 43, no. 1 (1982): 15–23.
The change in the string quartet from an emphasis on intimacy and subtlety to a heavier-textured "symphony in miniature." Musical examples.

2029. Hughes, Rosemary. *Haydn String Quartets*. London: British Broadcasting Corporation, 1966, 56 pp.
Brief descriptive overview, with analytic observations on Haydn's string quartet output. For the undergraduate student. Musical examples.

2030. Keller, Hans. *The Great Haydn Quartets: Their Interpretation*. New York: George Braziller, 1986, 268 pp.
Though meant for the performer, Keller's interpretative observations are based on analytic principles. Thorough review of forty-five quartets that comprise, in Keller's opinion, Haydn's "great" quartets. Musical examples.

2031. Moe, Orin. "Texture in Haydn's Early Quartets." *Music Review*, 35, no. 1 (1974): 4–22.

2032. Pauly, Reinhard. *Music in the Classic Period*, 150–157. Englewood Cliffs, NJ: Prentice-Hall, 1965.
General analytic observations are illustrated with muscial examples from specific works. The discussions are brief and general. For the undergraduate student.

2033. Robertson, Alex, ed. *Chamber Music*, 13–55. Baltimore: Penguin Books, 1957.

Thorough critical and analytic review of Haydn's string-quartet output. Observations on innovations and stylistic growth. Musical examples.

2034. Rosen, Charles. *The Classical Style: Haydn, Mozart, Beethoven.* Rev. ed, 111–142. London: Faber and Faber, 1976.
Analytic comments on many different works—usually on first movements. Comment on harmonic and thematic structure, rhythm, and the "Classical" style. Musical examples.

2035. Somfai, Laszlo. "A Bold Enharmonic Modulatory Model in Joeph Haydn's String Quartets." In *Studies in Eighteenth-Century Music.* Edited by H. C. Robbins Landon, 370–381. London: Allen and Unwin, 1970.
Advanced discussion of Haydn's harmonic experiments. Musical examples.

2036. Tovey, Donald Francis. *The Main Stream of Music and Other Essays,* 1–64. New York: Oxford University Press, 1949.
Excellent discourse on Haydn's role in the string quartet as a medium and on his stylistic traits. Specific works are discussed. Musical examples.

2037. Ulrich, Homer. *Chamber Music.* 2d ed., 154–185. New York: Columbia University Press, 1966.
Thorough critical summation, with historical background. Musical examples.

2038. Ulrich, Homer. "Haydn's String Quartets: A Few Observations—A Birthday Offering in His Honor." *American Music Teacher,* 31, no. 5. (1982): 16 + .
General observations on stylistic traits such as thematic development, melodic chromaticism, and the placement of the minuet. Influence of Mozart on Haydn considered briefly. Musical examples.

2039. Webster, James. "Freedom of Form in Haydn's Early String Quartets." In *Haydn Studies.* Edited by Jens Peter Larsen, Howard Serwer, and James Webster, 522–530. Proceedings of the International Haydn Conference. New York: W. W. Norton, 1981.
Formal procedures such as false recapitulation, variation of material upon its return, continual variation of a theme throughout a movement, and recomposition of the recapitulation explored. Suggests that many of Haydn's "unconventional" formal devices had early origins. Musical examples.

Quartets for Strings, Op. 33

2040. Rosen, Charles. *The Classical Style: Haydn, Mozart, Beethoven.*
Rev. ed., 115–119. London: Faber and Faber, 1976.
 Analytic comments describing the beginning of the classical style.
Musical examples.

Quartet for Strings, Op. 2, No. 2 in E Major

2041. Rosen, Charles. *Sonata Forms*, 143–146. New York: W. W.
Norton, 1980.
 Identification of the themes in the exposition and the development
of the first movement. Musical examples.

Quartet for Strings, Op. 9, No. 4 in D Minor

2042. Keller, Hans. "Today's Tomorrow." *Music Review*, 26, no. 3
(1965): 247–251.
 Descriptive commentary, with analytic remarks and suggestions
for performance. Musical examples.

Quartet for Strings, Op. 20, No. 1 in E-Flat Major

2043. Keller, Hans. "The String Quartet and Its Relatives." *Music
Review*, 26, no. 4 (1965): 340–344.
 Using this quartet as a starting point, Keller demonstrates
Haydn's mature sytle by comparing it to the later quartets. Ana-
lytic remarks and musical examples.

Quartet for Strings, Op. 20, No. 2 in C Major

2044. Keller, Hans. "The String Quartet and Its Relatives." *Music
Review*, 27, no. 1 (1966): 59–62.
 Analytic remarks and descriptive commentary on this quartet
demonstrating Haydn's maturing compositional style. Musical examples.

Quartet for Strings, Op. 20, No. 3 in G Minor

2045. Keller, Hans. "The String Quartet and Its Relatives." *Music
Review*, 27, no. 3 (1966): 228–232.

Structural and tonal analytic remarks, with descriptive commentary demonstrating Haydn's maturing compositional style. Musical examples.

Quartet for Strings, Op. 20, No. 4 in D Major

2046.   Keller, Hans. "The String Quartet and Its Relatives." *Music Review*, 27, no. 3 (1966): 232–235.
Descriptive commentary, with analytic remarks demonstrating Haydn's maturing compositional style. Musical examples.

Quartet for Strings, Op. 50, No. 3 in E-Flat Major

2047.   Rosen, Charles. *Sonata Forms*, 150–154. New York: W. W. Norton, 1980.
Discussion of the unusual structure of the first movement. Musical examples.

Quartet for Strings, Op. 54, No. 1 in G Major

2048.   Warburton, A. O. "Set Works for 'O' Level, GCE." *Music Teacher*, 48 (July 1969): 9–10.
Analysis of the form and thematic development of each movement.

Quartet for Strings, Op. 64, No. 5 in D Major

2049.   Tepping, Susan. "Form in the Finale of Haydn's String Quartet, Op. 64, No. 5." *Indiana Theory Review*, 4, no. 2 (1981): 51–68.
Advanced Schenkerian analysis.

Quartet for Strings, Op. 76, No. 2 in D Minor

2050.   Barret-Ayres, Reginald. "The Quinten." *Music Teacher*, 58 (April 1979): 22–23.
Discusses formal and thematic components of this quartet, with brief comments on the contrast of major and minor.

2051.   Warburton, A. O. "Set Works for 'O' Level, GCE." *Music Teacher*, 52 (May 1973): 21–22.
Thorough analysis for the undergraduate student. Musical examples.

Quartet for Strings, Op. 76, No. 3 in C Major

2052. Warburton, A. O. "Set Works for 'O' Level, GCE." *Music Teacher*, 48 (July 1969): 9–10.
Brief analytic remarks on the second movement (Variations).

Quartet for Strings, Op. 76, No. 4 B-Flat Major ("Sunrise")

2053. Ulrich, Homer. *Music: A Design for Listening*, 258–260. New York: Harcourt, Brace, 1957.
Descriptive breakdown, with analytic observations by measures. Musical examples.

Quartet for Strings, Op. 76, No. 5 in D Major

2054. Randall, J. K. "Haydn: String Quartet in D Major, Op. 76." *Music Review*, 21, no. 2 (1960): 94–105.
Analysis with emphasis on tonal aspects and key relationships. Provides charts with tonal progression. Score in hand recommended.

2055. Tischler, Hans. *The Perceptive Music Listener*, 286–290. Englewood Cliffs, NJ: Prentice-Hall, 1955.
Analysis, with musical examples.

Quartet for Strings, Op. 76, No. 6 in B Major

2056. Salzer, Felix. "Haydn's Fantasia from the String Quartet, Op. 76, No. 6." In *The Music Forum*. Vol. 4. New York: Edited by Felix Salzer and Carl Schachter, 161–194. Columbia University Press, 1976.
Thorough analysis of the Fantasia movement of this work. Advanced. Musical examples.

Seasons

2057. Hadden, J. Cuthbert. *Haydn*, 116–127. London: J. M. Dent and Sons, 1934.
Brief summary and critical discussion of the *Creation* and *Seasons*. For the undergraduate student.

2058. Tovey, Donald Francis. *Essays in Musical Analysis*. Vol. 5, 146–161. London: Oxford University Press, 1937.
Thorough analytic and critical commentary for the informed student. Musical examples.

2059. Young, Percy M. *The Choral Tradition*, 182–190. New York: W. W. Norton, 1971.

Highlights significant musical elements. Background and descriptive remarks on both the *Creation* and the *Seasons*. Musical examples.

Sinfonia Concertante, Op. 84 in B-Flat Major

2060. Landon, H. C. Robbins. *Haydn: Chronicle and Works:* Vol. 3, *Haydn in England, 1791–1795*, 536–541. Bloomington: Indiana University Press, 1976.

Critical and analytic discussion of the *Sinfonia Concertante*. Musical examples.

Sonatas for Piano

2061. Brown, A. Peter. "The Structure of the Exposition of Haydn's keyboard Sonatas." *Music Review*, 36, no. 2 (1975): 102–129.

Thorough analyses focusing on the exposition. Musical examples.

2062. Fillion, Michelle. "Sonata-Exposition Proceedings in Haydn's Keyboard Sonatas." In *Haydn Studies*. Edited by Jens Peter Larsen, Howard Serwer, and James Webster, 475–481. Proceedings of the International Haydn Conference. New York: W. W. Norton, 1981.

An analytical study of the tonal organization of the sonata expositions in all the sonata-form first movements.

2063. Fisher, Fred. "Humor in the Haydn Sonatas." *Piano Teacher*, 7, no. 1 (1964): 13–17.

Identification and brief analysis of many "humorous" passages.

2064. Landon, H. C. Robbins. *Essays on the Viennese Classical Style: Gluck, Haydn, Mozart, Beethoven*, 44–67. London: Barrie and Rockliff, 1970.

Thorough review, showing stylistic traits. Critical remarks with musical examples.

2065. Matthews, Denis, ed. *Keyboard Music*, 108–141. New York: Praeger, 1972.

Background, historical perspective, stylistic traits, critical, and analytic observations on specific pieces. Musical examples.

2066. Pauly, Reinhard. *Music in the Classic Period.* 2d ed., 110–113. Englewood Cliffs, NJ: Prentice-Hall, 1973.

Brief overview of stylistic traits, with specific sonatas discussed in detail. Musical examples.

2067.   Radcliffe, Philip. "Keyboard Music." In *The New Oxford History of Music.* Vol. 7, *The Age of Enlightenment, 1745–1790.* Edited by Egon Wellesz and F. W. Sternfeld, 596–602. London: Oxford University Press, 1973.

> Brief overview, highlighting important stylistic characteristics. Musical examples.

2068.   Shamgar, Beth. "Rhythmic Interplay in the Retransition of Haydn's Piano Sonatas." *Journal of Musicology,* 3, no. 1 (1984): 55–68.

Sonata for Piano No. 37 in D Major

2069.   Bryant, Celia M. "Claiming our Musical Heritage." *Clavier,* 8, no. 3 (1969): 35–39

> Performer's analysis of first movement. Score included.

Sonata for Piano No. 48 in C Major

2070.   Cole, William. *The Form of Music: An Outline of Musical Designs Used by the Great Composers,* 48–49. London: Associated Board of the Royal Schools of Music, n.d.

> Brief outline of the structure in table form.

Sonata for Piano No. 49 in E-Flat Major

2071.   Schenker, Heinrich. *Five Graphic Music Analyses,* 40–43. New York: Dover Publications, 1969.

> Purely graphic analysis for the advanced student. There is no accompanying analytic commentary. Score necessary.

Sonata for Piano No. 52 in E-Flat Major

2072.   Moss, Lawrence K. "Haydn's Sonata Hob. XVI:52 (CHL. 62) in E♭ major: An Analysis of the First Movement." In *Haydn Studies.* Edited by Jens Peter Larsen, Howard Serwer, and James Webster, 496–501. Proceedings of the International Haydn Conference. New York: W. W. Norton, 1981.

> Measure-by-measure analysis. Some musical examples, but score needed to follow analysis.

2073.   Ratner, Leonard. *Classic Music: Expression, Form, and Style,* 412–421. New York: Schirmer Books, 1980.

Detailed analytic discussion. Topics covered include the combination of various styles, rhetorical character, texture, harmonic structure, forms. Musical examples.

2074.   Tovey, Donald Francis. *Essays in Musical Analysis: Chamber Music,* 93–105. London: Oxford University Press, 1944.
Analysis with musical examples.

Symphonies

2075.   Cole, Malcolm S. "Haydn's Symphonic Rondo Finales: Their Structural and Stylistic Evolution." *Haydn Yearbook,* 13 (1982): 113–142.

2076.   Fisher, Stephen C. "Sonata Procedures in Haydn's Symphonic Rondo Finales of the 1770's." In *Haydn Studies.* Edited by Jens Peter Larsen, Howard Serwer, and James Webster, 481–487. Proceedings of the International Haydn Conference. New York: W. W. Norton, 1981.
Refutes argument that Mozart influenced Haydn in the use of the sonata-rondo concept. Author provides clues supporting the view that Haydn had begun to conceive the idea of the sonata-rondo before he knew any of Mozart's works.

2077.   Hodgson, Antony. *The Music of Joseph Haydn: The Symphonies.* London: Tantivy Press, 1976, 222 pp.
Commentaries in a program-note style on all the symphonies. Includes general analytical comments on style and form—but no very thorough analyses. Musical examples.

2078.   Landon, H. C. Robbins. *Haydn: Chronicle and Works.* Vol. 3, 490–617. Bloomington: Indiana University Press, 1976.
Thorough discourse on the *Salomon* Symphonies (Nos. 96–104) and *Sinfonia Concertante.* Critical and analytic with musical examples.

2079.   Landon, H. C. Robbins. *Haydn Symphonies.* Seattle: University of Washington Press, 1969, 64 pp.
Critical and analytic commentary intended for the undergraduate student.

2080.   Pauly, Reinhard. *Music in the Classic Period,* 98–105. Englewood Cliffs, NJ: Prentice-Hall, 1965.
General analytic observations are illustrated with musical examples from specific works. The discussions are brief and general.

2081.   Rosen, Charles. *The Classical Style: Haydn, Mozart, Beethoven.* Rev. ed., 143–163. London: Faber and Faber, 1976.
Numerous analytic comments on structure, themes, and other unifying factors. Comments especially on Symphonies 46 and 92. Musical examples.

2082.   Sternfeld, Frederick W. "Instrumental Masterworks and Aspects of Formal Design." In *The New Oxford History of Music.* Vol. 7, *The Age of Enlightenment, 1745–1790.* Edited by Egon Wellesz and F. W. Sternfeld, 615–624. London: Oxford University Press, 1973.
Overview of Haydn's symphonic achievement. Musical examples.

2083.   Wolf, Eugene K. "The Recapitulations in Haydn's London Symphonies." *Musical Quarterly,* 52, no. 1 (1966): 71–89.
Advanced, close examination of Haydn's musical procedures in the recapitulations. Musical examples.

Symphony No. 6 in D Major ("Le Matin")

2084.   Stedman, Preston. *The Symphony,* 34–36. Englewood Cliffs, NJ: Prentice-Hall, 1979.
Brief description of form, thematic materials, instrumental and concerto elements. Musical examples and diagrams.

Symphony No. 31 in D Major ("Hornsignal")

2085.   Rosen, Charles. *Sonata Forms,* 217–221. New York: W. W. Norton, 1980.
Discussion of the use of instrumentation to articulate form in the first movement. Musical examples.

Symphony No. 44 in E Minor ('Trauersinfonie")

2086.   Stedman, Preston. *The Symphony,* 41–44. Englewood Cliffs, NJ: Prentice-Hall, 1979.
Brief description of form, orchestration, use of canon, and motivic organization. Musical examples and diagrams.

Symphony No. 45 in F-Sharp Minor ("Farewell")

2087.   Rosen, Charles. *Sonata Forms,* 156–160. New York: W. W. Norton, 1980.
Discussion of the structure of the first movement. Musical examples.

285

Symphony No. 55 in E-Flat Major

2088.   Rosen, Charles. *Sonata Forms*, 264–268. New York: W. W. Norton, 1980.
Identification of the "premature," "false," and "real" reprises in the first movement. Musical examples.

Symphony No. 88 in G Major

2089.   Haggin, B. H. *A Book of the Symphony*, 28–32. London: Oxford University Press, 1937.
Straightforward description dealing with formal plan only. Brief background remarks, with no discussion of tonality, rhythm, or texture. For the musical amateur or undergraduate student concerned with form. Musical examples.

2090.   Kerman, Joseph. *Listen*, 171–175. New York: Worth Publishers, 1972.
Analysis, with musical examples. For the undergraduate student.

2091.   Nadeau, Roland. *The Symphony: Structure and Style*, 64–71. Boston: Crescendo, 1973.
Measure-by measure analysis.

2092.   Tovey, Donald Francis. *Essays in Musical Analysis.* Vol. 1, 140–143. London: Oxford University Press, 1935.
Brief descriptive and critical commentary for the undergraduate student. A few analytic observations on form and motives. Musical examples.

Symphony No. 92 in G Major ("Oxford")

2093.   Haggin, B. H. *A Book of the Symphony*, 33–37. London: Oxford University Press, 1937.
Straightforward description dealing with formal plan only. Brief background remarks, with no discussion of tonality, rhythm, or texture. For the musical amateur or undergraduate student concerned with form. Musical examples.

2094.   Rosen, Charles. *The Classical Style: Haydn, Mozart, Beethoven*, 159–163. New York: Viking Press, 1971.
Analytic comments, with special emphasis on Haydn's treatment of sonata form. Musical examples.

2095. Tovey, Donald Francis. *Essays in Musical Analysis.* Vol. 1, 143–147. London: Oxford University Press, 1935.
   Descriptive and analytic commentary on form, themes, and orchestral color. Musical examples.

Symphony No. 94 in G Major ("Surprise")

2096.   Haggin, B. H. *A Book of the Symphony,* 38–44. London: Oxford University Press, 1937.
   Straightforward description dealing with formal plan only. Brief background remarks, with no discussion of tonality, rhythm, or texture. For the musical amateur or undergraduate student concerned with form. Musical examples.

2097.   Johns, Donald C. "In Defence of Haydn: The *Surprise* Symphony Revisited." *Music Review,* 24, no. 4 (1963): 305–312.
   Detailed analysis highlighting unusual features. Musical examples.

2098.   Machlis, Joseph. *The Enjoyment of Music.* 3d ed., 248–252. New York: W. W. Norton, 1970.
   Compact analysis for the undergraduate student. Musical examples.

2099.   Tovey, Donald Francis. *Essays in Musical Analysis.* Vol. 1, 147–148. London: Oxford University Press, 1935.
   Brief descriptive commentary intended for the undergraduate student. Analytic observations on form and themes. Musical examples.

Symphony No. 95 in C Minor

2100.   Tovey, Donald Francis. *Essays in Musical Analysis.* Vol. 1, 149–150. London: Oxford University Press, 1935.
   Brief descriptive overview of form. Musical examples.

Symphony No. 97 in C Major

2101.   Haggin, B. H. *A Book of the Symphony,* 45–49. London: Oxford University Press, 1937.
   Straightforward description dealing with formal plan only. Brief background remarks, with no discussion of tonality, rhythm, or texture. For the musical amateur or undergraduate student concerned with form. Musical examples.

Symphony No. 98 in B-Flat Major

2102. Tovey, Donald Francis. *Essays in Musical Analysis.* Vol. 1, 150–156. London: Oxford University Press, 1935.

Commentary on style, form, and themes for the undergraduate student. Musical examples.

Symphony No. 99 in E-Flat Major

2103. Cuyler, Louise. *The Symphony,* 30–34. New York: Harcourt Brace Jovanovich, 1973.

Measure-by-measure analysis.

2104. Tovey, Donald Francis. *Essays in Musical Analysis.* Vol. 1, 156–159. London: Oxford University Press, 1935.

Brief examination of the form and themes of this symphony. Musical examples.

Symphony No. 100 in G Major ("Military")

2105. Haggin, B. H. *A Book of the Symphony,* 50–64. London: Oxford University Press, 1937.

Straightforward description dealing with formal plan only. Brief background remarks, with no discussion of tonality, rhythm, or texture. For the musical amateur or undergraduate student concerned with form. Musical examples.

2106. Tovey, Donald Francis. *Essays in Musical Analysis.* Vol. 1, 159–162. London: Oxford University Press, 1935.

Descriptive commentary on form and themes. Musical examples.

2107. Warburton, A. O. "Set Works for 'O' Level, GCE." *Music Teacher,* 48 (August 1969): 11–12.

Measure-by-measure analysis for the intermediate student.

Symphony No. 101 in D Major ("Clock")

2108. Haggin, B. H. *A Book of the Symphony,* 55–60. London: Oxford University Press, 1937.

Straightforward description dealing with formal plan only. Brief background remarks, with no discussion of tonality, rhythm, or texture. For the musical amateur or undergraduate student concerned with form. Musical examples.

2109.   Ratner, Leonard. *Classic Music: Expression, Form, and Style,* 203–206. New York: Schirmer Books, 1980.
Detailed analysis of the first reprise of the Menuetto. Musical examples.

2110.   Tovey, Donald Francis. *Essays in Muscial Analysis.* Vol. 1, 162–164. London: Oxford University Press, 1935.
Descriptive commentary with analytic observations on form and themes. Musical examples.

Symphony No. 102 in B-Flat Major

2111.   Domek, Richard C. "Comment: Berry's Remarks on Tonality as Established by Means of a Melody with a General Reaction to His *Structural Functions in Music.*" *In Theory Only,* 2 (December 1976): 31–35.
Advanced analytic discussion, with musical examples.

2112.   Tovey, Donald Francis. *Essays in Musical Analysis.* Vol. 1, 164–170. London: Oxford University Press, 1935.
Descriptive and analytic comments on background, form, and themes. Musical examples.

Symphony No. 103 in E-Flat Major ("Drum Roll")

2113.   Boyden, David B. *An Introduction to Music.* 2d ed., 74–83. New York: Alfred A. Knopf, 1970.
Thorough analysis, with musical examples.

2114.   Cole, Malcolm S. "Momigny's Analysis of Haydn's Symphony No. 103." *Music Review,* 30, no. 4 (1969): 261–284.
A contemporary analysis (1806) of Haydn's symphony with modern commentary. Musical examples.

2115.   Geiringer, Karl, ed. *Franz Joseph Haydn: Symphony No. 103 in E-Flat Major.* Norton Critical Scores. New York: W. W. Norton, 1974, 116 pp.
Complete score, with historical background, analysis, views, and comments.

2116.   Haggin, B. H. *A Book of the Symphony,* 61–65. London: Oxford University Press, 1937.
Straightforward description dealing with formal plan only. Brief

background remarks, with no discussion of tonality, rhythm, or texture. For the musical amateur or undergraduate student concerned with form. Musical examples.

2117. Tovey, Donald Francis. *Essays in Musical Analysis.* Vol. 1, 170–173. London: Oxford University Press, 1935.
Brief commentary on background, form, and themes. Musical examples.

Symphony No. 104 in D Major ("London")

2118. Haggin, B. H. *A Book of the Symphony,* 66–71. London: Oxford University Press, 1937.
Straightforward description dealing with formal plan only. Brief background remarks, with no discussion of tonality, rhythm, or texture. For the musical amateur or undergraduate student concerned with form. Musical examples.

2119. Livingstone, Ernest F. "Unifying Elements in Haydn's Symphony No. 104." In *Haydn Studies.* Edited by Jens Peter Larsen, Howard Serwer, and James Webster, 493–496. Proceedings of the International Haydn Conference. New York: W. W. Norton, 1981.
Measure-by-measure analysis. Score needed.

2120. Stedman, Preston. *The Symphony,* 56–61. Englewood Cliffs, NJ: Prentice-Hall, 1979.
Brief description of formal structure, treatment of themes, and meter. Musical examples and diagrams.

2121. Tovey, Donald Francis. *Essays in Musical Analysis.* Vol. 1, 174–176. London: Oxford University Press, 1935.
Brief commentary on form and themes. Musical examples.

Trios for Baryton

2122. Wollenberg, Susan. "Haydn's Baryton Trios and the 'Gradus.'" *Music and Letters,* 54, no. 2 (1973): 170–178.
Fugal finales of these Trios examined for their close association with Fux's *Stylus Antiquus.* Musical examples.

Trios for Piano

2123. Rosen, Charles. *The Classical Style: Haydn, Mozart, Beethoven,* Rev. ed., 351–365. London: Faber and Faber, 1976.
Analytic and critical comments. Musical examples.

DISSERTATIONS AND THESES

General

2124.   Trimmer, Maud Alice. "Texture and Sonata Form in the Late String Chamber Music of Haydn and Mozart." Ph.D., City University of New York, 1981, 594 pp., DA 42-3805A-6A.

2125.   Wheelock, Gretchen Ann. "Wit, Humor, and the Instrumental Music of Joseph Haydn." Ph.D., Yale University, 1979, 322 pp., DA 43-2827A.

Quartets for Strings

2126.   Demaree, Robert William, Jr. "The Structural Proportions of the Haydn Quartets." Ph.D., Indiana University, 1973, 264 pp., DA 34-6682-3A.

Sonatas for Piano

2127.   Anderson, Charles Allen. "Some Aspects of Melodic Structure and Style in the Early and Middle-Period Keyboard Sonatas of Joseph Haydn." D.M.A., University of Illinois at Urbana, 1970, 183 pp., DA 31-4812A.

Symphonies

2128.   Bawel, Frederick Henry. "A Study of Developmental Techniques in Selected Haydn Symphonies." Ph.D., Ohio State University, 1972, 258 pp., DA 33-4450A-51A.

2129.   Butcher, Norma Perkins. "A Comparative-Analytical Study of Sonata-Allegro Form in the First Movements of the *London* Symphonies of Franz Joseph Haydn." Ph.D., University of Southern California, 1971, 179 pp., DA 32-4647A.

2130.   Grim, William Edward. "Form, Process, and Morphology in the *Sturm und Drang* Symphonies of Franz Joseph Haydn." Ph.D., Kent State University, 1985, 354 pp., Da 47-13A.

Trio for Piano, Violin, and Violoncello No. 26 in F Major

2131.   McGeary, George L. "A Structural and Interpretive Analysis and Performance of Piano Trios by Haydn, Schubert, and Ravel." Ed.D., Columbia University, 1973, 247 pp., DA 34-3702A.

HAYDN, JOHANN MICHAEL, 1737–1806

Concerto for Organ, Viola, and Strings in C Major

2132. Stout, K. I. "The Organ Works of Johann Michael Haydn." *Diapason*, 75 (May 1984): 8–9.
Stylistic traits of Haydn's organ writing and a brief analysis of the organ concerto. Musical examples and bibliography.

HENZE, HANS WERNER, 1926–

General

2133. Griffiths, Paul. *Modern Music: The Avant-Garde Since 1945*, 249–255. New York: George Braziller, 1981.
A brief analytic survey of the operas.

2134. Whittall, Arnold. *Music Since the First World War*, 255–260. London: J. M. Dent and Sons, 1977.
Analytic comments on Henze's output.

Bassarids

2135. Griffiths, Paul. "Hans Werner Henze Talks to Paul Griffiths." *Musical Times*, 115 (October 1974): 831–832.
Henze discusses *Bassarids'* libretto, musical form, and structural unity.

2136. Helm, Everett. "The *Bassarids:* Current Chronicle." *Musical Quarterly*, 53, no. 3 (1967): 408–413.
Description and analysis of various aspects of the opera, such as production, libretto, and form. Musical examples.

2137. Henderson, Robert. "Henze's Progress: From *Boulevard Solitude* to *The Bassarids*." *Opera*, 25 (October 1974): 851–857.
The place of *Bassarids* in Henze's creative output. Some discussion of the music.

Muzen Siziliens

2138. Helm, Everett. "*Muzen Siziliens:* Current Chronicle." *Musical Quarterly*, 53, no. 3 (1967): 413–415.
Mainly descriptive commentary with analytic observations. The work is viewed as Neoclassical. Musical examples.

HINDEMITH, PAUL, 1895–1963

General

2139. Beechey, Gwilyn. "Hindemith's Motets." *Musical Times*, 114 (December 1973): 1276–1277.
Brief descriptive commentary, with background information.

2140. Carner, Mosco. "Music in the Mainland of Europe: 1918–1939." In *The New Oxford History of Music.* Vol. 10, *The Modern Age: 1890–1960.* Edited by Martin Cooper, 327–338. London: Oxford University Press, 1974.
Stylistic overview discussing influences on Hindemith, his "utility" or *Gebrauchmusik*, and compositional idiom. *Mathis der Maler* and *Cardillac* among the works discussed specifically. Musical examples.

2141. Evans, Peter. "Music of the European Mainstream: 1940–1960." In *The New Oxford History of Music.* Vol. 10, *The Modern Age: 1890–1960.* Edited by Martin Cooper, 402–408. London: Oxford University Press, 1974.
Brief stylistic overview of Hindemith's later works (1940–1960), with analytic remarks on *Ludus Tonalis, The Four Temperaments, Die Harmonie der Welt,* and the revision of the song cycle *Das Marienleben.* Musical examples.

2142. Ferguson, Donald N. *Image and Structure in Chamber Music,* 292–296. Minneapolis: University of Minnesota Press, 1964.
Brief critical and analytic remarks on the chamber music.

2143. Gibson, Emily C. "A Study of the Major Organ Works of Paul Hindemith." *Diapason,* 62 (February 1971): 22–24.
Describes basic stylistic features with complete analyses of the three sonatas and two concertos. Musical examples.

2144. Kemp, Ian. *Hindemith.* London: Oxford University Press, 1971, 58 pp.
Brief critical and analytic overview of Hindemith's output. Musical examples.

2145. Klyce, Stephen W. "Hindemith's Madrigals: Some Analytical Comments." *American Choral Review,* 14, no. 2 (1972): 3–13.
Analytic remarks on the five-voiced madrigals.

2146.   Mason, Colin. "Some Aspects of Hindemith's Chamber Music." *Music and Letters*, 41, no. 2 (1960): 150–155.
General discussion touching on playability of Hindemith's works; offers general formal analysis as well.

2147.   Matthews, Denis, ed. *Keyboard Music*, 330–332. New York: Praeger, 1972.
Brief critical overview. Musical examples.

2148.   Neumeyer, David. *The Music of Paul Hindemith.* New Haven, CT: Yale University Press, 1986, 294 pp.
Thorough analytic survey of Hindemith's output. Chapter on the stages of the compositional process, the author's analytic method, followed by extensive analyses of the principal works. Musical examples.

2149.   Ulrich, Homer. *Chamber Music.* 2d ed., 359–362. New York: Columbia University Press, 1966.
Mainly about the quartets. A discussion of style and idiom.

2150.   Whittal, Arnold. *Music Since the First World War*, 69–75. London: J. M. Dent and Sons, 1977.
Very brief survey of style.

Concert Music for Strings and Brass

2151.   Stedman, Preston. *The Symphony*, 333–337. Englewood Cliffs, NJ: Prentice-Hall, 1979.
Description and analytic breakdown by section, supported by musical examples and diagram.

Ludus Tonalis: "Fuga Undecima in B"

2152.   Forte, Allen. *Contemporary Tone-Structures*, 91–106. New York: Columbia University Press, 1955.
Thorough analysis dealing with formal structure, tonality, internal relationships, and general stylistic characteristics. Musical examples and analytic sketches.

Mathis der Maler

2153.   Clendenin, William R. "The Spirit of Grünewald in Hindemith's Orchestral Suite *Mathis der Maler.*" *American Music Teacher*, 17, no. 4 (1968): 16–18.
Examines relationship of *Mathis der Maler* to Grünewald's *Isenheim Altar* paintings, which form the basis for Hindemith's opera.

2154. George, Graham. *Tonality and Musical Structure,* 194–197. London: Faber and Faber, 1970.
  Tonal analysis. Charts.

2155. Hansen, Peter. *An Introduction to Twentieth Century Music.* 2d ed., 267–270. Boston: Allyn and Bacon, 1967.
  Descriptive commentary, with analytic insights. For the undergraduate student. Musical examples.

2156. Machlis, Joseph. *Introduction to Contemporary Music,* 204–208. New York: W. W. Norton, 1961.
  Descriptive commentary for the undergraduate student. Musical examples.

2157. Watkins, Glenn. *Soundings: Music in the Twentieth Century,* 342–348. New York: Schirmer Books, 1987.
  Background, descriptive, and analytic commentary focusing on tonal plan. Hindemith's harmonic theory described and the works utilizing this principle identified. Musical examples.

Quartets for Strings

2158. Deri, Otto. *Exploring Twentieth-Century Music,* 395–410. New York: Holt, Rinehart, and Winston, 1968.
  Analysis with musical examples.

2159. Dorfman, J. "Thematic Organization in the String Quartets of Paul Hindemith." *Orbis Musicae: Studies in Musicology,* 6 (1978): 43–58.
  An examination of melodic and rhythmic elements of motives and themes for Quartets 4, 5, and 6 in particular. Includes comments on *Ludus Tonalis.* Musical examples.

Quartet for Strings No. 3

2160. Whittall, Arnold. *Music Since the First World War,* 71–73. London: J. M. Dent and Sons, 1977.
  Brief analytic comments. Musical examples.

Quartet for Strings No. 5

2161. Ferguson, Donald N. *Image and Structure in Chamber Music,* 294–295. Minneapolis: University of Minnesota Press, 1964.
  Brief analysis.

Serenaden, Op. 35: "Gute Nacht"

2162. Neumeyer, David. "Letter-Name Mottoes in Hindemith's *Gute nacht.*" *In Theory Only,* 2 (November 1976): 5–19.
   Deals with *Gute Nacht* section of this work only. Discusses counterpoint and pitch structure by way of examining the letter-name mottoes used in this section.

Sonata for Clarinet for Piano

2163. Kidd, James C. "Aspects of Mensuration in Hindemith's Clarinet Sonata." *Music Review,* 38, no. 3 (1977): 211–222.
   A discussion of the fourteenth-century compositional techniques Hindemith adopted for use in this sonata. Musical examples.

Sonata for Organ

2164. Milner, Arthur. "The Organ Sonatas of Paul Hindemith." *Musical Opinion,* 87 (June 1964): 533+.
   Brief critical overview, with musical examples.

Sonata for Organ No. 1

2165. Gibbs, Alan. "Organ Music of Our Century." *Musical Times,* 105 (February 1964): 134–135.
   Descriptive and analytic remarks with musical examples.

Sonata for Organ No. 3

2166. Trevor, Caleb H. "Hindemith's Third Sonata." *Musical Times,* 102 (January 1961): 44–45.
   Brief descriptive commentary from a performance standpoint, suggesting suitable registrations for each movement. Musical examples.

Sonata for Piano No. 2

2167. Bryant, Celia M. "Neo-classicism: Antique Style with a Modern Twist." *Clavier,* 7, no. 1 (1968): 21–23.
   Background and analysis. Musical examples.

Sonata for Violin, Op. 11, No. 2 in D Major

2168.   Ferguson, Donald N. *Image and Structure in Chamber Music,* 293–294. Minneapolis: University of Minnesota Press, 1964.
Brief analysis.

Symphonic Metamorphoses on Themes by Weber

2169.   Fenton, John. "Hindemith's *Symphonic Metamorphoses. Music Teacher,* 57 (February 1978): 19–21.
Analytic essay. Identifies the Weber pieces on which the *Symphonic Metamorphoses* are based and describes the formal structures and the tonal, harmonic, and thematic modifications of the originals. Musical examples.

Symphony for Band in B-Flat Major

2170.   Gallagher, Charles. "Hindemith's Symphony for Band." *Journal of Band Research,* 2, no. 1 (1966): 19–27.
An analysis of all three movements, identifying forms and themes.

Symphony in E-Flat

2171.   Steadman, Preston. *The Symphony,* 329–330. Englewood Cliffs, NJ: Prentice-Hall, 1979.
Brief description of formal structure.

Trio for Strings, No. 2

2172.   Redlich, Hans. "Paul Hindemith: A Reassessment." *Music Review,* 25, no. 3 (1964): 247–253.
An analysis emphasizing its static harmonic and tonal characteristics. Musical examples.

When Lilacs Last in the Dooryard Bloom'd

2173.   Robertson, Alec. *Requiem: Music of Mourning and Consolation,* 252–259. New York: Praeger Publishers, 1968.
Background, descriptive and critical commentary. Musical examples.

DISSERTATIONS AND THESES

General

2174.   Koper, Robert Peter. "A Stylistic and Performance Analysis of the Bassoon Music of Paul Hindemith." Ed.D., University of Illinois at Urbana, 1972, 364 pp., DA 33-349A.

2175.   Walker, Alvah John. "The A Capella Choral Music of Paul Hindemith." Ph.D., University of Rochester, Eastman School of Music, 1971, 416 pp., DA 32-7036A.

Harmonie der Welt

2176.   D'Angelo, James P. "Tonality and Its Symbolic Associations in Paul Hindemith's Opera *Die Harmonie der Welt*." Ph.D., New York University, 1983, 599 pp., DA 44-1966A.

Mass for Mixed Choir A Capella

2177.   Vantine, Bruce Lynn. "Four Twentieth-Century Masses: An Analytical Comparison of Style and Compositional Technique." D.M.A., University of Illinois at Urbana, 1982, 427 pp., DA 43-583 A-4A.

Quartets for Strings

2178.   Epsey, Jule Adele (Sister). "Formal, Tonal, and Thematic Structure of the Hindemith String Quartets." Ph.D., Indiana University, 1973, 193 pp., DA 34-6683A-4A.

Sonatas for Organ

2179.   Bolitho, Albert George. "The Organ Sonatas of Paul Hindemith." Ph.D., Michigan State University, 1968, 157 pp., DA 30-353A-4A.

Sonata for Piano No. 3

2180.   Thurston, Viscount Francis. "Hindemith's Third Piano Sonata: A New Assessment." D.M.A., Ohio State University, 1984, 51 pp., DA 45-1570A.

Sonatas for Wind Instruments

2181. Payne, Dorothy Katherine. "The Accompanied Wind Sonatas of Hindemith: Studies in Tonal Counterpoint." Ph.D., University of Rochester, Eastman School of Music, 1974, 227 pp., DA 35-2325A.

Symphony for Band in B-Flat Major

2182. Ferguson, Thomas Clarence. "An Analysis of Four American Symphonies for Band." Ph.D., University of Rochester, Eastman School of Music, 1971, 388 pp., DA 33-347A.

When Lilacs Last in the Dooryard Bloom'd

2183. Kovalenko, Susan Chaffins. "The Twentieth-Century Requiem: An Emerging Concept." Ph.D., Washington University, 1971, 336 pp., DA 34-6023A-4A.

HOFFMANN, E. T. A, 1776–1822

Undine

2184. Garlington, Aubrey S., Jr. "Notes on Dramatic Motives in Opera; Hoffmann's *Undine.*" *Music Review*, 32, no. 2 (May 1971): 136–145.
   Remarks on Hoffmann's use of leitmotiv and his influence on Weber. Musical examples.

HOLST, GUSTAV, 1874–1934

General

2185. Head, Raymond. "Holst and India: Maya to Sita." *Tempo*, 158 (September 1986): 2–7; 160 (March 1987): 27–37.
   A study of Indian influences on Holst and his music. Discusses sources, compositional style, and the cultural context. The most important works considered are *Sita* and *Savitri* (operas), *The Cloud Messenger* (cantata), and *Hymns from the Rig Veda*. Musical examples.

2186. Holst, Imogen. *The Music of Gustav Holst.* London: Oxford University Press, 1968, 169 pp.
   Mainly descriptive commentary and background. Some analytic insights. Special section on *The Planets*. Musical examples.

2187.   Holst, Imogen. *The Music of Gustav Holst/Holst's Music Reconsidered.* 3d ed. Oxford: Oxford University Press, 1985, 178 pp.
This book is a combination of Imogen Holst's two previous books, the first in a shortened revised edition and the latter simply reprinted. Essays on all the major works, with musical examples. The essays tend to be descriptive rather than analytic. Includes an index of works and chronology.

2188.   Hutchings, Arthur. "Music in Britain, 1916–1960." In *The New Oxford History of Music.* Vol. 10, *The Modern Age: 1890–1960.* Edited by Martin Cooper, 513–519. London: Oxford University Press, 1974.
Brief critical assessment and stylistic overview. Analytic remarks on *Hymn of Jesus.* Musical examples.

2189.   Lloyd, Stephen, and Edmund Rubbra, eds. *Edmund Rubbra's Collected Essays on Gustav Holst,* 23–39. London: Triad Press, 1974.
Brief analytic comments on a number of works. Musical examples.

Hymn of Jesus

2190.   Boyer, Daniel R. "Holst's *The Hymn of Jesus." Music Review,* 36, no. 4 (1975): 272–283.
Holst's use of devices such as plainsong, dance elements, spoken words, and harmony to suggest mysticism. Musical examples.

2191.   Wiles, Edward. "Holst: *The Hymn of Jesus." Music Teacher,* 55 (October 1976): 22–23.
Analysis of the themes and form.

Planets

2192.   Warburton, A. O. "Set Works for 'O' Level, GCE." *Music Teacher,* 49 (November 1970): 13–14 +.
"Mars" and "Venus" movements analyzed.

Savitri

2193.   Parrott, Ian. "Holst's *Savitri* and Bitonality." *Music Review,* 28, no. 4 (1967): 323–328.
Compares Holst with other composers and analyzes the bitonal aspects of the work. Musical examples.

Suite for Military Band No. 1, Op. 28a in E-Flat Major

2194.   Fennell, Frederick. "The Holst Suite in E-Flat." *Instrumentalist*, 29 (April 1975): 27–33.
Interspersed in a discussion of performance problems are several analytic remarks on each movement. Musical examples.

2195.   Udell, Budd. "Gustav Holst's First Suite in E-Flat Major for Military Band." *Music Educators Journal*, 69 (December 1982): 27–30.
Analysis weighted toward the first movement's chaconne. Interspersed with performance suggestions. Musical examples.

DISSERATIONS AND THESES

General

2196.   Mitchell, Jon Ceander. "Gustav Holst: The Works for Military Band." Ed.D., University of Illinois at Urbana, 1980, 314 pp., DA-41-5019A.

Hymn of Jesus

2197.   Boyer, Daniel Royce. "Gustav Holst's *The Hymn of Jesus.*" D.M.A., University of Texas at Austin, 1968, 142 pp., DA 29-3629A.

HONEGGER, ARTHUR, 1892–1955

General

2198.   Koopman, John. "Honegger As a Song Composer." *NATS Bulletin*, 32, no. 2 (1975): 12–14.
Honegger's philosophy as a composer, his style, and musical techniques in the songs briefly discussed. Bibliography.

Symphony No. 5

2199.   Hansen, Peter. *An Introduction to Twentieth Century Music.* 2d ed., 145–148. Boston: Allyn and Bacon, 1967.
Short analysis, with musical examples.

2200.   Machlis, Joseph. *Introduction to Contemporary Music,* 229–232. New York: W. W. Norton, 1961.
Descriptive, program-note style commentary with analytic observations.

HOVHANESS, ALAN, 1911–

DISSERTATIONS AND THESES

General

2201.   Rosner, Arnold. "An Analytical Survey of the Music of Alan Hovhaness." Ph.D., State University of New York at Buffalo, 1972, 377 pp., DA 33-779A.

Symphony No. 4

2202.   Ferguson, Thomas Clarence. "An Analysis of Four American Symphonies for Band." Ph.D., University of Rochester, Eastman School of Music, 1971, 388 pp., DA 33-347A.

HUMMEL, JOHANN NEPOMUK, 1778–1837

General

2203.   Brock, David G. "The Church Music of Hummel." *Music Review*, 31, no. 3 (1970): 249–254.
   Critical assessment. Not an analysis.

DISSERTATIONS AND THESES

Mass in B-Flat Major

2204.   Westlund, John Otto. "The Mass Settings of Johann Nepomuk Hummel: A Conductor's Analysis of the Mass in B-Flat." D.M.A., University of Iowa, 1975, 264 pp., DA 36-7726A-7A.

INDY, VINCENT D', 1851–1931

Symphony No. 2 in B-Flat Major

2205.   Cooper, Martin. *French Music: From the Death of Berlioz to the Death of Fauré*, 158–161. London: Oxford University Press, 1951.
   Comments on program and thematic structure.

ISAAC, HEINRICH, c. 1450–1517

General

2206.   Novack, Saul. "Fusion of Design and Tonal Order in Mass and Motet: Josquin Desprez and Heinrich Isaac." In *The Music Forum*, Vol. 2. Edited by William J. Mitchell and Felix Salzer, 187–263. New York: Columbia University Press, 1970.
   Formal design in various works analyzed. Advanced. Musical examples.

Alla Battaglia

2207.   McGee, Timothy J. "Vocal Music for a Renaissance Military Ceremony." *American Choral Review*, 25, no. 3 (1983): 3–11.
   Background, descriptive, and analytic commentary. Musical examples.

Missa Carminum

2208.   Novack, Saul. "Fusion of Design and Tonal Order in Mass and Motet: Josquin Desprez and Heinrich Isaac." In *The Music Forum*, Vol. 2. Edited by William J. Mitchell and Felix Salzer, 231–251. New York: Columbia University Press, 1970.
   Extensive analysis probing the relationship of design to tonality. Musical examples.

IVES, CHARLES, 1874–1954

General

2209.   Alexander, Michael J. "Bad Resolutions or Good?: Ives's Piano 'Take-Offs.' " *Tempo*, 158 (September 1986): 8–14.
   A brief consideration of Ives's experimental piano music. Discusses compositional technique, aesthetics, and style. Musical examples.

2210.   Bader, Yvette. "The Chamber Music of Charles Edward Ives." *Music Review*, 33, no. 4 (1972): 292–299.
   Descriptive and analytic commentary. Works discussed include *Central Park in the Dark; From the Steeples and the Mountains;* Violin Sonatas Nos. 1–4; and String Quartets Nos. 1 and 2.

303

2211.   Boatwright, Helen. "The Songs." *Music Educators Journal*, 61 (October 1974): 42–47.
Background and general stylistic traits examined.

2212.   Cowell, Henry, and Sidney Cowell. *Charles Ives and His Music.* 1955. Reprint. London: Oxford University Press, 1969, 253 pp.
Descriptive and analytic discussion of most of Ives's music. *Paracelsus, Concord* Sonata, and *Universe* Symphony discussed in detail. Musical examples.

2213.   Echols, Paul C. "The Music for Orchestra." *Music Educators Journal*, 61 (October 1974): 29–41.
Overview, with remarks on style. Musical examples.

2214.   Hinson, Maurice. "The Solo Piano Music of Charles Ives (1874–1954)." *Piano Quarterly*, 23, no. 88 (1974–1975): 32–35.
Descriptive and analytic overview.

2215.   Hitchcock, H. Wiley. *Ives.* New York: Oxford University Press, 1977, 96 pp.
Brief descriptive and analytic commentary on Ives's output. Musical examples.

2216.   Kumlien, Wendell C. "The Music for Chorus." *Music Educators Journal*, 61 (October 1974): 48–52.
An overview of selected choral works, including some general analytic comments.

2217.   Lamb, Gordon H. "Charles Ives, 1874–1954." *Choral Journal*, 15, no. 2 (1974): 12–13.
Brief critical remarks on the choral works.

2218.   Matthews, Denis, ed. *Keyboard Music*, 353–355. New York: Praeger, 1972.
Brief critical appraisal. Musical examples.

2219.   McCrae, Elizabeth. "The Piano Music." *Music Educators Journal*, 61 (October 1974): 53–57.
Comparison of several piano works with interspersed analytic comments. Musical examples.

2220.   Perry, Rosalie Sandra. *Charles Ives and the American Mind.* Kent, OH: Kent State University Press, 1974, 137 pp.
Discussion of Ives's total output from the standpoint of its place in American culture. Musical examples.

2221. Smith, Gregg. "Charles Ives: The Man and His Music." *Choral Journal*, 15, no. 3 (1974): 17–20.
Critical overview of Ives's choral works.

2222. Starr, Lawrence. "Charles Ives: The Next Hundred years—Towards a Method of Analysing the Music." *Music Review*, 38, no. 2 (1977): 101–111.
Since Ives's music is not stylistically homogeneous, it defies traditional analysis. If Ives's many styles are perceived as part of the form, an approach to a suitable method of analysis will have been made. Specific works analyzed. Musical examples.

2223. Tipton, Julius R. "Some Observations on the Choral Style of Charles Ives." *American Choral Review*, 12, no. 3 (1970): 99–105.
Brief analytic comments on Psalm XXIV and Three Harvest Chorales. Musical examples.

2224. Wuellner, Guy S. "The Smaller Piano Works of Charles Ives." *American Music Teacher*, 22, no. 5 (1973): 14–16.
Descriptive overview of the *Three-Page Sonata, Some South-Paw Pitching (1908), Three Protests*, and Three Quarter-Tone Pieces. Not analytic.

Ann Street

2225. Starr, Lawrence. "Style and Substance: *Ann Street* by Charles Ives." *Perspectives of New Music*, 15, no. 2 (1977): 23–33.
Analysis showing that the style of this piece is derived from its substance, or subject matter. Musical examples.

Celestial Country

2226. Balshaw, Paul A. *The Celestial Country.*" *Choral Journal*, 15, no. 7 (1975): 16–20.
Analysis, with musical examples.

Fourth of July

2227. Nelson, Mark D. "Beyond Mimesis: Transcendentalism and Processes of Analogy in Charles Ives' *The Fourth of July.*" *Perspectives of New Music*, 22, nos. 1–2 (1984): 353+.
Examination of how Ives "paints" the total experience of the Fourth of July by using musical devices suggesting the acoustic and psychological essence of the holiday. Musical examples.

General Booth Enters into Heaven

2228. Perry, Rosalie Sandra. *Charles Ives and the American Mind*, 36–39. Kent, OH: Kent State University Press, 1974.

An attempt to place Ives in the context of American intellectual history. Not principally about the music, but the musical examples chosen to illustrate the text do contain analytic insights. Musical examples.

Paracelsus

2229. Cowell, Henry, and Sidney Cowell. *Charles Ives and His Music*, 182–190. New York: Oxford University Press, 1955.

Analytic discussion. Musical examples.

Piano Study No. 22

2230. Dumm, Robert. "Performer's Analysis of an Ives Piano Piece." *Clavier*, 13, no. 7 (1974): 21–25.

Psalm 90

2231. Grantham, Donald. "A Harmonic Leitmotif System in Ives's Psalm 90." *In Theory Only*, 5 (May–June 1979): 3–14.

An examination of the assignment of particular harmonies to specific, captioned sections of the piece in the manner of leitmotives. Musical examples.

Serenity

2232. Green, Douglass M. "Exempli Gratia: A Chord Motive." *In Theory Only*, 4 (October 1978): 20–21.

A brief analysis of the function of the harmonic accompaniment. Also examines tonal centering. For the advanced student. Musical examples.

Sonata for Piano No. 1

2233. Boretz, Benjamin, and E. T. Cone, eds. *Perspectives on American Composers*, 14–24. New York: W. W. Norton, 1971.

Ives's use of hymn tunes in the scherzo movement of this work. Musical examples.

Sonata for Piano No. 2 ("Concord")

2234.   Burk, James M. "Ives' Innovations in Piano Music." *Clavier,* 13, no. 7 (1974): 14–16.
Good capsule commentary on Ives's new musical ideas and devices. Musical examples.

2235.   Clark, Sondra R. "The Element of Choice in Ives's *Concord* Sonata." *Musical Quarterly,* 60, no. 2 (1974): 167–186.
Demonstrates that Ives intended the performer to play an integral role in the creative process of the Sonata. Musical examples.

2236.   Clark, Sondra R. "Ives and the Assistant Soloist." *Clavier,* 13, no. 7 (1974): 17–20.
The composer's intentions examined with special focus on Ives's suggestion to use an "assistant soloist" to assist in technically difficult passages. Musical examples.

2237.   Cowell, Henry, and Sidney Cowell. *Charles Ives and His Music.* 190–201. New York: Oxford University Press, 1955.
Thorough analysis with musical examples.

2238.   Dahlhaus, Carl. *Nineteenth-Century Music.* Translated by J. Bradford Robinson, 385–386. Berkeley: University of California Press, 1989.
Brief but concentrated analytic remarks dwelling on dissonance and motives. Advanced.

2239.   Fisher, Fred. "Ives' *Concord* Sonata." *Piano Quarterly,* 24, no. 92 (1975–1976): 23–27.
Background and analytic remarks. Musical examples.

2240.   Hansen, Peter. *An Introduction to Twentieth Century Music.* 2d ed., 82–84. Boston: Allyn and Bacon, 1967.
Good descriptive commentary showing Ives's intentions. For the undergraduate student. Musical examples.

2241.   Perry, Rosalie Sandra. *Charles Ives and the American Mind,* 21–23, 31–35, 47–48, 52, 64–67, 94 +. Kent, OH: Kent State University Press, 1974.
An attempt to place Ives in the context of American intellectual history. Not principally about the music, but the musical examples chosen to illustrate the text do have some analytic comments associated with them.

2242. Reti, Rudolph. *Tonality, Atonality, Pantonality: A Study of Some Trends in Twentieth Century Music*, 63–65, 149–151. London: Rockliff, 1958.

Brief analytic comments on harmonic structure. Fourth movement only. Musical examples.

Sonatas for Violin and Piano

2243. Gratovich, Eugene. "The Violin Sonatas." *Music Educators Journal*, 61 (October 1974): 58–63.

A brief analysis of Sonatas Nos. 1 and 4. Musical examples.

2244. Gratovich, Eugene. "The Violin Sonatas of Charles E. Ives." *Strad*, 85 (December 1974): 471 + .

Background and analyses of the four violin sonatas and the hymn tunes used are identified. Musical examples.

Sonata for Violin and Piano No. 4

2245. Perry, Rosalie Sandra. *Charles Ives and the American Mind*, 44–46, 67. Kent, OH: Kent State University Press, 1974.

An attempt to place Ives in the context of American intellectual history. Not principally about the music, but the musical examples chosen to illustrate the text do contain some analytic insights. Musical examples.

Symphony No. 2

2246. Buechner, Alan. "Ives in the Classroom: A Teaching Guide to Two Compositions." *Music Educators Journal*, 61 (October 1974): 64–70.

Easy analysis for the undergraduate student.

2247. Charles, Sydney Robinson. "The Use of Borrowed Material in Ives' Second Symphony." *Music Review*, 28, no. 2 (May 1967): 102–111.

Traces the appearances of borrowed material and discusses Ives's use of them as structural elements.

2248. Sterne, Colin. "The Quotations in Charles Ives' Second Symphony." *Music and Letters*, 52, no. 1 (1971): 39–45.

Lists tunes Ives quoted in this Symphony and provides analytic commentary.

Symphony No. 4

2249.   Cyr, Gordon. "Intervallic Structural Elements in Ives's Fourth Symphony." *Perspectives of New Music*, 10, no. 1 (1971): 291–303.

2250.   Stone, Kurt. "Ives' Fourth Symphony: A Review." *Musical Quarterly*, 52, no. 1 (1966): 1–16.
A thorough discussion and description, citing American melodies Ives used throughout this symphony.

2251.   Watkins, Glenn. *Soundings: Music in the Twentieth Century*, 438–441. New York: Schirmer Books, 1987.
Brief description identifying borrowed hymns and tunes. Musical examples.

Three Places in New England

2252.   Machlis, Joseph. *Introduction to Contemporary Music*, 463–465. New York: W. W. Norton, 1961.
Brief descriptive commentary, with musical examples. For the undergraduate student.

Three Quarter-Tone Pieces for Two Pianos

2253.   Pappastavrou, George. "Ives' Quarter-Tone Pieces." *Clavier*, 13, no. 7 (1974): 31–32.
Descriptive commentary focusing on performance problems.

Universe Symphony

2254.   Cowell, Henry, and Sidney Cowell. *Charles Ives and His Music*, 201–203. New York: Oxford University Press, 1955.
Brief descriptive commentary.

Variations on America

2255.   Buechner, Alan. "Ives in the Classroom: A Teaching Guide to Two Compositions." *Music Educators Journal*, 61, no. 2 (1974): 64–70.
Analysis and background. Musical examples.

DISSERTATIONS AND THESES

General

2256.   Gingerich, Lora Louise. "Processes of Motivic Transformation in the Keyboard and Chamber Music of Charles E. Ives." Ph.D., Yale University, 1983, 288 pp., DA 44-2617A.

2257. Hurst, Rolland Wood. "A Study, Analysis, and Performance of Selected Songs by Charles Ives." Ed.D., Columbia University, 1971, 169 pp., DA 32-752A.

2258. Kumlien, Wendel Clark. "The Sacred Choral Music of Charles Ives: A Study in Style Development." D.M.A., University of Illinois, 1969, 576 pp., DA 30-2061A.

2259. Schoffman, Nachum. "The Songs of Charles Ives." Ph.D., Hebrew University of Jerusalem, 1977, 456 pp., DA 39-5205A.

2260. Winters, Thomas Dyer. "Additive and Repetitive Techniques in the Experimental Works of Charles Ives." Ph.D., University of Pennsylvania, 1986, 348 pp., DA 86-24038.

Quartet for Strings No. 2

2261. Cantrick, Susan Birdsall. "Charles Ives's String Quartet No. 2: An Analysis and Evaluation." M.M., Peabody Conservatory of Music, 1983, 153 pp., DA 22-280A.

Robert Browning Overture

2262. Hilliard, John Stanley. ". . . Charles Ives' *Robert Browning* Overture: Style and Structure." D.M.A., Cornell University, 1983, 167 pp., DA 44-317A.

Sonata for Piano No. 2 ("Concord")

2263. Albert, Thomas Russell. "The Harmonic Language of Charles Ives' *Concord* Sonata." D.M.A., University of Illinois at Urbana, 1974, 109 pp., DA 35-4580A.

2264. Clark, Sondra Rae. "The Evolving *Concord* Sonata: A Study of Choices and Variants in the Music of Charles Ives." Ph.D., Stanford University, 1972, 382 pp., DA 32-7027A.

2265. Palmer, Kenneth Robert. "A Performer's Guide to Charles Ives' Piano Sonata No. 2, *Concord*, Mass., 1840–1860." Ph.D., Washington University, 1986, 135 pp., DA 47-4228A.

Symphonies

2266. Badolato, James Vincent. "The Four Symphonies of Charles Ives: A Critical, Analytical Study of the Musical Style of Charles Ives." Ph.D., Catholic University of America, 1978, 231 pp., DA 39-1912A.

2267. Eiseman, David. "Charles Ives and the European Symphonic Tradition: A Historical Reapprasial." Ph.D., University of Illinois at Urbana, 1972, 279 pp., DA 33-347A.

2268. Magers, Roy Vernon. "Aspects of Form in the Symphonies of Charles E. Ives." Ph.D., Indiana University, 1975, 392 pp., DA 36-2482A.

Symphony No. 4

2269. Brooks, William Fordyce. "Sources and Errata List for Charles Ives' Symphony No. 4, Movement 2." D.M.A., University of Illinois at Urbana, 1976, 170 pp., DA 37/05-A

2270. Lipkis, Larry Alan. "Aspects of Temporality in Debussy's *Jeux* and Ives's Symphony No. 4, Fourth Movement." Ph.D., University of California at Santa Barbara, 1984, 100 pp., DA 45-2689A.

Three Places in New England

2271. Stein, Alan. "The Musical Language of Charles Ives' *Three Places in New England.*" D.M.A., University of Illinois at Urbana, 1975, 231 pp., DA 36-6362LA-3A.

Three-Page Sonata

2272. Joyce, Sister Mary Ann. "Charles E. Ives: An Analysis and a Corrected Version." Ph.D., Washington University, 1970, 122 pp., DA 31-6099A.

2273. Shelton, Gregory Allard. "An Analysis of Charles Ives's *Three-Page* Sonata for Piano." M.A., American University, 1985, 238, pp., DA 23-415A.

JANÁČEK LEOŠ, 1854–1928

General

2274. Abraham, Gerald. *Slavonic and Romantic Music,* 86–98. London: Faber and Faber, 1968.
Discussion of "realism" in Janáček's operas, with analytic comments and musical examples.

2275. Chisholm, Erik. *The Operas of Leoš Janáček.* London: Oxford University Press, 1971, 390 pp.
Thorough treatment of the operas, including background, sources, synopses, and analyses. Musical examples.

2276. Ewans, Michael. *Janáček's Tragic Operas.* London: Faber and Faber, 1977, 284 pp.
Extended discussion of the plot, music, dramatic techniques, and musical characterization. The discussions focus on the dramaturgy and the ways in which Janáček supports it through orchestration, thematic ideas, texture, and other musical devices. Musical examples.

2277. Hollander, Hans. *Leoš Janáček: His Life and Work,* 124–153. Translated by Paul Hamburger. London: John Calder, 1963.
General discussion of musical and dramatic elements as well as Janáček's choice of libretti. An overview of all his operas.

2278. Tyrrell, John. "Janácek and the Speech-Melody Myth." *Musical Times,* 111 (August 1970): 793–796.
Author argues that Janáček often fitted text to previously composed music, rather than the reverse procedure. Musical examples.

2279. Vogel, Jaroslav. *Leoš Janáček: His Life and Works.* Translated by G. Thomsen-Muchova. London: Hamlyn, 1962, 426 pp.
A descriptive overview, with analytic observations on Janáček's output. Traces motifs in the operas. Musical examples.

2280. Whittall, Arnold. *Music Since the First World War,* 101–104. London: J. M. Dent and Sons, 1977.
Analytic observations. Musical examples.

Excursions of Mr. Broucek

2281. Matejcek, Jan. "Janáček's *Excursions.*" *Opera,* 21 (August 1970): 721–726.
Critical commentary, with discussion of Janáček's "speech-melody" theory and musical styles.

Jenufa

2282. Freeman, John. "Born of Suffering." *Opera News,* 39 (December 21, 1974): 20–21.
Brief descriptive remarks, with musical examples.

2283. Robinson, Harlow. "The Folk-Connection." *Opera News,* 50 (January 4, 1986): 18 + .
Brief discussion of Janáček's theory of following the melodic curves of speech ("speech-song").

Kát'a Kabanová

2284.   Tyrrell, John. *Leoš Janáček: "Kát'a Kabanová."* Cambridge: Cambridge University Press, 1982, 234 pp.
Book-length treatment, with sections on the libretto, compositional history, stage history, and reception, interpretations, and analysis of the music. Musical examples.

DISSERTATIONS AND THESES

General

2285.   Acord, Thomas Wadsworth. "An Examination of Leoš Janáček's Compositions for Solo Voice and Piano." D.M.A., University of Texas at Austin, 1981, 302 pp., DA 42-1042A.

2286.   Kaderavek, Milan Robert. "Stylistic Aspects of the Late Chamber Music of Leoš Janáček: An Analytic Study." D.M.A., University of Illinois at Urbana, 1970, 284 pp., DA 31-6649A.

JOACHIM, JOSEPH, 1831–1907

Concerto for Violin, Op. 11 in D Major ("Hungarian")

2287.   Swalin, Benjamin F. *The Violin concerto: A Study in German Romanticism,* 82–87. Chapel Hill: University of North Carolina Press, 1941.
Critical and analytic remarks. Musical examples.

JOSQUIN DESPREZ, c. 1440–1521

General

2288.   Bridgman, Nanie. "The Age of Ockeghem and Josquin." In *The new Oxford History of Music.* Vol. 3, *Ars Nova and the Renaissance, 1300–1540.* Edited by Dom Anselm Hughes and Gerald Abraham, 262–272. London: Oxford University Press, 1960.
Critical overview of the masses, motets, and secular music. Musical examples.

2289.   Mattfeld, Jacquelyn A. "Some Relationships Between Texts and Cantus Firmi in the Liturgical Motets of Josquin des Pres." *Jour-*

nal of the American Musicological Society, 14, no. 2 (1961): 159–183.
In-depth study of sources and setting of Josquin's motets. Includes analytic comments and detailed historic commentary.

2290. Novack, Saul. "Fusion of Design and Tonal Order in Mass and Motet: Josquin Desprez and Heinrich Isaac." In *The Music Forum.* Vol. 2. Edited by William J. Mitchell and Felix Salzer, 187–263. New York: Columbia University Press, 1970.
Formal design in various works analyzed. For the advanced student. Musical examples.

2291. Reese, Gustave. *Music in the Renaissance.* Rev. ed., 228–260. New York: W. W. Norton, 1959.
Detailed analytic description of Josquin's output, arranged by genre. Musical examples.

2292. Ruff, Lillian M. "Some Formal Devices in Josquin's Motets." *Consort*, 25 (1968–1969): 362–372.
In-depth study of Josquin's motets by type and number of voices. In each category, the setting of the text, compositional devices, and formal considerations, including cadences, are examined. Musical examples.

Ave Maria, gratia plena

2293. Judd, Christle C. "Some Problems of Pre-Baroque Analysis: An Examination of Josquin's *Ave Maria.*" *Music Analysis*, 4, no. 3 (1985): 201–239.
An analytical essay exploring aspects of the text, mode, articulation of structure, pitch organization, and tonal structure. For the advanced student. Musical examples, tables, and diagrams.

In Illo Tempore Assumpsit Jesus Duodecim Discipulos

2294. Novack, Saul. "Fusion of Design and Tonal Order in Mass and Motet: Josquin Desprez and Heinrich Isaac. " In *The Music Forum.* Vol. 2. Edited by William J. Mitchell and Felix Salzer, 196–200. New York: Columbia University Press, 1970.
Brief but concentrated analysis revealing the relationship of design to tonality. Musical examples.

Masses

2295. Wagner, Roger. "An Introduction to Three Masses of Josquin." *Caecilia*, 85 (February 1958): 15–39.

Describes the use of the cantus firmus in each work under discussion: *Missa Hercules dux Ferrariae, Missa L'Homme Armé Sexti Toni, Missa Ave Maris Stella.* Also describes formal divisions and polyphonic devices used by Josquin. Musical examples.

Miserere Mei, Deus

2296.   Novack, Saul. "Fusion of Design and Tonal Order in Mass and Motet: Josquin Desprez and Heinrich Isaac." In *The Music Forum.* Vol. 2. Edited by William J. Mitchell and Felix Salzer, 251–263. New York: Columbia University Press, 1970.
Concentrated analysis probing the relationship of design to tonality. Musical examples.

Missa Da Pacem

2297.   Ulrich, Homer. *Music: A Design for Listening,* 198–200. New York: Harcourt, Brace, 1957.
Analytic breakdown by measure. Score needed to follow analysis.

Missa L'Homme Armé: Benedictus

2298.   Cogan, Robert, and Pozzi Escot. *Sonic Design: The Nature of Sound and Music,* 17–24, 254–258. Englewood Cliffs, NJ: Prentice-Hall, 1976.
An analysis of spatial aspects and the relationship between the voices. Includes a rhythmic reduction of the piece for purposes of analysis.

Missa Pange Lingua

2299.   Kerman, Joseph. *Listen.* 2d ed., 64–66. New York: Worth Publishers, 1976.
Brief analysis for the undergraduate student. Musical examples.

2300.   Novack, Saul. "Fusion of Design and Tonal Order in Mass and Motet: Josquin Desprez and Heinrich Isaac." In *The Music Forum.* Vol. 2. Edited by William J. Mitchell and Felix Salzer, 206–231. New York: Columbia University Press, 1970.
Extensive analysis probing the relationship of design to tonality. Musical examples.

Plus nulz regretz

2301.   Aldrich, Putnam. "An Approach to the Analyses of Renaissance Music." *Music Review*, 30, no. 1 (1969): 2 + .
Thorough analysis. Musical examples.

2302.   Reynolds, Christopher. "Musical Evidence of Compositional Planning in the Renaissance: Josquin's *Plus nulz regretz.*" *Journal of the American Musicological Society*, 40, no. 1 (1987): 53–81.
A detailed discussion of the structure of the chanson. Examines structural and motivic relationships between the text and the music and hypothesizes on Josquin's use of proportion to plan the structure. For the advanced student. Musical examples and tables.

Sancti Dei Omnes

2303.   Novack, Saul. "Fusion of Design and Tonal Order in Mass and Motet: Josquin Desprez and Heinrich Isaac." In *The Music Forum.* Vol. 2. Edited by William J. Mitchell and Felix Salzer, 195–196. New York: Columbia University Press, 1970.
Brief examination of the relationship of design to tonality. Musical examples.

KABALEVSKY, DMITRI, 1904–1987

Easy Variations, Op. 40, No. 1 in D Major

2304.   Warburton, A. O. "Set Works for 'O' Level, GCE." *Music Teacher*, 53 (January 1974): 14–15.
A brief description of important features of each variation.

DISSERTATIONS AND THESES

Requiem

2305.   Kovalenko, Susan Chaffins. "The Twentieth-Century Requiem: An Emerging Concept." Ph.D., Washington University, 1971, 336 pp., DA 34-6023A-4A.

KAY, ULYSSES, 1917–

Choral Triptych

2306.   Herrema, Robert D. "The Choral Works of Ulysses Kay." *Choral Journal*, 11, no. 4 (1970): 5–10.

An interview with the composer and a general analysis of his *Choral Triptych*, a setting of two psalms. Includes form, instrumentation, rhythm, and melodic features. Musical examples.

DISSERTATIONS AND THESES

General

2307. Hadley, Richard Thomas. "The Published Choral Music of Ulysses Simpson Kay—1943 to 1968." Ph.D., University of Iowa, 1972, 358 pp., DA 33-3694A-5A.

2308. Hayes, Laurence Melton. "The Music of Ulysses Kay, 1939–1963." Ph.D., University of Wisconsin, 1971, 405 pp., DA 32-3351A.

Fantasy Variations

2309. Wyatt, Lucius Reynolds. "The Mid-Twentieth-Century Orchestral Variation, 1953–1963." Ph.D., University of Rochester, Eastman School of Music, 1974, 504 pp., DA 34-7273A.

Jubilee

2310. Davidson, Celia Elizabeth. "Operas by Afro-American Composers: A Critical Survey and Analysis of Selected Works." Ph.D., Catholic University of America, 1980, 526 pp., DA 41-452A.

KODÁLY, ZOLTÁN, 1882–1967

General

2311. Eösze, Laszlo. *Zoltán Kodály: His Life and Work.* Translated by I. Farkas and G. Gulyas. London: Collet's, 1962, 183 pp.
Analytic overview of Kodály's output. Musical examples.

2312. Jolly, Cynthia. "The Art Songs of Kodály." *Tempo*, 63 (Winter 1962–1963): 2–12.
Stylistic observations on a selection of songs. Musical examples.

2313. Mason, Colin. "Kodály and Chamber Music." *Studia Musicologica*, 3, nos. 1–4 (1962): 251–254.
A brief, general survey with a few analytical remarks.

317

2314. Stevens, Halsey. "The Choral Music of *Zoltán Kodály.*" *Musical Quarterly*, 54, no. 2 (1968): 147–168.

Examination of various choral styles, with some focus on stylistic inconsistencies in larger works. Includes historical background and origin of texts. Musical examples.

Dances of Galanta

2315. Sarosi, Balint. "Instrumental Folk Music in Kodály's Works: The *Galanta* and *Marosszék* Dances." *Studia Musicologica*, 25, nos. 1–4 (1983): 23–38.

Background and commentary about the original dances and Kodály's adaptation of them in this composition. Occasional analytic remarks. Musical examples.

Háry János Suite

2316. Brown, Alan. "Set Works for 'O' Level, GCE. *Music Teacher*, 54 (July 1975): 12–13.

Brief remarks on the programmatic aspects of this work.

Missa Brevis

2317. Pickar, Catherine J. "An Analytical Process Applied to Kodály's *Missa Brevis.*" *Choral Journal*, 26, no. 3 (1985): 7–12.

Pange Lingua

2318. Mahaffy, Dorothy. "Kodály's Legacy to Organ Students." *Clavier*, 21, no. 10 (1982): 32–33.

Brief analytic and descriptive remarks. Musical examples.

Psalmus Hungaricus

2319. Warburton, A. O. "Set Works for 'O' Level, GCE." *Music Teacher*, 50 (January 1971): 15–26.

Background and analysis.

Symphony in C Major

2320. Weissman, John S. "Kodály's Symphony: A Morphological Study." *Tempo*, 60 (Winter 1961–1962): 19–22 +.

Extended analytical observations. Includes musical examples and discussion of the work's position in Kodály's output.

DISSERTATIONS AND THESES

General

2321. Steen, Philip Lewis. "Zoltán Kodály's Choral Music for Children and Youth Choirs." Ph.D., University of Michigan, 1970, 225 pp., DA 31-6653A.

KOECHLIN, CHARLES, 1867–1950

General

2322. Cooper, Frank. "Sleeping Beauty—The Pianistic Legacy of Charles Koechlin." *Clavier*, 8, no. 9 (1969): 18–25.
Brief analytic and critical overview of Koechlin's piano output. The *Sonatines, School of Legato Playing, Landscapes and Seascapes,* and *Persian Hours* are some of the pieces discussed.

Jungle Book

2323. Kirk, Elise E. "Koechlin's Neglected *Le Livre de la Jungle.*" *Musical Quarterly*, 64, no. 2 (1978): 229–237.
Background, critical appraisal, and descriptive commentary.

Paysages et marines, Op. 63

2324. Sharon, Boaz. "Music of Charles Koechlin." *Clavier*, 20, no. 2 (1981): 14–19.
Stylistic and analytic commentary. Musical examples and bibliography.

DISSERTATIONS AND THESES

General

2325. Kirk, Elise Kuhl. "The Chamber Music of Charles Koechlin (1867–1950)." Ph.D., Catholic University of America, 403 pp., DA 38-1728A-9A.

KRENEK, ERNEST, 1900–

General

2326. Riedel, Johannes. "A Twelve Tone Setting of the Mass." *Sacred Music*, 103, no. 2 (1976): 24–31.
A discussion of the row and its varied appearance in different parts of the Mass. Musical examples.

Karl V

2327.   Zenck, Claudia M. "The Ship Loaded with Faith and Hope: Krenek's *Karl V* and the Viennese Politics of the Thirties." *Musical Quarterly,* 71, no. 2 (1985): 116–134.

Krenek's political viewpoints on Vienna in the 1930s, with analysis of twelve-tone style in this work and its relation to the text. Also, brief performance history.

Suite for Cello Solo, Op. 84

2328.   Perle, George. *Serial Composition and Atonality: An Introduction to the Music of Schoenberg, Berg, and Webern.* 5th ed., rev., 64–67. Berkeley: University of California Press, 1981.

Analysis of pitch content.

LALO, EDOUARD, 1823–1892

Roi d'ys

2329.   Cooper, Martin. *French Music: From the Death of Berlioz to the Death of Fauré,* 36–37. London: Oxford University Press, 1951.

Short, critical remarks on Wagner's influence and Lalo's distinctive musical contribution to French opera.

LASSUS, ORLANDO, 1532–1594

General

2330.   Coates, Henry, and Gerald Abraham. "The Perfection of the A Capella Style." In *The New Oxford History of Music.* Vol. 4, *The Age of Humanism, 1540–1630.* Edited by Gerald Abraham, 333–350. London: Oxford University Press, 1968.

Masses, motets, psalms, and *Magnificat* of Lassus are discussed critically and analytically. Musical examples.

2331.   Einstein, Alfred. *The Italian Madrigal.* Vol. 2. Translated by Alexander H. Krappe, Roger H. Sessions, and Oliver Strunk, 477–498. Princeton, NJ: Princeton University Press, 1949.

Excellent discourse on the madrigals for the more advanced student. Musical examples.

2332.   Roche, Jerome. *Lassus.* London: Oxford University Press, 1982, 58 pp.

A detailed and technical study of Lassus's music. Organization is by genre: motets, masses, other liturgical music, madrigals, villanellas, chansons, and *Lieder.* Includes a source-list of books. Musical examples.

2333.   Sternfeld, Frederick W., et al., eds. *Essays on Opera and English Music in Honour of Sir Jack Westrup,* 84–102. Oxford: Blackwell, 1975.

Stylistic analysis to show how Lassus anticipates monodic style even in his sacred works. Musical examples.

2334.   Van den Borren, Charles. "The French Chanson." In *The New Oxford History of Music.* Vol. 4, *The Age of Humanism, 1540–1630.* Edited by Gerald Abraham, 21–25. London: Oxford University Press, 1968.

Brief assessment of Lassus's unique contribution to the chanson.

"Bon jour, mon coeur"

2335.   Cogan, Robert, and Pozzi Escot. *Sonic Design: The Nature of Sound and Music,* 130–141. Englewood Cliffs, NJ: Prentice-Hall, 1976.

Harmonic analysis of this chanson. Includes reduction score examples and musical examples.

Masses

2336.   Scheibert, Beverly. "Orlando di Lasso and His Masses." *American Organist,* 16 (March 1982): 48–50.

Background, parody techniques, stylistic traits discussed. Musical examples and bibliography.

Prophetiae Sibyllarum

2337.   Berger, Karol. "Tonality and Atonality in the Prologue to Orlando di Lasso's *Prophetiae Sibyllarum." Musical Quarterly,* 66, no. 4 (1980): 484 + .

LAWES, HENRY, 1596–1662

General

2338.   Spink, Ian. *English Songs: Dowland to Purcell,* 74–79. London: B. T. Batsford, 1974.

321

An analytic discussion of the songs. Places the composer in historical context, identifies stylistic traits and relationships between text and music. Musical examples.

LEONIN, fl. 1163–1190

General

2339.   Harman, Alec. *Man and His Music: Medieval and Renaissance Music*, 53–64. New York: Schocken Books, 1969.
Overview of Leonin's style, technique, and importance. Leonin compared briefly to Perotin. Musical examples.

LIGETI, GYÖRGY, 1923–

General

2340.   Griffiths, Paul. *György Ligeti.* London: Robson Books, 1983, 128 pp.
An introduction to the music of Ligeti through an examination of ideas and techniques. The commentaries are more descriptive than analytic, but there are many musical examples, details of compositional techniques, and analytic comments. There are chapters dedicated to major works, *Atmosphères, Aventures, Le Grand Macabre,* with other works being grouped in the remaining chapters.

2341.   Thomas, Janet. "Ligeti's Organ Music." *Musical Times,* 124 (May 1983): 319+.
An overview of Ligeti's small output for organ, focusing on its textural and sonorous aspects. Musical examples.

2342.   Whittall, Arnold. *Music Since the First World War*, 242–246. London: J. M. Dent and Sons, 1977.
Brief analytic comments on a variety of works. One musical example from *Lontano.*

Etudes for Organ

2343.   Collins, D. "Avant-Garde Techniques in the Organ Works of György Ligeti." *Diapason,* 73 (January 1982): 10–11.
Stylistic features of Ligeti's writing and innovative compositional techniques discussed. Musical examples and bibliography.

Lontano

2344. Rollin, Robert L. "The Genesis of the Technique of Canonic Sound Mass in Ligeti's *Lontano.*" *Indiana Theory Review*, 2, no. 2 (1979): 23–33.

Requiem

2345. Nordwall, Ove. "Current Chronicle: Sweden." *Musical Quarterly*, 52, no. 1 (1966): 109–113.
Review of a performance, with analytic observations on style and symbolism.

DISSERTATIONS AND THESES

General

2346. Yannay, Yehuda. "Toward an Open-Ended Method of Analysis of Contemporary Music: A Study of Selected Works by Edgard Varèse and György Ligeti." D.M.A., University of Illinois at Urbana, 1974, 163 pp., DA 35-7952A-3A.

Atmosphères

2347. Van der Slice, John DeWitt. "An Analysis of György Ligeti's *Atmosphères.*" D.M.A., University of Illinois at Urbana, 1980, 51pp., DA 41-457A.

LISZT, FRANZ, 1811–1886

General

2348. Bakken, Howard. "Liszt and the Organ." *Diapason*, 60 (May 1969): 27–29.
Ad nos Salutarem, Mass for Organ, Zwei Kirchenhymnen analyzed. Musical examples and bibliography.

2349. Beckett, Walter. *Liszt.* London: J. M. Dent and Sons, 1963, 185 pp.
Descriptive and critical commentary intended for the intelligent layman and undergraduate student. Musical examples.

2350.   Brendel, Alfred. "Liszt's 'Bitterness of Heart' (Late Piano Pieces)." *Musical Times,* 122 (April 1981): 234–235.
Brief discussion of the late piano peices, showing how they herald the music of the twentieth century.

2351.   Collet, Robert. "Works for Piano and Orchestra." In *Franz Liszt: The Man and His Music.* Edited by Alan Walker, 258–273. New York: Taplinger, 1970.
Full descriptive, critical, and analytic treatment. Musical examples.

2352.   Dale, Kathleen. *Nineteeth-Century Piano Music: A Handbook for Pianists.* London: Oxford University Press, 1954, 320 pp.
Highlights stylistic traits and unique contribution to the literature of the piano. Form, harmony, and other musical aspects discussed in relation to style.

2353.   Douglas, John. "Franz Liszt As a Song Composer." *NATS Journal,* 43, no. 4 (1987): 4–15.
Descriptive introduction to Liszt's songs. More a description of general characteristics than a detailed analysis. Musical examples.

2354.   Einstein, Alfred. *Music in the Romantic Era,* 209–212. New York: W. W. Norton, 1947.
Specific works not discussed in detail, but Liszt's romantic impulse well portrayed.

2355.   Fowler, Andrew. "Multilevel Motivic Projection in Selected Piano Works of Liszt." *Journal of the American Liszt Society,* 16 (1984): 20–34.
Analysis for the advanced student. Derived from Schenker's concept of "hidden repetitions" and Schoenberg's "Grundgestalt." Works discussed are *Funérailles, Pensée des Morts, Sonetto 47 del Petrarca, Après une Lecture du Dante.*

2356.   Hsu, Dolores M. "The French Melodies of Franz Liszt." *NATS Bulletin,* 34, no. 2 (1977): 25–29.
A discussion of Liszt's songs employing French texts. Background, descriptive, and analytic commentary. Musical examples and bibliography.

2357.   Hutchins, Farley K. "Organ Music of Franz Liszt." *Clavier,* 18, no. 2 (1979): 27–31 +.
Overview focusing on background, stylistic characteristics, and borrowed material. No musical examples.

2358. Kaplan, Richard. "Sonata Form in the Orchestral Works of Liszt: The Revolutionary Reconsidered." *Nineteenth Century Music,* 8, no. 2 (1984): 142–152.

> The *Faust* Symphony, *Tasso, Les Préludes, Orpheus,* and *Prometheus* discussed and analyzed. Musical examples.

2359. Matthews, Denis, ed. *Keyboard Music,* 243–253. New York: Praeger, 1972.

> Background, historical perspective, critical observations, and capsule commentaries on many pieces. Musical examples.

2360. Pisk, Paul A. "Elements of Impressionism and Atonality in Liszt's Last Piano Pieces." *Radford Review,* 23 (Summer 1969): 170–176.

> Structural and harmonic analyses of seven piano pieces (written during or after 1880) in which Liszt experimented with new devices.

2361. Plantinga, Leon. *Romantic Music,* 180–189. New York: W. W. Norton, 1984.

> Analytic comments on the piano music. Musical examples.

2362. Searle, Humphrey. "Liszt's Organ Music." *Musical Times,* 112, (June 1971): 597–598.

> An overview showing Liszt's stylistic evolution toward the suspension of tonality. Musical examples.

2363. Searle, Humphrey. *The Music of Liszt.* 2d ed., rev. New York: Dover Publications, 1966, 207 pp.

> Overview with descriptive, critical, and analytic commentary. Musical examples.

2364. Sutter, Milton. "Liszt, and His Role in the Development of Nineteenth Century Organ Music." *Music (AGO),* 9 (January 1975): 35–39.

2365. Walker, Alan, ed. *Franz Liszt: The Man and His Music.* New York: Taplinger, 1970, 471 pp.

> Thorough overview of all Liszt's works. Critical, descriptive, and analytic, with musical examples.

2366. Walker, Alan. "Liszt and the Schubert Song Transcriptions." *Musical Quarterly,* 67, no. 1 (1981): 50–63.

> A description of Liszt's method and purpose in writing these transcriptions. Musical examples.

Album d'un Voyageur

2367. Kirby, Frank E. "Liszt's Pilgrimage." *Piano Quarterly*, 23, no. 89 (1975): 17–21.

Background and analytic observations on this model for *Années de Pèlerinage*. No musical examples.

2368. Main, Alexander. "Liszt's Lyon: Music and the Social Conscience." *Nineteenth Century Music*, 4, no. 3 (1981): 228–243.

Background with evaluative and descriptive commentary. Musical examples.

Après une lecture du Dante

2369. Dahlhaus, Carl. *Nineteenth-Century Music.* Translated by J. Bradford Robinson. Berkeley: University of California Press, 1989, 135–136.

Brief but concentrated examination of form, sytle, motives and variations to demonstrate Liszt's absorption of Paganini's virtuoso technique. Musical examples. Advanced.

2370. Newman, William S. *The Sonata Since Beethoven.* 3d ed., 369–372. New York: W. W. Norton, 1983.

Brief but compact analysis accompanied by chart displaying themes, keys, tempos, and dynamics of this work from the second year of *Années de Pèlerinage*. For the advanced undergraduate and graduate student. Musical examples.

2371. Robert, Walter. "*Après une lecture du Dante* (Fantasia Quasi Sonata)." *Piano Quarterly*, 23, no. 89 (1975): 22–24.

From *Années de Pèlerinage*, second year, this work is examined for Liszt's conception of Dante's poem, from which it draws its inspiration. Symbolism in the music briefly discussed. Musical examples.

Bagatelle sans Tonalité

2372. Dumm, Robert. "Liszt Lives." *Piano Quarterly*, 17, no. 66 (1968–1969): 22–23 + .

Analytic and descriptive commentary highlighting sections of the piece, displaying its underlying tonality. Musical examples.

Blume and Duft

2373. Cinnamon, Howard. "Tonal Structures and Voice-Leading in Liszt's *Blume und Duft*." *In Theory Only*, 6 (April 1982): 12–24.

2374.   Hantz, Edwin. "Motivic and Structural Unity in Liszt's *Blume und Duft.*" *In Theory Only,* 6 (April 1982): 3–11.

Christus

2375.   Orga, Ates. "Liszt's Life of Christ." *Music and Musicians,* 19 (January 1971): 44–45.
Background and critical assessment. Musical examples.

2376.   Orr, N. Lee. "Liszt, *Christus,* and the Transformation of the Oratorio." *Journal of the American Liszt Society,* 9 (1981): 4–18.
An historical study of Liszt's transformation of the oratorio from the eighteenth-century model based on opera seria into a symphonic work, which incorporates dramatic elements. Some analytic observations on style.

Concertos

2377.   Hill, Ralph, ed. *The Concerto,* 179–186. London: Penguin Books, 1952.
Critical and analytic commentary for the undergraduate student. Musical examples.

2378.   Veinus, Abraham. *The Concerto,* 199–213. Rev. ed. New York: Dover Publications, 1964.
Liszt's innovations in the concerto form, his musical lineage traced, and critical remarks on his music included. Concise discussion of Liszt's place in music history.

Concerto for Piano No. 1 in E-Flat Major

2379.   Nelson, Wendell. *The Concerto,* 53–55. Dubuque, IA: William C. Brown, 1969.
Brief analysis, with critical observations. Musical examples.

2380.   Pascall, Robert. "Liszt's Piano Concerto No. 1 in E flat (Set by the London Board)." *Music Teacher,* 56 (February 1977): 14–15.
Brief summary of the four movements of this concerto, which follows the plan of the classical symphony. Shows themes heard in first movement recurring in later movements.

Dante Symphony

2381.   Knight, Ellen. "The Harmonic Foundation of Liszt's *Dante* Symphony." *Journal of the American Liszt Society,* 10 (1981): 56–63.
Discussion of the work's genesis, structure, and harmony. Musical examples.

Fantasy and Fugue for Organ on Ad Nos, Ad Salutarem Undam

2382. Eggert, John. "Liszt's *Ad Nos*: A Guide for the Performer." *Diapason*, 73 (November 1982): 4–5.
Though meant for the performer, the article is useful to the student for its analysis of the work. Musical examples and bibliography.

2383. Todd, Ralph L. "Liszt, Fantasy and Fugue for Organ on *Ad Nos, Ad Salutarem Undam*." *Nineteenth Century Music*, 4, no. 3 (1981): 250–261.
Extensive analysis showing how Liszt modified sonata form. Musical examples.

Faust Symphony

2384. Stedman, Preston. *The Symphony*, 136–143. Englewood Cliffs, NJ: Prentice-Hall, 1979.
Description, movement by movement, of thematic transformation, harmonic basis, motives, and orchestration. Musical examples and diagram.

Festival Mass for Gran Cathedral

2385. Dahlhaus, Carl. *Nineteenth-Century Music.* Translated by J. Bradford Robinson, 187–188. Berkeley: University of California Press, 1989.
Brief but concentrated remarks on symphonic techniques, form, and thematic transformations. Musical examples. Advanced.

Harmonies poétiques et religieuses

2386. Backus, Joan. "Liszt's *Harmonies poétiques et religieuses*: Inspiration and the Challenge of Form." *Journal of the American Liszt Society*, 21 (January–June 1987): 3–21.
A discussion of harmonic, motivic, and formal aspects of this work. Investigates conflict between improvisation and cogent formal design in Liszt's music. Musical examples.

Les Morts

2387. Stewart, Arthur. "*La Notte* and *Les Morts*: Investigations into Progressive Aspects of Franz Liszt's Style." *Journal of the American Liszt Society*, 18 (1985): 67–106.

A technical investigation of progressive stylistic traits. These piano pieces are arrangements of two of the orchestral pieces of *Trois Odes Funèbres*. An historical introduction places these works in the context of Liszt's other compositions; progressive aspects of melody, rhythm, harmony, and form are discussed. Relates the pieces to the poems on which they are based. Musical examples.

La Notte

2388. Stewart, Arthur. *"La Notte* and *Les Morts*: Investigations into Progressive Aspects of Franz Liszt's Style." *Journal of the American Liszt Society*, 18 (1985): 67–106. See annotation in item no. 2387, above.

Nuages gris

2389. Decarsin, Franco. "Liszt's *'Nuages gris* and Kagel's *Unguis Incarnatus est*: A Model and Its Issue." *Music Analysis*, 4. no. 3 (1985): 259–263.
Explores melodic, harmonic, and textural connections between *Unguis Incarnatus est* (Kagel) and *Nuages gris* (Liszt), on which it is based. Musical examples and tables.

Orpheus

2390. Taylor, Karen. *Orpheus*, Symphonic Poem No. 4." *Journal of the American Liszt Society*, 11 (1982): 97–100.
Review of a score with a general analysis by Humphrey Searle in the introduction. Refers to major structural divisions by measure numbers.

Les Préludes

2391. Pascall, Robert. "Liszt's Symphonic Poem: *Les Préludes.*" *Music Teacher*, 55 (February 1976): 15–16.
Analysis of themes and form.

Prelude and Fugue on the Name B-A-C-H

2392. Ferre, Susan I. "Liszt's Prelude and Fugue on B-A-C-H: An Analysis." *Diapason*, 69 (April 1978): 12–13.

2393. Saffle, Michael. "New Light on Liszt's Prelude and Fugue on B-A-C-H." *American Organist*, 16 (November 1982): 44–49.
Though meant for the performer, this article contains analytic observations and a bibliography useful to the undergraduate music student. Musical examples.

Prometheus

2394. Nordquist, John. "Liszt's *Prometheus*: Greek Mythology Through a Romantic Prism." *Journal of the American Liszt Society*, 14 (1983): 130–134.
A general analysis of thematic and formal features. Musical examples.

Sonata for Piano in B Minor

2395. Longyear, Rey M. "Liszt's B Minor Sonata: Precedents for a Structural Analysis." *Music Review*, 34, nos. 3–4 (1973): 198–209.
Advanced analysis, with musical examples.

2396. Longyear, Rey M. *Nineteenth-Century Romanticism in Music*, 108–112. Englewood Cliffs, NJ: Prentice-Hall, 1969.
Brief, but complete analysis. Chart and musical examples.

2397. Longyear, Rey M. "The Text of Liszt's B Minor Sonata." *Musical Quarterly*, 60, no. 3 (1974): 435–450.
Background and textual problems considered, but many analytic insights along the way. Musical examples.

2398. Newman, William S. *The Sonata Since Beethoven*. 3d. ed., 371–378. New York: W. W. Norton, 1983.
Detailed analysis accompanied by chart displaying form, tempos, tonal centers, and thematic elements. For the advanced undergraduate and graduate student. Musical examples.

2399. Ott, Bertrand. "An Interpretation of Liszt's Sonata in B Minor." *Journal of the American Liszt Society*, 10 (1981): 30–38.
A description of those passages of the sonata that correlate to events in Geothe's *Faust*. Musical examples. Article continued below. (see item no 2400).

2400. Ott, Bertrand. "An Interpretation of Liszt's Sonata in B Minor." *Journal of the American Liszt Society*, 11 (1982): 40–41.
Evidence that this work is based on Goethe's *Faust*. Continuation of article cited above. (see item no. 2399).

2401.   Saffle, Michael. "Liszt's Sonata in B Minor: Another Look at the Double Function Question." *Journal of the American Liszt Society,* 11 (1982): 28–39.

The author contends that Liszt "unquestionably organized his Sonata to imply an interlocking multi-movement structure within this unusually intriguing and attractive single-movement composition."

2402.   Sandresky, Margaret V. "Tonal Design in Liszt's Sonata in B Minor." *Journal of the American Liszt Society,* 10 (1981): 15–29.

2403.   Sutton, Wadham. "Liszt: Piano Sonata in B Minor." *Music Teacher,* 52 (September 1973): 16–17.

Brief analytic remarks.

2404.   Szasz, Tibor. "Liszt's Symbols for the Divine and Diabolical: Their Revelation of a Program in the B Minor Sonata." *Journal of the American Liszt Society,* 15 (1984): 39–95.

The author claims to have decoded the program of this Sonata into Original Sin, Crucifixion, and Last Judgment, based on motivic elements and their correspondence with music of other composers.

Sonetto 47 del Petrarca

2405.   Banowetz, Joseph. "A Liszt Sonetto: Sonnet 47 of Petrarch." *Clavier,* 17, no. 3 (1978): 12–22.

This work is from the second year of Liszt's *Années de Pèlerinage.* Analytic and interpretive comments for the pianist. Score and Petrach's Sonnet 47 included.

2406.   Dahlhaus, Carl. *Nineteenth-Century Music.* Translated by J. Bradford Robinson, 150–152. Berkeley: University of California Press, 1989.

Brief but concentrated analytic observations on the music's relationship to the poem upon which it is based, tonalities, and motives. Advanced.

2407.   Fowler, Andrew. "Franz Liszt's *Petrarch Sonnets*: The Persistent Poetic Problem." *Indiana Theory Review,* 7, no. 2 (1986): 48–68.

Compares two versions (one for piano solo, the other for baritone voice and piano), identifying subsurface motivic relationships that unite the pieces despite the dissimilar surface elements, tonal and formal designs, and structural voice leading. Includes diagrams of form, musical examples, and voice-leading diagrams. For the advanced student.

Sonetto 104 del Petrarca

2408. Cinnamon, Howard. "Chromaticism and Tonal Coherence in Liszt's *Sonetto 104 del Petrarca*." *In Theory Only*, 7 (August 1983): 3–19.

Analytic essay for the advanced student on this work from Liszt's second year of the *Années de Pèlerinage*.

2409. Neumeyer, David. "Liszt's *Sonetto 104 del Petrarca*: The Romantic Spirit and Voice-Leading." *Indiana Theory Review*, 2, no. 2 (1979): 2–22.

A discussion of Liszt's three early settings of this sonnet, with particular emphasis on the final and fourth version, which appears in his *Années de Pèlerinage* (second year). For this final version, the author provides an in-depth analysis, examining motivic details, harmonic progression at different levels, and aspects of the voice leading. Musical examples.

Un Sospiro

2410. Hantz, Edwin. "Exempli Gratia: Leave It to Liszt." *In Theory Only*, 1 (August 1975): 32.

Discusses Liszt's use of the dominant-seventh resolution in this Etude. Advanced. Musical examples.

Transcendental Etudes

2411. Banowetz, Joseph. "Liszt, *Etudes d'exécution transcendante*." *American Music Teacher*, 20, no. 3 (1971): 18–19+.

Background and descriptive commentary.

Venezia e Napoli

2412. Schenkman, Walter. "The *Venezia e Napoli* Tarantella: Genesis and Metamorphosis; The Specifics of the Change Between Tarantelles and Tarantella." *Journal of the American Liszt Society*, 8 (1980): 44–59.

A discussion of Liszt's revision of this work, including observations on thematic changes, phrase structure, and form. Musical examples.

Via Crucis

2413.   Hill, Cecil. "Liszt's *Via Crucis.*" *Music Review*, 25, no. 3 (1964): 202–208.
Description and analysis of this sacred choral work. Musical examples and chart of tonal structure.

2414.   Robertson, Alec. *Requiem: Music of Mourning and Consolation*, 154–158. New York: Praeger, 1968.
Descriptive commentary, with critical assessment. Musical examples.

Weinen, Klagen, Sorgen, Zagen

2415.   Wait, Mark. "Liszt, Scriabin, and Boulez; Considerations of Form." *Journal of the American Liszt Society*, 1 (June 1977): 12.
Brief analysis. Musical examples.

DISSERTATIONS AND THESES

Années de Pèlerinage

2416.   Cinnamon, Howard. "Third-Relations As Structural Elements in Book II of Liszt's *Années de Pèlerinage.*" Ph.D., University of Michigan, 1984, 302 pp., DA 45-3475A.

Grand Etudes After Paganini

2417.   Altman, Ian Henry. "Liszt's Grand Etudes After Paganini: A Historical and Analytic Study." D.M.A., University of Cincinnati, 318 pp., DA 45-1565A.

Masses

2418.   White, Charles Willis. "The Masses of Franz Liszt." Ph.D., Bryn Mawr College, 1973, 457 pp., DA 34- 6694A.

Sonata for Piano in B Minor

2419.   Rea, John Rocco. "Franz Liszt's New Path of Composition: The Sonata in B Minor As Paradigm." Ph.D., Princeton University, 1978, 447 pp. DA 39-3217A.

Waltzes

2420. Hunt, Mary Angela. "Franz Liszt: The *Mephisto* Waltzes." D.M.A., University of Wisconsin at Madison, 1979, 176 pp., DA 40-2971A.

LULLY, JEAN BAPTISTE, 1632–1687

General

2421. Anthony, James R. *French Baroque Music from Beaujoyeulx to Rameau.* New York: W. W. Norton, 1974, 429 pp.
   A study of French Baroque style elements seen in historical context. Specific works in different genres discussed. Musical examples.

DISSERTATIONS AND THESES

2422. Newman, Joyce E. "Formal Structure and Recitative in the Tragedies Lyriques of Jean-Baptiste de Lully." Ph.D., University of Michigan, 1974, 389 pp., DA 35-5450A.

LUTOSLAWSKI, WITOLD, 1913–

General

2423. Whittall, Arnold. *Music Since the First World War*, 235–239. London: J. M. Dent and Sons, 1977.
   Analytic comments.

Quartet for Strings

2424. Selleck, John. "Pitch and Duration As Textural Elements." *Perspectives of New Music*, 13, no. 2 (1975): 150–161.

MACDOWELL, EDWARD, 1861–1908

Sonatas for Piano

2425. Kaiserman, David. "Edward MacDowell—The *Celtic* and *Eroica* Piano Sonatas." *Music Journal*, 24 (February 1966): 51+.
   Descriptive commentary with background. Mainly for the performer.

MACHAUT, GUILLAUME DE, c. 1300–1377

General

2426. Harman, Alec. *Man and His Music: Medieval and Renaissance Music.* 129–154. New York: Schocken Books, 1969.
Overview of Machaut's contribution in historical context. Isorhythmic motet, innovative techniques, and style discussed. Musical examples.

2427. Hoppin, Richard, H. *Medieval Music,* 396–432. New York: W. W. Norton, 1978.
Extended essay focusing on Machaut's importance, forms employed, melodic and rhythmic style, and isorhythmic motets. Machaut's output discussed in sections grouped by genre. Musical examples.

2428. Reaney, Gilbert. "Ars Nova in France." In *The New Oxford History of Music.* Vol. 3, *Ars Nova and the Renaissance, 1300–1540.* Edited by Dom Anselm Hughes and Gerald Abraham, 15–29. London: Oxford University Press, 1960.
Masses, motets, and secular polyphony of Machaut reviewed. His harmony and stylistic traits examined. Musical examples.

2429. Reaney, Gilbert. *Guillaume de Machaut.* London: Oxford University Press, 1971, 76 pp.
This is the best complete survey of Machaut's music to date. After chapters on Machaut as a musician-poet and his musical style, there are separate chapters on each genre of composition. Reaney describes the forms in detail and Machaut's treatment of them; motivic and harmonic structures; text setting; rhythmic treatment; texture. Musical examples.

2430. Reese, Gustave. *Music in the Middle Ages,* 347–359. New York: W. W. Norton, 1940.
Background and analytic descriptions of Machaut's output, including the rondeaux, virelais, motets, and masses. Musical examples.

Ballades

2431. DeLone, Richard P. "Machaut and the Ballade Style." *Indiana Theory Review,* 2, no. 1 (1978): 15–28.
A general discussion of the stylistic attributes of the ballade, in

cluding the treatment of the cantus, cadences, linear features, counterpoint, suspensions. Discusses *De Toutes Flours* in some detail. Musical examples.

Lais

2432. Bellamy, Sister Laurette. "Some Comments on the Lais of Guillaume de Machaut." *Indiana Theory Review*, 2, no. 1 (1978): 41–53.

Discusses historical and stylistic aspects of Machaut's lais. Analyzes *Le Lay Mortel* with respect to its overall strophic organization as well as the makeup of individual strophes resulting from the poetry. Musical examples and table.

Notre Dame Mass

2433. Cogan, Robert, and Pozzi Escot. *Sonic Design: The Nature of Sound and Music*, 228–238. Englewood Cliffs, NJ: Prentice-Hall, 1976.

A detailed discussion of pulse and rhythm.

2434. Keitel, Elizabeth A. "The So-Called Cyclic Mass of Guillaume de Machaut: New Evidence for an Old Debate." *Musical Quarterly*, 68, no. 3 (1982): 307–323.

Historical and analytic observations indicate that the Mass was not composed as a unit.

2435. Wilkins, Nigel. *Music in the Age of Chaucer*, 12–16. Totowa, NJ: Rowman and Littlefield, 1979.

Concise analysis. Musical examples.

Plus dure que in dyamant

2436. Cogan, Robert, and Pozzi Escot. *Sonic Design: The Nature of Sound and Music*, 114–124. Englewood Cliffs, NJ: Prentice-Hall, 1976.

Discusses mode, intervallic sonority, and syllabic and musical rhythm.

Rose, lis

2437. Leech-Wilkinson, Daniel. "Machaut's *Rose, lis* and the Problem of Early Music Analysis." *Music Analysis*, 3, no. 1 (1984): 9–28.

Discusses problems inherent in the analysis of early music. Includes voice-leading reductions and analysis of *Rose, lis*. For the advanced student.

DISSERTATIONS AND THESES

General

2438. Zipay, Terry Lee. "Closure in the Motets of Machaut." Ph.D., State University of New York at Buffalo, 1983, 299 pp., DA 44-12A.

MAHLER, GUSTAV, 1860–1911

General

2439. Barford, Philip. *Mahler Symphonies and Songs.* Seattle: University of Washington Press, 1970, 64 pp.
  Brief descriptive and critical remarks with musical examples. For the undergraduate student.

2440. Gartenberg, Egon. *Mahler: The Man and His Music.* New York: Schirmer Books, 1978, 406 pp.
  Background, remarks on programmatic elements, and analytic discussion of Mahler's output. Musical examples.

2441. James, Burnett. *The Music of Gustav Mahler.* Rutherford, NJ: Fairleigh Dickinson University Press, 1985, 230 pp.
  Discussion of Mahler's music for the informed listener. Commentary, with music examples, that identifies main themes, forms stylistic characteristics, and nonmusical associations.

2442. Kennedy, Michael. *Mahler.* London: J. M. Dent and Sons, 1974, 196 pp.
  Descriptive and analytic overview of Mahler's output. For the undergraduate student. Musical examples.

2443. Kravitt, Edward F. "The Ballad As Conceived by Germanic Composers of the Late Romantic Period." *Studies in Romanticism,* 12, no. 2 (1973): 499–515.
  The attraction of the romantic ballad to composers such as Mahler, Wolf, and Strauss. Discusses their techniques of word painting. Musical examples.

2444. La Grange, Henry-Louis de. *Mahler.* Vol. 1. New York: Doubleday, 1973. 982 pp.
  Background with structural analyses of various works. Musical examples.

2445. Mitchell, Donald. *Gustav Mahler: The Early Years.* Rev. ed. Berkeley: University of California Press, 1980, 338 pp.

Extended analytic essays with background on works written up to 1880.

2446. Mitchell, Donald. *Gustav Mahler: Songs and Symphonies of Life and Death.* London: Faber and Faber, 1985, 659 pp.

The third volume in Mitchell's series, providing extended analytic essays on Mahler's works. The late works, including *Das Lied von der Erde, Fünf Lieder nach Rückert, Kindertotenlieder,* and the Eighth Symphony are treated here.

2447. Mitchell, Donald. *Gustav Mahler: The Wunderhorn Years.* Boulder, CO: Westview Press, 1975, 461 pp.

Extended analytic essays including background. *Songs of a Wayfarer,* Symphonies 1–4, and other works written during the years 1880–1900 discussed. Musical examples.

2448. Redich, Hans. *Bruckner and Mahler,* 77–105. London: J. M. Dent and Sons, 1955.

Descriptive and critical commentary intended for the undergraduate student. Some analytic insights and comments on style. Musical examples.

2449. Roman, Zoltan. "The Chorus in Mahler's Music." *Music Review,* 43, no. 1 (1982): 31–43.

An examination of the treatment and function of the chorus in Mahler's music. Musical examples.

2450. Roman, Zoltan. "Structure As a Factor in the Genesis of Mahler's Songs." *Music Review,* 35, no. 2 (1974): 157–166.

Structural points emphasized to show Mahler's approach to text. Musical examples.

2451. Whaples, Miriam K. "Mahler and Schubert's A Minor Sonata, D. 784." *Music and Letters,* 65, no. 3 (1984): 255–263.

A discussion of how Schubert's Sonata for Piano in A Minor, D. 784, influenced Mahler ("much of it unconsciously") for thirty years. Musical examples.

Des Knaben Wunderhorn

2452. La Grange, Henry-Louis de. *Mahler.* Vol. 1, 758–780. New York: Doubleday, 1973.

Thorough, methodical treatment. Background, form, and other pertinent information with musical examples.

Kindertotenlieder

2453.   Agawu, V. Kofi. "The Musical Language of *Kindertotenlieder* No. 2." *Journal of Musicology*, 2, no. 1 (1983): 81–93.
Extensive analysis focusing on relationship of text to music, the melodic process, and the tonal/harmonic structure. Musical examples.

2454.   Dahlhaus, Carl. *Nineteenth-Century Music.* Translated by J. Bradford Robinson, 375–376. Berkeley: University of California Press, 1989.
Brief but concentrated analytic remarks on the last song of this cycle, *In diesem Wetter,* dwelling on motives, tonality, and text setting. Musical example. Advanced.

2455.   Kravitt, Edward F. "Mahler's Dirges for His Death: February 24, 1901." *Musical Quarterly*, 64, no. 3 (1978): 329–353.
Psychological background of the *Kindertotenlieder.*

2456.   Mitchell, Donald. *Gustav Mahler: Songs and Symphonies of Life and Death,* 74–108. London: Faber and Faber, 1985.
Extended analytic essays including background, analyses, musical examples, tables, diagrams.

Das Klagende Lied

2457.   Diether, Jack. "Mahler's *Klagende Lied*—Genesis and Evolution." *Music Review*, 29, no. 4 (1966): 268–287.
Background and conception of the *Klagende Lied.* Some discussion of the music. Musical examples.

2458.   La Grange, Henry-Louis de. *Mahler.* Vol. 1, 735–738. New York: Doubleday, 1973.
Background with descriptive and analytic remarks.

2459.   Mitchell, Donald. *Gustav Mahler: The Early Years.* Rev. ed., 141–196. Berkeley: University of California Press, 1980.
Extended analytic essay with background. Musical examples.

Das Lied von der Erde

2460.   Carner, Mosco. *Major and Minor,* 52–55. New York: Holmes and Meier, 1980.
Brief analytic remarks on formal structure to show symphonic conception of this work. Musical examples.

2461. Mitchell, Donald. *Gustav Mahler: Songs and Symphonies of Life and Death*, 162–432. London: Faber and Faber, 1985.

     Extended analytic essays including background, analyses, musical examples, tables, diagrams.

2462. Tischler, Hans. *The Perceptive Music Listener*, 166–172. Englewood Cliffs, NJ: Prentice-Hall, 1955.

     Descriptive and analytic commentary, with emphasis on form. Musical examples.

2463. Wenk, Arthur. "The Composer As Poet in *Das Lied von der Erde.*" *Nineteenth Century Music*, 1, no. 1 (1977): 33–47.

     A study of the relationship between music and text in this work. Relates changes that Mahler made to the original texts to accommodate their musical setting. Tables, musical examples.

Songs

2464. Mitchell, Donald. *Gustav Mahler: Songs and Symphonies of Life and Death*, London: Faber and Faber, 1985, 659 pp.

     Detailed studies of *Fünf Lieder nach Rückert, Kindertotenlieder, Das Lied von der Erde;* and the Eighth Symphony. Includes discussions of the textual sources, structure, rhythm, tonality, relationships between music and text. Musical examples.

Songs from Rückert

2465. Mitchell, Donald. *Gustav Mahler: Songs and Symphonies of Life and Death*, 54–74. Faber and Faber, 1985.

     Extended analytic essays, including background, analyses, musical examples, tables, diagrams.

Songs of a Wayfarer

2466. La Grange, Henry-Louis de. *Mahler.* Vol. 1, 741–746. New York: Doubleday, 1973.

     Full background, with analytic insights.

2467. Mitchell, Donald. *Gustav Mahler: The Wunderhorn Years*, 91–112. Boulder, CO: Westview Press, 1975.

     Extended analytic essay with background. Musical examples.

Symphonies

2468. Ballantine, Christopher. *Twentieth Century Symphony*, 107–109. London: Dennis Dobson, 1983.

     Brief comments on key symbolism. Musical examples.

2469.   Barford, Philip. *Mahler Symphonies and Songs,* 18–64. Seattle: University of Washington Press, 1970.
Descriptive, critical, and analytic commentary for the student. Musical examples.

2470.   Cardus, Neville. *Gustav Mahler, His Mind and His Music.* Vol. 1. New York: St. Martin's Press, 1965, 191 pp.
Analyses of Symphonies 1–5. Musical examples.

2471.   Greene, David B. *Mahler, Consciousness and Temporality.* New York: Gordon and Breach Science Publishers, 1984, 314 pp.
Detailed analyses of Symphonies 3, 5, 8, and 9 (a chapter on each), with an introduction. The nature of the structural unit of each movement of each symphony is discussed in turn. The major aim of the book is to compare musical and phenomenological analyses of these works. The writings of Husserl, Heidegger, and Sartre are drawn upon in this context. For the advanced student. Musical examples.

2472.   La Grange, Henry-Louis de. *Mahler.* Vol. 1, 746–823. New York: Doubleday, 1973.
Full background with structural analyses of Symphonies 1–4. Musical examples.

2473.   Mitchell, Donald. *Gustav Mahler: Songs and Symphonies of Life and Death.* London: Faber and Faber, 1985, 659 pp.
Detailed studies of *Fünf Lieder nach Rückert, Kindertotenlieder, Das Lied von der Erde,* and the Eighth Symphony. Includes discussions of the textual sorces, structure, rhythm, tonality, relationships between music and text. Musical examples.

2474.   Murphy, Edward W. "Sonata-Rondo Form in the Symphonies of Gustav Mahler." *Music Review,* 36, no. 1 (1975): 54–62.

2475.   Simpson, Robert, ed. *The Symphony.* Vol. 2, 29–51. New York: Drake Publishers, 1972.
Overview of Mahler's symphonies, concentrating on stylistic development and significant features of the symphonies.

2476.   Williamson, John. "Mahler and *Veni Creator Spiritus.*" *Music Review,* 44, no. 1 (1983): 25–35.
Formal and tonal characteristics of the symphonies.

Symphony No. 1 in D Major

2477.   Roman, Zoltan. "Connotative Irony in Mahler's *Todtenmarch in Callot's Manier.*" *Musical Quarterly,* 59, no. 2 (1973): 207–222.

Discussion of the creative impulse behind the funeral march (third movement) and relationship of this work to the *Songs of a Wayfarer*.

2478. Small, Christopher. "Mahler: Symphony No. 1." *Music in Education*, 38, no. 369 (1974): 215–217.
Brief but concentrated analytic discussion. Musical examples.

Symphony No. 2 in C Minor ("Resurrection")

2479. Franklin, Peter. "Funeral Rites—Mahler and Mickiewicz." *Music and Letters*, 55, no. 2 (1974): 203–208.
Influence of the Polish Romantic poet Adam Mickiewecz on the *Totenfeier* movement.

2480. Grant, Parks. "Mahler's Second Symphony." *Chord and Discord*, 2, no. 8 (1958): 76–85.
Thorough analysis, with musical examples.

Symphony No. 3 in D Minor

2481. Franklin, Peter R. "The Gestation of Mahler's Third Symphony." *Music and Letters*, 58, no. 4 (1977): 439–446.
Conception and compositional history of the Third Symphony. Musical examples.

Symphony No. 4 in G Major

2482. Cuyler, Louise. *The Symphony*, 130–133. New York: Harcourt Brace Jovanovich, 1973.
Concentrated musical analysis.

Symphony No. 5 in C-Sharp Minor

2483. Ballantine, Christopher. *Twentieth Century Symphony*, 88–89. London: Dennis Dobson, 1983.
Brief summary of the scherzo movement's form.

2484. Baxendale, Carolyn. "The Finale of Mahler's Fifth Symphony: Long-Range Musical Thought." *Journal of the Royal Musical Association*, 112, no. 2 (1987): 257–279.

Advanced analytic discussion, focusing in detail on structure to help explain how such an extended movement is held together and given shape. Musical examples and charts. Final movement only.

2485.   Forte, Allen. "Middleground Motives in the 'Adagietto' of Mahler's Fifth Symphony." *Nineteenth Century Music*, 8, no. 2 (1984): 153–163.

Tracing the motives in detail reveals a superstructure of motives (middle ground) lending structural unity. Musical examples.

2486.   Grant, Parks. "Mahler's Fifth Symphony." *Chord and Discord*, 2, no. 10 (1963): 125–137.

Thorough musical analysis, with many musical examples.

2487.   Stedman, Preston. *The Symphony*, 238–246. Englewood Cliffs, NJ: Prentice-Hall, 1979.

Description and full analytic breakdown of each movement, supported by musical examples and diagrams.

Symphony No. 6 in A Minor

2488.   Ratz, Erwin. "Musical Form in Gustav Mahler: An Analysis of the Finale of the Sixth Symphony." *Music Review*, 29, no. 1 (1968): 34–48.

Symphony No. 7 in E Minor

2489.   Dahlhaus, Carl. *Nineteenth-Century Music.* Translated by J. Bradford Robinson, 364–365. Berkeley: University of California Press, 1989.

Brief but concentrated analytic remarks dwelling on sonata form elements. Advanced.

2490.   Williamson, John. "The Structural Premises of Mahler's Introductions: Prolegomena to an Analysis of the First Movement of the Seventh Symphony." *Music Analysis*, 5, no. 1 (1986): 29–57.

Analytic discussion of the opening of Mahler's symphonies. Examines Symphony No. 1 briefly and then Symphony No. 7 in great detail (measures 1–50 only). Uses Schenkerian terminology and notation. Musical examples. For the advanced student.

Symphony No. 8 in E-Flat Major ("Symphony of a Thousand")

2491.   Mitchell, Donald. *Gustav Mahler: Songs and Symphonies of Life and Death*, 501–549. London: Faber and Faber, 1985.

Extended analytic essay including background, analysis, musical examples, tables, diagrams.

Symphony No. 9 in D Major

2492.   Diether, Jack. "The Expressive Content of Mahler's Ninth: An Interpretation." *Chord and Discord*, 2, no. 10 (1963): 69–107.

Exhaustive analysis, focusing on Mahler's expressive devices. Cites allusions to songs and other examples of musical symbolism. For the advanced student.

2493.   Lewis, Christopher Orlo. *Tonal Coherence in Mahler's Ninth Symphony*. Ann Arbor: UMI Research Press, 1984, 130 pp.

Published doctoral thesis offering a detailed analytic exploration. Advanced. Musical examples.

Symphony No. 10 (Unfinished)

2494.   Bergquist, Peter. "The First Movement of Mahler's Tenth Symphony: An Analysis and an Examination of the Sketches." In *The Music Forum*, Vol. 5. Edited by Felix Salzer and Carl Schachter, 335–394. New York: Columbia University Press, 1980.

Advanced analytic essay according to Schenker's principles.

2495.   Cooke, Deryck. "Correspondence: Mahler's Tenth Symphony." *Music Review*, 24, no. 1 (1963): 95–96.

Cooke's defense of Malloch's criticism (*see* item no. 2501).

2496.   Cooke, Deryck. "The Facts Concerning Mahler's Tenth Symphony." *Chord and Discord*, 2, no. 10 (1963): 3–27.

Background and analysis of Mahler's unfinished Tenth Symphony.

2497.   Cooke, Deryck. "Mahler's Tenth Symphony." *Musical Times*, 117 (July 1976): 563 + ; (August 1976): 645 + .

Complete history and background of the performing version of Mahler's unfinished, but sketched, Tenth Symphony.

2498.   Cooke, Deryck. "Mahler's Tenth Symphony: Artistic Morality and Musical Reality." *Musical Times*, 102 (June 1961): 351–354.

Analytical remarks on the incomplete manuscript intended to support the viability of the author's completion of the work.

2499.   Kaplan, Richard A. "The Interaction of Diatonic Collections in the Adagio of Mahler's Tenth Symphony." *In Theory Only*, 6 (November 1981): 29–39.

2500.   Kaplan, Richard A. "Interpreting Surface Harmonic Connections in the Adagio of Mahler's Tenth Symphony." *In Theory Only*, 4 (May–June 1978): 32–44.

2501.   Malloch, William. "Deryck Cooke's Mahler Tenth: An Interim Report." *Music Review,* 23, no. 4 (1962): 292–304.
Malloch offers a critique of Cooke's broadcast of the symphony with respect to what he terms misconceptions and misrepresentations of the work. Musical examples.

2502.   Reid, Charles. "Mahler's Tenth (Deryck Cooke's Realization)." *Music Review,* 26, no. 4 (1965): 318–325.
Supports Cooke's realization with analysis and historical commentary. Musical examples.

DISSERTATIONS AND THESES

General

2503.   Bruner, Ellen Carole. "The Relationship of Text and Music in the *Lieder* of Hugo Wolf and Gustav Mahler." Ph.D., Syracuse University, 1974, 389 pp., DA 35-7340A.

Symphonies

2504.   Sine, Nadine. "The Evolution of Symphonic Worlds: Tonality in the Symphonies of Gustav Mahler with Emphasis on the First, Third, and Fifth." Ph.D., New York University, 1983, 308 pp., DA 44-3538A.

Symphony No. 1 in D Major

2505.   Jones, Robert Frederick. "Thematic Development and Form in the First and Fourth Movements of Mahler's First Symphony." Ph.D., Brandeis University, 1980, 123 pp., DA 41-1827A.

Symphony No. 2 in C Minor ("Resurrection")

2506.   Schram, Albert-George." "Gustav Mahler: Symphony No. 2 (C Minor): A Historical Background and Analysis. " D.M.A., University of Washington, 1985, 172 pp., DA 46-2852A.

Symphony No. 9 in D Major

2507.   Lewis, Christopher. "Tonality and Structure in the Ninth Symphony of Gustav Mahler." Ph.D., University of Rochester, Eastman School of Music, 1983, 257 pp., DA 44-101A.

MARENZIO, LUCA, 1553–1599

General

2508. Arnold, Denis. *Marenzio.* London: Oxford University Press, 1965, 45 pp.

> Descriptive, critical, and analytic commentary with historical perspective. For the undergraduate student. Musical examples.

2509. Dent, Edward J. "The Sixteenth Century Madrigal." In *The New Oxford History of Music.* Vol. 4, *The Age of Humanism, 1540–1630.* Edited by Gerald Abraham, 62–67. London: Oxford University Press, 1968.

> Brief examination of Marenzio's place and stylistic characteristics of the madrigals. Musical examples.

2510. Einstein, Alfred. *The Italian Madrigal.* Translated by Alexander H. Krappe, Roger H. Sessions, and Oliver Strunk. 3 vols. Princeton, NJ: Princeton University Press, 1949.

> Historical perspective, stylistic characterization, relationship of text to music, and the function of the music for its time discussed. For the advance student. Musical examples.

MARTIN, FRANK, 1890–1974

DISSERTATIONS AND THESES

Concerto for Piano No. 2

2511. Dellinger, Michael Eldon. "An Analysis of Frank Martin's Second Piano Concerto." D.M.A., Ohio State University, 1985, 143 pp., DA 46-549A.

Mass for Double Choir A Cappella

2512. Vantine, Bruce Lynn. "Four Twentieth-Century Masses: An Analytical Comparison of Style and Compositional Techniques." D.M.A., University of Illinois at Urbana, 1982, 427 pp., DA 43-583A-4A.

Petite Symphonie Concertante

2513. Adams, Byron. ". . . Part 2: Frank Martin's *Petite Symphonie Concertante*: An Analysis." D.M.A., Cornell University, 1984, 64 pp., DA 45-1905A.

MARTINU, BOHUSLAV, 1890–1959

General

2514.   Clapham, John. "Martinu's Instrumental Works." *Music Review*, 24, no. 2 (1963): 158–167.

Symphonies

2515.   Ballantine, Christopher. *Twentieth Century Symphony*, 124–126. London: Dennis Dobson, 1984.
    Brief analytic comments on form in the first movements of Symphonies 4 and 5.

2516.   Evans, Peter. "Martinu the Symphonist." *Tempo*, 55–56 (Autum–Winter 1960): 19–33.
    Observations on the structural methods, with some comments on style in Symphonies 1, 2, 4, 5, and 6.

DISSERTATIONS AND THESES

General

2517.   Pettyway, B. Keith. "The Solo and Chamber Compositions for Flute by Bohuslav Martinu." D.M.A., University of Southern Mississippi, 1980, 154 pp., DA 41-4537A.

Trios for Piano

2518.   Cable, Susan Lee. "The Piano Trios of Bohuslav Martinu (1890–1959)." D.A., University of Northern Colorado, 1984, 203 pp., DA 45-3022A.

MASCAGNI, PIETRO, 1863–1945

Cavalleria Rusticana

2519.   Kestner, Joseph. "Out of the Tinder Box." *Opera News*, 42, (April 8, 1978): 10–14.
    Literary background to the "Verismo" movement launched in music by this work.

MASSENET, JULES, 1842–1912

General

2520.   Finck, Henry. *Massenet and His Operas.* New York: John Lane, 1910, 245 pp.
   Old, but still useful for its full discussion of the operas.

2521.   Harding, James. *Massenet.* London: J. M. Dent and Sons, 1970, 229 pp.
   Book-length discussion of the life of Massenet, background of the operas, characterization, staging, musical style.

Esclarmonde

2522.   Davis, Peter G. "In San Francisco: A Major Massenet Revival." *Opera News,* 39 (September 1974): 41–44.
   Background, history, and descriptive remarks on this seldom-performed work.

2523.   Lawrence, Robert. "Magic Carpet." *Opera News,* 41 (December 11, 1976): 32–33.
   Brief critical commentary, with musical examples.

Manon

2524.   John, Nicholas, ed. *Manon.* London: John Calder, 1984, 112 pp.
   An introduction to the opera for the general public. Analytic comments, background information, and discussion of characterization and drama. Musical examples.

Werther

2525.   Dahlhaus, Carl. *Nineteenth-Century Music.* Translated by J. Bradford Robinson, 278–279. Berkeley: University of California Press, 1989.
   Brief but concentrated analytic remarks dwelling on musical devices to portray dramatic action. Advanced.

2526.   Stocker, Leonard. *"Werther:* The Novel and the Opera." *Opera Journal,* 6, no. 4 (1973): 23–30.
   Background, tracing the story from Goethe's novel to Massenet. Not a discussion of the music.

DISSERTATIONS AND THESES

Werther

2527.   Stocker, Leonard L. "The Treatment of the Romantic Literary hero in Verdi's *Ernani* and in Massenet's *Werther.*" Ph.D., Florida State University, 1969, 188 pp, DA 32-3358A.

MATTHESON, JOHANN, 1681–1764

General

2528.   Schenkman, Walter. "Mattheson's Forty-Eight and Their Commentaries." *Music Review,* 42, no. 1 (1981): 9–21.
   Full descriptive and analytic commentary on this work, which anticipates Bach's treatment of equal temperament by several years. Musical examples.

MAXWELL DAVIES, PETER, 1934–

General

2529.   Davies, Lyn. "Maxwell Davies' Organ Music." *Musical Times,* 125 (September 1984): 525–527.
   Critical overview. Not analytic. Musical examples.

2530.   Griffiths, Paul. *Peter Maxwell Davies.* London: Robson Books, 1981, 196 pp.
   Analytic remarks, compositional techniques, and comments by the composer. Musical examples.

2531.   Pruslin, Stephen. *Peter Maxwell Davies: Studies from Two Decades.* London: Boosey and Hawkes, 1979, 102 pp.
   Consists of articles that first appeared in the journal *Tempo.* The articles are analytic in nature and comment on works from the period 1957–1978. Each article serves as an analytic introduction to the work under discussion. Musical examples.

Antechrist

2532.   Schwartz, Elliott. "Reviews of Records: Peter Maxwell Davies: *Antechrist.*" *Musical Quarterly,* 62, no. 2 (1976): 302–305.
   Brief critical remarks included in this record review.

From Stone to Thorn

2533.   Schwartz, Elliott. "Reviews of Records: Peter Maxwell Davies: *From Stone to Thorn.*" *Musical Quarterly,* 62, no. 2 (1976): 302–305.
Brief critical remarks are included in this record review.

Hymnos

2534.   Schwartz, Elliott. "Reviews of Records: Peter Maxwell Davies: *Hymnos.*" *Musical Quarterly,* 62, no. 2 (1976): 302–305.
Brief critical remarks included in this record review.

Missa Super L'Homme Armé

2535.   Schwartz, Elliott. "Reviews of Records: Peter Maxwell Davies: *Missa Super l'Homme Armé.*" *Musical Quarterly,* 62, no. 2 (1976): 302–305.
Brief critical remarks included in this record review.

Second Fantasia on an In Nomine of John Taverner

2536.   Whittall, Arnold. "Post-Twelve-Note Analysis." *Proceedings of the Royal Musical Association,* 94 (1967–1968): 8–12.
A brief study of the structure and thematic content of this work and relationships with Taverner theme. Musical examples.

Taverner

2537.   Foreman, Lewis, ed. *British Music Now—A Guide to the Work of Younger Composers,* 71–85. London: Paul Elek, 1975.
Commentary on style and technique, with an analysis of *Taverner.*

2538.   Harbison, John. "*Taverner.*" *Perspectives of New Music,* 11, no. 1 (1972): 233–240.
Background and critical remarks on this opera about John Taverner. Musical examples.

2539.   Northcott, Bayan. "*Taverner.*" *Music and Musicians,* 21 (September 1972): 62–64.
Critical impressions. Not analytic.

MEDTNER, NIKOLAI, 1880–1951

Sonata for Piano, Op. 22 in G Minor

2540. **Truscott, Harold.** "Medtner's Sonata in G Minor, Op. 22." *Music Review*, 22, no. 2 (1961): 112–123.
  Full analysis, with musical examples.

MENDELSSOHN, FELIX, 1809–1847

General

2541. **Butler, Douglas L.** "The Organ Works of Felix Mendelssohn Bartholdy." *Diapason*, 69, (February 1978): 4–6; (March 1978): 1+; (June 1978): 1+.
  Stylistic traits discussed and brief analytic observations on pieces written between 1820–1821. Musical examples and bibliography.

2542. **Dale, Kathleen.** *Nineteenth-Century Piano Music: A Handbook for Pianists*. London: Oxford University Press, 1954, 320 pp.
  Highlights stylistic traits and unique contribution to the literature of the piano. Form, harmony, and other musical aspects discussed in relation to style.

2543. **Ferguson, Donald N.** *Image and Structure in Chamber Music*, 156–163. Minneapolis: University of Minnesota Press, 1964.
  Overview of the chamber music, with brief analyses. Musical examples.

2544. **Horton, John.** *Mendelssohn Chamber Music*. Seattle: University of Washington Press, 1972, 64 pp.
  Descriptive and analytic commentary for the undergraduate student. Musical examples.

2545. **Jacob, Heinrich Eduard.** *Felix Mendelssohn and His Times*. Translated by Richard Winston and Clara Winston. 1963. Reprint. Westport, CT: Greenwood Press, 1973, 356 pp.
  Background, descriptive, critical, and analytic commentary. Musical examples.

2546. **Plantinga, Leon.** *Romantic Music*, 248–254. New York: W. W. Norton, 1984.
  Analytic comments. Musical examples.

2547. Pritchard, Brian W. "Mendelssohn's Chorale Cantatas: An Appraisal." *Musical Quarterly*, 62, no. 1 (1976): 1–24.
Thorough presentation of background with descriptive and analytic commentary on the chorale cantatas. Musical examples.

2548. Radcliffe, Philip. *Mendelssohn.* London: J. M. Dent, 1976, 214 pp.
Descriptive and critical overview for the undergraduate student. Musical examples.

2549. Robertson, Alec, ed. *Chamber Music*, 175–182. Baltimore: Penguin Books, 1957.
Critical and analytic remarks. Musical examples.

2550. Sabatier, Francois. "Mendelssohn's Organ Works." *American Organist*, 16 (January 1982): 46–56.
Background and analyses of the preludes, fugues, and sonatas for organ. Musical examples and bibliography.

2551. Todd, Larry R. "Mendelssohn's Ossianic Manner, with a New Source—*On Lena's Gloomy Heath*." In *Mendelssohn and Schumann: Essays on Their Music and Its Context.* Edited by Jon W. Finson and Larry R. Todd, 136–160. Durham: Duke University Press, 1984.
Discusses background, provides brief analytic comments, and suggests programmatic interpretations for three works: *Fingal's Cave Overture* (pp. 140–149); *Scottish* Symphony (pp. 149–153); and *On Lena's Gloomy Heath* (unpublished).

2552. Werner, Eric. *Mendelssohn.* Translated by Dika Newlin. New York: Free Press of Glencoe, 1963, 545 pp.
Descriptive, critical, analytic. Musical examples.

2553. Werner, Eric. "Mendelssohn's Choral Music." *American Choral Review*, 7, no. 2 (1964): 1–4.
Descriptive and critical commentary, with musical examples.

Concertos

2554. Hill, Ralph, ed. *The Concerto*, 154–161. London: Penguin Books, 1952.
Critical and analytic commentary for the undergraduate student. Musical examples.

2555. Veinus, Abraham. *The Concerto.* Rev. ed., 183–191. New York: Dover Publications, 1964.
An assessment of Mendelssohn's art in comparison to Mozart's. Critical remarks on specific works.

Concerto for Violin, Op. 64 in E Minor

2556. Jacob, Heinrich Eduard. *Felix Mendelssohn and His Times.* Translated by Richard and Clara Winston. 1963. Reprint, 304–306. Westport, CT: Greenwood Press, 1973.
Brief critical commentary. Musical examples.

2557. Machlis, Joseph. *The Enjoyment of Music.* 3d ed., 164–166. New York: W. W. Norton, 1970.
Brief analysis for the student. Musical examples.

2558. Nelson, Wendell. *The Concerto,* 56–59. Dubuque, IA: William C. Brown, 1969.
Brief analysis with critical observations. Musical examples.

2559. Swalin, Benjamin F. *The Violin Concerto: A Study in German Romanticism,* 62–74. Chapel Hill: University of North Carolina Press, 1941.
Full treatment, providing background, analysis, and critical remarks. Musical examples.

2560. Tovey, Donald Francis. *Essays in Musical Analysis.* Vol. 3, 178–181. London: Oxford University Press, 1936.
Background and analytical remarks, with musical examples.

Elijah

2561. Mintz, David. "Mendelssohn's *Elijah* Reconsidered." *Studies in Romanticism,* 3, no. 1 (1963): 1–9.
Discussion centering on text and musical style.

2562. Werner, Jack. *Mendelssohn's "Elijah."* London: Chappell, 1965, 109 pp.
Background, performance history, analyses of all the movements and revisions. Musical examples.

Fingal's Cave Overture

2563. Riedel, Johannes. *Music of the Romantic Period,* 43–44. Dubuque, IA: William C. Brown, 1969.
Brief analytic description.

353

2564. Todd, Larry R. "Mendelssohn's Ossianic Manner, with a New Source—*On Lena's Gloomy Heath.*" In *Mendelssohn and Schumann: Essays on Their Music and Its Context.* Edited by Jon W. Finson and Larry R. Todd, 140–149. Durham: Duke University Press, 1984.

Analytic comments, with discussion of background and possible programmatic interpretation.

2565. Tovey, Donald Francis. *Essays in Musical Analysis.* Vol. 4, 90–93. London: Oxford University Press, 1969.

Critical and analytic study, with musical examples. For the undergraduate student.

Melusine Overture

2566. Tovey, Donald Francis. *Essays in Musical Analysis.* Vol. 6, 37–40. London: Oxford University Press, 1969.

Critical and analytic, with musical examples. For the undergraduate student.

Midsummer Night's Dream

2567. Tovey, Donald Francis. *Essays in Musical Analysis.* Vol. 4, 102–109. London: Oxford University Press, 1969.

Critical and analytic study, with musical examples. For the undergraduate student.

Midsummer Night's Dream Overture

2568. Tovey, Donald Francis. *Essays in Musical Analysis.* Vol. 4, 97–102. London: Oxford University Press, 1969.

Critical and analytic study, with musical examples. For the undergraduate student.

Ruy Blas Overture

2569. Laycock, Ralph. "Score Analysis—The *Ruy Blas* Overture." *Instrumentalist,* 22 (May 1968): 96–99.

"Thematic skeleton" of the entire work, with brief explanatory comments. Intended for the conductor, but useful for the student as well.

2570. Tovey, Donald Francis. *Essays in Musical Analysis.* Vol. 4, 94–97. London: Oxford University Press, 1969.

Critical and analytic study, with musical examples. For the student.

Sonatas for Organ, Op. 65

2571. Butler, Douglas L. "The Organ Works of Mendelssohn: Chorale and Fugal Usage in the Six Sonatas, Op. 65." *Diapason*, 70 (November 1979): 6+.
Analysis, with musical examples and bibliography.

Sonata for Organ, Op. 65, No. 3

2572. Moorehead, Douglas M. "Mendelssohn's Organ Sonatas: A Look at No. 3." *Music (AGO)*, 9 (November 1975): 28–33.
Mendelssohn's style, historical background, and an analysis of the sonatas, performance practice. Extensive bibliography.

Songs Without Words

2573. Duncan, James L. "Words in Defense of *Songs Without Words*." *Music Educators Journal*, 56 (March 1970): 69–70+.
Evaluative remarks.

Songs Without Words, No. 6 in F-Sharp Minor

2574. Walton, Charles W. *Basic Forms in Music*, 27–29. Port Washington, NY: Alfred Publishing Co., 1974.
Condensed analysis, with full musical quotation. Complete score included.

Symphonies

2575. Werner, Eric. *Mendelssohn.* New York: Free Press of Glencoe, 1963, 545 pp.
Brief analyses, mainly of Symphonies 3, 4, and 5, highlighting the most significant features.

Symphony No. 3, Op. 56 in A Minor ("Scottish")

2576. Longyear, Rey M. "Cyclic Form and Tonal Relationships in Mendelssohn's *Scottish* Symphony." *In Theory Only*, 4 (January 1979): 38–48.

2577. Todd, Larry R. "Mendelssohn's Ossianic Manner, with a New Source—*On Lena's Gloomy Heath.*" In *Mendelssohn and Schumann:*

Essays on Their Music and Its Context. Edited by Jon W. Finson and Larry R. Todd, 149–153. Durham: Duke University Press, 1984.
  Brief analytic comments, with discussion of background and possible programmatic interpretation.

Symphony No. 4, Op. 90 in A Major ("Italian")

2578. Kerman, Joseph. *Listen,* 286–290. New York: Worth Publishers, 1972.
  Analysis, with musical examples. Intended for the undergraduate student.

2579. Laming, Frank M. "Set Works for 'O' Level, GCE." *Music Teacher,* 54 (November 1975): 15–16.
  Analysis, with musical examples.

2580. Machlis, Joseph. *The Enjoyment of Music.* 3d ed., 139–142. New York: W. W. Norton, 1970.
  Analytic overview for the undergraduate music student. Musical examples.

2581. Stedman, Preston. *The Symphony,* 109–114. Englewood Cliffs, NJ: Prentice-Hall, 1979.
  Description of form, tonality, thematic activity, and instrumentation. Musical examples and diagram.

2582. Tovey, Donald Francis. *Essays in Musical Analysis.* Vol. 1, 218–223. London: Oxford University Press, 1935.
  Lucid commentary and analytic remarks. Musical examples.

DISSERTATIONS AND THESES

General

2583. Butler, Douglas Lamar. "The Organ Works of Felix Mendelssohn-Bartholdy." D.M.A., University of Oregon, 1973, 268 pp., DA 34-6020A.

2584. Filosa, Albert James. "The Early Symphonies and Chamber Music of Felix Mendelssohn Bartholdy." Ph.D., Yale University, 1970, 229 pp., DA 31-6646A.

2585. Jessop, Craig Don. "An Analytical Survey of the Unaccompanied Choral Works for Mixed Voices by Felix Mendelssohn-Bartholdy." D.M.A., Stanford University, 1981, 111 pp., DA 41-4536A.

2586. Stoner, Thomas Alan. "Mendelssohn's Published Songs." Ph.D., University of Maryland, 1972, 440 pp., DA 33-6956A.

2587. Vitercik, Gregory John. "The Early Works of Felix Mendelssohn: A Study in the Romantic Sonata Style." Ph.D., State University of New York at Stony Brook, 1985, 508 pp., DA 47-344A.

2588. Woodward, Francis Lewis. "The Solo Songs of Felix Mendelssohn." D.M.A., University of Texas at Austin, 1972, 233 pp., DA 33-5229A.

Concertos for Two Pianos

2589. Roennfeld, Peter John. "The Double Piano Concertos of Felix Mendelssohn." D.M.A., University of Cincinnati, 1985, 169 pp., DA 46-2851A.

Elijah

2590. Ellison, Ross Wesley. "Unity and Contrast in Mendelssohn's *Elijah*." Ph.D., University of North Carolina at Chapel Hill, 1978, 381 pp., DA 40-16A-17A.

Symphonies

2591. Holt, Marilyn Barnes. "Developmental Procedures in the Sonata Form Movements of the Symphonies of Beethoven, Schubert, Mendelssohn, and Schumann." Ph.D., Case Western Reserve, 1973, 359 pp., DA 34-7807A.

MENNIN, PETER, 1923–1983

Symphony No. 3

2592. Machlis, Joseph. *Introduction to Contemporary Music*, 528–530. New York: W. W. Norton, 1961.
Brief analysis for the undergraduate student.

MESSIAEN, OLIVIER, 1908–

General

2593. Avery, James. "Olivier Messiaen—An Introduction to His Piano Music." *Contemporary Keyboard*, 5 (August 1979): 36–40+.
Overview of the piano works for the performer, with interspersed analytic comments. Musical examples.

2594. Bernard, Jonathan W. "Messiaen's Synaesthesia: The Correspondence Between Color and Sound Structure in His Music." *Music Perception,* 4, no. 1 (1986): 41–68.

A general study of sound/color correspondences in Messiaen's music. Examples are drawn from many works from the years 1929–1974. Uses Forte's set theory labels. For the advanced student. Musical examples.

2595. Evans, Peter. "Music of the European Mainstream: 1940–1960." In *The New Oxford History of Music.* Vol. 10, *The Modern Age: 1890–1960.* Edited by Martin Cooper, 428–434. London: Oxford University Press, 1974.

Brief overview of Messiaen's stylistic development, with analytic observations on *Mode de Valeurs et d'Intensités, Oiseaux Exotiques, Quatuor Pour la Fin du Temps,* and *Visions de L'Amen.* Musical examples.

2596. Griffiths, Paul. *Olivier Messiaen and the Music of Time.* London: Faber and Faber, 1985, 274 pp.

A study of the music of Messiaen. Discusses the style and techniques of the composer, with many musical examples. Of particular interest is discussion of Eastern influences on his music and those stylistic elements placing Messiaen outside the mainstream Western tradition.

2597. Johnson, Robert Sherlaw. *Messiaen.* Berkeley: University of California Press, 1975, 221 pp.

Thorough analytic overview of Messiaen's output. Musical examples.

2598. Lee, John M. "Harmony in the Solo Piano Works of Olivier Messiaen: The First Twenty Years." *College Music Symposium,* 23, no. 1 (1983): 65–80.

2599. Matthews, Denis, ed. *Keyboard Music,* 337–340. New York: Praeger, 1972.

Critical and analytic remarks. Musical examples.

2600. Nichols, Roger. *Messiaen.* London: Oxford University Press, 1975, 79 pp.

A detailed technical study of Messiaen's music. The book is short, but the discussions technical. Analytical comments on many different works and different compositional techniques. Modes of limited transposition, nonretrograde rhythms, and Hindu influences examined. Musical examples.

2601. Whittall, Arnold. *Music Since the First World War*, 216–219; 226–231. London: J. M. Dent and Sons, 1977.
Brief analytic discussion. Musical examples.

Méditations sur le Mystère de la Sainte Trinité

2602. Whittall, Arnold. *Music Since the First World War*, 227–231. London: J. M. Dent and Sons, 1977.
Analytic comments. Studies the seventh movement in detail. Musical examples and table.

Mode de valeurs et d'intensités

2603. Brindle, Reginald Smith. *The New Music: The Avant-Garde Since 1945*, 23–25. London: Oxford University Press, 1975.
Brief analytic commentary. Musical examples.

2604. Evans, Peter. "Music of the European Mainstream: 1940–1960." In *The New Oxford History of Music.* Vol. 10, *The Modern Age: 1890–1960.* Edited by Martin Cooper, 438–441. London: Oxford University Press, 1974.
Brief analytic remarks on specific highlights of the work. Musical examples.

2605. Griffiths, Paul. *Modern Music: The Avant-Garde Since 1945*, 47–49. New York: George Braziller, 1981.
Analyzes serialization of pitch, duration, and dynamics. Musical examples.

Poèmes pour Mi

2606. Griffiths, Paul. *"Poèmes* and *Haiku*—A Note on Messiaen's Development." *Musical Times*, 112 (September 1971): 851–852.
Brief overview showing stylistic changes.

Preludes for Piano

2607. Lee, J. M. "A Look at Olivier Messiaen: The Man, His Philosophy, and His Piano Preludes." *Piano Quarterly*, 33, no. 128 (1984–1985): 52 +.

Structures

2608. Brindle, Reginald Smith. *The New Music: The Avant-Garde Since 1945*, 26–34. London: Oxford University Press, 1975.
Compact analysis with charts and musical examples dealing with form, dynamics, note durations, and ordering of the note series.

Trois petites liturgies de la Présence Divine

2609. Davies, Laurence. "Three Aspects of God." *Music and Musicians,* 19 (March 1971): 26–27.
Background, descriptive commentary, and brief analyses.

DISSERTATIONS AND THESES

General

2610. Barrington, Clyde. "The Organ Works of Olivier Messiaen and Their Importance in His Total Oeuvre." S.M.D., Union Theological Seminary, 1974, 593 pp., DA 35-1686A-7A.

Cinq Rechants

2611. Davidson, Audrey Jean Ekdahl. "Olivier Messiaen's *Tristan Trilogy*: Time and Transcendence." Ph.D., University of Minnesota, 1975, 433 pp., DA 36-3199A.

Couleurs de la Cité Céleste

2612. Quilling, Howard Lee. "An Analysis of Olivier Messiaen's *Couleurs de la Cité Céleste.*" Ph.D., University of California, Santa Barbara, 1984, 346 pp., DA 45-3477A.

Harawi, chant d'amour et de Mort

2613. Davidson, Audrey Jean Ekdahl. "Olivier Messiaen's *Tristan Trilogy*: Time and Transcendence." Ph.D., University of Minnesota, 1975, 433 pp., DA 36-3199A.

Méditations sur le Mystère de la Sainte Trinité

2614. Gilmer, Carl DuVall. "Messiaen's Musical Language in *Méditations sur le Mystère de la Sainte Trinit.*" D.M.A., Memphis State University, 1978, 68 pp., DA 39-3905A.

Turangalîla-Symphonie

2615. Davidson, Audrey Jean Ekdahl. "Olivier Messiaen *Tristan Trilogy*: Time and Transcendence." Ph.D., University of Minnesota, 1975, 433 pp., DA 36-3199A.

MEYERBEER, GIACOMO, 1791–1864

Le Prophète

2616.   Thomson, Joan. "Pathbreaker: Analyzing *Le Prophète.*" *Opera News*, 41 (January 29, 1977): 36–37.
Brief descriptive and critical commentary. Musical examples.

MIASKOVSKY, NIKOLAI, 1881–1950

Concerto for Violoncello

2617.   Dale, S. S. "Contemporary Cello Concerti: Myaskovsky and Glière." *Strad*, 86 (July 1975): 193 + .
Brief analytic remarks.

MILHAUD, DARIUS, 1892–1974

Concerto for Percussion

2618.   Larrick, Geary. "Milhaud's Concerto for Percussion—Analysis and Performance." *School Musician*, 45 (February 1974): 8 + ; (April 1974): 14 + .

Concerto for Violin

2619.   Dale, S. S. "Contemporary Cello Concerti." *Strad*, 86 (March 1976): 807–809.
Brief background and analysis.

Création du Monde

2620.   Hansen, Peter. *An Introduction to Twentieth Century Music.* 2d ed., 136–139. Boston: Allyn and Bacon, 1967.
Brief descriptive commentary, with a few analytic remarks. For the undergraduate student. Musical examples.

2621.   Machlis, Joseph. *Introduction to Contemporary Music*, 222–225. New York: W. W. Norton, 1961.
Descriptive commentary, with musical examples. For the undergraduate student.

Une Journée "Midi"

2622.   Forte, Allen. *Contemporary Tone-Structures*, 39–47. New York: Columbia University Press, 1955.
Thorough analysis dealing with formal structure, tonality, internal relationships, and general stylistic characteristics. Musical examples and analytic sketches.

Septet for Strings

2623.   Puronne, Kevin. "The Septuor a Cordes of Darius Milhaud." *Indiana Theory Review*, 3, no. 3 (1980): 36–61.
A thorough analysis of each movement, discussing the compositional procedures of each. Additional comments on harmonic and structural properties of the work as a whole. Musical examples.

DISSERTATIONS AND THESES

Preludes for Organ

2624.   Goetz, Wilhelm A. "An Analytical Study of Milhaud's Neuf Preludes for Organ." Ed.D., Columbia University Teachers College, 1976, 110 pp., DA 37-1289A.

Symphonies

2625.   Swickard, Ralph James. "The Symphonies of Darius Milhaud: An Historical Perspective and Critical Study of Their Musical Content, Style, and Form." Ph.D., University of California at Los Angeles, 1973, 459 pp., DA 34-3458A.

MOMPOU, FEDERICO, 1893–1987

DISSERTATIONS AND THESES

Canciones y Danzas

2626.   Bendell, Christine Jean. "Federico Mompou: An Analytical and Stylistic Study of the *Canciones y Danzas* for Piano." D.A., University of Northern Colorado, 1983, 223 pp., DA 44-2283A.

MONTEVERDI, CLAUDIO, 1567–1643

General

2627. **Arnold, Denis.** *Monteverdi.* 2d ed. London: J. M. Dent and Sons, 1975, 212 pp.
A "Master Musician" series treatment intended for the student. Deals with the entire range of Monteverdi's output, focusing on specific pieces for critical and analytic observations. Monteverdi's life, historical significance, and influences are discussed. Musical examples.

2628. **Arnold, Denis.** "Monteverdi's Church Music: Some Venetian Traits." *Monthly Musical Record,* 88 (May–June 1958): 83–91.
Examines some elements of style and form that relate Monteverdi's music to that of his contemporaries. Examines form and style of the *Sonata sopra Sancta Maria.*

2629. **Arnold, Denis, and Nigel Fortune, eds.** *The New Monteverdi Companion.* London: Faber and Faber, 1985, 361 pp.
Analytic discussion of style, influence of other composers on Monteverdi, historical context, Monteverdi's influence on other composers, operatic predecessors and structure. Full treatment of the Venetian operas and the later madrigals with regard to style, structure, music, and text relationships. Musical examples.

2630. **Fortune, Nigel.** "Duet and Trio in Monteverdi." *Musical Times,* 108 (May 1967): 417–419+.
An examination of Monteverdi's writing in polyphonic textures as opposed to the fashionable monodic style of the time. Musical examples.

2631. **Hoover, Kathleen.** "Prophet of Music." *Opera News,* 26 (March 10, 1962): 9–13.
Overview of Monteverdi's achievement and innovation in dramatic music.

2632. **Pinter, Emoke.** "New Elements of Vocal Style in the First Half of the Seventeenth Century: Monteverdi and His Contemporaries." *Studia Musicologica,* 22, no. 1–4 (1980): 205–253.
Describes new style (called "concertos" in Madrigal Book VII) and its use in various works. Identifies rhythmic and motivic procedures and discusses relationship with contemporary composers.

2633. **Prunières, Henry.** *Monteverdi: His Life and Work.* Translated by Marie D. Mackie. New York: Dover Publications, 1972, 293 pp.

Excellent survey of Monteverdi's music for the student. Musical and dramatic features are singled out and Monteverdi's innovations seen in historical context.

2634. Redlich, Hans. *Claudio Monteverdi: Life and Works,* 94–116. London: Oxford University Press, 1952.
The place of Monteverdi's innovations in music history is stressed, along with specific comments on affective devices. Musical examples.

2635. Schrade, Leo. *Monteverdi: Creator of Modern Music.* New York: W. W. Norton, 1950, 348 pp.
Background, descriptive, and critical commentary on all Monteverdi's operas. Special mention of the forms and innovations. Musical examples.

2636. Stevens, Denis. *Monteverdi: Sacred, Secular, and the Occasional Music.* Rutherford, NJ: Fairleigh Dickinson University Press, 1978, 147 pp.
Brief discussions of Monteverdi's output. The organization of the book is by genre. The discussions include background and comments on texture, thematic content, harmony, general style characteristics, and text setting. Musical examples.

2637. Stevens, Denis. "Monteverdi's Venetian Church Music." *Musical Times,* 108 (May 1967): 414+.
An overview with remarks on style. Musical examples.

Madrigals

2638. Arnold, Denis. *Monteverdi Madrigals.* Seattle: University of Washington Press, 1967, 61 pp.
Thorough critical and analytic discussion for the student. Musical examples.

2639. Bukofzer, Manfred. *Music in the Baroque Era,* 33–38. New York: W. W. Norton, 1947.
Brief commentary focusing on the changes that Monteverdi wrought on the madrigal form. Musical examples.

2640. Dent, Edward J. "The Sixteenth Century Madrigal." In *The New Oxford History of Music.* Vol. 4, *The Age of Humanism, 1540–1630.* Edited by Gerald Abraham, 69–73. London: Oxford University Press, 1968.
Brief overview focusing on stylistic characteristics. Musical examples.

2641.   Einstein, Alfred. *The Italian Madrigal.* Vol. 2. Translated by Alexander H. Krappe, Roger H. Sessions, and Oliver Strunk, 717–728; 850–872. Princeton, NJ: Princeton University Press, 1949.
Historical perspective, stylistic characteristics, relationship of text to music, and function of the music for its time discussed. For the more advanced student. Musical examples.

2642.   Reese, Gustave. *Music in the Renaissance.* Rev. ed., 437–443. New York: W. W. Norton, 1959.
Detailed descriptive overview with musical examples.

Madrigali Guerrieri, et Amorosi

2643.   Stevens, Denis. *"Madrigali Guerrieri, et Amorosi*—A Reappraisal for the Quatercentenary." *Musical Quarterly,* 53, no. 2 (1967): 161–187.
Historical commentary, with analysis. Musical examples.

Mass in G Minor

2644.   Brindle, Reginald Smith. "Monteverdi's G Minor Mass: An Experiment in Construction." *Musical Quarterly,* 54, no. 3 (1968): 352–360.
Criticism and analysis with musical examples.

Messe et Salmi

2645.   Roche, Jerome. "Monteverdi—An Interesting Example of Second Thoughts." *Music Review,* 32, no. 3 (1971): 193–204.
Background, descriptive, and critical commentary. Musical examples.

Orfeo

2646.   Donington, Robert. *The Opera,* 22–30. New York: Harcourt Brace Jovanovich, 1978.
Full discussion of the dramatic and musical action, with remarks on historical importance.

2647.   George, Graham. "The Structure of Dramatic Music, 1607–1909." *Musical Quarterly,* 52, no. 4 (1966): 471–472.
Tonal and structural analysis of the work, with commentary on the use of symbolism through keys.

2648.   George, Graham. *Tonality and Musical Structure*, 33–36. London: Oxford University Press, 1970.
Tonality as it relates to the dramatic structure of *Orfeo*. Chart.

2649.   Schuller, Gunther. *Musings: The Musical World of Gunther Schuller*, 208–213. New York: Oxford University Press, 1986.
Analytic discussion.

2650.   Whenham, John. *Claudio Monteverdi: Orfeo.* New York: Cambridge University Press, 1986, 116 pp.
This volume contains little concrete analysis of the music. Some analytic observations are to be found in the synopsis (John Whenham, "Five Acts: One Action," pp. 48–77) and in an article called "Recreating *Orfeo* for the Modern Stage: Solving the Musical Problems," pp. 138–155). Musical examples.

Sfogave con le stelle

2651.   Horsely, Imogene. "Monteverdi's Use of Borrowed Material in *Sfogave con le stelle." Music and Letters*, 59, no. 3 (1978): 316–328.
An examination of how Monteverdi used Caccini's monody as the basis for his madrigal. Musical examples.

Vespro della Beata Vergine

2652.   Bonta, Stephen. "Liturgical Problems in Monteverdi's *Marian* Vespers." *Journal of the American Musicological Society*, 20, no. 1 (1967): 87–106.
Advanced discussion. Musical examples.

2653.   Lowell, John. "Aspects of Psalmody and Text Setting in Monteverdi's *Marian* Vespers." *Musical Analysis*, 2, no. 2 (1974): 14–26.
Analyzes the influence of psalmody on structure, melody, and music-text relationship. Musical examples and tables.

2654.   Stevens, Denis. "Where Are the Vespers of Yesteryear?" *Musical Quarterly*, 47, no. 3 (1961): 315–330.
Historical analysis demonstrating the lack of stylistic and liturgical unity of Monteverdi's vespers. Descriptive and critical commentary follows mentioning structural and tonal characteristics. Musical examples.

MOZART, WOLFGANG AMADEUS, 1756–1791

General

2655.   Abert, Anna Amalie. "The Operas of Mozart." In *The New Oxford History of Music*, Vol. 7, *The Age of Enlightenment, 1745–1790.*

Edited by Egon Wellesz and F. W. Sternfeld, 97–172. London: Oxford University Press, 1973.
Survey of Mozart's operas, showing stylistic growth both musically and dramatically. Musical examples.

2656. Abraham, Gerald. "The Operas." In *The Mozart Companion.* Edited by H. C. Robbins Landon, 283–323. New York: W. W. Norton, 1969.
Excellent overview, with many critical remarks on specific operas. Assesses Mozart's unique contribution to the opera as a form.

2657. Beaujean, Alfred. "Mozart's Church Sonatas." *Music* (AGO), 11, (June 1977): 47–48.
Background and descriptive commentary, with analytic observations.

2658. Blom, Eric. *Mozart.* London: J. M. Dent and Sons, 1974, 388 pp.
Descriptive and critical, with occasional analytic observations on Mozart's output for the undergraduate student or musical amateur. Musical examples.

2659. Dent, Edward J. *Mozart's Operas: A Critical Study.* 2d ed. London: Oxford University Press, 1947, 276 pp.
Extremely detailed treatment of the dramatic aspects. The music is lightly treated, and then only as an adjunct to the drama. Influences on Mozart examined.

2660. Einstein, Alfred. *Mozart: His Character, His Work.* Translated by Arthur Mendel and Nathan Broder. London: Oxford University Press, 1945, 292 pp.
Scholarly discourse on Mozart's output with special focus on influences and style. Not analytic. Musical examples.

2661. Ferguson, Donald N. *Image and Structure in Chamber Music,* 46–74. Minneapolis: University of Minnesota Press, 1964.
Overview of the chamber music, with brief analyses. Musical examples.

2662. Geiringer, Karl. "The Rise of Chamber Music." In *The New Oxford History of Music,* Vol. 7, *The Age of Enlightenment, 1745–1790.* Edited by Egon Wellesz and F. W. Sternfeld, 539–545; 569–572. London: Oxford University Press, 1973.
Very brief descriptive overview of the violin sonatas, piano trios, and piano quintets. Analytic remarks on the Piano Quintet, K. 516 (pp. 569–572). Musical examples.

2663. Gianturco, Carolyn. *Mozart's Early Operas.* London: B. T. Batsford, 1981, 216 pp.

Historical background, plot summaries, and analytic account of each opera. Comments cover orchestration, form, characterization, and motivic elements. Musical examples.

2664. Hughes, Spike. *Famous Mozart Operas.* 2d ed., rev. New York: Dover Publications, 1972, 238 pp.

Abduction from the Seraglio, Marriage of Figaro, Don Giovanni, Così fan Tutte, and *Magic Flute* discussed analytically, with musical examples.

2665. King, Alexander Hyatt. *Mozart Chamber Music.* London: British Broadcasting Corporation, 1968, 68 pp.

Mainly descriptive overview intended for undergraduate students. Some analytic remarks. Musical examples.

2666. Landon, H. C. Robbins, and Donald Mitchell, eds. *The Mozart Companion.* New York: W. W. Norton, 1956, 397 pp.

Critical and analytic survey by different authors on Mozart's output. Musical examples.

2667. Liebner, Janos. *Mozart on the Stage.* New York: Praeger, 1972, 254 pp.

Excellent treatment of Mozart as dramatist. Specific musical elements are highlighted with regard to dramatic action.

2668. Mann, William. *The Operas of Mozart.* New York: Oxford University Press, 1977, 656 pp.

Thorough discussion of all the operas, including background, synopses, and analytic observations on the music. Musical examples.

2669. Matthews, Denis, ed. *Keyboard Music,* 143–165. New York: Praeger, 1972.

Background, historical perspective, stylistic traits, and analytic remarks on specific works. Musical examples.

2670. Moberly, Robert B. *Three Mozart Operas: "Figaro," "Don Giovanni," "The Magic Flute."* New York: Dodd, Mead, 1968, 303 pp.

Detailed descriptive commentary of the "blow-by-blow" variety. Little analytic commentary, but useful for dramatic sources and background.

2671. Noske, Frits. *The Signifier and the Signified: Studies in the Operas of Mozart and Verdi.* The Hague: M. Nijhoff, 1977, 418 pp.

Detailed analytic discussions of *Marriage of Figaro, Don Giovanni,* and *Così fan Tutte.*
Analyses go beyond the surface to encompass the musico-dramatic relationships. Musical examples.

2672. Olleson, Edward. "Solo Song." In *The New Oxford History of Music.* Vol. 7, *The Age of Enlightenment, 1745–1790.* Edited by Egon Wellesz and F. W. Sternfeld, 359–363. London: Oxford University Press, 1973.
Brief remarks on Mozart's *Lieder* and concert arias. Musical examples.

2673. Osborne, Charles. *The Complete Operas of Mozart.* London: Victor Gollancz, 1978, 349 pp.
Background, plot summary, and analysis. Very thorough. Musical examples.

2674. Pauly, Reinhard. *Music in the Classic Period.* 2d ed., 129–139. Englewood Cliffs, NJ: Prentice-Hall, 1973.
Descriptive and critical overview of Mozart's output. Mentions stylistic features and Mozart's contribution in historical context. Musical examples.

2675. Radcliffe, Philip. "Keyboard Music." In *The New Oxford History of Music,* Vol. 7, *The Age of Enlightenment, 1745–1790.* Edited by Egon Wellesz and F. W. Sternfeld, 602–610. London: Oxford University Press, 1973.
Overview, highlighting important stylistic characteristics of the keyboard music. Musical examples.

2676. Robertson, Alec, ed. *Chamber Music,* 60–93. Baltimore: Penguin Books, 1957.
The trios, quartets, and quintets explored from various musical points of view; harmony, form, technique, use of counterpoint and rhythm. Musical examples.

2677. Rosen, Charles. *The Classical Style: Haydn, Mozart, Beethoven,* 288–325. New York: Viking Press, 1971.
Mozart's comic operas explored for underlying sonata-form principles. Demonstrates techniques of classical balance even in highly dramatic moments. Musical examples.

2678. Sadie, Stanley. *Mozart,* 145–164. New York: Grossman, 1970.
Brief overview of the operas, with critical commentary.

2679. Thomson, Katharine. *The Masonic Thread in Mozart.* London: Lawrence and Wishart, 1977, 207 pp.

Masonic symbolism discussed first as background, then examined in detail in specific works. *The Marriage of Figaro, The Magic Flute,* and some of the piano concertos looked at closely.

2680. Ulrich, Homer. *Chamber Music.* 2d ed., 186–216. New York: Columbia University Press, 1966.
Thorough survey of the chamber works, their background, influences, and stylistic growth. Musical examples.

2681. Wolff, Konrad. *Masters of the Keyboard: Individual Style Elements in the Piano Music of Bach, Haydn, Mozart, Beethoven, and Schubert,* 76–109. Bloomington: Indiana University Press, 1983.
Discussion of keyboard style meant for performers. Undergraduate students will find the discussion useful for its interspersed analytic comments. Musical examples.

Abduction from the Seraglio

2682. Abert, Anna Amalie. "The Operas of Mozart." In *The New Oxford History of Music.* Vol. 7, *The Age of Enlightenment, 1745–1790.* Edited by Egon Wellesz and F. W. Sternfeld, 141–147. London: Oxford University Press, 1973.
Focuses on Mozart's characterization and growth as a dramatist.

2683. Liebner, Janos. *Mozart on the Stage,* 72–93. London: John Calder, 1975.
Descriptive and analytic commentary, with observations on characterization. Musical examples.

Adagio and Allegro for Clock Organ in F Minor, K. 594.

2684. Richner, Thomas and E. Shay. "Mozart's Three Pieces for Clock Organ." *Music (AGO),* 11 (June 1977): 44–46.
Background and descriptive commentary. Musical examples.

Andante for Clock Organ in F Major, K. 616

2685. Richner, Thomas, and E. Shay. "Mozart's Three Pieces for Clock Organ." *Music (AGO),* 11 (June 1977): 44–46.
Background and descriptive commentary. Musical examples.

La Clemenza di Tito

2686. Bloomfield, Theodore. "Mozart's Last Opera." *Music and Musicians,* 22 (April 1974): 30–32 +.
Background and critical commentary assessing this opera's historical lack of popularity.

2687. Heartz, Daniel. *La Clemenza di Sarastro*: Masonic Benevolence in Mozart's Last Operas." *Musical Times,* 124 (March 1983): 152–157.
Masonic symbolism traced in this opera, as well as in *Magic Flute.* Musical examples.

2688. Heartz, Daniel. "Mozart's Overture to *Titus* as Dramatic Argument." *Musical Quarterly,* 64, no. 1 (1978): 29–49.
Traces the relationship of the overture to the opera and how it sums up the dramatic action of the entire work. Musical examples.

2689. Sadie, Stanley. "Mozart's Last Opera." *Opera,* 20 (October 1969): 837–843.
Circumstances under which this work was written and a critical discussion.

Concertos

2690. King, Alexander Hyatt. *Mozart String and Wind Concertos.* London: British Broadcasting Corporation, 1978.
Brief, mainly descriptive commentary, with occasional analytic observations on the Clarinet Concerto, Horn Concertos, *Sinfonie Concertanti,* Oboe and Flute Concertos, Violin Concertos, Bassoon Concertos, and Concertone for two Violins. Musical examples.

2691. Rosen, Charles. *The Classical Style: Haydn, Mozart, Beethoven,* 185–263. New York: Viking Press, 1971.
Discussion of the concerto as a form and Mozart's approach to it as a dramatic expression. Mentions most of the concertos, but treats the Piano Concerto No. 20, K. 466, at length. Historic, critical, and analytic with musical examples.

2692. Simon, Eric J. "Sonata into Concerto: A Study of Mozart's First Seven Concertos." *Acta Musicologica,* 31, nos. 3–4 (1959): 170–185.
Description and analytic remarks on those concertos that were adapted from sonatas.

2693. Tischler, Hans. *A Structural Analysis of Mozart's Piano Concertos.* New York: Institute of Medieval Music, 1966, 140 pp.
Detailed, coded analyses of all the piano concertos. Some general discussion of Mozart's style and method as well. Musical examples.

2694. Veinus, Abraham. *The Concerto.* Rev. ed., 72–126. New York: Dover Publications, 1964.

General discussion of the growth of the concerto form under Mozart, the influence of the evolving piano on the concerto, and stylistic traits of Mozart and Beethoven. Good treatment of historical perspective.

Concerto for Clarinet in A Major, K. 622

2695. Etheridge, David E. *Mozart's Clarinet Concerto: The Clarinetist's View.* Gretna, LA: Pelican, 1983, 192 pp.

Though mainly a discussion of various clarinetist's interpretations of this concerto, there is a description of the formal structure with diagrams. Musical examples.

2696. Hacker, Alan. "Mozart and the Basset Clarinet." *Musical Times,* 110 (April 1969): 359–362.

The evidence pointing to the basset clarinet as the instrument Mozart had in mind for this concerto. Musical examples.

2697. Tovey, Donald Francis. *Essays in Musical Analysis.* Vol. 3, 52–53. London: Oxford University Press, 1936.

Brief descriptive and critical remarks. Notes Mozart's influence on the clarinet. Musical examples.

Concertos for Flute

2698. Tovey, Donald Francis. *Essays in Musical Analysis.* Vol. 3, 47–51. London: Oxford University Press, 1936.

Brief analytic remarks on Concertos Nos. 1 and 2 (K. 313 and 314). Musical examples.

Concerto for Flute and Harp in C Major, K. 299

2699. Tovey, Donald Francis. *Essays in Musical Analysis.* Vol. 3. London: Oxford University Press, 1936, 60–62.

Background and descriptive remarks with musical examples.

Concerto for Horn No. 3 in E-Flat Major, K. 447

2700. Newbould, Brian. "Mozart, the Hand Horn, and K. 447." *Music Teacher,* 57 (September 1978): 17–18.

Brief analysis with musical examples.

Concertos for Piano

2701. Forman, Denis. *Mozart's Concerto Form: The First Movements of the Piano Concertos.* New York: Praeger, 1971, 303 pp.
   Examination of form in the first movements of Mozart's piano concertos. Describes the development of the form, and takes issue with analyses based on "sonata form." Contains musical examples, thematic index, and numerous tables and diagrams showing formal structures.

2702. Girdlestone, Cuthbert. *Mozart and His Piano Concertos.* Norman: University of Oklahoma Press, 1952, 511 pp.
   Thorough treatment of all the piano concertos, observations on Mozart's artistic growth and development of the concerto form. Musical examples.

2703. Grout, Donald Jay. *A History of Western Music,* 466–467. New York: W. W. Norton, 1960.
   General remarks on salient musical characteristics and basic formal scheme of the piano concertos.

2704. Hill, Ralph, ed. *The Concerto,* 49–118. London: Penguin Books, 1952.
   Critical and analytic commentary for the undergraduate student. Musical examples.

2705. Hutchings, Arthur. *A Companion to Mozart's Piano Concertos.* 2d ed. London: Oxford University Press, 1951, 211 pp.
   Descriptive and analytic commentary on all the piano concertos, emphasizing formal structure, tonality, and themes. Brief background information is provided for each concerto. Mozart's contribution to the concerto form and the keyboard concerto before Mozart are examined. Musical examples.

2706. Kimbell, David R. "Variation Form in the Piano Concertos of Mozart." *Music Review,* 44, no. 2 (1983): 95–103.
   A survey of variation techniques in the concertos, tracing stylistic development from mere ornamentation to virtuoso variations.

2707. Meyer, John A. "The Operatic Basis of Mozart's Keyboard Concertos." *Musicology,* 6 (1980): 62–65.
   Identifies operatic influence in the concertos, with K. 453 taken as a special example. One table, no musical examples.

2708.   Pauly, Reinhard. *Music in the Classic Period,* 142–146. Englewood Cliffs, NJ: Prentice-Hall, 1965.

General analytic observations are illustrated with musical examples from specific works. The discussions are brief and general.

2709.   Radcliffe, Philip. *Mozart Piano Concertos.* London: British Broadcasting Corporation, 1978, 72 pp.

A "BBC Music Guide" designed for the listener rather than the analyst. Generally descriptive rather than analytic treatment. All the concertos are discussed in turn, dwelling on forms, keys, major themes, and stylistic characteristics. Musical examples.

2710.   Rosen, Charles. *The Classical Style: Haydn, Mozart, Beethoven.* Rev. ed., 185–263. London: Faber and Faber, 1976.

An extensive and detailed analytic discussion of Mozart's piano concertos. Describes the development of Mozart's style in this genre. Detailed analytic treatment is given to K. 271 and K. 466. Substantive analytic comments on the *Sinfonia Concertante,* K. 364, and several other of Mozart's piano concertos. Musical examples.

2711.   Simon, Eric J. "Sonata into Concerto: A Study of Mozart's First Seven Concertos." *Acta Musicologica,* 31, nos. 3–4 (1959): 170–185.

Stylistic observations on K. 21a, K. 37, K. 39, K. 40, and K. 41—all based on preexisting music by other composers. Musical examples.

Concerto for Piano No. 9 in E-Flat Major, K. 271

2712.   Cobin, Marian. "Aspects of Stylistic Evolution in Two Mozart Concertos: K. 271 and K. 482." *Music Review,* 31, no. 1 (1970): 1–20.

Analytic examination to show specific factors contributing to the sense of greater maturity and depth in K. 482 over K. 271. Objective analysis with musical examples.

2713.   Nelson, Wendell. *The Concerto,* 25–28. Dubuque, IA: William C. Brown, 1969.

Brief analysis with critical remarks. Musical examples.

2714.   Warburton, A. O. *Analyses of Musical Classics.* Book 4, 84–96. London: Longman, 1974.

Full measure-by-measure analysis. Score necessary.

2715.   Warburton, A. O. "Set Works for 'O' Level, GCE." *Music Teacher,* 52 (June 1973): 18–19+.

Compact analysis.

Concerto for Piano No. 12 in A Major, K. 414

2716. Tovey, Donald Francis. *Essays in Musical Analysis.* Vol. 3, 27–30. London: Oxford University Press, 1936.
Brief analysis, with critical remarks and musical examples.

Concerto for Piano No. 15 in B-Flat Major, K. 450

2717. Tovey, Donald Francis. *Essays in Musical Analysis.* Vol. 3, 30–33. London: Oxford University Press, 1936.
Brief analytic remarks and critical observations. Musical examples.

Concerto for Piano No. 17 in G Major, K. 453

2718. Cole, William. *The Form of Music: An Outline of Musical Designs Used by the Great Composers,* 69–74. London: Associated Board of the Royal Schools of Music, n.d.
Brief outline of the structure in table form.

2719. Tovey, Donald Francis. *Essays in Musical Analysis.* Vol. 3, 33–36. London: Oxford University Press, 1936.
Brief analytic insights and lucid critical observations. Musical examples.

Concerto for Piano No. 20 in D Minor, K. 466

2720. Davie, Cedric Thorpe. *Musical Structure and Design,* 110–114. New York: Dover Publications, 1966.
Compact measure-by-measure analysis. Musical examples.

2721. Green, Douglass M. *Form in Tonal Music,* 243–244. New York: Holt, Rinehart, and Winston, 1965.
General stylistic characteristics discussed, followed by a chart-outline summary analyzing the entire last movement.

2722. Hopkins, Antony. *Talking About Concertos,* 12–23. London: Heinemann, 1964.
Extended analytic essay describing tonal, thematic, and formal events.

2723. Stadlen, Peter. "Thoughts on Musical Continuity." *Score,* 26 (January 1960): 52–62.

Traces Mozart's creative process through examination of the original manuscripts. Phrases that are today accepted as part of the natural flow of ideas are shown as inserted afterthoughts. Musical examples.

2724. Ulrich, Homer. *Music: A Design for Listening,* 268–270. New York: Harcourt, Brace, 1957.
Descriptive breakdown by measure, with analytic observations. Musical examples.

Concerto for Piano No. 21 in C Major, K. 467

2725. Machlis, Joseph. *The Enjoyment of Music.* 3d ed., 269–272. New York: W. W. Norton, 1970.
Compact analysis for the undergraduate music student. Musical examples.

Concerto for Piano No. 22 in E-Flat Major, K. 482

2726. Cobin, Marian. "Aspects of Stylistic Evolution in Two Mozart Concertos: K. 271 and K. 482." *Music Review,* 31, no. 1 (1970): 1–20.
Analytic examination to show specific factors contributing to the sense of greater maturity and depth of K. 482 over K. 271. Objective analysis with musical examples.

Concerto for Piano No. 23 in A Major, K. 488

2727. Green, Douglass M. *Form in Tonal Music,* 245. New York: Holt, Rinehart, and Winston, 1965.
Chart outline analyzing entire last movement.

2728. Hopkins, Antony. *Talking About Concertos,* 24–34. London: Heinemann, 1964.
Extended analytic essay describing tonal, thematic, and formal events.

2729. Nelson, Wendell. *The Concerto,* 29–31. Dubuque, IA: William C. Brown, 1969.
Brief analysis, with critical remarks. Musical examples.

2730. Tovey, Donald Francis. *Essays in Musical Analysis.* Vol. 3, 37–42. London: Oxford University Press, 1936.
Critical commentary, with analytic insights. Musical examples.

Concerto for Piano No. 24 in C Minor, K. 491

2731.   Green, Douglass M. *Form in Tonal Music,* 234–240. New York: Holt, Rinehart, and Winston, 1965.
   Compact analysis, with charts, symbols, and musical examples. First movement only.

2732.   Meyer, John A. "Mozart's Pathetique Concerto." *Music Review,* 39, no. 3 (1978): 196–210.
   Chromaticism and the Neapolitan sixth are the focus of this analysis, to show that though apparently disruptive in character, they unify the work. Musical examples.

2733.   Nelson, Wendell. *The Concerto,* 31–33. Dubuque, IA: William C. Brown, 1969.
   Brief analysis, with critical remarks. Musical examples.

2734.   Stadlen, Peter. "Thoughts on Musical Continuity." *Score,* 26 (January 1960): 52–62.
   Traces Mozart's creative process through examination of the original manuscripts. Phrases that are today accepted as part of the natural flow of ideas are shown to be inserted afterthoughts. Musical examples.

2735.   Tischler, Hans. *The Perceptive Music Listener,* 322–326. Englewood, Cliffs, NJ: Prentice-Hall, 1955.
   Analysis, with musical examples.

2736.   Tovey, Donald Francis. *Essays in Musical Analysis.* Vol. 3, 42–46. London: Oxford University Press, 1936.
   Brief but solid discussion of formal principles and emotional content. Musical examples.

Concerto for Piano No. 25 in C Major, K. 503

2737.   Kerman, Joseph, ed. *Wolfgang Amadeus Mozart: Piano Concerto in C Major, K. 503.* Norton Critical Scores. New York: W. W. Norton, 1970, 202 pp.
   Historical background and analytic essays by Alfred Einstein, Donald Francis Tovey, C. M. Girdlestone, and Hans Keller. Full score provided.

Concerto for Piano No. 26 in D Major, K. 537. ("Coronation")

2738.   Reynolds, R. G. "K. 537: Regression or Progression?" *Music Review,* 35, no. 2 (1974): 142–148.

Tonal relationships as a clue to understanding K. 537. Author feels that the expanded tonal range in this work is in keeping with the musical trends of the time and does not reflect a lapse in musical taste, as many critics maintain.

Concerto for Piano No. 27 in B-Flat Major, K. 595

2739.   Rosen, David. "The Composer's 'Standard Operating Procedure' as Evidence of Intention: The Case of a Formal Quirk in Mozart's K. 595." *Journal of Musicology*, 5, no. 1 (1987): 79–90.
   Discusses this concerto against the background of formal procedures (the "standard operating procedures") evident in other concertos and offers reasons for Mozart's addition of seven measures. The discussion necessarily includes some analytic comments on the first movement. For the advanced student.

Concertos for Violin

2740.   Pauly, Reinhard. *Music in the Classic Period*, 138–142. Englewood Cliffs, NJ: Prentice-Hall, 1965.
   General analytic observations are illustrated with musical examples from specific works. The discussions are brief.

Concerto for Violin No. 4 in D Major, K. 218

2741.   George, Graham. *Tonality and Musical Structure*, 129–132. London: Oxford University Press, 1970.
   Analysis focusing on tonal relations. Musical examples.

2742.   Nelson, Wendell. *The Concerto*, 22–25. Dubuque, IA: William C. Brown, 1969.
   Brief remarks on influences, form, and style with musical examples.

2743.   Tovey, Donald Francis. *Essays in Musical Analysis*. Vol. 3, 54–56. London: Oxford University Press, 1936.
   Descriptive and critical commentary. Musical examples.

Concerto for Violin No. 5 in A Major, K. 219

2744.   Tovey, Donald Francis. *Essays in Musical Analysis*. Vol. 3, 56–59. London: Oxford University Press, 1936.
   Remarks on authenticity, style, and form. Musical examples.

Così fan Tutte

2745. Hughes, Spike. "Così Is Like That." *Opera News*, 29 (February 20, 1965): 24–25.
Brief remarks on Mozart's ability to portray the characters through music.

2746. Keahey, Delores Jerde. "*Così fan Tutte*: Parody or Irony?" In *Paul A. Pisk: Essays in His Honor.* Edited by John Glowacki, 116–130. Austin: University of Texas Press, 1966.
Detailed discussion on dramatic intentions of *Così*.

2747. Liebner, Janos. *Mozart on the Stage*, 198–215. London: John Calder, 1975.
Descriptive and analytic commentary. Musical examples.

2748. Livermore, Ann. "*Così fan Tutte*, A Well-Kept Secret." *Music and Letters*, 46, no. 4 (1965): 316–321.
A discussion of the origins of Da Ponte's libretto in the works of Tirso de Molina and Molière.

2749. Sandow, Gregory. "On Gentle Winds." *Opera News*, 49 (December 22, 1984): 24 + .
Descriptive commentary with analytic insights into the trio from Act I.

2750. Steptoe, Andrew. *The Mozart–Da Ponte Operas.* Oxford: Clarendon Press, 1988, 273 pp.
Places *Marriage of Figaro, Don Giovanni,* and *Così fan Tutte* in the context of their time. The audience's understanding of the operas, Mozart's position in society, Da Ponte's attitudes, compositional history, staging, stylistic framework, and the music itself are discussed. Analyses are an important part of the author's presentation. Advanced. Musical examples.

2751. Wadsworth, Stephen. "The Course of Love." *Opera News*, 40 (December 20–27, 1975): 14–16.
Critical commentary on structure and characterization. Musical examples.

2752. Williams, Bernard. "Passion and Cynicism: Remarks on *Così fan Tutte.*" *Musical Times*, 114 (April 1973): 361 + .
General discussion, with critical remarks.

Così fan Tutte Overture

2753. Tovey, Donald Francis. *Essays in Musical Analysis.* Vol. 6, 30–31. London: Oxford University Press, 1969.
Brief remarks. For the undergraduate student.

Divertimenti

2754. Meyer, Eve. "The Viennese Divertimento." *Music Review*, 29, no. 3 (1968): 166–170.
  Basic stylistic characteristics of the form as Mozart used it. Very general.

Divertimento in E-Flat Major, K. 563

2755. Salzer, Felix. "The Variation Movement of Mozart's Divertimento, K. 563." In *The Music Forum*. Vol. 5. Edited by Felix Salzer and Carl Schachter, 257–315. New York: Columbia University Press, 1980.
  In-depth Schenkerian analysis, with musical examples.

Don Giovanni

2756. Abert, Hermann. *Mozart's Don Giovanni.* Translated by Peter Gellhorn. London: Eulenberg Books, 1976.
  Thorough treatment, including compositional history, historical background of story, remarks on characterization and analysis. Musical examples.

2757. Allanbrook, Wye J. "Metric Gesture as a Topic in *Le Nozze di Figaro* and *Don Giovanni*." *Musical Quarterly*, 67, no. 1 (1981): 94–112.
  Mozart's use of meter was intended to infuse the singers with the physical bearing to match the mood of the character. The author demonstrates that meters have, over the course of time, gained identifiable connotations that help support characterization on the stage. Musical examples. Author later develops this thesis in the book *Rhythmic Gesture in Mozart* (*see* item no. 2758, below).

2758. Allanbrook, Wye J. *Rhythmic Gesture in Mozart: "Le Nozze di Figaro" and "Don Giovanni."* Chicago: University of Chicago Press, 1983, 396 pp.
  The role of rhythm in conveying gesture, the key to character portrayal. Thorough descriptive and analytic commentary on rhythmic and other devices to convey mood and character. Musical examples.

2759. Einstein, Alfred. "Concerning Some Recitatives in *Don Giovanni*." *Music and Letters*, 19 (1938): 417–425.

Warns against feeling that Mozart's last version is the most authentic. Describes the many changes Mozart made merely to accommodate singers or the public. Also two recitatives not written by Mozart are uncovered in a later version.

2760.   Gounod, Charles. *Mozart's "Don Giovanni": A Commentary.* 3d ed. Translated by Windeyer Clark and J. T. Hutchinson. 1895. Reprint. New York: Da Capo Press, 1970, 144 pp.
  Of interest because of its author and detailed treatment.

2761.   Henning, Cosmo. "Thematic Metamorphosis in *Don Giovanni.*" *Music Review,* 30, no. 1 (1969): 22–26.
  Analysis of motives and their transformations to depict characterization. Shows how Mozart began with motives and arrived at themes—the reverse of the symphonic process.

2762.   Jefferson, Alan. *"Don Giovanni,* James Bond & Co." *Opera,* 16 (December 1965): 864–867.
  The concept of "hero" as seen in *Don Giovanni.*

2763.   Jenkins, Speight. "The Unrelated." *Opera News,* 33 (January 4, 1969): 24–25.
  Brief remarks on characterization and how the music helps to depict personality.

2764.   Liebner, Janos. *Mozart on the Stage,* 138–197. London: John Calder, 1975.
  Background, dramatic structure, and musical analysis. Musical examples.

2765.   Moberly, Robert B. *Three Mozart Operas: "Figaro," "Don Giovanni," "The Magic Flute."* New York: Dodd, Mead, 1967, 303 pp.
  Detailed commentary. The drama is analyzed, almost measure-by-measure, with many analytical comments on the music.

2766.   Noske, Frits. *"Don Giovanni:* Musical Affinities and Dramatic Structure." *Studia Musicologica,* 12, nos. 1–4 (1970): 167–203.
  Discussion of musical techniques, such as motifs and musical characterization, to heighten the dramatic unity of the opera. Musical examples.

2767.   Ratner, Leonard. *Classic Music: Expression, Form, and Style,* 397–411. New York: Schirmer Books, 1980.
  Examines the opera as the synthesis of the mature classic style. Topics discussed include *seria* and *buffa* elements, association of certain keys with plot situations, forms, overall structure, and harmonic structure. There is a detailed analytic discussion of the opera.

2768. Rosen, Charles. *The Classical Style: Haydn, Mozart, Beethoven.* Rev. ed., 296–302. London: Faber and Faber, 1976.
Formal analysis demonstrating underlying sonata form principles in the Sextet of Act II. Musical examples.

2769. Rushton, Julian. *W. A. Mozart: "Don Giovanni."* Cambridge: Cambridge University Press, 1981.
Chapters on various aspects of the opera: a synopsis of the plot (including differences between the Prague and Vienna versions); musical and literary predecessors of the opera; analysis of the librettos; a detailed analysis of the Quartet No. 9 (Elvira: "Non ti Fidor, O Misera, di quel Rebaldo Cor"); a discussion of musical characterization; a discussion of the large-scale musical structure; a discussion of other literature on the opera; discography. Musical examples.

2770. Sandow, Gregory. "Enigma Variations." *Opera News,* 48 (March 3, 1984): 14–17.
Though the plot is riddled with inconsistencies, raising many unanswered questions, the music succeeds in holding the drama together. Author demonstrates some of the musical binding forces at work.

2771. Sargeant, Winthrop. "Force of Nature (Don Giovanni As an Archetype)." *Opera News,* 42 (March 18, 1978): 18–21.
Interpretive views of the general public, E. T. A. Hoffmann, Kierkegaard, and Sargeant on the meaning of the drama.

2772. Steptoe, Andrew. *The Mozart–Da Ponte Operas.* Oxford: Clarendon Press, 1988, 273 pp.
Places *Marriage of Figaro, Don Giovanni,* and *Così fan Tutte* in the context of their time. The audience's understanding of the operas, Mozart's position in society, Da Ponte's attitudes, compositional history, staging stylistic framework, and the music itself are discussed in this holistic approach. Analyses are an important part of the author's presentation. Advanced. Musical examples.

2773. Warburton, A. O. *Analyses of Musical Classics.* Book 4, 103–107. London: Longman, 1974.
Descriptive remarks on Act I, Scene V. No musical examples.

2774. Wellesz, Egon. *"Don Giovanni* and the 'Drama Giocoso.' " *Music Review,* 4 (1943): 121–126.
Builds case for considering *Don Giovanni* to be a tragic opera with comic elements, rather than the reverse.

Don Giovanni: "Finch' han dal vino"

2775. Youens, Susan. "The Champagne Aria Reconsidered." *Opera Journal*, 17, no. 2 (1984): 19–30.
Describes enigmatic quality of Giovanni's character. Analysis of rhythmic structure, phrase structure, motivic structure, and harmony in this aria shows that the music reveals the Don "en vrai caractère" (in true character).

Fantasia for Clock Organ in F Minor, K. 608

2776. Richner, Thomas, and E. Shay. "Mozart's Three Pieces for Clock Organ." *Music (AGO)*, 11 (June 1977): 44–46.
Background and descriptive commentary. Musical examples.

Fantasy in C Minor, K. 475

2777. Badura-Skoda, Paul. "A Master Lesson on Mozart's Fantasy in C Minor (K. 475) Composed May–June 1785." *Piano Quarterly*, 32, no. 125 (1984): 36–39.
Brief analysis for performer. Musical examples.

2778. Demus, Joerg. "Two Fantasies." *Piano Quarterly*, 27, no. 104 (1978–1979): 9–17.
Analysis of the relationship between Mozart's Fantasy, K. 475, and Schubert's Largo for Harpsichord, D. 993. Includes reproduction of the Schubert work in full. Musical examples.

2779. Museus, Betty C. "Mozart's Fantasia in C Minor, K. 475." *American Music Teacher*, 26, no. 2 (1976): 31–32.
Brief analysis, detailing the salient features of each section. For the undergraduate student or musical amateur.

2780. Rosen, Charles. *The Classical Style: Haydn, Mozart, Beethoven,* 91–93. New York: Viking Press, 1971.
Analytic observations on form and key relationships. Musical examples.

2781. Tischler, Hans. *The Perceptive Music Listener,* 207–209. Englewood, Cliffs, NJ: Prentice-Hall, 1955.
Descriptive and analytic discussion with musical examples.

Idomeneo

2782. Abert, Anna Amalie. "The Operas of Mozart." In *The New Oxford History of Music.* Vol. 7, *The Age of Enlightenment, 1745–1790.*

Edited by Egon Wellesz and F. W. Sternfeld, 135–140. London: Oxford University Press, 1973.
  Idomeneo's place in Mozart's stylistic growth. Mentions influences of Gluck on this early opera. Musical examples.

2783. Heartz, Daniel. "The Genesis of Mozart's *Idomeneo." Musical Quarterly,* 55, no. 1 (1969): 1–19.
  A detailed history of *Idomeneo.* Identifies Mozart's source for the libretto and how it was adapted.

2784. Heartz, Daniel. "The Great Quartet in Mozart's *Idomeneo."* In *The Music Forum,* Vol. 5. Edited by Felix Salzer and Carl Schachter, 233–256. New York: Columbia University Press, 1980.
  In-depth Schenkerian analysis, with musical examples.

2785. Heartz, Daniel. "Tonality and Motif in *Idomeneo." Musical Times,* 115 (May 1974): 382–386.
  Motivic relationships and their bearing on the tonal structure of *Idomeneo* explored. Musical examples.

2786. Liebner, Janos. *Mozart on the Stage,* 40–71. London: John Calder, 1975.
  Background, plot summary, descriptive and analytic commentary with discussion of characterization. Musical examples.

2787. Sadie, Stanley. "*Idomeneo* and Its Textural History." *Opera,* 25 (May 1974): 389–398.
  Historical background focusing on the opera's textual history and preparations for the premiere performance.

Impresario Overture

2788. Tovey, Donald Francis. *Essays in Musical Analysis.* Vol. 4, 21–23. London: Oxford University Press, 1969.
  Brief critical and analytic remarks. Musical examples. For the undergraduate student.

Magic Flute

2789. Batley, E. M. "Textual Unity in *Die Zauberflöte." Music Review,* 27, no. 2 (1966): 81–92.
  A detailed study to disprove theories that the libretto we are accustomed to is an alteration of the original plot.

2790. Chailley, Jacques. *"The Magic Flute,"* Masonic Opera: An Interpretation of the Libretto and the Music. Translated by Herbert Weinstock. 1971. Reprint. New York: Da Capo Press, 1982, 347 pp.
Background on the libretto, Mozart's freemasonry, and Mozart and the *Singspiel*. Also focuses on Masonic symbolism in *Magic Flute*.

2791. Cole, Malcolm S. "The Magic Flute and the Quatrain." *Journal of Musicology*, 3, no. 2 (1984): 157–176.
Identification and analysis of quatrains in the *Magic Flute*.

2792. Donington, Robert. *The Opera*, 98–105. New York: Harcourt Brace Jovanovich, 1978.
Discussion of dramatic and musical action, as well as place of *Magic Flute* in operatic history. Musical examples.

2793. Eckelmeyer, Judith A. "Structure As Hermeneutic Guide to *The Magic Flute*." *Musical Quarterly*, 72, no. 1 (1986): 51–73.
The author argues that a study of the overall structure of *Magic Flute* aids in discerning the meaning of the work. Argues against tendency to reorder musical numbers for performance because it seriously disrupts the musical organization. Charts of tonality and structure.

2794. Eckelmeyer, Judith A. "Two Complexes of Recurrent Melodies Related to *Die Zauberflöte*." *Music Review*, 41, no. 1 (1980): 11–25.
A glimpse into Mozart's creative process by way of examination of recurrent melodies in his works. Musical examples.

2795. Elenor, John. "Masonic Mediants: Notes on a Three-Keyed Opera." *Musical Times*, 128 (June 1987): 327–328.
Tonal relationships seen as Masonic symbolism. No musical examples.

2796. Faust, Carl R. "Seven Keys to the *Flute*." *Opera News*, 34 (January 17, 1970): 22–23.
A brief study of Mozart's use of key in this work. Musical examples.

2797. Godwin, Joscelyn R. "Layers of Meaning in *The Magic Flute*." *Musical Quarterly*, 65, no. 4 (1979): 471 + .
Detailed examination of the symbolism in the story as seen from a Masonic point of view.

2798. Haldeman, L. W. "The Triumph of Papageno." *Opera Journal*, 1, no. 1 (1968): 11–15.
Analysis of plot and characters. Not a discussion of the music.

2799. Heartz, Daniel. *"La Clemenza di Sarastro*: Masonic Benevolence in Mozart's Last Operas." *Musical Times*, 124 (March 1983): 152–157.
Masonic symbolism traced in this opera, as well as in *La Clemenza di Tito*. Musical examples.

2800. Hughes, Spike. "Gift of Surprise." *Opera News*, 31 (March 4, 1967): 24–25.
Musical characterization and element of freshness and surprise examined. Musical examples.

2801. King, Alexander Hyatt. *Mozart in Retrospect: Studies in Criticism and Bibliography*, 141–163. London: Oxford University Press, 1955.
Traces Mozart's borrowing of melodies from himself and other composers in the composition of *Magic Flute*. Thesis is not Mozart's poverty of invention, but rather the importance of association that the melodies had for Mozart.

2802. Lee, M. Owen. "A Delicate Balance." *Opera News*, 38 (December 15, 1973): 28–29.
Critical remarks on characterization and meaning of plot.

2803. Liebner, Janos. *Mozart on the Stage*, 221–252. London: John Calder, 1975.
Background, dramatic structure, descriptive, and analytic commentary. Musical examples.

2804. Moberly, Robert B. *Three Mozart Operas: "Figaro," "Don Giovanni," "The Magic Flute."* New York: Dodd, Mead, 1967, 303 pp.
Detailed commentary. The drama is analyzed, almost measure-by-measure, with many analytical comments on the music.

2805. Thomson, Katherine. "Mozart and Freemasonry." *Music and Letters*, 57, no. 1 (1976): 25–46.
A close examination of the Masonic elements in Mozart's music and, in particular, the *Magic Flute*. Musical examples.

Magic Flute Overture

2806. Tovey, Donald Francis. *Essays in Musical Analysis*. Vol. 4, 23–25. London: Oxford University Press, 1969.
Critical and analytic essay with musical examples. For the undergraduate student.

Marriage of Figaro

2807.   Abert, Anna Amalie. "The Operas of Mozart." In *The New Oxford History of Music.* Vol. 7, *The Age of Enlightenment, 1745–1790.* Edited by Egon Wellesz and F. W. Sternfeld, 149–154. London: Oxford University Press, 1973.

Characterization, musical features, and the models Mozart drew upon are the main focus.

2808.   Allanbrook, Wye J. "Metric Gesture As a Topic in *Le Nozze di Figaro* and *Don Giovanni.*" *Musical Quarterly,* 67, no. 1 (1981): 94–112.

Mozart's use of meter was intended to infuse the singers with the physical bearing to match the mood of the character. The author demonstrates that meters have, over the course of time, gained identifiable connotations that help support characterization on the stage. Musical examples. Author develops this thesis in his book *Rhythmic Gesture in Mozart* (*see* item no. 2809, below).

2809.   Allanbrook, Wye J. *Rhythmic Gesture in Mozart: "Le Nozze di Figaro" and "Don Giovanni."* Chicago: University of Chicago Press, 1983, 396 pp.

The role of rhythm in conveying gesture, the key to character portrayal. Thorough descriptive and analytic commentary of rhythmic and other devices to convey mood and character. Musical examples.

2810.   Blom, Eric. "The Literary Ancestry of *Figaro.*" *Musical Quarterly,* 13, no. 4 (1927): 528–539.

Traces sources for libretto of *Figaro* in detail. Not a discussion of the music.

2811.   Brophy, Brigid. "*Figaro* and the Limitations of Music." *Music and Letters,* 51, no. 1 (1970): 26–36.

A response to Noske's article cited below (*see* item no 2820), in which he attributes to music the power to characterize, whereas Brophy feels the text performs that function more ably.

2812.   Downes, Edward. "A Tender Irony." *Opera News,* 29 (January 2, 1965): 24–25.

Brief remarks on the musical characterization. Musical examples.

2813.   George, Graham. "The Structure of Dramatic Music, 1607–1909." *Musical Quarterly,* 52, no. 4 (1966): 474–477.

Tonal and structural analysis, with comparisons to other works.

2814.   George, Graham. *Tonality and Musical Structure,* 46–51. London: Oxford University Press, 1970.

Tonal structure and the structure of the arias and ensembles examined. Chart.

2815.   Levarie, Siegmund. *Mozart's "Le Nozze di Figaro": A Critical Analysis.* 1952. Reprint. New York: Da Capo Press, 1977, 270 pp.

Book-length, measure-by-measure analysis of the entire opera, exclusive of recitative. Also, structure and characterization of the opera as a whole discussed. Musical examples and diagrams.

2816.   Liebner, Janos. *Mozart on the Stage,* 94–137. London: John Calder, 1975.

Background, descriptive, and analytic commentary with observations on characterization. Musical examples.

2817.   Mackerras, Charles. "What Mozart Really Meant." *Opera,* 16 (April 1965): 240–246.

Delves into the differences between Mozart's first version of *Figaro* and the many later versions designed to suit a singer or public taste. Musical examples.

2818.   Moberly, Robert B. *Three Mozart Operas: "Figaro," "Don Giovanni," "The Magic Flute."* New York: Dodd, Mead, 1967, 303 pp.

Detailed commentary. The drama is analyzed almost measure-by-measure, with many analytical comments on the music.

2819.   Noske, Frits. "Musical Quotation As a Dramatic Device: The Fourth Act of *Le Nozze di Figaro.*" *Musical Quarterly,* 54, no. 2 (1968): 185–198.

Mozart's parodies and alterations of tunes in *Figaro* as a means of heightening dramatic effect. Elevated discussion with musical examples.

2820.   Noske, Frits. "Social Tensions in *Le Nozze di Figaro.*" *Music and Letters,* 50, no. 1 (1969): 45–62.

Examination of *Figaro's* dramatic forces from a sociological point of view. Mozart was keenly aware of social customs and exploited their full dramatic potential. Musical examples.

2821.   Rosen, Charles. *The Classical Style: Haydn, Mozart, Beethoven.* Rev. ed., 290–295. London: Faber and Faber, 1976.

Formal analysis of sextet, showing use of sonata form in Act III. Musical examples.

2822.   Steptoe, Andrew. *The Mozart–Da Ponte Operas.* Oxford: Clarendon Press, 1988.

Places *Marriage of Figaro, Don Giovanni,* and *Così fan Tutte* in the context of their time. The audience's understanding of the operas, Mozart's position in society, Da Ponte's attitudes, compositional history, staging, stylistic framework, and the music itself are discussed in this holistic approach. Analyses are an important part of the author's presentation. Advanced. Musical examples.

2823.   Warburton. A. O. *Analyses of Musical Classics.* Book 4, 96–103. London: Longman, 1974.
Compact analysis of Act III.

2824.   Warburton. A. O. "Set Works for 'O' Level, GCE." *Music Teacher,* 51 (June 1972): 12–13.
Analysis for the undergraduate student.

Mass in C Major, K. 66

2825.   Young, Percy M. *The Choral Tradition.* Rev. ed., 166–171. New York: W. W. Norton, 1981.
Brief analytic remarks. Musical examples.

Mass in C Major, K. 317 ("Coronation")

2826.   Ratner, Leonard. *Classic Music: Expression, Form, and Style,* 174–178. New York: Schirmer Books, 1980.
Identifies some of the *galant* elements. Musical examples.

2827.   Young, Percy M. *The Choral Tradition.* Rev. ed., 166–171. New York: W. W. Norton, 1981.
Brief descriptive and analytic remarks. Musical examples.

2828.   Young, Percy M. *The Choral Tradition,* 168–170. New York: W. W. Norton, 1971.
Brief descriptive and analytic remarks. Older edition than above with similar coverage. Musical examples.

Menuetto for Piano in D Major, K. 355 (594a)

2829.   Boatwright, Howard, and Ernst Oster. "Analysis Symposium." *Journal of Music Theory,* 10, no. 1 (1966): 18–52.
Two complete analyses of this piece. The whole piece is reproduced on pp. 20–22. Boatwright's article occupies pp. 22–31; Oster's, pp. 32–52. Boatwright's approach is more traditional—dealing with chromaticism, motives and their development,

rhythmic relationships, harmony, and tonality. Oster discusses similar topics, but the emphasis is on voice-leading progressions; that is, a Schenkerian approach. Musical examples in both.

Missa Brevis, K. 192

2830.   Young, Percy M. *The Choral Tradition.* Rev. ed., 166–171. New York: W. W. Norton, 1981.
Brief analytic comments. Musical examples.

Octets for Wind Instruments

2831.   Leeson, Daniel N., and David Whitwell. "Mozart's 'Spurious' Wind Octets." *Music and Letters,* 53, no. 4 (1972): 377–399.
On the authenticity of these works. Musical examples.

Les Petits Riens

2832.   Warburton, A. O. "Set Works for 'O' Level, GCE." *Music Teacher,* 48 (September 1969): 25 + .
Brief analytic comments.

Quartet for Piano and Strings in G Minor, K. 478

2833.   Cone, Edward T. "Communications." *Perspectives of New Music,* 1, no. 2 (1963): 206–210.
Discusses the rhythm in an eleven-measure extract from this work. This is a reply to a comment in P. Westergaard, (*see* item no. 2834, below). Musical examples.

2834.   Westergaard, Peter. "Some Problems in Rhythmic Theory and Analysis." *Perspectives of New Music,* 1, no. 1 (1962): 180–191.
Advanced theoretical analysis. See E. T. Cone's comment on this (*see* item no. 2833, above).

Quartets for Strings

2835.   Cuyler, Louis E. "Mozart's Six Quartets Dedicated to Haydn." In *The Commonwealth of Music.* Edited by Gustave Reese and Rose Brandel, 293–299. New York: Free Press, 1965.
Mainly descriptive commentary with analytic observations on K. 387, K. 421, K. 428, K. 458, K. 464, and K. 465, the "Haydn" quartets.

2836. Dunhill, Thomas F. *Mozart's String Quartets.* 1927. Reprint. Westport, CT: Greenwood Press, 1970, 44 pp.

Descriptive and analytic commentary for the undergraduate student. Musical examples.

Quartet for Strings in D Minor, K. 421

2837. Grave, Floyd. "Interpretation Through Style Analysis." *College Music Symposium,* 18 (1978): 56–71.

An examination of the first movement, largely based on Jan La Rue's *Guidelines for Style Analysis.* The author includes a style analysis of the large, medium, and small dimensions. Score included.

2838. Mitchell, William J. "Giuseppe Sarti and Mozart's Quartet, K. 421." *Current Musicology,* 9 (1969): 147–153.

Examination of some older criticism in the light of modern analysis. Advanced. Musical examples.

2839. Warburton, A. O. "Set Works for 'O' Level, GCE." *Music Teacher,* 49 (July 1970): 10 + .

Background, descriptive, and analytic commentary for the undergraduate student.

Quartet for Strings in B-Flat Major, K. 458. ("Hunt")

2840. Warburton, A. O. "Set Works for 'O' Level, GCE." *Music Teacher,* 52 (July 1973): 21 + .

Analysis for the undergraduate student. To be used with score in hand.

Quartet for Strings in C Major, K. 465 ("Dissonant")

2841. DeFotis, William. "Rehearings: Mozart, Quartet in C, K. 465." *Nineteenth Century Music,* 6, no. 1 (1982): 31–38.

Extensive analysis showing how the adagio relates to the work as a whole. Musical examples.

2842. Vertrees, Julie A. "Mozart's String Quartet, K. 465: The History of a Controversy." *Current Musicology,* 17 (1974): 96–114.

History and discussion of criticism directed at this controversial work. Musical examples.

Quintet for Clarinet and Strings in A Major, K. 581

2843.   Kerman, Joseph. *Listen.* 2d ed., 180–183. New York: Worth Publishers, 1976.
Background and analysis with musical examples. For the undergraduate student.

2844.   Tischler, Hans. *The Perceptive Music Listener,* 291–295. Englewood Cliffs, NJ: Prentice-Hall, 1955.
Analysis with musical examples.

Quintet for Piano and Winds in E-Flat Major, K. 452

2845.   Tovey, Donald Francis. *Essays in Musical Analysis: Chamber Music,* 106–120. London: Oxford University Press, 1944.
Thorough discussion with musical examples for the undergraduate student.

Quintet for Strings in C Major, K. 515

2846.   Rosen, Charles. *The Classical Style: Haydn, Mozart, Beethoven.* Rev. ed., 266–274. London: Faber and Faber, 1976.
A detailed analytic discussion, concentrating on the first movement. Overall proportions, tonal structure, and rhythmic questions are discussed. Musical examples.

Quintet for Strings in G Minor, K. 516

2847.   Keller, Hans. "Functional Analysis of Mozart's G Minor Quintet." *Music Analysis,* 4, nos. 1–2 (1985): 73–94.
Advanced analysis.

2848.   Ratner, Leonard. *Classic Music: Expression, Form, and Style,* 253–254. New York: Schirmer Books, 1980.
Brief analysis of form in the Finale. Musical examples.

2849.   Rosen, Charles. *The Classical Style: Haydn, Mozart, Beethoven.* Rev. ed., 274–280. London: Faber and Faber, 1976.
A general discussion with analytic observations. Focuses mainly on the Finale. Musical examples.

2850.   Rosen, Charles. *Sonata Forms,* 121–125. New York: W. W. Norton, 1980.
Description of the structure of the Finale. Musical examples.

Quintet for Strings in D Major, K. 593

2851. Lerdahl, Fred, and Ray Jackendorff. *A Generative Theory of Tonal Music*, 269–273. Cambridge, MA: M.I.T. Press, 1983.
A prolongational reduction with analytic comments on the first movement, development section. Diagrams and musical examples.

2852. Rosen, Charles. *The Classical Style: Haydn, Mozart, Beethoven.* Rev. ed., 283–286. London: Faber and Faber, 1976.
Identifies the background scheme of descending thirds, which provides the basis for each movement. Musical examples.

Quintet for Strings in E-Flat Major, K. 614

2853. Ratner, Leonard. *Classic Music: Expression, Form, and Style*, 237–246. New York: Schirmer Books, 1980.
Analysis of the style and structure in the first movement. Musical examples.

2854. Stokes, Jeffrey L. "Motivic Unity in Mozart's String Quintet, K. 614." *Studies in Musicology (Canada)*, 2 (1977): 22–30.

Requiem

2855. Blume, Friedrich. "Requiem but No Piece." *Musical Quarterly*, 47, no. 2 (1961): 147–169.
Scholarly discourse on authenticity. Not an analytic discussion.

2856. Landon, H. C. Robbins. *Essays on the Viennese Classical Style: Gluck, Haydn, Mozart, Beethoven*, 82–122. London: Barrie and Rockliff, 1970.
Thorough discussion of the Requiem, covering background, composition history, Süssmayer's and Eybler's participation, style, motivic unity, and critical assessment. Musical examples.

2857. Robertson, Alec. *Requiem: Music of Mourning and Consolation*, 64–74. New York: Praeger, 1968.
Thorough background and extensive discussion of the music. Musical examples.

2858. Slotterback, Floyd. "Mozart's Requiem: History and Performance." *American Choral Review*, 26, no. 2 (1984): Entire issue.
Background, analysis, scoring, editions, and text.

2859. Vanson, Frederic. "Mozart's Final Masterpiece: The Requiem in D Minor, K. 626." *Choir*, 55 (August 1964): 146–147.
Background and brief critical commentary.

2860. Young, Percy M. *The Choral Tradition*, 178–182. New York: W. W. Norton, 1971.
Brief background and descriptive commentary.

Rondo in F Major, K. 494

2861. Cole, William. *The Form of Music: An Outline of Musical Designs Used by the Great Composers*, 46–47. London: Associated Board of the Royal Schools of Music, n.d.
Brief outline of the structure in table form. Example of sonata-rondo form.

Rondo in A Minor, K. 511

2862. Forte, Allen. "Generative Chromaticism in Mozart's Music: The Rondo in A Minor, K. 511." *Musical Quarterly*, 66, no. 4 (1980): 459–483.
A detailed examination of the structural ramifications of the chromaticism in this piece. Musical examples.

Sinfonia Concertante in E-Flat Major, K. 364

2863. Smith, Edwin. "Mozart: Sinfonia Concertante, K. 364." *Music Teacher*, 55 (October 1976): 19–21.
Thematic and formal analysis for the undergraduate student.

Sonatas for Piano

2864. Elder, Dean. "Lili Kraus—On Mastering Mozart." *Clavier*, 10, no. 4 (1971): 10–16.
Performer's remarks on style in Mozart. Critical observations on K. 332 and K. 333.

2865. Kraus, Lili. "Making Mozart Live." *Clavier*, 10, no. 5 (1971): 12–18.
Notes for performance, but useful here for its analytic remarks. Musical examples.

2866. Pauly, Reinhard. *Music in the Classic Period*, 119–128. Englewood Cliffs, NJ: Prentice-Hall, 1965.
General analytic observations are illustrated with musical examples from specific works. The discussions are brief and general.

2867. Richner, Thomas. *Orientation for Interpreting Mozart's Piano Sonatas.* New York: Teachers College, Columbia University, 1953, 96 pp.
A guide for performers and teachers. Each sonata receives a brief analysis. The analyses are limited to descriptions of the forms and characterizations of the themes.

2868. Tobin, Joseph Raymond. *Mozart and the Sonata Form.* 1916. Reprint. New York: Da Capo Press, 1971, 156 pp.
Measure-by-measure analysis of each sonata. Since no musical examples are provided, a score is necessary.

Sonata for Piano No. 4 in E-Flat Major, K. 282

2869. Hormes, Linda. "Exempli Gratie: A Singular Perversion of Second Inversion." *In Theory Only*, 3 (August 1977): 30–31.
Advanced technical discussion on two different but consecutive six-four chords in measures 7 and 9. Score.

Sonata for Piano No. 5 in G Major, K. 283

2870. Kresky, Jeffrey. *Tonal Music: Twelve Analytic Studies*, 108–119. Bloomington: Indiana University Press, 1977.
In-depth analysis of the first movement dealing with sonata form, melodic analysis, and tonality. Advanced. Musical examples and diagrams.

2871. Lester, Joel. "Articulation of Tonal Structures As a Criterion for Analytic Choices." *Music Theory Spectrum*, 1 (1979): 69–73.
Demonstrates that the tightly controlled structure of this work is seen in the first ten measures. Musical examples and graphs.

Sonata for Piano No. 6 in D Major, K. 284

2872. Walton, Charles W. *Basic Forms in Music*, 174–175. Port Washington, NY: Alfred Publishing Co., 1974.
Brief outline with full musical quotation. First movement only.

Sonata for Piano No. 10 in C Major, K. 309

2873. Bryant, Celia M. "The Music Lesson: Acquire Sophistication Through Mozart." *Clavier*, 9, no. 9 (1970): 24–32.
Performer's analysis, with musical examples.

Sonata for Piano No. 12 in F Major, K. 332

2874. Mason, Wilton. "Melodic Unity in Mozart's Piano Sonata, K. 332." *Music Review*, 22, no. 1 (1961): 28–33.
Analysis showing melody to be the major unifying force in this work. Musical examples.

2875. Warburton, A. O. "Set Works for 'O' Level, GCE." *Music Teacher*, 48 (October 1969): 19–20.
Brief analysis for the undergraduate student. Musical examples.

Sonata for Piano No. 13 in B-Flat Major, K. 333

2876. Ricci, Robert. "The Division of the Pulse: Progressive and Retrogressive Rhythmic Forces." *In Theory Only*, 1 (November 1975): 13–19.
Advanced technical discussion of differing stress areas of the pulse. Musical examples.

2877. Warburton, A. O. "Set Works for 'O' Level, GCE." *Music Teacher and Piano Student*, 46 (September 1967): 12.
Brief analytic summary for the undergraduate student.

Sonata for Piano No. 14 in C Minor, K. 457

2878. Newman, William S. "K. 457 and Op. 13—Two Related Masterpieces in C Minor." *Music Review*, 28, no. 1 (1967): 38–44.
Shows Mozart's K. 457 as the true direct ancestor of Beethoven's *Pathétique* Sonata. Musical examples.

Sonata for Piano No. 15 in C Major, K. 545

2879. Beach, David. "Motive and Structure in th Andante Movement of Mozart's Piano Sonata K. 545." *Music Analysis*, 3, no. 3 (1984): 227–241.

2880.   Hiller, Lejaren, and Calvert Bean. "Information Theory Analyses of Four Sonata Expositions." *Journal of Music Theory*, 10, no. 1 (1966): 96–137.
For the advanced and mathematically minded student.

Sonata for Piano No. 17 in D Major, K. 576

2881.   Warburton, A. O. "Set Works for 'O' Level, GCE." *Music Teacher*, 50 (June 1971): 13–14.
Background and analysis.

Sonatas for Violin

2882.   Pauly, Reinhard. *Music in the Classic Period*, 128–132. Englewood Cliffs, NJ: Prentice-Hall, 1965.
General analytic observations are illustrated with musical examples from specific works. The discussions are brief and general.

Symphonies

2883.   Blom, Eric. *Mozart*, 189–210. London: J. M. Dent and Sons, 1935.
Descriptive, critical, and analytic commentary designed for the undergraduate student. Focuses mainly on the later symphonies. Musical examples.

2884.   Cuyler, Louise. *The Symphony*, 40–47. New York: Harcourt Brace Jovanovich, 1973.
Concentrated analyses of Symphonies 39, 40, and 41.

2885.   Dearling, Robert. *The Music of Wolfgang Amadeus Mozart: The Symphonies.* Cranbury, NJ: Associated University Presses, 1982, 224 pp.
All the symphonies discussed. The earlier works are more briefly treated, with summaries of style and form, than the later works. Chapters dealing with the later symphonies contain analytic comments on individual works. Musical examples.

2886.   Einstein, Alfred. *Mozart: His Character, His Work.* Translated by Arthur Mendel and Nathan Broder, 215–236. London: Oxford University Press, 1945.
Traces influences and deals with Mozart's stylistic traits and contribution to the symphony as a form.

2887. Landon, H. C. Robbins, ed. *The Mozart Companion*, 156–198. New York: Oxford University Press, 1956.
Light discussion of Mozart's evolving symphonic style.

2888. Maycock, John. "The Significance of Mozart's Last Symphonies." *Musical Opinion*, 96 (January 1973): 179.
Brief view of the last three symphonies as one conception, even though they are different in character.

2889. Pauly, Reinhard. *Music in the Classic Period.* 2d ed., 99–107. Englewood Cliffs, NJ: Prentice-Hall, 1973.
General discussion of classicism in the symphonies. Musical examples.

2890. Saint-Foix, Georges de. *The Symphonies of Mozart.* London: Dennis Dobson, 1947, 118 pp.
Analytic insights on all the symphonies and Mozart's stylistic growth as evidenced within the music.

2891. Sternfeld, Frederick W. "Instrumental Masterworks and Aspects of Formal Design." In *The New Oxford History of Music.* Vol. 7, *The Age of Enlightenment, 1745–1790.* Edited by Egon Wellesz and F. W. Sternfeld, 629–635. London: Oxford University Press, 1973.
Brief analytic remarks on background and general stylistic traits of the later symphonies. Musical examples.

2892. Tischler, Hans. *The Perceptive Music Listener*, 344–347. Englewood Cliffs, NJ: Prentice-Hall, 1955.
Compact analysis with musical examples.

2893. Tovey, Donald Francis. *Essays in Musical Analysis.* Vol. 1, 183–198. London: Oxford University Press, 1935.
Thorough analytic commentary meant for the undergraduate student on Symphonies 36, 39, 40, and 41. Musical examples.

Symphony No. 1 in E-Flat Major, K. 16

2894. Stedman, Preston. *The Symphony*, 37–39. Englewood Cliffs, NJ: Prentice-Hall, 1979.
Brief description of thematic construction, form, and orchestration. Musical examples and diagrams.

Symphony No. 29 in A Major, K. 201

2895. Stedman, Preston. *The Symphony*, 45–48. Englewood Cliffs, NJ: Prentice-Hall, 1979.

Brief description of form, motivic activity, and texture. An example of Mozart's middle stylistic period. Musical examples and diagram.

Symphony No. 34 in C Major, K. 338

2896. Haggin, B. H. *A Book of the Symphony*, 72–79. London: Oxford University Press, 1937.
Straightforward description dealing with formal plan only. Brief background remarks, with no discussion of tonality, rhythm, or texture. For the musical amateur or undergraduate student concerned with form. Musical examples.

Symphony No. 35 in D Major K. 385 ("Haffner")

2897. Haggin, B. H. *A Book of the Symphony*, 80–85. London: Oxford University Press, 1937.
Straightforward description dealing with formal plan only. Brief background remarks, with no discussion of tonality, rhythm, or texture. For the musical amateur or undergraduate student concerned with form. Musical examples.

2898. Schachter, Carl. "Rhythm and Linear Analysis, Durational Reduction." In *The Music Forum*. Vol. 5. Edited by Felix Salzer and Carl Schachter, 210–215 +. New York: Columbia University Press, 1980.

Symphony No. 36 in C Major, K. 425 ("Linz")

2899. Haggin, B. H. *A Book of the Symphony*, 86–91. London: Oxford University Press, 1937.
Straightforward description dealing with formal plan only. Brief background remarks, with no discussion of tonality, rhythm, or texture. For the musical amateur or undergraduate student concerned with form. Musical examples.

Symphony No. 38 in D Major, K. 504 ("Prague")

2900. Haggin, B. H. *A Book of the Symphony*, 92–97. London: Oxford University Press, 1937.
Straightforward description dealing with formal plan only. Brief background remarks, with no discussion of tonality, rhythm, or texture. For the musical amateur or undergraduate student concerned with form. Musical examples.

2901. Rosen, Charles. *Sonata Forms,* 194–217. New York: W. W. Norton, 1980.

Discussion of the structure of the first movement. Musical examples.

Symphony No. 39 in E-Flat Major, K. 543

2902. Haggin, B. H. *A Book of the Symphony,* 98–106. London: Oxford University Press, 1937.

Straightforward description dealing with formal plan only. Brief background remarks, with no discussion of tonality, rhythm or texture. For the musical amateur or undergraduate student concerned with form. Musical examples.

2903. Taylor, Clifford. "The Contemporaneity of Music in History." *Music Review,* 24, no. 3 (1963): 205–217.

Music viewed in historical context. Comparison of Berg's methods (in the Violin Concerto) with those of Mozart (in the Symphony No. 39) to illustrate how the period affected the music. Largely a philosophical discussion of style.

2904. Wen, Eric. "A Tritone Key Relationship: The Bridge Sections of the Slow Movement of Mozart's thirty-ninth Symphony." *Music Analysis,* 5, no. 1 (1986): 59–84.

An analytic essay on this movement with special emphasis on the bridge sections. The form is "sonata without development." Uses Schenkerian techniques and terminology. Musical examples and table of formal structure.

Symphony No. 40 in G Minor, K. 550

2905. Berry, Wallace. "Analysis Symposium Subject: Mozart, Symphony in G Minor, K. 550, Movement I." *In Theory Only,* 1 (October 1975): 8–25.

Advanced analysis of the first movement.

2906. Broder, Nathan, ed. *Mozart: Symphony in G Minor, K. 550.* Norton Critical Scores. New York: W. W. Norton, 1967, 114 pp.

Full score provided, with historical background, analysis, and criticism.

2907. Haggin, B. H. *A Book of the Symphony,* 107–113. London: Oxford University Press, 1937.

Straightforward description dealing with formal plan only. Brief background remarks, with no discussion of tonality, rhythm, or texture. For the musical amateur or undergraduate student concerned with form. Musical examples.

2908.   Hendrickson, Hugh. "Mozart's Symphony No. 40/IV, Second Theme: A Study of Chromaticism and Harmonic Association." *In Theory Only*, 3 (July 1977): 27–37.

2909.   Kerman, Joseph. *Listen*, 186–187. New York: Worth Publishers, 1972.
Brief analytic summary for the undergraduate student. Musical examples.

2910.   Lerdahl, Fred, and Ray Jackendorff. *A Generative Theory of Tonal Music*, 21–25; 85–87; 258–260. Cambridge, MA: M.I.T. Press, 1983.
Analytic comments on the rhythm. Time-span and prolongational reductions, with analytic comments. Diagrams and musical examples of measures 1–22 of the first movement. Advanced.

2911.   Machlis, Joseph. *The Enjoyment of Music.* 3d ed., 265–269. New York: W. W. Norton, 1970.
Compact analysis intended for the undergraduate student. Musical examples.

2912.   Nadeau, Roland. *The Symphony: Structure and Style.* Shorter ed., rev., 76–83. Boston: Crescendo, 1973.
Straight measure-by-measure analysis.

2913.   Smith, F. Joseph. "Mozart Revisited, K. 550: The Problem of Survival of Baroque Figures in the Classical Era." *Music Review*, 31, no. 3 (1970): 201–214.
Discussion of the use of old Baroque figures in Classical music that convey a different effect than the original figure did in the Baroque era.

2914.   Stedman, Preston. *The Symphony*, 49–54. Englewood Cliffs, NJ: Prentice-Hall, 1979.
Description of formal structure, orchestral technique, texture, and harmony. An example of Mozart's late stylistic period. Musical examples and diagrams.

Symphony No. 41 in C Major, K. 551 ("Jupiter")

2915.   Haggin, B. H. *A Book of the Symphony*, 114–120. London: Oxford University Press, 1937.

Straightforward description dealing with formal plan only. Brief background remarks, with no discussion of tonality, rhythm, or texture. For the musical amateur or undergraduate student concerned with form. Musical examples.

2916.   Klenz, William. " 'Per Aspera Ad Astra' or the Stairway to Jupiter." *Music Review,* 30 (1969): 169–210.
Mozart's use of the main theme of this symphony in other works.

2917.   Rogers, John E. "Pitch Class Sets in Fourteen Measures of Mozart's *Jupiter* Symphony." *Perspectives of New Music,* 10, no. 1 (1971): 209–231.
Advanced analytic discussion. Musical examples.

2918.   Stevenson, Patric. "A Notation of Thematic Structure." *Music in Education,* 29, no. 315– (1965): 223–226; no. 316 (1965): 273–276.
Article in two parts: the first outlines a method for notating the thematic structure of musical works; the second demonstrates the method using the Symphony No. 41. Advanced analysis in graph form showing mathematical relationships.

2919.   Warburton, A. O. "Set Works for 'O' Level, GCE." *Music Teacher and Piano Student,* 46 (October 1967): 11 + .
Analysis for the undergraduate student.

2920.   Wollenberg, Susan. "The *Jupiter* Theme: New Lights on Its Creation." *Musical Times,* 116 (September 1975): 781–783.
The famous *Jupiter* theme traced back to Fux as a possible source. Musical examples.

Trio for Clarinet, Viola, and Piano in E-Flat, K. 498

2921.   Giokas, Dennis G. "Mozart's Trio, K. 498: An Interpretive Study of Themes." *Clarinet,* 5, no. 2 (1978): 12–13.
Analysis using the concepts presented by Rudolf Réti in *The Thematic Process in Music.* Traces thematic transformations and relationships between the movements.

Vesperae de Dominica, K. 321

2922.   Young Percy M. *The Choral Tradition.* Rev. ed., 166–171. New York: W. W. Norton, 1981.
Brief analytic remarks. Musical examples.

Vesperae Solennes de Confessore in C Major, K. 339.

2923.   Young, Percy M. *The Choral Tradition.* Rev. ed., 166–171. New York: W. W. Norton, 1981.
   Brief analytic remarks. Musical examples.

DISSERTATIONS AND THESES

General

2924.   Trimmer, Maud Alice. "Texture and Sonata Form in the Late String Chamber Music of Haydn and Mozart." Ph.D., City University of New York, 1981, 594 pp., DA 42-3805A-6A.

2925.   Whitlock, Prentice Earle. "The Analysis, Development of Form, and Interpretation of the Epistle Sonatas of Wolfgang Amadeus Mozart (1756–1791)." Ph.D., New York University, 1985, 262 pp., DA 46-643A.

Litaniens

2926.   Kazenas, Bruno. "The *Litaniens* of Wolfgang Amadeus Mozart: A Comparative Analysis." D.M.A., University of Cincinnati, 1985, 182 pp., DA 46-1773A.

Magic Flute

2927.   Malloy, Joseph Thomas. "Musico-Dramatic Irony in Mozart's *Magic Flute.*" Ph.D., University of Virginia, 1985, 224 pp., DA 47-539-40A.

Mass in C Minor, K. 427

2928.   Crabb, Richard Paul. "Wolfgang Amadeus Mozart's Grand Mass in C Minor K. 427/417a: A History and Comparative Analyses of Performance Editions." Ph.D., Florida State University, 1984, 174 pp., DA 45-1677A.

Sonatas for Piano (Four Hands)

2929.   Hankla, Jesse R. "Mozart's Fourhand Piano Sonatas with a Theoretical and Performance Analysis of K. 358 in B-Flat Major and K. 497 in F Major." D.M.A., University of Oklahoma, 1986, 156 pp., DA 47-3231A.

MUSSORGSKY, MODEST, 1839–1881

General

2930. Calvocoressi, M. D. *Modest Mussorgsky.* London: Rockliff, 1956, 322 pp.

Mussorgsky's technique, influences, and musical style discussed. Musical examples.

2931. Calvocoressi, M. D. *Mussorgsky.* London: J. M. Dent and Sons, 1974, 216 pp.

Descriptive and critical commentary, with occasional analytic observations on Mussorgsky's entire output. For the student. Musical examples.

2932. Riesemann, Oskar von. *Mussorgsky.* Translated by Paul England, 181–273. New York: Alfred A. Knopf, 1929.

Full historical account of the development of *Boris* and *Khovanstchina.* Story adaptations, revisions, and sources discussed, but very little commentary on the music.

Boris Godunov

2933. Abraham, Gerald. *Slavonic and Romantic Music,* 178–194. New York: St. Martin's Press, 1968.

Comparison of Mussorgsky's *Boris* with Pushkin's original text. Also traces Mussorgsky's reworking of material from *Salammbo* into *Boris.* Shows how music intended for a completely different opera was adapted to suit *Boris.*

2934. Carr, Maureen A. "The Sound of Mussorgsky." *Opera News,* 39 (January 25, 1975): 24–25.

Brief discussion of the modal quality of *Boris* and the reduction of the use of modes in the 1872 version to make the opera more acceptable to the Imperial Theatre Committee. Musical examples.

2935. Dahlhaus, Carl. *Nineteenth-Century Music.* Translated by J. Bradford Robinson, 295–297. Berkeley: University of California Press, 1989.

Brief but concentrated analytic remarks dwelling on form, motives, and harmonic associations as unifying forces. Musical examples. Advanced.

2936. Goldovsky, Boris. "Boris G. on Boris G." *Opera News,* 42 (February 18, 1978): 36–40.

Concise discussion of the versions of *Boris.*

2937.   Jacobs, Arthur. "Will the Real Boris Godunov Please Stand Up?" *Opera*, 22 (May 1971: 388–396.
Rimsky-Korsakov's version of *Boris* is compared with Mussorgsky's original. Also discusses the many options among Mussorgsky's revisions.

2938.   Kerman, Joseph. "The Puzzle of *Boris*: What Makes Mussorgsky's Original the Strongest?." *Opera News*, 39 (January 25, 1975): 9–12.
Untangles the history of the different versions of *Boris* and offers a critical evaluation.

2939.   Machlis, Joseph. *The Enjoyment of Music.* 3d ed., 203–207. New York: W. W. Norton, 1970.
Analytic overview, with musical examples.

2940.   Taruskin, Richard. "Musorgsky vs. Musorgsky: The Version of *Boris Godunov.*" *Nineteenth Century Music*, 8, no. 2 (1984): 91–118.
A detailed examination of the unique qualities of the many versions of *Boris*. Musical examples.

Night on Bald Mountain

2941.   Wiles, Edward. "*A Night on Bald Mountain.*" *Music Teacher*, 57 (March 1978): 13–14.
Description of the work and its program followed by an analysis. Musical examples.

The Nursery

2942.   Agawu, V. Kofi. "Pitch Organizational Procedures in Mussorgsky's *Nursery.*" *Indiana Theory Review*, 5, no. 1 (1981): 23–59.

Pictures at an Exhibition

2943.   Calvocoressi, M. D. *Mussorgsky.* Translated by A. Eaglefield Hull, London: Kegan Paul, n.d. 79–87.
Descriptive and critical commentary. Musical examples.

2944.   Kerman, Joseph. *Listen.* 2d ed., 272–273. New York: Worth Publishers, 1976.
Background and analysis for the undergraduate student.

2945. Matthews, Denis, ed. *Keyboard Music,* 309–310. New York: Praeger, Publishers, 1972.
Critical and analytic comments. Musical examples.

2946. Riesemann, Oskar von. *Moussorgsky,* 290–293. New York: Alfred A. Knopf, 1929.
Program note–type description.

2947. Tischler, Hans. *The Perceptive Music Listener,* 155–156. Englewood Cliffs, NJ: Prentice-Hall, 1955.
Brief descriptive and analytic remarks. Musical examples.

2948. Warburton, A. O. "Set Works for 'O' Level, GCE." *Music Teacher,* 50 (September 1971): 19–20.
Background and analysis for the undergraduate student.

Songs and Dances of Death

2949. Middaugh, Bennie. "Modest Mussorgsky's *Songs and Dances of Death.*" *NATS Bulletin,* 26, no. 2 (1969): 2 + .
Brief analytic discussion focusing on the musical means by which Mussorgsky achieved realism. Musical examples and brief bibliography.

Sunless

2950. Walker, James G. "Mussorgsky's *Sunless* Cycle in Russian Criticism: Focus of Controversy." *Musical Quarterly,* 67, no. 3 (1981): 382–391.
An examination of opinions about *Sunless* contained in the memoirs of Mussorgsky's friends and critics to demonstrate stylistic changes and their possible relationship to the ideological struggle between Czarist and Soviet Russia.

DISSERTATIONS AND THESES

Boris Godunov

2951. Carr, Maureen Ann. "Keys and Modes Functions and Progressions in Mussorgsky's *Boris Godounov.*" Ph.D., University of Wisconsin, 1972, 410 pp., DA 33-5762A.

NANCARROW, CONLON, 1912–

Study for Player Piano, No. 27

2952.   **Jarvlepp, Jan.** "Conlon Nancarrow's Study No. 27 for Player Piano Viewed Analytically." *Perspectives of New Music,* 22, nos. 1–2 (1984): 218+.

DISSERTATIONS AND THESES

General

2953.   **Carlsen, Philip Caldwell.** "The Player Piano Music of Conlon Nancarrow: An Analysis of Selected Studies. Ph.D., City University of New York, 1986, 188 pp., DA 47-1525A.

NIELSEN, CARL, 1865–1931

General

2954.   **Miller, Mina F.** "Carl Nielsen's Tonal Language: An Examination of the Piano Music." *College Music Symposium,* 22, no. 1 (1982): 32–45.

Symphonies

2955.   **Ballantine, Christopher.** *Twentieth Century Symphony,* 164–166; 206–212. London: Dennis Dobson, 1983.
  Analytic comments on Symphonies 3, 4, and 6. Musical examples.

2956.   **Simpson, Robert.** *Carl Nielsen: Symphonist, 1865–1931,* 124–135. London: J. M. Dent and Sons, 1952.
  Full discussion, critical and analytic, with musical examples.

Symphony No. 4 ("Inextinguishable")

2957.   **Simpson, Robert, ed.** *The Symphony.* Vol. 2, 61–71. New York: Drake Publishers, 1972.
  Thorough analysis.

Symphony No. 5

2958.   Whittall, Arnold. *Music Since the First World War*, 11–18, London: J. M. Dent and Sons, 1977.
Analytic discussion. Musical examples and diagrams.

Symphony No. 6

2959.   Ballantine, Christopher. *Twentieth Century Symphony*, 164–166. London: Dennis Dobson, 1984.
Brief analytic comments on the first movement.

DISSERTATIONS AND THESES

General

2960.   Hiatt, James Smith. "Form and Tonal Organization in the Late Instrumental Works of Carl Nielsen." Ph.D., Indiana University, 1986, 131 pp., DA 47-2790A.

2961.   Krenek, Thomas B. "An Examination and Analysis of the Choral Music of Carl Nielsen (1865–1931)." D.M.A., University of Cincinnati, 1984, 96 pp., DA 45-2298A.

2962.   Miller, Mina Florence. "The Solo Piano Music of Carl Nielsen: An Analysis for Performance." Ph.D., New York University, 1978, 328 pp., DA 39-4585.

2963.   Schindler, Christopher John. "A Stylistic Analysis of the Piano Music of Carl Nielsen." D.M.A., University of Oregon, 1984, 193 pp., DA 45-680A.

Symphonies

2964.   Jones, William Isaac, Jr. "A Study of Tonality in the Symphonies of Carl Nielsen," Ph.D., Florida State University, 1973, 80 pp., DA 34-1951A-2A.

NONO, LUIGI, 1924–1990

General

2965.   Evans, Peter. "Music of the European Mainstream: 1940–1960." In *The New Oxford History of Music*. Vol. 10, *The Modern Age:*

1890–1960. Edited by Martin Cooper, 469–477. London: Oxford University Press, 1974.

Brief overview of Nono's contribution, focusing on *Il Canto Sospeso* and *Composizione 2.* Musical examples.

Il Canto Sospeso

2966. Brindle, Reginald Smith. *The New Music: The Avant-Garde Since 1945,* 38–40. London: Oxford University Press, 1975.

Brief analytic observations on the principle of using rhythmic cells to establish rhythmic patterns of the music through a set (or sets) of number proportions. Musical examples.

2967. Griffiths, Paul. *Modern Music: The Avant-Garde Since 1945,* 103–104. New York: George Braziller, 1981.

Brief analytic remarks. Musical examples.

2968. Stockhausen, Karlheinz. "Music and Speech." *Reihe,* 6 (1964): 40–64.

An examination of text/music relationships, including discussion of poetry, phonetics, rhythm, and instrumentation. Many musical examples, graphs, tables. For the advanced student.

OBRECHT, JACOB, c. 1450–1505

Masses

2969. Todd, Ralph L. "Retrograde, Inversion, Retrograde Inversion, and Related Techniques in the Masses of Jacobus Obrecht." *Musical Quarterly,* 64, no. 1 (1978): 50–78.

Missa Sine Nomine

2970. Noblitt, Thomas. "Obrecht's *Missa Sine Nomine* and Its Recently Discovered Model." *Musical Quarterly,* 68, no. 1 (1982): 102–127.

Extensive analysis, with musical examples.

Missa Sub Tuum Praesidium

2971. Lockwood, Lewis. "A Note on Obrecht's Mass *Sub Tuum Praesidium.*" *Revue Belge de Musicologie,* 14, nos. 1–4 (1960): 30–39.

Identifies the preconceived formal plan of the work.

OCKEGHEM, JOHANNES, 1425–1495

General

2972. Bridgman, Nanie. "The Age of Ockeghem and Josquin." In *The New Oxford History of Music.* Vol. 3, *Ars Nova and the Renaissance, 1300–1540.* Edited by Dom Anselm Hughes and Gerald Abraham, 239–260. London: Oxford University Press, 1960.
  Overview of Ockeghem's place, forms used, musical style, and influence. Musical examples.

ORFF, CARL, 1895–1982

General

2973. Liess, Andreas. *Carl Orff.* Translated by Adelheid and Herbert Parkin, 77–157. London: John Calder, 1966.
  Detailed coverage with many analytic observations.

ORNSTEIN, LEO, 1892–

DISSERTATIONS AND THESES

Danse Sauvage

2974. Darter, Thomas Eugene. "The Futurist Piano Music of Leo Ornstein," D.M.A., Cornell University, 1979, 222 pp., DA 39-6386A.

PACHELBEL, JOHANN, 1653–1706

Christ Lag in Todesbanden

2975. Thoburn, Crawford R. "Pachelbel's *Christ Lag in Todesbanden*: A Possible Influence on Bach's Work." *American Choral Review,* 19, no. 1 (1977): 3–16.
  Melody, structure, instrumental forces, setting, and treatment of voice considered in comparing Bach's setting of this text with Pachelbel's. Musical examples.

PAGANINI, NICCOLÒ, 1782–1840

Concertos

2976. Swalin, Benjamin F. *The Violin Concerto: A Study in German Romanticism*, 34–41. Chapel Hill: University of North Carolina Press, 1941.
  Critical and analytic remarks with background. Musical examples.

2977. Veinus, Abraham. *The Concerto.* Rev. ed., 162–169. New York: Dover Publications, 1964.
  General discussion of Paganini's contribution to the form, rather than an analysis of individual works.

PAINE, JOHN KNOWLES, 1839–1906

General

2978. Schmidt, John C. *The Life and Works of John Knowles Paine.* Ann Arbor: UMI Research Press, 1981, 756 pp.
  The most detailed study of this composer to date. Published version of a dissertation. Each work is discussed in detail: background, orchestration, style, text setting, formal structure, and harmony. Musical examples.

PAISIELLO, GIOVANNI, 1740–1816

General

2979. Hunt, Juno L. "The Keyboard Works of Giovanni Paisiello." *Musical Quarterly*, 61, no. 2 (1975): 213–232.
  Overview of Paisiello's keyboard output, including concertos as well as solo works.

PALESTRINA, GIOVANNI, c. 1525–1594

General

2980. Andrews, Herbert K. *An Introduction to the Technique of Palestrina.* London: Novello, 1958, 256 pp.
  The largest single study of Palestrina's style to date. Mode, rhythm, time signature, melodic line, consonance and dissonance, contrapuntal techniques, texture, form, structure, and word setting discussed. Musical examples.

2981. Boyd, Malcolm. *Palestrina's Style.* London: Oxford University Press, 1973, 61 pp.

An analytical discussion of Palestrina's style. Many brief analytic examples with chapters on modality, rhythm, harmony, and texture.

2982.   Coates, Henry. *Palestrina.* London: J. M. Dent and Sons, 1948, 243 pp.
Critical guide for the undergraduate student or musical amateur. Musical examples.

2983.   Coates, Henry, and Gerald Abraham. "The perfection of the A Capella Style." In *The New Oxford History of Music.* Vol. 4, *The Age of Humanism, 1540–1630.* Edited by Gerald Abraham, 312–333. London: Oxford University Press, 1968.
Palestrina's style, masses, and motets examined. Musical examples.

2984.   Jeppesen, Knud. *The Style of Palestrina and the Dissonance.* 1946. Reprint. New York: Dover Publications, 1970, 306 pp.
Thorough examination of Palestrina's style and treatment of dissonance. Musical examples.

2985.   Novack, Saul. "Tonality and the Style of Palestrina." In *Music and Civilization: Essays in Honor of Paul Henry Lang.* Edited by Edmond Strainchamps and Maria Rika Maniates, 428–443. New York: W. W. Norton, 1984.
A study of those elements of Palestrina's technique leading to tonality. Opening imitation at the fifth, tonal prolongation, and voice leading are some of the techniques studied in detail. Musical examples.

2986.   Reese, Gustave. *Music in the Renaissance.* Rev. ed., 455–481. New York: W. W. Norton, 1959.
Detailed analytic description of Palestrina's output by genre. Musical examples.

2987.   Roche, Jerome. *Palestrina.* London: Oxford University Press, 1971, 60 pp.
A detailed and technical study of Palestrina's music. The organization is by genre: chapters on masses, motets, other liturgical music and madrigals. Musical examples.

Magnificats

2988.   Lamb, Gordon H. "The Psalm Tone Technique and Palestrina's Magnificat Settings." *American Choral Review,* 17, no. 1 (1975): 3–11.

Palestrina's use of psalm tones and their influence on the structure of the Magnificats. Musical examples.

Masses

2989. Marshall, Robert L. "The Paraphrase Technique of Palestrina in His Masses Based on Hymns." *Journal of the American Musicological Society*, 16, no. 3 (1963): 347–372.

Advanced, technical discussion of the use of borrowed themes. Musical examples.

Pope Marcellus Mass

2990. Godt, Irving. "A New Look at Palestrina's *Missa Papae Marcelli.*" *College Music Symposium*, 23, no. 1 (1983): 22–49.

The author inquires as to whether or not there are unifying features in freely composed settings of the Ordinary. He concludes that in this Mass, thematic unity exists between the beginning and late portions of several movements, thereby creating "families." This also creates similarities in rhythm at beginnings and endings of phrases. Tables.

2991. Lockwood, Lewis, ed. *"Pope Marcellus Mass."* Norton Critical Scores. New York: W. W. Norton, 1975.

Background, history, analysis, and critical commentary. Full score provided.

PEETERS, FLOR, 1903–1986

General

2992. Hesford, Bryan. "The Organ Works of Flor Peeters." *Musical Opinion*, 100 (September 1977): 603; 101 (November 1977): 49–51, 53, 55.

A survey with many analytical observations.

PENDERECKI, KRZYSZTOF, 1933–

St. Luke Passion

2993. Newell, Robert. "Penderecki's *Passio*—A Structure and Performance." *American Choral Review*, 16, no. 3 (1974): 13–19.

Analysis with musical examples.

2994.   Robinson, Ray, and Allen Winold. *A Study of the Penderecki "St. Luke" Passion.* Celle: Moeck, 1983, 124 pp.
Thorough book-length study including background, text, musical analysis, and comparison of the *St. Luke* Passion with works of other composers. Musical examples.

Threnody for the Victims of Hiroshima

2995.   Machlis, Joseph. *The Enjoyment of Music.* 5th ed., 580–581. New York: W. W. Norton, 1984.
Brief remarks on background accompanied by descriptive commentary. For the undergraduate student.

DISSERTATIONS AND THESES

Da Natura Sonoris

2996.   Albers, Bradley Gene. *"Da Natura Sonoris* I and II by Krysztof Penderecki: A Comparative Analysis." D.M.A., University of Illinois at Urbana, 116 pp., DA 39-2605A.

PERGOLESI, GIOVANNI, 1710–1736

La Serva Padrona

2997.   Henning, Cosmo. "Where Comic Opera Was Born." *Opera,* 20 (April 1969): 294–301.
Examines Pergolesi's role in the establishment of comic opera (opera buffa). Some standard comic effects mentioned. Musical examples.

PEROTIN, c. 1155–1200

General

2998.   Harman, Alec. *Man and His Music: Medieval and Renaissance Music,* 57–66. New York: Schocken Books, 1969.
Overview of Perotin's style, technique, and importance. Perotin compared briefly with Leonin. Musical examples.

2999.   Reese, Gustave. *Music in the Middle Ages,* 298–305. New York: W. W. Norton, 1940.

Focus on Perotin's chief contributions in the *Clausalae*. Analytic descriptions of the *Clausalae* with comparisons to Leonin's technique. Musical examples.

PERSICHETTI, VINCENT, 1915–1987

Do Not Go Gentle

3000. Shackelford, Rudolph. "Notes on the Recent Organ Music of Vincent Persichetti." *Diapason*, 67 (November 1976): 5–9.
Background and analysis. Musical examples and bibliography.

Parable IV for Organ, Op. 117

3001. Shackelford, Rudolph. "Notes on the Recent Organ Music of Vincent Persichetti." *Diapason*, 67 (November 1976): 5–9.
Background and analysis. Musical examples and bibliography.

Shimah B'koli (Psalm 130)

3002. Shackelford, Rudolph. "Vincent Persichetti's *Shimah B'koli* (Psalm 130) for Organ—An Analysis." *Diapason*, 66 (September 1975): 3–8+.

Sonata for Organ, Op. 86

3003. Shackelford, Rudolph. "Vincent Persichetti's Sonata for Organ and Sonatine for Organ, Pedals Alone—An Analysis." *Diapason*, 65 (May 1974): 4–7; (June 1974): 4–7.

Sonatine for Organ, Pedals Alone, Op. 11

3004. Shackelford, Rudolph. "Vincent Persichetti's Sonata for Organ and Sonatine for Organ, Pedals Alone—An Analysis." *Diapason*, 65 (May 1974): 4–7 (June 1974): 4–7.

DISSERTATIONS AND THESES

General

3005. Barnard, Jack Richard. "The Choral Music of Vincent Persichetti: A Descriptive Analysis." Ph.D., Florida State University, 1974, 300 pp., DA 35-7940A.

415

Parables

3006. Nelson, Mark Allan. "The Brass Parables of Vincent Persichetti." D.M.A., Arizona State University, 1985, 120 pp., DA 46-1124A.

PFITZNER, HANS, 1869–1949

General

3007. Truscott, Harold. "Pfitzner's Orchestral Music." *Tempo*, 104 (1973): 2–10.
Analytic overview, with special emphasis on his Violin Concerto. Musical examples.

Concerto for Violoncello Op. 42, No. 1 in G Major

3008. Dale, S. S. "Contemporary Cello Concerti." *Strad*, 86 (March 1986): 801 + .
Background and analysis.

PICCINI, NICCOLÒ, 1728–1800

Griselda

3009. Hunter, Mary. "The Fusion and Juxtaposition of Genres in Opera Buffa, 1770–1800: Anelli and Piccini's *Griselda*." *Music and Letters*, 67, no. 4 (1986): 363–380.
Discusses general distinctions between opera seria and opera buffa in this period, illustrating ways in which this work combines elements of both genres. The designation is *dramma eroicomico*. Musical structures are discussed. Musical examples.

Iphigénie en Tauride

3010. Rushton, Julian. "*Iphigénie en Tauride*: The Operas of Gluck and Piccini." *Music and Letters*, 53, no. 4 (1972): 411–430.
A comparison of the settings of *Iphigénie* by Gluck and Piccini. Background and critical remarks on the drama and music. Musical examples.

PISTON, WALTER, 1894–1976

General

3011.   Taylor, Clifford. "Walter Piston: For His Seventieth Birthday." In *Perspectives on American Composers*. Edited by Benjamin Boretz and E. T. Cone, 171–183. New York: W. W. Norton, 1971.
Commentary on stylistic traits coupled with analytic observations on, among other pieces, his Violin Concerto, Partita for Violin, Viola, and Organ, and the Second and Seventh Symphonies. Musical examples.

Symphony No. 4

3012.   Hansen, Peter. *An Introduction to Twentieth Century Music*. 2d ed., 336–338. Boston: Allyn and Bacon, 1967.
Brief overview, with musical examples.

3013.   Machlis, Joseph. *Introduction to Contemporary Music*, 509–511. New York: W. W. Norton, 1961.
Brief analysis. Musical examples.

POULENC, FRANCIS, 1899–1963

General

3014.   Bernac, Pierre. *Francis Poulenc: The Man and His Songs.* Translated by Winifred Radford. New York: W. W. Norton, 1977, 233 pp.
Descriptive and analytic commentary on all the songs.

3015.   Bernac, Pierre. "The Songs of Francis Poulenc." *NATS Bulletin*, 21, no. 3 (1965): 2–6.
Extensive critical commentary with catalog of songs of Poulenc.

3016.   Daniel, Keith W. *Francis Poulenc: His Artistic Development and Musical Style.* Ann Arbor: UMI Research Press, 1982, 390 pp.
Revision of a dissertation. Chapters 1–5 are biographical. Chapter 6 is on "Style." Chapters 7–12 treat each genre separately (chamber music, concertos, piano music, choral music, songs, stage works). Numerous analytical comments, analytical discussion, and more extended analyses of major works. Many musical examples.

3017. Davies, Laurence. "The Piano Music of Poulenc." *Music Review*, 33, no. 3 (1972): 194–203.
   Overview of Poulenc's piano compositions, focusing on style with background remarks and critical evaluation. Musical examples.

3018. Werner, Warren K. "The Piano Music of Francis Poulenc." *Clavier*, 9, no. 3 (1970): 17–19.
   General remarks on style. Very brief.

3019. Wood, Vivian. *Poulenc's Songs: An Analysis of Style.* Jackson: University Press of Mississippi, 1979, 173 pp.
   A study of the musical style of Poulenc's songs. The various musical elements are discussed in different chapters: Text and Music; Melody; Harmony; Form; Piano Accompaniment. Musical examples and diagrams.

Banalités

3020. Weide, Marion S. "Poulenc's *Banalités*: A Surrealist Song Cycle." *NATS Bulletin*, 35, no. 3 (1979): 12–16.
   Background and descriptive commentary for the performer. Bibliography.

Dialogues of the Carmelites

3021. Freeman, John W. "Song of the Scaffold." *Opera News*, 30 (March 5, 1966): 14–15.
   Critical commentary supported by musical examples.

Mouvements Perpétuels

3022. Warburton, A. O. "Set Works for 'O' Level, GCE." *Music Teacher*, 50 (December 1971): 14–15.
   Analysis.

Mouvements Perpétuels No. 3

3023. Werner, Warren K. "Performer's Analysis of Poulenc's *Mouvements Perpétuels No. 3*." *Clavier*, 9, no. 3 (1970): 36–37.
   Performance hints with analytic remarks. Musical examples.

DISSERTATIONS AND THESES

General

3024.   Almond, Frank W. "Melody and Texture in the Choral Works of Francis Poulenc." Ph.D., Florida State University, 1970, 85 pp., DA 31-4811A.

3025.   Ebensberger, Gary Lee. "The Motets of Francis Poulenc." D.M.A., University of Texas at Austin, 1970, 200 pp., DA 31-3579A.

3026.   Romain, Edwin Philip. "A Study of Francis Poulenc's Fifteen Improvisations for Piano Solo." D.M.A., University of Southern Mississippi, 1978, 183 pp., DA 39-1920A.

3027.   Wood, Vivian Lee Poates. "Francis Poulenc's Songs for Voice and Piano." Ph.D., Washington University, 1973, 164 pp., DA 34-6031A.

PROKOFIEV, SERGEI, 1891–1953

General

3028.   Lloyd-Jones, David. "Prokofiev and the Opera." *Opera,* 13 (August 1962): 513–517.
   Concise overview of Prokofiev's operatic achievement. Some remarks on specific works.

3029.   Nestyev, Israel V. *Prokofiev.* Translated by Florence Jones. Stanford: Stanford University Press, 1960, 528 pp.
   Mainly background, accompanied by critical and descriptive remarks on the music.

3030.   Porter, Andrew. "Prokofiev's Late Operas." *Musical Times,* 108 (April 1967): 312–314.
   An overview of Prokofiev's later operatic achievement. Some critical commentary on the music and stylistic characteristics.

3031.   Whittall, Arnold. *Music Since the First World War,* 106–109. London: J. M. Dent and Sons, 1977.
   Analytic observations on the operas.

Children's Songs (Three), Op. 68

3032.   Blok, Vladimir, ed. *Sergei Prokofiev: Materials, Articles, Interviews,* 126–156. London: Progress/ Central Books, 1980.
   Analytic commentary. Musical examples.

Concertos

3033. Hill, Ralph, ed. *The Concerto,* 380–386. London: Penguin Books, 1952.
  Critical and analytic commentary for the undergraduate student. Musical examples.

Concerto for Piano No. 3 in C Major

3034. Hansen, Peter. *An Introduction to Twentieth Century Music.* 2d ed., 283–286. Boston: Allyn and Bacon, 1967.
  Brief remarks on important musical features. Musical examples.

3035. Machlis, Joseph. *The Enjoyment of Music.* 3d ed., 539–540. New York: W. W. Norton, 1970.
  Analytic overview for the undergraduate student. Musical examples.

3036. Nelson, Wendell. *The Concerto,* 98–100. Dubuque, IA: William C. Brown, 1969.
  Descriptive and critical commentary, with musical examples.

Concerto for Violin No. 2 in G Minor

3037. Hansen, Peter. *An Introduction to Twentieth Century Music.* 2d ed., 286–288. Boston: Allyn and Bacon, 1967.
  Brief descriptive and analytic remarks, with musical examples.

Fiery Angel

3038. Jefferson, Alan. "The Angel of Fire." *Music and Musicians,* 13 (August 1965): 32–35.
  Descriptive and analytic remarks, with musical examples.

3039. Payne, Anthony. "Prokofiev's *The Fiery Angel.*" *Tempo,* 74 (Autumn 1965): 21–23.
  A review with critical commentary.

Lieutenant Kijé

3040. Pilgrim, Jack. "Set Works for 'O' Level, GCE." *Music Teacher,* 53 (December 1974): 15–16.
  Descriptive and analytic comments on each movement. For the undergraduate student.

3041. Reynolds, Gordon. "Prokofiev: *Lieutenant Kijé.*" *Music in Education*, 38, no. 368 (1974): 171–173.
Synopsis of the story of the film, followed by analytic comments on each of the five movements of the Suite. Musical examples.

Music for Children, Op. 65

3042. Blok, Vladimir, ed. *Sergei Prokofiev: Materials, Articles, Interviews*, 126–156. London: Progress/Central Books, 1980.
Extended analytic discussion. Musical examples.

Peter and the Wolf

3043. Blok, Vladimir, ed. *Sergei Prokofiev: Materials, Articles, Interviews*, 126–156. London: Progress/Central Books, 1980.
Analytic commentary. Musical examples.

Sonatas for Piano

3044. Chaikin, Lawrence. "The Prokofieff Sonatas: A Psychograph." *Piano Quarterly*, 22, no. 86 (1974): 8–19.
Brief analyses of all the sonatas. Musical examples.

3045. Roseberry, Eric. "Prokofiev's Piano Sonatas." *Music and Musicians*, 19 (March 1971): 38–42 +.
Stylistic traits and analytic remarks both specific and general. Musical examples.

Sonata for Piano No. 8, Op. 84 in B-Flat Major

3046. Brown, Malcolm A. "Prokofieff's Eighth Piano Sonata." *Tempo*, 70 (Autum 1964): 9–15.
Advanced analysis. Musical examples.

Symphonies

3047. Simpson, Robert, ed *The Symphony.* Vol. 2, 166–180. New York: Drake Publishers, 1972.
Descriptive and critical overview with analytic insights. Musical examples.

3048. Whittall, Arnold. *Music Since the First World War*, 76–84. London: J. M. Dent and Sons, 1977.
Analytic discussions on Symphonies 6 and 7. Musical examples.

Symphony No. 1 in D Major, Op. 25 ("Classical")

3049. Austin, William W. *Music in the Twentieth Century*, 451–455. New York: W. W. Norton, 1966.
Analytic comments, with remarks on style. Musical examples.

3050. Elkin, Robert. "Prokofiev's *Classical* Symphony." *Music in Education*, 28, no. 310 (1964): 273–275.
Concentrated analysis, with musical examples.

3051. Nadeau, Roland. *The Symphony: Structure and Style.* Shorter ed., rev., 169–174. Boston: Crescendo, 1973.
Measure-by-measure analysis.

3052. Nestyev, Israel V. *Prokofiev*, 145–148. Stanford: Stanford University Press, 1960.
Descriptive commentary with remarks on Prokofiev's creative intention in the writing of the satirical work.

3053. Warburton, A. O. "Set Works for 'O' Level, GCE." *Music Teacher and Piano Student*, 44 (April 1965): 162–177.
An analysis of the form of each of the four movements; includes other analytical observations.

Symphony No. 5 in B-Flat Major

3054. Stedman, Preston. *The Symphony*, 289–298. Englewood Cliffs; NJ: Prentice-Hall, 1979.
Description and analytic breakdown of each movement, supported by musical examples and diagram.

Symphony No. 7

3055. Austin, William W. *Music in the Twentieth Century*, 468–471. New York: W. W. Norton, 1966.
Descriptive and analytic commentary for the undergraduate student.

War and Peace

3056. Brown, David. "Prokofiev's *War and Peace*." *Music and Musicians*, 21 (October 1972): 24–26.
Compositional history and critical commentary.

3057.   Brown, Malcolm H. "Prokofiev's *War and Peace*: A Chronicle." *Musical Quarterly*, 63, no. 3 (1977): 297–326.
   Extensive compositional history.

3058.   McAllister, Rita. "Prokofiev's Tolstoy Epic." *Musical Times*, 113 (September 1972): 851–855.
   Compositional history only.

3059.   Yarustovsky, Boris. "Prokofiev's *War and Peace*." *Music Journal*, 18 (April–May 1960): 32 + .
   Brief critical remarks.

Winter Bonfire, Op. 122

3060.   Blok, Vladimir, ed. *Sergei Prokofiev: Materials, Articles, Interviews*, 126–156. London: Progress/Central Books, 1980.
   Analytical commentary. Musical examples.

DISSERTATIONS AND THESES

Sonatas for Piano

3061.   Martin, Rebecca Gena. "The Nine Piano Sonatas of Sergei Prokofiev." D.M.A., University of Kentucky, 1982, 118 pp., DA 43-3749A.

3062.   Vlahcevic, Sonia Klosek. "Thematic-Tonal Organization in the Late Sonatas of Sergei Prokofiev." Ph.D., Catholic University of America, 1975, 251 pp., DA 36-1897A.

Sonata for Piano No. 7, Op. 83 in B-Flat Major

3063.   Mathes, James Robert. "Texture and Musical Structure: An Analysis of First Movements of Select Twentieth-Century Piano Sonatas." Ph.D., Florida State University, 1986, 271 pp., DA 47-2363A.

PUCCINI, GIACOMO, 1858–1924

General

3064.   Ashbrook, William. *The Operas of Puccini.* London: Oxford University Press, 1968, 269 pp.

Background, genesis, synopsis, and musical discussion of each opera. Musical discussion includes style, orchestration, tonality, thematic material, and voice types. Musical examples.

3065.   Carner, Mosco. *Puccini: A Critical Biography.* New York: Alfred A. Knopf, 1959, 500 pp.
Background, descriptive, critical, and analytic commentary on all of Puccini's operas. Musical examples.

3066.   MacDonald, Ray S. *Puccini: King of Verismo.* New York: Vantage Press, 1973, 211 pp.
A discussion of all the operas from the point of view of realistic dramatic treatment (*verismo* and the use of leitmotiv. Musical examples.

3067.   Osborne, Charles. *The Complete Operas of Puccini.* New York: Atheneum, 1982, 279 pp.
Background, composition history, plot summary, and descriptive commentary on the music, with analytic observations. For the undergraduate or concertgoer. Not as detailed as Ashbrook, whose comments on the music are more specific.

3068.   Plantinga, Leon. *Romantic Music,* 326–330. New York: W. W. Norton, 1984.
Brief analytic comments on the operas. Musical examples.

La Bohème

3069.   Downes, Edward. "The Feel of Reality." *Opera News,* 30 (April 16, 1966): 24–25.
Brief critical and analytic commentary for the general reader. Musical examples.

3070.   Hughes, Spike. *Famous Puccini Operas,* 51–82. New York: Dover Publications, 1972.
Discussion covers background, plot, characterization, themes, orchestration, dramatic function of themes, and analytic comments. For the undergraduate student or musical amateur.

La Fanciulla del West

3071.   Carner, Mosco. "How Puccini Won the West." *Music and Musicians,* 11 (December 1962): 10–12.
Background and critical commentary on the music and discussion of special effects.

3072.   Carner, Mosco. *"La Fanciulla del West."* Opera, 28 (May 1977): 426–433.
Puccini's "new" style examined, with reasons given for the changes in his compositional style. Musical examples.

3073.   Hughes, Spike. *Famous Puccini Operas*, 139–172. New York: Dover Publications, 1972.
Discussion covers background, plot, characterization, themes, orchestration, dramatic function of themes, and analytic comments for the amateur listener. Musical examples.

Gianni Schicci

3074.   Ashbrook, William. "A Sense of Promise." *Opera News*, 39 (February 22, 1975): 20–21.
Brief critical remarks on highlights. Musical examples.

3075.   Hughes, Spike. *Famous Puccini Operas*, 196–210. New York: Dover Publications, 1972.
Discussion covers background, plot characterization, themes, orchestration, dramatic function of themes, and analytic comments for the amateur listener. Musical examples.

Madama Butterfly

3076.   Ashbrook, William. "The Real Hero." *Opera News*, 29 (March 27, 1965): 24–25.
Musical characterization demonstrated. Musical examples.

3077.   Freeman, John. "A Wisp on the Horizon." *Opera News*, 32 (March 30, 1968): 24–25.
Focuses on Puccini's musical characterization.

3078.   Heath, Mary R. "Exoticism in Puccini: The Japanese Melodies in *Madama Butterfly*." *Opera Journal*, 13, no. 4 (1980): 21–28.
On the derivation of melodies from Japanese modes in this work. Musical examples.

3079.   Hughes, Spike. *Famous Puccini Operas*, 111–138. New York: Dover Publications, 1972.
Discussion covers background, plot, characterization, themes, orchestration, dramatic function of themes, and analytic comments for the amateur listener.

3080. John, Nicholas, ed. *Madama Butterfly.* London: John Calder, 1984, 128 pp.

Background articles and libretto. No analytic essays. There is a "thematic guide" of music examples indexed in the libretto.

Manon Lescaut

3081. Hughes, Spike. "The Charm of the Unexpected." *Opera News*, 32 (March 23, 1968): 24–25.

Brief remarks on Puccini's musical setting in two examples. Musical examples.

3082. Hughes, Spike. *Famous Puccini Operas*, 17–50. New York: Dover Publications, 1972.

Discussion covers background, plot, characterization, themes, orchestration, dramatic function of themes, and analytic comments for the amateur listener.

Suor Angelica

3083. Hughes, Spike. *Famous Puccini Operas*, 186–195. New York: Dover Publications, 1972.

Discussion covers background, plot, characterization, themes, orchestration, dramatic function of themes, and analytic comments for the amateur listener. Musical examples.

Il Tabarro

3084. Hughes, Spike. *Famous Puccini Operas*, 174–185. New York: Dover Publications, 1972.

Discussion covers background, plot, characterization, themes, orchestration, dramatic function of themes, and analytic comments for the amateur listener. Musical examples.

Tosca

3085. Ashbrook, William. "A Message of Love." *Opera News*, 43 (December 16, 1978): 26–27.

A deeper level of meaning is found to be associated with some principal motifs. Musical examples.

3086. Carner, Mosco. *Giacomo Puccini: "Tosca."* New York: Cambridge University Press, 1985, 165 pp.

A volume in the "Cambridge Opera Handbooks" series. Exhaustive treatment of *Tosca*, including synopsis, motifs, characterization, orchestration, tonality, harmony, dramatic structure, relationship of words to music. There is also a chapter-length analysis of Act I. Musical examples.

3087.   Hughes, Spike. *Famous Puccini Operas,* 83–110. New York: Dover Publications, 1972.
Discussion covers background, plot, characterization, themes, orchestration, dramatic function of themes, and analytic comments for the amateur listener. Musical examples.

3088.   Kleine-Ahlbrandt, Laird. "The Hero As Revolutionary." *Opera News,* 33 (February 15, 1969): 24–25.
Brief remarks on the plot and its historical accuracy.

Turandot

3089.   Haldeman, L. W. "Once Upon a Time." *Opera News,* 33 (March 22, 1969): 24–25.
Brief remarks on some reasons why Puccini's adaptation of Gozzi's *Turandotte* succeeded while other composers' settings failed.

3090.   Hughes, Spike. *Famous Puccini Operas,* 211–252. New York: Dover Publications, 1972.
Discussion covers background, plot, characterization, themes, orchestration, dramatic function of themes, and analytic comments for the amateur listener. Musical examples.

3091.   John, Nicholas, ed. *Turandot.* London: John Calder, 1984, 112 pp.
An introduction to the opera for the general public. Analytic comments on motifs, characterization, drama, and other musical features. Musical examples.

3092.   McDonald, Katherine Griffith. "The Sun and the Moon." *Opera News,* 25 (March 4, 1961): 21–23.
Analytic remarks and comments on influences in *Turandot.* Musical examples.

PURCELL, HENRY, 1659–1695

General

3093.   Gordon, Lewis W. "The Odes of Henry Purcell." *American Choral Review,* 26, no. 4 (1984): Entire issue.
Musical characteristics, descriptive commentary dealing with style, analytic observations, and critical appraisal. Musical examples.

3094. Holland, Arthur Keith. *Henry Purcell: The English Musical Tradition.* 1932. Reprint. New York: Books for Libraries Press, 1970, 248 pp.

Survey of Purcell's output, focusing on historical context, elements of musical style, and use of poetry.

3095. Laurie, Margaret. "Purcell's Extended Solo Songs." *Musical Times,* 125 (January 1984): 19–25.

Survey of the secular songs. Discusses declamation and modulation used to enhance the text.

3096. Lewis, Anthony. "Purcell and Blow's *Venus and Adonis.*" *Music and Letters,* 44, no. 3 (1963): 266–269.

Compares the Ground from Blow's work with the Air from *Fairy Queen* by Purcell. Suggests musical link between the two composers. Analysis comparing and contrasting the two works. Musical examples.

3097. Maxwell, Margaret R. "Sacred Solo Songs of Henry Purcell." *NATS Bulletin,* 35, no. 2 (1978): 27–30.

Texts, form, melody and rhythm, texture, and harmony discussed.

3098. Moore, Robert Etheridge. *Henry Purcell and the Restoration Theatre.* 1961. Reprint. Westport, CT: Greenwood Press, 1974, 223 pp.

Full treatment of all Purcell's dramatic works.

3099. Price, Curtis A. *Henry Purcell and the London Stage.* Cambridge: Cambridge University Press, 1984, 380 pp.

Thorough review of Purcell's music for the plays, comedies, and tragedies for the London stage as well as his operas *Dido and Aeneas, Dioclesian, King Arthur,* and the *Fairy Queen.* Musical examples.

3100. Spink, Ian. *English Songs: Dowland to Purcell.* London: B. T. Batsford, 1974.

An analytic discussion of the songs. Places the composer in historical context, identifies influences upon him and his influence on others, identifies stylistic traits, discusses musical techniques and relationships between text and music. Includes a critical assessment. Musical examples.

3101. Sternfeld, Frederick W., et al. eds. *Essays on Opera and English Music in Honour of Sir Jack Westrup,* 44–78. Oxford: B. Blackwell, 1975.

Analytic discussion of Purcell's style in his early church music and domestic sacred music. Musical examples.

3102. Tilmouth, Michael. "The Technique and Form of Purcell's Sonatas." *Music and Letters*, 40 (April 1959): 109–121. Focuses on the trio sonatas.

3103. Westrup, Jack. *Purcell.* London: J. M. Dent and Sons, 1975, 323 pp.
   Descriptive, critical, and analytic remarks for the undergraduate student. Musical examples.

3104. Zimmerman, Franklin B. "Purcell's Concerted Anthems: New Aesthetic Concepts." *American Choral Review*, 5, no. 2 (1963): 8–12. Stylistic observations. Musical examples.

3105. Zimmerman, Franklin B. "Purcell's Polyphonic Anthems: Styles, Media, and Interpretation." *American Choral Review*, 4, no. 4 (1962): 1, 3–6.
   Various analytical observations, with musical examples.

3106. Zimmerman, Franklin B. "Thematic Unity in Purcell's Grand Concerted Anthems." *American Choral Review*, 5, no. 4 (1963): 10–13; 6, no. 1 (1963): 3–4 + .
   Coherence and unity is demonstrated with many musical examples from various works.

Dido and Aeneas

3107. Arundell, Dennis. *Henry Purcell*, 67–71. New York: Books for Libraries Press, 1970.
   Brief but effective review of important features of *Dido*. Musical examples. Includes similar information on Purcell's other dramatic works.

3108. Arundell, Dennis. "New Light on *Dido and Aeneas*." *Opera*, 13 (July 1962): 445–448.
   Discussion of manuscript versions and where first performed. Informative background remarks.

3109. Kuchner, David Z. "Henry Purcell's *Dido and Aeneas*: An Analytical Discussion." *American Music Teacher*, 21, no. 1 (1971): 25–28.

3110. Price, Curtis A. ed. *Purcell: "Dido and Aeneas."* Norton Critical Scores. New York: W. W. Norton, 1986, 277 pp.
   Historical background, criticism, analysis, production, and interpretation. Full score provided.

Fantazia No. 4 in G Minor, Z. 735.

3111.   Warburton, A. O. "Set Works for 'O' Level, GCE." *Music Teacher and Piano Student,* 46 (June 1967): 10.
Brief analytic comments.

DISSERTATIONS AND THESES

Anthems

3112.   Anderson, William Woodrow. "The Stylistic Development of Henry Purcell As Revealed by His Sacred Verse Anthems." D.M.A., University of Kansas, 1980, 182 pp., DA 41-2818A.

RACHMANINOFF, SERGEI, 1873–1943

General

3113.   Crociata, Francis. "The Piano Music of Sergei Wassilievitch Rachmaninoff." *Piano Quarterly,* 21, no. 82 (1973): 27–33.
A survey of Rachmaninoff's piano works, which includes descriptive, historic, and analytic remarks. Musical examples.

3114.   Culshaw, John. *Rachmaninov: The Man and His Music.* New York: Oxford University Press, 1950, 174 pp.
Descriptive commentary, critical evaluations, and remarks on style. Musical examples.

3115.   Norris, Geoffrey. *Rakhmaninov.* London: J. M. Dent and Sons, 1976, 211 pp.
In the "Master Musician" series, this is a traditional "life and works" study. The "works" section surveys works grouped by genre and includes many analytic remarks on individual works. Musical examples.

3116.   Piggott, Patrick. *Rachmaninov Orchestral Music.* London: British Broadcasting Corporation, 1974, 60 pp.
Commentaries on the symphonies, piano concertos, and other orchestral music. The discussions are quite descriptive, but there are analytic comments on themes, motives, form, keys, and other unifying factors. For the layman or undergraduate student. Musical examples.

Concertos

3117. Coolidge, Richard. "Architectonic Technique and Innovation in the Rachmaninoff Piano Concertos." *Music Review*, 40, no. 3 (1979): 176–216.
Assessment of Rachmaninoff's position in the professional musical world as opposed to reception by the public. Highly detailed analyses of his four piano concertos and the Rhapsody on a Theme of Paganini. Musical examples.

3118. Hill, Ralph, ed. *The Concerto*, 289–300. London: Penguin Books, 1952.
Critical and analytic commentary for the undergraduate student. Musical examples.

3119. Veinus, Abraham. *The Concerto*. Rev. ed., 253–256. New York: Dover Publications, 1964.
General remarks, placing Rachmaninoff in historical perspective. Not analytic.

Concerto for Piano No. 3 in D Minor

3120. Hopkins, Antony. *Talking About Concertos*, 123–134. London: Heinemann, 1964.
Extended analytic essay describing tonal, thematic, and formal events.

3121. Yasser, Joseph. "The Opening Theme of Rachmaninoff's Third Piano Concerto and Its Liturgical Prototype." *Musical Quarterly*, 55, no. 3 (1969): 313–328.
Thorough discussion tracing liturgical and folkloric elements in the opening theme. Musical examples.

Preludes

3122. Slenczynka, Ruth. "Rachmaninoff's Preludes." *Clavier*, 2, no. 6 (1963): 27–30.
Discussion of the preludes from a performer's standpoint. Useful here for Rachmaninoff's remarks and descriptive commentary. Score included.

Rhapsody on a Theme of Paganini

3123. Coolidge, Richard. "Architectonic Technique and Innovation in the Rachmaninov Piano Concertos." *Music Review*, 40, no. 3 (1979): 176 + .

Assessment of Rachmaninoff's position in the professional musical world as opposed to his public reception. Detailed analyses of his four piano concertos and the Rhapsody. Musical examples.

Symphonies

3124. Maycock, Robert. "Rachmaninov the Symphonist." *Music and Musicians,* 21 (July 1973): 40–42 + .
As assessment of Rachmaninoff's symphonies highlighting stylistic characteristics.

3125. Simpson, Robert, ed. *The Symphony.* Vol. 2, 128–131. New York: Drake Publishers, 1972.
Brief descriptive and critical remarks. No analytic discussion.

Symphony No. 2, Op. 27 in E Minor

3126. Rubin, David. "Transformations of the 'Dies Irae' in Rachmaninov's Second Symphony." *Music Review,* 23 (1962): 132–136.
Traces variations of "Dies Irae" throughout the symphony and elucidates its structural significance.

DISSERTATIONS AND THESES

Vespers

3127. Prussing, Stephan Henry. "Compositional Techniques in Rachmaninoff's Vespers, Opus 37." Ph.D., Catholic University of America, 1980, 237 pp., DA 40-5644A.

RAMEAU, JEAN PHILIPPE, 1683–1764

General

3128. Anthony, James R. *French Baroque Music from Beaujoyeulx to Rameau.* New York: W. W. Norton, 1974, 429 pp.
A study of French Baroque style elements seen in historical context. Specific works in different genres discussed. Musical examples.

3129. Girdlestone, Cuthbert. *Jean-Philippe Rameau: His Life and Work.* Rev. ed., 14–37. New York: Dover Publications, 1969.
Descriptive and critical commentary. Musical examples.

DISSERTATIONS AND THESES

3130. Rice, Paul Francis. "The Fontainbleau Operas of Jean-Philippe Rameau: A Critical Study." Ph.D., University of Victoria (Canada), 1982, DA 43-2490A.

RAVEL, MAURICE, 1875–1937

General

3131. Davies, Laurence. *Ravel Orchestral Music.* Seattle: University of Washington Press, 1970, 64 pp.
Analytic guide for the undergraduate student. Musical examples.

3132. Demuth, Norman. *Ravel.* London: J. M. Dent and Sons, 1947, 214 pp.
Critical and analytic remarks, with musical examples. Shows Ravel's stylistic development.

3133. Matthews, Denis, ed. *Keyboard Music,* 280–285. New York: Praeger, 1972.
Critical overview, with discussion of influences. Musical examples.

3134. Myers, Rollo. *Ravel.* London: Duckworth, 1960, 239 pp.
Mainly descriptive commentary, with occasional analytic remarks. For the undergraduate student. Musical examples.

3135. Nichols, Roger. *Ravel.* London: J. M. Dent and Sons, 1977, 199 pp.
Descriptive and critical commentary for the undergraduate student. Musical examples.

3136. Orenstein, Arbie. *Ravel: Man and Musician.* New York: Columbia University Press, 1975. 291 pp.
Descriptive program note–style commentary, with occasional observations on important features such as structure, tonality, or rhythm. Useful here for its thorough inclusion of Ravel's works.

3137. Stuckenschmidt, H. H. *Maurice Ravel: Variations on His Life and Work.* Philadelphia: Chilton Book Co., 1968, 271 pp.
Descriptive commentary for the musical amateur. No analyses, but useful for students in search of background information.

Boléro

3138. Davies, Laurence. *Ravel Orchestral Music*, 41–43. Seattle: University of Washington Press, 1970.
   Descriptive and analytic commentary for the undergraduate student. Musical examples.

Chansons (Three) (1914–1915)

3139. Shearin, Arthur. "The Choral Music of Debussy and Ravel." *Choral Journal*, 19, no. 6 (1979): 7–9.
   A comparison of the setting of these medieval poems. Discusses texture, use of modality, phrase structure, vocal ranges.

Concertos for Piano

3140. Hill, Ralph, ed. *The Concerto*, 307–314. London: Penguin Books, 1952.
   Critical and analytic commentary for the undergraduate student. Musical examples.

Concerto for Piano for the Left Hand

3141. Davies, Laurence. *Ravel Orchestral Music*, 47–50. Seattle: University of Washington Press, 1970.
   Brief descriptive and analytic commentary. Musical examples.

Concerto for Piano in G Major

3142. Davies, Laurence. *Ravel Orchestral Music*, 45–47. Seattle: University of Washington Press, 1970.
   Brief descriptive and analytic commentary. Musical examples.

3143. Nelson, Wendell. *The Concerto*, 89–92. Dubuque, IA: William C. Brown, 1969.
   Descriptive and critical commentary, with musical examples.

Daphnis et Chloé

3144. Davies, Laurence. *Ravel Orchestral Music*, 26–32. Seattle: University of Washington Press, 1970.
   Descriptive and analytic commentary. Musical examples.

Daphnis et Chloé: Suite No. 2

3145. Machlis, Joseph. *Introduction to Contemporary Music,* 140–142. New York: W. W. Norton, 1961.
   Descriptive commentary, with musical examples. For the undergraduate student.

L' Enfant et les sortilèges

3146. Orenstein, Arbie. *Ravel: Man and Musician,* 193–195. New York: Columbia University Press, 1975.
   Condensed summary of the musical and plot characteristics.

Gaspard de la nuit

3147. Cooper, Martin. *French Music: From the Death of Berlioz to the Death of Fauré,* 130–133. London: Oxford University Press, 1969.
   Brief descriptive and analytic commentary. Musical examples.

Introduction and Allegro

3148. Warburton, A. O. "Set Works for 'O' Level, GCE." *Music Teacher,* 48 (April 1969): 16 + .
   Analytic description. Principal motives are identified; comments on tonality.

Ma Mère l'oye

3149. Austin, William W. *Music in the Twentieth Century,* 169–172. New York: W. W. Norton, 1966.
   Brief analysis of the *Pavane de la belle au bois dormant* from this set. Musical examples.

3150. Davies, Laurence. *Ravel Orchestral Music,* 18–21. Seattle: University of Washington Press, 1970.
   Descriptive and analytic commentary. Musical examples.

Menuet antique

3151. Davies, Laurence. *Ravel Orchestral Music,* 9–10. Seattle: University of Washington Press, 1970.
   Descriptive and analytic commentary. Musical examples.

Menuet sur le nom d'Haydn

3152. Montandon, Blaise. "A Twentieth-Century Minuet." *Clavier*, 11 (April 1972): 29–30.
　　Performer's notes, with analytic observations. Complete musical examples.

Pavane pour une infante défunte

3153. Davies, Laurence. *Ravel Orchestral Music*, 11–12. Seattle: University of Washington Press, 1970.
　　Brief descriptive and analytic commentary. Musical examples.

Poèmes de Stéphane Mallarmé

3154. Gronquist, Robert. "Raval's *Trois poèmes de Stéphane Mallarmé*." *Musical Quarterly*, 64, no. 4 (1978): 507–523.
　　Analytic discussion of the music's relationship to the text. Musical examples.

Quartet for Strings

3155. Ferguson, Donald N. *Image and Structure in Chamber Music*, 259–262. Minneapolis: University of Minnesota Press, 1964.
　　Brief analysis. Musical examples.

3156. Warburton, A. O. "Set Works for 'O' Level, GCE." *Music Teacher*, 50 (December 1971): 13–15.
　　Analysis for the undergraduate.

Rapsodie Espagnole

3157. Davies, Laurence. *Ravel Orchestral Music*, 12–16. Seattle: University of Washington Press, 1970.
　　Descriptive and analytic commentary. Musical examples.

Sonata for Violin (1897)

3158. Wen, Eric. "Rare Ravel." *Strad*, 94 (January 1984): 614–615 + .
　　Background and analysis.

Sonatine

3159.   Smith, Edwin. "Ravel: Sonatine." *Music Teacher*, 55 (March 1976): 13–15.
Analysis of thematic content and the form of each movement. Includes notes on nontonal (whole-tone, modal) harmonies.

Tombeau de Couperin

3160.   Davies, Laurence. *Ravel Orchestral Music*, 32–37. Seattle: University of Washington Press, 1970.
Descriptive and analytic commentary. Musical examples.

Trois chansons de France

3161.   Shearin, Arthur. "The Choral Music of Debussy and Ravel." *Choral Journal*, 19, no. 6 (1979): 7–9.
A comparison of the setting of these medieval poems. Discusses texture, use of modality, phrase structure, vocal range.

Tzigane

3162.   Davies, Laurence. *Ravel Orchestral Music*, 51–52. Seattle: University of Washington Press, 1970.
Brief descriptive and analytic commentary. Musical examples.

La Valse

3163.   Davies, Laurence. *Ravel Orchestral Music*, 37–41. Seattle: University of Washington Press, 1970.
Brief descriptive and analytic commentary. Musical examples.

Valses nobles et sentimentales

3164.   Davies, Laurence. *Ravel Orchestral Music*, 21–26. Seattle: University of Washington Press, 1970.
Brief descriptive and analytic commentary. Musical examples.

3165.   Hantz, Edwin. "Exempli Gratia: A Ravelled Labyrinth or 3 (5) = 3 (mod 12)." *In Theory Only*, 1 (September 1975): 21–23.
Measures 57–61 examined, which comprise a circle of fifths. For the advanced student. Graph.

DISSERTATIONS AND THESES

General

3166.   Russom, Philip Wade. "A Theory of Pitch Organization for the Early Works of Maurice Ravel." Ph.D., Yale University, 1985, 216 pp., DA 46-3188A.

L'Enfant et les sortilèges

3167.   Wilson, John Duane. "Ravel's *L'Enfant et les sortilèges*: Musical-Dramatic Analysis and Guide to Its Musical Preparation for College Opera Workshop Production." D.M.A., University of Rochester, Eastman School of Music, 1974, 304 pp., DA 35-3802A.

Gaspard de la nuit

3168.   Pohl, Norma Doris. "*Gaspard de la nuit* by Maurice Ravel: A Theoretical and Performance Analysis." Ph.D., Washington University, 1978, 283 pp., DA 40-23A.

Tombeau de Couperin

3169.   Koh, Bo Young Yum. "Ravel's *Le Tombeau de Couperin*: A Study of the Work and Its Historical Significance." D.M.A., University of Miami, 1986, 88 pp., DA 47-3903A.

Valses nobles et sentimentales

3170.   McCrae, Elizabeth. "Ravel's *Valses nobles et sentimentales*: Analysis, Stylistic Considerations, Performance Problems." D.M.A., Boston University, 1974, 196 pp., DA 35-1688A.

REGER, MAX, 1873–1916

General

3171.   Barker, John Wesley. "The Organ Works of Max Reger." *Miscellanea Musicologica*, 1 (March 1966): 56–73.
    Many analytical observations are included in this survey. Identifies distinctive uses of harmony, treatment of form, and other unifying factors.

3172.   Barker, John Wesley. "Reger's Organ Music." *Musical Times*, 109 (February 1968): 170-171.

Discusses Reger's adoption of intervallic cells as a primary compositional principle in his later organ works. The "cellular generation" (occurring after 1900) by characteristic intervals permeates his later organ works. Musical examples.

3173. Palmer, Christopher. "Reger's Orchestral Music." *Musical Times,* 114 (March 1973): 243–244.

Brief descriptive review of the orchestral music mentioning characteristic musical devices. Musical examples.

3174. Wuensch, Gerhard. "Max Reger's Choral Cantatas." *Music (AGO),* 6 (February 1972): 32–33 + .

Brief discussion of general style and structure. No real analysis. Musical examples.

Chorale Preludes, Op. 67

3175. Krentz, Michael E. "Max Reger's Op. 67." *American Organist,* 16 (August 1982): 34–36.

Remarks on importance of the chorale preludes in Reger's output, organization of the collection, and style. Interspersed with analytic observations. Bibliography.

Introduction, Variations, and Fugue on an Original Theme

3176. Mahnke, Allan. "Max Reger's Introduction, Variations, and Fugue in F-Sharp Minor, Op. 73." *American Organist,* 17 (April 1983): 46–48.

Analysis with musical examples.

Quartet for Strings, Op. 74 in D Minor

3177. Dahlhaus, Carl. *Nineteenth-Century Music.* Translated by J. Bradford Robinson, 339. Berkeley: University of Calfornia Press, 1989.

Brief analytic remarks on thematic contrast and sonata form elements as unifying forces. Advanced.

Serenade in G Major, Op. 95

3178. Tovey, Donald Francis. *Essays in Musical Analysis.* Vol. 6, 65–73. London: Oxford University Press, 1969.

Thorough critical and analytic discussion, with musical examples. For the undergraduate student.

Songs, Op. 70, No. 12

3179. Dahlhaus, Carl. *Nineteenth-Century Music.* Translated by J. Bradford Robinson, 371–372. Berkeley: University of California Press, 1989.
Brief but concentrated analytic remarks on "Dein Bild," dwelling on motivic structure, declamation, and harmony. Musical examples. Advanced.

DISSERTATIONS AND THESES

General

3180. Hopkins, William Thomas. "The Short Piano Compositions of Max Reger (1873–1916)." Ph.D., Indiana University, 1972, 259 pp., DA 32-6477A-8A.

Chorale Fantasias for Organ, Op. 52

3181. Maki, Paul-Martin. "The Three Chorale-Fantasias, Op. 52 of Max Reger: Commentary and a Practical Edition." D.M.A., University of Rochester, Eastman School of Music, 1975, 179 pp., DA 36-2483A.

REICH, STEVE, 1936–

General

3182. Schwarz, K. Robert. "Steve Reich: Music As a Gradual Process (Part 1)." *Perspectives of New Music,* 19, no. 1 (1980–1981): 373–392.
An explanation of Reich's music and the philosophy behind it. Specific works, such as *Octet (1978), Music for a Large Ensemble, It's Gonna Rain, Come Out,* and others are discussed. Followed by an excellent bibliography.

3183. Schwarz, K. Robert. "Steve Reich: Music As a Gradual Process (Part 2)." *Perspectives of New Music,* 20, nos. 1–2 (1981–1982): 225–286.
Analytic essay on the music of Steve Reich. Discusses many works, exploring the development of Reich's style. Musical examples.

Come Out

3184. **Schrader, Barry.** *Introduction to Electro-Acoustic Music*, 19–20. Englewood Cliffs, NJ: Prentice-Hall, 1982.
Brief analytic comments.

Pendulum Music

3185. **O'Grady, Terrence J.** "Aesthetic Value in Indeterminate Music." *Musical Quarterly*, 67, no. 3 (1981): 366–381.
The effect of the level of indeterminacy on the potential "value" of a piece. The music of John Cage and Terry Riley also discussed.

Piano Phase

3186. **Epstein, Paul.** "Pattern Structure and Process in Steve Reich's *Piano Phase*." *Musical Quarterly*, 72, no. 4 (1986): 494–502.
Advanced theoretical analysis. Musical examples.

RIMSKY-KORSAKOV, NIKOLAI, 1844–1908

General

3187. **Abraham, Gerald.** "Arab Melodies in Rimsky-Korsakov and Borodin." *Music and Letters*, 56, nos. 3–4 (1975): 313–318.
Historic and analytic survey of Rimsky-Korsakov's borrowing of Arab melodies from various sources and his treatment of those melodies. Musical examples.

3188. **Abraham, Gerald.** *Slavonic and Romantic Music*, 202–211. New York: St. Martin's Press, 1968.
Descriptive and critical overview of the songs. Musical examples.

3189. **Montagu-Nathan, Montagu.** *Rimsky-Korsakaov.* New York: Duffield and Co., 1917, 124 pp.
Descriptive and critical commentary, with musical examples.

Concerto for Piano in C-Sharp Minor

3190. **Garden, Edward.** "Three Russian Piano Concertos." *Music and Letters*, 69, no. 2 (1979): 172–174.

Historic and descriptive commentary with analysis. Briefly compares and contrasts this concerto to Tchaikovsky's Concerto for Piano No. 1 in B-Flat Minor. Musical examples.

Le Coq d'or

3191. Abraham, Gerald. "Satire and Symbolism in *The Golden Cockerel.*" *Music and Letters,* 52, no. 1 (1971): 46–54.

Mozart and Salieri

3192. Knutsen, Arvid J. "*Mozart and Salieri*: A Brief Critical and Analytic Study of Rimsky-Korsakov's Opera." *NATS Bulletin,* 39, no. 2 (1982): 15+.
Background, historical setting of Pushkin's play, theories on Mozart's death, setting of the text, form, and structure discussed. Bibliography.

ROCHBERG, GEORGE, 1918–

Quartet for Strings No. 3

3193. Linthicum, David. "Gramophone Records: George Rochberg: String Quartet No. 3." *Music Review,* 36, no. 2 (1975): 156–159.
A review of a recording of this work, which includes a general discussion of Rochberg's use of traditional compositional methods. The composer's comments on the record jacket are also discussed.

RORE, CIPRIANO DE, 1515–1565

Quando Signor Lasciaste

3194. Luoma, Robert G. "Relationships Between Music and Poetry." *Musica Disciplina,* 31 (1977): 135–154.
Examination of the effect of the text on the composition, including linear shape, sonorities, cadential patterns, tone painting, and mode.

ROREM, NED, 1923–

General

3195. Middaugh, Bennie. "The Songs of Ned Rorem—Aspects of Musical Style." *NATS Bulletin,* 24, no. 4 (1968): 36–39.

Book of Hours

3196.   Warren, Linda. "Ned Rorem's *Book of Hours*: Analysis and Study Guide." *American Harp Journal,* 7, no. 2 (1979): 27–29.

DISSERTATIONS AND THESES

General

3197.   Bloomquist, Marvin Robert. "Songs of Ned Rorem: Aspects of the Musical Settings of Songs in English for Solo Voice and Piano." D.M.A., University of Missouri at Kansas City, 1970, 104 pp., DA 31-4191A.

3198.   Davis, Deborah Louise Bodwin. "The Choral Works of Ned Rorem." Ph.D., Michigan State University, 1978, 243 pp., DA 40-730A.

3199.   Griffiths, Richard Lyle. "Ned Rorem: Music for Chorus and Orchestra." D.M.A., University of Washington, 1979, 200 pp., DA 40-526A-7A.

ROSSI, LUIGI, 1598–1653

Cantatas

3200.   Caluori, Eleonor. *The Cantatas of Luigi Rossi: Analysis and Thematic Index.* Vol. 1. Ann Arbor: UMI Research Press, 1982, 303 pp.

ROSSINI, GIOACCHINO, 1792–1868

General

3201.   Dent, Edward J. *The Rise of Romantic Opera,* 110–124. Cambridge: Cambridge University Press, 1976.
    Examination of Romantic traits and tendencies. Critical remarks on music and observations on style.

3202.   Harding, James. *Rossini.* London: Faber and Faber, 1971, 92 pp.
    Discussion of musical highlights from Rossini's works. For the undergraduate. Not analytic. Musical examples.

3203.   Meyerowitz, Jan. "How Seriously Can We Take Rossini's Operas?" *High Fidelity*, 18 (November 1968): 61–65.
Virtues and shortcomings of the serious operas examined. Reasons for their lack of popularity compared to the success of the comic operas.

3204.   Payne, Nicholas. "Rossini as Dramatist." *Opera*, 20 (March 1969): 186–193.
Mainly critical remarks on the drama. Some observations on Rossini's musical growth and style. Musical examples.

3205.   Sutherland, Edward H. *Rossini and His School.* London: Sampson, Low, Marston, n.d., 114 pp.
Thorough discussion of Rossini's operatic achievement, showing influences on him as well as his influence on other opera composers.

3206.   Toye, Francis. *Rossini: A Study in Tragi-Comedy.* New York: W. W. Norton, 1963, 269 pp.
Mainly a biography, but includes background and critical commentary on the operas. Not analytic.

Barber of Seville

3207.   Ashbrook, William. "Perspectives on an Aria: 'Una Voce Poco Fa.' " *Opera News*, 49 (December 8, 1984): 24 + .
Performance practices in the singing tradition of this aria. Some analytic observations.

3208.   Ashbrook, William. "The Ways of Wit: How Rossini Captures His Comic Characters." *Opera News*, 46 (March 13, 1982): 24.
Identifies some melodic and harmonic features used by Rossini to delineate his comic characters.

Le Comte Ory

3209.   Hammond, Tom. "Rossini and *Le Comte Ory*." *Opera*, 14 (February 1963): 76–79.
Background, plot and place of *Le Comte Ory* in Rossini's stylistic growth.

Elisabetta, Regina d'Inghilterra

3210.   Bellingardi, Luigi. "Rossini's *Queen Elizabeth*, Its Style and Originality." *Opera*, 23 (August 1972): 686–691.
Historical background and stylistic characteristics of the music.

La Gazza Ladra

3211. Hammond, Tom. "Rossini's Real-Life Opera." *Opera*, 17 (January 1966): 6–10.
Critical remarks.

L'Italiana in Algeri

3212. Freeman, John. "Fit for a Sultan." *Opera News*, 38 (December 8, 1973): 36–37.
Critical observations on Rossini's techniques of musical characterization and humor. Musical examples to illustrate points.

Mosè in Egitto

3213. Conati, Marcello. "Between Past and Future: The Dramatic World of Rossini in *Mosè in Egitto* and *Moise et Pharon*." *Nineteenth Century Music*, 4, no. 1 (1980): 32–47.
A comparison of the Neapolitan and Parisian versions of Rossini's opera. Contains some analytic comments. Musical examples.

Otello

3214. Klein, John W. "Verdi's *Otello* and Rossini's." *Music and Letters*, 45, no. 2 (1964): 130–140.
A comparison of plot treatment by Rossini and Verdi of Shakespeare's *Othello*.

Overtures

3215. Gossett, Philip. "The Overtures of Rossini." *Nineteenth Century Music*, 3, no. 1 (1979): 3–31.
The essential nature of Rossini's musical language is embodied in the archetypical Rossini overture. Using this archetype as a model, the authenticity of some of Rossini's overtures is questioned.

Siege of Corinth

3216. Dahlhaus, Carl. *Nineteenth-Century Music.* Translated by J. Bradford Robinson, 61–62. Berkeley: University of California Press, 1989.
Analysis of the *terzetto* in Act I, "Destin Terribile," showing it to be comprised of five sections that balance musical and dramatic elements; comments on form and its underlying psychological basis. Advanced.

3217.   Langford, Jeffrey. "Berlioz, Cassandra, and the French Tradition." *Music and Letters*, 62, nos. 3–4 (1981): 310 + .
Suggests that Berlioz borrowed material from Rossini's Finale to complete his opera, *Les Troyens*.

3218.   Mastroianni, J. F. "The Long and Thorny Saga of *L'Assedio di Corinto*." *Opera News*, 39 (April 19, 1975): 12–16.
Background and place of *Siege* in Rossini's output. Brief compositional history. Musical examples.

Tancredi

3219.   Gossett, Philip. "The 'Candeur Virginale' of *Tancredi*." *Musical Times*, 112 (April 1971): 326–329.
Compositional background and analytic commentary to demonstrate the purity of line, balance, and clarity of shape of this work. Musical examples.

William Tell Overture

3220.   Warburton, A. O. "Set Works for 'O' Level, GCE." *Music Teacher*, 50 (August 1971): 9–10.
Background and analysis for the undergraduate student.

DISSERTATIONS AND THESES

The Barber of Seville

3221.   Little, Ricky Ricardo. "A Comparative Study of . . . the Original Play, and the Two Operas, *Il Barbiere di Siviglia* by Giovanni Paisiello and Gioachino Rossini." D.M.A. Ohio State University, 1985, 103 pp., DA 46-2480A.

ROUSSEL, ALBERT, 1869–1937

General

3222.   Deane, Basil. *Albert Roussel.* London: Barrie and Rockliff, 1961, 188 pp.
Descriptive and critical commentary, with analytic observations. Musical examples.

3223. Demuth, Norman. *Albert Roussel: A Study.* London: United Music Publishers, n.d., 151 pp.

Descriptive, critical, and analytic discussion of Roussel's output. Musical examples.

Symphonies

3224. Simpson, Robert, ed. *The Symphony.* Vol. 2, 104–113. New York: Drake Publishers, 1972.

Descriptive and analytic commentary focusing on the Third and Fourth Symphonies. Musical examples.

Symphony No. 3, Op. 42 in G Minor

3225. Machlis, Joseph. *Introduction to Contemporary Music,* 244–246. New York: W. W. Norton, 1961.

Brief descriptive commentary for the undergraduate student. A few analytic observations. Musical examples.

RUBINSTEIN, ANTON, 1829–1894

Concertos for Piano

3226. Norris, Jeremy. "The Piano Concertos of Anton Rubinstein." *Music Review,* 46 (November 1985): 241–283.

Thorough critical appraisal, pointing out flaws in these compositions and Rubinstein's debt to other composers. Many analytic observations. Musical examples and bibliography.

RUGGLES, CARL, 1876–1971

Angels

3227. Dombek, Stephen. "A Study of Harmonic Interrelationships and Sonority Types in Carl Ruggles' *Angels.*" *In Theory Only,* 4, no. 1 (1980): 29–44.

SAINT-SAËNS, CAMILLE, 1835–1921

General

3228. Hervey, Arthur. Saint-Saëns. 1922. Reprint. New York: Books for Libraries Press, 1969, 159 pp.

Descriptive and analytic guide for the student. Musical examples.

3229. Lyle, Watson. *Camille Saint-Saëns: His Life and Art.* 1923. Reprint. Westport, CT: Greenwood Press, 1970, 210 pp.

    Descriptive commentary and background. Not analytic. Musical examples.

Concertos

3230. Hill, Ralph, ed. *The Concerto,* 206–218. London: Penguin Books, 1952.

    Critical and analytic commentary for the student. Musical examples.

3231. Veinus, Abraham. *The Concerto.* Rev. ed., 258–260. New York: Dover Publications, 1964.

    Brief critical remarks. Not analytic. No musical examples.

Concerto for Piano No. 4, Op. 44 in C Minor

3232. Tovey, Donald Francis. *Essays in Musical Analysis.* Vol. 3, 189–192. London: Oxford University Press, 1936.

    Description, critique, and analysis for the undergraduate student. Musical examples.

Concerto for Violoncello No. 1, Op. 33 in A Minor

3233. Tovey, Donald Francis. *Essays in Musical Analysis.* Vol. 3, 192–194. London: Oxford University Press, 1936.

    Brief critical and analytic remarks for the undergraduate student. Musical examples.

Phaeton

3234. Tovey, Donald Francis. *Essays in Musical Analysis.* Vol. 4, 19–21. London: Oxford University Press, 1969.

    Brief critical and analytic commentary with musical examples. For the undergraduate student.

Samson and Delila

3235. Ashbrook, William. "Saint-Saëns et Dalila—Music for Seduction." *Opera News,* 41 (April 16, 1977): 26–27.

    Background and analytic observations on some of the arias. Musical examples.

3236. McDonald, Katherine. "What Makes *Samson* Run." *Opera News,* 29 (December 26, 1964): 24–25.
Background and musical characterization. Musical examples.

Symphony No. 3, Op. 78 in C Minor

3237. Dahlhaus, Carl. *Nineteenth-Century Music.* Translated by J. Bradford Robinson, 289–291. Berkeley: University of California Press, 1989.
Brief but concentrated analytic remarks on the second movement, dwelling on thematic transformation. Advanced.

DISSERTATIONS AND THESES

General

3238. Scherperel, Loretta Fox. "The Solo Organ Works of Camille Saint-Saëns." D.M.A., University of Rochester, Eastman School of Music, 1978, 179 pp., DA 40-23A.

SALIERI, ANTONIO, 1750–1825

Les Horaces

3239. Rushton, Julian. "Salieri's *Les Horaces*: A Study of an Operatic Failure." *Music Review,* 37, no. 4 (1976): 266–282.
Special focus on the libretto for reasons for failure of this opera. Musical examples.

SAMMARTINI, GIOVANNI BATTISTA, 1701–1775

Symphonies

3240. Churgin, Bathia Dina. "G. B. Sammartini and the Symphony." *Musical Times,* 116 (January 1975): 26–29.
An examination of Sammartini's stylistic periods. Musical examples.

Symphony No. 1 in C Major

3241. Stedman, Preston. *The Symphony,* 26–28. Englewood Cliffs, NJ: Prentice-Hall, 1979.
Brief description of form and thematic organization. Musical examples and diagrams.

DISSERTATIONS AND THESES

Cantatas

3242. Marley, Marie Annette. "The Sacred Cantatas of Giovanni Battista Sammartini." Ph.D., University of Cinncinnati, 1978, 360 pp., DA 39-2610A.

Symphonies

3243. Churgin, Bathia Dina. "The Symphonies of G. B. Sammartini." Ph.D., Harvard University, 1963, 888 pp., DA 35-3790A-91A.

SATIE, ERIK, 1866–1925

General

3244. Fisher, Fred. "Erik Satie's Piano Music—A Centenary Survey." *Clavier*, 5, no. 5 (1966): 14–19.
Background remarks with descriptive overview of Satie's piano works. Complete musical example of a piece included.

3245. Gillman, Alan M. *Erik Satie.* Boston: Twayne Publishers, 1988, 387 pp.
Background with descriptive and analytic commentary on Satie's entire output. Musical examples.

3246. Templier, Pierre-Daniel. *Erik Satie.* Translated by Elena L. French and David S. French. Cambridge, MA: M.I.T. Press, 1969, 127 pp.
Descriptive and critical commentary.

Embryons desséchés No. 2

3247. Fisher, Fred. "A Lesson on Satie's *Desiccated Embryo* No. 2." *Clavier*, 5, no. 5 (1966): 25.
Brief analytic description. Complete musical example.

Parade

3248. Machlis, Joseph. *Introduction to Contemporary Music*, 213–216. New York: W. W. Norton, 1961.
Brief descriptive commentary, with musical examples. For the undergraduate student.

Rose + Croix

3249. Gowers, Patrick. "Satie's *Rose Croix* Music (1891–1895)." *Proceedings of the Royal Musical Association,* 92 (1965–1966): 1–25.
Detailed analysis of harmonic and formal devices used in these piano works.

Sports et divertissements

3250. Porter, David H. "Recurrent Motifs in Erik Satie's *Sports et divertissements.*" *Music Review,* 39, nos. 3–4 (1978): 227 + .
An analytic view of five different motifs in this work, accompanied by a chart. Score of one selection from this work with motifs marked.

DISSERTATIONS AND THESES

General

3251. Koon, Margery A. "Aspects of Harmonic Structure in Piano Works of Erik Satie." D.M.A., University of Wisconsin, 1974, 121, pp., DA 35-3038A.

Parade

3252. Axsom, Richard Hayden. "*Parade*: Cubism As Theater." Ph.D., University of Michigan, 1974, 196 pp., DA 35-7803A.

3253. DeBold, Conrad. "*Parade* and 'Le Spectacle Interieur': The Role of Jean Cocteau in an Avant-Garde Ballet." Ph.D., Emory University, 1982, 253 pp., DA 43-2139A.

SCARLATTI, ALESSANDRO, 1660–1725

General

3254. Dent, Edward J. *Alessandro Scarlatti: His Life and Works.* New York: St. Martin's Press, 1960, 252 pp.
Background, critical, and descriptive commentary. Musical examples.

3255. Poultney, David. "Alessandro Scarlatti and the Transformation of the Oratorio." *Musical Quarterly,* 59, no. 4 (1973): 584–601.
Historical and analytic approach to Scarlatti's role in the development of the oratorio. Musical examples.

3256. Swale, David. "The *Judith* Oratorios of Alessandro Scarlatti." *Miscellanea Musicologica*, 9 (1977): 145–155.

A discussion of the two *Judith* oratorios of Scarlatti. Synopses and comparison of the two works. Comments on style and orchestration.

Messa di Santa Cecilia

3257. Krist, Esther. "Alessandro Scarlatti's *Messa di Santa Cecilia.*" *American Choral Review*, 15, no. 3 (1973): 3–13.

Analytic comments and critical assessment. Style and texture discussed. Musical examples.

Toccatas

3258. Esteban, Julio. "On the Neglected Keyboard Compositions of Alessandro Scarlatti." *American Music Teacher*, 18, no. 3 (1969): 22–23.

A brief look at the keyboard contribution of Alessandro Scarlatti reveals as his innovations. Musical examples.

DISSERTATIONS AND THESES

Cantatas

3259. Freund, Cecilia Kathryn Van de Ramp. "Alessandro Scarlatti's Duet Cantatas with Obbligato instruments." Ph.D., Northwestern University, 1979, 740 pp., DA 40-2969A.

Motets

3260. Owens, Samuel Battie. ". . . Four Lenten Motets of Alessandro Scarlatti." D.M.A., George Peabody College for Teachers, 1974, 295 pp., DA 35-4597A-8A.

SCARLATTI, DOMENICO, 1685–1757

General

3261. Bogianckino, Massimo. *The Harpsichord Music of Domenico Scarlatti.* Translated by John Tickner. Rome: Edizioni de Santis, 1967, 138 pp.

Background and full treatment of the music. Musical examples.

3262.   Boyd, Malcolm. *Domenico Scarlatti—Master of Music.* London: Weidenfeld and Nicolson, 1986, 302 pp.

A "life and works" study that makes use of the large amount of new information made available since Ralph Kirkpatrick's book on Scarlatti (*see* item no. 3266). Analytic comments on the music, description of sources, and biographical chapters. Musical examples.

3263.   Clark, Jane. "Domenico Scarlatti and Spanish Folk Music: A Performer's Re-Appraisal." *Early Music,* 4, no. 1 (1976): 19–21.

Relationship of the sonatas to Spanish folk music.

3264.   DeVenney, David. "The Sacred Choral Music of Domenico Scarlatti." *American Organist,* 19 (October 1985): 98–102.

Background, analyses, and bibliography.

3265.   Hashimoto, Eiji. "Keyboard Works of Domenico Scarlatti." *American Music Teacher,* 35, no. 1 (1985): 14–15.

Brief overview of stylistic traits, harmonic techniques, and unique rhythmic treatments.

3266.   Kirkpatrick, Ralph. *Domenico Scarlatti.* Princeton: Princeton University Press, 1953, 473 pp.

The most definitive work to date. Thorough, in-depth treatment of Scarlatti's harpsichord music. Musical examples.

3267.   Williams, Peter. "*Figurae* in the Keyboard Works of Scarlatti, Handel, and Bach: An Introduction." In *Bach, Handel, Scarlatti: Tercentenary Essays.* Edited by Peter Williams, 327–346. London: Cambridge University Press, 1985.

Defines the term "figurae" (motifs, figures, *Figuren*), gives a brief background, and discusses their use in the keyboard works of the above composers. Musical examples.

Narcisso

3268.   McCredie, Andrew D. "Scarlatti and His Opera *Narcisso.*" *Acta Musicologica,* 33, no. 1 (1961): 19–29.

Observations on the style and orchestration. Musical examples.

Sonatas for Harpsichord

3269.   Hashimoto, Eiji. "Domenico Scarlatti, 1685–1757." *American Music Teacher,* 28, no. 6 (1979): 12–15.

Brief overview of formal characteristics of the sonatas as a whole. Little discussion of individual sonatas.

3270.   Smith, Edwin. "Set Works for 'O' Level, GCE." *Music Teacher*, 53 (June 1974): 20–21.

Brief analytic information provided for sonatas K. 96, K. 113, K. 159, K. 426 (Longo nos. 465, 345, 104, 128).

Sonata for Harpsichord in D Minor, L. 370

3271.   Bryant, Celia M. "Teach Scarlatti's Music." *Clavier*, 4, no. 6 (1965): 24–29.

Stylistic traits and analysis. Complete musical example provided.

Sonata for Harpsichord in D Minor, L. 413

3272.   Dumm, Robert. "A Performer's Analysis: A Scarlatti Sonata." *Clavier*, 14, no. 2 (1975): 27–30.

Analysis oriented toward the performer. Score included.

3273.   Schenker, Heinrich. "Essays from *Das Meisterwerk in der Musik*, Vol. 1 (1925)." *Music Analysis*, 5 (July–October 1986): 153–171.

Densely packed Schenkerian analysis for the advanced theory student. Musical examples.

Sonata for Harpsichord in G Major, L. 486

3274.   Schenker, Heinrich. "Essays from *Das Meisterwerk in der Musik*, Vol. 1 (1925)." *Music Analysis*, 5 (July–October 1986): 171–185.

Densely packed Schenkerian analysis for the advanced theory student. Musical examples.

DISSERTATIONS AND THESES

General

3275.   Borton, Bruce. "The Sacred Choral Works of Domenico Scarlatti." D.M.A., University of Cincinnati, 1983, 377 pp., DA 44-1617A.

SCHMITT, FLORENT, 1870–1958

DISSERTATIONS AND THESES

General

3276.   Maes, Lloyd Rodney. "The Choral Style of Florent Schmitt: An Analysis." D.M.A., Stanford University, 1983, 143 pp., DA 44-1967A.

SCHOECK, OTHMAR, 1886–1957

General

3277. Puffett, Derrick. *The Song Cycles of Othmar Schoeck.* Berne: Haupt, 1982, 482 pp.

Descriptive, stylistic, and analytic summary of Schoeck's song cycles. Musical examples.

SCHOENBERG, ARNOLD, 1874–1951

General

3278. Bailey, Walter B. *Programmatic Elements in the Works of Schoenberg.* Ann Arbor: UMI Research Press, 1983, 188 pp.

Traces extra musical or programmatic concepts behind Schoenberg's music, including many secret programs. For instance, the String Trio Op. 45 is based on Schoenberg's illness and includes specific musical references to his penicillin injections.

3279. Carner, Mosco. "Music in the Mainland of Europe: 1918–1939." In *The New Oxford History of Music.* Vol. 10, *The Modern Age: 1890–1960.* Edited by Martin Cooper, 340–362. London: Oxford University Press, 1974.

Stylistic overview discussing influences on Schoenberg and his progression towards atonality. His use of the tone row explored in works such as the Suite Op. 25, Third String Quartet Op. 30, *Von Heute auf Morgen*, Two Piano Pieces Op. 33, and the Fourth String Quartet. Musical examples.

3280. Carpenter, Patricia. "The Piano Music of Arnold Schoenberg." *Piano Quarterly,* 41 (Fall 1962): 26–31.

Analytic discussion, with musical examples.

3281. Carpenter, Patricia. "The Piano Music of Arnold Schoenberg." *Piano Quarterly,* 42 (Winter 1962–1963): 23–29.

Historic background on Schoenberg, as well as brief explanation of atonality. Descriptive and analytic commentary on Op. 25 and Op. 11. Musical examples. Continues article cited above (*see* item no. 3280).

3282. Ferguson, Donald N. *Image and Structure in Chamber Music,* 304–309. Minneapolis: University of Minnesota Press, 1964.

Brief critical and analytic remarks with musical examples.

3283.   Forte, Allen. "Schoenberg's Creative Evolution: The Path to Atonality." *Musical Quarterly,* 64, no. 2 (1978): 133–176.

Traces emergence of atonal style from its origins. Clues to his atonal style seen in the atonal harmonies found in his early tonal music. During his transition period tonality is momentarily suspended, but still tonal. His mature stage is fully atonal. Advanced analyses of representative works. Musical examples.

3284.   Forte, Allen. "Sets and Nonsets in Schoenberg's Atonal Music." *Perspectives of New Music,* 43, no. 1 (1972): 43–64.

Identifies "sets" of "pitch-classes" in works by Schoenberg. Serves to illustrate Forte's analytic method. Analytic observations on many works. Musical examples.

3285.   Friedheim, Philip. "The Solo Keyboard Works of Arnold Schoenberg." *Music Review,* 23, no. 1 (1962): 39–50.

Analyses of Opp. 11, 19, 23, 25, 33a, and 33b. Musical examples.

3286.   Gelles, George. "Schoenberg's Choruses, Op. 50." *American Choral Review,* 11, no. 1 (1968): 17–22.

Introduction and brief analytic comments. Musical examples.

3287.   Gradenwitz, Peter. "The Religious Works of Arnold Schoenberg." *Music Review,* 21, no. 1 (1960): 19–29.

How Schoenberg incorporated his religious beliefs into his "religious" works. Musical examples.

3288.   Harvey, Jonathan. "Schoenberg: Man or Woman?" *Music and Letters,* 56, nos. 3–4 (1975): 371–385.

Demonstrates Schoenberg's ability to be "both emotionally stirring" in the traditional sense and still be innovative enough to "fire the mind" as well. Thorough historic commentary and analysis of various works in support of the author's thesis. Musical examples.

3289.   Jacobson, Robert. "Eternal Revolutionary." *Opera News,* 39 (November 1974): 38–42.

Good layman's overview of Schoenberg's technique in vocal writing *(Sprechgesang).*

3290.   MacDonald, Malcolm. *Schoenberg.* London: J. M. Dent and Sons, 1976, 289 pp.

Analytic overview of Schoenberg's entire output. Most significant works singled out for closer examination. Musical examples.

3291.   Matthews, Denis, ed. *Keyboard Music,* 323–326. New York: Praeger, 1972.

Brief critical summary. Musical examples.

3292. Newlin, Dika. "Arnold Schoenberg As a Choral Composer." *American Choral Review,* 6, no. 4 (1964): 1+.
Brief descriptive and critical overview.

3293. Newlin, Dika. "The Piano Music of Arnold Schoenberg." *Piano Quarterly,* 27, no. 105 (1979): 38–43.
Descriptive commentary, with remarks on historical background and performance. Schoenberg's Opp. 11, 19, 23, 25, 33a, and 33b discussed. Musical examples. This article is written for the performer.

3294. Payne, Anthony. *Schoenberg.* London: Oxford University Press, 1968, 61 pp.
A short but very technical investigation of Schoenberg's music. Analytic discussions of many of Schoenberg's most important works. For the advanced student. Musical examples.

3295. Reich, Willi. *Schoenberg: A Critical Biography.* Translated by Leo Black. London: Longman, 1968, 268 pp.
Background, plot, and formal scheme are discussed in this overview of Schoenberg's output.

3296. Rosen, Charles. *Arnold Schoenberg.* New York: Viking Press, 1975, 113 pp.
No extended analyses. However, there are some useful remarks on the harmony in *Erwartung* on pp. 42–44 and on symmetrical patterns in two tone rows (Third Quartet, Variations for Orchestra) on pp. 89–91. Musical examples.

3297. Spies, Claudio. "The Organ Supplanted: A Case for Differentiations." *Perspectives of New Music,* 11, no. 2 (1973): 24–55.
Discusses Schoenberg's orchestration of each of these three works: J. S. Bach's Chorale Prelude for Organ on "Schmücke Dich, o liebe Seele" and Chorale Prelude for Organ on "Komm, Gott, Schöpfer, Heiliger Geist" and Johannes Brahms' Quartet for Piano and Strings Op. 25 in G Minor. Includes discussion of textures, doubling, register, and timbres. Each work is treated in turn.

3298. Stuckenschmidt, H. H. *Schoenberg: His Life, World, and Work.* Translated by Humphrey Searle. London: John Calder, 1977, 581 pp.
Generally not analytic. However the chapter titled "The Primal Cell" (pp. 525–534) contains a discussion of motivic cells in Schoenberg's music and his preference for keys based on D. Musical examples.

3299.   Ulrich, Homer. *Chamber Music.* 2d ed., 348–352. New York: Columbia University Press, 1966.
   Brief summation of style, method, and significance of the chamber works. Musical examples.

3300.   Wellesz, Egon. *Arnold Schoenberg.* Translated by W. H. Kerridge. 1925. Reprint. New York: Da Capo Press, 1969, 159 pp.
   Analytic commentary, with musical examples. For the intermediate student.

3301.   Whittall, Arnold. *Music Since the First World War,* 119–142. London: J. M. Dent, 1977.
   A discussion of the twelve-tone method of composition, and an analytic survey of Schoenberg's works composed using this method. Musical examples.

3302.   Whittall, Arnold. *Schoenberg Chamber Music.* Seattle: University of Washington Press, 1972, 64 pp.
   Guide for the undergraduate student. Surveys all the major chamber works, including *Transfigured Night.* Descriptive with analytic observations. Musical examples.

Ballades (Two), Op. 12

3303.   Harbinson, William G. "Rhythmic Structure in Schoenberg's *Jane Grey.*" *Journal of the Arnold Schoenberg Institute,* 7, no. 2 (1983): 222–237.

Book of the Hanging Gardens

3304.   Babbitt, Milton. "Three Essays on Schoenberg." In *Perspectives on Schoenberg and Stravinsky,* Rev. ed. Edited by Benjamin Boretz and E. T. Cone, 51–52. New York: W. W. Norton, 1972.
   Brief analytic commentary.

3305.   Boretz, Benjamin. "Meta-Variations, Part 4: Analytic Fallout (2)." *Perspectives of New Music,* 11, no. 2 (1973): 175–188.
   Highly technical analysis of measures 1–7 of the first piece of this set to "help locate the relevant syntactical basis" of the work. Musical examples.

3306.   Dean, Jerry. "Schoenberg's Vertical-Linear Relationships in 1908." *Perspectives of New Music,* 12, nos. 1–2 (1973–1974): 173–179.
   Advanced analysis of Nos. 2, 6, and 11 of this set.

3307.   Deri, Otto. *The Book of Hanging Gardens,* 292–297. New York: Holt, Rinehart, and Winston, 1968.
Brief analytic remarks. Musical examples.

3308.   Dill, Heinz F. "Schoenberg's *George-Lieder*: The Relationship Between Text and Music in Light of Some Expressionist Tendencies." *Current Musicology,* 17 (1974): 91–95.

3309.   Fisher, George. "Text and Music in Song 8 of *Das Buch der Hängenden Gaerten.*" *In Theory Only,* 6 (February 1982): 3–15.
Advanced analytic discussion of "Wenn ich heut nicht deinen Leib berühre" of this set.

3310.   Larson, Steve. "An Atonal Model of an 'Atonal' Piece: Schoenberg's Op. 15, No. 2." *Perspectives of New Music,* 25, nos. 1–2 (1987): 418–433.
An analysis that identifies a tonal background to this nominally atonal piece. Analysis is based on a series of recorded examples provided with the journal. Uses Schenkerian terminology. For the advanced student. Musical examples.

3311.   Lewin, David. "A Way into Schoenberg's Op. 15, No. 7." *In Theory Only,* 6, no. 1 (1981): 3–24.
A study of rhythm and pitch relationships in "Angst und Hoffen wechselnd mich beklemmen." Advanced.

3312.   Lewin, David. "Toward the Analysis of a Schoenberg Song (Op. 15, No. 11)." *Perspectives of New Music,* 12, nos. 1–2 (1973–1974): 43–86.

3313.   Stroh, Wolfgang M. "Schoenberg's Use of Text: The Text as a Musical Control in the fourteenth *Georgelied,* Op. 15." *Perspectives of New Music,* 6, no. 2 (1968): 35–44.
A discussion of the influence of the text on Schoenberg's compositional method in this song. Musical examples, tables.

Chamber Symphony, Op. 9

3314.   Ballantine, Christopher. *Twentieth Century Symphony,* 117–118. London: Dennis Dobson, 1983.
Describes structure. Table.

3315.   Payne, Anthony. *Schoenberg,* 11–16. London: Oxford University Press, 1969.
Analytic commentary with musical examples.

3316.   Schoenberg, Arnold. *Style and Idea: Selected Writings of Arnold Schoenberg.* Translated by L. Black. Edited by Leo Stein, 84–86. New York: St. Martin's Press, 1975.
Brief analytic remarks on thematic relationships. Musical examples.

3317.   Wellesz, Egon. *Arnold Schoenberg.* Translated by W. H. Kerridge. 1925. Reprint, 104–106. New York: Da Capo Press, 1969.
Analytic remarks. Musical examples.

Concerto for Piano

3318.   Bailey, Walter B. *Programmatic Elements in the Works of Schoenberg*, 136–151. Ann Arbor: UMI Research Press, 1984.
Brief comments on the program underlying this work.

3319.   Hansen, Peter. *An Introduction to Twentieth Century Music.* 2d ed., 198–201. Boston: Allyn and Bacon, 1967.
Brief analysis of this atonal work. Musical examples.

3320.   MacDonald, Malcolm. *Schoenberg*, 125–126. J. M. Dent and Sons, 1976.
Brief descriptive and analytic remarks for the undergraduate student. Musical examples.

3321.   Machlis, Joseph. *The Enjoyment of Music.* 3d ed., 519–521. New York: W. W. Norton, 1970.
Analytic overview for the undergraduate student. Musical examples.

3322.   Newlin, Dika. "Secret Tonality in Schoenberg's Piano Concerto." *Perspectives of New Music*, 13, no. 1 (1974): 137–139.
A way of viewing the Concerto from a tonal standpoint. Musical examples.

Concerto for Violin

3323.   Babbitt, Milton. "Three Essays on Schoenberg." In *Perspectives on Schoenberg and Stravinsky.* Rev. ed. Edited by Benjamin Boretz and E. T. Cone, 47–50. New York: W. W. Norton, 1972.
Analysis, with detailed examination of the twelve-tone set. Chart.

3324.   Keller, Hans. "No Bridge to Nowhere." *Musical Times*, 102 (March 1961): 156–158.

A descriptive and analytical introduction to this work, including a brief comparison of the twelve-tone technique to that of Stravinsky's Movements for Piano and Orchestra.

3325. Leibowitz, René. *Schoenberg and His School.* Translated by Dika Newlin, 120–124. New York: Philosophical Library, 1949.
Detailed analysis for the advanced student. Musical examples.

3326. Perle, George. "Babbitt, Lewin, and Schoenberg: A Critique." *Perspectives of New Music,* 2, no.1 (1963): 120–132.
Advanced discussion of the criticism of Schoenberg's Violin Concerto.

Erwartung

3327. Buchanan, Herbert H. "A Key to Schoenberg's *Erwartung* (Op. 17)." *Journal of the American Musicological Society,* 20, no. 3 (1967): 434–449.
Buchanan challenges the belief that this work is both "athematic" and "atonal." Supports his point by showing that *Erwartung* is actually based on an earlier composition by Schoenberg, "Am Wegrand," a song (Op. 6, No. 6). Shows thematic, tonal, and formal aspects of earlier work. Musical examples.

3328. Hartog, Howard, ed. *European Music in the Twentieth Century.* New York: Praeger, 1957, 88–91.
Brief analysis for the undergraduate student.

3329. Wellesz, Egon. *Arnold Schoenberg.* Translated by W. H. Kerridge. 1925. Reprint, 126–138. New York: Da Capo Press, 1969.
Condensed analysis. Musical examples.

Glückliche Hand

3330. Wellesz, Egon. *Arnold Schoenberg.* Translated by W. H. Kerridge. 1925. Reprint, 126–138. New York: Da Capo Press, 1969.
Condensed analysis. Musical examples.

Herzgewächse

3331. Carlson, David. "Exempli Gratia: Two Instances of 'Bilingual Text-Painting' in Schoenberg's *Herzgewäsche*, Op. 20," *In Theory Only,* 6 (November 1981): 25–28.

461

3332. Clifton, Thomas. "On Listening to *Herzgewächse*." *Perspectives of New Music*, 87, no. 2 (1973): 87–103.

An analytic essay. Including discussion of texture, shape and gesture, motives, and form. Musical examples, tables, diagrams.

3333. Hough, Bonny. "Schoenberg's *Herzgewächse and the 'Blaue Reiter' Almanac.*" *Journal of the Arnold Schoenberg Institute*, 7, no. 2 (1983): 197–221.

Analytic discussion focusing on how the shape and design of the song reflect the meaning and structure of the poem. Musical examples.

3334. Wood, Jeffrey. "Tetrachordal and Inversional Structuring in Arnold Schoenberg's *Herzgewächse*, Op. 20." *In Theory Only*, 7 (August 1983): 23–34.

In diesen Wintertagen, Op. 14

3335. Cinnamon, Howard. "Some Elements of Tonal and Motivic Structure in *In diesen Wintertagen*, Op. 14, No. 2 by A. Schoenberg: A Schoenbergian-Schenkerian Study." *In Theory Only*, 7, nos. 7–8 (1984): 23 + .

Jakobsleiter

3336. Stuckenschmidt, H. H. "Current Chronicle: Austria." *Musical Quarterly*, 47, no. 4 (1961): 534–539.

Background on the genesis of the idea for this composition, its place in Schoenberg's compositional development, and a critical and analytic discussion. *Jakobsleiter* demonstrates Schoenberg's development from free atonality to serial and twelve-tone methods.

3337. Stuckenschmidt, H. H. "Schoenberg's *Jacob's Ladder.*" *Tempo*, 75 (Winter 1965–1966): 21–22.

Description with brief mention of Schoenberg's technical procedures in this work.

Moses und Aron

3338. Babbitt, Milton. "Three Essays on Schoenberg." In *Perspectives on Schoenberg and Stravinsky*. Edited by Benjamin Boretz and E. T. Cone, 53–60. Princeton: Princeton University Press, 1968.

A useful descriptive guide with a detailed analysis of Act I, Scene I, on pages 61–67. For the advanced student.

3339. Freeman, John. "Voice in the Wilderness." *Opera News*, 30 (May 7, 1966): 14–16.
Analytic remarks supported by musical examples.

3340. Lewin, David. "Moses und Aron: Some General Remarks, and Analytic Notes for Act I." In *Perspectives on Schoenberg and Stravinsky*. Rev. ed. Edited by Benjamin Boretz and E. T. Cone, 61–77. New York: W. W. Norton, 1972.
Background and detailed analysis. Musical examples and diagrams.

3341. Lewin, David. "*Moses und Aron*: Some General Remarks and Analytic Notes for Act I, Scene I." *Perspectives of New Music*, 6, no. 1 (1967): 1–17.
Same article as cited above (*see* item no. 3340).

3342. Moss, Lawrence K., and Wayne D. Shirley. "Communications." *Perspectives of New Music*, 7, no. 1 (1968): 149.
Factual correction to the article by David Lewin cited above (*see* item no. 3340).

3343. Redlich, Hans. "Schoenberg's Religious Testament." *Opera*, 16, (June 1965): 401–407.
Discusses Schoenberg's religious convictions, the libretto and the plot, compositional technique (serial method), and general style.

3344. Stuckenschmidt, H. H. "An Introduction to Schoenberg's Opera *Moses and Aaron*." In *Paul A. Pisk: Essays in His Honor*. Edited by John Glowacki, 243–256. Austin: University of Texas Press, 1966.
Background and artistic development leading to *Moses*, followed by an analysis.

3345. Wörner, Karl H. *Schoenberg's "Moses and Aron."* Translated by Paul Hamburger. London: Faber and Faber, 1963, 208 pp.
Exhaustive treatment of the opera from many points of view. Musical analysis, religious elements, philosophic concepts. A bibliography of related materials is included. Musical examples.

3346. White, Pamela C. *Schoenberg and the God-Idea: The Opera "Moses und Aron."* Ann Arbor: UMI Research Press, 1985, 339 pp.
A study of the genesis of *Moses und Aron*, the development of Schoenberg's religious thought, sources for the text, and musical analysis. The analyses include a consideration of row forms, relationships between theme and derivation of motivic and thematic material, characterization and leitmotives. Musical examples, diagrams, and tables.

Orchestral Pieces (Five), Op. 16

3347. Bailey, Walter B. *Programmatic Elements in the Works of Schoenberg*, 131–132. Ann Arbor: UMI Research Press, 1984.
Brief comments on the program underlying this work.

3348. Burkhart, Charles. "Schoenberg's *Farben*: An Analysis of Op. 16, No. 3." *Perspectives of New Music*, 12, nos. 1–2 (1973–1974): 141–172.
Advanced analysis of *Farben* (*Colors*).

3349. Cogan, Robert, and Pozzi Escot. *Sonic Design; The Nature of Sound and Music*, 365–368, 372–374, 412–426. New Jersey: Prentice-Hall, 1976.
Detailed analysis of the timbres used, the spatial aspects, phrase structure, and voice leading of No. 3 of this set (*Colors*).

3350. Craft, Robert. "Schoenberg's Five Pieces for Orchestra." In *Perspectives on Schoenberg and Stravinsky*. Rev. ed. Edited by Benjamin Boretz and E. T. Cone, 8–24. New York: W. W. Norton, 1972.
Detailed analysis. Musical examples.

3351. Lansky, Paul. "Pitch-Class Consciousness." *Perspectives of New Music*, 13, no. 2 (1975): 30–56.
An analytic essay about pitches and pitch classes, taking this piece (*Vergangenes*, No. 2 of this set) as its example. For the very advanced student. Musical examples, diagrams, tables.

3352. Machlis, Joseph. *Introduction to Contemporary Music*, 354–357. New York: W. W. Norton, 1961.
Brief descriptive and analytic commentary with musical examples. For the undergraduate student.

3353. Payne, Anthony. *Schoenberg*, 20–28. London: Oxford University Press, 1969.
Thorough analysis with musical examples.

3354. Solomon, Larry. "The List of Chords, Their Properties and Use in Analysis." *Interface*, 11, no. 2 (1982): 61–107.

3355. Watkins, Glenn. *Soundings: Music in the Twentieth Century*, 32–36. New York: Schirmer Books, 1987.
Brief analytic observations dealing with tone color (*Klangfarbenmelodie*) used as a structural element. Musical examples.

Orchestral Songs (Four), Op. 22

3356. Dunsby, Jonathan. "Schoenberg's 'Premonition,' Op. 22, No. 4, in Retrospect." *Journal of the Arnold Schoenberg Institute,* 1, no. 3 (1977): 137–149.
   A comparison of Schoenberg's views on the aesthetics of song composition in "Vorgefuel," offering an analytic examination of formal processes and motivic development. Text/music relationship examined as well. Musical examples.

3357. Schoenberg, Arnold. "Analysis of the Four Orchestral Songs, Op. 22." *Perspectives of New Music,* 3, no. 2 (1965): 1–21.
   An analytic discussion by the composer. Includes description of motivic and thematic treatment, music/text relationship, and orchestration. Musical examples.

3358. Schoenberg, Arnold. "Analysis of the Four Orchestral Songs, Op. 22" In *Perspectives on Schoenberg and Stravinsky.* Rev. ed. Edited by Benjamin Boretz and E. T. Cone, 25–45. New York: W. W. Norton, 1972.
   Detailed analysis by the composer. Same article as cited above in *Perspectives of New Music* (*see* item no. 3357).

Orchestral Songs (Four), Op. 22, No. 1

3359. Simms, Bryan R. "Line and Harmony in the Sketches of Schoenberg's *Seraphita,* Op. 22, No. 1." *Journal of Music Theory,* 26, no. 2 (1982): 291 + .

Orchestral Songs (Four), Op. 22, No. 2

3360. Falck, Robert. "Schoenberg's (and Rilke's) 'Alle, welche dich suchen.' " *Perspectives of New Music,* 12, nos. 1–2 (1973–1974): 87–98.
   A detailed analysis of the vocal line only of this song. Discusses motives, music/text relationship, and rhythm. Musical examples.

Pelleas and Melisande

3361. Bailey, Walter B. *Programmatic Elements in the Works of Schoenberg,* 52–75. Ann Arbor: UMI Research Press, 1984.
   Discusses the programs, both explicit and implicit, of this work.

3362. Schoenberg, Arnold. *Style and Idea: Selected Writings of Arnold Schoenberg.* Translated by L. Black. Edited by Leo Stein, 82–84. New York: St. Martin's Press, 1975.
   Brief analytic remarks on extended tonality. Musical examples.

3363. Wellesz, Egon. *Arnold Schoenberg.* Translated by W. H. Kerridge. 1925. Reprint, 88–103. New York: Da Capo Press, 1969.
Descriptive, critical, and analytic with musical examples.

Phantasy for Violin with Piano Accompaniment, Op. 47.

3364. Forte, Allen. *Contemporary Tone-Structures,* 110–126. New York: Columbia University Press, 1955.
Thorough analysis dealing with formal structure, tonality, internal relationships, and general stylistic characteristics. Musical examples and analytic sketches.

Piano Pieces, Op. 11

3365. Leichtentritt, Hugo. *Musical Form,* 425–443. Cambridge, MA: Harvard University Press, 1959.
Exhaustive analysis, with musical examples.

3366. Salzman, Eric. *Twentieth Century Music: An Introduction.* 2d ed., 206. Englewood Cliffs, NJ: Prentice-Hall, 1974.
Identifies the use of simple interval structures. Musical examples.

Piano Pieces, Op. 11, No. 1

3367. Christensen, T. "Exempli Gratia: Interval Ordering and Re-ordering in Schoenberg's Op. 11, No. 1." *In Theory Only,* 4 (February–March 1979): 27–29.
Commentary on W. Benjamin's review of Allan Forte's *The Structure of Atonal Music* in *Perspectives of New Music* 13, No. 1 (Fall 1974): 170–190.

3368. Forte, Allen. "The Magical Kaleidoscope: Schoenberg's First Atonal Masterwork, Op. 11, No. 1." *Journal of the Arnold Schoenberg Institute,* 5, no. 2 (1981): 127–168.
A comprehensive analysis of the piece, including form, harmonic vocabulary, and thematic statements of hexachords. Short sections are presented in musical and diagrammatic notation.

3369. Ogdon, Will. "How Tonality Functions in Schoenberg's Op. 11, No. 1." *Journal of the Arnold Schoenberg Institute,* 5, no. 2 (1981): 179–181.
The author argues that tonality functions structurally in this piece, influencing tonal motion, form, thematic articulation, voice

leading, cadences, "suspended" harmony, and rhythm. Musical examples.

3370.   Wittlich, Gary. "Interval Set Structure in Schoenberg's Op. 11, No. 1." *Perspectives of New Music*, 13, no. 1 (1974): 41–55.
Analysis for the very advanced student. Musical examples.

Piano Pieces, Op. 11, No. 3

3371.   Dahlhaus, Carl. *Nineteenth-Century Music.* Translated by J. Bradford Robinson, 387–388. Berkeley: University of California Press, 1989.
Brief but concentrated analytic remarks dwelling on motives, atonal writing techniques and texture. Advanced.

3372.   Lewin, David. "Some Notes on Schoenberg's Op. 11." *In Theory Only*, 3 (April 1977): 3–7.
Analysis of the hexachord types found in No. 3 of this set, with reference to No. 1. Musical examples.

Piano Pieces, Op. 19

3373.   Forte, Allen. "Context and Continuity in an Atonal Work: A Set-Theoretic Approach." *Perspectives of New Music*, 1, no. 2 (1963): 72–82.
An analysis utilizing Forte's set-theory techniques. Only a partial analysis to illustrate his analytic techniques. Musical examples.

3374.   Leichtentritt, Hugo. *Musical Form*, 443–450. Cambridge, MA: Harvard University Press, 1959.
Brief analyses with musical examples.

Piano Pieces, Op. 19, No. 2

3375.   Goode, Daniel. "Reply." *Perspectives of New Music*, 6, no. 1 (1967): 158–160.
Response to the Travis article cited below (*see* item no. 3379). Goode agrees that there is directed motion in this piece, but it does not have a specific harmonic goal.

3376.   Guck, Marion A. " 'A Noir—A Miroir': Past Senses/ Reverses Nests (A Priori?)." *In Theory Only*, 2 (January 1977): 29–34.
A response to Stein's article (*see* item no. 3378) on voice leading and overall structure in this atonal work.

3377. Smith, Charles J. "Comment: Notes on 'Voice-Leading' in Schoenberg." *In Theory Only*, 2 (January 1977): 23–28.
A response to Stein's article (*see* item no 3378) on voice leading and overall structure in this atonal work.

3378. Stein, Deborah. "Schoenberg's Op. 19, No. 2: Voice-Leading and Overall Structure in an Atonal Work." *In Theory Only*, 2 (October 1976): 27–43.

3379. Travis, Roy. "Directed Motion in Schoenberg and Webern." *Perspectives of New Music*, 4, no. 2. (1966): 85–86.
An attempt to apply the concepts of Schenker to this piece to determine its directed motion.

3380. Travis, Roy. "Letters." *In Theory Only*, 2 (January 1977): 3.
A reply to Stein's article (*see* item no. 3378), in which voice leading and overall structure of this atonal work are discussed.

3381. Travis, Roy. "Letters to the Editor." *In Theory Only*, 3 (May 1977): 2–3.
A second response by this author to Stein's article (*see* item no. 3378) on voice leading and overall structure in this atonal work.

Piano Pieces, Op. 19, No. 3

3382. Lubet, Alex. "Vestiges of Tonality in a Work of Arnold Schoenberg." *Indiana Theory Review*, 5, no. 3 (1982): 11–21.

Piano Pieces, Op. 19, No. 6

3383. Cogan, Robert, and Pozzi Escot. *Sonic Design: The Nature of Sound and Music*, 49–59. Englewood Cliffs, NJ: Prentice-Hall, 1976.
A discussion of register and musical space. Musical examples and graphs.

Piano Pieces, Op. 23

3384. Graziano, John. "Serial Procedures in Schoenberg's Op. 23." *Current Musicology*, 13, (1972): 58–63.

3385. Hyde, Martha M. "Musical Form and the Development of Schoenberg's Twelve-Tone Method." *Journal of Music Theory*, 29, no. 1 (1985): 85–143.

An extended analytic discussion of the first four movements of Op. 23. Uses both serial and set theoretic terminology. For the advanced student. Diagrams and musical examples.

Piano Pieces, Op. 23, No. 1

3386.   Barkin, Elaine. "Registral Procedures in Schoenberg's Op. 23, No. 1." *Music Review*, 34, no. 2 (1973): 141–145.
Use of register as a structural device. Musical examples.

3387.   Barkin, Elaine. "A View of Schoenberg's Op. 23, No. 1." *Perspectives of New Music*, 12, nos. 1–2 (1973–1974): 99–127.
An analysis of form and pitch relationships. For the very advanced student. Musical examples, diagrams, tables.

3388.   Graziano, John. "Serial Procedures in Schoenberg's Op. 23." *Current Musicology*, 13 (1972): 58–63.
Analysis with musical examples.

3389.   Perle, George. *Serial Composition and Atonality: An Introduction to the Music of Schoenberg, Berg, and Webern.* 5th ed., rev., 10–15; 45–50. Berkeley: University of California Press, 1981.
Detailed analysis of the motivic structure, pitch content and rhythm of No. 1 of this set. Musical examples.

Piano Pieces, Op. 33a

3390.   Glofcheskie, John. " 'Wrong' Notes in Schoenberg's Op. 33a." *Studies in Music (Canada)*, 1 (1976): 88–104.
A detailed analysis of the piece to demonstrate the deviations from strict serial procedure. Musical examples. Diagrams. For the advanced student.

3391.   Graebner, Eric. "An Analysis of Schoenberg's *Klavierstück*, Op. 33a." *Perspectives of New Music*, 12, nos. 1–2 (1973–1974): 128–140.
Advanced analysis.

3392.   Jack, Adrian. "The Meaning of Serial." *Music and Musicians*, 22 (October 1973): 42–46 + .
For the undergraduate student somewhat familiar with twelve-tone theory. Takes the reader through a step-by-step introduction to serialism. Analytic material from Op. 33a to exemplify serialism. Musical examples.

3393. Perle, George. *Serial Composition and Atonality: An Introduction to the Music of Schoenberg, Berg, and Webern.* 5th ed., rev., 111–116. Berkeley: University of California Press, 1981.
Discussion of the relationship between the pitch structure (twelve-tone) and the formal structure. Musical examples.

3394. Salzman, Eric. *Twentieth Century Music: An Introduction.* 2d ed., 221–222. Englewood Cliffs, NJ: Prentice-Hall, 1974.
Brief analysis identifying row forms, the relationship between their use and the overall structure. Musical examples.

Piano Pieces, Op. 33b

3395. Bailey, Kathryn. "Row Anomalies in Understanding of the Serial Procedure." *Current Musicology*, 22 (1976): 42–60.

Pierrot Lunaire

3396. Austin, William W. *Music in the Twentieth Century*, 195–210. New York: W. W. Norton, 1966.
Analytic commentary for the undergraduate student. Musical examples.

3397. Bailey, Kathryn. "Formal Organization and Structural Imagery in Schoenberg's *Pierrot Lunaire*." *Studies in Musicology (Canada)*, 2 (1977): 93–107.

3398. Biringer, Gene. "Musical Metaphors in Schoenberg's 'Der kranke Mond.'" *In Theory Only*, 8, no. 7 (1985): 3–14.
Advanced analytic commentary on No. 7 of this set, "Der kranke Mond."

3399. Ferguson, Donald N. *Image and Structure in Chamber Music*, 309–320. Minneapolis: University of Minnesota Press, 1964.
Analysis with complete text in English.

3400. Keller, Hans. "Whose Fault Is the Speaking Voice?" *Tempo*, 75 (Winter 1965–1966): 12–17.
The relationship of atonality to the speaking voice part in *Pierrot*.

3401. Klein, Lothar. "Twentieth-Century Analysis: Essays in Miniature." *Music Educators Journal*, 53 (February 1967): 115–116.
Analytic commentary for the undergraduate student.

3402.   Perle, George. *"Pierrot Lunaire."* In *The Commonwealth of Music.* Edited by Gustave Reese and Rose Brandel, 307–312. New York: Free Press, 1965.

> Background and descriptive commentary, with analytic observations.

3403.   Stadlen, Peter. "Schoenberg's Speech Song." *Music and Letters,* 62, no. 1 (1981): 1–11.

> Historic commentary and detailed description of Schoenberg's technical advice in performing speech-song. Modern performance has overcome the problems Schoenberg foresaw in executing this piece.

Quartets for Strings

3404.   Bailey, Walter B. *Programmatic Elements in the Works of Schoenberg.* 130–131. Ann Arbor: UMI Research Press, 1984.
> Brief comments on the programs underlying String Quartets Nos. 1, 2, 3.

3405.   Keller, Hans. "Schoenberg: The Future of Symphonic Thought." *Perspectives of New Music,* 13, no. 1 (1974): 3–20.
> A general analytic essay on the String Quartets.

3406.   Payne, Anthony. "A Note on Schoenberg's String Quartets." *Musical Times,* 113 (March 1972): 266–267.
> A brief discussion of the salient structural features of each of Schoenberg's four Quartets.

Quartet for Strings No. 1, Op. 7 in D Minor

3407.   Frisch, Walter. *Brahms and the Principle of Developing Variation,* 163–169. Berkeley: University of California Press, 1984.
> Analytic discussion using Schoenberg's principle of "developing variation." For the advanced student. Musical examples.

3408.   Frisch, Walter. "Thematic Form and the Genesis of Schoenberg's D-Minor Quartet, Op. 7." *Journal of the American Musicological Society,* 41, no. 2 (1988): 289–314.
> Advanced analysis demonstrating thematic continuity and contrast between sections. Examines sketches for evidence of revised formal strategy to accommodate large design of work. Musical examples and chart of formal plan.

3409.   Leibowitz, René. *Schoenberg and His School.* Translated by Dika Newlin. 1949. Reprint, 61–65. New York: Da Capo Press, 1970.
Brief but solid report on Alban Berg's analytic observations on this work. Musical examples.

3410.   Reich, Willi. *Alban Berg.* Translated by Cornelius Cardew, 189–204. New York: Harcourt, Brace, and World, 1965.
Alban Berg's analysis titled: "Why Is Schoenberg's Music So Difficult to Understand?" Traces inner logic of the writing to prove its "rightness" despite its confusing impact on first hearings. Musical examples.

3411.   Samson, Jim. *Music in Transition: A Study of Tonal Expansion and Atonality, 1900–1920,* 94–98; 101–104. New York: W. W. Norton, 1977.
Concise tonal and formal analysis, with chart of formal plan and tonality.

3412.   Schoenberg, Arnold. *Style and Idea: Selected Writings of Arnold Schoenberg.* Translated by L. Black. Edited by Leo Stein, 61–67. New York: St. Martin's Press, 1975.
Brief analytic remarks. Musical examples.

3413.   Wintle, Christopher. "Schoenberg's Harmony: Theory and Practice." *Journal of the Arnold Schoenberg Institute,* 4, no. 1 (1980): 50–67.
In-depth analytic comments on the harmonic language of this piece. Also contains comparison with and analysis of examples from Schoenberg's textbook, *Harmonielehre.* For the advanced student. Musical examples.

Quartet for Strings No. 2, Op. 10

3414.   Deri, Otto. *Exploring Twentieth-Century Music,* 277–292. New York: Holt, Rinehart, and Winston, 1968.
Thorough analysis with musical examples.

3415.   Samson, Jim. *Music in Transition: A Study of Tonal Expansion and Atonality, 1900–1920,* 104–113. New York: W. W. Norton, 1977.
Analysis focusing on tonality, with observations on formal structure, rhythm, and Schoenberg's debt to Brahms in this work. Musical examples.

3416.   Watkins, Glenn. *Soundings: Music in the Twentieth Century,* 28–32. New York: Schirmer Books, 1987.
Brief description with analytic remarks on tonality. Musical examples and words to solo voice part in English and German included.

Quartet for Strings No. 3, Op. 30

3417. Ulrich, Homer. *Music: A Design for Listening*, 422–424. New York: Harcourt, Brace, 1957.
  Analytic breakdown by measures. Musical examples.

Quartet for Strings No. 4, Op. 37

3418. Babbitt, Milton. "Set Structure As a Compositional Determinant." *Journal of Music Theory*, 5, no. 1 (1961): 72–94.
  Analytic treatment of the initial measures of the third movement. Diagrams, no musical examples. Score necessary.

3419. Beach, David. "Segmental Invariance and the Twelve-Tone System." *Journal of Music Theory*, 20, no. 2 (1976): 157–184.

3420. Haimo, Ethan, and P. Johnson. "Isomorphic Partitioning and Schoenberg's Fourth String Quartet." *Journal of Music Theory*, 27, no. 2 (1984): 47–72.

3421. Lake, William E. "Structural Functions of Segmental Interval-Class 1 Dyads in Schoenberg's Fourth Quartet, First Movement." *In Theory Only*, 8, no. 2 (1984): 21–29.

3422. Mead, Andrew W. "Letter to the Editor: Reply." *In Theory Only*, 8, no. 3 (1984): 4–5.
  A reply to the article cited above (*see* item no. 3421) by William Lake on the "Structural Functions of Segmental Interval-Class 1 Dyads in Schoenberg's Fourth Quartet, First Movement."

3423. Whittall, Arnold. *Music Since the First World War*, 135–139. London: J. M. Dent and Sons, 1977.
  Brief analytic discussion. Musical examples.

Quintet for Winds, Op. 26

3424. Schoenberg, Arnold. *Style and Idea: Selected Writings of Arnold Schoenberg*. Translated by L. Black. Edited by Leo Stein, 227–232. New York: St. Martin's Press, 1975.
  Analytic discussion showing typical examples of the 12-tone technique of composition. Musical examples.

Sonata for Organ (1941)

3425. Bond, Timothy. "Schoenberg's Sonata for Organ." *Musical Times*, 119 (November 1978): 984–985 + .

Brief discussion of incomplete Sonata for Organ (1941). Concentrates on the first movement, which contains the most substantial fragment. Article requires a fundamental knowledge of twelve-tone terminology. Includes some historical background.

3426. Watkins, Glenn. "Schoenberg and the Organ." *Perspectives of New Music,* 4, no. 1 (1965): 119–135.

Discussion for the advanced student. Schoenberg's own analysis, with Watkins' comments. Same article as cited here in Boretz and Cone's *Perspectives on Schoenberg and Stravinsky,* (*see* item no. 3427). Musical examples.

3427. Watkins, Glenn. "Schoenberg and the Organ." In *Perspectives on Schoenberg and Stravinsky.* Rev. ed. Edited by Benjamin Boretz and E. T. Cone, 104–108. New York: W. W. Norton, 1972.

Schoenberg's analysis of this piece, with Watkins' comments. Same article as cited here in *Perspectives of New Music* (*see* item no. 3426). Musical examples.

Songs

3428. Bunting, Richard L. "Arnold Schoenberg's Songs with Piano Accompaniment: A Survey of Style Characterstics." *NATS Bulletin,* 27, no. 1 (1970): 26–31.

Compact analytic discussion, with musical examples and extensive bibliography. Advanced.

3429. Cone, Edward T. "Sound and Syntax: An Introduction to Schoenberg's Harmony." *Perspectives of New Music,* 13, no. 1 (1974): 21–40.

An analytic essay on the sound (i.e., the chordal vocabulary) and syntax (harmonic progression) in Schoenberg's music. Examples are drawn from Schoenberg's songs, Opp. 2, 3, 6, 14, 15, 48. Musical examples.

3430. Lessen, Alan Philip. *Music and Text in the Works of Arnold Schoenberg: The Critical Years, 1908-1922.* Ann Arbor, MI: UMI Research Press, 1979, 247 pp.

Analytic studies of text-based works focusing on relationship of text to music. Advanced. Musical examples.

Songs (Two), Op. 14, No. 1

3431. Dahlhaus, Carl. *Nineteenth-Century Music.* Trnaslated by J. Bradford Robinson, 377–379. Berkeley: University of California Press, 1989.

Brief but concentrated analytic remarks on "Ich darf nicht dank-end," dwelling on tonality, motives, and atonal implications. Advanced.

Suite for Chamber Ensemble, Op. 29

3432. Bailey, Walter B. *Programmatic Elements in the Works of Schoenberg*, 133–136. Ann Arbor: UMI Research Press, 1984.
Brief comments on the program underlying this work.

Suite for Piano, Op. 25

3433. Hyde, Martha M. "Musical Form and the Development of Schoenberg's Twelve-Tone Method." *Journal of Music Theory*, 29, no. 1 (1985): 85–143.
In-depth analysis with background on Opp. 23 and 24. Musical examples, charts, tables.

3434. Salzman, Eric. *Twentieth Century Music: An Introduction.* 2d ed., 219–221. Englewood Cliffs, NJ: Prentice-Hall, 1974.
Identifies the row forms used and illustrates them with examples. Musical examples.

3435. Schoenberg, Arnold. *Style and Idea: Selected Writings of Arnold Schoenberg.* Translated by L. Black. Edited by Leo Stein, 232–235. New York: St. Martin's Press, 1975.
Analytic discussion showing examples of the twelve-tone technique of composition used in this work. Musical examples.

Theme and Variations, Op. 43a.

3436. Roznoy, Richard. "Schoenberg's Theme and Variations, Op. 43a." *Instrumentalist*, 30 (February 1976): 40–42.
Written from the point of view of the conductor, the article includes commentary on the theme and its transformations.

Transfigured Night (Verklärte Nacht)

3437. Bailey, Walter B. *Programmatic Elements in the Works of Schoenberg*, 27–38. Ann Arbor: UMI Research Press, 1984.
Discusses the programs, both explicit and implicit, of this work.

3438. Machlis, Joseph. *Introduction to Contemporary Music*, 353–354. New York: W. W. Norton, 1961.

Brief descriptive commentary, with remarks on the significance of this work. For the undergraduate student. Musical examples.

3439.   Schoenberg, Arnold. *Style and Idea: Selected Writings of Arnold Schoenberg.* Translated by L. Black. Edited by Leo Stein, 80–82. New York: St. Martin's Press, 1975.
Brief analytic remarks on thematic construction and style. Musical examples.

3440.   Swift, Richard. "1/XII/99: Tonal Relations in Schoenberg's *Verklärte Nacht." Nineteenth Century Music,* 1, no. 1 (1977): 3–14.

"Traumleben," Op. 6, No. 1

3441.   Wintle, Christopher. "Schoenberg's Harmony: Theory and Practice." *Journal of the Arnold Schoenberg Institute,* 4, no. 1 (1980): 50–67.
In-depth analytic commentary on the harmonic language of this song. Also contains comparison with and analysis of examples from Schoenberg's textbook, *Harmonielehrer.* For the advanced student. Musical examples.

Trio for Strings, Op. 45

3442.   Bailey, Walter B. *Programmatic Elements in the Works of Schoenberg,* 151–157. Ann Arbor: UMI Research Press, 1984.
Brief comments on the program underlying this work.

3443.   Peel, John M. "On Some Celebrated Measures of the Schoenberg String Trio." *Perspectives of New Music,* 14, no. 2, 15, no. 1 (1976): 260–279.
A detailed analysis of measures 12–17 only. Pitch content and rhythm discussed in great detail. Musical examples, tables, and diagrams.

3444.   Salzman, Eric. *Twentieth Century Music: An Introduction.* 2d ed., 223–224. Englewood Cliffs, NJ: Prentice-Hall, 1974.
Description of the row techniques. Musical examples.

3445.   Whittall, Arnold. "Schoenberg and the 'True Tradition': Theme and Form in the String Trio." *Musical Times,* 115 (September 1974): 739–743.

Variations for Orchestra, Op. 31

3446.   Deri, Otto. *Exploring Twentieth-Century Music,* 301–309. New York: Holt, Rinehart, and Winston, 1968.
Analysis with musical examples.

3447.   Hansen, Peter. *An Introduction to Twentieth Century Music.* 2d ed., 193–197. Boston: Allyn and Bacon, 1967.
Descriptive commentary. For the undergraduate student. Musical examples.

3448.   Machlis, Joseph. *Introduction to Contemporary Music,* 357–363. New York: W. W. Norton, 1961.
Descriptive and analytic commentary, with musical examples. For the undergraduate student.

3449.   Schoenberg, Arnold. *Style and Idea: Selected Writings of Arnold Schoenberg.* Translated by L. Black. Edited by Leo Stein, 235–244. New York: St. Martin's Press, 1975.
Analytic discussion showing typical examples of the 12-tone technique of musical composition. Musical examples.

3450.   Watkins, Glenn. *Soundings: Music in the Twentieth Century,* 331–340. New York: Schirmer Books, 1987.
Brief descriptive and analytic commentary with a chart matrix of the forty-eight versions of the tone series Schoenberg employs in this work. Musical examples.

Variations on a Recitative for Organ, Op. 40

3451.   Folts, Martha. "Arnold Schoenberg's Variations on a Recitative, Op. 40—An Analysis." *Diapason,* 65 (September 1974): 4–9.
Advanced analysis. Musical examples.

3452.   Folts, Martha. "Arnold Schoenberg's Variations on a Recitative, Op. 40—An Analysis." *Diapason,* 66 (March 1975): 7–10+.
Advanced analysis, continued. Musical examples.

3453.   Gibbs, Alan. "Schoenberg's Variations on a Recitative." *Musical Times,* 103 (March 1962): 184–185.
Brief analytic commentary. Musical examples.

3454.   Milner, A. "Schoenberg's Variations for Organ." *Organ Yearbook,* 43, no. 172 (1964): 179–187.
A brief analysis of the complete work.

3455.   Walker, James G. "Schoenberg's Op. 40." *Music (AGO),* 4 (October 1970): 33–35+.
Thorough discussion covering influences on Schoenberg, an analysis, editions, performance, with an extensive bibliography. Musical examples.

3456. Watkins, Glenn. "Schoenberg and the Organ." *Perspectives of New Music,* 4, no. 1 (1965): 119–135.

Schoenberg's own analysis. Includes discussion of form, motivic/thematic treatment, and performance problems. Same article as below. Musical examples.

3457. Watkins, Glenn. "Schoenberg and the Organ." In *Perspectives on Schoenberg and Stravinsky.* Rev. ed. Edited by Benjamin Boretz and E. T. Cone, 98–104. New York: W. W. Norton, 1972. *See* item no. 3456 above.

Der Velorene Haufen

3458. Martin, Henry. "A Structural Model for Schoenberg's *Der verlorene Haufen,* Op. 12, No. 2." *In Theory Only,* 3 (June 1977): 4–22.

The first three measures analyzed reveal the overall structure of the piece.

Violin Fantasy

3459. Lewin, David. "A Study of Hexachord Levels in Schoenberg's Violin Fantasy." *Perspectives of New Music,* 6, no. 1 (1967): 18–32.

Analysis focusing on one element of structure in this piece. Same article as cited below (*see* item no. 3460). Musical examples and diagrams.

3460. Lewin, David. "A Study of Hexachord Levels in Schoenberg's Violin Fantasy." In *Perspectives on Schoenberg and Stravinsky.* Rev. ed. Edited by Benjamin Boretz and E. T. Cone, 78–92. New York: W. W. Norton, 1972.

Analysis focusing on one element of structure in the piece. Musical examples and diagrams.

Von Heute auf Morgen

3461. Whittal, Arnold. *Music Since the First World War,* 128–130. London: J. M. Dent and Sons, 1977.

Brief analytic discussion. Musical example.

DISSERTATIONS AND THESES

General

3462. Ballan, Harry Reuben. "Schoenberg's Expansion of Tonality, 1899–1908." Ph.D., Yale University, 1986, 230 pp., DA 47-2786A.

3463.   Crawford, John Charlton. "The Relationship of Text and Music in the Vocal Works of Schoenberg, 1908–1924." Ph.D., Harvard University, 1963, 376 pp., DA 29-4035A-6A.

3464.   Lohman, Peter Nathan. "Schoenberg's Atonal Procedures: A Non-Serial Analytic Approach to the Instrumental Works, 1908–1921." Ph.D., Ohio State University, 1981, 336 pp., DA 42-446A.

Book of the Hanging Gardens

3465.   Dean, Jerry Mac. "Schoenberg's *George* Songs, Op. 15." Ph.D., University of Michigan, 1971, 209 pp., DA 32-6474A-5A.

3466.   Silverton, Jann Jacobs. "A Grundgestalt Analysis of Op. 15, *Das Buch der Hängenden Gärten*, by Arnold Schoenberg on Poems by Stefan George." Ph.D., Northwestern University, 1986, 233 pp., DA 47-707A.

Concerto for Violin

3467.   Laporta, Mark Stevens. "Patterns of Invariance and Repetition As Structural Functions in Schoenberg's Op. 36." D.M.A., Cornell University, 1983, 188 pp., DA 44-1620A.

3468.   Watrous, John. "Harmonic and Transpositional Logic in the First Movement of Schoenberg's Violin Concerto." Ph.D., Brandeis University, 1986, 157 pp., DA 47-1528A.

Herzgewächse, Op. 20

3469.   Hough, Bonny Ellen. "Schoenberg's *Herzgewächse*, Op. 20: An Integrated Approach to Atonality Through Complementary Analyses." Ph.D., Washington University, 1982, 303 pp., DA 43-1341A.

Jakobsleiter

3470.   Christensen, Jean Marie. "Arnold Schoenberg's Oratorio *Die Jakobsleiter*." Ph.D., University of California at Los Angeles, 1979, 797 pp., DA 40-3612A.

Moses und Aron

3471.   Cherlin, Michael. "The Formal and Dramatic Organization of Schoenberg's *Moses und Aron*." Ph.D., Yale University, 1983, 413 pp., DA 47-1917A.

3472. Fleisher, Robert Jay. "Schoenberg, Dualism, and *Moses und Aron.*" D.M.A., University of Illinois at Urbana, 1980, 151 pp., DA 41-4534A.

3473. White, Pamela Cynthia. "Idea and Representation: Source-Critical and Analytical Studies of Music, Text, and Religious Thought in Schoenberg's *Moses und Aron.*" Ph.D., Harvard University, 1983, 518 pp., DA 44-3538A.

Moses und Aron: Act II, Scene V

3474. Anderson, Allen. "Recitative and Act II, Scene V, of Arnold Schoenberg's *Moses und Aron.*" Ph.D., Brandeis University, 1984, 156 pp., DA 45-1565A.

Piano Pieces, Op. 11

3475. Reible, John Joseph. "Tristan-Romanticism and the Expressionism of the Three Piano Pieces, Op. 11 of Arnold Schoenberg." Ph.D., Washington University, 1980, 381 pp., DA 41-846A.

Piano Pieces, Op. 19

3476. Boge, Claire Louise. "The Dyad As Voice in Schoenberg's Op. 19: Pitch and Interval Prolongations, Voice-Leading, and Relational Systems." Ph.D., University of Michigan, 1985, 354 pp., DA 46-3184A.

Piano Piece, Op. 23, No. 1

3477. Barkin, Elaine Radoff. "Pitch-Time Structure in Arnold Schoenberg's Op. 23, No. 1: A Contribution Toward a Theory of Non-Tonal Music." Ph.D., Brandeis University, 1971, 130 pp., DA 32-4041A.

Pierrot Lunaire

3478. Asarnow, Elliot Bruce. "Arnold Schoenberg's 'Heimweh' from *Pierrot Lunaire*: Registral Partitioning of the Harmonic Structure." Ph.D., Brandeis University, 1979, 109 pp., DA 7042A.

Quartet for Strings, No. 4

3479. Cubbage, John Rex. "Directed Pitch Motion and Coherence in the First Movement of Arnold Schoenberg's Fourth String Quartet." Ph.D., Washington University, 1979, 303 pp., DA 40-3613A.

3480. Phipps, Graham Howard. "Schoenberg's 'Grundgestalt' Principle: A New Approach with Particular Application to the Variations for Orchestra Op. 31." Ph.D., University of Cincinnati, 1976, 608 pp., DA 37-6133A.

Songs (Four), Op. 2

3481. Mizell, John. "Trends, Analysis, and Style of Specific Compositions by Twentieth Century Composers." D.M.A., University of Missouri, 1972, 83 pp., DA 33-2414A.

Suite for Piano, Op. 25

3482. Blasch, Robert Edward. "A Structural and Interpretive Analysis of the Suite for Piano, Op. 25." Ed.D., Columbia University, 1971, 169 pp., DA 32–1180A.

Theme and Variations for Band, Op. 43a.

3483. Garcia, David Manuel. "Tonality in Schoenberg's Theme and Variations for Band, Op. 43a, and Symphony for Band." D.M.A., Ohio State University, 1986, 113 pp., DA 47-2362A.

Theme and Variations for Band, Opp. 43a and 43b

3484. Plate, Stephen W. "A Study and Comparison . . . with Particular Attention to Instrumentation, Orchestration, and Variation Technique." D.M.A., University of Cincinnati, 1986, 200 pp., DA 47-2793A.

Trio for Strings, Op. 45

3485. Jordan, Roland Carroll, Jr. "Schoenberg's String Trio, Op. 45: An Analytic Study." Ph.D., Washington University, 1973, 279 pp., DA 34-7808A.

Variations for Orchestra, Op. 31

3486. Hicken, Kenneth Lambert. "Structure and Prolongations: Tonal and Serial Organization in the Introduction of Schoenberg's Variations for Orchestra." Ph.D., Brigham Young University, 1970, 192 pp., DA 31-5446A.

3487. Phipps, Graham Howard. "Schoenberg's *Grundgestalt* Principle: A New Approach with Particular Application to the Variations for Orchestra, Op. 31." Ph.D., University of Cincinnati, 1976, 608 pp., DA 37-6133A.

Variations on a Recitative for Organ, Op. 40

3488. Ore, Charles William. "Numbers and Number Correspondences in Op. 40 by Arnold Schoenberg: Pythagoras and the Quadrivium Revisited." D.M.A., University of Nebraska at Lincoln, 1986, 263 pp., DA 47-1109A.

SCHUBERT, FRANZ, 1797–1828

General

3489. Abraham, Gerald, ed. *The Music of Schubert.* New York: W. W. Norton, 1947. 342 pp.
  Critical, descriptive, and analytic discussions of Schubert's output. Musical examples.

3490. Bell, A. Craig. *The Songs of Schubert.* Lowestoft: Alston, 1964, 163 pp.
  Analytic commentaries on selected songs by Schubert. Includes a chapter on "The Song before Schubert." Appendixes include a complete chronological and alphabetical list of poets. Musical examples.

3491. Bie, Oskar. *Schubert: The Man.* 123–153. New York: Dodd, Mead, 1929.
  Mainly descriptive commentary. Musical examples.

3492. Brauner, Charles S. "Irony in the Heine *Lieder* of Schubert and Schumann." *Musical Quarterly*, 67, no. 2 (1981): 261–281.
  Discusses ways in which music can express, relate to, or deal with irony in song texts. Discusses both covert and overt irony in selected Heine settings of Schubert and Schumann. Musical examples.

3493. Brown, Maurice J. *Essays on Schubert.* New York: St. Martin's Press, 1966, 315 pp.
  Background, analytic commentary on Schubert's Ninth Symphony, part-songs for male voices, Fantasia in F Minor Op. 103, and *Lazarus, or the Feast of Resurrection.* Musical examples.

3494.   Brown, Maurice J. *Schubert: A Critical Biography.* London: Macmillan, 1958, 414 pp.
Overview of Schubert's entire output, concentrating on style. Occasional analytic comments. Musical examples.

3495.   Brown, Maurice J. "Schubert's Italian Overtures." *Music Review*, 26, no. 4 (1965): 303–307.
Historical background. No discussion of the music itself.

3496.   Brown, Maurice J. *Schubert's Variations.* London: Macmillan, 1954, 104 pp.
Critical remarks, focusing on Schubert's use of variations. "Impromptu" in B-Flat, Op. 142, No. 3, and Variations on a Theme by Anselm Hüttenbrenner and others are chosen for discussion. Musical examples.

3497.   Capell, Richard. *Schubert's Songs.* 2d ed., rev., New York: Basic Books, 1957, 292 pp.
Mainly descriptive and critical commentary on all the songs with some analytic observations. Musical examples.

3498.   Dale, Kathleen. *Nineteenth-Century Piano Music: A Handbook for Pianists.* London: Oxford University Press, 1954, 320 pp.
Highlights stylistic traits and unique contribution to the literature of the piano. Form, harmony, and other musical aspects discussed in relation to style.

3499.   Dent, Edward J. *The Rise of Romantic Opera,* 135–144. Cambridge: Cambridge University Press, 1976.
Examination of romantic traits and tendencies. Critical remarks on music and observations on style.

3500.   Duncan, Edmondstoune. *Schubert.* London: J. M. Dent and Sons, 1934, 244 pp.
Mainly critical and descriptive commentary with occasional analytic observations intended for the undergraduate student or musical amateur. Musical examples.

3501.   Duschak, Alice G. "The Influence of the Songs of Franz Schubert." *NATS Bulletin,* 29, no. 2 (1972): 30–31.
Survey of Schubert's influence on Schumann, Wagner and others. Certain stylistic and musical techniques examined. Musical examples.

3502.   Einstein, Alfred. *Schubert: A Musical Portrait.* New York: Oxford University Press, 1951, 343 pp.
Comments on style, forms, and orchestration. Musical examples.

3503.   Ferguson, Donald N. *Image and Structure in Chamber Music*, 134–155. Minneapolis: University of Minnesota Press, 1964.
Overview of the chamber music with brief analyses. Musical examples.

3504.   Ferguson, Donald N. *Piano Music of Six Great Composers*, 125–145. New York: Books for Libraries Press, 1947.
Descriptive and critical commentary, with some analytic insights. Musical examples.

3505.   Fischer-Dieskau, Dietrich. *Schubert: A Biographical Study of His Songs.* Translated and edited by Kenneth S. Whitton. London: Cassell, 1976, 331 pp.
Contains many analytical insights, but no isolated musical analyses.

3506.   Gal, Hans. *Franz Schubert and the Essence of Melody*, London: Victor Gollancz, 1974, 205 pp.
Descriptive, critical, and analytic. A thorough discussion of Schubert's musical process. Musical examples.

3507.   Gray, Walter. "The Classical Nature of Schubert's *Lieder.*" *Musical Quarterly*, 57, no. 1 (1971): 62–72.
Emphasis placed on Classical form in the songs, rather than the customary emphasis on Romantic traits.

3508.   Heider, Anne Harrington. "A Survey of Schubert's Part-Songs for Mixed Voices." *American Choral Review*, 22, no. 3 (1980): 3–17.
Background, stylistic traits, analytic observations. Musical examples.

3509.   Hoorickx, Reinhard Van. "Fugue and Counterpoint in Schubert's Piano Music." *Piano Quarterly*, 27, no. 105 (1979): 48–52.
Cites examples of counterpoint and fugue in Schubert's piano music in an attempt to prove Schubert's ability to write in this style. Includes historic and descriptive commentary as well as analytic remarks. Musical examples.

3510.   Hutchings, Arthur. *Schubert.* London: J. M. Dent and Sons, 1973, 233 pp.
Descriptive and critical, with analytic observations for the undergraduate student. Musical examples.

3511.   Kinsey, Barbara. "Schubert and the Poems of Ossian." *Music Review*, 34, no. 1 (1973): 22–29.
Descriptive and analytic commentary. Musical examples.

3512.   Matthews, Denis, ed. *Keyboard Music,* 185–198. New York: Praeger, 1972.

Background, critical evaluation, historical perspective, stylistic traits, and mention of specific works. Musical examples.

3513.   McKay, Elizabeth N. "Schubert's Music for the Theatre." *Proceedings of the Royal Musical Association,* 93 (1966–1967): 51–56.

A discussion of Schubert's operas—in particular, *Die Freunde von Salamanka, Die Zauberharfe, Alfonso und Estrella,* and *Fierrabras.* Discusses motivic techniques (leitmotives), style, and other unifying factors.

3514.   McNamee, Ann. "The Role of the Piano Introduction in Schubert's *Lieder.*" *Music Analysis,* 4, nos. 1–2 (1985): 95–107.

Schenkerian analyses of a selection of piano introductions to Schubert songs.

3515.   Newton, George. "The Songs of Franz Schubert." *NATS Bulletin,* 22, no. 1 (1965): 4–7.

Background and descriptive commentary, with special mention of the appoggiaturas in Schubert's songs. Musical examples.

3516.   Plantinga, Leon. *Romantic Music,* 104–126. New York: W. W. Norton, 1984.

Analytic comments on the piano music and the Lieder.

3517.   Porter, Ernest G. *Schubert's Song Technique.* London: Dennis Dobson, 1961, 152 pp.

A small book about Schubert's songs. Chapter headings include: Phrasing and Form; Key; Harmony; Modulation. There are analytical comments about individual songs—illustrating points made under these headings—but no complete analyses. Musical examples.

3518.   Porter, Ernest G. "Schubert's Song Workshop." *Music and Letters,* 39 (April 1958): 143–147.

Schubert's use of forms in his early songs.

3519.   Robertson, Alec, ed. *Chamber Music,* 140–190. Baltimore: Penguin Books, 1957.

Thorough critical and analytic overview, with musical examples.

3520.   Stein, Jack M. "Schubert's Heine Songs." *Journal of Aesthetics and Art Criticism,* 24, no. 4 (1966): 559–566.

Advanced discussion of the relationship of text and music. Musical examples.

3521.   Ulrich, Homer. *Chamber Music.* 2d ed., 263–298. New York: Columbia University Press, 1966.
>   Descriptive and analytic commentary for the undergraduate student. Musical examples.

3522.   Walker, Alan. "Liszt and the Schubert Song Transcriptions." *Musical Quarterly,* 67, no. 1 (1981): 50–63.
>   A description of Liszt's method and purpose in writing these transcriptions. Musical examples.

3523.   Westrup, Jack. *Schubert Chamber Music.* Seattle: University of Washington Press, 1969, 63 pp.
>   A "BBC Music Guide." Surveys all of Schubert's chamber music, describing style, form, tonalities, and other significant features of important works. Many analytic comments on individual pieces. Musical examples.

3524.   Whaples, Miriam K. "On Structural Integration in Schubert's Instrumental Works." *Acta Musicologica,* 40, no. 2 (1968): 186–195.
>   Advanced discussion of unifying elements. Musical examples.

3525.   Whaples, Miriam K. "Style in Schubert's Piano Music From 1817–1818." *Music Review,* 35, nos. 3–4 (1974): 260–280.
>   A stylistic analysis of the eight piano sonatas written during this period, with referral to the *Grazer* Fantasy, D. 605a, and its role in Schubert's stylistic development. Musical examples.

3526.   Wolff, Konrad. *Masters of the Keyboard: Individual Style Elements in the Piano Music of Bach, Haydn, Mozart, Beethoven, and Schubert,* 160–183. Bloomington: Indiana University Press, 1983.
>   A discussion of keyboard style of interest to performers. However, there are occasional analytic comments for undergraduate students. Musical examples.

Alfonso und Estrella

3527.   Brown, Maurice J. "Schubert's Two Major Operas: A Consideration of Actual Stage Production." *Music Review,* 20, no. 2 (1959): 104–118.
>   Detailed plot summary with musical examples. Critical commentary and reasons for lack of popularity explored.

Du bist die Ruh

3528.   Cogan, Robert, and Pozzi Escot. *Sonic Design: The Nature of Sound and Music,* 163–171. Englewood Cliffs, NJ: Prentice-Hall, 1976.
>   Discusses harmony and voice leading.

Duets for Piano

3529. Weekley, Dallas, and Nancy Arganbright. "Schubert: Master of the Piano Duet." *Piano Quarterly*, 27, no. 104 (1978–1979): 41–48.
Overview of the duets composed during three different development stages in Schubert's output. Historic, descriptive, and analytic commentary for the undergraduate and piano student. Musical examples.

Erlkönig

3530. Chittum, Donald. "Music Theory and Interpretation." *American Music Teacher*, 17, no. 4 (1968): 31 + .
Brief analysis intended for the undergraduate student.

3531. Cone, Edward T. *The Composer's Voice*, 1–29. Berkeley: University of California Press, 1974.
A discussion of the priority of importance: the poem or the music. Author concludes that what we hear in a song is the composer's voice interpreting the poem. Therefore, the music takes precedence but is affected by the poetry.

3532. Dickinson, A. E. F. "Fine Points in *The Erl King*." *Monthly Musical Record*, 88 (July–August 1958): 141–143.
Chiefly a comparison of the four versions. Contains some analytic observations.

3533. Siddons, James. "The Words and Music of the *Erlking*." *Musical Analysis*, 1, no. 2 (1972): 27–38.
An analytic comparison of settings of *Erlkönig* by Carl Loewe (1796–1869) and Schubert. Includes comments on settings by other composers and background information on the poem. Musical examples and tables.

Fantasia for Piano Four-Hands in F Minor, D. 940

3534. Smith, Edwin. "Schubert's F Minor Fantasia." *Music Teacher*, 59 (May 1980): 18–20.
Background, critical, descriptive, and analytic commentary. Musical examples.

Fantasy in C Major, D. 760

3535. Brody, Elaine. "Mirror of His Soul." *Piano Quarterly*, 27, no. 104 (1978–1979): 23–31.

Historic background, including derivation of melody. Analytic remarks as well as hints on performance of this work. Musical examples.

Fierrabras

3536. Brown, Maurice J. "Schubert's Two Major Operas: A Consideration of Actual Stage Production." *Music Review*, 20, no. 2 (1959): 104–118.
Detailed plot summary, with musical examples. Critical commentary and reasons for lack of popularity explored.

Ganymed, D. 544

3537. Frisch, Walter, ed. *Schubert: Critical and Analytic Studies*, 224–233. Lincoln: University of Nebraska Press, 1986.
Analysis focusing on harmonic devices relating music to text. Musical examples.

Gretchen am Spinnrade

3538. Pilgrim, Jack. "Set Works for 'O' Level, GCE." *Music Teacher*, 54 (August 1975): 12.
Brief background and analytic commentary.

Heidenröslein

3539. Kresky, Jeffrey. *Tonal Music: Twelve Analytic Studies*, 68–79. Bloomington: Indiana University Press, 1977.
In-depth analysis dealing with small formal divisions, tonality, and melody. Advanced. Musical examples and diagrams.

Impromptus for Piano, D. 899

3540. Dyke, Valerie. "Schubert Impromptus." *Music Teacher*, 58 (August 1979): 16–18.
Brief comments on formal structure for the performer of Op. 142, Nos. 2 and 3.

Impromptu for Piano, Op. 90, No. 2 in E-Flat Major, D. 899

3541. Schenkman, W. "A Lesson on a Schubert Impromptu." *Clavier*, 17, no. 7 (1978): 25–33.
Analytic and interpretive comments for the performer. Score included.

Ländler, D. 790

3542. Frisch, Walter, ed. *Schubert: Critical and Analytic Studies,* 32–47. Lincoln: University of Nebraska Press, 1986.
Analyses of these twelve German dances, demonstrating their unity as a group.

Largo for Harpsichord, D. 993

3543. Demus, Joerg. "Two Fantasies." *Piano Quarterly,* 27, no. 104 (1978–1979): 9–17.
Analysis of the relationship between Mozart's Fantasy, K. 475, and Schubert's Largo for Harpsichord, D. 993. Includes reproduction of the Schubert work in full. Musical examples.

Mass in E-Flat Major

3544. Dahlhaus, Carl. *Nineteenth-Century Music.* Translated by J. Bradford Robinson, 186–187. Berkeley: University of California Press, 1989.
Brief but concentrated examination of form, motivic variation, and symphonic conception. Advanced.

Meeres Stille, D. 216.

3545. Frisch, Walter, ed. *Schubert: Critical and Analytic Studies,* 210–215. Lincoln: University of Nebraska Press, 1986.
Analysis focusing on tonality and relationship of the music to the poem. Musical examples.

Moments Musicaux, Op. 94

3546. Reed, John. *Schubert: The Final Years,* 160–162. London: Faber and Faber, 1972.
Brief analytic remarks on the unity of all six pieces in this set. Musical examples.

3547. Warburton, A. O. "Set Works for 'O' Level, GCE." *Music Teacher,* 51 (August 1972): 16–18.
Brief analyses for the undergraduate student.

Moments Musicaux, Op. 94, No. 1 in C Major, D. 780

3548. Hughes, Matt, Lawrence Ross, and Carl Schachter. "Analysis Symposium—*Moments Musical,* Op. 94, Franz Schubert." *Journal of Music Theory,* 12, no. 2 (1968): 184–239.
Advanced analysis. Musical examples.

3549. Rothgeb, John. "Another View on Schubert's *Moment Musical,* Op. 94, No. 1." *Journal of Music Theory,* 13, no. 1 (1969): 128–139.
Advanced analysis. Musical examples.

Moments Musicaux, Op. 94, No. 2 in A-Flat Major, D. 780

3550. McCreless, Patrick. "Schubert's *Moment Musical* No. 2: The Interaction of Rhythmic and Tonal Structures." *In Theory Only,* 3 (July 1977): 3–11.

Moments Musicaux, Op. 94, No. 3 in F Minor, D. 780

3551. Feil, Arnold. "Two Analyses." In *Schubert: Critical and Analytic Studies,* Edited by Walter Frisch, 116–125. Lincoln: University of Nebraska Press, 1986.
Analysis examining meter and motive. Musical examples.

Moments Musicaux, Op. 94, No. 6 in A-Flat Major, D. 780

3552. Cone, Edward T. "Schubert's Promissory Note: An Exercise in Musical Hermeneutics." *Nineteenth Century Music,* 5, no. 3 (1982): 233–241.
A detailed analysis followed by an interpretation of the piece's expressive meaning. Hypothesizes that the tonal structure is related to Schubert's final illness and death. For the advanced student.

3553. Wittlich, Gary. "Compositional Premises in Schubert's Op. 94, No. 6." *In Theory Only,* 5 (September 1981): 31–43.
A detailed analysis—Schenkerian in nature. Includes Schenkerian graphs and a table. Discussion of harmonic and rhythmic structure. For the advanced student.

Nähe des Geliebten D. 162

3554. Frisch, Walter. "Schubert's *Nähe des Geliebten*: Transformation of the Volkston." In *Schubert: Critical and Analytic Studies.* Edited by Walter Frisch, 175–199. Lincoln: University of Nebraska Press, 1986.
A close examination of the interplay of content of the poem and form of the music. Musical examples.

Quartets for Strings

3555.   Coolidge, Richard A. "Form in the String Quartets of Franz Schubert." *Music Review,* 32, no. 4 (1971): 309–325.
Thorough analytic overview of form in the string quartets.

Quartet Movement for Strings in C Minor, D. 703

3556.   Bruce, Robert. "The Lyrical Element in Schubert's Instrumental Forms." *Music Review,* 30, no. 2 (1969): 131–137.
A comparison of this work to Beethoven's "Razumovsky" Quartet, Op. 59, No. 3, to show Schubert's lyrical emphasis in contrast to Beethoven's dramatic character.

Quartet for Strings in A Minor, D. 804

3557.   Tischler, Hans. *The Perceptive Music Listener,* 296–300. Englewood Cliffs, NJ: Prentice-Hall, 1955.
Analysis with musical examples.

Quartet for Strings in D Minor, D. 810 ("Death and the Maiden")

3558.   Brown, Maurice J. "Schubert's D Minor Quartet: A Footnote." *Musical Times,* 111 (October 1970): 985 + .
A study of the manuscript. Musical examples.

3559.   Truscott, Harold. "Schubert's D Minor String Quartet." *Music Review,* 19 (February 1958): 27–36.
Formal and structural overview.

Quartet for Strings in G Major, D. 887

3560.   Frisch, Walter, ed. *Schubert: Critical and Analytic Studies,* 1–12. Lincoln: University of Nebraska Press, 1986.
An examination of sonata form in the first movement. Shows how it deviates from Beethoven's model of sonata form.

3561.   Gillett, Judy. "The Problem of Schubert's G Major String Quartet (D. 887)." *Music Review,* 35, nos. 3–4 (1974): 281–292.
The composition is analyzed as a whole—including the "problem" last movement. Views of some critics considered. Musical examples.

3562. Truscott, Harold. "Schubert's String Quartet in G Major." *Music Review*, 20, (May 1959): 119–145.
> Overview of the quartet with an in-depth analysis and discussion of the work's place in Schubert's output. Musical examples.

Quintet for Strings in A Minor, D. 438

3563. Kerman, Joseph. *Listen.* 2d ed., 207–209. New York: Worth Publishers, 1976.
> Background and analysis, with musical examples. For the undergraduate student.

Quintet for Strings in C Major, D. 956

3564. Allen, Judith S. "Schubert's C Major String Quintet, Op. 163, No. 1: The Evolving Dominant." *In Theory Only*, 6 (July 1982): 3–16.
> A study of the harmonic structure of this movement. Musical examples and harmonic reductions. For the advanced student.

Rosamunde Overture

3565. Smith, Edwin. "Set Works for 'O' Level, GCE." *Music Teacher*, 49 (October 1974): 15–16.
> An outline of the overture by section and phrase structure.

Die Schöne Müllerin

3566. Dahlhaus, Carl. *Nineteenth-Century Music.* Translated by J. Bradford Robinson, 102. Berkeley: University of California Press, 1989.
> Brief but concentrated analysis of the third song in this cycle, "Halt." Examines sources of coherence, tonality, and mood. Advanced.

3567. Frisch, Walter, ed. *Schubert: Critical and Analytic Studies,* 215–218. Lincoln: University of Nebraska Press, 1986.
> Analysis focusing on tonality and texture in the twelfth song of this set ("Pause"). Musical examples.

3568. Lerdahl, Fred, and Ray Jackendorff. *A Generative Theory of Tonal Music,* 264–268. Cambridge, MA: M.I.T. Press, 1983.
> Time-span and prolongational reductions, with remarks on rhythmic and motivic structure of "Morgengruss" (No. 8) of this set. Diagrams and musical examples.

3569. Pazur, Robert. "An Interpretation of the Pitch-Structure of *Die schöne Müllerin.*" *In Theory Only*, 1 (September 1975): 9–13.
Advanced analytic discussion. Musical examples.

3570. Warburton, A. O. "Set Works for 'O' Level, GCE." *Music Teacher*, 47 (December 1968): 9–10.
Brief analyses of songs 7–12 of this cycle. For the undergraduate student.

3571. Youens, Susan. "Brief Reflections on the Two Mueller Cycles of Franz Schubert: *Die schöne Müllerin*, D. 795, and *Winterreise.*" *NATS Journal*, 43, no. 3 (1987): 16–18.
Contains brief analytic comments.

Schwanengesang

3572. Frisch, Walter, ed. *Schubert: Critical and Analytic Studies*, 48–64, 218–224. Lincoln: University of Nebraska Press, 1986.
In-depth analysis of the meaning of the unusual opening measures. Also an analysis of song No. 13 of this cycle ("Doppelgänger"), focusing on relationship of music to text. Musical examples.

3573. Kerman, Joseph. "A Romantic Detail in Schubert's *Schwanengesang.*" *Musical Quarterly*, 48, no. 1 (1962): 36–49.
Detailed analysis of the introduction to "Ihr Bild" of this cycle. Discussion of word-painting techniques. Musical examples.

3574. Kramer, Richard. "Schubert's Heine." *Nineteenth Century Music*, 8, no. 3 (1985): 213–225.
Examines the theory that the ordering of the Heine songs (Nos. 8–13) is wrong and that they actually comprise an independent cycle of their own. Concludes that the reordering was in fact Schubert's. Article includes analytical remarks on tonal, melodic, and harmonic structure and on the music/text relationships. Musical examples.

3575. Thomas, Jennifer H. "Schubert's Modified Strophic Songs with Particular Reference to *Schwanengesang.*" *Music Review*, 34, no. 2 (1973): 83–99.
Advanced discussion of form and tonality in the strophic songs. Musical examples.

Sonata for Arpeggione in A Minor, D. 821

3576. Geiringer, Karl. "Schubert's Arpeggione Sonata and the 'Super Arpeggio.'" *Musical Quarterly*, 65, no. 4 (1979): 513 + .
A discussion of the instrument (arpeggione) and its technique as applied to this composition.

Sonatas for Piano

3577. Brown, Maurice J. "Schubert's Piano Sonatas." *Musical Times*, 116 (October 1975): 873–875.
Brief critical overview, with comparisons to Beethoven's piano sonata style.

3578. Cone, Edward T. "Schubert's Beethoven." *Musical Quarterly*, 56, no. 4 (1970): 779–793.
Shows influence of Beethoven on Schubert. Musical examples.

3579. Elder, Dean. "Paul Badura-Skoda on the Schubert Sonatas." *Clavier*, 12, no. 3 (1973): 7–24.
Remarks on style and interpretation from the performer's point of view. Musical examples.

3580. Porter, Ernest G. "Schubert's Piano Works." *Music and Letters*, 62, nos. 3–4 (1981): 378.
Brief and basic analytic review for the undergraduate student. Musical examples.

3581. Radcliffe, Philip. *Schubert Piano Sonatas.* Seattle: University of Washington Press, 1971, 56 pp.
Well-written background, description, and analytical insights. Intended for the undergraduate student. Musical examples.

3582. Whaples, Miriam K. "Schubert's Piano Sonatas of 1817–1818." *Piano Quarterly*, 27, no. 104 (1978–1979): 34–37.
A survey of Schubert's sonatas from this period, with comparison to the styles of Haydn, Mozart, and Beethoven. Identifies stylistic elements that make Schubert's works unique. Harmonic and tonal aspects discussed as well as "bel canto" style.

Sonata for Piano in A Minor, D. 784

3583. Whaples, Miriam K. "Mahler and Schubert's A Minor Sonata D. 784." *Music and Letters*, 65, no. 3 (1984): 255–263.
A discussion of how this work influenced Mahler ("much of it unconsciously") for thirty years. Background and analysis with musical examples.

Sonata for Piano in A Minor, D. 845

3584. Newbould, Brian. "Schubert Sonata." *Music Teacher*, 56 (November 1977): 14–16.

Discussion of structure, phrase structure, harmony, texture, and thematic treatment, with emphasis on deviations from the normal in each category. Musical examples.

Sonata for Piano in G Major, D. 894

3585. Payne, Donald. "Achieving the Effect of Freedom in Musical Composition." *Piano Quarterly*, 20, no. 78 (1971–1972): 12–14 +.

The structure of the sonata is outlined and those aspects that exemplify the composer's freedom are discussed. Descriptive commentary, with some analytic remarks. Musical examples.

Sonata for Piano in A Major, D. 959

3586. Chusid, Martin. "Cyclicism in Schubert's Piano Sonata in A Major (D. 959)." *Piano Quarterly*, 27, no. 104 (1978–1979): 38–40.

A discussion of the unifying elements present in the work through descriptive, analytic, and historic commentary. Musical examples and reproductions of sketch fragments.

3587. Waldbauer, Ivan F. "Rehearing: Recurrent Harmonic Patterns in the First Movement of Schubert's Sonata in A Major, D. 959," *Nineteenth Century Music*, 12, no. 1 (1988): 64–73.

Sonata for Piano in B-Flat Major, D. 960

3588. Rosen, Charles. *Sonata Forms.* Rev. ed., New York: W. W. Norton, 1988, 415 pp.

Close examination of the three-key exposition and how Schubert modulates from B-flat major to F-sharp minor. Also discusses tonality in detail in the development section. Advanced.

3589. Sutton, Wadham. "Schubert: Piano Sonata in B-Flat (D. 960)." *Music Teacher*, 51 (November 1972): 11–12.

Brief background and analysis focusing on tonality, the slow movements, and the sonata's possible link with Beethoven.

3590. Wolff, Konrad. "Observations on the Scherzo of Schubert's B-Flat Sonata, Op. Posth. (D. 960)." *Piano Quarterly*, 24, no. 92 (1975–1976): 28–29.

A very brief analysis of the cyclic nature of the work. Offers examples that are detailed and analytic. Musical examples.

Sonata for Piano and Violin, Op. 137, No. 3 in G Minor, D. 408

3591. Rosen, Charles. *Sonata Forms*, 284–285. New York: W. W. Norton, 1980.
Description of the structure of the first movement. Musical examples.

Symphonies

3592. Brown, Maurice J. *Schubert Symphonies.* Seattle: University of Washington Press, 1971, 64 pp.
Essentially a concertgoers' guide, but does cover the main points of structure and thematic and tonal relationships, along with other unifying devices. Musical examples.

3593. Cuyler, Louise. *The Symphony*, 86–92. New York: Harcourt Brace Jovanovich, 1973.
Concentrated formal analysis of Symphonies Nos. 8 and 9. Musical examples.

3594. Plantinga, Leon. *Romantic Music*, 84–88. New York: W. W. Norton, 1984.
Analytic comments.

3595. Simpson, Robert, ed. *The Symphony.* Vol. 1, 188–208. New York: Drake Publishers, 1972.
Traces Schubert's stylistic development leading to the Eighth and Ninth Symphonies.

3596. Smith, Alexander Brent. *Schubert: The Symphonies.* London: Oxford University Press, 1926, 48 pp.
Thorough analytic discussion of both the Eighth and Ninth Symphonies. Musical examples. For the undergraduate student.

3597. Tovey, Donald Francis. *Essays in Musical Analysis.* Vol. 1, 205–218. London: Oxford University Press, 1935.
Short, but pointed analytic commentary on Symphonies Nos. Eight and Nine. Musical examples.

Symphony No. 7 (10), D. 729.

3598. Newbould, Brian. "Schubert Symphonic Realisation." *Music Teacher*, 57 (July 1978): 13–15.
Background and description of Newbould's realization of Schubert's sketch for a tenth symphony. Musical examples.

Symphony No. 8 in B Minor, D. 759 ("Unfinished")

3599.   Abraham, Gerald. "Finishing the *Unfinished.*" *Musical Times,* 112 (June 1971): 547–548.
Background of the composition, with theories on the intended last movement. Musical examples.

3600.   Chusid, Martin, ed. *Schubert: Symphony in B Minor, "Unfinished."* Norton Critical Scores. New York: W. W. Norton, 1967, 114 pp.
Historical background, analysis, criticism, with complete miniature score.

3601.   Haggin, B. H. *A Book of the Symphony,* 230–237. London: Oxford University Press, 1937.
Straightforward description dealing with formal plan only. Brief background remarks, with no discussion of tonality, rhythm, or texture. For the musical amateur or undergraduate student concerned with form. Musical examples.

3602.   Klein, John W. "Should One 'Tamper' with a Masterpiece?" *Musical Opinion,* 95 (May 1972): 403–405.
A response to Gerald Abraham's "completion" of this work and a look at the whole question of unfinished works.

3603.   Machlis, Joseph. *The Enjoyment of Music.* 3d ed., 301–304. New York: W. W. Norton, 1970.
Analysis for the undergraduate student. Musical examples.

3604.   Stedman, Preston. *The Symphony,* 102–105. Englewood Cliffs, NJ: Prentice-Hall, 1979.
Description of form, thematic treatment, tonality, and instrumentation. Musical examples and diagram.

3605.   Truscott, Harold. "Schubert's B Minor Symphony." *Music Review,* 23, no. 1 (1962): 1–16.
Analytic remarks emphasizing the importance of tonality as a structural feature in this work.

Symphony No. 9 in C Major, D. 944 ("The Great")

3606.   Brown, Maurice J. *Essays on Schubert,* 30–58. New York: St. Martin's Press, 1966.
Examination of the influences on Schubert and his artistic development, culminating in the Ninth Symphony.

3607. Haggin, B. H. *A Book of the Symphony*, 218–229. London: Oxford University Press, 1937.

Straightforward description dealing with formal plan only. Brief background remarks, with no discussion of tonality, rhythm, or texture. For the musical amateur or undergraduate student concerned with form. Musical examples.

3608. Reed, John. "How the *Great* C Major Was Written." *Music and Letters*, 56, no. 1 (1975): 18–25.

Shows that many of the ideas for this symphony were present before the final manuscript was completed. Disputes theory that it was written in haste just before Schubert's death and provides evidence that it was composed between 1818 and 1826.

3609. Reed, John. *Schubert: The Final Years*, 72–98. London: Faber and Faber, 1972.

Expanded treatment of Reed's articles cited above on the compositional history of this work. Provides evidence that this work was not written in haste just before Schubert's death, but was in the process of composition between 1818 and 1826. Author presents same thesis in article above. Musical examples.

Der Taucher, D. 77

3610. Gresch, Donald C. "The Nature of Schubert's Genius—Inspiration or Intelligence?" *NATS Bulletin*, 35, no. 2 (1978): 32–35.

By way of examining Schubert's revisions of this work, many analytic observations are made. Musical examples.

Trio for Violin, Violoncello, and Piano in B-Flat Major, D. 898

3611. Warburton, A. O. "Set Works for 'O' Level, GCE." *Music Teacher*, 48 (November 1969): 15–16.

Brief analysis for the undergraduate student. Musical examples.

Valses sentimentales, D. 779

3612. Lerdahl, Fred and Ray Jackendorff. *A Generative Theory of Tonal Music*, 250–253. Cambridge, MA: M.I.T. Press, 1983.

An analysis of the rhythmic structure of the A-Major Waltz (No. 13) of this set using theoretical concepts advanced by the authors. Diagrams and musical examples.

"Wandrers Nachtlied" ("Über allen Gipfeln ist Ruh"), D. 768

3613.   Frisch, Walter, ed. *Schubert: Critical and Analytic Studies,* 84–103. Lincoln: University of Nebraska Press, 1986.
Analysis of the structure of the poem and how Schubert drew inspiration from the same source as the poem, rather than super-imposing a new musical idea.

"Wehmut" ("Wenn ich durch Wald und Fluren geh"), D. 772

3614.   Cogan, Robert, and Pozzi Escot. *Sonic Design: The Nature of Sound and Music,* 159–163. Englewood Cliffs, NJ: Prentice-Hall, 1976.
Analysis of linear-harmonic motion.

Winterreise

3615.   Agawu, V. Kofi. "On Schubert's 'Der greise Kopf.' " *In Theory Only,* 8, no. 1 (1984): 3–21.
Advanced analysis. The discussion establishes the concept of a "highpoint," analyzes the song's structure and discusses the music/text relationship. Musical examples.

3616.   Frisch, Walter, ed. *Schubert: Critical and Analytic Studies,* 104–116, 126–152, 153–174. Lincoln: University of Nebraska Press, 1986.
Thorough analysis dealing with the music and the poetic content of "Im Dorfe" of this cycle. Also, analysis exploring the relation of musical structure to textual imagery and expressive meaning in "Auf dem Flusse" of this cycle. Musical examples.

3617.   Gauldin, Robert. "Intramusical Symbolism in the Last Strophe of Schubert's 'Der Wegweiser.' " *In Theory Only,* 3 (March 1978): 3–6.

3618.   Greene, David B. "Schubert's *Winterreise*: A Study in the Aesthetics of Mixed Media." *Journal of Aesthetics and Art Criticism,* 29, no. 2 (1970): 181–193.
Advanced discussion of the relationship of text and musical form. Word painting examined. Musical examples.

3619.   Kerman, Joseph. *Listen.* 2d ed., 211–213. New York: Worth Publishers, 1976.
Background and analysis with musical examples. For the under-graduate student.

3620. Lewin, David. " 'Auf dem Flusse': Image and Background in a Schubert Song." *Nineteenth Century Music*, 6, no. 1 (1982): 47–59.
  Examines the relation of musical structure to textual imagery in this song. Includes general comments about the relation of text and music in Schubert; a detailed discussion of tonal and rhythmic structure; and a conclusion concerning the interpretation of the textual and musical images. Utilizes Schenkerian techniques of analysis. Musical examples and table.

3621. Marshall, H. Lowen. "Symbolism in Schubert's *Winterreise.*" *Studies in Romanticism*, 12, no. 3 (1973): 607–632.
  Thorough treatment of word painting and symbols used to portray text. Musical examples.

3622. McKay, Elizabeth N. "Schubert's *Winterreise* Reconsidered." *Music Review*, 38, no. 2 (1977): 94–100.
  Textual problems considered, descriptive commentary, and some analytic observations. Musical examples.

3623. Youens, Susan. "Brief Reflections on the Two Müller Cycles of Franz Schubert: *Die schöne Müllerin*, D. 795, and *Winterreise.*" *NATS Journal*, 43, no. 3 (1987): 16–18.
  Contains brief analytic comments.

3624. Youens, Susan. "Poetic Rhythm and Musical Meter in Schubert's *Winterreise.*" *Music and Letters*, 65, no. 1 (1984): 28–40.
  How Müller's poetic rhythms reflect and heighten the mood of the text. Also how Schubert transforms those effects by musical means into metrical and rhythmic patterns that fuse the poetry and music into an artistic whole.

3625. Youens, Susan. "Retracing a Winter Journey: Reflections on Schubert's *Winterreise.*" *Nineteenth Century Music*, 9, no. 2 (1985): 128–135.
  An essay that discusses the text rather than the music. Sections on "Realism," "Madness," "The Wanderer As Musician."

3626. Youens, Susan. "*Wegweiser* in *Winterreise.*" *Journal of Musicology*, 5, no. 3 (1987): 357–379.
  Examines recurring "journeying" (*Wegweiser*) figure for its role in cyclic unification and interdependence of songs in this work. Musical examples.

DISSERTATIONS AND THESES

General

3627. Andrus, John Clarke. "Schubert and His Public: The Songs from 1817 to 1828." Ph.D., University of California at Santa Barbara, 1974, 224 pp., DA 42-4193A-4A.

3628. Citron, Marcia Judith. "Schubert's Seven Complete Operas: A Musico/Dramatic Study." Ph.D., University of North Carolina at Chapel Hill, 1971, 232 pp., DA 32-5262A.

3629. Kranz, Kathleen Nee. "Structural Functions of Rests in Franz Schubert's Works for Piano." Ph.D., University of California at San Diego, 1985, 148 pp., DA 46-1774A.

Sonata for Piano in A Major, D. 959

3630. Prescott, Elliot Jordan. "A Study, Analysis, and Recital of the Last Two Piano Sonatas of Franz Schubert: A Major (D. 959); B-Flat Major (D. 960)." Ed.D., Columbia University Teachers College, 1976, 183 pp., DA 37-2046A.

Sonata for Piano in B-Flat Major, Op. Posthumous, D. 960

3631. Bante-Knight, Mary Martha. "Tonal and Thematic Coherence in Schubert's Piano Sonata in B-Flat (D. 960)." Ph.D., Washington University, 1983, 125 pp., DA 44-3197A.

3632. Prescott, Elliot Jordan. "A Study, Analysis, and Recital of the Last Two Piano Sonatas of Franz Schubert: A Major (D. 959); B-Flat Major (D. 960)." Ed.D., Columbia University Teachers College, 1976, 183 pp., DA 37-2046A.

Symphonies

3633. Holt, Marilyn Barnes. "Developmental Procedures in the Sonata Form Movements of the Symphonies of Beethoven, Schubert, Mendelssohn, and Schumann." Ph.D., Case Western Reserve, 1973, 359 pp., DA 34-7807A.

Trio for Piano and Strings in B-Flat Major, D. 898

3634. McGeary, George L. "A Structural and Interpretive Analysis and Performance of Piano Trios by Haydn, Schubert, and Ravel." Ed.D., Columbia University Teachers College, 1973, 247 pp., DA 34-3702A.

SCHULLER, GUNTHER, 1925–

Concerto for Contrabassoon and Orchestra (1978)

3635. Schuller, Gunther. *Musings: The Musical World of Gunther Schuller*, 194–196. New York: Oxford University Press, 1986.
Analytic comments.

In Praise of Winds (1981)

3636. Schuller, Gunther. *Musings: The Musical World of Gunther Schuller*, 196–197. New York: Oxford University Press, 1986.
Analytic comments.

On Light Wings for Piano Quartet (1984)

3637. Schuller, Gunther. *Musings: The Musical World of Gunther Schuller*, 197–198. New York: Oxford University Press, 1986.
Analytic comments.

Shapes and Designs (1969)

3638. Schuller, Gunther. *Musings: The Musical World of Gunther Schuller*, 199–200. New York: Oxford University Press, 1986.
Analytic comments. Diagrams

Symphony (1965)

3639. Schuller, Gunther. *Musings: The Musical World of Gunther Schuller*, 141–150. New York: Oxford University Press, 1986.
Analytic discussion. Musical examples. Table.

DISSERTATIONS AND THESES

Studies on Themes of Paul Klee

3640. Cowen, Carol Vanrandwyk. "Analogical Observations: Gunther Schuller's Settings of *Artworks* by Paul Klee." M.M., Michigan State University, 1984, 81 pp., DA 23-9A.

SCHUMAN, WILLIAM, 1910–

General

3641. Schreiber, Flora Rheta, and Vincent Persichetti. *William Schuman.* New York: G. Schirmer, 1954, 139 pp.
The *American Festival* Overture and *Undertow* discussed in detail. Musical examples.

Carols of Death

3642.   Griffin, Malcolm J. "William Schuman's *Carols of Death*—An Analysis." *Choral Journal,* 17, no. 6 (1977): 17–18.

Symphony No. 3

3643.   Stedman, Preston. *The Symphony,* 358–366. Englewood Cliffs, NJ: Prentice-Hall, 1979.
   Description and analytic breakdown of all the sections with commentary on Schuman's style. Musical examples and diagram.

SCHUMANN, ROBERT, 1810–1856

General

3644.   Abraham, Gerald, ed. *Schumann: A Symposium.* London: Oxford University Press, 1952, 319 pp.
   Thorough discussions including background, descriptive, critical, and analytic commentaries by experts in the field. Musical examples.

3645.   Brauner, Charles S. "Irony in the Heine *Lieder* of Schubert and Schumann." *Musical Quarterly,* 67, no. 2 (1981): 261–281.
   Comments on the ways in which music can express, relate to, or deal with irony in song texts. Discusses both covert and overt irony in seleted Heine settings of Schubert and Schumann. Musical examples.

3646.   Chissel, Joan. *Schumann.* London: J. M. Dent and Sons, 1967, 257 pp.
   Critical and analytic discussion of Schumann's output. Musical examples.

3647.   Chissel, Joan. *Schumann Piano Music.* London: British Broadcasting Corporation, 1972, 72 pp.
   Descriptive and analytic observations on all Schumann's piano works. Musical examples.

3648.   Cooper, Frank. "Operatic and Dramatic Music." In *Robert Schumann: The Man and His Music.* Edited by Alan Walker, 324–349. London: Barrie and Jenkins, 1972.
   Good critical overview of Schumann's dramatic output. Musical examples.

3649.   Dale, Kathleen. *Nineteenth-Century Piano Music: A Handbook for Pianists.* London: Oxford University Press, 1954, 320 pp.
Highlights stylistic traits. Form, harmony, and other musical aspects discussed in relation to style.

3650.   Elder, Dean. "Cortot on Schumann." *Clavier,* 3, no. 5 (1964): 14–18.
Remarks on style with a view toward performance. Score included.

3651.   Ferguson, Donald N. *Image and Structure in Chambr Music,* 164–174. Minneapolis: University of Minnesota Press, 1964.
Overview of the chamber music, with brief analyses. Musical examples.

3652.   Ferguson, Donald N. *Piano Music of Six Great Composers,* 147–181. New York: Books for Libraries Press, 1947.
Descriptive and critical commentary showing Schumann's stylistic traits. Musical examples.

3653.   Gal, Hans. *Schumann Orchestral Music.* London: British Broadcasting Corporation, 1978, 64 pp.
Analytic overview of the symphonies, overtures, and concertos for the undergraduate student. Musical examples.

3654.   Longyear, Rey M. *Nineteenth-Century Romanticism in Music,* 66–71. Englewood Cliffs, NJ: Prentice-Hall, 1969.
Overview with descriptive and critical remarks intended for the undergraduate student. Musical examples.

3655.   Matthews, Denis, ed. *Keyboard Music,* 230–242. New York: Praeger, 1972.
Background, historical perspective, forms stylistic traits with discussion of specific pieces. Musical examples.

3656.   Obenshain, Kathryn. "Schumann As Symphonist." *American Music Teacher,* 23, no. 6 (1974): 31–33.
Brief remarks on Schumann's symphonic works, including the overtures. Reviews earlier "authorities" and general criticism, then describes each work in general terms to support a more positive assessment. Analytic comments are very general.

3657.   Patterson, Annie. *Schumann.* London: J. M. Dent and Sons, 1934, 238 pp.
Descriptive and critical overview, with occasional analytic remarks. Musical examples.

3658.   Plantinga, Leon. *Romantic Music,* 225–246. New York: W. W. Norton, 1984.

Analytic comments. Musical examples.

3659.   Robertson, Alec, ed. *Chamber Music,* 183–190. Baltimore: Penguin Books, 1957.

Critical and analytic remarks. Musical examples.

3660.   Sams, Eric. *The Songs of Robert Schumann.* 2d ed., London: Eulenberg Books, 1975, 228 pp.

The bulk of this book consists of a chronological history of the songs, giving dates, translations, and commentaries for each one. There is also discussion of music/text relationships, the use of melodic motifs, and rhythmic and harmonic patterns. Musical examples.

3661.   Siegel, Linda. "The Piano Cycles of Schumann and the Novels of Jean Paul Richter." *Piano Quarterly,* 18, no. 69 (1969): 16–22.

Siegel discusses the intricate connection between Richter's novels and Schumann's *Carnaval* and *Papillon.* Contains many passages from Richter's works, as well as some musical examples. More descriptive than analytic.

3662.   Walker, Alan, ed. *Robert Schumann: The Man and His Music.* London: Barrie and Jenkins, 1972, 489 pp.

Thorough critical and analytic discussions of Schumann's output by various authors. Musical examples.

3663.   Walsh, Stephen. *The Lieder of Schumann.* London: Cassell, 1971, 128 pp.

Thorough critical and analytic discussion. Musical examples.

Album for the Young

3664.   Lester, Joel. "Substance and Illusion in Schumann's *Erinnerung,* Op. 68: A Structural Analysis and Pictorial (*Geistliche*) Description." *In Theory Only,* 4 (April 1978): 9–17.

Carnaval

3665.   Elder, Dean. "Master Lesson: Seven Pieces from Schumann's *Carnaval.*" *Clavier,* 7, no. 2 (1968): 21–28.

Performance-oriented remarks, useful here for their characterization of the pieces under discussion. Musical examples.

3666.   Leichtentritt, Hugo. *Musical Form*, 323–325. Cambridge, MA: Harvard University Press, 1959.

Condensed analysis, focusing on variation technique. Musical examples.

3667.   Tischler, Hans. *The Perceptive Music Listener*, 150–155. Englewood Cliffs, NJ: Prentice-Hall, 1955.

Brief analysis of each section. Musical examples.

Concertos

3668.   Hill, Ralph, ed. *The Concerto*, 170–178. London: Penguin Books, 1952.

Critical and analytic commentary for the undergraduate student. Musical examples.

3669.   Veinus, Abraham. *The Concerto*. Rev. ed., 194–199. New York: Dover Publications, 1964.

An assessment of Schumann's style as well as specific remarks on individual works. Some comments on formal scheme.

Concerto for Piano, Op. 54 in A Minor

3670.   Hopkins, Antony. *Talking About Concertos*, 74–84. London: Heinemann, 1964.

Extended analytic essay describing tonal, thematic, and formal events.

3671.   Kerman, Joseph. *Listen*. 2d ed., 237–238. New York: Worth Publishers, 1976.

Brief analysis, with musical examples. For the undergraduate student.

3672.   Machlis, Joseph. *The Enjoyment of Music*. 3d ed., 167–168. New York: W. W. Norton, 1970.

Compact analysis for the undergraduate student, touching on highlights only. Musical examples.

3673.   Nelson, Wendell. *The Concerto*, 63–66. Dubuque, IA: William C. Brown, 1969.

Analysis with critical commentary. Musical examples.

3674.   Tovey, Donald Francis. *Essays in Musical Analysis*. Vol. 3, 182–184. London: Oxford University Press, 1936.

Brief critical commentary with musical examples.

3675. **Ulrich, Homer.** *Music: A Design for Listening,* 330–332. New York: Harcourt, Brace, 1957.
Descriptive/analytic breakdown by measures. Musical examples.

Concerto for Violin in D Minor

3676. **Swalin, Benjamin F.** *The Violin Concerto: A Study in German Romanticism,* 76–82. Chapel Hill: University of North Carolina Press, 1941.
Background and analysis, with musical examples.

Davidsbündlertänze

3677. **Fiske, Roger.** "A Schumann Mystery." *Musical Times,* 105 (August 1964): 574–578.
A thematic analysis that relates the work to Schumann biography.

Dichterliebe

3678. **Agawu, V. Kofi.** "Structural 'Highpoints' in Schumann's *Dichterliebe.*" *Music Analysis,* 3, no. 2 (1984): 159–180.

3679. **Hallmark, Rufus E.** *The Genesis of Schumann's "Dichterliebe": A Source Study.* Ann Arbor: UMI Research Press, 1979, 208 pp.
Sources, compositional history of the individual songs, and analytic observations. Musical examples.

3680. **Hardin, Philip W.** "Robert Schumann and the *Dichterliebe.*" *NATS Bulletin,* 28, no. 2 (1971): 19+.
Brief commentary focusing on stylistic characteristics and critical evaluation for performance. Brief bibliography.

3681. **Herbert, Rembert B.** "The Narrator and the Drama of Schumann's *Dichterliebe.*" *NATS Bulletin,* 31, no. 4 (1975): 15–20.
A discussion of the drama of Heine's poetry and the musical devices used by Schumann to reflect that drama. Bibliography.

3682. **Horton, Charles T.** "A Structural Function of Dynamics in Schumann's 'Ich grolle nicht.' " *In Theory Only,* 4 (February–March 1979): 30–47.

3683. **Komar, Arthur, ed.** *Schumann: "Dichterliebe" Op. 48.* Norton Critical Scores. New York: W. W. Norton, 1971, 136 pp.
Historical background, analytic essays, modern and nineteenth-century critical commentary. Full score included. Bibliography.

507

3684.   Large, John, and Klaus Weissenberger. "The Irony of the Allusions in *Dichterliebe.*" *NATS Bulletin*, 27, no. 1 (1970): 22–25.
The ironic intent behind Heine's allusions to familiar landmarks and art in these songs. Bibliography.

3685.   Rothgeb, John. "A Structural Function of Dynamics in Schumann's 'Ich grolle nicht': Comment: On the form of 'Ich grolle nicht.' " *In Theory Only*, 5 (May–June 1979): 15–17.

Fantasiestücke, Op. 12

3686.   Smith, Edwin. "Fantasiestücke." *Music Teacher*, 58 (March 1979): 23–25.
Outlines the form of each of the eight pieces of this set, highlighting salient features of each. For the undergraduate student.

Fantasy for Piano, Op. 17 in C Major

3687.   Rosen, Charles. *The Classical Style: Haydn, Mozart, Beethoven*, 451–453. New York: Viking Press, 1971.
Analytic observations on the essence of Romanticism in this work. Musical examples.

3688.   Walker, Alan. "Schumann, Liszt, and the C Major Fantasie Op. 17: A Declining Relationship." *Music and Letters*, 60, no. 2 (1979): 156–165.
Essay on Schumann's relationship with Liszt and the history of the Fantasie's dedication to Liszt.

Frauenliebe und Leben

3689.   Tischler, Hans. *The Perceptive Music Listener*, 157–166. Englewood Cliffs, NJ: Prentice-Hall, 1955.
Analytic commentary with emphasis on form. Musical examples.

Genoveva

3690.   Siegel, Linda. "A Second Look at Schumann's *Genoveva.*" *Music Review*, 36, no. 1 (1975): 17–41.
Mainly an historical account of the "fate" of *Genoveva* (the failure of the work) with a look into text and symbolic themes. Musical examples.

Introduction and Allegro Appassionato, Op. 92

3691. Longyear, Rey M. "Introduction and Allegro Appassionato, Op. 92." *In Theory Only*, 3 (March 1978): 22–30.
Examines the unusual treatment of tonal relationships. Analytic remarks on the tonal structures. Tables of keys and modulations. Advanced.

Kinderscenen

3692. Warburton, A. O. "Set Works for 'O' Level, GCE." *Music Teacher and Piano Student*, 46 (November 1967): 10+.
Brief analysis of each piece. For the undergraduate student.

Liederkreis

3693. McCreless, Patrick. "Song Order in the Song Cycle: Schumann's *Liederkreis* Op. 39." *Music Analysis*, 5, no. 1 (1986): 5–28.
Discusses various possible song orderings in this cycle and examines evidence (literary, structural, and musical) suggesting Schumann's reasons for choosing the order he did. Includes tables showing overall structure; possible song ordering, and many analytic observations. Musical examples.

Nachtstück, Op. 23, No. 4 in F Major

3694. Walton, Charles W. *Basic Forms in Music*, 37–40. Port Washington, NY: Alfred Publishing Co., 1974.
Condensed analysis, with full musical quotation. No score needed.

Novellette No. 8, Op. 21 in F-Sharp Minor

3695. Tovey, Donald Francis. *Essays in Musical Analysis: Chamber Music*, 142–149. London: Oxford University Press, 1944.
Critical observations and analyses, with musical examples. For the undergraduate student.

Overture, Scherzo, and Finale, Op. 52

3696. Tovey, Donald Francis. *Essays in Musical Analysis*. Vol. 6, 40–44. London: Oxford University Press, 1969.
Critical and analytic remarks, with musical examples. For the undergraduate student.

Quartets for Strings, Op. 41

3697.   Correll, Linda. "Structural Revisions in the String Quartets Op. 41 of Robert Schumann." *Current Musicology*, 7 (1968): 87–95.
A study of the sketches to show Schumann's creative process. Musical examples.

3698.   Longyear, Rey M. "Unusual Tonal Procedures in Schumann's Sonata Type Cycles." *In Theory Only*, 3 (March 1978): 22–30.
Examines the unusual treatment of tonal relationships. Analytic remarks on the tonal structures, tables of keys, and modulations.

Quintet for Piano and Strings, Op. 44 in E-Flat Major

3699.   Longyear, Rey M. "Unusual Tonal Procedures in Schumann's Sonata Type Cycles." *In Theory Only*, 3 (march 1978): 22–30.
Examines the unusual treatment of tonal relationships. Analytic remarks on the tonal structures, tables of keys, and modulations.

3700.   Tovey, Donald Francis. *Essays in Musical Analysis: Chamber Music*, 149–154. London: Oxford University Press, 1944.
Critical and analytic remarks with musical examples. For the undergraduate student.

3701.   Warburton, A. O. "Set Works for 'O' Level, GCE." *Music Teacher and Piano Student*, 46 (January 1967): 15+.
Background and analysis for the undergraduate student. To be used with score.

Sonata for Piano, Op. 11 in F-Sharp Minor

3702.   Harwood, Gregory. "Robert Schumann's Sonata in F-Sharp Minor: A Study of Creative Process and Romantic Inspiration." *Current Musicology*, 29 (1980): 17–30.
Discusses the sketches for the work (titled "Fandango"), extramusical references in the work (including those to Clara Wieck), and the form of the work. Musical examples. Table giving form of the first movement.

3703.   Longyear, Rey M. "Unusual Tonal Procedures in Schumann's Sonata Type Cycles." *In Theory Only*, 3 (March 1978): 22–30.
Examines the unusual treatment of tonal relationships. Analytic remarks on the tonal structures, tables of keys, and modulations.

3704. Rosen, Charles. *Sonata Forms*, 296–314. New York: W. W. Norton, 1980.

Analysis of the sonata-form structures in the first movement and the Finale. Musical examples.

Sonata for Piano, Op. 22 in G Minor

3705. Sutton, Wadham. "Schumann: Piano Sonata in G Minor, Op. 22." *Music Teacher*, 52 (April 1973): 14–15.

Brief analytic remarks.

Symphonies

3706. Smith, Raymond R. "Motivic Procedure in Opening Movements of the Symphonies of Schumann, Bruckner, and Brahms." *Music Review*, 36, no. 2 (1975): 130–134.

Advanced discussion of motivic treatment as an important element of sonata form.

3707. Tovey, Donald Francis. *Essays in Musical Analysis.* Vol. 2, 45–62. London: Oxford University Press, 1935.

Thorough, intelligent, musical analysis for the undergraduate student of Symphonies 1, 3, and 4. Musical examples.

Symphony in G Minor ("Jugendsinfonie", 1832–1833)

3708. Abraham, Gerald. *Slavonic and Romantic Music*, 272–280. New York: St. Martin's Press, 1968.

Discussion of background and sketches, with analytic commentary on this early sketch for a symphony. Musical examples.

Symphony No. 1, Op. 38, in B-Flat Major ("Spring")

3709. Nadeau, Roland. *The Symphony: Structure and Style.* Shorter ed., rev., 111–113. Boston: Crescendo, 1973.

Measure-by-measure analysis.

3710. Stedman, Preston. *The Symphony*, 117–122. Englewood Cliffs, NJ: Prentice-Hall, 1979.

Description of form, motivic activity, tonality, and orchestral technique. Musical examples and diagram.

Symphony No. 2, Op. 61, in C Major

3711. Newcomb, Anthony. "Once More Between Absolute and Program Music: Schumann's Second Symphony." *Nineteenth Century Music*, 7, no. 3 (1984): 233–250.

Discusses the initial reception and interpretation of the symphony in the nineteenth century. Summarizes the opinions of twentieth-century authors. The ninteenth-century opinion tended to be polite; twentieth-century opinion has tended to be negative. There follows a brief analysis of the first three movements and a detailed study of the Finale. Musical examples.

Symphony No. 4, Op. 120, in D Minor

3712. Abraham, Gerald. *Slavonic and Romantic Music*, 281–287. New York: St. Martin's Press, 1968.

Discussion of the three versions of this symphony. Provides an insight into Schumann's creative process. Musical examples.

3713. Cuyler, Louise. *The Symphony*, 96–103. New York: Harcourt Brace Jovanovich, 1973.

Concentrated analysis with musical examples.

3714. Maniates, Maria Rika. "The D Minor Symphony of Robert Schumann." In *Festschrift für Walter Wiora*. Compiled by Ludwig Finscher and Christoph-Helmut Mehling, 441–447. Kassel: Bärenreiter, 1967.

Discussion of the creative impulse behind this symphony. On an advanced level, but many analytic insights available to the undergraduate student.

3715. Ulrich, Homer. *Music: A Design for Listening*, 327–329. New York: Harcourt, Brace 1957.

Brief outline of the formal structure. Musical examples.

DISSERTATIONS AND THESES

General

3716. Ashley, Douglas Daniels. "The Role of the Piano in Schumann's Songs." Ph.D., Northwestern University, 1973, 375 pp., DA 34-3449A.

3717. Campbell, Lawrence Bracey. "A Study of Selected Vocal Chamber Music of Robert Schumann." Ed.D., Columbia University, 1973, 334 pp., DA 34-3110A-11A.

3718.   Paul, Sharon June. "Robert Schumann's Choral Music for Women's Voices." D.M.A., Stanford University, 1984, 172 pp., DA 45-3023A.

3719.   Vancil, Gregory Kent. "A Study of Robert Schumann's 'Adventlied' and 'Neujahrslied,' with English Translations." D.M.A., University of Southern California, 1983, DA 44-1969A.

Abegg Variations, Op. 1

3720.   Jacobson, Allan S. "A Study of . . . *Abegg* Variations, Op. 1, by Robert Schumann." D.M.A., University of Wisconsin at Madison, 1982, 84 pp., DA 43-3451A.

Concerto for Piano, Op. 54 in A Minor

3721.   Earle, Diane Kay. "An Analytical Study of the Piano Concerto in A Minor, Op. 54 of Robert Schumann." D.M.A., Ohio State University, 1984, 189 pp., DA 45-1566A.

Kreisleriana

3722.   Arnsdorf, Mary Hunter. "Schumann's *Kreisleriana*, Op. 16: Analysis and Performance." Ed.D., Columbia University Teachers College, 1976, 193 pp., DA 37-1284A.

Liederkreis, Op. 39

3723.   Jack, Dwight Christian. "Two Romantic Song Cycles: An Analytical Description of the Schumann-Eichendorff *Liederkreis II* Op. 39, and the Brahms-Tieck *Romanzen aus Magelone*." D.M.A., University of Miami, 1973, 131 pp., DA 35-500A.

Sonatas for Piano

3724.   Kim, Kyoung-Im. "A Critical Analysis of the First Movements of Schumann's Piano Sonatas." D.M.A., University of Oklahoma, 1980, 204 pp., DA 40-6062A.

Symphonies

3725.   Holt, Marilyn Barnes. "Developmental Procedures in the Sonata Form Movements of the Symphonies of Beethoven, Schubert,

Mendelssohn, and Schumann." Ph.D., Case Western Reserve, 1973, 359 pp., DA 34-7807A.

SCHÜTZ, HEINRICH, 1585–1672

General

3726. Bukofzer, Manfred. *Music in the Baroque Era*, 88–95. New York: W. W. Norton, 1947.
   Brief overview focusing on formal and stylistic characteristics as well as Schütz's place in music history. Musical examples.

3727. Gérold, Théodore. "Protestant Music on the Continent." In *The New Oxford History of Music*, Vol. 4, *The Age of Humanism, 1540–1630*. Edited by Gerald Abraham, 461–464. London: Oxford University Press, 1968.
   Brief assessment of Schütz's place in music history and his unique contribution. Musical examples.

3728. Moser, Hans Joachim. *Heinrich Schütz: His Life and Work.* Translated by Carl Pfatteicher. St. Louis: Concordia, 1959, 740 pp.
   Long the standard "life and works" study. The section on his works includes information on background, composition, and an analytical discussion of each work. Musical examples.

3729. Palisca, Claude. *Baroque Music*, 93–102. Englewood Cliffs, NJ: Prentice-Hall, 1968.
   Concise summation, with remarks on specific musical features. Musical examples.

3730. Steinitz, Paul. "German Church Music." In *The New Oxford History of Music*. Vol. 5, *Opera and Church Music, 1630–1750*. Edited by Anthony Lewis and Nigel Fortune, 600–604, 625–628, 665–668. London: Oxford University Press, 1975.
   Brief critical evaluation with discussion of Schütz's setting of text and his unique contribution to German sacred music. Musical examples.

Cantiones Sacrae

3731. Bray, Roger. "The *Cantiones Sacrae* of Heinrich Schütz Reexamined." *Music and Letters*, 52, no. 3 (1971): 299–305.
   Stylistic traits examined. Musical examples.

Musicalische Exequien

3732. Bernick, Thomas. "Modal Digressions in the *Musicalische Exequien* of Heinrich Schütz." *Music Theory Spectrum*, 4 (1982): 51–65.
Study of the modes used and "digressions" from them. Includes discussion of overall tonal organization. For the advanced student.

3733. Robertson, Alec. *Requiem: Music of Mourning and Consolation*, 171–175. New York: Praeger, 1968.
Descriptive and critical commentary with musical examples.

Psalms of David

3734. Arnold, Denis. "Schütz's *Venetian* Psalms." *Musical Times*, 113 (November 1972): 1071–1073.
Descriptive and analytic remarks. Musical examples.

DISSERTATIONS AND THESES

Symphoniae Sacrae

3735. Faulkner, Quentin. "The *Symphoniae Sacrae* of Heinrich Schütz: A Manual for Performance." S.M.D., Union Theological Seminary, 1975, 405 pp., DA 36-17A.

SCRIABIN, ALEXANDER, 1872–1915

General

3736. Baker, James. *The Music of Alexander Scriabin*. New Haven: Yale University Press, 1986, 289 pp.
Thorough, in-depth analytic overview of Scriabin's output. For the advanced student. Musical examples.

3737. Bowers, Faubion. "How to Play Scriabin." *Piano Quarterly*, 19, no. 74 (1970–1971): 12–18.
Stylistic traits and technical problems discussed. Musical examples.

3738. Bowers, Faubion. *The New Scriabin: Enigma and Answers*. New York: St. Martin's Press, 1973, 210 pp.
Discusses the ten piano sonatas at length and Scriabin's style and harmonic system. Musical examples.

3739.   Bowers, Faubion. *Scriabin.* 2 vols. Palo Alto: Kodansha International, 1969.
> Mainly treats Scriabin's life, but does include descriptive and critical commentary on the music.

3740.   Hull, A. Eaglefield. *A Great Russian Tone-Poet: Scriabin.* 1918. Reprint. New York: AMS Press, 1970, 304 pp.
> Summation of Scriabin's piano output. Critical and analytic remarks. Musical examples.

3741.   MacDonald, Hugh. *Skryabin.* London: Oxford University Press, 1978, 71 pp.
> Overview of Scriabin's output. Descriptive commentary with analytic observations. Special emphasis on *Divine Poem, Poem of Ecstasy* and *Prometheus.* Musical examples.

3742.   Randlett, Samuel. "Elements of Scriabin's Keyboard Style." *Piano Quarterly,* 20, no. 78 (1971–1972): 26–30.
> Stylistic traits and technical problems discussed. Mainly for the pianist. Musical examples.

3743.   Reise, Jay. "Late Skriabin: Some Principles Behind the Style." *Nineteenth Century Music,* 6, no. 3 (1983): 220–231.
> Examines the use of whole-tone and octatonic scales in Scriabin's works and the resulting melodic and harmonic structure. Examines *Poème,* Op. 69, No. 1, and *Etrangeté,* Op. 63, No. 2, in particular. Musical examples.

Albumleaf, Op. 45, No. 1

3744.   Austin, William W. *Music in the Twentieth Century,* 70–72. New York: W. W. Norton, 1966.
> Brief analysis. Musical examples.

Fantastic Poem for Piano, Op. 45, No. 2 in C Major

3745.   Talley, Howard. "Scriabine the Inscrutable: Or, Making the Complicated Simple—Analysis of the *Fantastic Poem* in C." *Clavier,* 3, no. 5 (1964): 28–31.
> Analysis of harmony and form. Complete musical example.

Preludes (Five) for Piano, Op. 74

3746.   Perle, George. "Scriabin's Self-Analyses." *Music Analysis,* 3, no. 2 (1984): 101–122.
> The octatonic system and notational practice of Scriabin is discussed. For the advanced student.

Sonata for Piano No. 3, Op. 23 in F-Sharp Minor

3747.   William, Sister M. "Scriabin—The Mystic." *Clavier*, 4, no. 6 (1965): 35–37.
  Descriptive and analytic remarks. Complete musical example.

Sonata for Piano No. 4, Op. 30 in F-Sharp Major

3748.   Samson, Jim. *Music in Transition: A Study of Tonal Expansion and Atonality, 1900–1920*, 82–85. New York: W. W. Norton, 1977.
  Concise analysis focusing on tonality and the composition's place in Scriabin's development. Musical examples.

Sonata for Piano No. 5, Op. 53 in F-Sharp Major

3749.   Samson, Jim. *Music in Transition: A Study of Tonal Expansion and Atonality, 1900–1920*, 88–90. New York: W. W. Norton, 1977.
  Concise analysis focusing on tonality. Musical examples.

Sonata for Piano No. 7, Op. 64 in F-Sharp Major ("White Mass")

3750.   Perle, George. *Serial Composition and Atonality: An Introduction to the Music of Schoenberg, Berg, and Webern.* 5th ed., rev., 41–43. Berkeley: University of California Press, 1981.
  Brief comments on the pitch structure. Musical examples.

3751.   Perle, George. "Scriabin's Self-Analyses." *Music Analysis*, 3, no. 2 (1984): 101–122.
  The octatonic system and notational practice of Scriabin is discussed in the article. The Sonata is dealt with briefly—the Preludes are discussed at great length. For the advanced student.

Sonata for Piano No. 10, Op. 70

3752.   Wait, Mark. "Liszt, Scriabin, and Boulez: Considerations." *Journal of the American Liszt Society*, 1 (June 1977): 12–13.
  Brief analysis. Musical examples.

Symphony No. 5, Op. 60 ("Prometheus, the Poem of Fire")

3753.   Peacock, Kenneth. "Synesthetic Perception: Alexander Scriabin's Color Hearing." *Music Perception*, 2, no. 4 (1985): 483–505.

Discussion of the "Tastiera per Luce," which uses projected colored light. Also provides the key to the harmonic and structural organization of the work.

3754. Watkins, Glenn. *Soundings: Music in the Twentieth Century,* 164–168. New York: Schirmer Books, 1987.
Brief examination of the philosophy behind Scriabin's vision, the relationship between music and color in this work, and the "mystic chord" as its harmonic foundation.

DISSERTATIONS AND THESES

General

3755. Goldwire, Bettsylynn Dunn. "Harmonic Evolution in the Piano Poems of Alexander Scriabin." D.M.A., University of Texas at Austin, 1984, 57 pp., DA 45-1908A.

Preludes

3756. Meeks, John Samuel. "Aspects of Stylistic Evolution in Scriabin's Piano Preludes." D.M.A., Peabody Conservatory of Music, 1975, 344 pp., DA 37-1866A-7A.

Prometheus (Poem of Fire)

3757. Peacock, Kenneth John. "Alexander Scriabin's *Prometheus*: Philosophy and Structure." Ph.D., University of Michigan, 1976, 269 pp., DA 37-1291A.

Sonatas for Piano

3758. Rinehart, Arthur Edward. "The Factors Present in the Transitional Musical Vocabulary of Alexander Nikolayevitch Scriabin Which Suggest Later Compositional Techniques." D.M.A., University of Missouri, 1975, 82 pp., DA 36-7037A.

3759. Woolsey, Timothy Dwight. "Organizational Principles in Piano Sonatas of Alexander Scriabin." D.M.A., University of Texas at Austin, 1977, 167 pp., DA 38-2408A.

Sonata for Piano, No. 5, Op. 53 in F-Sharp Major

3760. Bellardo, Samarah J. "A Study, Analysis, and Performance of Selected One-Movement Piano Sonatas of the Nineteenth and Twentieth Centuries." Ed.D., Columbia University Teachers College, 1973, 126 pp., DA 34-1471A.

SESSIONS, ROGER, 1896–1985

General

3761.   Imbrie, Andrew. "Roger Sessions: In Honor of His Sixty-Fifth Birthday." In *Perspectives on American Composers.* Edited by Benjamin Boretz and E. T. Cone, 59–89. New York: W. W. Norton, 1971.
    Critical evaluation of Sessions, focusing on the opening phrases of his Concerto for Violin and his Quintet to demonstrate the composer's technique and style. Musical examples.

3762.   Olmstead, Andrea. *Roger Sessions and His Music.* Ann Arbor: UMI Research Press, 1985, 218 pp.
    Comments on Sessions the man, placing the music in context. The works are discussed in detail: background, compositional techniques, formal divisions, performance histories. Musical examples.

Mass for Unison Choir and Organ

3763.   Stevens, Denis. "Roger Sessions' 'Mass.' " *Musical Times,* 102 (November 1961): 696–697.
    A brief analytical/critical overview of the work.

My Diary No. 3

3764.   Forte, Allen. *Contemporary Tone-Structures,* 48–61. New York: Columbia University Press, 1955.
    Thorough analysis dealing with formal structure, tonality, internal relationships, and general stylistic characteristics. Musical examples and analytic sketches.

Symphony No. 1

3765.   Machlis, Joseph. *Introduction to Contemporary Music,* 585–586. New York: W. W. Norton, 1961.
    Brief analytical remarks.

Symphony No. 2

3766.   Hansen, Peter. *An Introduction to Twentieth Century Music.* 2d ed., 340–342. Boston: Allyn and Bacon, 1967.
    Brief analysis, with musical examples.

DISSERTATIONS AND THESES

General

3767.   Gorelick, Brian Lee. "Movement and Shape in the Choral Music of Roger Sessions." D.M.A., University of Illinois at Urbana-Champaign, 1985, 296 pp., DA 46-1772A.

3768.   Wheeler, William Scott. "Harmonic Motion in the Music of Roger Sessions." Ph.D., Brandeis University, 1984, 93 pp., DA 45-15A.

Montezuma

3769.   Mason, Charles Norman. "A Comprehensive Analysis of Roger Sessions' Opera *Montezuma*." D.M.A., University of Illinois at Urbana, 1982, 179 pp., DA 43-3452A.

Quintet for Strings

3770.   Sheeler, William Scott. "Movement 1. Harmonic Motion in the Music of Roger Sessions." Ph.D., Brandeis University, 1984, 93 pp., DA 45-15A.

Sonata for Piano No. 3

3771.   Merryman, Marjorie Jane. "Aspects of Phrasing and Pitch Usage in Roger Sessions' Piano Sonata No. 3." Ph.D., Brandeis University, 1981, 53 pp., DA 42-3803A.

SHAPEY, RALPH, 1921–

Dimensions

3772.   Henahan, Donal. "Current Chronicle: Chicago." *Musical Quarterly*, 53, no. 2 (1967): 249–250.
General descriptive commentary and formal overview in this review of a performance of *Dimensions*.

SHOSTAKOVICH, DMITRI, 1906–1975

General

3773.   Kay, Norman. *Shostakovich*. London: Oxford University Press, 1971, 80 pp.
Brief critical and analytic overview for the undergraduate student. Musical examples.

3774.   Martynov, Ivan. *Dmitri Shostakovich: The Man and His Work.* Translated by T. Guralsky. New York: Greenwood Press, 1947, 197 pp.
   Brief descriptive and critical remarks.

3775.   Norris, Christopher, ed. *Shostakovich: The Man and His Music.* London: Lawrence and Wishart, 1982, 233 pp.
   Mainly descriptive commentary of the program-note variety, with a few analytic observations. Musical examples.

3776.   Ottaway, Hugh. "Shostakovich: Some Later Works." *Tempo,* 50 (Winter 1959): 2–12.
   Substantial commentary on Symphonies 10 and 11. Brief comments on the program, structure and style of the Violin Concerto (1955). Musical examples.

Concerto for Violin No. 2

3777.   Kay, Norman. "Shostakovich's Second Violin Concerto." *Tempo,* 83 (Winter 1967–1968): 21–23.
   Brief critical and analytic remarks. Musical examples.

3778.   Orga, Ates. "Shostakovich's New Concerto." *Music and Musicians,* 16 (January 1968): 23–25.
   Analysis with musical examples.

Concerto for Violoncello, Op. 107 in E-Flat Major

3779.   McVeagh, Diana. "Shostakovich's Concerto." *Musical Times,* 101 (November 1960): 701–703.
   Brief critical and analytic remarks. Musical examples.

Lady Macbeth of Mtsensk

3780.   Carter, Elliott. "Current Chronicle: Germany." *Musical Quarterly,* 46, no. 3 (1960): 367–371.
   Review of a performance. Critical and descriptive commentary.

Preludes (Twenty-Four)

3781.   Martynov, Ivan. *Dmitri Shostakovich: The Man and His Work,* 53–55. New York: Greenwood Press, 1969.
   Very brief evaluation of the Twenty-four Preludes. Mainly descriptive commentary.

3782. Matthews, Denis, ed. *Keyboard Music,* 313–314. New York: Praeger, 1972.

Brief critical remarks. Musical examples.

Quartets for Strings

3783. Barry, Malcolm. "Shostakovich's Quartets." *Music and Musicians,* 27 (February 1979): 28–30+.

A discussion of stylistic influences and musical language. Some brief analytic comments about formal and thematic processes.

3784. Norris, Christopher. "The String Quartets of Shostakovich." *Music and Musicians,* 23 (December 1974): 26–28+.

Analytic overview, with remarks on political atmosphere during the composition of the quartets. Musical examples.

3785. O'Loughlin, Niall. "Shostakovich's String Quartets." *Tempo,* 87 (Winter 1968–1969): 9–16.

Analytic overview. Musical examples.

3786. O'Loughlin, Niall. "Shostakovich's String Quartets." *Musical Times,* 115 (September 1974): 744–746.

Critical and stylistic review of the quartets. Some analytic observations.

Quartet for Strings, No. 8

3787. Fenton, John. "Thematic Unity in Shostakovich's Eighth Quartet." *Music Teacher,* 58 (May 1979): 18–21.

Quartet for Strings, No. 9

3788. Hopkis, G. W. "Shostakovich's Ninth String Quartet." *Tempo,* 75 (Winter 1965–1966): 23–25.

Description. Not analytic, no musical examples.

Quartet for Strings, No. 12

3789. Keller, Hans. "Shostakovich's Twelfth Quartet." *Tempo,* 94 (Autumn 1970): 6–15.

Thorough analysis. Musical examples.

Symphonies

3790. Gow, David. "Shostakovich's *War* Symphonies." *Musical Times*, 105 (March 1964): 191–193.
Relationships between Symphonies 7 and 8 examined. Musical examples.

3791. Simpson, Robert, ed. *The Symphony.* Vol. 2, 199–217. New York: Drake Publishers, 1972.
A descriptive overview of stylistic development in the symphonies. Musical examples.

Symphony No. 1 in F Major

3792. Kay, Norman. *Shostakovich,* 100–116. London: Oxford University Press, 1971.
Influences, stylistic traits, and descriptive remarks. Not analytical. Musical examples.

Symphony No. 2 in C Major ("October")

3793. Lawson, Stephen P. "Shostakovich's Second Symphony." *Tempo,* 91 (Winter 1969–1970): 14–15.
Brief descriptive, critical, and analytic commentary. Musical examples.

Symphony No. 4

3794. Ballantine, Christopher. *Twentieth Century Symphony,* 127–129. London: Dennis Dobson, 1984.
Brief analytic comments and table of the structure. First movement only.

3795. Souster, Tim. "Shostakovich at the Crossroads." *Tempo,* 78 (Autumn 1966): 2–9.
Analytical observations and comparison with the Symphony No. 5. Musical examples.

Symphony No. 5 in D Minor

3796. Machlis, Joseph. *Introduction to Contemporary Music,* 289–292. New York: W. W. Norton, 1961.
Descriptive commentary, with musical examples.

3797.   Souster, Tim. "Shostakovich at the Crossroads." *Tempo*, 78 (Autumn 1966): 2–9.
   Analytical observations and comparison with the Symphony No. 4. Musical examples.

3798.   Stedman, Preston. *The Symphony*, 309–317. Englewood Cliffs, NJ: Prentice-Hall, 1979.
   Description and analytic breakdown of each movement, supported by musical examples and diagram.

3799.   Whittall, Arnold. *Music Since the First World War*, 84–89. London: J. M. Dent and Sons, 1977.
   Brief analytic comments. Musical example.

Symphony No. 7 ("Leningrad")

3800.   Ottaway, Hugh. "Shostakovich's 'Fascist' Theme." *Musical Times*, 111 (March 1970): 274.
   Objections to the commonly held idea that the theme in the first movement is meant to represent the approach of Nazi invaders.

Symphony No. 10

3801.   Ballantine, Christopher. *Twentieth Century Symphony*, 166–168. London: Dennis Dobson, 1983.
   Analytic comments.

3802.   Ottaway, Hugh. "Shostakovich: Some Later Works." *Tempo*, 50 (Winter 1959): 2–14.
   A brief analytical overview of the program, the structure, and the style. Musical examples.

Symphony No. 11

3803.   Ottaway, Hugh. "Shostakovich: Some Later Works." *Tempo*, 50 (Winter 1959): 2–14.
   A brief analytical overview of the program, the structure, and the style. Musical examples.

Symphony No. 14

3804.   Kay, Norman. "Shostakovich's Fourteenth Symphony." *Tempo*, 92 (Spring 1970): 20–21.
   Brief analytical sketch. Musical examples.

3805.   Whittall, Arnold. *Music Since the First World War*, 84–89. London: J. M. Dent and Sons, 1977.
Brief analytic comments. Musical example.

Symphony No. 15

3806.   Kay, Norman. "New Music: Shostakovich's Fifteenth Symphony." *Tempo*, 100 (1972): 36–40.
Analysis. Musical examples.

DISSERTATIONS AND THESES

Preludes for Piano, Op. 34

3807.   Aster, Samuel Sheah. "An Analytical Study of Selected Preludes from Shostakovich's Twenty-Four Preludes for Piano, Op. 34." Ed.D., Columbia University, 1975, 304 pp., DA 36-1361A-2A.

Quartets for Strings

3808.   Fay, Auarel Elizabeth. "The Last Quartets of Dmitri Shostakovich: A Stylistic Investigation." Ph.D., Cornell University, 1978, 158 pp., DA 39-3905A.

3809.   Smith, Arthur Dove. "Recurring Motives and Themes As a Means to Unity in Selected String Quartets of Dmitri Shostakovich." D.Mus. Ed., University of Oklahoma, 1976, 480 pp., DA 37-2487-8A.

Symphonies

3810.   Huband, Joseph Dance. "The First Five Symphonies of Dmitri Shostakovich." D.A., Ball State University, 1984, 172 pp., DA 2296A-7A.

3811.   Kazakova, Tatyana. "Orchestral Style Development in the Symphonies of Dmitri Shostakovich." M.A., California State University at Fullerton, 1983, 268 pp., DA 21-237A.

SIBELIUS, JEAN, 1865–1957

General

3812.   Abraham, Gerald, ed. *The Music of Sibelius*. New York: W. W. Norton, 1947, 218 pp.

Excellent guide for the undergraduate student through all the forms of Sibelius's output. Features a discussion of Sibelius the man, analyses of the music, and Sibelius's stylistic characteristics. Musical examples.

3813.   Gould, Glenn. "Sibelius and the Post-Romantic Piano Style." *Piano Quarterly,* 25, no. 99 (1977): 22–27.

Critique of the post-Romantic piano style, with descriptive commentary and analytic remarks on the Sonatinas Op. 67 and *Kyllikki* Op. 41. The entire second movement of the latter work is reproduced in the article.

3814.   Morin, Robert. "The Songs of Jean Sibelius." *American Music Teacher,* 15, no. 2 (1965): 16–17+.

A general introduction covering style, influences and relationship to his music in other genres. No analyses of individual songs, but a few general analytic remarks.

3815.   Simpson, Robert, ed. *The Symphony.* Vol. 2, 86–130. New York: Drake Publishers, 1972.

Analytic discussion of all the symphonies, with emphasis on stylistic growth.

3816.   Tawaststjerna, Erik. *The Pianoforte Compositions of Sibelius.* Helsinki: Kustannusosoakeyhtiö Otava, 1957, 104 pp.

A descriptive and critical assessment of Sibelius's piano compositions. Forms, general stylistic characteristics, and other notable features are discussed for each piece. Musical examples.

3817.   Tawaststjerna, Erik. *Sibelius: 1856–1905.* Vol. 1. Berkeley: University of California, 1976, 316 pp.

A "life and works" treatment, with thorough analyses of Symphonies 1 and 2 and the Violin Concerto. Musical examples.

Concerto for Violin

3818.   Hill, Ralph, ed. *The Concerto,* 276–281. London: Penguin Books, 1952.

Critical and analytic commentary for the undergraduate student. Musical examples.

3819.   James, Burnett. *The Music of Jean Sibelius.* London: Associated University Presses, 1983, 174 pp.

Descriptive and critical review, with analytic observations of Sibelius's output. Musical examples.

3820.   Layton, Robert. *Sibelius.* London: J. M. Dent and Sons, 1965, 210 pp.
Overview with descriptive and critical commentary intended for the undergraduate student. Occasional analytic remarks. Musical examples.

3821.   Payne, Anthony. "The Scope of Sibelius." *Music and Musicians,* 14 (December 1965): 20–23.
A look at Sibelius's orchestral technique and style as a clue to some limitations in his emotional scope. Unifying devices identified in some tone poems and symphonies. Musical examples.

3822.   Ringbom, Nils-Erik. *Jean Sibelius.* Norman: University of Oklahoma Press, 1954, 196 pp.
Descriptive and critical commentary on Sibelius's entire output. Musical examples.

3823.   Tovey, Donald Francis. *Essays in Musical Analysis.* Vol 3, 211–215. London: Oxford University Press, 1936.
Critique and analysis, with musical examples.

3824.   Warburton, A. O. "Set Works for 'O' Level, GCE." *Music Teacher,* 52 (October 1973): 12–13.
Background and thorough analysis for the undergraduate student.

Lemminkäinen and the Maidens of the Island

3825.   Jacobs, Robert L. "Lemminkäinen and the Maidens of Saari." *Music Review,* 24, no. 2 (1963): 146–157.
Thorough analysis and discussion showing Sibelius's use of "evolutionary thematicism" and the thematic affinities of this work with some of the later symphonies.

Symphonies

3826.   Collins, M. Stuart. "Germ Motives and Guff." *Music Review,* 23, no. 3 (1962): 238–243.
Analytic argument showing that Sibelius must be judged on his own terms. Views of other critics considered. Musical examples.

3827.   Gray, Cecil. *Sibelius: The Symphonies.* 1935. Reprint. New York: Books for Libraries Press, 1970, 77 pp.
Guide for the musical amateur or undergraduate student seeking basic information on the symphonies.

3828. Parmet, Simon. *The Symphonies of Sibelius.* Translated by Kingsley A. Hart. London: Cassell, 1959.

A survey of the Sibelius symphonies for the general reader. Includes analytic discussion of style, form, and melodic treatment.

3829. Sutton, Wadham. "Sibelius and the Symphony: A Centenary Tribute." *Music in Education,* 29 (1965): 221–222.

An overview, with a characterization of Sibelius's symphonic style.

3830. Whittall, Arnold. *Music Since the First World War,* 18–20. London: J. M. Dent and Sons, 1977.

Brief analytic comments on Symphonies 5 and 6. Musical examples.

Symphony No. 1, Op. 39 in E Minor

3831. Pike, Lionel. *Beethoven, Sibelius, and the "Profound Logic": Studies in Symphonic Analysis,* 170–178. London: Athlone Press, 1978.

Analysis focusing on tonal, stylistic, and rhythmic elements. Musical examples.

Symphony No. 2, Op. 43 in D Major

3832. Ballantine, Christopher. *Twentieth Century Symphony,* 146–152. London: Dennis Dobson, 1984.

Analytic discussion. Musical examples.

3833. Machlis, Joseph. *Introduction to Contemporary Music,* 96–99. New York: W. W. Norton, 1961.

Descriptive and analytic comments, with musical examples. For the undergraduate student.

3834. Nadeau, Roland. *The Symphony: Structure and Style.* Shorter ed., rev., 160–164. Boston: Crescendo, 1973.

Measure-by-measure analysis.

3835. Pike, Lionel. *Beethoven, Sibelius, and the "Profound Logic": Studies in Symphonic Analysis,* 87–98. London: Athlone Press, 1978.

Analysis demonstrating Sibelius's expansion of tonality in symphonic music. Musical examples.

Symphony No. 3, Op. 52 in C Major

3836. Ballantine, Christopher. *Twentieth Century Symphony* , 149–151. London: Dennis Dobson, 1984

Brief analytic comments on the first movement.

3837. Pike, Lionel. *Beethoven, Sibelius, and the "Profound Logic":
Studies in Symphonic Analysis,* 98–106. London: Athlone Press, 1978.
Tonal analysis demonstrating Sibelius's use of the tritone as a
unifying device. Musical examples.

Symphony No. 4, Op. 63 in A Minor

3838. Dahlhaus, Carl. *Nineteenth-Century Music.* Translated by
J. Bradford Robinson, 367. Berkeley: University of California Press,
1989.
Brief remarks on motivic "germ cells," thematic transformation,
keys, and rhythmic patterns as unifying forces. Advanced.

3839. Pike, Lionel. *Beethoven, Sibelius, and the "Profound Logic":
Studies in Symphonic Analysis,* 106–116. London: Athlone Press, 1978.
Tonal analysis demonstrating Sibelius's use of the tritone to in-
terrupt the tonal and rhythmic flow of the symphony. Musical
examples.

3840. Stedman, Preston. *The Symphony,* 259–268. Englewood Cliffs,
NJ: Prentice-Hall, 1979.
Description and full analytic breakdown of each movement, sup-
ported by musical examples and diagram.

Symphony No. 5, Op. 82 in E-Flat Major

3841. Ballantine, Christopher. *Twentieth Century Symphony,* 115–
116, 157–158. London: Dennis Dobson, 1984.
Brief analytic comments. Musical examples.

3842. Pike, Lionel. *Beethoven, Sibelius, and the "Profound Logic":
Studies in Symphonic Analysis,* 130–145. London: Athlone Press, 1978.
Extended analytic essay focusing on rhythmic structure as the
crucial unifying force in this symphony. Musical examples.

3843. Tovey, Donald Francis. *Essays in Musical Analysis.* Vol. 2,
128–129. London: Oxford University Press, 1935.
Brief analytic remarks for the undergraduate student. Musical
examples.

Symphony No. 6, Op. 104 in D Minor

3844. Pike, Lionel. *Beethoven, Sibelius, and the "Profound Logic":
Studies in Symphonic Analysis,* 188–202. London: Athlone Press, 1978.

Extended analytic essay probing Sibelius's use of the Dorian modes, the influence of Renaissance polyphony, and their respective effects on the formal structure of the work. Musical examples.

3845. Pike, Lionel. "Sibelius's Debt to Renaissance Polyphony." *Music and Letters*, 55, no. 3 (1974): 317–326.
   Advanced discussion of Sibelius's use of ancient modes. Musical examples.

Symphony No. 7, Op. 105 in C Major

3846. Ballantine, Christopher. "The Symphony in the Twentieth Century: Some Aspects of Its Tradition and Innovation." *Music Review*, 32, no. 3 (1971): 226–228.
   Brief remarks on Sibelius's unifying devices. Musical examples.

3847. Ballantine, Christopher. *Twentieth Century Symphony*, 170–172. London: Dennis Dobson, 1984.
   Very brief analytic commentary.

3848. Pike, Lionel. *Beethoven, Sibelius, and the "Profound Logic": Studies in Symphonic Analysis*, 203–213. London: Athlone Press, 1978.
   Analysis focusing on treatment of dissonance, tonality, and the influence of Renaissance music on Sibelius. Musical examples.

3849. Whittall, Arnold. *Music Since the First World War*, 20–23. London: J. M. Dent and Sons, 1977.
   Brief analytic discussion for the undergraduate student. Musical examples.

Tapiola

3850. Payne, Anthony. "The Scope of Sibelius." *Music and Musicians*, 14 (December 1965): 20–23.
   Analytic observations, with specific musical examples.

3851. Tovey, Donald Francis. *Essays in Musical Analysis.* Vol. 6, 93–95. London: Oxford University Press, 1969.
   Critical and analytic discussion with musical examples. For the undergraduate student.

3852. Whittall, Arnold. "Sibelius's Eighth Symphony." *Music Review*, 25, no. 3 (1964): 239–240.
   Critical commentary on the main formal principle at work.

Voces Intimae

3853. **Ringbom, Nils-Erik.** *Jean Sibelius.* Translated by G. I. C. de Courcy, 97–116. Norman: University of Oklahoma Press, 1954.
Thorough analysis, with musical examples.

DISSERTATIONS AND THESES

Symphonies

3854. **Jordan, Alan T.** "Harmonic Style in Selected Sibelius Symphonies." Ph.D., Indiana University, 1984, 229 pp., DA 46-14A.

3855. **Shanks, Marilyn E.** "Sibelius Symphonies 3 Through 6: Degrees of Departure from Traditional Sonata-Allegro Structure." M.M., Duquesne University, 1984, 68 pp., DA 23-11A.

Symphony No. 1, Op. 39 in E Minor

3856. **Bates, Karen Anne.** "Harmonic Language in the First Symphony of Jean Sibelius." M.Mus., University of Arizona, 1984, 141 pp., DA 23-319A.

SMETANA, BEDŘICH, 1824–1884

General

3857. **Clapham, John.** *Smetana.* New York: Octagon Books, 1972, 161 pp.
Descriptive and critical overview for the undergraduate student. More analytic slant given to Smetana's considerable operatic output. Musical examples.

3858. **Ferguson, Donald N.** *Image and Structure in Chamber Music,* 225–226. Minneapolis: University of Minnesota Press, 1964.
Brief analytic remarks on the chamber music.

3859. **Large, Brian.** *Smetana.* London: Duckworth, 1970, 473 pp.
Critical and analytic observations with musical examples. Fullest treatment given to the operas, discussing musical techniques, plots, and background.

3860. **Robertson, Alec, ed.** *Chamber Music,* 202–206. Baltimore: Penguin Books, 1957.
Brief critical remarks on the chamber music. Musical examples.

The Bartered Bride

3861.   Abraham, Gerald. *Slavonic and Romantic Music*, 28–39. New York: St. Martin's Press, 1968.
Discusses the genesis of the opera and offers analytical comments. Musical examples.

Má Vlast

3862.   Dahlhaus, Carl. *Nineteenth-Century Music.* Translated by J. Bradford Robinson, 243–244. Berkeley: University of California Press, 1989.
Brief but concentrated analytic remarks dwelling on form and motivic transformation. Advanced.

3863.   Large, Brian. *Smetana*, 260–288. London: Duckworth, 1970.
Background, critical, and descriptive commentary, with musical examples.

The Moldau

3864.   Burns, Mary T. "An Analysis of Selected Folk-Style Themes in the Music of Bedrich Smetana and Aaron Copland." *American Music Teacher*, 25, no. 2 (1975): 8–10.
Comparison of type and use of folk melody used in the *Moldau* and *Appalachian Spring*. Musical examples.

Quartet for Strings in E Minor ("From My Life")

3865.   Ferguson, Donald N. *Image and Structure in Chamber Music*, 225–226. Minneapolis: University of Minnesota Press, 1964.
Brief analysis.

SOLER, PADRE ANTONIO, 1729–1783

DISSERTATIONS AND THESES

Sonatas for Keyboard

3866.   Dieckow, Almarie. "A Stylistic Analysis of the Solo Keyboard Sonatas of Antonio Soler." Ph.D., Washington University, 1971, 281 pp., DA 33-346A.

SORABJI, KAIKHOSRU SHAPURJI, 1892–1988

DISSERTATIONS AND THESES

Le Jardin Parfumé

3867.   Habermann, Michael R. "A Style Analysis of the Nocturnes for Solo Piano by Kaikhosru Shapurji Sorabji with Special Emphasis on *Le Jardin Parfumé*." D.M.A., Peabody Conservatory of Music, 1985, 292 pp., DA 46-550A.

SPOHR, LOUIS, 1784–1859

General

3868.   Brown, Clive. *Louis Spohr: A Critical Biography*. Cambridge: Cambridge University Press, 1984, 364 pp.
   Includes overview of Spohr's output with descriptive, critical, and analytic remarks, with heavy emphasis on stylistic traits. Musical examples.

Concertos for Violin

3869.   Swalin, Benjamin F. *The Violin Concerto: A Study in German Romanticism*, 8–33. Chapel Hill: University of North Carolina Press, 1941.
   Background, analyses and critical remarks. Musical examples.

DISSERTATIONS AND THESES

Concertos for Clarinet

3870.   Johnston, Stephen Keith. "The Clarinet Concertos of Louis Spohr." D.M.A., University of Maryland, 1972, 164 pp., DA 33-2413A-14A.

STAMITZ, JOHANN, 1717–1757

Symphonies

3871.   Wolf, Eugene. *The Symphonies of Johann Stamitz*. Utrecht: Bohn, Scheltema and Holkema, 1981, 500 pp.

An extensive and detailed study. Analyses of style and structure occupy the bulk of the book. Separate chapters devoted to the early, middle, and late symphonies. Musical examples.

STOCKHAUSEN, KARLHEINZ, 1928–

General

3872. Evans, Peter. "Music of the European Mainstream: 1940–1960." In *The New Oxford History of Music.* Vol. 10, *The Modern Age: 1890–1960.* Edited by Martin Cooper, 454–468. London: Oxford University Press, 1974.
Discussion of Stockhausen's idiom with analytic commentary on *Klavierstücke I–IV, Zeitmasze* and *Klavierstück XI.* Musical examples.

3873. Harvey, Jonathan. *The Music of Stockhausen: An Introduction.* Berkeley: University of California Press, 1975, 144 pp.
Analytic discussion of Stockhausen's output. Musical examples.

3874. Maconie, Robin. *The Works of Karlheinz Stockhausen.* London: Oxford University Press, 1976, 341 pp.
Thorough analytic summary of Stockhausen's output. Musical examples.

3875. Whittall, Arnold. *Music Since the First World War,* 260–263. London: J. M. Dent and Sons, 1977.
Brief, general analytic comments to characterize Stockhausen's place in music history.

3876. Wörner, Karl H. *Stockhausen: Life and Work.* Translated and edited by B. Hopkins. Berkeley: University of California Press, 1973, 270 pp.
Thorough overview with discussion of Stockhausen's concepts and development.

Aus den sieben Tagen

3877. Johl, J. "Serial Determinis and 'Intuitive Music': An Analysis of Stockhausen's *Aus den sieben Tagen." In Theory Only,* 3 (March 1978): 7–19.

Donnerstag

3878. Britton, Peter. "Stockhausen's Path to Opera." *Musical Times,* 126 (September 1985): 515–521.
Analysis with musical examples.

Gesang der Jünglinge

3879.   Griffiths, Paul. *Modern Music: The Avant-Garde Since 1945,* 101–103. New York: George Braziller, 1981.
Brief analytic remarks.

3880.   Schrader, Barry. *Introduction to Electro-Acoustic Music,* 94–96. Englewood Cliffs, NJ: Prentice-Hall, 1982.
Analytic comments.

3881.   Stockhausen, Karlheinz. "Music and Speech." *Reihe,* 6 (1964): 40–64.
An examination of text/music relationships in this work, including discussion of poetry, phonetics, rhythm, and instrumentation. Musical examples, graphs, tables. For the advanced student.

Gruppen

3882.   Smalley, Roger. "Stockhausen's *Gruppen.*" *Musical Times,* 108 (September 1967): 794–797.
An overview of the background and structure of the work, including tone rows. Musical examples.

Hymnen

3883.   Griffiths, Paul. *Modern Music: The Avant-Garde Since 1945.* 210–211. New York: George Braziller, 1981.
Brief analytic remarks.

3884.   Harvey, Jonathan. "Stockhausen's *Hymnen.*" *Musical Times,* 116 (August 1975): 705 +.
Brief description accompanied by analytic commentary.

Konkrete Etüde

3885.   Toop, Richard. "Stockhausen's *Konkrete Etüde.*" *Music Review,* 37, no. 4 (1976): 295–300.
Mainly a discussion of the evolution of Stockhausen's compositional discoveries in this work. Stockhausen's own comments on this work are quoted, some analysis, and a "sound graph."

Kontakte

3886.   Griffiths, Paul. *Modern Music: The Avant-Garde Since 1945,* 144-147. New York: George Braziller, 1981.
Analytic commentary. Musical examples.

Kontra-Punkte

3887. Griffiths, Paul. *Modern Music: The Avant-Garde Since 1945*, 81–84. New York: George Braziller, 1981.
Analytic observations. Musical examples.

Kreuzspiel

3888. Griffiths, Paul. *Modern Music: The Avant-Garde Since 1945*, 50–55. New York: George Braziller, 1981.
The serial method of composition is identified and other influences are discussed. Musical examples.

Mantra

3889. Griffiths, Paul *Modern Music: The Avant-Garde Since 1945*, 287–289. New York: George Braziller, 1981.
Analytic discussion.

Momente

3890. Griffiths, Paul. *Modern Music: The Avant-Garde Since 1945*, 147–148. New York: George Braziller, 1981.
Brief analytic remarks. Musical examples.

Piano Pieces

3891. Smalley, Roger. "Stockhausen's Piano Pieces: Some Notes for the Listener." *Musical Times*, 110 (January 1969): 30–32.
Analysis, with musical examples.

Piano Pieces V

3892. Harvey, Jonathan. "Stockhausen: Theory and Music." *Music Review*, 29, no. 2 (1968): 134–141.
In-depth analysis, with critical commentary. Musical examples.

Study II (1954)

3893. Schrader, Barry. *Introduction to Electro-Acoustic Music*, 83–88. Englewood Cliffs, NJ: Prentice-Hall, 1982.
Analytic discussion. Describes techniques of composition. Includes graphs, diagrams, and tables.

DISSERTATIONS AND THESES

Klavierstück XI

3894. Truelove, Nathan M. "Karlheinz Stockhausen's *Klavierstück XI*: An Analysis of Its Composition . . . and the Translation of Rhythm into Pitch." D.M.A., University of Oklahoma, 1984, 200 pp., DA 45-2301A.

STRAUSS, RICHARD, 1864–1949

General

3895. Del Mar, Norman. *Richard Strauss: A Critical Commentary on His Life and Works.* 3 vols. London: Barrie and Jenkins, 1962–1972.
Background, descriptive, and critical commentary focusing on style and use of motifs. Musical examples.

3896. Jefferson, Alan. *The Lieder of Richard Strauss.* London: Cassell, 1971, 134 pp.
Descriptive overview of Strauss's *Lieder*, with occasional analytic observations. Musical examples.

3897. Kennedy, Michael. *Richard Strauss.* London: J. M. Dent and Sons, 1976, 274 pp.
Full coverage of Strauss's entire output, with critical commentary on orchestration, opera plots, symbolism, and form. Musical examples.

3898. Krause, Ernst. *Richard Strauss: The Man and His Work,* 277–475. London: Collett's, 1964.
Lengthy treatment of all Strauss's operas, with some critical commentary. Not strongly analytic, but focuses on background and aesthetics.

3899. Mann, William. *Richard Strauss: A Critical Study of the Operas.* London: Cassell, 1964, 402 pp.
Full background given on plot sources and compositional inspiration, followed by a detailed descriptive commentary. Musical examples support comments on leitmotivs.

3900. Marek, George. *Richard Strauss: The Life of a Non-Hero.* New York: Simon and Schuster, 1967, 350 pp.
All the operas discussed, focusing on background and political influences. Very little music criticism. For the amateur music listener.

3901.   Newman, Ernest. *Richard Strauss.* 1908. Reprint. New York: Books for Libraries Press, 1969, 144 pp.
    Brief descriptive overview with critical remarks. Some discussion of Strauss's use of leitmotivs. Musical examples.

Also sprach Zarathustra

3902.   Murphy, Edward. "Tonal Organization in Five Strauss Tone Poems." *Music Review,* 44, nos. 3–4 (1983): 223 + .

Arabella

3903.   Jefferson, Alan. "An Introduction to *Arabella.*" *Opera,* 16 (January 1965): 9–12.
    Background and critical remarks.

Ariadne auf Naxos

3904.   Forsyth, Karen. *"Ariadne auf Naxos" by Hugo von Hofmannsthal and Richard Strauss: Its Genesis and Meaning.* New York: Oxford University Press, 1982, 291 pp.
    A very detailed study (originally a doctoral dissertation) that concentrates on the genesis and later alterations of the opera. The emphasis is more literary than musical, but in chapter 3, "The Genesis of the Opera," there is discussion of musical characterization and many analytical observations. For the advanced student.

3905.   Owen, M. Lee. "Death and Transfiguration." *Opera News,* 34 (March 28, 1970): 24–25.
    Brief remarks on a central idea in *Ariadne*—transformation. Musical examples illustrate word painting.

Capriccio

3906.   Whittall, Arnold. *Music Since the First World War,* 93–97. London: J. M. Dent and Sons, 1977.
    Brief analytic observations. Musical examples.

Concerto for Violin in D Minor

3907.   Swalin, Benjamin F. *The Violin Concerto: A Study in German Romanticism,* 119–121. Chapel Hill: University of North Carolina Press, 1941.
    Analysis, with musical examples.

Death and Transfiguration

3908. Longyear, Rey M. "Schiller, Moszkowski, and Strauss: Joan of Arc's 'Death and Transfiguration.'" *Music Review*, 28, no. 3 (1967): 209–217.

A discussion of Moszkowski's composition, *Jeanne d'Arc* and the possible influence that it had on Strauss's *Death and Transfiguration*. Background information on Schiller's drama included. Musical examples.

3909. Murphy, Edward. "Tonal Organization in Five Strauss Tone Poems." *Music Review*, 44, nos. 3–4 (1983): 223+.

Don Juan

3910. Kerman, Joseph. *Listen.* 2d ed., 250–251. New York: Worth Publishers, 1976.

Analysis, with musical examples. For the undergraduate student.

3911. Murphy, Edward. "Tonal Organization in Five Strauss Tone Poems." *Music Review*, 44, nos. 3–4 (1983): 223+.

3912. Tovey, Donald Francis. *Essays in Musical Analysis.* Vol. 4, 154–158. London: Oxford University Press, 1969.

Critical and analytic study with musical examples. For the undergraduate student.

Elektra

3913. Ashbrook, William. "The Shock of Recognition." *Opera News*, 40 (January 10, 1976): 24–25.

Brief discussion of Strauss's use of motives to enhance the "recognition scene" in this work. Musical examples.

3914. Breuer, Robert. "Of Timeless Passions." *Opera News*, 31 (December 10, 1966): 24–25.

Elektra as an expression of its time. Brief look at some leitmotives, with musical examples.

3915. Carner, Mosco. "Witches' Cauldron." *Opera News*, 35 (February 27, 1971): 24–26.

Place of *Elektra* in Strauss's output, its characterization, motives, and musical devices to depict text.

3916. Rotter, John, and Suzanne Rotter. "Prophetic Avenger." *Opera News*, 44 (February 9, 1980): 16–18.

Descriptive summary of the dramatic action. Motifs characterizing some of the dramatic points are briefly examined. Musical examples.

Four Last Songs

3917. Garlington, Aubrey S., Jr. "Richard Strauss's *Vier letzte Lieder*: The Ultimate *Opus Ultimatum*." *Musical Quarterly*, 73, no. 1 (1989): 79–93.

Discussion of Alfred Einstein's concept of *opus ultimum* and its application to Strauss' *Vier letzte lieder*. Reviews Strauss's career and output to demonstrate that this work is truly a culminating work. Descriptive commentary on each of the songs. Advanced.

Die Frau ohne Schatten

3918. Ashbrook, William. "Shadow and Substance." *Opera News*, 42 (April 1, 1978): 28–29.

Comparisons with Mozart's *Magic Flute* and brief observations on Struass's use of motivs. Musical examples.

3919. Jenkins, Speight. "Kaleidoscope." *Opera News*, 31 (December 17, 1966.): 25–27.

An examination of the leitmotiv. Musical examples.

3920. Mann, William. "How I Got Rid of Monstrous Mildred." *Opera News*, 33 (March 8, 1969): 24–25.

Brief explanation of the opera's symbolism, reasons for lengthy second act and lack of aria writing.

3921. Snook, Lynn. "The Myth and the 'Shadow.' " *Opera*, 18 (June 1967): 454–459.

Explores plot for psychological-mythical meaning.

Ein Heldenleben

3922. Murphy, Edward. "Tonal Organization in Five Strauss Tone Poems." *Music Review*, 44, nos. 3–4 (1983): 223 + .

3923. Ulrich, Homer. *Music: A Design for Listening*, 404–406. New York: Harcourt, Brace, 1957.

Descriptive/analytic breakdown by measures. Musical examples.

Der Rosenkavalier

3924. Jefferson, Alan. *Richard Strauss: Der Rosenkavalier*. Cambridge: Cambridge University Press, 1985, 152 pp.

Contains articles on genesis, sources, synopsis and analysis, staging the opera, critical view, interpretation. Musical examples.

STRAUSS, RICHARD, 1864–1949   3932

3925. Lee, M. Owen. "When Time Stands Still." *Opera News,* 37 (April 14, 1973): 22–23.
Brief discussion of the character of the Marschallin. Musical examples.

3926. Rockwell, John. "Something Old, Something New." *Opera News,* 33 (February 8, 1969): 24–25.
Brief discussion of the music focusing on its stylistic roots, melodic writing, musical depiction, and harmonic invention. Musical examples.

Salome

3927. Lee, M. Owen. "The Moon Is Like the Moon." *Opera News,* 36 (March 18, 1972): 24–25.
Some examples of how Strauss portrays Wilde's text in music. Musical examples.

3928. McDonald, Katherine. "Daughter of Desperation." *Opera News,* 26 (February 17, 1962): 23–25.
Examples of Strauss' tone-painting techniques. Musical examples.

3929. Schmidgal, Gary. "Imp of Perversity." *Opera News,* 41 (February 12, 1977): 10–13.
Strauss's musical methods of portraying mental states such as fixation, mania, perverse and erratic energy discussed. Musical examples.

Die Schweigsame Frau (Silent Woman)

3930. Feasy, Norman. *"The Silent Woman—*An Introduction." *Opera,* 12 (November 1961): 692–697.
Background, synopsis, and some critical remarks on the music.

Symphony, Op. 12 in F Minor

3931. Bloomfield, Theodore. "A Case of Neglect: Richard Strauss' Symphony in F Minor." *Music and Musicians,* 22 (January 1974): 24–28 + .
Descriptive commentary, with analytic remarks. A defense of the symphony. Musical examples.

Till Eulenspiegel's Merry Pranks

3932. Murphy, Edward. "Tonal Organization in Five Strauss Tone Poems." *Music Review,* 44, nos. 3–4 (1983): 223 + .

3933. Stedman, Preston. *The Symphony*, 218–224. Englewood Cliffs, NJ: Prentice-Hall, 1979.
Description and analytic breakdown, section by section. Musical examples and diagram.

3934. Warburton, A. O. "Set Works for 'O' Level, GCE." *Music Teacher*, 49 (January 1970): 15–16.
Brief analysis for the undergraduate student.

DISSERTATIONS AND THESES

General

3935. Thurston, Richard Elliott. "Musical Representation in the Symphonic Works of Richard Strauss." Ph.D., University of Texas at Austin, 1971, 384 pp., DA 32-5832A-3A.

3936. Wilde, Denis Gerard. "Melodic Process in the Tone Poems of Richard Strauss." Ph.D., Catholic University of America, 1984, 436 pp., DA 45-1571A.

Daphne

3937. Gilliam, Bryan Randolph. "Richard Strauss's *Daphne*: Opera and Symphonic Continuity." Ph.D., Harvard University, 1984, 329 pp., DA 45-1908A.

Domestic Symphony

3938. Koska, Linda Jean "The Structure and Harmonic Language of the *Domestic* Symphony by Richard Strauss." M.M., University of Arizona, 1986, 77 pp., DA 24-319A.

Elektra

3939. Kaplan, Richard Andrew. "The Musical Language of *Elektra*: A Study in Chromatic Harmony." Ph.D., University of Michigan, 1985, 190 pp., DA 46-832A.

Four Last Songs

3940. Colson, William Wilder. *"Four Last Songs* by Richard Strauss." D.M.A., University of Illinois at Urbana, 1975, 187 pp., DA 36-16A-17A.

3941.   Strickert, Jane Elizabeth Bernsten. "Richard Strauss' *Vier letzte Lieder*: An Analytical Study." Ph.D., Washington University, 1975, 240 pp., DA 36-5632A-3A.

STRAVINSKY, IGOR, 1882–1971

General

3942.   Carner, Mosco. "Music in the Mainland of Europe: 1918–1939." In *The New Oxford History of Music.* Vol. 10, *The Modern Age: 1890–1960.* Edited by Martin Cooper, 210–229. London: Oxford University Press, 1974.
> Stylistic overview of the music composed after the *Rite of Spring.* Stravinsky's Neo-classicism explored, as well as his later style in the *Symphony of Psalms* and Concerto for Two Pianos. Musical examples.

3943.   Evans, Peter. "Music of the European Mainstream: 1940–1960." In *The New Oxford History of Music.* Vol. 10, *The Modern Age: 1890–1960.* Edited by Martin Cooper, 389–402. London: Oxford University Press, 1974.
> Stravinsky's style analytically traced during his later years (1940–1960) from the traditional forms of the *Ebony* Concerto, the Two Piano Sonata, and the Symphony in C to serial works such as *In Memoriam Dylan Thomas, Canticum Sacrum,* and Movements for Piano and Orchestra. Musical examples.

3944.   Evenson, David. "The Piano Works in the Compositions of Igor Stravinsky." *Piano Quarterly,* 30, no. 118 (1982): 26–33.
> A brief survey of Stravinsky's works for piano. Includes descriptive commentary and analytic remarks. Mainly, a pianist's reactions to Stravinsky's writing for the piano. Musical examples.

3945.   Friedberg, Ruth C. "The Solo Vocal Works of Igor Stravinsky: A Review." *NATS Bulletin,* 23, no. 1 (1966): 6–8, 10, 12–13.
> A complete list, with brief analytical notes for each work.

3946.   Joseph, Charles M. *Stravinsky and the Piano.* Ann Arbor: UMI Research Press, 1983, 304 pp.
> Analytic overview of the piano music. Advanced. Musical examples.

3947.   Lacy, Gene M. "Stravinsky's Orchestral Technique in His Russian Period." *American Music Teacher,* 22, no. 5 (1973): 17–22.
> Stravinsky's techniques of orchestration highlighted. Musical examples.

3948. Maconie, Robin. "Stravinsky's Final Cadence." *Tempo*, 103 (1972): 18–23.

Analysis of Stravinsky's transcriptions of Wolf songs. Musical examples.

3949. Mason, Colin. "Stravinsky and Gesualdo." *Tempo*, 55–56 (Autumn–Winter 1960): 39–48.

A description of Stravinsky's recomposition of Gesauldo's madrigals. Musical examples.

3950. Moffet, Maureen C. "Stylistic Consistency in Three Choral Works of Stravinsky." *Choral Journal*, 23, no. 6 (1983): 11–14.

Three choral works from three stylistic periods discussed: *Noces, Oedipus Rex,* and *Threni.* Despite stylistic differences, Stravinsky was consistent in his use of analogous openings and closings, symmetrical layouts, ostinato figures, and cellular processes to achieve unity.

3951. Nelson, Robert U. "Stravinsky's Concept of Variations." In *Stravinsky: A New Appraisal of His Work.* Edited by Paul Henry Lang, 61–73. New York: W. W. Norton, 1963.

Explores Stravinsky's variation technique in the Concerto for Two Pianos and *Ebony* Concerto. Other discussions center on *Oedipus* and *Fairy's Kiss,* with analyses of other selected works. Musical examples.

3952. Newlin, Dika. "The Piano Music of Igor Stravinsky." *Piano Quarterly*, 27, no. 106 (1979): 27+.

A brief survey of Stravinsky's piano literature, which includes structural analyses of various works as well as an assessment of their level of difficulty to perform.

3953. Perle, George. *Serial Composition and Atonality: An Introduction to the Music of Schoenberg, Berg, and Webern.* 5th ed., rev., 54–59. Berkeley: University of California Press, 1981.

Brief analytic comments on Stravinsky's serial (but not twelve-tone) works. The Cantata, Septet, *Three Songs From William Shakespeare,* and *In Memoriam Dylan Thomas* discussed. Musical examples.

3954. Purswell, Joan. "Stravinsky's Piano Music." *Clavier*, 18, no. 1 (1979): 24–25+.

Brief overview focusing on sound and color. Musical examples and bibliography.

3955. Routh, Francis. *Stravinsky.* London: J. M. Dent and Co., 1975, 202 pp.

Brief critical and analytic commentary for the undergraduate student. Musical examples.

3956. Tangeman, Robert. "Stravinsky's Two-Piano Works." *Modern Music*, 12, no. 2 (1945): 93–98.
Brief descriptive and analytic commentary. Musical examples.

3957. Tansman, Alexandre. *Igor Stravinsky: The Man and His Music.* Translated by Therese Bleefield and Charles Bleefield. New York: G. P. Putnam's Sons, 1949, 295 pp.
Brief descriptive and critical commentary. Special remarks on *Soldier's Tale.*

3958. Troup, Malcolm. "Serial Stravinsky: The 'Granite Period' (1956–1966)." In *Twentieth Century Music.* Edited by Rollo Myers, 45–62. London: Calder and Boyers, 1968.
Some analytic comments on Stravinsky's serial works from 1956–1966.

3959. Vlad, Roman. *Stravinsky.* Translated by Frederick Fuller and Ann Fuller. 2d ed., 50–66. London: Oxford University Press, 1967.
Background and critical commentary, with musical examples. Includes discussion of *L'Histoire du Soldat (Soldier's Tale).*

3960. White, Eric Walter. *Stravinsky: The Composer and His Works.* Berkeley: University of California Press, 1966, 608 pp.
Thorough discussion of the works, providing background, critical, and analytic commentary. Musical examples.

3961. Whittall, Arnold. Music Since the First World War, 51–68, 177–183. London: J. M. Dent and Sons, 1977.
Brief analytic and stylistic comments on specific works, including those of Stravinsky's serial period.

Abraham and Isaac

3962. Payne, Anthony. "Stravinsky's *Abraham and Isaac* and *Elegy for J. F. K.*" *Tempo*, 73 (Summer 1965): 12–15.
Description of the work. Musical examples.

3963. Spies, Claudio. "Notes on Stravinsky's *Abraham and Isaac.*" In *Perspectives on Schoenberg and Stravinsky.* Rev. ed. Edited by Benjamin Boretz and E. T. Cone, 186–209. New York: W. W. Norton, 1972.
Thorough analysis for the advanced student. Musical examples.

3964. Thomas, Janet. "The Use of Color in Three Chamber Works of the Twentieth Century." *Indiana Theory Review*, 4, no. 3 (1981): 24–40.
Reveals Webern's influence on Stravinsky's later style in his adoption of the *Klangfarbenmelodie.* Musical examples.

3965. Whittall, Arnold. "Thematicism in Stravinsky's *Abraham and Isaac.*" *Tempo*, 89 (Summer 1969): 12–16.
Analysis for the advanced student. Musical examples.

Agon

3966. Machlis, Joseph. *Introduction to Contemporary Music*, 403–407. New York: W. W. Norton, 1961.
Descriptive and analytic commentary, with musical examples. For the undergraduate student.

3967. Wiesel, Meir. "Motivic Unity in Stravinsky's *Agon.*" *Orbis Musicae: Studies in Musicology*, 7 (1980–1981): 119–124.

Canticum Sacrum

3968. Deri, Otto. *Exploring Twentieth-Century Music*, 208–212. New York: Holt, Rinehart, and Winston, 1968.
Analysis of salient features of this work. Musical examples.

3969. Klein, Lothar. "Twentieth-Century Analysis: Essays in Miniature, Stravinsky: *Canticum Sacrum. Music Educators Journal*, 54 (December 1967): 51–52.
General analytical discussion of the entire work.

3970. Zinar, Ruth. "Stravinsky and His Latin Texts." *College Music Symposium*, 18, no. 2 (1978): 186–187.
A brief analysis of selected passages illustrating word-music relationships.

Concerto for Piano and Wind Instruments

3971. Benjamin, William E. "Tonality Without Fifths: Remarks on the First Movement of Stravinsky's Concerto for Piano and Wind Instruments." *In Theory Only*, 2 (February–March 1977): 53–70; 3 (May 1977): 9–31.
An extended analytical essay. Discusses the extent to which the concerto is tonal. For the advanced student.

3972. Morgan, Robert P. "Dissonant Prolongations, Perfect Fifths, and Major Thirds in Stravinsky's Piano Concerto." *In Theory Only*, 4 (August–September 1978): 3–7.
A reply to Benjamin's article (*see* item no. 3977). For the advanced student.

Concerto for Two Solo Pianos

3973. James, Thomas S. "Communications." *Perspectives of New Music*, 10, no. 1 (1971): 358–361.
Analytic remarks for the advanced student.

Double Canon in Memoriam Raoul Dufy (1959)

3974. Goldman, Richard Franko. "Current Chronicle: New York." *Musical Quarterly*, 46, no. 2 (1960): 260–264.
Review of a performance. Descriptive and critical commentary with remarks on form and historical significance.

3975. Mason, Charles Norman. "Stravinsky's Newest Works." *Tempo*, 53–54 (Spring–Summer 1960): 3–4.
Analytical observations.

Easy Pieces for Piano

3976. Chadabe, Joel "Stravinsky and His *Easy Duets* for Piano." *Piano Quarterly*, 42 (Winter 1962–1963): 14–17.
Analytical remarks on *Three Easy Pieces* (1915) and *Five Easy Pieces* (1917) for piano duet.

Elegy for J. F. K.

3977. Payne, Anthony. "Stravinsky's *Abraham and Isaac* and *Elegy for J. F. K.*" *Tempo*, 73 (Summer 1965):12–15.
Description of the work. Musical examples.

Epitaphium for the Grave of Prince Max Egon of Fürstenberg

3978. Mason, Charles Norman. "Stravinsky's Newest Works." *Tempo*, 53–54 (Spring–Summer 1960): 2–3.
Brief analysis with musical examples.

Fairy's Kiss

3979. Lang, Paul Henry, ed. *Stravinsky: A New Appraisal of His Work*, 47–60. New York: W. W. Norton, 1963.

An examination of the source material Stravinsky derived from Tchaikovsky for this ballet. Some fourteen pieces by Tchaikovsky are identified as positive sources. Musical examples.

Firebird

3980. Antokoletz, Elliott. "Interval Cycles in Stravinsky's Early Ballets." *Journal of the American Musicological Society*, 39, no. 3 (1986): 579–589.

Analytic discussion of intervallic structure. Author identifies passages in which cyclic partitions of the octave are generated from a basic cell. For the advanced student. Musical examples.

Five Fingers: "Larghetto"

3981. Forte, Allen. *Contemporary Tone-Structures*, 25–38. New York: Columbia University Press, 1955.

Thorough analysis dealing with formal structure, tonality, internal relationships, and general stylistic characteristics. Musical examples and analytic sketches.

The Flood

3982. Payne, Anthony. "Stravinsky's *The Flood*." *Tempo*, 70 (Autumn 1964): 2–8.

Analytical overview of the work. Musical examples.

Histoire du Soldat (Soldier's Tale)

3983. Craft, Robert. "*Histoire du Soldat.*" *Musical Quarterly*, 66, no. 3 (1980): 321–338.

Mainly historical information on revisions of score. Also includes evolution of the libretto and discussion of the musical sketches. Musical examples.

3984. Heyman, Barbara B. "Stravinsky and Ragtime." *Musical Quarterly*, 68, no. 4 (1982): 543–562.

Traces Stravinsky's use of ragtime prior to 1918 (*L'Histoire du Soldat*). Some analytic discussion of this work. Musical examples.

3985. Warburton, A. O. "Set Works for 'O' Level, GCE." *Music Teacher and Piano Student*, 46 (April 1967): 12.

Background, descriptive, and analytic commentary of the Suite for the undergraduate student. No musical examples.

3986.   Zur, Menachem. "Tonal Ambiguities As a Constructive Force in the Language of Stravinsky." *Musical Quarterly*, 68, no. 4 (1982): 516–526.

A detailed analytical survey, with focus on pitch relationships. Musical examples.

In Memoriam Dylan Thomas

3987.   Clemmons, W. Ronald. "The Coordination of Motivic and Harmonic Elements in the 'Dirge Canons' of Stravinsky's *In Memoriam Dylan Thomas*." *In Theory Only*, 3 (April 1977): 8–21.

3988.   Gauldin, Robert, and W. Benson. "Structure and Numerology in Stravinsky's *In Memoriam Dylan Thomas*." *Perspectives of New Music*, 23, no. 2 (1985): 166–185.

Investigates the significance of the number 5 in the structure of this work, the use of the five-tone row, and its possible origin in terms of the poem itself. Diagrams. Musical examples.

3989.   Robertson, Alec. *Requiem: Music of Mourning and Consolation*, 220–225. New York: Praeger, 1968.

Descriptive and analytic commentary. Musical examples.

Introitus (In Memoriam T. S. Eliot)

3990.   Spies, Claudio. "Some Notes on Stravinsky's Requiem Settings." In *Perspectives on Schoenberg and Stravinsky*. Rev. ed. Edited by Benjamin Boretz and E. T. Cone, 223–249. New York: W. W. Norton, 1972.

Advanced analytic commentary. Same article as cited below. Discusses the *Introitus*, as well as *Elegy for J. F. K.*, Requiem, and *Threni*. Musical examples, charts, diagrams.

3991.   Spies, Claudio. "Some Notes on Stravinsky's Requiem Settings." *Perspectives of New Music*, 5, no. 2 (1967): 98–123. *See* item no. 3990 above.

3992.   White, Eric Walter. "Two New Memorial Works by Stravinsky." *Tempo*, 74 (Autumn 1965): 20–21.

Brief remarks with musical examples.

Mavra

3993.   Campbell, Stuart. "The *Mavras* of Pushkin, Kochno, and Stravinsky." *Music and Letters*, 58, no. 3 (1977): 304–317.

Identifies similarities among the play by Pushkin, the libretto by Kochno, and *Mavra* by Stravinsky. Some analytic observations. Musical examples.

Movements for Piano and Orchestra

3994.   Boykan, Martin. " 'Neo-Classicism' and Late Stravinsky." *Perspectives of New Music*, 1, no. 2 (1963): 155–166.
A discussion of serial techniques, harmony, tonal suggestions in these works. Musical examples.

3995.   Goldman, Richard Franko. "Current Chronicle: New York." *Musical Quarterly*, 46, no. 2 (1960): 260–264.
In this review of a performance, the intent and place of Movements and the *Double Canon* in Stravinsky's artistic development and to music in general is assessed. Some comments on structure accompanied by historical observations.

3996.   Keller, Hans. "No Bridge to Nowhere." *Musical Times*, 102 (March 1961): 156–158.
A descriptive and analytical introduction to this work, including a brief comparison of the twelve-tone technique to that of the Schoenberg Violin Concerto.

3997.   Mason, Colin. "Stravinsky's Newest Works." *Tempo*, 53–54 (Spring–Summer 1960): 4–10.
Brief analyses of all five movements. Musical examples.

Les Noces

3998.   Lanchbery, John. "Stravinsky Peasants and Pianos." *About the House*, 2, no. 2 (1966): 40–42.
Historical background, genesis, thematic correspondences with other works, and analytical observations. Musical examples.

Oedipus Rex

3999.   Deri, Otto. *Exploring Twentieth-Century Music*, 196–200. New York: Holt, Rinehart, and Winston. 1968.
Analytic remarks on selected sections of this work. Musical examples.

4000.   Holmberg, Arthur. "Too Deep for Tears (Sophocles' *Oedipus Tyrannus* and Stravinsky's Music)." *Opera News*, 48 (February 18, 1984): 30–33.
An examination of Stravinsky's setting of Sophocles' play, focusing on the reasons behind the choice of a Latin text. Verdi's influ-

ence examined, as well as how the music succeeds in capturing and translating the mood of fifth-century Athens to the twentieth century.

4001. Lang, Paul Henry, ed. *Stravinsky: A New Appraisal of His Work,* 35–46. New York: W. W. Norton, 1963.
Thorough discussion and analysis for the undergraduate student. Musical examples.

4002. Mellers, Wilfrid. "Stravinsky's *Oedipus* As Twentieth-Century Hero." *Musical Quarterly,* 48, no. 3 (1962): 300–312.
Traces symbolism present in *Oedipus Rex* by means of tonal analysis. Philosophic discussion of how Stravinsky's style reflects the artistic problems of the twentieth century. Musical examples.

4003. Sessions, Roger. "On *Oedipus Rex.*" *Modern Music,* 3 (March–April 1928): 9–15.
Mainly critical commentary by a distinguished composer. Some analytic observations. Musical examples.

4004. Whittall, Arnold. *Music Since the First World War,* 57–61. London: J. M. Dent, 1977.
Analytic discussions focusing on form and tonality. Musical examples.

4005. Zinar, Ruth. "Stravinsky and His Latin Texts." *College Music Symposium,* 18, no. 2 (1978): 178–181.
A brief analysis of selected passages illustrating word-music relationships of the score

Petrushka

4006. Antokoletz, Elliott. "Interval Cycles in Stravinsky's Early Ballets." *Journal of the American Musicological Society,* 39, no. 3 (1986): 589–600.
Analytic discussion of intervallic structure. Author identifies passages in which cyclic partitions of the octave are generated from a basic cell. For the advanced student. Musical examples.

4007. Boretz, Benjamin. "Meta-Variations, Part 4: Analytic Fallout (2)." *Perspectives of New Music,* 11, no. 2 (Spring–Summer 1973): 167–175.
Highly technical analysis to "help locate the relevant syntactical basis" of the work. Musical examples.

4008. Deri, Otto. *Exploring Twentieth-Century Music*, 172–182. New York: Holt, Rinehart, and Winston, 1968.
> Full, descriptive commentary, with analytic observations. Musical examples.

4009. Forte, Allen. *Contemporary Tone-Structures*, 128–138. New York: Columbia University Press, 1955.
> Thorough analysis dealing with formal structure, tonality, internal relationships, and general stylistic characteristics. Musical examples and analytic sketches.

4010. Warburton, A. O. "Set Works for 'O' Level, GCE." *Music Teacher*, 47 (January 1968): 10 + .
> Brief analytic commentary for the undergraduate student.

Piano-Rag-Music

4011. Heyman, Barbara B. "Stravinsky and Ragtime." *Musical Quarterly*, 68, no. 4 (1982): 543–562.
> Traces Stravinsky's use of ragtime prior to 1918 (*L'Histoire du Soldat*). Overview of ragtime form, analysis of *Piano-Rag-Music*. Musical examples.

4012. Joseph, Charles M. "Structural Coherence in Stravinsky's *Piano-Rag-Music*." *Music Theory Spectrum*, 4 (1982): 76–91.
> An examination of set-theoretic relationships (Forte set names are used). For the advanced student.

Piano Scherzo (1902)

4013. Joseph, Charles M. "Stravinsky's Piano Scherzo (1902) in Perspective: A New Starting Point." *Musical Quarterly*, 67, no. 1 (1981): 82–93.
> Mainly historical background, with some analysis on how this work affected later works. Musical examples.

Pieces (Three) for String Quartet

4014. Cogan, Robert, and Pozzi Escot. *Sonic Design: The Nature of Sound and Music*, 276–285. Englewood Cliffs, NJ: Prentice-Hall, 1976.
> Discussion of tempo, pulse, and rhythm. Second movement only.

The Rake's Progress

4015. Cooke, Deryck. "*The Rake* and the Eighteenth Century." *Musical Times*, 103 (January 1962): 20–23.
> Analytical remarks with musical examples. Also, critical appraisal of Stravinsky's imitation of eighteenth-century musical style.

4016. Griffiths, Paul. *Igor Stravinsky: "The Rake's Progress."* London: Cambridge University Press, 1982, 107 pp.

The composer's own views; Robert Craft on the libretto; a synopsis, performance history and analysis of Act III, Scene II (Graveyard Scene). Musical examples, bibliography, discography.

4017. Watkins, Glenn. *Soundings: Music in the Twentieth Century,* 320–326. New York: Schirmer Books, 1987.

Background, descriptive, and analytic commentary. Musical examples.

Requiem Canticles

4018. Payne, Anthony. "Requiem Canticles." *Tempo,* 81 (Summer 1967): 10–19.

A general discussion of the work, including analytic observations about the structure of the tone rows and their use as the motivic material of the composition. Musical examples.

4019. Salzman, Eric. "Current Chronicle: Princeton." *Musical Quarterly,* 53, no. 1 (1967): 80–86.

Light analysis comparing earlier works. Musical examples.

4020. Souvtchinsky, Pierre. "Thoughts on Stravinsky's Requiem Canticles." *Tempo,* 86 (Autumn 1986): 6–7.

Brief critical remarks.

4021. Spies, Claudio. "Communications." *Perspectives of New Music,* 6, no. 1 (1967): 160.

Corrections and further insights to Spies's article cited below (*see* item no. 4022).

4022. Spies, Claudio. "Some Notes on Stravinsky's Requiem Settings." In *Perspectives on Schoenberg and Stravinsky.* Rev. ed. Edited by Benjamin Borez and E. T. Cone, 223–249. New York: W. W. Norton, 1972.

Advanced analytic commentary. Musical examples, charts, diagrams.

4023. White, Eric Walter. "Stravinsky's Requiem Canticles." *Tempo,* 79 (Winter 1966–1967): 10–19.

Thorough analysis, with musical examples. Advanced.

The Rite of Spring

4024. Antokoletz, Elliott. "Interval Cycles in Stravinsky's Early Ballets." *Journal of the American Musicological Society,* 39, no. 3 (1986): 600–614.

Analytic discussion of intervallic structure. Author identifies passages in which cyclic partitions of the octave are generated from a basic cell. For the advanced student. Musical examples.

4025.   Craft, Robert. *"The Rite of Spring*: Genesis of a Masterpiece."* *Perspectives of New Music*, 5, no. 1 (1969): 20–36.
Background and performance history. Some analytic remarks.

4026.   Forte, Allen. *The Harmonic Organization of "The Rite of Spring"*. New Haven: Yale University Press, 1978, 151 pp.
Book-length advanced theoretical analysis. Musical examples.

4027.   Hansen, Peter. *An Introduction to Twentieth Century Music.* 2d ed., 48–55. Boston: Allyn and Bacon, 1967.
Clear descriptive commentary demonstrating how Stravinsky achieves his effects. For the undergraduate student. Musical examples.

4028.   Kerman, Joseph. *Listen.* 2d ed., 330–333. New York: Worth Publishers, 1976.
Analysis with musical examples. For the undergraduate student.

4029.   Machlis, Joseph. *Introduction to Contemporary Music*, 174–177. New York: W. W. Norton, 1961.
Brief descriptive commentary, with musical examples. For the undergraduate student.

4030.   Morton, Lawrence. "Footnotes to Stravinsky Studies: *Le Sacre du Printemps.*" *Tempo*, 128 (March 1979): 9–16.
The idea for *The Rite of Spring* traced to its origins and the folk melodies within identified. Musical examples and bibiliography.

4031.   Siddons, James. "Rhythmic Structures in *Le Sacre du Printemps (Danse Sacrale).*" *Musical Analysis*, 1, no. 1 (1972): 6–11.

4032.   Taruskin, Richard. "Russian Folk Melodies in *The Rite of Spring.*" *Journal of the American Musicological Society*, 33, no. 3 (1980): 501–543.

4033.   Travis, Roy. "Towards a New Concept of Tonality?" *Journal of Music Theory*, 3 (November 1959): 257–284.
Deals with tonality and structure in the first nine measures. For the beginning student.

4034.   Warburton, A. O. "Set Works for 'O' Level, GCE." *Music Teacher*, 51 (January 1972): 13–15; (December 1972): 20–21.
Analysis for the undergraduate student. No musical examples.

4035. Watkins, Glenn. *Soundings: Music in the Twentieth Century,* 211–221. New York: Schirmer Books, 1987.

Literary background, composition history, and analytic observations on some musically significant sections. Analytic overview by section concludes the volume. Musical examples.

4036. Whittall, Arnold. "Music Analysis As Human Science? *Le Sacre du Printemps* in Theory and Practice." *Music Analysis,* 1, no. 1 (1981): 33–53.

Analytic observations on the technique of generating dissonance or conflict within diatonicism. Musical examples.

Serenade in A Major

4037. Schmid, Angeline. "Stravinsky's Serenade en La." *Clavier,* 21, no. 10 (1982): 29–30.

Brief analytic and descriptive commentary. Musical examples.

A Sermon, a Narrative, and a Prayer

4038. Austin, William W. *Music in the Twentieth Century,* 528–531. New York: W. W. Norton, 1966.

Brief analysis with chart and musical examples.

4039. Boykan, Martin. " 'Neoclassicism' and Late Stravinsky." *Perspectives of New Music,* 1, no. 2 (1963): 155–169.

A discussion of serial techniques, harmony, tonal references, in this work and other works of this period. Musical examples.

4040. Clifton, Thomas. "Types of Symmetrical Relations in Stravinsky's *A Sermon, a Narrative, and a Prayer.*" *Perspectives of New Music,* 9, no. 1 (1970): 96–112.

4041. Mason, Charles Norman. "Stravinsky's New Work." *Tempo,* 59 (Autumn 1961): 5–14.

Serial analyses of all three movements. Musical examples.

4042. Morton, Lawrence. "Current Chronicle: Ojai, California." *Musical Quarterly,* 48, no. 3 (1962): 392–396.

Analytic remarks with musical examples.

4043. Wilkey, Jay W. "Igor Stravinsky's Cantata *A Sermon, a Narrative, and a Prayer.*" *Choral Journal,* 10, no. 2 (1969): 14–19.

An examination of the work for the choral conductor, including stylistic characteristics. Discusses "structural form" and "inner form." Musical examples.

Sonata for Piano (1924)

4044.   Rajna, Thomas. "Stravinsky's Piano Works." *Composer* (London), 29 (Autumn 1968): 6–7.
   Brief analytic commentary.

Sonata for Two Pianos

4045.   Burkhart, Charles. "Stravinsky's Revolving Canon." *Music Review*, 29, no. 3 (1968): 161–164.
   An analysis of the "mirror canon" in the theme of the "Theme and Variations" movement (second movement). Musical examples.

4046.   Johns, D. C. "An Early Serial Idea of Stravinsky." *Music Review*, 23, no. 4 (1962): 305–313.
   An analysis of the second movement ("Theme and Variations"). Musical examples.

Songs (Three) from William Shakespeare

4047.   Hantz, Edwin. "Exempli Gratia: What You Hear Is What You Get." *In Theory Only*, 2 (April–May 1976): 51–54.
   Advanced analytic commentary. Musical examples.

Symphonies of Wind Instruments

4048.   Bowles, R. W. "Stravinsky's Symphonies of Wind Instruments for Twenty-Three Winds: An Analysis." *Journal of Band Research*, 15, no. 1 (1979): 32–37.

4049.   Cone, Edward T. "Stravinsky: The Progress of a Method." In *Perspectives on Schoenberg and Stravinsky*. Rev. ed. Edited by Benjamin Boretz and E. T. cone, 159–160. New York: W. W. Norton, 1972.
   Brief but dense analysis for the advanced theory student.

4050.   Somfai, Laszlo. "Symphonies for Wind Instruments (1920)— Observations on Stravinsky's Organic Construction." *Studia Musicologica*, 14, nos. 1–4 (1972): 355–383.

4051.   Tyra, Thomas. "An Analysis of Stravinsky's Symphonies of Wind Instruments." *Journal of Band Research*, 8, no. 2 (1972): 6–39.
Discussion of derivation of thematic material, melodic and harmonic devices, and structural problems. Formal analysis included. Musical examples.

4052.   White, Eric Walter. *Stravinsky: The Composer and His Works*, 253–260. Berkeley: University of California Press, 1966.
Solid analytic commentary.

Symphony in C

4053.   Dahl, Ingolf. "Stravinsky in 1946." *Modern Music*, 12, no. 3 (1946): 159–165.
Analysis. Musical examples.

4054.   Lang, Paul Henry, ed. *Stravinsky: A New Appraisal of His Work*, 25–30. New York: W. W. Norton, 1963.
Full, detailed analysis.

4055.   Vlad, Roman. *Stravinsky.* Translated by Frederick Fuller and Ann Fuller. 2d ed., 136–146. London: Oxford University Press, 1967.
Detailed analysis, with musical examples.

4056.   White, Eric Walter. *Stravinsky: The Composer and His Works*, 364–370. Berkeley: University of California Press, 1966.
Background and analysis. Musical examples.

4057.   Whittall, Arnold. *Music Since the First World War*, 61–64. London: J. M. Dent, 1977.
Analytic discussion focusing on form and tonality.

4058.   Williams, B. M. "Time and the Structure of Stravinsky's Symphony in C." *Musical Quarterly*, 59, no. 3 (1973): 355–369.

Symphony in E Flat

4059.   White, Eric Walter. *Stravinsky: The Composer and His Works*, 138–139. Berkeley: University of California Press, 1966.
Brief descriptive remarks.

Symphony in Three Movements

4060.   Austin, William W. *Music in the Twentieth Century*, 337–341. New York: W. W. Norton, 1966.
Brief analytic commentary, with chart outlining chief motifs and unifying tonal elements. Musical examples.

4061. Stedman, Preston. *The Symphony*, 320–325. Englewood Cliffs, NJ: Prentice-Hall, 1979.
Description and analytic breakdown of each movement. Musical examples and diagram.

4062. White, Eric Walter. *Stravinsky: The Composer and His Works*, 389–397. Berkeley: University of California Press, 1966.
Analytic commentary. Musical examples.

Symphony of Psalms

4063. Austin, William W. *Music in the Twentieth Century*, 333–335. New York: W. W. Norton, 1966.
Brief but concentrated analysis.

4064. Burnau, John. "Stravinsky's Symphony of Psalms." *Instrumentalist*, 23 (December 1968): 60–62.
Analytic observations with musical examples.

4065. Chittum, Donald. "Compositional Similarities in Beethoven and Stravinsky." *Music Review*, 30, no. 4 (1969): 285–290.
Discussion of the similarity of motivic and harmonic plan of Beethoven's Ninth Symphony and Stravinsky's Symphony of Psalms. Musical examples.

4066. Cone, Edward T. "Stravinsky: The Progress of a Method." In *Perspectives on Schoenberg and Stravinsky*. Rev. ed. Edited by Benjamin Boretz and E. T. Cone, 161–162. New York: W. W. Norton, 1972.
Brief but concentrated analysis focusing on stratification. For the advanced student.

4067. Hansen, Peter. *An Introduction to Twentieth Century Music*. 2d ed., 169–173. Boston: Allyn and Bacon, 1967.
Compositional history, scoring, texts, and counterpoint discussed in this brief descriptive commentary. For the undergraduate student. Musical examples.

4068. Machlis, Joseph. *Introduction to Contemporary Music*, 180–183. New York: W. W. Norton, 1961.
Descriptive and analytical comments for the undergraduate student and musical amateur.

4069. Mellers, Wilfrid. "1930: Symphony of Psalms." *Tempo*, 97 (1971): 19–27.
Extensive analysis, with musical examples.

4070. Salzman, Eric. *Twentieth Century Music: An Introduction.* 2d ed. 208–214. Englewood Cliffs, NJ: Prentice-Hall, 1974.
  Brief analysis outlining the tonal structure of each movement. Musical examples.

4071. Stephens, Howard. "Stravinsky: The Symphony of Psalms." *Music Teacher*, 55 (November 1976): 14–15.
  Analysis of forms and thematic content. For the undergraduate student.

4072. Stravinsky, Igor, and Robert Craft. "A Quintet of Dialogues." *Perspectives of New Music*, 1, no. 1 (1962): 15–17.
  Stravinsky's remarks on the *Symphony of Psalms*.

4073. Ulrich, Homer. *Music: A Design for Listening*, 434–436. New York: Harcourt, Brace, 1957.
  Analytic/descriptive breakdown by measures. Musical examples.

4074. Vlad, Roman. *Stravinsky.* Translated by Frederick Fuller and Ann Fuller. 2d ed., 154–164. London: Oxford University Press, 1967.
  Detailed analysis, with musical examples.

4075. Walsh, Stephen. "Stravinsky's Choral Music." *Tempo*, 81 (Summer 1967): 41–51.
  An overview of Stravinsky's choral music, with emphasis on this work. Musical examples.

4076. Watkins, Glenn. Soundings: Music in the Twentieth Century, 467–470. New York: Schirmer Books, 1987.
  Brief remarks on structure. Musical examples.

4077. White, Eric Walter. *Stravinsky: The Composer and His Works*, 320–328. Berkeley: University of California Press, 1966.
  Solid analytic commentary.

4078. Young, Percy M. *The Choral Tradition*, 300–304. New York: W. W. Norton, 1971.
  Background and brief analysis, with musical examples.

4079. Zinar, Ruth. "Stravinsky and His Latin Texts." *College Music Symposium*, 18, no. 2 (1978): 181–183.
  Brief analysis of selected passages illustrating word-music relationships of the score.

Threni

4080.   Zinar, Ruth. "Stravinsky and His Latin Texts." *College Music Symposium*, 18, no. 2 (1978): 183–185.
A brief analysis of selected passages illustrating word-music relationships of the score. Musical examples.

Variations (In Memoriam Aldous Huxley)

4081.   Kohl, Jerome. "Exposition in Stravinsky's Orchestral Variations." *Perspectives of New Music*, 18, nos. 1–2 (1980–1981): 391 +.
A detailed examination of pitch organization in the first variation. For the advanced student. Musical examples.

4082.   Phillips, Paul S. "The Enigma of Variations: A Study of Stravinsky's Final Work for Orchestra." *Music Analysis*, 3, no. 1 (1984): 69–89.
Analyzes the eleven variations, as well as the composite structure. For the advanced student.

4083.   Spies, Claudio. "Notes on Stravinsky's Variations." In *Perspectives on Schoenberg and Stravinsky*. Rev. ed. Edited by Benjamin Boretz and E. T. Cone, 210–222. New York: W. W. Norton, 1972.
Same article as cited below (*see* item no. 4084).

4084.   Spies, Claudio. "Notes on Stravinsky's Variations." *Perspectives of New Music*, 4, no. 1 (1965): 62–74.
Thorough analysis for the advanced student. Musical examples, charts, diagrams.

DISSERTATIONS AND THESES

General

4085.   Brantley, John Paul. "The Serial Choral Music of Igor Stravinsky." Ph.D., University of Iowa, 1978, 453 pp., DA 39-4577A-8A.

4086.   Reade, Eugene Walter. "A Study of Rhythm in the Serial Works of Igor Stravinsky." Ph.D., Indiana University, 1979, 287 pp., DA 40-1743A.

4087.   Wolterink, Charles Paul. "Harmonic Structure and Organization in the Early Works of Igor Stravinskii, 1952–1957." Ph.D., Stanford University, 1979, 373 pp., DA 39-7050A.

Abraham and Isaac

4088.   Buell, Timothy John. "Aspects of Stravinsky's *Abraham and Isaac*. Ph.D., University of Pittsburgh, 1986, 81 pp., DA 47-4225A.

Agon

4089.   Wilson, Mark Edwards. "An Analysis of Igor Stravinsky's *Agon*." Ph.D., University of California at Los Angeles, 1974, 89 pp., DA 35-5458A.

Octet for Wind Instruments

4090.   Kielian-Gilbert, Marianne Catherine. "Pitch-Class Function, Centricity, and Symmetry As Transposition Relations in Two Works of Stravinsky." Ph.D., University of Michigan, 1981, 278 pp., DA 42-908A.

Petrushka

4091.   Hallquist, Robert Nels, Jr. "Stravinsky and the Transcriptional Process: An Analytical and Historical Study of *Petrouchka*." D.M.A., North Texas State, 1979, 74 pp., DA 40–1142A.

Pieces (Three) for String Quartet

4092.   Kielian-Gilbert, Marianne Catherine. "Pitch-Class Function, Centricity, and Symmetry as Transposition Relations in Two Works of Stravinsky." Ph.D., University of Michigan, 1981, 278 pp., DA 42-908A.

The Rake's Progress

4093.   Danes, Robert Harold. "Stravinsky's *The Rake's Progress*: Paradigm of Neoclassic Opera." Ph.D., Washington University, 1972, 242 pp., DA 33-4452A.

Requiem Canticles

4094.   Cole, Vincent Lewis. "Analyses of *Symphony of Psalms* (1930, rev. 1948) and Requiem Canticles (1966) by Igor Stravinsky." Ph.D., University of California at Los Angeles, 1980, 143 pp., DA 41-4879A.

4095.   Kresky, Jeffrey Jay. "Requiem Canticles: A Study in Analysis." Ph.D., Princeton University, 1974, 125 pp., DA 35-3038A.

4096.   Lockwood, Larry Paul. "Rhythmic Analysis: A Theory, a Methodology, and a Study of Stravinsky's Requiem Canticles." D.M.A., Cornell University, 1975, 113 pp., DA 36-1893A-4A.

Symphony in Three Movements

4097.   Tashjian, Beatrice Chapman. "Stravinsky's Symphony in Three Movements: An Analysis." D.M., Northwestern University, 1985, 63 pp., DA 46-838A.

Symphony of Psalms

4098.   Cole, Vincent Lewis. "Analyses of Symphony of Psalms (1930, rev. 1948) and Requiem Canticles (1966)." Ph.D., University of California at Los Angeles, 1980, 143 pp., DA 41-4879A.

SUBOTNICK, MORTON, 1933–

Serenade No. 1

4099.   Perkins, John M. "Morton Subotnick: Serenade No. 1." *Perspectives of New Music*, 2, no. 2 (1964): 100–105.
   An analytic discussion. Musical examples.

Touch

4100.   Schrader, Barry. *Introduction to Electro-Acoustic Music*, 131–134. Englewood Cliffs, NJ: Prentice-Hall, 1982.
   Analytic comments.

SWEELINCK, JAN, 1562–1621

General

4101.   Curtis, Alan. *Sweelinck's Keyboard Music*. London: Oxford University Press, 1969, 243 pp.
   Background, historical significance of Sweelinck's music, and a discussion of his style. Musical examples.

DISSERTATIONS AND THESES

4102.   Spacht, Thomas. "Sweelinck's Organ Music: A Study of Structure and Style." D.M.A., University of Rochester, Eastman School of Music, 1975, 82 pp., DA 38-1109A.

SZYMANOWSKI, KAROL, 1882–1937

General

4103.   Beechey, Gwilyn. "Karol Szymanowski (1882–1937) and His Piano Music." *Musical Opinion*, 106 (October 1982): 5–16 + .
An overview of Szymanowski's piano works, with interspersed analytic comments.

4104.   Martin, Walter. "Karol Szymanowski: The Unknown Song Composer." *NATS Bulletin*, 39, no. 2 (1982): 18–23 + .
Extensive overview focusing on stylistic traits. Many analytic observations. Musical examples and bibliography.

Mazurkas, Op. 50

4105.   McNamee, Ann. "Bitonality, Mode, and Interval in the Music of Karol Szymanowski." *Journal of Music Theory*, 29, no. 1 (1985): 61–84.

DISSERTATIONS AND THESES

General

4106.   Kosakowski, Ann Louise. "Karol Szymanowski's Mazurkas: Cyclic Structure and Harmonic Language." Ph.D., Yale University, 1980, 329 pp., DA 43-2488A.

Masques, Op. 34

4107.   Fletcher, Marylynn Louise. "Pitch Constructions in the Masques, Op. 34 of Karol Szymanowski." D.M.A., University of Texas at Austin, 1984, 85 pp., DA 45-1907A.

Masque No. 3

4108.   Coulter, Beverly Norton. "The Affective Nature of the Harmonic Content in the Third Masque of Karol Szymanowski." D.M.A., University of Miami, 1985, 73 pp., DA 47-341A.

Sonatas for Piano

4109.   Godes, Catherine Anne. "Stylistic Evolution in Szymanowski's Three Piano Sonatas." D.M.A., University of Cincinnati, 1984, 97 pp., DA 46-550A.

TAKEMITSU, TORU, 1930–

Water Music

4110.   Schrader, Barry. *Introduction to Electro-Acoustic Music*, 47–49. Englewood Cliffs, NJ: Prentice-Hall, 1982.
   Analytic comments.

TALLIS, THOMAS, c. 1505–1585

General

4111.   Doe, Paul. *Tallis.* London: Oxford University Press, 1968, 71 pp.
   Part of the "Oxford Studies of Composers," this volume provides an analytic overview of the music. Chapters on: The Old Tradition; Ritual Music of the Mid-Century; The Elizabethan Motets; English Church Music; Instrumental Music. For the intermediate to advanced undergraduate student. Musical examples.

4112.   Kerman, Joseph. "Byrd, Tallis, and the Art of Imitation." In *Aspects of Medieval and Renaissance Music: A Birthday Offering to Gustave Reese.* Edited by Jan La Rue, 519–537. New York: W. W. Norton, 1966.
   Graduate and faculty level discussion of the use of imitation as compared to Tallis's use of the technique. Musical examples.

DISSERTATIONS AND THESES

General

4113.   Hansard, Mary Ethyl Patricia. "The Vocal Polyphonic Style of the Latin Church Music by Thomas Tallis (c. 1505–1585)." D.M.A., University of Kentucky, 1974, 211 pp., DA 32-5266A-7A.

Anthems

4114.   Mayer, Karl Eby. "The Anthems of Thomas Tallis." D.M.A., University of Rochester, Eastman School of Music, 1980, 472 pp., DA 41-2347A.

Lamentations

4115.   Klimisch, Sister Mary Jane. "The Music of the Lamentations: Historical and Analytical Aspects." Ph.D., Washington University, 1971, 200 pp., DA 32-5268A.

TAVERNER, JOHN, c. 1490–1545

General

4116.   Hand, Colin. *John Taverner: His Life and Music.* London: Eulenberg, 1978, 128 pp.
The music, as found in the approximately forty surviving sacred works, is analyzed.

4117.   Josephson, David S. *John Taverner: Tudor Composer.* Ann Arbor: UMI Research Press, 1979, 283 pp.
A published doctoral dissertation dealing with Taverner's life and works. Taverner's church music and songs are discussed analytically with musical examples. Advanced.

TCHAIKOVSKY, PYOTR ILYICH, 1840–1893

General

4118.   Abraham, Gerald, ed. *The Music of Tchaikovsky.* New York: W. W. Norton, 1946, 277 pp.
Thorough discussion of Tchaikovsky's output, with background and analytic commentary. Musical examples and charts showing structure.

4119.   Abraham, Gerald. *Slavonic and Romantic Music,* 116–177. New York: St. Martin's Press, 1968.
Survey of all ten Tchaikovsky operas, including plot action and description of musical characteristics. Musical influences on Tchaikovsky are mentioned.

4120. Evans, Edwin. *Tchaikovsky.* 1906. Reprint. London: J. M. Dent and Sons, 1966, 266 pp.
Brief descriptive commentary, with remarks on structure, themes, and other general musical features. Musical examples.

4121. Ferguson, Donald N. *Image and Structure in Chamber Music,* 222–225. Minneapolis: University of Minnesota Press, 1964.
Brief analytic remarks.

4122. Garden, Edward. *Tchaikovsky.* London: J. M. Dent and Sons, 1973, 194 pp.
Critical and analytic commentary for the undergraduate student. Musical examples.

4123. Mason, Colin. "The Chamber Music." In *The Music of Tchaikovsky.* Edited by Gerald Abraham, 104–113. New York: W. W. Norton, 1946.
Critical and analytic commentary, with musical examples.

4124. Newmarch, Rosa. *Tchaikovsky.* London: William Reeves, 1908, 418 pp.
Background, descriptive commentary, with analytic observations suitable for the musical amateur or beginning student. Musical examples.

Album for Children: Twenty-Four Easy Pieces, Op. 39

4125. Brown, David. *Tchaikovsky: A Biographical and Critical Study.* Vol. 2, *The Crisis Years (1874–1878),* 277–278. New York: W. W. Norton, 1982.
Brief analytic and critical remarks. Musical examples.

Children's Songs (Sixteen)

4126. Brown, David. *Tchaikovsky: A Biographical and Critical Study.* Vol. 3, *The Years of Wandering (1878–1885),* 236–238. London: Victor Gollancz, 1986.
Brief analytic comments. Musical examples.

Concert Fantasia for Piano and Orchestra in G Major, Op. 56

4127. Brown, David. *Tchaikovsky: A Biographical and Critical Study.* Vol. 3, *The Years of Wandering (1878–1885),* 278–282. London: Victor Gollancz, 1986.
Brief analytic comments. Musical examples.

Concertos

4128.   Hill, Ralph, ed. *The Concerto*, 219–233. London: Penguin Books, 1952.
Critical and analytic commentary for the undergraduate student. Musical examples.

4129.   Veinus, Abraham. *The Concerto.* Rev. ed., 243–252. New York: Dover Publications, 1964.
General remarks of a historical and critical nature. Not analytic.

4130.   Warrack, John. *Tchaikovsky: Symphonies and Concertos.* Seattle: University of Washington Press, 1969, 65 pp.
Analytic and critical commentary intended for the undergraduate student. Musical examples.

Concerto for Piano No. 1, Op. 23 in B-Flat Minor

4131.   Brown, David. *Tchaikovsky: A Biographical and Critical Study.* Vol. 2, *The Crisis Years (1874–1878)*, 15–27. New York: W. W. Norton, 1982.
Background, analysis and critical assessments. Diagram of the form of the first movement. Musical examples.

4132.   Friskin, James. "The Text of Tchaikovsky's B-Flat Minor Concerto." *Music and Letters*, 50, no. 2 (1969): 246–251.
The Dannreuther revisions of the second edition are discussed. Not an analysis.

4133.   Garden, Edward. "A Note on Tchaikovsky's First Piano Concerto." *Musical Times*, 122 (April 1981): 238–239.
A brief speculation on thematic unity in the first movement. Musical examples.

4134.   Garden, Edward. "Three Russian Piano Concertos." *Music and Letters*, 60, no. 2 (1979): 174–179.
Historic and descriptive commentary on this work, with analytic remarks. Musical examples.

Concerto for Piano No. 2, Op. 44 in G Major

4135.   Brown, David. *Tchaikovsky: A Biographical and Critical Study.* Vol. 3, *The Years of Wandering (1878–1885)*, 81–89. London: Victor Gollancz, 1986.

Analytic discussion and critical assessment. Includes discussion of melodic invention, structure, and tonality. Diagram and musical examples.

Concerto for Violin, Op. 35 in D Major

4136. Brown, David. *Tchaikovsky: A Biographical and Critical Study.* Vol. 2, *The Crisis Years (1874–1878)*, 261–269. New York: W. W. Norton, 1982.

Description of the structure, with analytic and critical commentary. Musical examples.

4137. Nelson, Wendell. *The Concerto,* 77–79. Dubuque, IA: William C. Brown, 1969.

Analysis with critical commentary. Musical examples.

Eugen Onegin

4138. Abraham, Gerald. *Slavonic and Romantic Music,* 142–149. New York: St. Martin's Press, 1968.

Plot synopsis, including discussion of revision. Analytic comments.

4139. Brown, David. *Tchaikovsky: A Biographical and Critical Study.* Vol. 2, *The Crisis Years (1874–1878)*, 176–219. New York: W. W. Norton, 1982.

Extended discussion, including compositional history, an account of the first performance and critical reaction, plot, summary, analytic and critical commentary. Includes discussion of tonalities, characterization, and of recurrent themes and motifs. Musical examples.

Francesca da Rimimi

4140. Brown, David. *Tchaikovsky: A Biographical and Critical Study.* Vol. 2, *The Crisis Years (1874–1878)*, 106–116. New York: W. W. Norton, 1982.

Background, assessment of stylistic debt to Wagner, and a critical and analytic discussion. Musical examples.

Iolanthe

4141. Abraham, Gerald. *Slavonic and Romantic Music,* 173–177. New York: St. Martin's Press, 1968.

Plot synopsis and analytic commentary. Musical examples.

4142. Lloyd-Jones, David. "A Background to *Iolanthe*." *Musical Times*, 109 (March 1968): 225–226.

Background and performance history. A few critical remarks on the music.

Liturgy of St. John Chrysostom, Op. 40

4143. Brown, David. *Tchaikovsky: A Biographical and Critical Study.* Vol. 2, *The Crisis Years (1874–1878)*, 283–286. New York: W. W. Norton, 1982.

Brief analytic and critical discussion. Musical examples.

Maid of Orleans

4144. Abraham, Gerald. *Slavonic and Romantic Music*, 149–155. New York: St. Martin's Press, 1968.

Plot synopsis and analytic comments. Musical examples.

4145. Brown, David. *Tchaikovsky: A Biographical and Critical Study.* Vol. 3, *The Years of Wandering (1878–1885)*, 37–61. London: Victor Gollancz, 1986.

Plot synopsis; discussion of dramatic effectiveness; musical characterization; harmony and tonality discussed. Musical examples.

Manfred Symphony

4146. Brown, David. *Tchaikovsky: A Biographical and Critical Study.* Vol. 3, *The Years of Wandering (1878–1885)*, 306–321. London: Victor Gollancz, 1986.

Analytic discussion of themes, structure, program, and thematic evolution. Musical examples.

Mazeppa

4147. Abraham, Gerald. *Slavonic and Romantic Music*, 155–160. New York: St. Martin's Press, 1968.

Plot synopsis and analytic commentary. Musical examples.

4148. Brown, David. *Tchaikovsky: A Biographical and Critical Study.* Vol. 3, *The Years of Wandering (1878–1885)*, 179–204. London: Victor Gollancz, 1986.

Plot synopsis. Discussion of relationship to Pushkin's poem, Tchaikovsky's use of folksong, tonality, and characterization. Musical examples.

Moscow

4149. Brown, David. *Tchaikovsky: A Biographical and Critical Study.* Vol. 3, *The Years of Wandering (1878–1885)*, 214–218. London: Victor Gollancz, 1986.

Analytic comments. Musical examples.

The Nutcracker Suite

4150. Wiles, Edward. "Tchaikovsky's *Casse Noisette.*" *Music Teacher*, 56 (June 1977): 15–17.

Discusses each piece of this suite for thematic treatment, harmony, and form.

Oprichnik

4151. Abraham, Gerald. *Slavonic and Romantic Music*, 128–133. New York: St. Martin's Press, 1968.

Plot synopsis and analytic comments. Musical examples.

4152. Brown, David. *Tchaikovsky: A Biographical and Critical Study.* Vol. 2, *The Crisis Years (1874–1878)*, 221–245. New York: W. W. Norton, 1982.

Background, analysis, and critical assessment. Musical examples.

Quartet for Strings No. 1, Op. 11 in D Major

4153. Brown, David. *Tchaikovsky: A Biographical and Critical Study.* Vol. 1, *The Early Years (1840–1874)*, 216–220. New York: W. W. Norton, 1978.

Background, analysis, and critical assessment. Musical examples.

Quartet for Strings No. 2, Op. 22 in F Major

4154. Brown, David. *Tchaikovsky: A Biographical and Critical Study.* Vol. 1, *The Early Years (1840–1874)*, 298–305. New York: W. W. Norton, 1978.

Analytic and critical commentary, with a chart of structure. Musical examples.

Quartet for Strings No. 3, Op. 30 in E-Flat Minor

4155. Brown, David. *Tchaikovsky: A Biographical and Critical Study.* Vol. 2, *The Crisis Years (1874–1878)*, 61–66. New York: W. W. Norton, 1982.

Analytic and critical commentary. Musical examples.

The Queen of Spades

4156. Abraham, Gerald. *Slavonic and Romantic Music,* 166–173. New York: St. Martin's Press, 1968.
Plot synopsis and analytic comments. Musical examples.

4157. Jefferson, Alan. "Tchaikovsky's Card-Sharp Countess." *Music and Musicians,* 15 (October 1966): 16–17.
Brief background and critical commentary, with musical examples.

Romances, Opp. 25, 27, 28, 38

4158. Brown, David. *Tchaikovsky: A Biographical and Critical Study.* Vol. 2, *The Crisis Years (1874–1878),* 30–40, 281–282. New York: W. W. Norton, 1982.
Critical commentary, with analytic observations and musical examples.

Romances (Seven), Op. 47

4159. Brown, David. *Tchaikovsky: A Biographical and Critical Study.* Vol. 3, *The Years of Wandering (1878–1885),* 109–112. London: Victor Gollancz, 1986.
Brief analytic comments. Musical examples.

Romances (Six), Op. 63

4160. Brown, David. *Tchaikovsky: A Biographical and Critical Study.* Vol. 3, *The Years of Wandering (1878–1885),* 288–290. London: Victor Gollancz, 1986.
Brief analytic comments. Musical examples.

Romeo and Juliet

4161. Brown, David. *Tchaikovsky: A Biographical and Critical Study.* Vol. 1, *The Early Years (1840–1874),* 180–197. New York: W. W. Norton, 1978.
Thorough treatment including background, compositional history, analytic comparison of preliminary and completed versions, diagram of structure, and critical appraisal. Musical examples and chart.

Serenade for Strings, Op. 48

4162. Brown, David. *Tchaikovsky: A Biographical and Critical Study.* Vol. 3, *The Years of Wandering (1878–1885)*, 122–125. London: Victor Gollancz, 1986.
  Comments on structure and style. Musical examples.

The Snow Maiden

4163. Abraham, Gerald *Slavonic and Romantic Music*, 133–136. New York: St. Martin's Press, 1968.
  Plot synopsis and analytic comments. Musical examples.

4164. Brown, David. *Tchaikovsky: A Biographical and Critical Study.* Vol. 1, *The Early Years (1840–1874)*, 284–290. New York: W. W. Norton, 1978.
  Analytic and critical commentary. Musical examples.

Sonata for Piano in G Major

4165. Brown, David. *Tchaikovsky: A Biographical and Critical Study.* Vol. 2, *The Crisis Years (1874–1878)*, 273–276. New York: W. W. Norton, 1982.
  Analytic and critical commentary. Musical examples.

The Sorceress

4166. Abraham, Gerald. *Slavonic and Romantic Music*, 160–166. New York: St. Martin's Press, 1968.
  Plot synopsis and analytic comments. Musical examples.

The Storm

4167. Brown, David. *Tchaikovsky: A Biographical and Critical Study.* Vol. 1, *The Early Years (1840–1874)*, 75–80. New York: W. W. Norton, 1978.
  Background, critical evaluation, and comments on structure, orchestration, and tonality.

Suite No. 1 in D Major, Op. 43

4168. Brown, David. *Tchaikovsky: A Biographical and Critical Study.* Vol. 3, *The Years of Wandering (1878–1885)*, 22–23, 62–63. London: Victor Gollancz, 1986.
  Brief description of style, with suggested programmatic associations. Musical examples.

Suite No. 2 in C Major, Op. 53.

4169. Brown, David. *Tchaikovsky: A Biographical and Critical Study.* Vol. 3, *The Years of Wandering (1878–1885),* 226–233, 242–243. London: Victor Gollancz, 1986.
Analytic discussion of structure, style, orchestral color. Musical examples.

Suite No. 3 in G Major, Op. 55

4170. Brown, David. *Tchaikovsky: A Biographical and Critical Study.* Vol. 3, *The Years of Wandering (1878–1885),* 268–273. London: Victor Gollancz, 1986.
Analytic discussion. Musical examples.

Swan Lake

4171. Brown, David. *Tchaikovsky: A Biographical and Critical Study.* Vol. 2, *The Crisis Years (1874–1878),* 67–86. New York: W. W. Norton, 1982.
Background, account of the first performance, description and contemporary critical reaction, plot summary, account of later versions, followed by an extended critical and analytic commentary. Musical examples.

Symphonies

4172. Cuyler, Louise. *The Symphony,* 153–157. New York: Harcourt Brace Jovanovich, 1973.
Short but compact analyses of Symphonies 4 and 6.

4173. Warrack, John. *Tchaikovsky: Symphonies and Concertos.* Seattle: University of Washington Press, 1969, 65 pp.
Background with descriptive and critical remarks. Musical examples.

Symphony No. 1, Op. 13 in G Minor ("Winter Dreams")

4174. Brown, David. *Tchaikovsky: A Biographical and Critical Study.* Vol. 1, *The Early Years (1840–1874),* 99–115. New York: W. W. Norton, 1978.
Background, compositional history, analysis, and critical evaluation. Musical examples and chart.

Symphony No. 2, Op. 17 in C Minor ("Little Russian")

4175. **Brown, David.** *Tchaikovsky: A Biographical and Critical Study.* Vol. 1, *The Early Years (1840–1874),* 256–273. New York: W. W. Norton, 1978.

Thorough discussion including compositional history, analysis, and critical assessment. Musical examples and chart.

Symphony No. 3, Op. 29 in D Major ("Polish")

4176. **Brown, David.** *Tchaikovsky: A Biographical and Critical Study.* Vol. 2, *The Crisis Years (1874–1878),* 41–50. New York: W. W. Norton, 1982.

Description and critical assessment with analytic observations. Musical examples.

Symphony No. 4, Op. 36 in F Minor

4177. **Blom, Eric.** *Tchaikovsky: Orchestral Works.* 1927. Reprint, 23–41. Westport, CT: Greenwood Press, 1970.

Descriptive, critical, and analytic commentary for the undergraduate student. Musical examples.

4178. **Brown, David.** *Tchaikovsky: A Biographical and Critical Study.* Vol. 2, *The Crisis Years (1874–1878),* 159–176. New York: W. W. Norton, 1982.

Compositional history, discussion of the symphony's "program," comments on dramatic influences from Wagner, critical and analytic commentary including a diagram of thematic, formal, and tonal relationships in the first movement.

4179. **Dahlhaus, Carl.** *Nineteenth-Century Music.* Translated by J. Bradford Robinson, 266–268. Berkeley: University of California Press, 1989.

Brief but concentrated analytic remarks on Tchaikovsky's struggle with symphonic form in this work. Use of thematic transformation, rather than formal design, holds the work together. Advanced.

4180. **Haggin, B. H.** *A Book of the Symphony,* 283–293. London: Oxford University Press, 1937.

Straightforward description dealing with formal plan only. Brief background remarks, with no discussion of tonality, rhythm, or texture. For the musical amateur or undergraduate student concerned with form. Musical examples.

4181.   Stedman, Preston. *The Symphony*, 172–178. Englewood Cliffs, NJ: Prentice-Hall, 1979.
Extensive description focusing on formal plan, meter, tonality, motivic activity, and orchestral technique. For the undergraduate student. Musical examples and diagrams.

4182.   Ulrich, Homer. *Music: A Design for Listening*, 352–355. New York: Harcourt, Brace, 1957.
Descriptive/analytic breakdown by measures. Musical examples.

4183.   Weinstock, Herbert. *Tchaikovsky*, 172–178. New York: Alfred A. Knopf, 1943.
Background and critical remarks. Not analytic.

Symphony No. 5, Op. 64 in E Minor

4184.   Haggin, B. H. *A Book of the Symphony*, 294–302. London: Oxford University Press, 1937.
Straightforward description dealing with formal plan only. Brief background remarks, with no discussion of tonality, rhythm, or texture. For the musical amateur or undergraduate student concerned with form. Musical examples.

Symphony No. 6, Op. 74 in B Minor ("Pathétique")

4185.   Bernstein, Leonard. *The Infinite Variety of Music*, 171–193. New York: Simon and Schuster, 1966.
Analysis, similar to Bernstein's television talks. For the musical amateur and beginning student. Musical examples.

4186.   Haggin, B. H. *A Book of the Symphony*, 303–310. London: Oxford University Press, 1937.
Straightforward description dealing with formal plan only. Brief background remarks, with no discussion of tonality, rhythm, or texture. For the musical amateur or undergraduate student concerned with form. Musical examples.

4187.   Machlis, Joseph. *The Enjoyment of Music*. 3d ed., 156–158. New York: W. W. Norton, 1970.
Compact analysis for the undergraduate student. Musical examples.

4188.   Tovey, Donald Francis. *Essays in Musical Analysis*. Vol. 2, 84–89. London: Oxford University Press, 1935.
Analytic guide for the musical amateur and undergraduate student. Comments on structure and tonality. Musical examples.

Tempest, Op. 18

4189.   Brown, David. *Tchaikovsky: A Biographical and Critical Study.* Vol. 1, *The Early Years (1840–1874),* 295–298. New York: W. W. Norton, 1978.

> Brief analytic and critical commentary. Musical examples.

Trio for Piano and Strings, Op. 50

4190.   Brown, David. *Tchaikovsky: A Biographical and Critical Study.* Vol. 3, *The Years of Wandering (1878–1885),* 152–161. London: Victor Gollancz, 1986.

> Critical assessment. Analytic discussion of formal structure, thematic relationships, tonality, rhythm. Musical examples and diagram.

Vakula the Smith

4191.   Abraham, Gerald. *Slavonic and Romantic Music,* 136–142. New York: St. Martin's Press, 1968.

> Plot synopsis and analytic commentary. Musical examples.

4192.   Brown, David. *Tchaikovsky: A Biographical and Critical Study.* Vol. 1, *The Early Years (1840–1874),* 308–336. New York: W. W. Norton, 1978.

> Compositional history, plot synopsis with analytic and critical commentary.

Variations on a Rococo Theme, Op. 33

4193.   Brown, David. *Tchaikovsky: A Biographical and Critical Study.* Vol. 2, *The Crisis Years (1874–1878),* 117–123. New York: W. W. Norton, 1982.

> Critical and analytic discussion, with a table comparing the structures of the original and revised versions. Musical examples.

Voyevoda

4194.   Abraham, Gerald. *Slavonic and Romantic Music,* 120–126. New York: St. Martin's Press, 1968.

> Analytic comments. Musical examples.

4195.   Brown, David. *Tchaikovsky: A Biographical and Critical Study.* Vol. 1, *The Early Years (1840–1874),* 134–155. New York: W. W. Norton, 1978.

Background, compositional history, analytic commentary on the music, and plot summary, followed by a critical assessment. Musical examples.

TCHEREPNIN, ALEXANDER, 1899–1977

Bagatelles, Op. 5

4196.   Wuellner, Guy. "Alexander Tcherepnin in Youth and Maturity: Bagatelles, Op. 5 and *Expressions* Op. 81." *Journal of the American Liszt Society,* 9 (1981): 88–94.

Brief remarks on style.

Expressions, Op. 81

4197.   Wuellner, Guy. "Alexander Tcherepnin in Youth and Maturity: Bagatelles, Op. 5 and *Expressions* Op. 81." *Journal of the American Liszt Society,* 9 (1981): 88–94.

A brief overview of the style of this piece.

TELEMANN, GEORG PHILIPP, 1681–1767

General

4198.   Petzoldt, Richard. *Georg Philipp Telemann.* Translated by H. Fitzpatrick. New York: Oxford University Press, 1974.

Telemann's works are surveyed by genre. Includes background, historical information on each genre (suites, concerti, keyboard music, *Lieder,* opera, cantatas, oratorios, passions), and an analytical/critical discussion of Telemann's music. Includes chapters on Telemann's style and attitude, and on the reception of his music today. Musical examples.

Concertos

4199.   Hutchings, Arthur. *The Baroque Concerto,* 237–251. New York: W. W. Norton, 1961.

Observations on historical context and musical style of Telemann's concertos. Musical examples.

DISSERTATIONS AND THESES

General

4200. Peckham, Mary Adelaide. "The Operas of Georg Philipp Telemann." Ph.D., Columbia University, 1972, 309 pp., DA 33-2415A.

THOMPSON, RANDALL, 1899–1984

Alleluia

4201. Urrows, David F. "Randall Thompson on Choral Composition: Essays and Reflections." *American Choral Review*, 22, no. 2 (1980): 24–27.
   Descriptive commentary with analytic observations. Musical examples.

Long Songs (Five)

4202. Urrows, David F. "Randall Thompson on Choral Composition: Essays and Reflections." *American Choral Review*, 22, no. 2 (1980): 28–38.
   Descriptive commentary with analytic observations. Musical examples.

THOMSON, VIRGIL, 1896–1989

General

4203. Dickinson, Peter. "Stein Satie Cummings Thomson Berners Cage: Toward a Context for the Music of Virgil Thomson." *Musical Quarterly*, 72, no. 3 (1986): 394–409.
   A discussion of the connections and influences among these composers and writers. Contains some discussion of Thomson's style and some analytic comments. Musical examples.

4204. Hoover, Kathleen, and John Cage. *Virgil Thomson: His Life and Music.* New York: Thomas Yoseloff, 1959, 288 pp.
   Composer John Cage offers a critical and analytic perspective on Thomson's output and Kathleen Hoover deals with Thomson's life. Musical examples.

Missa Pro Defunctis

4205. Wolf, Robert E. "Current Chronicle: France." *Musical Quarterly*, 47, no. 3 (1961): 400–407.
A review of a performance, with descriptive commentary. Musical examples.

Portraits for Piano

4206. Tommasini, Anthony Carl. *Virgil Thomson's "Musical Portraits."* N.Y.: Pendragon Press, 1986.
Genesis of the idea of musical portraits: Gertrude Stein's library portraits as a model for Thomson described, Thomson's procedures in composing musical portraits, a stylistic survey, and an analysis of four portraits. Musical examples. Based on the author's doctoral dissertations cited here.

DISSERTATIONS AND THESES

General

4207. Anagnost, Dean Z. "The Choral Music of Virgil Thomson." Ed.D., Columbia University Teachers College, 1977, 200 pp., DA 38-1962A-3A.

Four Saints in Three Acts

4208. Jeffers, Grant Lyle. "Non-Narrative Music Drama: Settings by Virgil Thomson, Ned Rorem, and Earl Kim of Plays by Gertrude Stein and Samuel Beckett." Ph.D., University of California at Los Angeles, 1983, 168 pp., DA 44-3201A.

4209. Ward, Kelly Mac. "An Analysis of the Relationship Between Text and Musical Shape and an Investigation of the Relationship Between Text and Surface Rhythmic Detail." Ph.D., University of Texas at Austin, 1978, 387 pp., DA 39-3912A-13A.

Portraits for Piano

4210. Tommasini, Anthony Carl. "The *Portraits for Piano* by Virgil Thomson." D.M.A., Boston University School for the Arts, 1982, 219 pp., DA 43-970A.

TIPPETT, SIR MICHAEL, 1905–

General

4211.   Bowen, Meirion. *Michael Tippett.* New York: Universe, 1982, 196 pp.
Analytic overview of Tippett's output. Musical examples.

4212.   Kemp, Ian. *The Composer and His Music.* London: Eulenberg Books, 1984, 516 pp.
A comprehensive study of the music of Tippett up to the composition of *The Ice Break* (1973–1976). A postscript mentions later works, such as Symphony No. 4, String Quartet No. 4, Triple Concerto, and *The Mask of Time.* However, there is no detailed discussion of these. Compositional techniques, Tippett's attitudes, and his style discussed, and his major works are treated in an analytic manner. Musical examples and tables.

4213.   Matthews, David. *Michael Tippett: An Introductory Study.* London: Faber and Faber, 1979, 112 pp.
Descriptive overview, with analytic remarks on Tippett's output. Musical examples.

4214.   White, Eric Walter. *Tippett and His Operas.* London: Barrie and Jenkins, 1979, 142 pp.
Mainly a discussion of plot, dramatic action, and background, with occasional analytic remarks on the music.

4215.   Whittall, Arnold. *The Music of Britten and Tippett: Studies in Themes and Techniques.* Cambridge: Cambridge University Press, 1982, 314 pp.
A collection of essays on the music of these two composers. Analytic discussions on a wide range of works by both composers, with certain works singled out for detailed analytic study. Musical examples.

4216.   Whittall, Arnold. *Music Since the First World War,* 212–216, 222–226. London: J. M. Dent and Sons, 1977.
Brief analytic discussion. Musical examples.

Ice Break

4217.   Gellhorn, Peter. "Tippett's Operas: A Musical Survey." *Composer* (London), 70 (Summer 1980): 9–12.
A brief descriptive overview of the opera, highlighting important vocal, textural, formal, and harmonic events.

King Priam

4218.   Gellhorn, Peter. "Tippett's Operas: A Musical Survey." *Composer* (London), 70 (Summer 1980): 4–6.
A brief descriptive overview of the opera, highlighting important vocal, textural, formal, and harmonic events.

Knot Garden

4219.   Gellhorn, Peter. "Tippett's Operas: A Musical Survey." *Composer* (London), 70 (Summer 1980): 6–8.
A brief descriptive overview of the opera, highlighting important vocal, textural, formal, and harmonic events.

Midsummer Marriage

4220.   Gellhorn, Peter. "Tippett's Operas: A Musical Survey." *Composer* (London), 70 (Summer 1980): 1–4.
A brief descriptive overview of the opera, highlighting important vocal, textural, formal, and harmonic events.

Quartet for Strings No. 2 in F-Sharp Major

4221.   Clements, Andrew. "Tippett's Fourth Quartet." *Music and Musicians*, 27 (May 1979): 28–29.
Brief summary of form.

4222.   Puffett, Derrick. "The Fugue from Tippett's Second String Quartet." *Music Analysis*, 5, nos. 2–3 (1986): 233–264.
An analytic essay revealing connections with Purcell and Beethoven, followed by a Schenkerian analysis. Table of formal structure, a Schenkerian graph of the movement, the complete score of the movement and musical examples. Last movement only. Advanced.

4223.   Warburton, A. O. "Set Works for 'O' Level, GCE." *Music Teacher*, 52 (February 1973): 14–16.
Thorough analysis for the undergraduate student.

Quartet for Strings No. 4

4224.   Clements, A. "Tippett's Fourth Quartet." *Music and Musicians*, 27 (May 1979): 28–30.
Description of the work, with some analytic observations about formal and melodic schemes.

Symphonies

4225.   Ballantine, Christopher. *Twentieth Century Symphony*, 127–129, 186–194. London: Dennis Dobson, 1983.
Analytic comments on Symphonies 1 and 2. Musical examples.

Symphony No. 3

4226.   Clarke, Symon. "The Blues in Tippett's Third Symphony." *Composer* (London), 70 (Summer 1980): 17–21.
Brief critical remarks, followed by analytic observations on the Finale, which incorporates elements from the blues and from Beethoven's Ninth Symphony.

4227.   Rodda, Richard E. "Genesis of a Symphony: Tippett's Symphony No. 3" *Music Review*, 39, no. 2 (1978): 110–116.
Compositional background and source of inspiration examined.

DISSERTATIONS AND THESES

Symphonies

4228.   Rodda, Richard Earl. "The Symphonies of Michael Tippett." Ph.D., Case Western Reserve, 1979, 533 pp., DA 40-3621A.

TOCH, ERNST, 1887–1964

General

4229.   Mason, Wilton, "The Piano Music of Ernst Toch." *Piano Quarterly*, 41 (Fall 1962): 22–25.
A brief introduction to the piano works. General description, with some analytic observations about each group of pieces.

TOMKINS, THOMAS, 1572–1656

General

4230.   Stevens, Denis. *Thomas Tomkins, 1572–1656.* New York: St. Martin's Press, 1957, 214 pp.
Discussion of sources, chronology, style, points and figurations, forms, relationships between text and music, harmony, key relationships, and other unifying factors. Musical examples.

TORELLI, GIUSEPPE, 1658–1709

General

4231.   Bukofzer, Manfred. *Music in the Baroque Era*, 226–229. New York: W. W. Norton, 1947.
   Torelli's role in the establishment of the Baroque concerto form. Descriptive and critical remarks on his style.

Concertos

4232.   Talbot, Michael. "The Concerto Allegro in the Early Eighteenth Century." *Music and Letters*, 52 (1971): 8–18, 159–172.
   The development of the concerto form by Italian composers up to 1720, including Torelli. Advanced-level discussion.

Concerto Grosso, Op. 8, No. 8 in C Minor

4233.   Cole, William. *The Form of Music: An Outline of Musical Designs Used by the Great Composers*, 59–61 London: Associated Board of the Royal Schools of Music, n.d.
   Brief outline of the structure in table form. An example of ritornello form.

TURINA, JOAQUIN, 1882–1949

Danses Gitanes, Op. 55, No. 5 (Sacro-Monte)

4234.   Kuehl, Olga L. "Turina's *Sacro-Monte*: A Master Lesson." *Clavier*, 22, no. 5 (1983): 26–27.
   Brief analysis. Musical examples.

USSACHEVSKY, VLADIMIR, 1911–1990

A Piece for Tape Recorder

4235.   Schrader, Barry. *Introduction to Electro-Acoustic Music*, 36–37. Englewood Cliffs, NJ: Prentice-Hall, 1982.
   Analytic comments.

Of Wood and Brass

4236.   Schrader, Barry. *Introduction to Electro-Acoustic Music,* 50–51. Englewood Cliffs, N.J.: Prentice-Hall, 1982.
Analytic comments.

VARÈSE, EDGARD, 1883–1965

General

4237.   Babbitt, Milton. "Edgard Varèse: A Few Observations of His Music." In *Perspectives on American Composers.* Edited by Benjamin Boretz and E. T. Cone, 40–48. New York: W. W. Norton, 1971.
Critical and analytic commentary on Varèse's stylistic characteristics, mentioning *Intégrales, Density 21.5, Octandre,* and *Déserts.*

4238.   Bernard, Jonathan W. "Pitch/Register in the Music of Edgard Varèse." *Music Theory Spectrum,* 3 (1981): 1–25.
The application of the geometric properties of symmetry to the works of Varèse. Many examples, graphs, pictorial representations. For the advanced student.

4239.   Chung, Chou Wen. "Open Rather Than Bounded." In *Perspectives on American Composers.* Edited by Benjamin Boretz and E. T. Cone, 49–54. New York: W. W. Norton, 1971.
An assessment of Varèse's innovations.

4240.   Cox, David Harold. "Thematic Interrelationships Between the Works of Varèse." *Music Review,* 49, no. 3 (1988): 205–217.
Varèse's use of thematic quotations to create links between his works. Focuses on three specific occasions in which Varèse uses thematic cross-references to link pieces. Reference to his own and other composers' works explored. Advanced. Musical examples.

4241.   Oullette, Fernand. *Edgard Varèse, Composer.* Translated by D. Coltman. New York: Orion, Goosman, 1968, 270 pp.
Overview of Varèse's output, with discussion of background, performance history, and analytic details.

4242.   Van Solkema, Sherman, ed. *The New Worlds of Edgard Varèse: A Symposium.* New York: Institute for Studies in American Music, 1979, 90 pp.
General analytic commentary on Varèse's output, with special emphasis on *Ionisation,* which is thoroughly analyzed. Charts, musical examples.

4243. Whittall, Arnold. *Music Since the First World War*, 197–205. London: J. M. Dent and Sons, 1977.
    Analytic survey of works. Musical examples.

Density 21.5

4244. Baron, Carol K. "Varèse's Explication of Debussy's *Syrinx* in *Density 21.5* and an Analysis of Varèse's Composition: A Secret Model Revealed." *Music Review*, 43, no. 2 (1982): 121–134.

4245. Bernard, Jonathan W. "On *Density 21.5*: A Response to Nattiez." *Music Analysis*, 5 (July–October 1986): 207–231.
    A response to an article in *Music Analysis* cited below (*see* item no. 4247). Author refutes Nattiez's analytic technique and, in so doing, provides his own advanced-level analysis of this work. Musical examples.

4246. Guck, Marion. "A Flow of Energy: *Density 21.5*." *Perspectives of New Music*, 23, no. 1 (1984): 334–347.
    Analysis with musical examples.

4247. Nattiez, Jean Jacques. "Varèse's *Density 21.5*: A Study in Semiological Analysis." *Music Analysis*, 1, no. 3 (1982): 243–340.

4248. Siddons, James. "On the Nature of Melody in Varèse's *Density 21.5*." *Perspectives of New Music*, 23, no. 1 (1984): 296+.

Grand Sommeil Noir

4249. Stempel, Larry. "Not Even Varèse Can Be an Orphan." *Musical Quarterly*, 60, no. 1 (1974): 46–60.
    Analytic discussion of Varèse's style, demonstrating his debt to Debussy and Machaut. Musical examples.

Intégrales

4250. Strawn, John. "The *Intégrales* of Edgard Varèse: Space, Mass, Element, and Form." *Perspectives of New Music*, 17, no. 1 (1978): 138–160.
    An analysis using Varèse's own terms as a starting point ("space," "mass," "elements"). Discusses each term in turn and interprets them. Deals with problems of form of the piece. Musical examples and tables.

Ionisation

4251.   Takashi, Koto. "Basic Cells and Combinations in Varèse's *Ionisation.*" *Sonus,* 7, no. 2 (Spring 1987): 35–45.
Identification and discussion of the use and development of the basic rhythmic/timbral cells in *Ionisation.* Also relates the cells and timbres to the overall structure. Musical examples and diagram of the structure.

DISSERTATIONS AND THESES

General

4252.   Bloch, David Reed. "The Music of Edgard Varèse." Ph.D., University of Washington, 1973, 288 pp., DA 34-6018A-19A.

4253.   Yannay, Yehuda. "Toward an Open-Ended Method of Analysis of Contemporary Music: A Study of Selected Works by Edgard Varèse and György Ligeti." D.M.A., University of Illinois at Urbana, 1974, 163 pp., DA 35-7952A-3A.

Arcana

4254.   Conely, James Hannon, Jr. "An Analysis of Form in *Arcana* of Edgard Varèse and *Trilogy* of Samuel Beckett," Ed.D., Columbia University, 1968, 157 pp., DA 29-3606A-7A.

Hyperprism

4255.   Wood, Darrell Elroy. "A Paradigm for the Study and Performance of *Intégrales* and *Hyperprism,* Two Instrumental Works by Edgard Varèse." D.A., Ball State University, 1974, 179 pp., DA 35-6188A-9A.

Intégrales

4256.   Ramsier, Paul. "An Analysis and Comparison of the Motivic Structure of *Octandre* and *Intégrales,* Two Instrumental Works by Edgard Varèse." Ph.D., New York University, 1972, 206 pp., DA 33-1772A.

4257.   Wood, Darrell Elroy. "A Paradigm for the Study and Performance of *Intégrales* and *Hyperprism,* Two Instrumental Works by Edgard Varèse." D.A., Ball State University, 1974, 179 pp., DA 35-6188A-9A.

Octandre

4258. Ramsier, Paul. "An Analysis and Comparison of the Motivic Structure of *Octandre* and *Intégrales*, Two Instrumental Works by Edgard Varèse." Ph.D., New York University, 1972, 206 pp., DA 33-1772A.

VAUGHAN WILLIAMS, RALPH, 1872–1958

General

4259. Day, James. *Vaughan Williams.* London: J. M. Dent and Sons, 1975, 228 pp.
  Descriptive, critical, and analytic commentary on Vaughan Williams's entire output. Musical examples.

4260. Dickinson, A. E. F. *An Introduction to the Music of Ralph Vaughan Williams.* London: Oxford University Press, 1928, 83 pp.
  Descriptive and critical commentary for the student. Musical examples.

4261. Dickinson, A. E. F. *Vaughan Williams.* London: Faber and Faber, 1963, 540 pp.
  Analytic commentary, with musical examples.

4262. Foss, Hubert. *Ralph Vaughan Williams: A Study.* New York: Oxford University Press, 1950, 219 pp.
  Brief critical remarks on Vaughan Williams's entire output.

4263. Howes, Frank. *The Music of Ralph Vaughan Williams.* London: Oxford University Press, 1954, 372 pp.
  Descriptive and critical commentary, with occasional analytic observations. Musical examples.

4264. Hutchings, Arthur. "Music in Britain, 1916–1960." In *The New Oxford History of Music.* Vol. 10, *The Modern Age: 1890–1960.* Edited by Martin Cooper, 507–513. London: Oxford University Press, 1974.
  Critical assessment and stylistic overview, with brief analytic commentary on the *Pastoral* Symphony and Symphonies 4 and 5. Musical examples.

4265. Kennedy, Michael. *The Works of Ralph Vaughan Williams.* London: Oxford University Press, 1964, 776 pp.
  Brief background, descriptive, and analytic commentary on Vaughan Williams's output. Musical examples.

4266. Pakenham, Simona. *Ralph Vaughan Williams: A Discovery of His Music.* London: Macmillan, 1957, 205 pp.
  Descriptive and critical commentary.

Benedicte

4267. Warburton, A. O. "Set Works for 'O' Level, GCE." *Music Teacher,* 48 (March 1969): 18 + .
  Analysis for the undergraduate student.

Fantasia on a Theme of Tallis

4268. Warburton, A. O. "Set Works for 'O' Level, GCE." *Music Teacher and Piano Student,* 39 (March 1960): 128–155.
  Brief analytical comments for the undergraduate student.

Serenade to Music

4269. Warburton, A. O. "Set Works for 'O' Level, GCE." *Music Teacher,* 51 (October 1972): 22–23 + .
  Background and thorough analysis.

Symphonies

4270. Dickinson, A. E. F. "The Vaughan Williams Symphonies." *Musical Opinion,* 96 (December 1972): 123 + .
  An overview, highlighting salient features of each symphony.

4271. Ottaway, Hugh. *Vaughan Williams Symphonies.* Seattle: University of Washington Press, 1973, 64 pp.
  Descriptive, critical, and analytic guide for the undergraduate student. Musical examples.

4272. Schwartz, Elliott. *The Symphonies of Ralph Vaughan Williams.* Amherst: University of Massachusets Press, 1964, 242 pp.
  Describes the structure of each symphony and identifies the main themes. Discussions are mainly descriptive. Contains a chapter that summarizes various aspects of the symphonies: forms, melody, harmony, counterpoint, rhythm, orchestration, tonality. There is also a chapter on the sources of Vaughan Williams's style.

4273. Simpson, Robert, ed. *The Symphony.* Vol. 2, 114–127. New York: Drake Publishers, 1972.
  Brief descriptive and analytic remarks on Symphonies 1 through 9. Musical examples.

Symphony No. 1 ("A Sea Symphony")

4274.   Clarke, F. R. C. "The Structure of Vaughan Williams's *Sea Symphony*." *Music Review*, 34, no. 1 (1973): 58–61.

4275.   Hurd, Michael. "Vaughan Williams's *Sea Symphony*: An Analysis." *Music in Education*, 29, no. 311 (1965): 27–28; no. 312 (1965): 83–84.
  A thematic analysis of the complete work. Includes a discussion of the relationship of the music to Whitman's poetry.

Symphony No. 2 ("London")

4276.   Cuyler, Louise. *The Symphony*, 191–196. New York: Harcourt Brace Jovanovich, 1973.
  Short but efficient musical analysis, with musical examples.

4277.   Machlis, Joseph. *Introduction to Contemporary Music*, 299–301. New York: W. W. Norton, 1961.
  Analytic highlights intended for the undergraduate student.

Symphony No. 4 in F Minor

4278.   Whittall, Arnold. *Music Since the First World War*, 25–28. London: J. M. Dent and Sons, 1977.
  Analytic discussion. Musical examples.

Symphony No. 5 in D Major

4279.   Ballantine, Christopher. *Twentieth Century Symphony*, 161–163. London: Dennis Dobson, 1984.
  Analytic comments. Musical examples.

4280.   Ottaway, Hugh. "VW 5—A New Analysis." *Musical Times*, 105 (May 1964): 354–356.
  An analysis of the key structure of the first movement. Takes issue with earlier commentators.

Symphony No. 6 in E Minor

4281.   Hansen, Peter. *An Introduction to Twentieth Century Music*. 2d ed. 306–308. Boston: Allyn and Bacon, 1967.
  "Minianalysis" of entire symphony. Musical examples.

4282. Stedman, Preston. *The Symphony,* 277–283. Englewood Cliffs, NJ: Prentice-Hall, 1979.
Description and analytic breakdown of each movement, supported by musical examples and diagram.

Symphony No. 9 in E Minor

4283. Frogley, Alain. "Vaughan Williams and Thomas Hardy: *Tess* and the Slow Movement of the Ninth Symphony." *Music and Letters,* 68, no. 1 (1987): 42–59.
An analytic essay on the slow movement of the Ninth Symphony. Introductory remarks discuss background and genesis. Analytic discussion is on pp. 50–59. Hardy's *Tess of the d'Urbervilles* is identified as the programmatic basis; parallels between the story and the music are identified. Structure described. Musical examples.

Toward the Unknown Region

4284. Warburton, A. O. "Set Works for 'O' Level, GCE." *Music Teacher,* 51 (October 1972): 22–23+.
Background and analysis.

VERDI, GIUSEPPE, 1813–1901

General

4285. Aycock, Roy E. "Shakespeare, Boito, and Verdi." *Musical Quarterly,* 58, no. 4 (1972): 588–604.
Traces adaptation of plots, mainly *Othello* and *Falstaff,* from the original Shakespeare to Boito and, finally, Verdi. No discussion of the music.

4286. Bonavia, Ferruccio. Verdi. London: Oxford University Press, 1930, 161 pp.
Mainly background on Verdi's composition of the operas. Some remarks on Verdi's style and influence. Not analytic.

4287. Budden, Julian. *The Operas of Verdi.* 3 vols. New York: Oxford University Press, 1979–1986.
Thorough analytic discussion of each opera. Musical examples.

4288. Gatti, Carlo. *Verdi: The Man and His Music.* Translated by Elisabeth Abbott. New York: Putnam's Sons, 1955, 371 pp.
Provides full history of the writing of the operas, but no real musical analysis.

4289. Godefroy, Vincent. *The Dramatic Genius of Verdi: Studies of Selected Operas.* New York: St. Martin's Press, 1975, 287 pp.
Critical studies of a selection of Verdi's operas. Discusses genesis, background, characterization, style, and critical assessment of Verdi's development. Musical examples.

4290. Hussey, Dynely. *Verdi.* London: J. M. Dent and Sons, 1948, 355 pp.
Thorough treatment of style, drama, and characterization. For the undergraduate student. Musical examples.

4291. Kerman, Joseph. "Verdi's Use of Recurring Themes." In *Studies in Music History: Essays for Oliver Strunk.* Edited by Harold Powers, 495–510. Princeton NJ: Princeton University Press, 1968.
Verdi's use of leitmotives and their role in the structure of the operas.

4292. Kimbell, David. *Verdi in the Age of Italian Romanticism.* Cambridge: Cambridge University Press, 1981, 703 pp.
An extended study of many issues surrounding the operas of Verdi. Contains many analytic observations on various selected operas. Principally *Nabucco, Ernani, I Due Foscari, Il Corsaro, Macbeth, La Battaglia de Legnano, Rigoletto, La Traviata, I Masnadieri,* and *Luisa Miller.* Musical examples.

4293. Martin, George. *Verdi: His Music, Life and Times.* New York: Dodd, Mead, 1963, 633 pp.
Mainly background of the composition of the operas and Verdi's life, but some discussion of the music throughout.

4294. Noske, Frits. "Ritual Scenes in Verdi's Operas." *Music and Letters,* 54, no. 4 (1973): 415–439.
Traces Verdi's use of ritual to heighten dramatic effect. Musical devices used in connection with ritual scenes are mentioned. Musical examples.

4295. Noske, Frits. *The Signifier and the Signified: Studies in the Operas of Mozart and Verdi.* The Hague: M. Nijhoff, 1977, 418 pp.
Detailed analytic discussion of *Otello, Simon Boccanegra,* and *Don Carlos.* Analyses not from the musical point of view alone, but from the musico-dramatic process as well. Musical examples.

4296. Osborne, Charles. *The Complete Operas of Verdi.* New York: Alfred A. Knopf, 1970, 472 pp.
Thorough discussion of all the operas, with plot synopsis, musical commentary, and influences of other composers evident in Verdi's writing.

591

4297. Plantinga, Leon. *Romantic Music,* 299–323. New York: W. W. Norton, 1984.
Analytic comments on the operas. Musical examples.

4298. Toye, Francis. *Giuseppe Verdi: His Life and Works.* New York: Alfred A. Knopf, 1931, 495 pp.
Background, influences, and critical appraisal of Verdi's music. Musical examples.

Aida

4299. Downes, Edward. "The Kindling Word." *Opera News,* 29, (March 20, 1965): 24–25.
Discusses characterization and mood painting. Musical examples.

4300. Machlis, Joseph. *The Enjoyment of Music.* 3d ed., 179–182. New York: W. W. Norton, 1970.
Brief overview, with analytic remarks for the undergraduate student. Musical examples.

4301. Osborne, Charles. "The Plot of *Aida.*" *Musical Times,* 110 (October 1969): 1034–1036.
Discussion of sources used to write the libretto.

Attila

4302. Matheson, Johann. "*Attila* and Verdi's Dramatic Form." *Opera,* 14 (November 1963): 737–740.
Discussion of the formal scheme of the drama and some critical remarks on the music.

Un Ballo in Maschera

4303. Levarie, Siegmund. "Key Relations in Verdi's *Un Ballo in Maschera.*" *Nineteenth Century Music,* 2, no. 2 (1978): 143–147.
An investigation of key relationships and their influence on structure, characterization, and the drama. Tables.

4304. Parker, Roger, and M. Brown. "Motivic and Tonal Interaction in Verdi's *Un Ballo in Maschera.*" *Journal of the American Musicological Society,* 36, no. 2 (1983): 243–265.
Analysis focusing on motivic and tonal interaction in this work. Musical examples.

Il Corsaro

4305.   Town, Stephen. "Observations on a Cabaletta from Verdi's *Il Corsaro.*" *Current Musicology,* 32 (1981): 59–75.
An examination of one cabaletta, beginning "S'avvicina il Tuo Momento." This is a manuscript study of the revisions made to the piece. A few analytic remarks. Musical examples.

Don Carlos

4306.   Freeman, John. "A Play of Light and Shade." *Opera News,* 34 (February 14, 1970): 24–25.
Brief discussion of subtlety of relationships and psychological nuance as they are reflected in the music.

4307.   McDonald, Katherine. "Dark Brilliance." *Opera News,* 28 (March 7, 1964): 24–25.
Descriptive commentary, with musical examples. Special focus on the atmosphere of *Don Carlos.*

4308.   Porter, Andrew. "A Sketch for *Don Carlos.*" *Musical Times,* 111 (September 1970): 882–885.
A study of the sketches for the libretto.

Ernani

4309.   Parker, Roger. "Levels of Motivic Definition in Verdi's *Ernani.*" *Nineteenth Century Music,* 6, no. 2 (1982): 141–150.
Examines recurring melodic motives in *Ernani* and analyzes Elvira's Act I scene, "Surta è la Notte," in this context. Includes a discussion of phrase structure, harmony and tonality. Musical examples.

4310.   Weaver, William. "The Irresistable *Ernani.*" *Opera,* 18 (March 1967): 184–191.
Background, performance history, and critical remarks on style and form.

Falstaff

4311.   Alderson, Richard. "Is Music Really Comic?" *Opera Journal,* 6, no. 1 (1973): 13–22.
Detailed comparison of musical figures in *Falstaff* and *Otello* to show their similarity. Author feels music is not inherently comic, but depends on plot for humor. Musical examples.

4312. Downes, Edward. *Music That Laughs and Capers."* *Opera News*, 32 (December 16, 1967): 24–25.

Verdi's musical depiction of comic events explored in a few examples. Musical examples.

4313. Hepokoski, James A. *Giuseppe Verdi: "Falstaff."* Cambridge: Cambridge University Press, 1983.

Full treatment of the opera, including synopsis, compositional history, analysis, stage history, bibliography, and discography. Musical examples.

4314. Lelash, Marjorie. "He Who Laughs Last." *Opera News*, 28 (March 21, 1964): 24–26.

Descriptive and critical commentary, with musical examples. Special mention of Verdi's use of leitmotive.

4315. McElroy, George. "Forebears of Falstaff." *Opera News*, 29 (January 23, 1965): 24–25.

Background on the sources of the libretto. Compares, briefly, Shakespeare's Falstaff in the *Merry Wives of Windsor* with Boito's treatment of the character.

4316. Potter, John, and Richard Brett. "Verdi's Comic Vision." *Opera News*, 39 (April 15, 1975): 13–14.

Brief descriptive remarks supported by musical examples. Highlights musical devices that enhance the comic element.

La Forza del Destino

4317. John, Nicholas, ed. *La Forza del Destino.* London: John Calder, 1983, 112 pp.

Background articles and complete libretto. The article "The Music of *The Force of Destiny,"* on pp. 17–33 contains many analytic observations of characterization and dramatic structure. Thematic guide on pp. 54–57.

4318. McDonald, Katherine. "Three Under Stress." *Opera News*, 29 (February 6, 1965): 24–25.

Brief remarks on musical characterization and depiction. Musical examples.

Luisa Miller

4319. Larkey, Lionel. "Love and Intrigue." *Opera News*, 32 (February 17, 1968): 22–23.

Place of *Luisa* in Verdi's output examined, remarks on musical form and characterization. Musical examples.

4320. Tuggle, Robert A. "Why *Luisa Miller?" Opera News,* 36 (December 11, 1971): 21–24.

Descriptive overview, highlighting musical features of special interest. Musical examples.

Macbeth

4321. Alper, Clifford D. "Verdi's Use of the Minor Second Interval in *Macbeth." Opera Journal,* 4, no. 4 (1971): 10–14.

The use of the minor second for a particular dramatic effect identified. Musical examples.

4322. Antokoletz, Elliott. "Verdi's Dramatic Use of Harmony and Tonality in *Macbeth." In Theory Only,* 4 (November–December 1978): 17–28.

4323. Chusid, Martin. "Evil, Guilt, and the Supernatural in Verdi's *Macbeth*: Toward an Understanding of the Tonal Structure and Key Symbolism." In *Verdi's "Macbeth": A Sourcebook.* Edited by David Rosen and Andrew Porter, 249–260. New York: W. W. Norton, 1984.

4324. Freeman, John. "The Path to Power." *Opera News,* 37 (February 3, 1973): 20–21.

Brief discussion of the opera, with analytic remarks and musical examples.

4325. Hughes, Spike. "An Introduction to Verdi's *Macbeth." Opera,* 11 (April 1960): 247–256.

Describes general musical character of the opera; its genesis; the Paris version, revision; and contains many analytic comments. Not an attempt at a complete analysis.

4326. Knowles, John. "The Banquet Scene from Verdi's *Macbeth*: An Experiment in Large-Scale Musical Form." In *Verdi's "Macbeth": A Sourcebook.* Edited by David Rosen and Andrew Porter, 284–292. New York: W. W. Norton, 1984.

4327. McDonald, Katherine. "In Tune with Shakespeare." *Opera News,* 26 (March 24, 1962): 24–27.

Verdi's methods of characterization with music. Musical examples.

4328. Rosen, David, and Andrew Porter, eds. *Verdi's "Macbeth": A Sourcebook.* New York: W. W. Norton, 1984, 527 pp.

Analytic essays, discussion of sources, editions, publication history, early reviews and performance history. Bibliography and musical examples.

4329. Sabbeth, Daniel. "On the Tonal Organization of *Macbeth* 2." In *Verdi's "Macbeth": A Sourcebook*. Edited by David Rosen and Andrew Porter, 261–269. New York: W. W. Norton, 1984.

4330. Tomlinson, Gary. "Macbeth, Attila, and Verdi's Self-Modeling." In *Verdi's "Macbeth": A Sourcebook*. Edited by David Rosen and Andrew Porter, 270–283. New York: W. W. Norton, 1984.

A look at some musical ideas in *Macbeth* that had their origins in *Attila*. Musical examples.

Otello

4331. Archibald, Bruce. "Tonality in *Otello*." *Music Review*, 35, no. 1 (1974): 23–28.

A discussion of Verdi's use of tonality in four tonal units of Act I (the opening "storm scene"; the chorus, "Fuoco di Gioia"; the "Drinking Song"; and the final duet). Special emphasis on the love duet. Musical examples.

4332. Dahlhaus, Carl. *Nineteenth-Century Music*. Translated by J. Bradford Robinson, 215–217. Berkeley: University of California Press, 1989.

Brief but concentrated analytic remarks on phrase structure and melodic prolongation. Musical examples. Advanced.

4333. Harrison, John. "The Beast in the Mud: 'Otello' from 'Othello.' " *Opera Journal*, 5, no. 4 (1972): 26–28.

A comparison of Shakespeare's character, Othello, with Verdi's Otello. Some mention of musical devices in characterization.

4334. Hauger, George. "*Othello* and *Otello*." *Music and Letters*, 50, no. 1 (1969): 76–85.

Both Boito's libretto and Verdi's music are discussed in this comparison of the opera with the Shakespeare play from which it was adapted.

4335. Lawton, David. "On the 'Bacio' Theme in *Otello*." *Nineteenth Century Music*, 1, no. 3 (1978): 211–220.

An analysis of the theme using a Schenkerian technique, followed by a detailed study of its tonal and dramatic associations. The implications of this relationship between tonality and drama are examined for their effect on the drama as a whole. Musical examples.

4336. Parker, Roger, and Matthew Brown. " 'Ancora un Bacio': Three Scenes from *Otello*." *Nineteenth Century Music*, 9, no. 1 (1985): 50–62.

Analyses, using Schenkerian techniques, of the "storm scene" and "love scene" from Act I, and the final scene of Act IV. Includes critiques of approaches by other scholars. For the advanced student. Musical examples.

4337.   Youens, Susan. "The Quartet in Act II of Verdi's *Otello*." *Opera Journal*, 16, no. 1 (1983): 2–15.
Discussion of how musical motives reflect dramatic action.

Requiem

4338.   Robertson, Alec. *Requiem: Music of Mourning and Consolation*, 96–110. New York: Praeger, 1968.
Background, descriptive, and analytic commentary on the music. Musical examples.

4339.   Rosen, David. "Verdi's *Liber Scriptus* Rewritten." *Musical Quarterly*, 55, no. 2 (1969): 151–169.
The musical reasons for Verdi's rewriting of the *Liber Scriptus*.

4340.   Tovey, Donald Francis. *Essays in Musical Analysis.* Vol. 2, 195–209. London: Oxford University Press, 1937.
Thorough analytic and critical commentary for the informed student. Musical examples.

4341.   Young, Percy M. *The Choral Tradition.* Rev. ed., 248–256. New York: W. W. Norton, 1981.
Brief analytic discussion.

Rigoletto

4342.   Downes, Edward. "His Hand on His Heart." *Opera News*, 28 (February 22, 1964): 24–26.
Special focus on the dramatic quality of the music. Musical examples.

Simon Boccanegra

4343.   Klein, John W. "Some Reflections on Verdi's *Simon Boccanegra*." *Music and Letters*, 43, no. 2 (1962): 115–122.
Traces the revisions of *Simon* from its early form to the finished opera. Musical examples.

4344. Powers, Harold S. "By Design: The Architecture of *Simon Boccanegra.*" *Opera News,* 49 (December 22, 1984): 16–18 + .
Scene-by-scene descriptive commentary of the dramatic action of the opera. Mention is made of musical features such as motives, modes, and tempi.

4345. Tuggle, Robert A. "The Measure of a Man." *Opera News,* 33 (December 14, 1968): 24–25.
Brief observations on musical characterizations in the arias. Musical examples.

Te Deum

4346. Warburton, A. O. "Set Works for 'O' Level, GCE." *Music Teacher,* 51 (September 1972): 16–18.
Background and analysis for the undergraduate student.

La Traviata

4347. Borroff, Edith. "Verisimilitude and the Operatic Set Piece." *College Music Symposium,* 24, no. 1 (1984): 123–126.
Detailed descriptive commentary on several arias, with remarks on their role in the overall dramatic structure. Author compares Wagner and Verdi in their treatment of action and drama.

4348. Machlis, Joseph. *The Enjoyment of Music.* 3d ed., 175–179. New York: W. W. Norton, 1970.
Brief overview, with analytic remarks. Musical examples.

Il Trovatore

4349. Klein, Howard. "At White Heat." *Opera News,* 30 (December 4, (1965): 24–25.
Explores Verdi's use of tonality in *Trovatore.* Musical examples.

4350. Parker, Roger. "The Dramatic Structure of *Il Trovatore.*" *Music Analysis,* 1, no. 2 (1982): 155–167.

4351. Petrobelli, Pierluigi. "Towards an Explanation of the Dramatic Structure of *Il Trovatore.*" *Music Analysis,* 1, no. 2 (1982): 129–141.

I Vespri Siciliani

4352. Freeman, John. "Things to Come." *Opera News,* 38 (March 9, 1974): 20–21.
Vespri's place in Verdi's output, with descriptive commentary. Musical examples.

DISSERTATIONS AND THESES

General

4353.   Rindo, John Patrick. "A Structural Analysis of Giuseppe Verdi's Early Operas and Their Influence on the Italian Risorgimento." Ph.D., University of Oregon, 1984, 333 pp., DA 45-1922A.

Ernani

4354.   Stocker, Leonard L. "The Treatment of the Romantic Literary Hero in Verdi's *Ernani* and in Massenet's *Werther.*" Ph.D., Florida State University, 1969, 188 pp., DA 32-3358A.

Falstaff

4355.   Sabbeth, Daniel Paul. "Principles of Tonal and Dramatic Organization in Verdi's *Falstaff.*" Ph.D., City University of New York, 1976, 234 pp., DA 37-3980A.

Otello

4356.   Grace, Irwin. "An Analysis of the Dramatic Content of the Music of Verdi's *Otello.*" Ed.D., Columbia University, 1969, 275 pp., DA 32-999A-100A.

VIERNE, LOUIS, 1870–1937

Symphonies for Organ

4357.   Long, P. C. "Vierne and His Six Organ Symphonies." *Diapason*, 21 (June 1970): 23–25; (July 1970): 7–9; (August 1970): 8–10. Thorough study, including historical background and analyses. Musical examples and bibliography.

VILLA-LOBOS, HEITOR, 1887–1959

Bachianas Brasileiras

4358.   Béhague, Gerard. *Music in Latin America: An Introduction,* 197–201. Englewood Cliffs, NJ: Prentice-Hall 1979. Brief analytic overview. Musical examples.

Choros

4359. Béhague, Gerard. *Music in Latin America: An Introduction*, 193–197. Englewood Cliffs, NJ: Prentice-Hall 1979.
Brief analytic overview. Musical examples.

Rudepoema for Piano

4360. Béhague, Gerard. *Music in Latin America: An Introduction*, 189–192. Englewood Cliffs, NJ: Prentice-Hall, 1979.
Brief analytic overview. Musical examples.

DISSERTATIONS AND THESES

Symphonies

4361. Enyart, John William. "The Symphonies of Heitor Villa-Lobos." Ph.D., University of Cincinnati, 1984, 501 pp., DA 45-1907A.

VIVALDI, ANTONIO, 1678–1741

General

4362. Bukofzer, Manfred. *Music in the Baroque Era*, 229–231. New York: W. W. Norton, 1947.
Brief but compact assessment of Vivaldi's part in the history of the concerto form. Stylistic features mentioned with musical examples.

4363. Cross, Eric. "The Relationship Between Text and Music in the Operas of Vivaldi." In *Opera and Vivaldi*. Edited by Michael Collins and E. K. Kirk, 279–307. Austin: University of Texas Press, 1984.
Discussion includes treatment of tonality, rhythm, chromaticism, instrumentation, and figuration.

4364. Kolneder, Walter. *Antonio Vivaldi: His Life and Work*. Translated by B. Hopkins. Berkeley: University of California Press, 1970, 228 pp.
Historical, descriptive and analytic overview of Vivaldi's output. Musical examples.

4365. Pincherle, Marc. *Vivaldi: Genius of the Baroque*. Translated by Christopher Hatch. New York: W. W. Norton, 1962, 278 pp.
"Life and works" study. The section on his works deals primarily with style and form. The general analytic observations about Vivaldi's music (principally his instrumental music) are supported

by many musical examples taken from specific pieces. Very short chapter on the operatic and sacred music.

4366. Talbot, Michael. *Vivaldi.* London: J. M. Dent and Sons, 1978, 275 pp.
"Master Musician" series treatment. Background, descriptive, and analytic commentary intended for the undergraduate student. Musical examples.

Beatus Vir

4367. Mahrt, William P. "Antonio Vivaldi (1678–1741) and His Sacred Music." *Sacred Music,* 105, no. 4 (1978): 7–19.
An overview of Baroque forms, followed by a brief analysis with commentary on the adoption of secular forms to sacred works. Musical examples.

Concertos

4368. Grout, Donald Jay. *A History of Western Music,* 371–375. New York: W. W. Norton, 1960.
General remarks on salient musical characteristics and basic formal structure found in the concertos.

4369. Hutchings, Arthur. *The Baroque Concerto,* 133–173. New York: W. W. Norton, 1961.
Extensive remarks on stylistic traits and Vivaldi's contribution to the concerto form. Musical examples.

4370. Palisca, Claude. *Baroque Music,* 149–152. Englewood Cliffs, NJ: Prentice-Hall, 1968.
Critical remarks on specific concertos as well as commentary on Vivaldi's handling of the new form. Musical examples.

4371. Seidler, R. "Vivaldi's Concertos for Bassoon or Oboe." *NACWPI,* 25, no. 4 (1977): 3–23.
Descriptive and analytic commentary of nine concertos for bassoon or oboe. Musical examples and bibliography.

4372. Veinus, Abraham. *The Concerto.* Rev. ed., 21–26. New York: Dover Publications, 1964.
General remarks on the stylistic traits of the music. Mainly descriptive and background remarks.

Concerto Grosso, Op. 3, No. 8 in A Minor (RV 522)

4373. Green, Douglass M. *Form in Tonal Music*, 228–231. New York: Holt, Rinehart, and Winston, 1965.
> Very close analysis, with elaborate graphs and musical examples. First movement only.

4374. Stedman, Preston. *The Symphony*, 11–13. Englewood Cliffs, NJ: Prentice-Hall, 1979.
> Brief description of form and solo materials. Musical examples.

4375. Ulrich, Homer. *Music: A Design for Listening*, 220–221. New York: Harcourt, Brace, 1957.
> Descriptive breakdown by measures. Musical examples.

Concerto for Violoncello, Op. 3, No. 6 in C Major (RV 399)

4376. Green, Douglass M. *Form in Tonal Music*, 231–232. New York: Holt, Rinehart, and Winston, 1965.
> Brief but compact analysis, with graph. Some general observations on characteristics shared by most Vivaldi first and last movements of concertos. Last movement only.

Griselda

4377. Cross, Eric. *The Late Operas of Antonio Vivaldi, 1727–1738.* 2 vols. Ann Arbor: UMI Research Press, 1981.
> Background, overall structure, libretto, melody, harmony, phrase structure, rhythm discussed thoroughly. Full musical examples.

4378. Cross, Eric. "Vivaldi as Opera Composer: *Griselda.*" *Musical Times*, 119 (May 1978): 411–413+.
> A discussion of Vivaldi's dramatic use of modulation and distant keys.

Orlando Furioso

4379. Harris, Ellen. "Eighteenth Century Orlando: Hero, Satyr, and Fool." In *Opera and Vivaldi*. Edited by Michael Collins and E. K. Kirk, 120–124. Austin: University of Texas Press, 1984.
> Analytic comments on thematic structure of the arias.

Seasons

4380. Talbot, Michael. "Vivaldi's *Four Seasons.*" *Music Teacher*, 59 (February 1980): 16–18.
> Background and critical commentary, with an analysis. Musical examples and brief bibliography.

Stabat Mater

4381.   Mahrt, William P. "Antonio Vivaldi (1648–1741) and His Sacred Music." *Sacred Music*, 105, no. 4 (1978): 7–19.
An overview of Baroque forms, followed by a general discussion on the adoption of secular forms to sacred works with particular reference to this piece. Musical examples.

DISSERTATIONS AND THESES

Concertos for Bassoon

4382.   Seidler, Richard David. "The Bassoon Concertos of Antonio Vivaldi." Ph.D., Catholic University of America, 1974, 787 pp., DA 34-7811A-12A.

WAGNER, RICHARD, 1813–1883

General

4383.   Adorno, Theodor. *In Search of Wagner.* Translated by R. Livingston. New York: Schocken Books, 1981, 159 pp.
Free-ranging analytic essays in chapters on "Gesture," "Motiv," "Sonority," "Color," and "Music Drama."

4384.   Bekker, Paul. *Richard Wagner: His Life in His Work.* Translated by M. M. Bozman. New York: Books for Libraries Press, 1970, 522 pp.
All the operas surveyed. Analytic remarks.

4385.   Cooke, Deryck. *Vindications: Essays on Romantic Music,* 25–36. London: Faber and Faber, 1982.
Detailed exploration into the expressive content of Wagner's leitmotivs. Musical examples.

4386.   Dahlhaus, Carl. *Richard Wagner's Music Dramas.* Translated by M. Whittall. Cambridge: Cambridge University Press, 1979.
A view of the *Ring* as a whole, from its conception, its use of myth, poetic form, and leitmotivs. Background and analytic remarks on the music dramas outside the *Ring* cycle as well.

4387.   Henderson, William J. *Richard Wagner: His Life and His Dramas.* 1923. Reprint. 2d ed., rev. New York: AMS Press, 1971, 504 pp.
Orderly overview of the operas, giving background, plot and all the leitmotivs. Handy guide for the undergraduate student.

4388.   Jacobs, Robert L. *Wagner.* London: J. M. Dent and Sons, 1965, 278 pp.

Brief and accessible treatment of Wagner's stylistic growth. Musical examples.

4389.   Millington, Barry. *Wagner.* London: J. M. Dent and Sons, 1984, 342 pp.

Traces stylistic development in the early operas, reserving fuller treatment for the *Ring* cycle, *Tristan, Meistersinger,* and *Parsifal.* For these, sources, libretto, compositional history, musical analysis, and orchestration are discussed. Other instrumental and vocal works are also considered. Musical examples.

4390.   Newcomb, Anthony. "The Birth of Music Out of the Spirit of Drama: An Essay in Wagnerian Formal Analysis." *Nineteenth Century Music,* 5, no. 1 (1981): 38–66.

An extended and detailed essay on the analysis of Wagner's music. Summarizes older analytic approaches, discusses the meaning of the term "form," Wagner's use of traditional formal schemes, his use of tempo, instrumentation, dramatic structure of text, rhythmic structure, motives, and tonality. Includes a critique of recent analytic approaches and concludes with analyses of three specific works: *Siegfried, Tristan,* and *Walküre.*

4391.   Newman, Ernest. *Wagner As Man and Artist.* New York: Tudor Publishing Co., 399 pp.

Explores Wagner's theories as they apply to his music.

4392.   Timbrell, Charles W. "Wagner's Piano Music." *American Music Teacher,* 23, no. 5 (1974): 5–9; (1974): 6–9.

Examination of all the extant piano music of Wagner. Comments on style, form, harmony, rhythm, and other unifying factors. Includes a brief background of each piece and a catalog of the piano compositions. Musical examples.

Adagio for Clarinet and Strings

4393.   Newhill, John P. "The Adagio for Clarinet and Strings by Wagner/Baermann." *Music and Letters,* 55, no. 2 (1974): 167–171.

Reveals the true composer of the work and cites its source. Descriptive commentary and analytic remarks, as well as background information. Musical examples.

Die Feen

4394. Williamson, Avery. "Early, Early Wagner." *Opera News*, 32 (January 27, 1968): 8–12.
Brief descriptive overview of some special musical effects and characterization. Musical examples.

The Flying Dutchman

4395. Dahlhaus, Carl. *Richard Wagner's Music Dramas*, 7–20. Cambridge: Cambridge University Press, 1979.
Background and analytic observations. Musical examples.

4396. Downes, Edward. "Wings of the Storm." *Opera News*, 29 (February 13, 1965): 24–26.
Musical depiction and leitmotivs briefly discussed. Musical examples.

4397. Granville Barker, Frank, ed. *The Flying Dutchman: English National Opera Guide 12.* London: John Calder, 1982, 80 pp.
Essays by John Warrack (background), John Deathridge (analytical introduction to the opera), William Vaughan (on the legend), and Richard Wagner (on the overture and on how to perform the work). Also contains the complete libretto and table of themes referred to in the articles.

Die Götterdämmerung (Twilight of the Gods)

4398. Dahlhaus, Carl. *Richard Wagner's Music Dramas*, 131–141. Cambridge: Cambridge University Press, 1979.
Background and analytic observations. Musical examples.

4399. Jenkins, Speight. "Wagner's Grand Opera." *Opera News*, 38 (March 23, 1974): 24–25.
Wagner's new theories and maturity as a composer are demonstrated in this brief essay by examining his use of motives. Musical examples.

4400. Kinderman, William. "Dramatic Recapitulation in Wagner's *Götterdämmerung*." *Nineteenth Century Music*, 4, no. 2 (1980): 101–112.
An investigation of the dramatic implications of recapitulations in *Götterdämmerung*—including detailed observations of tonal relations. Musical examples, tables.

4401.   Raphael, Robert. *Richard Wagner.* New York: Twayne, 1969, 153 pp.

Focus is on Wagner's literary and philosophical achievements. Discussion of the music as well.

4402.   Ryde, Peter John. *"Götterdämmerung*—Possible Solutions to Some Wagner Problems." *Opera,* 22 (January 1971): 26–31.

A new interpretation of the *Ring* cycle story. Explains basic story inconsistency.

Gedichte (Five) für eine Frauenstimme

4403.   Gauldin, Robert. "Wagner's Parody Technique: *Traeume* and the *Tristan* Love Duet." *Music Theory Spectrum,* 1 (1979): 35–42.

Analytic observations, tracing its influence on Wagner's later work, the love duet from *Tristan.* Graphs, musical examples.

Das Liebesverbot

4404.   Badacsonyi, George. "Wagner's Shakespearian Opera." *Opera,* 16 (February 1965): 89–92.

Critical evaluation of this little-performed early opera.

4405.   Williamson, Avery. "Early, Early Wagner." *Opera News,* 32 (January 27, 1968): 8–12.

Brief descriptive overview of some special musical effects and characterization. Musical examples.

Lohengrin

4406.   Dahlhaus, Carl. *Richard Wagner's Music Dramas,* 35–48. Cambridge: Cambridge University Press, 1979.

Extended commentary on background, plot, and music. Many analytic observations. Musical examples.

4407.   McDonald, Katherine. "Study in Black and White." *Opera News,* 32 (February 10, 1968): 24–25.

Analytic commentary, with musical examples.

Lohengrin: "Elsa's Dream"

4408.   Darcy, Warren. " 'Elsa's Dream': A Dramatic Musical Analysis." *NATS Bulletin,* 38, no. 3 (1982): 14–19.

Extensive analysis, with musical examples.

Die Meistersinger

4409.   Atterberg, Kurt. "Midsummer Mood." *Opera News,* 36 (January 15, 1972): 21–23.
Brief examples of how Wagner portrays mood through musical devices. Musical examples.

4410.   Dahlhaus, Carl. *Richard Wagner's Music Dramas,* 65–79. Cambridge: Cambridge University Press, 1979.
Extended commentary on background, plot, and music. Many analytic observations. Musical examples.

4411.   Donington, Robert. *The Opera,* 160–164. New York: Harcourt Brace Jovanovich, 1978.
Brief overview of dramatic and musical action. Musical examples.

4412.   George, Graham. "The Structure of Dramatic Music, 1607–1909." *Musical Quarterly,* 52, no. 4 (1966): 467–471 +.
Survey focusing on *Die Meistersinger,* with a detailed analysis of Act III.

4413.   George, Graham. *Tonality and Musical Structure,* 53–71. New York: Praeger, 1970.
Tonal structure examined in detail. Chart.

4414.   John, Nicholas, ed. *Die Meistersinger.* London: John Calder, 1984, 128 pp.
An introduction to the opera for the general public. Analytic comments on the leitmotivs, characterization, drama, and other musical features. Musical examples.

4415.   Kerman, Joseph. "Night Music." *Opera News,* 31 (January 14, 1967): 24–25.
A look at some of the many special and ingenious effects of the opera. The "nightwatchman" scene is the focus of the discussion. Musical examples.

4416.   Lee, M. Owen. "Baptism of Song." *Opera News,* 33 (December 28, 1968): 24–25.
Brief observations on the images and metaphors in the text. Bird motives as well as references to shoes, hammering, cobblers have metaphorical implications.

4417.   Raynor, Robert. *Wagner and "Die Meistersinger."* London: Oxford University Press, 1940, 263 pp.
Thorough treatment, showing sources, creative development, and a descriptive commentary with musical examples of leitmotivs.

Parsifal

4418. Beckett, Lucy. " 'Parsifal' As Drama." *Music and Letters*, 52, no. 3 (1971): 259–271.
Extended discussion of the symbolism in the story and the story's relationship to religion. No discussion of the music.

4419. Beckett, Lucy. *Richard Wagner: "Parsifal."* New York: Cambridge University Press, 1981, 163 pp.
Thorough discussion of the music, sources, text, stage history, critical assessments, and interpretation. Bibliography and discography.

4420. Dahlhaus, Carl. *Richard Wagner's Music Dramas*, 142–155. Cambridge: Cambridge University Press, 1979.
Background and analytic observations. Musical examples.

4421. Honig, Joel. "Transfigured Knight." *Opera News*, 30 (April 2, 1966): 26–27.
Analytic remarks on the Prelude to *Parsifal*.

4422. Sutcliffe, James H. "*Parsifal*: Summation of a Musical Lifetime, Part 1." *Opera*, 33 (July 1982): 686–692.
Dwelling mainly on the relationship between *Parsifal* and *Tristan*, musical threads from other Wagner operas are traced. Musical examples.

4423. Sutcliffe, James H. *Parsifal*, Summation of a Musical Lifetime, Part 2." *Opera*, 33 (August 1982): 805–812.
Motifs in *Parsifal* examined for their relationship to *Tristan*. Continuation of article cited above (*see* item no. 4422). Musical examples.

Das Rheingold

4424. Dahlhaus, Carl. *Richard Wagner's Music Dramas*, 110–118. Cambridge: Cambridge University Press, 1979.
Full background on plot sources, composer's inspiration, and the music. Many analytic observations. Musical examples.

4425. Downes, Edward. "Bridge to a New World." *Opera News*, 33 (February 22, 1969): 24–25.
Brief discussion of the principal motifs that form the foundation for *Das Rheingold* and perhaps the entire *Ring* cycle. Musical examples.

Rienzi

4426.   Scherman, Thomas. "The Riddle of *Rienzi.*" *Music Journal,* 21 (November 1963): 26–28.
Background, brief descriptive and critical remarks.

The Ring of the Nibelung

4427.   Chapman, Kenneth G. "Siegfried and Brünnhilde and the Passage of Time in Wagner's *Ring.*" *Current Musicology,* 32 (1981): 43–58.
A discussion of the question: "How much time is meant to have passed between the end of *Siegfried* and the beginning of *Götterdämmerung?*" Textual and musical evidence is considered, with analytic comments on the music. Musical examples.

4428.   Cooke, Deryck. *I Saw the World End: A Study of Wagner's "Ring,"* 37–73. London: Oxford University Press, 1979.
A critique of previous musical analyses based on leitmotivs, principally those of Hans Wolzogen. Many musical examples and numerous analytic observations on the *Ring.*

4429.   Dahlhaus, Carl. *Richard Wagner's Music Dramas,* 80–109. Cambridge: Cambridge University Press, 1979.
A view of the *Ring* as a whole from its conception, its use of myth, poetic form and leitmotivs.

4430.   DiGaetani, John L., ed. *Penetrating Wagner's Ring: An Anthology.* Rutherford, NJ: Fairleigh Dickinson University Press, 1978, 453 pp.
Interpretation, historical influences, literary sources, the music of the individual operas analyzed, performance discussed in thorough articles by various authors. Musical examples.

4431.   Donington, Robert. *The Opera,* 144–157. New York: Harcourt Brace Jovanovich, 1978.
Overview of the dramatic and musical action in *Das Rheingold, Die Walküre, Siegfried, Die Götterdämmerung,* with leading motives and their connections. Musical examples.

4432.   Donington, Robert. *Wagner's "Ring" and Its Symbols.* London: Faber and Faber, 1974, 342 pp.
The story of the *Ring* perceived on a symbolic level. Psychological forces and ancient myths based on these forces are called into play in Wagner's story. A chart of leitmotivs is provided.

4433. Hamilton, David. "How Wagner Forged His *Ring*." *Opera News*, 39, no. 15 (February 15–March 1975): 21–26.
General remarks on Wagner's grand time scale, sense of structure and genius for transition. Motives mentioned. Musical examples.

4434. Jacobs, Robert L. "A Freudian View of *The Ring*." *Music Review*, 26, no. 3 (1965): 201–219.
A psychoanalytic view of the dramatic forces of the *Ring* story. Little mention of the music.

4435. Loveday, Lillian F. "Sieglinde's Sorrow." *Opera News*, 37 (December 16, 1972): 24–25.
Brief description of the character of Sieglinde and how the music is associated with her. Motives are included in musical examples.

4436. Plantinga, Leon. *Romantic Music*, 272–285. New York: W. W. Norton, 1984.
Analytic comments. Musical examples.

Siegfried

4437. Dahlhaus, Carl. *Richard Wagner's Music Dramas*, 126–133. Cambridge: Cambridge University Press, 1979.
Background and analytic observations. Musical examples.

4438. John, Nicholas, ed. *Siegfried*. London: John Calder, 1984, 128 pp.
An introduction to the opera for the general public. Analytic comments on leitmotivs, characterization, drama, and other musical features. Musical examples.

4439. McCreless, Patrick. *Wagner's "Siegfried": Its Drama, History, and Music*. Ann Arbor: UMI Research Press, 1982, 248 pp.
Thorough, book-length analysis dealing with the dramatic, comic, tonal, and formal structure. Genesis of *Siegfried* and dramatic structure of the *Ring* as a whole also discussed. Musical examples and charts.

Siegfried (Act III, Scene I, "Wotan and Erde")

4440. Newcomb, Anthony. "The Birth of Music Out of the Spirit of Drama: An Essay in Wagnerian Formal Analysis." *Nineteenth Century Music*, 5, no. 1 (1981): 58–64.

An extended and detailed essay on the analysis of Wagner's music. Summarizes older analytic approaches, defines the term "form," and provides a critique of recent approaches. Includes analyses based on principles discussed at beginning of article.

Tannhäuser

4441.   Lawrence, Robert. "Hymn to Venus." *Opera News,* 42 (January 21, 1978): 8–13.
A comparison of the Paris and Dresden versions. Musical examples.

Tannhäuser: Venusberg Music

4442.   Dahlhaus, Carl. *Richard Wagner's Music Dramas,* 21–34. Cambridge: Cambridge University Press, 1979.
Extended essay providing background on plot, plot sources, and composer's inspiration. Many analytic observations. Musical examples.

4443.   Tovey, Donald Francis. *Essays in Musical Analysis.* Vol. 6, 114–116. London: Oxford University Press, 1969.
Critical and analytic with musical examples. For the undergraduate student.

Tristan and Isolde

4444.   Beeson, Roger. "The 'Tristan' Chord and Others; Harmonic Analysis and Harmonic Explanation." *Soundings,* 5 (1975): 55–72.

4445.   Cone, Edward T. " 'Yet Once More, O Ye Laurels.' " *Perspectives of New Music,* 14, no. 2, 15, no. 1 (1976): 294–306.
A discussion of how the opening measures of *Tristan* provide all the motivic material that underlies the whole work. Musical examples.

4446.   Dahlhaus, Carl. *Richard Wagner's Music Dramas,* 49–64. Cambridge: Cambridge University Press, 1979.
Full discussion of the opera, including background, plot, and analytic observations on the music. Musical examples.

4447.   Enix, Margery. "Formal Expansion Through Fusion of Major and Minor: A Study of Tonal Structure in *Tristan and Isolde,* Act I." *Indiana Theory Review,* 1, no. 2 (1978): 28–34.

4448. Gauldin, Robert. "Wagner's Parody Technique: *Träume* and the *Tristan* Love Duet." *Music Theory Spectrum*, 1 (1979): 35–42.
A discussion of the love duet. Motivic features, tonal scheme, thematic material show the influence of Wagner's earlier song *Träume*. Musical examples, graph.

4449. Knapp, Raymond "The Tonal Structure of *Tristan and Isolde*: A Sketch." *Music Review*, 45, no. 1 (1984): 11–25.
Harmonic analysis of the "Tristan chord" and discussion of the tonal structure of the opera. Musical examples.

4450. Machlis, Joseph. *The Enjoyment of Music.* 3 ed., 192–194. New York: W. W. Norton, 1970.
Brief analytic overview with musical examples. For the undergraduate student.

4451. Nattiez, Jean Jacques. "The Concepts of Plot and Seriation Process in Music Analysis." *Music Analysis*, 4, nos. 1–2 (1985): 107 + .
Advanced analysis. Includes discussion of the "Tristan" chord. Musical examples.

4452. Plantinga, Leon. *Romantic Music*, 286–291. New York: W. W. Norton, 1984.
Analytic comments. Musical examples.

4453. Raymond, Joely. "The Leitmotiv and Musical-Dramatic Structure in Tristan's Third Narration of the Delirium." *Indiana Theory Review*, 3, no. 3 (1980): 3–17.

4454. Rudolf, Max. "A Stroke of Genius." *Opera News*, 38 (January 26, 1974): 24–25.
Brief analysis of the solo violin motive in Act III to show Wagner's genius for transition. Musical examples.

4455. Tovey, Donald Francis. *Essays in Musical Analysis.* Vol. 4, 124–126. London: Oxford University Press, 1969.
Critical and analytic study with musical examples. For the undergraduate student.

4456. Truscott, Harold. "Wagner's *Tristan* and the Twentieth Century." *Music Review*, 24, no. 1 (1963): 75–85.
Refutes theory that the *Tristan* Prelude has the basis of twelve-tone music within it. Author sees it as thoroughly tonal and holds false the claim that twelve-tone music is a natural step from Wagner's *Tristan* Prelude.

Tristan and Isolde (Act II, Scene II, "Love Duet")

4457. Newcomb, Anthony. "The Birth of Music Out of the Spirit of Drama: An Essay in Wagnerian Formal Analysis." *Nineteenth Century Music*, 5, no. 1 (1981): 56–58.

An extended and detailed essay on the analysis of Wagner's music. Summarizes older analytic approaches, defines the term "form," and provides a critique of recent approaches. Includes analyses based on principles discussed at beginning of article.

Tristan and Isolde: Prelude

4458. Barford, Philip T. "The Way of Unit: A Study of *Tristan and Isolde.*" *Music Review*, 20 (August–November 1959): 253–263.

A discussion of the mythical and the musical in the opera, and how the two relate to each other.

4459. Friedheim, Philip. "The Relationship Between Tonality and Musical Structure." *Music Review*, 27, no. 1 (1966): 44–53.

An examination of the tonal structure of *Tristan*. Musical examples.

4460. Hill, Cecil. "That Wagner-Tristan Chord." *Music Review*, 45, no. 1 (1984): 7–10.

Harmonic analysis, with musical examples.

4461. Jackson, Roland. "Leitmotive and Form in the *Tristan* Prelude." *Music Review*, 36, no. 1 (1975): 42–53.

Analysis of the Prelude, with particular emphasis on the treatment of leitmotiv. Also traces earlier appearances (before Wagner) of the so-called "Tristan" chord.

4462. Mitchell, William J. "The *Tristan* Prelude: Techniques and Structure." In *The Music Forum*. Vol. 1. Edited by William J. Mitchell and Felix Salzer, 162–203. New York: Columbia University Press, 1967.

Exhaustive Schenkerian analysis, with musical examples. For the advanced student.

Tristan and Isolde: Prelude and Liebestod

4463. Bailey, Robert, ed. *Richard Wagner: Prelude and Transfiguration from "Tristan and Isolde."* Norton Critical Scores. New York: W. W. Norton, 1985. 306 pp.

613

Background, descriptive commentary, criticism of the work during Wagner's lifetime to current critical commentary and analysis. Full score included.

4464. Kerman, Joseph. *Listen.* 2d ed., 256–257. New York: Worth Publishers, 1976.
Brief analysis, with musical examples. For the undergraduate student.

Die Walküre

4465. Abraham, Gerald. *A Hundred Years of Music*, 122–129. London: Duckworth, 1949.
Detailed analysis of the entire first act. Mainly from a formal point of view, rather than harmonic or rhythmic. Motivs identified. Musical examples.

4466. Dahlhaus, Carl. *Richard Wagner's Music Dramas*, 119–125. Cambridge: Cambridge University Press, 1979.
Background and analytic observations. Musical examples.

4467. Downes, Edward. "The Subject Is Love." *Opera News*, 33 (March 1, 1969): 24–25.
Brief discussion of the music, its maturity over *Das Rheingold*, and Wagner's technique in using motivs. Musical examples.

4468. John, Nicholas, ed. *The Valkyrie.* London: John Calder, 1984, 112 pp.
An introduction to the opera for the general public. Describes the leitmotiv technique and identifies the major themes. Contains other analytic comments. Musical examples.

4469. Machlis, Joseph. *The Enjoyment of Music.* 3d ed., 187–192. New York: W. W. Norton, 1970.
Brief overview, with analytic remarks. For the undergraduate student. Musical examples.

4470. Sandow, Gregory. "Uninterrupted Flow." *Opera News*, 47 (March 26, 1983): 12 + .
Brief examination of the technique behind Wagner's art of seamless musical transitions.

4471. Sutcliffe, James H. "Mortal Coils." *Opera News*, 32 (February 24, 1968): 24–25.
Brief remarks on *Walküre's* place in the *Ring* cycle and the stage of artistic development it represents.

Die Walküre (Act II, Scene I, "Frika's Lament")

4472. Newcomb, Anthony. "The Birth of Music Out of the Spirit of Drama: An Essay in Wagnerian Formal Analysis." *Nineteenth Century Music*, 5, no. 1 (1981): 55–56.
An extended and detailed essay on the analysis of Wagner's music. Summarizes older analytic approaches, defines the term "form," and provides a critique on recent approaches. Includes analyses based on principles discussed at beginning of article.

WALKER, GEORGE, 1922–

General

4473. Lerma, Dominique-René de. "The Choral Works of George Walker." *American Choral Review*, 23, no. 1 (1981): Entire issue. Overview with descriptive and analytic commentary, along with chronological list of works. Musical examples.

WALTON, WILLIAM, 1902–1983

General

4474. Hutchings, Arthur. "Music in Britain, 1916–1960." In *The New Oxford History of Music*. Vol. 10, *The Modern Age: 1890–1960*. Edited by Martin Cooper, 526–531. London: Oxford University Press, 1974.
Critical assessment and stylistic overview. Analytic comments on the Symphony No. 1. Musical examples.

4475. Palmer, Christopher. "Walton's Film Music," *Musical Times*, 113 (March 1972): 249–253.
Critical review of Walton's film scores, with analytic remarks on style and characteristic musical devices. Musical examples.

4476. Tierney, Neil. *William Walton: His Life and Music.* Dover, NH: Longwood, 1985, 303 pp.
Descriptive overview of Walton's output, dealing with his works by genre: Symphonies, Concertos, Film Music, Stage Music. Discussions tend to be limited to background, plots, formal outlines, tempos, and generalizations about style.

Belshazzar's Feast

4477. Bartlett, Ian. "Set Works for 'O' Level: A Second Look at Walton's *Belshazzar's Feast*," *Music Teacher*, 61 (March 1982): 20–21.
Brief analysis for the undergraduate student.

Concerto for Violin

4478. Dale, S. S. "Twentieth Century Violin Concertos." *Strad*, 91 (December 19890): 571–572.
 Brief descriptive and analytic commentary.

Facade

4479. Driver, Paul. "*Facade* Revisited." *Tempo*, 133–4 (September 1980): 3–9.
 Critical and analytic discussion.

Symphony No. 1

4480. Ballantine, Christopher. *Twentieth Century Symphony*, 158–161. London: Dennis Dobson, 1983.
 Analytic comments. Musical examples.

4481. Simpson, Robert, ed. *The Symphony.* Vol. 2, 189–196. Drake Publishers, 1972.
 Descriptive and critical discussion, with analytic observations on form, motives, and harmony. Musical examples.

Symphony No. 2

4482. Woodham, Ronald. "Walton's Second Symphony." *Music Review*, 22, no. 3 (1961): 251–253.
 Descriptive commentary with analytic remarks. Musical examples.

DISSERTATIONS AND THESES

Concertos

4483. De Zeeuw, Anne Marie. "Tonality and the Concertos of William Walton." Ph.D., University of Texas at Austin, 1983, 432 pp., DA 45-677A.

WARLOCK, PETER (PHILIP HESELTINE), 1894–1930

General

4484. Copely, Ian A. *The Music of Peter Warlock.* London: Dennis Dobson, 1981, 334 pp.

Revision of a dissertation. Brief treatment of Warlock's life, but extended discussion of his music. Chapters on style, songs, vocal chamber music, choral music, and instrumental music. Analytic comments with extended discussions of the larger pieces. Also discusses Warlock's work as an editor.

4485. **Copley, Ian A.** "Peter Warlock's Vocal Chamber Music." *Music and Letters*, 44, no. 4 (1963): 358–370.
Descriptive commentary, historic background, and analytic remarks on many of the cycles. Musical examples.

4486. **Hold, Trevor.** "Peter Warlock: The Art of the Song-Writer." *Music Review*, 36, no. 4 (1975): 284–299.
An assessment of Warlock as a song writer, with analyses of five of his songs. Musical examples.

Curlew

4487. **Teague, Thomas S.** "Peter Warlock's *The Curlew*." *NATS Bulletin*, 29, no. 1 (1972): 18–21+.
Analytic commentary. Musical examples and bibliography.

Sweet and Twenty

4488. **Warburton, A. O.** "Set Works for 'O' Level, GCE." *Music Teacher*, 51 (February 1972): 13.
Brief analysis.

Yarmouth Fair

4489. **Warburton, A. O.** "Set Works for 'O' Level, GCE." *Music Teacher*, 51 (February 1972): 13.
Brief analysis.

WEBER, CARL MARIA VON, 1786–1826

General

4490. **Dale, Kathleen.** *Nineteenth-Century Piano Music: A Handbook for Pianists.* London: Oxford University Press, 1954, 320 pp.
Highlights stylistic traits and unique contribution to the literature of the piano. Form and harmony and other musical aspects discussed in relation to style.

4491. Dent, Edward J. *The Rise of Romantic Opera*, 145–161. Cambridge: Cambridge University Press, 1976.
> Examination of Romantic traits and tendencies. Critical remarks on music and observations on style.

4492. Einstein, Alfred. *Music in the Romantic Era*, 111–116. New York: W. W. Norton, 1947.
> Brief overview of Weber's historical position in Romantic opera. Mention made of his musical characteristics and influence on Wagner.

4493. Langley, Robin. "Weber and the Piano." *Musical Times*, 127 (November 1986): 604–608.
> Stylistic overview, with analytic observations. Musical examples.

4494. Saunders, William. *Weber*. 1940. Reprint. New York: Da Capo Press, 1970, 384 pp.
> Critical overview, with focus on musical technique and characteristics.

4495. Warrack, John. *Carl Maria von Weber*. London: Hamish Hamilton, 1968, 377 pp.
> Full discussion of all Weber's operas, with musical characteristics and influences highlighted. Musical examples.

Der Freischütz

4496. Donington, Robert. *The Opera*, 113–117. New York: Harcourt Brace Jovanovich, 1978.
> Brief discussion of the dramatic and musical action. Musical examples.

4497. McDonald, Katherine. "Fresh from the Forest." *Opera News*, 36 (April 15, 1972): 24–25.
> Brief descriptive remarks, with musical examples. Discusses characterization and the early Romantic atmosphere of the opera.

4498. Plantinga, Leon. *Romantic Music*, 158–165. New York: W. W. Norton, 1984.
> Analytic discussion. Musical examples.

Overtures

4499. Tovey, Donald Francis. *Essays in Musical Analysis*, 52–60. London: Oxford University Press, 1969.

Critical and analytic studies with musical examples. Discusses *Euryanthe, Freischütz,* and *Oberon* Overtures. For the undergraduate student.

Oberon Overture

4500.   Warburton, A. O. "Set Works for 'O' Level, GCE." *Music Teacher,* 49 (September 1970): 19–20.
Background, descriptive, and analytic commentary.

Preciosa

4501.   Hsu, Dolores M. "Carl Maria von Weber's *Preciosa*: Incidental Music on a Spanish Theme." *Music Review,* 26, no. 2 (1965): 97–103.
Musical sources examined. Not analytic. Musical examples.

The Three Pintos

4502.   Dean, Winton. *"The Three Pintos." Musical Times,* 103 (June 1962): 409–410.
Review of a performance. Includes a brief critical overview of the work in its completion by Mahler.

DISSERTATIONS AND THESES

Euryanthe

4503.   Tusa, Michael Charles. "Carl Maria von Weber's *Euryanthe*: A Study of Its Historical Context, Genesis, and Reception." Ph.D., Princeton University, 1983, 614 pp., DA 43-3453A.

Der Freischütz

4504.   Gras, Alfred H. "A Study of *Der Freischütz* by Carl Maria von Weber." Ph.D., Northwestern University, 1968, DA 31-1832A.

Sonatas for Piano

4505.   Kang, Nakcheung Paik. "An Analytical Study of the Piano Sonatas of Carl Maria von Weber." Ph.D., New York University, 1978, 222 pp., DA 39-4582A.

4506. Marinaro, Stephen John. "The Four Piano Sonatas of Carl Maria von Weber." D.M.A., University of Texas at Austin, 1980, 54 pp., DA 41-2823A.

WEBERN, ANTON, 1883–1945

General

4507. Bracanin, Philip K. "The Palindrome: Its Applications in the Music of Anton Webern." *Miscellanea Musicologica*, 6 (1972): 38–47.

4508. Carner, Mosco. "Music in the Mainland of Europe: 1918–1939." In *The New Oxford History of Music*. Vol. 10, *The Modern Age: 1890–1960*. Edited by Martin Cooper, 372–386. London: Oxford University Press, 1974.
  Stylistic overview tracing Webern's development from the pre-dodecaphonic works to the most concentrated serial works. Analytic remarks on many works, including the Symphony Op. 21, the String Trio Op. 20, Quartet Op. 22, and Concerto Op. 24. Musical examples.

4509. Charles, Henry. "The Posthumous Songs of Anton Webern." *NATS Bulletin*, 28, no. 1 (1971): 21–23 + .
  Critical and analytic commentary, with musical examples.

4510. Kabbash, Paul. "Aggregate-Derived Symmetry in Webern's Early Works." *Journal of Music Theory*, 28, no. 2 (1983): 225–250.
  Advanced theoretical discussion. Musical examples.

4511. Kolneder, Walter. *Anton Webern: An Introduction to His Works*. Translated by Humphrey Searle. Berkeley: University of California Press, 1968, 232 pp.
  Clear analytic and critical discussion with musical examples.

4512. Moldenhauer, Hans, comp. *Anton von Webern: Perspectives*. Seattle: University of Washington Press, 1966, 191 pp.
  A collection of essays by various authors, dealing with early orchestral works, the *Dehmel Lieder*, choral works, and symphonic works. Analytic comments and observations on compositional technique. Musical examples.

4513. Moldenhauer, Hans, and Rosalien Moldenhauer. *Anton von Webern: A Chronicle of His Life and Work*. New York: Alfred A. Knopf, 1979, 803 pp.

Mainly an extensive narrative on Webern's life, with background on the compositions. However, interspersed analytic remarks (many Webern's own) may be found through the book's index of compositions.

4514. Whittall, Arnold. *Music Since the First World War,* 157–176. London J. M. Dent, 1977.
An analytic survey of his works.

Bagatelles for String Quartet, Op. 9

4515. Chrisman, Richard. "Anton Webern's Six Bagatelles for String Quartet, Op. 9: The Unfolding of Intervallic Successions." *Journal of Music Theory,* 23, no. 1 (1979): 81 + .
Advanced analysis.

Bagatelles for String Quartet, Op. 9, No. 1

4516. Hasty, Christopher. "Phase Formation in Post-Tonal Music." *Journal of Music Theory,* 28, no. 2 (1983): 179–186.

Cantata No. 1, Op. 29

4517. Hartwell, Robin. "Duration and Mental Arithmetic: The First Movement of Webern's First Cantata." *Perspectives of New Music,* 23, no. 1 (1984): 348–359.
Advanced analysis.

4518. Jone, Hildegard. "A Cantata." *Reihe,* 2 (1958): 7–8.
Brief analytic comments on the closing section of this work, "Verwandlung der Chareten." No musical examples.

4519. Kramer, Jonathan. "The Row As Structural Background and Audible Foreground: The First Movement of Webern's First Cantata." *Journal of Music Theory,* 15, nos. 1–2 (1971): 158–181.
Advanced analysis.

4520. Phipps, Graham H. "Tonality in Webern's Cantata 1." *Music Analysis,* 3, no. 2 (1984): 124–158.
Advanced analysis.

4521. Saturen, David. "Symmetrical Relationships in Webern's First Cantata." *Perspectives of New Music,* 6, no. 1 (1967): 142–143.
Advanced analysis with musical examples.

Concerto for Nine Instruments, Op. 24

4522.   Beach, David. "Segmental Invariance and the Twelve-Tone System."*Journal of Music Theory*, 20, no. 2 (1976): 157–184.

4523.   Cohen, David. "Anton Webern and the Magic Square." *Perspectives of New Music*, 13, no. 1 (1974): 213–215.
Detailed analytic discussion of measures 56–70, showing the presence of trichords that form interlocking palindromes. Musical examples, as well as reproduction of Latin word square that fascinated Webern.

4524.   Gauldin, Robert. "The Magic Squares of the Third Movement of Webern's Concerto Op. 24." *In Theory Only*, 2 (February–March 1977): 32–42.

4525.   Gauldin, Robert. "Pitch Structure in the Second Movement of Webern's Concerto, Op. 24." *In Theory Only*, 2 (January 1977): 8–22.
Advanced analysis.

4526.   Hansen, Peter. *An Introduction to Twentieth Century Music.* 2d ed., 226–228. Boston: Allyn and Bacon, 1967.
Brief analysis of this nine-minute composition. Musical examples.

4527.   Hasty, Christopher. "Segmentation and Process in Post-Tonal Music." *Music Theory Spectrum*, 3 (1981): 54 + .
Advanced analysis of the second movement.

4528.   Polansky, Larry. "Temporal Gestalt Perception in Music." *Journal of Music Theory*, 24, no. 2 (1980): 227–230.

4529.   Posseur, Henri. "The Question of Order in New Music." *Perspectives of New Music*, 5, no. 1 (1966): 106–108.
Webern's use of symmetry discussed. Musical examples.

4530.   Salzman, Eric. *Twentieth Century Music: An Introduction.* 2d ed., 226–227. Englewood Cliffs, NJ: Prentice-Hall, 1974.
Description of the row techniques. Musical examples.

4531.   Small, Christopher. "Webern: Concerto for Nine Instruments." *Music in Education*, 39 (1975): 19–22.
Analytic comments on all three movements. Describes the internal structure of the row and gives examples from each movement. Musical examples.

4532. Smalley, Roger. "Webern's Sketches." *Tempo,* 112 (March 1975): 2–12.
　An examination of the genesis of the work, based on the sketches. Includes some analytic comments. Musical examples.

4533. Spinner, Leopold. "Analysis of a Period." *Reihe,* 2 (1958): 46–50.
　Concentrated, advanced analysis of the first part (theme) of the second movement. Musical examples.

4534. Wintle, Christopher. "Analysis and Performance: Webern's Concerto Op. 24, No. 2." *Music Analysis,* 1, no. 1 (1981): 73–99.
　Advanced analysis.

Little Pieces (Three), Op. 11

4535. Baststone, Philip. "Musical Analysis As Phenomenology." *Perspectives of New Music,* 7, no. 2 (1969): 97–108.
　Analysis with musical examples.

4536. Kolneder, Walter. *Anton Webern.* Translated by Humphrey Searle, 78–80. Berkeley: University of California, 1968.
　Brief but concentrated analysis. Musical examples.

4537. Westergaard, Peter. "On the Problems of 'Reconstruction from a Sketch': Webern's *Kunfttag III* and *Leise Düfte.*" *Perspectives of New Music,* 11, no. 2 (1973): 104–121.
　An account of the author's efforts in reconstructing these pieces from sketches. Not analytic.

Little Pieces (Three), Op. 11, No. 1

4538. Marra, James. "Interrelations Between Pitch and Rhythmic Structure in Webern's Op. 11, No. 1." *In Theory Only,* 7 (June 1983): 3–33.

Little Pieces (Three), Op. 11, No. 3

4539. Cogan, Robert, and Pozzi Escot. *Sonic Design: The Nature of Sound and Music,* 184–189. Englewood Cliffs, NJ: Prentice-Hall, 1976.
　Discusses chromatic pitch aggregates.

4540. Perle, George. *Serial Composition and Atonality: An Introduction to the Music of Schoenberg, Berg, and Webern.* 5th ed., rev., 21–23. Berkeley: University of California Press, 1981.
　Commentary on structure, pitch, and motive content. Score included.

4541.   Wintle, Christopher. "An Early Version of 'Derivation': Webern's Op. 11, No. 3" *Perspectives of New Music*, 13, no. 2 (1975): 166–177.
Analysis for the advanced student. Musical examples.

Movements (Five) for String Quartet, Op. 5

4542.   Beach, David. "Pitch Structure and the Analytic Process in Atonal Music: An Interpretation of the Theory of Sets." *Music Theory Spectrum*, 1, (1979): 7–22.

4543.   Boretz, Benjamin. "Meta-Variations, Part 4: Analytic Fallout." *Perspectives of New Music*, 11, no. 1 (1972): 217–223.
Technical discussion for the very advanced.

4544.   Ferguson, Donald N. *Image and Structure in Chamber Music*, 302–304. Minneapolis: University of Minnesota Press, 1964.
Analysis. Musical examples.

4545.   Kolneder, Walter. *Anton Webern.* Translated by Humphrey Searle, 53–58. Berkeley: University of California, 1968.
Concentrated analysis of all five movements. Musical examples.

4546.   Persky, Stanley. "A Discussion of Compositional Choices in Webern's *Fünf Sätze für Streichquartett* Op. 5." *Current Musicology*, 13 (1972): 68–74.
Discusses the melodic and harmonic aspects of pitch structure. For the advanced student.

Movements (Five) for String Quartet, Op. 5, No. 1

4547.   Reti, Rudolph. *Tonality, Atonality, Pantonality: A Study of Some Trends in Twentieth Century Music*, 75–76, 78–79, 103, 144–145. London: Rockliff, 1958.
Brief analytic comments. Musical examples.

Movements (Five) for String Quartet, Op. 5, No. 2

4548.   Archibald, Bruce. "Some Thoughts on Symmetry in Early Webern: Op. 5, No. 2." *Perspectives of New Music*, 10, no. 2 (1972): 159–163.
Principle of symmetry as a unifying device studied in the second movement of this work.

4549. Lewin, David. "Transformational Techniques in Atonal and Other Music Theories." *Perspectives of New Music*, 21, nos. 1–2 (1982): 312 + .

Movements (Five) for String Quartet, Op. 5, No. 4

4550. Boretz, Benjamin. "Meta-Variations, Part 4: Analytic Fallout." *Perspectives of New Music*, 11, no. 1 (1972): 217–223.
Analysis viewing pitch-set relations with reference to *Tristan*. Advanced. Musical examples.

4551. Burkhart, Charles. "The Symmetrical Source of Webern's Op. 5, No. 4." In *The Music Forum*. Vol 5. Edited by Felix Salzer and Carl Schachter, 317–334. Columbia University Press, 1980.
Extended analysis for the advanced student identifying a single "symmetrical construct" that functions as the piece's most crucial unifying source. Musical examples.

4552. Perle, George. *Serial Composition and Atonality: An Introduction to the Music of Schoenberg, Berg, and Webern*. 5th ed., rev., 16–19. Berkeley: University of California Press, 1981.
Commentary on the pitch structure. Score included.

Orchestral Pieces (Six), Op. 6

4553. Baker, J. J. "Coherence in Webern's Six Pieces for Orchestra." *Music Theory Spectrum*, 4 (1982): 1–27.
Advanced discussion of the unifying factors in this work.

4554. Leibowitz, René. *Schoenberg and His School*. Translated by Dika Newlin. 1949. Reprint, 197–202. New York: Da Capo Press, 1970.
Analysis with comparisons to Schoenberg and Berg. Musical examples.

Orchestral Pieces (Six), Op. 6, No. 1

4555. Barkin, Elaine. "Analysis Symposium: Webern, Orchestra Pieces (1913): Movement 1 ("Bewegt")." *Journal of Music Theory*, 19, no. 1 (1975): 48–64.
Advanced theoretical analysis dwelling on motivic features and intervallic design. Musical examples.

4556. Elston, Arnold, et al. "Some Views of Webern's Op. 6, No. 1: The Formal Structure." *Perspectives of New Music*, 6, no. 1 (1967): 63–78.
Advanced analysis.

Orchestral Pieces (Six), Op. 6, No. 3

4557.   Crotty, John E. "A Preliminary Analysis of Webern's Op. 6, No. 3." *In Theory Only*, 5 (May–June 1979): 23–32.
Advanced analysis.

Orchestral Pieces (Five), Op. 10

4558.   Kerman, Joseph. *Listen.* 2d ed., 319–321. New York: Worth Publishers, 1976.
Background and analysis, with musical examples. For the undergraduate student.

4559.   Machlis, Joseph. *Introduction to Contemporary Music*, 388–390. New York: W. W. Norton, 1961.
Descriptive commentary for the beginning student. Musical examples.

4560.   Underwood, James. "Time and Activities in Webern's Op. 10: A Composer's Viewpoint." *Indiana Theory Review*, 3, no. 2 (1980): 31–38.
Analysis of temporal aspects and their relationship to form.

Orchestral Pieces (Five), Op. 10, No. 1

4561.   Benjamin, William E. "Ideas of Order in Motivic Music." *Music Theory Specturm*, 1 (1979): 23–34.
Advanced discussion on unifying principles.

4562.   Forte, Allen, and Roy Travis. "Analysis Symposium: Webern, Orchestra Pieces (1913): Movement 1 ("Bewegt")." *Journal of Music Theory*, 18, no. 1 (1974): 2–43.
Forte analyzes the movement ("Bewegt") according to form, segmentation, hexachordal structure, and order relations. For the advanced theory student. Graphs, score, tables.

4563.   Olson, Christine. "Tonal Remnants in Early Webern: The First Movement of Orchestral Pieces (1913)." *In Theory Only*, 5 (May–June 1979): 34–46.

4564.   Snarrenberg, Robert. "Hearings of Webern's 'Bewegt.' " *Perspectives of New Music*, 24, no. 2 (1986): 386–404.
Advanced analysis of the author's aural impressions of this work. A look at its overall architecture as well. Musical examples and bibliography.

Orchestral Pieces (Five), Op. 10, No. 3

4565.   Beach, David. "Pitch Structure and the Analytic Process in Atonal Music: An Interpretation of the Theory of Sets." *Music Theory Spectrum,* 1 (1979): 7–22.

Orchestral Pieces (Five), Op. 10, No. 4

4566.   Johnson, Peter. "Symmetrical Sets in Webern's Op. 10, No. 4." *Perspectives of New Music,* 17, no. 1 (1978): 219–229.
   Advanced analysis. Musical examples.

4567.   Salzman, Eric. *Twentieth Century Music: An Introduction.* 2d ed., 207–208. Englewood Cliffs, NJ: Prentice-Hall, 1974.
   Brief analysis. Musical examples.

Passacaglia for Orchestra, Op. 1

4568.   Leibowitz, René. *Schoenberg and His School.* Translated by Dika Newlin. 1949. Reprint, 189–195. New York: Da Capo Press, 1970.
   Analysis with comparisons to Berg and Schoenberg. Musical examples.

4569.   Nelson, Robert U. "Webern's Path to the Serial Variation." *Perspectives of New Music,* 7, no. 2 (1969): 73–76.
   Analysis with musical examples.

Quartet for Clarinet, Violin, Saxophone, and Piano, Op. 22

4570.   Fennelly, Brian. "Structure and Process in Webern's Op. 22." *Journal of Music Theory,* 10, no. 2 (1966): 300–328.
   Analysis for the advanced student. Musical examples, charts, and tables of sets and rows.

4571.   Leibowitz, René. *Schoenberg and His School.* Translated by Dika Newlin. 1949. Reprint, 218–221. New York: Da Capo Press, 1970.
   Brief analysis focusing on contrapuntal devices, variations, and color. Musical examples.

4572.   Thomas, Janet. "The Use of Color in Three Chamber Works of the Twentieth Century." *Indiana Theory Review,* 3 (1981): 24–40.
   Discusses how Webern used his technique of *Klangfarbenmelodie* and the element of color in the composition of this quartet. Demonstrates Webern's exploitation of the color characteristics of the instruments used. Musical examples.

Quartet for Strings, Op. 28

4573.   Bracanin, Philip. "Analysis of Webern's Twelve-Note Music— Fact and Fantasy." *Studies in Music* (Australia), 2 (1968): 108–110.

4574.   Eimert, Herbert. "Interval Proportions." *Reihe*, 2 (1958): 93– 99.
> Concentrated, advanced analysis of the first movement. Musical examples, charts, and tables.

4575.   Huff, Jay A. "Webern's Op. 28: Serial Organisation of Time Spans in the Last Movement." *Music Review*, 31, no. 3 (1970): 255– 256.
> Brief technical analysis.

4576.   Leibowitz, René. *Schoenberg and His School.* Translated by Dika Newlin. 1949. Reprint, 241–251. New York: Da Capo Press, 1970.
> Thorough analysis for the intermediate student. Formal structure, tone rows, unifying devices, texture, and harmonic structure discussed. Musical examples.

4577.   Small, Christopher. "Webern: String Quartet Op. 28." *Music in Education*, 39, no. 373 (1975): 114–119.
> Analysis of the whole work. Traces the forms of the row, discusses canonic structure, form, and symmetrical properties. Musical examples.

4578.   Spinner, Leopold. "The Abolition of Thematicism and the Structural Meaning of the Method of Twelve-Tone Composition." *Tempo*, 146 (September 1983): 7–8.

4579.   Stockhausen, Karlheinz. "Structure and Experiential Time." *Reihe*, 2 (1958): 64–74.
> Concentrated, advanced analysis exploring the sense of time in this work. Musical examples, chart.

4580.   Whittall, Arnold. *Music Since the First World War*, 170–174. London: J. M. Dent and Sons, 1977.
> Analytic discussion. Musical examples and tables showing structures and row forms.

Songs (Five) from "Der Siebente Ring," Op. 3

4581.   Raney, Carolyn. "Atonality and Serialism: A Comparison of Webern's Op. 3 and Op. 23." *NATS Bulletin*, 25, no. 1 (1968): 12 +.
> Analytic commentary with musical examples.

Songs (Sacred), Op. 15, No. 4

4582.   Metzger, Heinz-Klaus. "Analysis of the Sacred Song Op. 15, No. 4." *Reihe*, 2 (1958): 75–80.
Concentrated, advanced analysis. Musical examples.

Songs (Three) from 'Viae Inviae', Op. 23

4583.   Raney, Carolyn. "Atonality and Serialism: A Comparison of Webern's Op. 3 and Op. 23." *NATS Bulletin*, 25, no. 1 (1968): 12 + .
Analytic commentary with musical examples.

Songs (Three), Op. 25

4584.   Chittum, Donald. "Some Observations on the Row Technique in Webern's Op. 25." *Current Musicology*, 12 (1971): 96–101.
Analytic commentary. Advanced. Musical examples.

4585.   Sturhahn, Gertrude E. "An Aesthetic Evaluation of Anton Webern's *Drei Lieder*, Op. 25." *NATS Bulletin*, 25, no. 4 (1969): 34–36.
Analysis focusing on musical tension and resolution. Musical examples and brief bibliography.

Songs (Three), Op. 25, No. 1

4586.   Lewin, David. "Some Applications of Communication Theory to the Study of Twelve-Tone Music." *Journal of Music Theory*, 12, no. 1 (1968): 76–80.
Highly advanced twelve-tone theoretical analysis. Score necessary.

Symphony for Chamber Orchestra, Op. 21

4587.   Austin, William W. *Music in the Twentieth Century*, 357–367. New York: W. W. Norton, 1966.
Analysis with musical examples.

4588.   Ballantine, Christopher. *Twentieth Century Symphony*, 194–201. London: Dennis Dobson, 1983.
Analytic discussion. Musical examples.

4589.   Borris, Siegfried. "Structural Analysis of Webern's Symphony Op. 21." In *Paul A. Pisk: Essays in His Honor*. Edited by John Glowacki, 231–242. Austin: University of Texas Press, 1966.
Thorough analysis with diagrams and musical examples.

629

4590. Brindle, Reginald Smith. *The New Music: The Avant-Garde Since 1945*, 11–12. London: Oxford University Press, 1975.
Short paragraph, but offers key to formal structure. Musical examples.

4591. Dagnes, Edward P. "Symmetrical Structures in Webern: An Analytical Overview of the *Symphonie*, Movement 2, Variation 3." *In Theory Only*, 1 (December–January 1976–1977): 33–51.

4592. Deri, Otto. *Exploring Twentieth-Century Music*, 377. New York: Holt, Rinehart, and Winston, 1968.
Concentrated description of formal structure.

4593. Hiller, Lejaren, and Ramon Fuller. "Structure and Information in Webern's *Symphonie*, Op. 21." *Journal of Music Theory*, 11, no. 1 (1967): 60–115.
Complete structural analysis and an information theory analysis of the first movement only. Graphs and tables.

4594. Hitchcock, H. Wiley. "Colloquy and Review: A Footnote on Webern's Variations." *Perspectives of New Music*, 8, no. 2 (1970): 123–126.
Argument against doubts introduced by Nelson's article cited below (*see* item no. 4599) that the entire second movement is palindromic. Musical examples.

4595. Kerr, Elizabeth. "The Variations of Webern's Symphony Op. 21: Some Observations on Rhythmic Organization and the Use of Numerology." *In Theory Only*, 8, no. 2 (1984): 5–14.

4596. Kolneder, Walter. *Anton Webern: An Introduction to His Works.* Translated by Humphrey Searle, 113–119. Berkeley: University of California Press, 1968.
Analysis with musical examples.

4597. Leibowitz, René. *Schoenberg and His School.* Translated by Dika Newlin. 1949. Reprint, 211–218. New York: Da Capo Press, 1970.
Analysis discussing contrapuntal devices, formal scheme, motives, and development. Importance of this work in Webern's output assessed. Musical examples.

4598. Machlis, Joseph. *Introduction to Contemporary Music*, 391–397. New York: W. W. Norton, 1961.
Full treatment, dealing with complex elements in a style accessible to the undergraduate student. Musical examples.

4599.   Nelson, Robert U. "Webern's Path to Serial Variation." *Perspectives of New Music*, 7, no. 2 (1969): 76–82.
Advanced analysis with musical examples.

4600.   Perle, George. *Serial Composition and Atonality: An Introduction to the Music of Schoenberg, Berg, and Webern.* 5th ed., rev., 118–126. Berkeley: University of California Press, 1981.
Discussion of the pitch structure, form, rhythm, texture, and the relationships between these elements. Musical examples.

4601.   Smith, Charles J. "Comment on Dagnes." *In Theory Only*, 1 (December–January 1976–1977): 53–54.
A response to Dagnes's article cited above.

4602.   Spinner, Leopold. "The Abolition of Thematicism and the Structural Meaning of the Method of Twelve-Tone Composition." *Tempo*, 146 (September 1983): 4–7.

4603.   Starr, Mark. "Colloquy and Review: Webern's Palindrome." *Perspectives of New Music*, 8, no. 2 (1970): 127–142.
Further explanation of the palindromic second movement. Musical examples. See articles by Hitchcock and Nelson cited here (item nos. 4594 and 4599).

Trio for Strings, Op. 20

4604.   Deri, Otto. *Exploring Twentieth-Century Music*, 374–376. New York: Holt, Rinehart and Winston, 1968.
Analysis with musical examples.

4605.   Haimo, Ethan. "Secondary and Disjunct Order-Position Relationships in Webern's Op. 20." *Perspectives of New Music*, 24, no. 2 (1986): 406–419.

4606.   Leibowitz, René. *Schoenberg and His School.* Translated by Dika Newlin. 1949. Reprint, 206–209. New York: Da Capo Press, 1970.
Brief analysis. Musical examples.

4607.   Perle, George. *Serial Composition and Atonality: An Introduction to the Music of Schoenberg, Berg and Webern.* 5th ed., rev., 118–119. Berkeley: University of California Press, 1981.
Brief outline of relationship between the use of twelve-tone sets and formal structure.

Variations for Orchestra, Op. 30

4608. Austin, William W. *Music in the Twentieth Century,* 367–370. New York: W. W. Norton, 1966.
  Analysis with chart.

4609. Bailey, K. "Formal and Rhythmic Procedures in Webern's Op. 30," *CAUSM Journal,* 2, no. 1 (1972): 34–52.

4610. Cogan, Robert, and Pozzi Escot. *Sonic Design: The Nature of Sound and Music,* 189–204. Englewood Cliffs, NJ: Prentice-Hall, 1976.
  Discusses the serial technique in detail.

4611. Deri, Otto. *Exploring Twentieth-Century Music,* 380–385. New York: Holt, Rinehart, and Winston, 1968.
  Analysis with musical examples. For the intermediate student.

4612. Nelson, Robert U. "Webern's Path to Serial Variation." *Perspectives of New Music,* 7, no. 2 (1969): 87–93.
  Analysis with musical examples.

4613. Reid, John W. "Properties of the Set Explored in Webern's Variations Op. 30." *Perspectives of New Music,* 12, nos. 1–2 (1973–1974): 344–350.

4614. Spinner, Leopold. "The Abolition of Thematicism and the Structural Meaning of the Method of Twelve-Tone Composition." *Tempo,* 146 (September 1983): 4.

Variations for Piano, Op. 27

4615. Fiore, Mary E. "Webern's Use of Motive." In *The Computer and Music,* Edited by Harry Lincoln, 115–122. New York: Cornell University Press, 1970.
  Computer analysis showing the first twelve measures of the third movement as the theme. For the advanced student.

4616. Hasty, Christopher. "Rhythm in Post-Tonal Music: Preliminary Questions of Duration and Motion." *Journal of Music Theory,* 25, no. 2 (1981): 183 + .

4617. Jones, James Rives. "Some Aspects of Rhythm and Meter in Webern's Op. 27." *Perspectives of New Music,* 7, no. 1 (Fall–Winter 1968): 103–109.
  Rhythmic analysis of the first fourteen measures of the third movement. For the advanced student.

4618.   Klammer, Armin. "Webern's Piano Variations Op. 27." *Reihe,* 2 (1958): 81–92.
> Advanced, concentrated analysis of the third movement. Tables, musical examples.

4619.   Kolneder, Walter. *Anton Webern: An Introduction to His Works.* Translated by Humphrey Searle, 140–144. Berkeley: University of California Press, 1968.
> Analysis with musical examples.

4620.   Leibowitz, René. *Schoenberg and His School.* Translated by Dika Newlin. 1949. Reprint, 226–241. New York: Da Capo Press, 1970.
> Thorough analysis for the intermediate student. Musical examples.

4621.   Lewin, David. "Forte's Interval Vector, My Interval Function, and Regener's Common-Note Function." *Journal of Music Theory,* 21, no. 2 (1977): 194–237.

4622.   Lewin, David. "A Metrical Problem in Webern's Op. 27." *Journal of Music Theory,* 6, no. 1 (1962): 124–132.
> Concentrates on measures 1–6 in the second movement from a rhythmic point of view. Shows difficulties in attaining a sense of the 2/4 meter. Score necessary.

4623.   Nelson, Robert U. "Webern's Path to Serial Variation." *Perspectives of New Music,* 7, no. 2 (1969): 83–87.
> Analysis with musical examples.

4624.   Ogdon, Will. "A Webern Analysis." *Journal of Music Theory,* 6, no. 1 (1962): 133–138.
> Analysis with special emphasis on the second movement. Score necessary.

4625.   Riley, Hugh. "A Study in Constructivist Procedures: Webern's Variations for Piano Op. 27, First Movement." *Music Review,* 27, no. 3 (1966): 207–210.
> A detailed analysis of this movement, with a perspective on Webern's influence on later composers. Musical examples.

4626.   Travis, Roy. "Directed Motion in Schoenberg and Webern." *Perspectives of New Music,* 4, no. 2 (1966): 87–88.
> An attempt to apply concepts of Heinrich Schenker to this piece to determine its directed motion.

4627.   Westergaard, Peter. "Some Problems in Rhythmic Theory and Analysis." *Perspectives of New Music,* 1, no. 1 (1962): 180–191.

Analysis focusing on "the differential role of rhythm in creating pitch relationships" and "some ways in which pitch relationships create a sense of rhythm, particularly large scale rhythm." Musical examples.

4628. Westergaard, Peter. "Webern and 'Total Organization': An Analysis of the Second Movement of Piano Variations Op. 27." *Perspectives of New Music,* 1, no. 2 (1963): 107–120.
Detailed analysis of form in the second movement. Advanced. Musical examples.

DISSERTATIONS AND THESES

General

4629. Kabbash, Paul Andrew. "Form and Rhythm in Webern's Atonal Works." Ph.D., Yale University, 1983, 175 pp., DA 44-2618A.

4630. Woodward, Gregory S. "Non-Pitch Aspects As Structural Determinants in the Atonal Works of Anton Webern." D.M.A., Cornell University, 1986, 123 pp., DA 47–2368A.

Canons (Five), Op. 16

4631. Nelson, Gary Lee. "Anton Webern's Five Canons, Op. 16: A Test Case for Computer-Aided Analysis and Synthesis of Musical Style." Ph.D., Washington University, 1974, 237 pp., DA 35-2324A-5A.

Movements (Five) for String Quartet, Op. 5

4632. Vander Weg, John Dean. "Symmetrical Pitch and Equivalence Class Set Structure in Anton Webern's Op. 5." Ph.D., University of Michigan, 1983, 161 pp., DA 44-1969A.

Quartet for Violin, Clarinet, Saxophone, and Piano, Op. 22

4633. O'Leary, Jane Strong. "Aspects of Structure in Webern's Quartet, Op. 22." Ph.D., Princeton University, 1978, 98 pp., DA 39-3214A-15A.

Songs

4634. Trembath, Shirley Elizabeth. "Text and Texture in the Solo Vocal Works, Opp. 14–25 of Anton Webern." Ph.D., University of Texas at Austin, 1985, 337 pp., DA 46-3532A.

WEELKES, THOMAS, c. 1576–1623

General

4635. Brown, David. *Thomas Weelkes: A Biographical and Critical Study.* London: Faber and Faber, 1969, 223 pp.
Descriptive, critical, and analytic commentary on Weelkes' entire output. Musical examples.

WEILL, KURT, 1900–1950

Three Penny Opera

4636. Whittall, Arnold. *Music Since the First World War,* 98–101. London: J. M. Dent and Sons, 1977.
Very brief analytic observations. Musical examples.

WIDOR, CHARLES MARIE, 1844–1937

DISSERTATIONS AND THESES

Symphonies for Organ

4637. Anthony, Jimmy Jess. "Charles-Marie Widor's Symphonies *Pour Orgue*: Their Artistic Context and Cultural Antecedents." D.M.A., University of Rochester, Eastman School of Music, 1986, 293 pp., DA 47-1102A-3A.

WOLF, HUGO, 1860–1903

General

4638. Carner, Mosco. *Hugo Wolf Songs.* London: British Broadcasting Corporation, 1982, 72 pp.
Brief descriptive and critical commentary. Musical examples.

4639. Kravitt, Edward F. "The Ballad As Conceived by Germanic Composers of the Late Romantic Periods." *Studies in Romanticism,* 12, no. 2 (1973): 499–515.
The attraction of the Romantic ballad to composers such as Mahler, Wolf, and Strauss. Discusses their technique of word painting.

4640.   Maconie, Robin. "Stravinsky's Final Cadence." *Tempo,* 103 (1972): 18–23.

Analysis of Stravinsky's transcription of Wolf songs. Musical examples.

4641.   Newman, Ernest. *Hugo Wolf.* 1907. Reprint. New York: Dover Publications, 1966, 279 pp.

The first English-language "life and works" study of Wolf. The "works" section surveys the songs and operas separately, with occasional analytic comments. Musical examples.

4642.   Sams, Eric. *The Songs of Hugo Wolf.* 2d ed. London: Eulenberg Books, 1983, 401 pp.

The bulk of this book consists of a chronological history of the songs, giving a date, translation, and a brief commentary for each one. Also discussion of text/music relationships, melody, rhythm and harmony, and a list of rhythm and melodic motives found in the songs. Musical examples.

4643.   Stein, Deborah J. *Hugo Wolf's "Lieder" and Extensions of Tonality.* Ann Arbor: UMI Research Press, 1985, 237 pp.

Thorough, in-depth analytic survey of Wolf's song output. Advanced. Musical examples.

4644.   Walker, Frank. *Hugo Wolf.* New York: Alfred A. Knopf, 1968, 522 pp.

Background with analytic commentary and musical examples on the larger works, such as *Penthesilea.*

"Italienisches Liederbuch," No. 10

4645.   Hantz, Edwin. "Exempli Gratia: le dernier cri (?): Wolf's Harmony Revisited." *In Theory Only,* 5 (May 1981): 29–32.

Analytic remarks on the treatment of traditional functional harmony in this song. Musical examples.

Kennst du das Land?

4646.   Ivey, Donald. "Comparative Analysis—An Approach to Style." *NATS Bulletin,* 22, no. 2 (1965): 18–21.

A stylistic comparison of settings of Goethe's lyrics by Wolf, Schubert, Schumann, and Liszt.

Mörike Lieder

4647. Stein, Jack M. "Poem and Music in Hugo Wolf's *Mörike* Songs." *Musical Quarterly*, 53, no. 1 (1967): 22–38.
  Thorough critical treatment of the relationship of music and text. Musical examples.

Songs (Three Michelangelo Settings)

4648. Dahlhaus, Carl. *Nineteenth-Century Music.* Translated by J. Bradford Robinson, 369–370. Berkeley: University of California Press, 1989.
  Brief but concentrated analytic discussion dwelling on relationship of music to text, motives, and tonality. Advanced.

Songs (Three) from Michelangelo, No. 2

4649. Youens, Susan. " 'Alles endet, was entstehet': The Second of Hugo Wolf's 'Michelangelo-*Lieder*.' " *Studies in Music* (Australia), 14 (1980): 87–103.
  Detailed study of this song. Discusses melodic, harmonic and rhythmic elements. Traces the pervasive use of a four-note motivic figure. Includes discussion of text. Musical examples.

DISSERTATIONS AND THESES

General

4650. Stein, Deborah Jane. "Extended Tonal Procedures in the *Lieder* of Hugo Wolf." Ph.D., Yale University, 1982, 421 pp., DA 45-2690A.

Mörike Lieder

4651. Loewen, Wesley James. "The Relationship of Text and Vocal Aspects in the *Mörike* Songs of Hugo Wolf." D.M.A., University of Missouri at Kansas City, 1983, 377 pp., DA 44-607A.

WOLPE, STEFAN, 1902–1972

General

4652. Levy, Edward. "Stefan Wolpe: For His Sixtieth Birthday." In *Perspectives on American Composers*. Edited by Benjamin Boretz and E. T. Cone, 184–198. New York: W. W. Norton, 1971.

Commentary on stylistic traits, coupled with analytic observations on his Piece for Two Instrumental Units (1962), Passacaglia (1936), and Violin Sonata (1949). Musical examples.

WUORINEN, CHARLES, 1938–

DISSERTATIONS AND THESES

Trio for Strings

4653.   Kuchera-Morin, Joann. "Structure in Charles Wuorinen's String Trio." Ph.D., University of Rochester, Eastman School of Music, 1984, 111 pp., DA 45-1568A.

XENAKIS, IANNIS, 1922–

General

4654.   Whittall, Arnold. *Music Since the First World War*, 239–242. London: J. M. Dent and Sons, 1977.
   Brief comments on style and technique.

ZANDONAI, RICCARDO, 1883–1944

Francesca da Rimini

4655.   Conrad, Peter. "A Woman in Flames." *Opera News*, 48 (March 31, 1984): 14–16.
   The influence of Wagner on the librettist, D'Annunzio, and the composer, Zandonai.

BIBLIOGRAPHY

BOOKS

Abert, Hermann. *Mozart's "Don Giovanni."* Translated by Peter Gellhorn. London: Eulenberg Books, 1976.

Abraham, Gerald. *Borodin: The Composer and His Music.* London: William Reeves, n.d.

———. *Chopin's Musical Style.* London: Oxford University Press, 1960.

———. *A Hundred Years of Music.* London: Duckworth, 1949.

———. *Slavonic and Romantic Music.* New York: St. Martin's Press, 1968.

———, ed. *Grieg: A Symposium.* Norman: University of Oklahoma Press, 1950.

———, ed. *Handel: A Symposium.* London: Oxford University Press, 1954.

———, ed. *The Music of Schubert.* New York: W. W. Norton, 1947.

———, ed. *The Music of Sibelius.* New York: W. W. Norton, 1947.

———, ed. *The Music of Tchaikovsky.* New York: W. W. Norton, 1946.

———, ed. *The New Oxford History of Music.* Vol. 4, *The Age of Humanism, 1540–1630.* London: Oxford University Press, 1968.

———, ed. *The New Oxford History of Music.* Vol. 8, *The Age of Beethoven, 1790–1830.* London: Oxford University Press, 1982.

———, ed. *Schumann: A Symposium.* London: Oxford University Press, 1952.

Adorno, Theodor. *In Search of Wagner.* Translated by R. Livingston. New York: Schocken Books, 1981.

Allanbrook, Wye J. *Rhythmic Gesture in Mozart: "Le Nozze di Figaro" and "Don Giovanni."* Chicago: University of Chicago Press, 1983.

Andrews, Herbert K. *An Introduction to the Technique of Palestrina.* London: Novello, 1958.

———. *The Technique of Byrd's Vocal Polyphony.* London: Oxford University Press, 1966.

Anthony, James R. *French Baroque Music from Beaujoyeulx to Rameau.* New York: W. W. Norton, 1974.

Antokoletz, Elliott. *The Music of Béla Bartók: A Study of Tonality and*

Progression in Twentieth-Century Music. Berkeley: University of California Press, 1984.

Aprahamian, Felix. *Bax: A Composer and His Times.* London: Scolar Press, 1983.

Arnold, Denis. *Giovanni Gabrieli.* London: Oxford University Press, 1974.

———. *Giovanni Gabrieli and the Music of the Venetian High Renaissance.* London: Oxford University Press, 1979.

———. *Marenzio.* London: Oxford University Press, 1965.

———. *Monteverdi.* 2d ed. London: J. M. Dent and Sons, 1975.

———. *Monteverdi Madrigals.* Seattle: University of Washington Press, 1967.

Arnold, Denis, and Nigel Fortune, eds. *The Beethoven Companion.* London: Faber and Faber, 1971.

———, eds. *The New Monteverdi Companion.* London: Faber and Faber, 1985.

Arundell, Dennis. *Henry Purcell.* New York: Books for Libraries Press, 1970.

Ashbrook, William. *Donizetti.* London: Cassell, 1965.

———. *The Operas of Puccini.* London: Oxford University Press, 1968.

Austin, William W. *Music in the Twentieth Century.* New York: W. W. Norton, 1966.

———, ed. *Debussy: "Prelude to the Afternoon of a Faun."* Norton Critical Scores. New York: W. W. Norton, 1971.

Bailey, Robert, ed. *Richard Wagner: Prelude and Transfiguration from "Tristan and Isolde."* Norton Critical Scores. New York: W. W. Norton, 1985.

Bailey, Walter B. *Programmatic Elements in the Works of Schoenberg.* Ann Arbor: UMI Research Press, 1984.

Baker, James. *The Music of Alexander Scriabin.* New Haven: Yale University Press, 1986.

Ballantine, Christopher. *Twentieth Century Symphony.* London: Dennis Dobson, 1984.

Balough, Teresa, ed. *A Musical Genius From Australia.* Nedlands: University of Western Australia Press, 1982.

Barbour, James M. *The Church Music of William Billings.* Michigan: Michigan State University Press, 1960.

Barford, Philip. *Bruckner Symphonies.* Seattle: University of Washington Press, 1978.

———. *The Keyboard Music of C. P. E. Bach.* New York: October House, 1966.

———. *Mahler Symphonies and Songs.* Seattle: University of Washington Press, 1970.

Barret-Ayres, Reginald. *Joseph Haydn and the String Quartet.* New York: Schirmer Books, 1974.

Barricelli, Jean-Pierre, and Leo Weinstein. *Ernest Chausson.* Norman: University of Oklahoma Press, 1955.

Barzun, Jacques. *Berlioz and the Romantic School.* Boston: Little, Brown, 1950.

Beaumont, Antony. *Busoni the Composer.* London: Faber and Faber, 1985.

Beckett, Lucy. *Richard Wagner: "Parsifal."* New York: Cambridge University Press, 1981.

Beckett, Walter. *Liszt.* London: J. M. Dent and Sons, 1963.

Beecham, Sir Thomas. *Frederick Delius.* New York: Alfred A. Knopf, 1960.

Béhague, Gerard. *Music in Latin America: An Introduction.* Englewood Cliffs, NJ: Prentice-Hall, 1979.

Bekker, Paul. *Beethoven.* Translated and adapted from the German by M. M. Bozman. London: J. M. Dent and Sons, 1925.

———. *Richard Wagner: His Life in His Work.* Translated by M. M. Bozman. New York: Books for Libraries Press, 1970.

Bell, A. Craig. *The Songs of Schubert.* Lowestoft: Alston, 1964.

Bent, Margaret. *Dunstaple.* London: Oxford University Press, 1981.

Berger, Arthur. *Aaron Copland.* New York: Oxford University Press, 1963.

Bernac, Pierre. *Francis Poulenc: The Man and His Songs.* Translated by Winifred Radford. New York: W. W. Norton, 1977.

Bernstein, Leonard. *The Infinite Variety of Music.* New York: Simon and Schuster, 1966.

———. *The Joy of Music.* New York: Simon and Schuster, 1959.

Bidou, Henri. *Chopin.* Translated by Catherine Alison Phillips. New York: Alfred A. Knopf, 1927.

Bie, Oskar. *Schubert: The Man.* New York: Dodd, Mead, 1929.

Blok, Vladimir, ed. *Sergei Prokofiev: Materials, Articles, Interviews.* London: Progress/Central Books, 1980.

Blom, Eric. *Beethoven's Pianoforte Sonatas Discussed.* 1938. Reprint. New York: Da Capo Press, 1968.

———. *Classics Major and Minor: With Some Other Musical Ruminations.* London: J. M. Dent and Sons, 1958.

———. *Mozart.* London: J. M. Dent and Sons, 1974.

———. *Tchaikovsky: Orchestral Works.* 1927. Reprint. Westport, CT: Greenwood Press, 1970.

Bogianckino, Massimo. *The Harpsichord Music of Domenico Scarlatti.* Translated by John Tickner. Rome: Edizioni de Santis, 1967.

Bonavia, Ferruccio. *Verdi.* London: Oxford University Press, 1930.

Boretz, Benjamin, and E. T. Cone, eds. *Perspectives on American Composers.* New York: W. W. Norton, 1971.

————, eds. *Perspectives on Schoenberg and Stravinsky.* Rev. ed. New York: W. W. Norton, 1972.

Bowen, Meirion. *Michael Tippett.* New York: Universe, 1982.

Bowers, Faubion. *The New Scriabin: Enigma and Answers.* New York: St. Martin's Press, 1973.

————. *Scriabin.* 2 vols. Palo Alto: Kodansha International, 1969.

Boyd, Malcolm. *Bach.* London: J. M. Dent and Sons, 1983.

————. *Bach's Instrumental Counterpoint.* London: Barrie and Rockliff, 1967.

————. *Domenico Scarlatti—Master of Music.* London: Weidenfeld and Nicolson, 1986.

————. *Palestrina's Style.* London: Oxford University Press, 1973.

Boyden, David B. *An Introduction to Music.* 2d ed. New York: Alfred A. Knopf, 1970.

Branson, David. *John Field and Chopin.* New York: St. Martin's Press, 1972.

Brenet, Michael. *Haydn.* Translated by C. Leonard Leese. London: Oxford University Press, 1926.

Brett, Philip, ed. *Benjamin Britten: "Peter Grimes."* Cambridge: Cambridge University Press, 1983.

Brindle, Reginald Smith. *The New Music: The Avant-Garde Since 1945.* London: Oxford University Press, 1975.

Broder, Nathan. *Samuel Barber.* New York: G. Schirmer, 1954.

————, ed. *Mozart: Symphony in G Minor, K. 550.* Norton Critical Scores. New York: W. W. Norton, 1967.

Brown, A. Peter. *Joseph Haydn's Keyboard Music: Sources and Style.* Bloomington: Indiana University Press, 1986.

Brown, Clive. *Louis Spohr: A Critical Biography.* Cambridge: Cambridge University Press, 1984.

Brown, David. *Mikhail Glinka: A Biographical and Critical Study.* London: Oxford University Press, 1974.

————. *Tchaikovsky: A Biographical and Critical Study.* 3 vols. New York: W. W. Norton, 1978–1986.

————. *Thomas Weelkes: A Biographical and Critical Study.* London: Faber and Faber, 1969.

Brown, Maurice J. *Essays on Schubert.* New York: St. Martin's Press, 1966.

642

———. *Schubert Symphonies.* Seattle: University of Washington Press, 1971.

———. *Schubert's Variations.* London: Macmillan, 1954.

———. *Schubert: A Critical Biography.* London: Macmillan, 1958.

Budden, Julian. *The Operas of Verdi.* 3 vols. New York: Oxford University Press, 1979–1986.

Bukofzer, Manfred. *Music in the Baroque Era.* New York: W. W. Norton, 1947.

Burk, John N. *The Life and Works of Beethoven.* New York: Random House, 1943.

Burley, Rosa, and Frank C. Carruthers. *Edward Elgar: The Record of a Friendship.* London: Barrie and Jenkins, 1972.

Butterworth, Neil. *The Music of Aaron Copland.* London: Toccata Press, 1985.

Caluori, Eleonor. *The Cantatas of Luigi Rossi: Analysis and Thematic Index.* Vol. 1. Ann Arbor: UMI Research Press, 1982.

Calvocoressi, M. D. *Modest Mussorgsky.* London: Rockliff, 1956.

———. *Mussorgsky.* Translated by A. Eaglefield Hull. London: Kegan Paul, n.d.

Capell, Richard. *Schubert's Songs.* 2d ed., rev. New York: Basic Books, 1957.

Cardus, Neville. *Gustav Mahler, His Mind and His Music.* Vol. 1. New York: St. Martin's Press, 1965.

Carner, Mosco. *Alban Berg: The Man and the Work.* New York: Holmes and Meier, 1975.

———. *Giacomo Puccini: "Tosca."* New York: Cambridge University Press, 1985.

———. *Hugo Wolf Songs.* London: British Broadcasting Corporation, 1982.

———. *Major and Minor.* New York: Holmes and Meier, 1980.

———. *Puccini: A Critical Biography. New York: Alfred A. Knopf, 1959.*

Carrel, Norman. *Bach's "Brandenburg" Concertos.* London: George Allen and Unwin, 1963.

Chailley, Jacques. *"The Magic Flute," Masonic Opera: An Interpretation of the Libretto and the Music.* Translated by Herbert Weinstock. 1971. Reprint. New York: Da Capo Press, 1982.

Charlton, David. *Grétry and the Growth of Opéra-Comique.* Cambridge: Cambridge University Press, 1986.

Chisholm, Erik. *The Operas of Leos Janácek.* London: Oxford University Press, 1971.

Chissel, Joan. *Schumann.* London: J. M. Dent and Sons, 1967.

————. *Schumann Piano Music.* London: British Broadcasting Corporation, 1972.

Chusid, Martin, ed. *Schubert: Symphony in B Minor, "Unfinished."* Norton Critical Scores. New York: W. W. Norton, 1967.

Clapham, John. *Antonín Dvořák: Musician and Craftsman.* New York: St. Martin's Press, 1966.

————. *Smetana.* New York: Octagon Books, 1972.

Clinkscale, Edward H., and Claire Brook, eds. *A Musical Offering: Essays in Honor of Martin Bernstein.* New York: Pendragon Press, 1977.

Coates, Henry. *Palestrina.* London: J. M. Dent and Sons, 1948.

Cogan, Robert, and Pozzi Escot. *Sonic Design: The Nature of Sound and Music.* Englewood Cliffs, NJ: Prentice-Hall, 1976.

Cole, William. *The Form of Music: An Outline of Musical Designs Used by the Great Composers.* London: Associated Board of the Royal Schools of Music, n.d.

Colles, Henry C. *The Chamber Music of Brahms.* London: Oxford University Press, 1933.

Collins, Michael, and E. K. Kirk, eds. *Opera and Vivaldi.* Austin: University of Texas Press, 1984.

Cone, Edward T. *The Composer's Voice.* Berkeley: University of California Press, 1974.

————, ed. *Hector Berlioz: "Fantastic Symphony."* Norton Critical Scores. New York: W. W. Norton, 1971.

Cooke, Deryck. *I Saw the World End: A Study of Wagner's "Ring."* London: Oxford University Press, 1979.

————. *Vindications: Essays on Romantic Music.* London: Faber and Faber, 1982.

Cooper, Martin. *Beethoven: The Last Decade, 1817–1827.* London: Oxford University Press, 1970.

————. *French Music: From the Death of Berlioz to the Death of Fauré.* London: Oxford University Press, 1951.

————. *Georges Bizet.* London: Oxford University Press, 1938.

————, ed. *The New Oxford History of Music. Vol. 10, The Modern Age: 1890–1960.* London: Oxford University Press, 1974.

Copley, Ian A. *The Music of Peter Warlock.* London: Dennis Dobson, 1981.

Cortot, Alfred. *French Piano Music.* Translated by Hilda Andrews. London: Oxford University Press, 1932.

Cowell, Henry, and Sidney Cowell. *Charles Ives and His Music.* 1955. Reprint. London: Oxford University Press, 1969.

Cox, David V. *Debussy Orchestral Music*. Seattle: University of Washington Press, 1975.

Crichton, Ronald. *Falla*. Seattle: University of Washington Press, 1983.

Cross, Eric. *The Late Operas of Antonio Vivaldi, 1727–1738*. Ann Arbor: UMI Research Press, 1981.

Crow, Todd, ed. and comp. *Bartók Studies*. Detroit: Information Coordinators, 1976.

Culshaw, John, *Rachmaninov: The Man and His Music*. New York: Oxford University Press, 1950.

Cunningham, Walker. *The Keyboard Music of John Bull*. Ann Arbor: UMI Research Press, 1984.

Curtis, Alan. *Sweelinck's Keyboard Music*. London: Oxford University Press, 1969.

Cuyler, Louise. *The Symphony*. New York: Harcourt Brace Jovanovich, 1973.

Dahlhaus, Carl. *Richard Wagner's Music Dramas*. Translated by M. Whittall. Cambridge: Cambridge University Press, 1979.

———. *Nineteenth-Century Music*. Translated by J. Bradford Robinson. Berkeley: University of California Press, 1989.

Dale, Kathleen. *Nineteenth-Century Piano Music: A Handbook for Pianists*. London: Oxford University Press, 1954.

Daniel, Keith W. *Francis Poulenc: His Artistic Development and Musical Style*. Ann Arbor: UMI Research Press, 1982.

David, Hans T. *J. S. Bach's "Musical Offering"; A History, Interpretation, and Analysis*. New York: G. Schirmer, 1945.

Davies, Cedric Thorpe. *Musical Structure and Design*. New York: Dover Publications, 1966.

Davies, Laurence. *César Franck and His Circle*. London: Barrie and Jenkins. 1970.

———. *Franck*. London: J. M. Dent and Sons, 1973.

———. *Paths to Modern Music: Aspects of Music From Wagner to the Present Day*. London: Barrie and Jenkins, 1971.

———. *Ravel Orchestral Music*. Seattle: University of Washington Press, 1970.

Dawes, Frank. *Debussy's Piano Music*. London: British Broadcasting Corporation, 1969.

Day, James. *Vaughan Williams*. London: J. M. Dent and Sons, 1975.

Dean, Winton. *Georges Bizet: His Life and Work*. Rev. ed. London: J. M. Dent and Sons, 1965.

————. *Handel and the Opera Seria*. London: Oxford University Press, 1970.

————. *Handel's Dramatic Oratorios and Masques*. London: Oxford University Press, 1959.

Dean, Winton, and John Merrill Knapp. *Handel's Operas: 1704–1726*. Oxford: Clarendon Press, 1987.

Deane, Basil. *Albert Roussel*. London: Barrie and Rockliff, 1961.

————. *Cherubini*. London: Oxford University Press, 1965.

Dearling, Robert. *The Music of Wolfgang Amadeus Mozart: The Symphonies*. Cranbury, NJ: Associated University Presses, 1982.

Del Mar, Norman. *Richard Strauss: A Critical Commentary on His Life and Works*. 3 vols. London: Barrie and Jenkins, 1962–1972.

Demarquez, Suzanne. *Manuel de Falla*. Translated from the French by Salvator Attanasio. Philadelphia: Chilton Book Co., 1968.

Demuth, Norman. *Albert Roussel: A Study*. London: United Music Publishers, n.d.

————. *César Franck*. London: Dennis Dobson, 1949.

————. *Ravel*. London: J. M. Dent and Sons, 1947.

Dent, Edward J. *Alessandro Scarlatti: His Life and Works*. New York: St. Martin's Press, 1960.

————. *Mozart's Operas: A Critical Study*. 2d ed. London: Oxford University Press, 1947.

————. *The Rise of Romantic Opera*. Cambridge: Cambridge University Press, 1976.

Deri, Otto. *The Book of Hanging Gardens*. New York: Holt, Rinehart, and Winston, 1968.

————. *Exploring Twentieth-Century Music*. New York: Holt, Rinehart, and Winston, 1968.

DiGaetani, John L., ed. *Penetrating Wagner's "Ring": An Anthology*. Rutherford, NJ: Fairleigh Dickinson University Press, 1978.

Dianin, Serge. *Borodin*. Translated from the Russian by Robert Lord. London: Oxford University Press, 1963.

Dickinson, A. E. F. *Bach's Fugal Works: With an Account of Fugue Before and After Bach*. London: Sir Isaac Pitman and Sons, 1956.

————. *Beethoven*. London: Thomas Nelson and Sons, 1941.

————. *An Introduction to the Music of Ralph Vaughan Williams*. London: Oxford University Press, 1928.

————. *The Music of Berlioz*. New York: St. Martin's Press, 1972.

————. *Vaughan Williams*. London: Faber and Faber, 1963.

Dixon, Graham. *Carissimi*. Oxford: Oxford University Press, 1986.

Doe, Paul. *Tallis*. London: Oxford University Press, 1968.

Donington, Robert. *The Opera*. New York: Harcourt Brace Jovanovich, 1978.

———. *Wagner's "Ring" and Its Symbols*. London: Faber and Faber, 1974.

Duffy, John. *The Songs and Motets of Alfonso Ferrabosco, the Younger (1575–1628)*. Ann Arbor: UMI Research Press, 1980.

Duncan, Edmonstoune. *Schubert*. London: J. M. Dent and Sons, 1934.

Dunhill, Thomas F. *Mozart's String Quartets*. 1927. Reprint. Westport, CT: Greenwood Press, 1970.

Dunsby, Jonathan. *Structural Ambiguity in Brahms*. Ann Arbor: UMI Research Press, 1981.

Einstein, Alfred. *Gluck*. Translated by Eric Blom. London: J. M. Dent and Sons, 1936.

———. *The Italian Madrigal*. Vol. 2. Translated by Alexander H. Krappe, Roger H. Sessions, and Oliver Strunk. Princeton, NJ: Princeton University Press, 1949.

———. *Mozart: His Character, His Work*. Translated by Arthur Mendel and Nathan Broder. London: Oxford University Press, 1945.

———. *Music in the Romantic Era*. New York: W. W. Norton, 1947.

———. *Schubert: A Musical Portrait*. New York: Oxford University Press, 1951.

Eldridge, Muriel T. *Thomas Campion: His Poetry and Music*. New York: Vantage Press, 1971.

Elliot, John H. *Berlioz*. London: J. M. Dent and Sons, 1967.

Eösze, Laszlo. *Zoltán Kodály: His Life and Work*. Translated by I. Farkas and G. Gulyas. London: Collet's, 1962.

Etheridge, David E. *Mozart's Clarinet Concerto: The Clarinetist's View*. Gretna, LA: Pelican, 1983.

Evans, Edwin. *Historical, Descriptive, and Analytic Account of the Entire Works of Johannes Brahms*. London: William Reeves, 1912.

———. *Tchaikovsky*. 1906. Reprint. London: J. M. Dent and Sons, 1966.

Evans, Peter. *The Music of Benjamin Britten*. Minneapolis: University of Minnesota Press, 1979.

Ewans, Michael. *Janáček's Tragic Operas*. London: Faber and Faber, 1977.

Ewen, David. *A Journey to Greatness*. Englewood Cliffs, NJ: Prentice-Hall, 1970.

Fallows, David. *Dufay*. London: J. M. Dent and Sons, 1982.

647

Fellowes, Edmund H. *William Byrd.* 2d ed. London: Oxford University Press, 1948.

Ferguson, Donald N. *Image and Structure in Chamber Music.* Minneapolis: University of Minnesota Press, 1964.

——. *Piano Music of Six Great Composers.* New York: Books for Libraries Press, 1947.

Finck, Henry. *Massenet and His Operas.* New York: John Lane, 1910.

Finscher, Ludwig, and Christoph-Helmut Mehling, comps. *Festschrift für Walter Wiora.* Kassel: Bärenreiter, 1967.

Finson, Jon W., and Larry R. Todd, eds. *Mendelssohn and Schumann: Essays on Their Music and Its Context.* Durham: Duke University Press, 1984.

Fischer, Edwin. *Beethoven's Pianoforte Sonatas.* London: Faber and Faber, 1959.

Fischer-Dieskau, Dietrich. *Schubert: A Biographical Study of His Songs.* Translated and edited by Kenneth S. Whitton. London: Cassell, 1976.

Fischl, Viktor, ed. *Antonín Dvořák: His Achievement.* Westport, CT: Greenwood Press, 1970.

Fiske, Roger. *Beethoven Concertos and Overtures.* Seattle: University of Washington Press, 1970.

——. *Beethoven's "Missa Solemnis."* London: Paul Elek, 1979.

Forbes, Elliott, ed. *Ludwig van Beethoven: Symphony No. 5 in C Minor.* Norton Critical Scores. New York: W. W. Norton, 1971.

Foreman, Lewis, ed. *British Music Now—A Guide to the Work of Younger Composers.* London: Paul Elek, 1975.

——. *The Percy Grainger Companion.* London: Thames Publishing, 1981.

Forman, Denis. *Mozart's Concerto Form: The First Movements of the Piano Concertos.* New York: Praeger, 1971.

Forsyth, Karen. *"Ariadne auf Naxos" by Hugo von Hofmannsthal and Richard Strauss: Its Genesis and Meaning.* New York: Oxford University Press, 1982.

Forte, Allen. *The Compositional Matrix.* New York: Music Teachers National Association, 1961.

——. *Contemporary Tone-Structures.* New York: Columbia University Press, 1955.

——. *The Harmonic Organization of "The Rite of Spring."* New Haven: Yale University Press, 1978.

Foss, Hubert. *Ralph Vaughan Williams: A Study.* New York: Oxford University Press, 1950.

Friedlaender, Max. *Brahms' Lieder.* Translated by C. Leonard Leese. London: Oxford University Press, 1928.

648

Frisch, Walter. *Brahms and the Principle of Developing Variation.* Berkeley: University of California Press, 1984.

————, ed. *Schubert: Critical and Analytic Studies.* Lincoln: University of Nebraska Press, 1986.

Fuller-Maitland, John A. *The "48": Bach's "Wohltemperirtes Clavier."* 1925. Reprint. 2 vols. New York: Books for Libraries Press, 1970.

Gal, Hans. *Franz Schubert and the Essence of Melody.* London: Victor Gollancz, 1974.

————. *Schumann Orchestral Music.* London: British Broadcasting Corporation, 1978.

Garden, Edward. *Balakirev.* New York: St. Martin's Press, 1967.

————. *Tchaikovsky.* London: J. M. Dent and Sons, 1973.

Gartenberg, Egon. *Mahler: The Man and His Music.* New York: Schirmer Books, 1978.

Gatti, Carlo. *Verdi: The Man and His Music.* Translated from the Italian by Elisabeth Abbott. New York: Putnam's Sons, 1955.

Geiringer, Karl. *Brahms: His Life and Work.* 2d. ed. New York: Oxford University Press, 1947.

————. *Haydn: A Creative Life in Music.* Berkeley: University of California Press, 1968.

————, ed. *Franz Joseph Haydn: Symphony No. 103 in E-Flat Major.* Norton Critical Scores. New York: W. W. Norton, 1974.

George, Graham. *Tonality and Musical Structure.* New York: Praeger, 1970.

Gianturco, Carolyn. *Mozart's Early Operas.* London: B. T. Batsford, 1981.

Gillman, Alan M. *Erik Satie.* Boston: Twayne, 1988.

Gilman, Lawrence. *Debussy's "Pelléas et Mélisande."* New York: G. Schirmer, 1907.

Girdlestone, Cuthbert. *Jean-Philippe Rameau: His Life and Work.* Rev. ed. New York: Dover Publications, 1969.

————. *Mozart and His Piano Concertos.* Norman: University of Oklahoma Press. 1952.

Glover, Jane. *Cavalli.* London: B. T. Batsford, 1978.

Glowacki, John, ed. *Paul A. Pisk: Essays in His Honor.* Austin: University of Texas Press, 1966.

Godefroy, Vincent. *The Dramatic Genius of Verdi: Studies of Selected Operas.* New York: St. Martin's Press, 1975.

Goldberg, Isaac. *George Gershwin: A Study in American Music.* New York: Frederick Ungar, 1958.

Gossett, Philip. *"Anna Bolena" and the Artistic Maturity of Gaetano Donizetti.* London: Oxford University Press, 1985.

Gounod, Charles. *Mozart's "Don Giovanni": A Commentary.* Translated from the 3d French edition by Windeyer Clark and J. T. Hutchinson. 1895. Reprint. New York: Da Capo Press, 1970.

Grace, Harvey. *The Organ Works of Bach.* London: Novello, n.d.

Granville Barker, Frank. *The Flying Dutchman: English National Opera Guide 12.* London: John Calder, 1982.

Gray, Cecil. *The Forty-Eight Preludes and Fugues of J.S. Bach.* London: Oxford University Press, 1952.

———. *Sibelius: The Symphonies.* 1935. Reprint. New York: Books for Libraries Press, 1970.

Grayson, David A. *The Genesis of Debussy's "Pelléas et Mélisande."* Ann Arbor: UMI Research Press, 1986.

Green, Douglass M. *Form in Tonal Music.* New York: Holt, Rinehart, and Winston, 1965.

Greene, David B. *Mahler, Consciousness, and Temporality.* New York: Gordon and Breach Science Publishers, 1984.

———. *Temporal Processes in Beethoven's Music.* New York: Gordon and Breach Science Publishers, 1982.

Grew, Eva, and Syndey Grew. *Bach.* London: J. M. Dent and Sons, 1947.

Griffiths, Paul. *Bartók.* London: J. M. Dent and Sons, 1984.

———. *Cage.* London: Oxford University Press, 1981.

———. *György Ligeti.* London: Robson Books, 1983.

———. *Igor Stravinsky: "The Rake's Progress."* London: Cambridge University Press, 1982.

———. *Modern Music: The Avant-Garde Since 1945.* New York: George Braziller, 1981.

———. *Olivier Messiaen and the Music of Time.* London: Faber and Faber, 1985.

———. *Peter Maxwell Davies.* London: Robson Books, 1981.

Grout, Donald Jay. *A History of Western Music.* New York: W. W. Norton, 1960.

Grove, George. *Beethoven and His Nine Symphonies.* 3d ed. 1898. Reprint. New York: Dover Publications, 1962.

Hadden, J. Cuthbert. *Haydn.* London: J. M. Dent and Sons, 1934.

Haggin, B. H. *A Book of the Symphony.* London: Oxford University Press, 1937.

Hallmark, Rufus E. *The Genesis of Schumann's "Dichterliebe": A Source Study.* Ann Arbor: UMI Research Press, 1979.

650

Hammond, Frederick. *Girolamo Frescobaldi: His Life and Music.* Cambridge, MA: Harvard University Press, 1983.

Hand, Colin. *Jchn Taverner: His Life and Music.* London: Eulenberg, 1978.

Hansen, Peter. *An Introduction to Twentieth Century Music.* 2d ed. Boston: Allyn and Bacon, 1967.

Harding, James. *Gounod.* New York: Stein and Day, 1973.

———. *Massenet.* London: J. M. Dent and Sons, 1970.

———. *Rossini.* London: Faber and Faber, 1971.

Harman, Alec. *Man and His Music: Medieval and Renaissance Music.* New York: Schocken Books, 1969.

Harris, Ellen. *Handel and the Pastoral Tradition.* London: Oxford University Press, 1980.

Harrison, Julius. *Brahms and His Four Symphonies.* 1939. Reprint. New York: Da Capo Press, 1971.

Harrison, Max. *The Lieder of Brahms.* London: Cassell, 1972.

Hartog, Howard, ed. *European Music in the Twentieth Century.* London: Routledge and Kegan Paul, 1957.

Harvey, Jonathan. *The Music of Stockhausen: An Introduction.* Berkeley: University of California Press, 1975.

Haydn Yearbook. Vol. 4. Bryn Mawr, PA: Theodore Presser, n.d.

Hedley, Arthur. *Chopin.* London: J. M. Dent and Sons, 1974.

Heinrich, Adel. *Bach's "Die Kunst der Fuge": A Living Compendium of Fugal Procedures with a Motivic Analysis of All the Fugues.* Landam, MD: University Press of America, 1983.

Henderson, William J. *Richard Wagner: His Life and His Dramas.* 1923. Reprint, 2d ed., rev. New York: AMS Press, 1971.

Hepokoski, James A. *Giuseppe Verdi: "Falstaff."* Cambridge: Cambridge University Press, 1983.

Hervey, Arthur. *Saint-Saens.* 1922. Reprint. New York: Books for Libraries Press, 1969.

Herz, Gerhard. *Essays on J. S. Bach.* Ann Arbor: UMI Research Press, 1985.

———, ed. *Cantata No. 140, "Wachet auf, ruft uns die Stimme."* Norton Critical Scores. New York: W. W. Norton, 1972.

Heseltine, Philip, and Cecil Gray. *Carlo Gesualdo, Prince of Venosa.* 1926. Reprint. Westport, CT: Greenwood Press, 1971.

Heyworth, Peter, ed. *Berlioz, Romantic and Classic: Writings by Ernest Newman.* London: Victor Gollancz, 1972.

Higgins, Thomas, ed. *Frédéric Chopin: Preludes, Opus 28.* Norton Critical Scores. New York: W. W. Norton, 1973.

Hill, Ralph, ed. *The Concerto.* London: Penguin Books, 1952.

651

————, ed. *The Symphony*. Harmondsworth: Penguin Books, 1950.

Hitchcock, H. Wiley. *Ives*. New York: Oxford University Press, 1977.

Hodgson, Antony. *The Music of Joseph Haydn: The Symphonies*. London: Tantivy Press, 1976.

Holland, Arthur Keith. *Henry Purcell: The English Musical Tradition*. 1932. Reprint. New York: Books for Libraries Press, 1970.

Hollander, Hans. *Leos Janáček: His Life and Work*. Translated by Paul Hamburger. London: John Calder, 1963.

Holst, Imogen. *The Music of Gustav Holst*. London: Oxford University Press, 1968.

————. *The Music of Gustav Holst/Holst's Music Reconsidered*. 3d ed. Oxford: Oxford University Press, 1985.

Hoover, Kathleeen, and John Cage. *Virgil Thomson: His Life and Music*. New York: Thomas Yoseloff, 1959.

Hopkins, Antony. *The Nine Symphonies of Beethoven*. London: Heinemann. 1981.

————. *Talking About Concertos*. London: Heinemann, 1964.

Hoppin, Richard H. *Medieval Music*. New York: W. W. Norton, 1978.

Horton, John. *Brahms Orchestral Music*. London: British Broadcasting Corporation, 1968.

————. *César Franck*. London: Oxford University Press, 1946.

————. *Grieg*. London: J. M. Dent and Sons, 1974.

————. *Mendelssohn Chamber Music*. Seattle: University of Washington Press, 1972.

Howard, Patricia. *Gluck and the Birth of Modern Opera*. London: Barrie and Rockliff, 1963.

————. *The Operas of Benjamin Britten: An Introduction*. 1969. Reprint. Westport, CT: Greenwood Press, 1976.

————, ed. *C. W. von Gluck: Orfeo*. Cambridge: Cambridge University Press, 1981.

————, ed. *The Turn of the Screw*. Cambridge: Cambridge University Press, 1985.

Howat, Roy. *Debussy in Proportion: A Musical Analysis*. Cambridge: Cambridge University Press, 1983.

Howes, Frank. *The Music of Ralph Vaughan Williams*. London: Oxford University Press, 1954.

Hughes, Dom Anselm, and Gerald Abraham, eds. *The New Oxford History of Music*. Vol. 3, *Ars Nova and the Renaissance, 1300–1540*. London: Oxford University Press, 1960.

Hughes, Gervase. *Dvořák: His Life and Music*. New York: Dodd, Mead, 1967.

Hughes, Rosemary. *Haydn*. London: J. M. Dent and Sons, 1962.

————. *Haydn String Quartets.* London: British Broadcasting Corporation, 1966.

Hughes, Spike. *Famous Mozart Operas.* 2d rev., ed. New York: Dover Publications, 1972.

————. *Famous Puccini Operas.* New York: Dover Publications, 1972.

Hull, A. Eaglefield. *A Great Russian Tone-Poet: Scriabin.* 1918. Reprint. New York: AMS Press, 1970.

Humphreys, David. *The Esoteric Structure of Bach's "Clavierübung III."* Cardiff: University College, 1983.

Hussey, Dynely. *Verdi.* London: J. M. Dent and Sons, 1948.

Hutchings, Arthur. *A Companion to Mozart's Piano Concertos.* 2d ed. London: Oxford University Press, 1951.

————. *The Baroque Concerto.* New York: W. W. Norton, 1961.

————. *Delius.* London: Macmillan, 1949.

————. *Schubert.* London: J. M. Dent and Sons, 1973.

Iliffe, Frederick. *Bach's Forty-Eight Preludes and Fugues: Analyzed for Students by Frederick Iliffe.* 2 vols. Kent: Novello, n.d.

Jacob, Heinrich Eduard. *Felix Mendelssohn and His Times.* Translated from the German by Richard Winston and Clara Winston. 1963. Reprint. Westport, CT: Greenwood Press, 1973.

Jacobs, Robert L. *Wagner.* London: J. M. Dent and Sons, 1965.

James, Burnett. *Brahms: A Critical Study.* New York: Praeger, 1972.

————. *The Music of Gustav Mahler.* Rutherford, NJ: Fairleigh Dickinson University Press, 1985.

————. *The Music of Jean Sibelius.* London: Associated University Presses, 1983.

Jarman, Douglas. *The Music of Alban Berg.* Berkeley: University of California Press, 1979.

Jarocinski, Stephen. *Debussy: Impressionism and Symbolism.* Translated by R. Myers. London: Eulenberg Books, 1976.

Jefferson, Alan. *Delius.* London: J. M. Dent and Sons, 1972.

————. *The Lieder of Richard Strauss.* London: Cassell, 1971.

————. *Richard Strauss: Der Rosenkavalier.* Cambridge: Cambridge University Press, 1985.

Jeppesen, Knud. *The Style of Palestrina and the Dissonance.* 1946. Reprint. New York: Dover Publications, 1970.

John, Nicholas, ed. *La Forza del Destino.* London: John Calder, 1983.

————. *Madama Butterfly.* London: John Calder, 1984.

————. *Manon.* London: John Calder, 1984.

————. *Die Meistersinger.* London: John Calder, 1984.

————. *Turandot.* London: John Calder, 1984.

Johnson, Robert Sherlaw. *Messiaen.* Berkeley: University of California Press, 1975.

Joseph, Charles M. *Stravinsky and the Piano.* Ann Arbor: UMI Research Press, 1983.

Josephson, David S. *John Taverner: Tudor Composer.* Ann Arbor: UMI Research Press, 1979.

Kárpáti, János. *Bartók's String Quartets.* Translated by F. Macnicol. London: Barrie and Jenkins, 1975.

Kay, Norman, *Shostakovich.* London: Oxford University Press, 1971.

Keller, Hans. *The Great Haydn Quartets: Their Interpretation.* New York: George Braziller, 1986.

Keller, Hermann. *The Organ Works of Bach.* Translated from the German by Helen Hewitt. New York: C. F. Peters, 1967.

————. *The Well-Tempered Clavier by Johann Sebastian Bach.* Translated by L. Gerdine. New York: W. W. Norton, 1976.

Kelley, Edgar Stillman. *Chopin the Composer.* New York: G. Schirmer, 1913.

Kemp, Ian. *The Composer and His Music.* London: Eulenberg Books, 1984.

————. *Hindemith.* London: Oxford University Press, 1971.

Kennedy, Michael. *Britten.* London: J. M. Dent and Sons, 1981.

————. *Elgar Orchestral Music.* London: British Broadcasting Corporation, 1970.

————. *Mahler.* London: J. M. Dent and Sons, 1974.

————. *Portrait of Elgar.* London: Oxford University Press, 1968.

————. *Richard Strauss.* London: J. M. Dent and Sons, 1976.

————. *The Works of Ralph Vaughan Williams.* London: Oxford University Press, 1964.

Kenton, Egon. *Life and Works of Giovanni Gabrieli.* Netherlands: American Institute of Musicology, 1967.

Kerman, Joseph. *The Beethoven Quartet.* New York: Alfred A. Knopf, 1967.

————. *Listen.* 2d ed. New York: Worth Publishers, 1976.

————. *The Masses and Motets of William Byrd.* Berkeley: University of California Press, 1981.

————, ed. *Wolfgang Amadeus Mozart: Piano Concerto in C Major, K. 503.* Norton Critical Scores. New York: W. W. Norton, 1970.

Keys, Ivor. *Brahms Chamber Music.* London: British Broadcasting Corporation, 1974.

Kimbell, David. *Verdi in the Age of Italian Romanticism*. Cambridge: Cambridge University Press, 1981.

King, Alexander Hyatt. *Mozart Chamber Music*. London: British Broadcasting Corporation, 1968.

———. *Mozart in Retrospect: Studies in Criticism and Bibliography*. London: Oxford University Press, 1955.

———. *Mozart String and Wind Concertos*. London: British Broadcasting Corporation, 1978.

Kirkpatrick, Ralph. *Domenico Scarlatti*. Princeton: Princeton University Press, 1953.

Kolneder, Walter. *Anton Webern: An Introduction to His Works*. Translated by Humphrey Searle. Berkeley: University of California Press, 1968.

———. *Antonio Vivaldi: His Life and Work*. Translated by B. Hopkins. Berkeley: University of California Press, 1970.

Kolodin, Irving. *The Interior Beethoven*. New York: Alfred A. Knopf, 1975.

Komar, Arthur, ed. *Schumann: "Dichterliebe" Op. 48*. Norton Critical Scores. New York: W. W. Norton, 1971.

Krause, Ernst. *Richard Strauss: The Man and His Work*. London: Collett's, 1964.

Krenek, Ernst. *Exploring Music*. Translated by Margaret Sheffield and Geoffrey Skelton. New York: October House, 1966.

Kresky, Jeffrey. *Tonal Music: Twelve Analytic Studies*. Bloomington: Indiana University Press, 1977.

Kroó, György. *A Guide to Bartók*. Translated by R. Pataki and M. Steiner. London: Clematis Press, 1974.

La Grange, Henry-Louis de. *Mahler*. Vol. 1 New York: Doubleday, 1973.

La Rue, Jan, ed. *Aspects of Medieval and Renaissance Music: A Birthday Offering to Gustave Reese*. New York: W. W. Norton, 1966.

Lam, Basil. *Beethoven String Quartets*. 2 vols. London: British Broadcasting Corporation, 1976.

Landon, H. C. Robbins. *Essays on the Viennese Classical Style: Gluck, Haydn, Mozart, Beethoven*. London: Barrie and Rockliff, 1970.

———. *Haydn: Chronicle and Works*. 5 vols. Bloomington: Indiana University Press, 1976.

———. *Haydn Symphonies*. Seattle: University of Washington Press, 1969.

———, ed. *The Mozart Companion*. New York: W. W. Norton, 1969.

———. *Studies in Eighteenth-Century Music*. London: George Allen and Unwin, 1970.

Landon, H. C. Robbins, and David Wyn Jones. *Haydn: His Life and Music*. Bloomington: Indiana University Press, 1988.

Lang, Paul Henry. *George Frideric Handel*. New York: W. W. Norton, 1966.

————, ed. *The Creative World of Beethoven*. New York: W. W. Norton, 1971.

————, ed. *Stravinsky: A New Appraisal of His Work*. New York: W. W. Norton, 1963.

Large, Brian. *Smetana*. London: Duckworth, 1970.

Larsen, Jens Peter. *Handel's "Messiah": Origins, Composition, Sources*. 2d ed. New York: W. W. Norton, 1972.

Larsen, Jens Peter, Howard Serwer, and James Webster, eds. *Haydn Studies*. Proceedings of the International Haydn Conference. New York: W. W. Norton, 1981.

Latham, Peter. *Brahms*. London: J. M. Dent and Sons, 1975.

Layton, Robert. *Dvořák Symphonies and Concertos*. Seattle: University of Washington Press, 1978.

————. *Sibelius*. London: J. M. Dent and Sons, 1965.

Leibowitz, Rene. *Schoenberg and His School*. Translated from the French by Dika Newlin. 1949. Reprint. New York: Da Capo Press, 1970.

Leichtentritt, Hugo. *Musical Form*. Cambridge, MA: Harvard University Press, 1959.

Lendvai, Erno. *Béla Bartók: An Analysis of His Music*. London: Kahn and Averill, 1971.

Lerdahl, Fred, and Ray Jackendorff. *A Generative Theory of Tonal Music*. Cambridge: M.I.T. Press, 1983.

Lesznai, Lajos. *Bartók*. Translated by P. M. Young. London: J. M. Dent and Sons, 1973.

Levarie, Siegmund. *Mozart's "Le Nozze di Figaro": A Critical Analysis*. 1952. Reprint. New York: Da Capo Press, 1977.

Lewis, Anthony, and Nigel Fortune, eds. *The New Oxford History of Music*. Vol. 5, *Opera and Church Music, 1630–1750*. London: Oxford University Press, 1975.

Lewis, Christopher Orlo. *Tonal Coherence in Mahler's Ninth Symphony*. Ann Arbor: UMI Research Press, 1984.

Liebich, Louise. *Claude Achille Debussy*. London: John Lane, 1918.

Liebner, Janos. *Mozart on the Stage*. New York: Praeger, 1972.

Liess, Andreas. *Carl Orff*. Translated by Adelheid Parkin and Herbert Parkin. London: John Calder, 1966.

Lincoln, Harry, ed. *The Computer and Music*. New York: Cornell University Press, 1970.

Lloyd, Stephen, and Edmund Rubbra, eds. *Edmund Rubbra's Collected Essays on Gustav Holst.* London: Triad Press, 1974.

Lockspeiser, Edward. *Debussy.* London: J. M. Dent and Sons, 1972.

———. *Debussy: His Life and Mind.* New York: Macmillan, 1962.

Lockwood, Lewis, ed. *"Pope Marcellus Mass."* Norton Critical Scores. New York: W. W. Norton, 1975.

Lockwood, Lewis, and Phyllis Benjamin, eds. *Beethoven Essays: Studies in Honor of Elliot Forbes.* Cambridge, MA: Harvard University Press, 1984.

Long, Marguerite. *At the Piano with Debussy.* Translated by Olive Senior-Ellis. London: J. M. Dent and Sons, n.d.

Longyear, Rey M. *Nineteenth-Century Romanticism in Music.* Englewood Cliffs, NJ: Prentice-Hall, 1969.

Lyle, Watson. *Camille Saint-Saens: His Life and Art.* 1923. Reprint. Westport, CT: Greenwood Press, 1970.

MacDonald, Hugh. *Berlioz.* London: J. M. Dent and Sons, 1982.

———. *Berlioz Orchestral Music.* London: British Broadcasting Corporation, 1969.

———. *Skryabin.* London: Oxford University Press, 1978.

MacDonald, Malcolm. *Schoenberg.* London: J. M. Dent and Sons, 1976.

———. *The Symphonies of Havergal Brian.* 3 vols. London: Kahn and Averill, 1973–1983.

MacDonald, Ray S. *Puccini: King of Verismo.* New York: Vantage Press, 1973.

Machlis, Joseph. *The Enjoyment of Music.* 3d ed., New York: W. W. Norton, 1970.

———. *The Enjoyment of Music.* 5th ed., New York: W. W. Norton, 1984.

———. *Introduction to Contemporary Music.* New York: W. W. Norton, 1961.

Maconie, Robin. *The Works of Karlheinz Stockhausen.* London: Oxford University Press, 1976.

Maisel, Edward. *Charles T. Griffes.* Rev. ed. New York: Alfred A. Knopf, 1984.

Mann, William. *The Operas of Mozart.* New York: Oxford University Press, 1977.

———. *Richard Strauss: A Critical Study of the Operas.* London: Cassell, 1964.

Marek, George. *Richard Strauss: The Life of a Non-Hero.* New York: Simon and Schuster, 1967.

Marliave, Joseph de. *Beethoven's Quartets.* New York: Dover Publications, 1961.

657

Marshall, Robert L. *The Music of Johann Sebastian Bach.* New York: Schirmer Books, 1989.

Martin, George. *Verdi: His Music, Life and Times.* New York: Dodd, Mead, 1963.

Martynov, Ivan. *Dmitri Shostakovich: The Man and His Work.* Translated from the Russian by T. Guralsky. New York: Greenwood Press, 1947.

Mason, Daniel Gregory. *The Chamber Music of Brahms.* New York: Macmillan, 1933.

Matthews, David. *Michael Tippett: An Introductory Study.* London: Faber and Faber, 1979.

Matthews, Denis. *Beethoven Piano Sonatas.* Seattle: University of Washington Press, 1969.

————. *Brahms Piano Music.* Seattle: University of Washington Press, 1978.

————, ed. *Keyboard Music.* New York: Praeger, 1972.

McCabe, John. *Bartók Orchestral Music.* London: British Broadcasting Corporation, 1975.

McCreless, Patrick. *Wagner's "Siegfried": Its Drama, History, and Music.* Ann Arbor: UMI Research Press, 1982.

Mellers, Wilfrid. *Bach and the Dance of God.* London: Faber and Faber, 1980.

————. *Beethoven and the Voice of God.* London: Faber and Faber, 1983.

————. *François Couperin and the French Classical Tradition.* 1950. Reprint. New York: Dover Publications, 1968.

————. *Music in a New Found Land.* New York: Alfred A. Knopf, 1965.

Meyer, Leonard B. *Emotion and Meaning in Music.* Chicago: University of Chicago Press, 1956.

Millington, Barry. *Wagner.* London: J. M. Dent and Sons, 1984.

Misch, Ludwig. *Beethoven Studies.* Norman: University of Oklahoma Press, 1953.

Mitchell, Donald. *Gustav Mahler: The Early Years.* Rev. ed. Berkeley: University of California Press, 1980.

————. *Gustav Mahler: Songs and Symphonies of Life and Death.* London: Faber and Faber, 1985.

————. *Gustav Mahler: The Wunderhorn Years.* Boulder, CO: Westview Press, 1975.

Mitchell, Donald, and Hans Keller, eds. *Benjamin Britten: A Commentary on His Works from a Group of Specialists.* London: Rockliff, 1952.

Mitchell, William J., Felix Salzer, and Carl Schacter, eds. *The Music Forum*. 5 vols. New York: Columbia University Press, 1967–1980.

Moberly, Robert B. *Three Mozart Operas: "Figaro," "Don Giovanni," "The Magic Flute."* New York: Dodd, Mead, 1968.

Moldenhauer, Hans, comp. *Anton von Webern: Perspectives*. Seattle: University of Washington Press, 1966.

Moldenhauer, Hans, and Rosalien Moldenhauer. *Anton von Webern: A Chronicle of His Life and Work*. New York: Alfred A. Knopf, 1979.

Montagu-Nathan, Montagu. *Rimsky-Korsakov*. New York: Duffield, 1917.

Moore, Jerrold N. *Edward Elgar: A Creative Life*. London: Oxford University Press, 1984.

Moore, Robert Etheridge. *Henry Purcell and the Restoration Theatre*. 1961. Reprint. Westport, CT: Greenwood Press, 1974.

Moser, Hans Joachim. *Heinrich Schütz: His Life and Work*. Translated by Carl Pfatteicher. St. Louis: Concordia, 1959.

Musgrave, Michael. *The Music of Brahms*. London: Routlege and Kegan Paul, 1985.

Myers, Rollo. *Emmanuel Chabrier and His Circle*. London: J. M. Dent and Sons, 1969.

———. *Ravel*. London: Duckworth, 1960.

———, ed. *Twentieth Century Music*. London: Calder and Boyers, 1968.

Nadeau, Roland. *The Symphony: Structure and Style*. Boston: Crescendo, 1973.

Neighbour, Oliver. *The Consort and Keyboard Music of William Byrd*. Berkeley: University of California Press, 1978.

Nelson, Wendell. *The Concerto*. Dubuque, IA: William C. Brown, 1969.

Nestyev, Israel V. *Prokofiev*. Translated from the Russian by Florence Jones. Stanford: Stanford University Press, 1960.

Nettel, Reginald. *Havergal Brian and His Music*. London: Dennis Dobson, 1976.

Neumeyer, David. *The Music of Paul Hindemith*. New Haven: Yale University Press, 1986.

The New Grove Dictionary of Music and Musicians. Edited by Stanley Sadie. Vol. 18. London: Macmillan, 1980.

Newman, Ernest. *Gluck and the Opera: A Study in Musical History*. London: Victor Gollancz, 1964.

———. *Hugo Wolf*. 1907. Reprint. New York: Dover Publications, 1966.

————. *Richard Strauss.* 1908. Reprint. New York: Books for Libraries Press, 1969.

————. *Wagner as Man and Artist.* New York: Tudor Publishing Co., 1924.

Newman, William S. *The Sonata Since Beethoven.* 3d ed. New York: W. W. Norton, 1983.

Newmarch, Rosa. *Tchaikovsky.* London: William Reeves, 1908.

Nichols, Roger. *Debussy.* London: Oxford University Press, 1973.

————. *Messiaen.* London: Oxford University Press, 1975.

————. *Ravel.* London: J. M. Dent and Sons, 1977.

Niecks, Frederick. *Frederick Chopin As a Man and Musician.* 2 vols. London: Novello, 1902.

Niemann, Walter. *Brahms.* Translated by Catherine Alison Phillips. New York: Cooper Square, 1969.

Norris, Christopher., ed. *Shostakovich: The Man and His Music.* London: Lawrence and Wishart, 1982.

Norris, Geoffrey. *Rakhmaninov.* London: J. M. Dent and Sons, 1976.

Noske, Frits. *The Signifier and the Signified: Studies in the Operas of Mozart and Verdi.* The Hague: M. Nijhoff, 1977.

Olmstead, Andrea. *Roger Sessions and His Music.* Ann Arbor: UMI Research Press, 1985.

Orenstein, Arbie. *Ravel: Man and Musician.* New York: Columbia University Press, 1975.

Orledge, Robert. *Debussy and the Theatre.* Cambridge: Cambridge University Press, 1983.

————. *Gabriel Fauré.* New York: Da Capo Press, 1982.

Orrey, Leslie. *Bellini.* New York: Farrar, Straus, and Giroux, 1969.

Osborne, Charles. *The Complete Operas of Mozart.* London: Victor Gollancz, 1978.

————. *The Complete Operas of Puccini.* New York: Atheneum, 1982.

————. *The Complete Operas of Verdi.* New York: Alfred A. Knopf, 1970.

Osmond-Smith, David. *Playing on Words: A Guide to Luciano Berios's Sinfonia.* London: Royal Musical Association, 1985.

Ottaway, Hugh. *Vaughan Williams Symphonies.* Seattle: University of Washington Press, 1973.

Oullette, Fernand. *Edgard Varèse, Composer.* Translated by D. Coltman. New York: Orion, Goosman, 1968.

Pakenham, Simona. *Ralph Vaughan Williams: A Discovery of His Music.* London: Macmillan, 1957.

Palisca, Claude. *Baroque Music*. Englewood Cliffs, NJ: Prentice-Hall, 1968.

Palmer, Christopher. *Delius: Portrait of a Cosmopolitan*. New York: Holmes and Meier, 1976.

———. *Impressionism in Music*. London: Hutchinson, 1973.

———, ed. *The Britten Companion*. London: Faber and Faber, 1984.

Parker, Robert L. *Carlos Chávez, Mexico's Modern-Day Orpheus*. Boston: Twayne, 1983.

Parmet, Simon. *The Symphonies of Sibelius*. Translated by Kingsley A. Hart. London: Cassell, 1959.

Parrott, Ian. *Elgar*. London: J. M. Dent and Sons, 1971.

Pascall, Robert, ed. *Brahms: Biographical, Documentary, and Analytical Studies*. Cambridge: Cambridge University Press, 1983.

Patterson, Annie. *Schumann*. London: J. M. Dent and Sons, 1934.

Pauly, Reinhard. *Music in the Classic Period*. Englewood Cliffs, NJ: Prentice-Hall, 1965.

Payne, Anthony. *Frank Bridge: Radical and Conservative*. London: Thames Publishing, 1984.

———. *Schoenberg*. London: Oxford University Press, 1969.

Perle, George. *The Operas of Alban Berg*. Vol. 1, *"Wozzeck."* Berkeley: University of California Press, 1980.

———. *The Operas of Alban Berg*. Vol. 2, *"Lulu."* Berkeley: University of California Press, 1984.

———. *Serial Composition and Atonality: An Introduction to the Music of Schoenberg, Berg, and Webern*. 5th ed., rev. Berkeley: University of California Press, 1981.

Perry, Rosalie Sandra. *Charles Ives and the American Mind*. Kent, OH: Kent State University Press, 1974.

Petzoldt, Richard. *Georg Philipp Telemann*. Translated by H. Fitzpatrick. New York: Oxford University Press, 1974.

Peyser, Joan. *Boulez*. New York: Schirmer Books, 1976.

Piggot, Patrick. *The Life and Music of John Field: 1782–1837*. Berkeley: University of California Press, 1973.

———. *Rachmaninov Orchestral Music*. London: British Broadcasting Corporation, 1974.

Pike, Lionel. *Beethoven, Sibelius and the "Profound Logic": Studies in Symphonic Analysis*. London: Athlone Press, 1978.

Pincherle, Marc. *Corelli: His Life, His Work*. Translated from the French by Hubert E. M. Russell. New York: W. W. Norton, 1956.

———. *Vivaldi: Genius of the Baroque*. Translated from the French by Christopher Hatch. New York: W. W. Norton, 1962.

Pirro, Andre. *J. S. Bach.* Translated from the French by Mervyn Savill. New York: Orion Press, 1957.

Plantinga, Leon. *Clementi: His Life and Music.* London: Oxford University Press, 1977.

———. *Romantic Music.* New York: W. W. Norton, 1984.

Porter, Ernest G. *Schubert's Song Technique.* London: Dennis Dobson, 1961.

Poulton, Diana. *John Dowland.* 2d ed. Berkeley: University of California Press, 1982.

Powers, Harold, ed. *Studies in Music History: Essays for Oliver Strunk.* Princeton: Princeton University Press, 1968.

Price, Curtis A. *Henry Purcell and the London Stage.* Cambridge: Cambridge University Press, 1984.

———, ed. *Purcell: "Dido and Aeneas."* Norton Critical Scores. New York: W. W. Norton, 1986.

Primmer, Brian. *The Berlioz Style.* London: Oxford University Press, 1973.

Prunières, Henry. *Monteverdi: His Life and Work.* Translated from the French by Marie D. Mackie. New York: Dover Publications, 1972.

Pruslin, Stephen. *Peter Maxwell Davies: Studies From Two Decades.* London: Boosey and Hawkes, 1979.

Puffett, Derrick. *The Song Cycles of Othmar Schoeck.* Berne: Haupt, 1982.

Radcliffe, Philip. *Beethoven's String Quartets.* London: Hutchinson, 1965.

———. *Mendelssohn.* London: J. M. Dent and Sons, 1976.

———. *Mozart Piano Concertos.* London: British Broadcasting Corporation, 1978.

———. *Schubert Piano Sonatas.* Seattle: University of Washington Press, 1971.

Raphael, Robert. *Richard Wagner.* New York: Twayne, 1969.

Ratner, Leonard. *Classic Music: Expression, Form, and Style.* New York: Schirmer Books, 1980.

Raynor, Robert. *Wagner and "Die Meistersinger."* London: Oxford University Press, 1940.

Reaney, Gilbert. *Guillaume de Machaut.* London: Oxford University Press, 1971.

Redlich, Hans. *Alban Berg: The Man and His Music.* London: John Calder, 1957.

———. *Bruckner and Mahler.* London: J. M. Dent and Sons, 1955.

————. *Claudio Monteverdi: Life and Works.* London: Oxford University Press, 1952.

Redwood, Christopher, ed. *A Delius Companion.* London: John Calder, 1976.

Reed, John. *Schubert: The Final Years.* London: Faber and Faber, 1972.

Reese, Gustave. *Music in the Middle Ages.* New York: W. W. Norton, 1940.

————. *Music in the Renaissance.* Rev. ed. New York: W. W. Norton, 1959.

Reese, Gustave, and Rose Brandel, eds. *The Commonwealth of Music.* New York: Free Press, 1965.

Reich, Willi. *Alban Berg.* Translated by Cornelius Cardew. New York: Harcourt, Brace, and World, 1965.

————. *Schoenberg: A Critical Biography.* Translated by Leo Black. London: Longman, 1968.

Reti, Rudolph. *Thematic Patterns in Sonatas of Beethoven.* New York: Macmillan, 1967.

————. *Tonality, Atonality, Pantonality: A Study of Some Trends in Twentieth Century Music.* London: Rockliff, 1958.

Richner, Thomas. *Orientation for Interpreting Mozart's Piano Sonatas.* New York: Teachers College, Columbia University, 1953.

Riedel, Johannes. *Music of the Romantic Period.* Dubuque, IA: William C. Brown, 1969.

Riesemann, Oskar von. *Moussorgsky.* New York: Alfred A. Knopf, 1929.

Riezler, Walter. *Beethoven.* Translated by G. D. Pitcock. 1936. Reprint. New York: Vienna House, 1972.

Ringbom, Nils-Erik. *Jean Sibelius.* Norman: University of Oklahoma Press, 1954.

Robertson, Alec. *The Church Cantatas.* New York: Praeger, 1972.

————. *Dvořák.* Rev. ed. London: J. M. Dent and Sons, 1964.

————. *Requiem: Music of Mourning and Consolation.* New York: Praeger, 1968.

————, ed. *Chamber Music.* Baltimore: Penguin Books, 1957.

Robinson, Ray, and Allen Winold. *A Study of the Penderecki "St. Luke" Passion.* Celle: Moeck, 1983.

Roche, Jerome. *Lassus.* London: Oxford University Press, 1982.

————. *Palestrina.* London: Oxford University Press, 1971.

Rolland, Romain. *Handel.* Translated by A. Eaglefield Hull. New York: Henry Holt, 1916.

Rosen, Charles. *Arnold Schoenberg.* New York: Viking Press, 1975.

————. *The Classical Style: Haydn, Mozart, Beethoven.* Rev. ed. London: Faber and Faber, 1976.

————. *Sonata Forms.* New York: W. W. Norton, 1980.

————. *Sonata Forms.* Rev. ed. New York: W. W. Norton, 1988.

Rosen, David, and Andrew Porter, eds. *Verdi's "Macbeth": A Sourcebook.* New York: W. W. Norton, 1984.

Routh, Francis. *Stravinsky.* London: J. M. Dent and Sons, 1975.

Rushton, Julian. *W. A. Mozart: "Don Giovanni."* Cambridge: Cambridge University Press, 1981.

Sadie, Stanley. *Beethoven.* London: Faber and Faber, 1967.

————. *Handel Concertos.* London: British Broadcasting Corporation, 1973.

————. *Mozart.* New York: Grossman, 1970.

Saint-Foix, Georges de. *The Symphonies of Mozart.* London: Dennis Dobson, 1947.

Salzman, Eric. *Twentieth Century Music: An Introduction.* 2d ed. Englewood Cliffs, NJ: Prentice-Hall, 1974.

Sams, Eric. *Brahms' Songs.* Seattle: University of Washington Press, 1972.

————. *The Songs of Hugo Wolf.* 2d ed. London: Eulenberg Books, 1983.

————. *The Songs of Robert Schumann.* 2d ed. London: Eulenberg Books, 1975.

Samson, Jim. *The Music of Chopin.* London: Routledge and Kegan Paul, 1985.

————. *Music in Transition: A Study of Tonal Expansion and Atonality, 1900–1920.* New York: W. W. Norton, 1977.

Saunders, William. *Weber.* 1940. Reprint. New York: Da Capo Press, 1970.

Schenker, Heinrich. *Five Graphic Music Analyses.* New York: Dover Publications, 1969.

————. *J. S. Bach's Chromatic Fantasy and Fugue: Critical Edition with Commentary.* Translated and edited by Hedi Siegel. New York: Longman, 1984.

Scherman, Thomas K., and Louis Biancolli, eds. *The Beethoven Companion.* New York: Doubleday, 1972.

Schiff, David. *The Music of Elliott Carter.* New York: Da Capo Press, 1983.

Schjelderup-Ebbe, Dag. *Edvard Grieg 1858–1867, with Special Reference to the Evolution of His Harmonic Style.* London: Allen and Unwin, 1964.

Schmalfeldt, Janet. *Berg's "Wozzeck": Harmonic Language and Dramatic Design.* New Haven: Yale University Press, 1983.

Schmidt, John C. *The Life and Works of John Knowles Paine.* Ann Arbor: UMI Research Press, 1981.

Schmitz, E. Robert. *The Piano Works of Claude Debussy.* New York: Duell, Sloan and Pearce, 1950.

Schoenberg, Arnold. *Style and Idea: Selected Writings of Arnold Schoenberg.* Translated by L. Black. Edited by Leo Stein. New York: St. Martin's Press, 1975.

Schrade, Leo. *Monteverdi: Creator of Modern Music.* New York: W. W. Norton, 1950.

Schrader, Barry. *Introduction to Electro-Acoustic Music.* Englewood Cliffs, NJ: Prentice-Hall, 1982.

Schreiber, Flora Rheta, and Vincent Persichetti. *William Schuman.* New York: G. Schirmer, 1954.

Schulenberg, David. *The Instrumental Music of Carl Philipp Emanuel Bach.* Ann Arbor: UMI Research Press, 1984.

Schuller, Gunther. *Musings: The Musical World of Gunther Schuller.* New York: Oxford University Press, 1986.

Schwartz, Charles M. *Gershwin: His Life and Music.* Indianapolis: Bobbs-Merrill, 1973.

Schwartz, Elliott. *The Symphonies of Ralph Vaughan Williams.* Amherst: University of Massachusetts Press, 1964.

Schweitzer, Albert. *J. S. Bach.* Translated by Ernest Newman. 2 vols. London: Breitkopf and Härtel, 1911.

Scott, Marion M. *Beethoven.* Revised by Sir Jack Westrup. London: J. M. Dent and Sons, 1974.

Scott-Sutherland, Colin. *Arnold Bax.* London: J. M. Dent and Sons, 1973.

Searle, Humphrey. *The Music of Liszt.* 2d ed., rev. New York: Dover Publications, 1966.

Seiber, Mátyás. *Béla Bartók: A Memorial Review.* New York: Boosey and Hawkes, 1950.

Simpson, Robert. *Beethoven Symphonies.* Seattle: University of Washington Press, 1971.

———. *Carl Nielsen: Symphonist, 1865–1931.* London: J. M. Dent and Sons, 1952.

———, ed. *The Symphony.* Vol. 2. New York: Drake Publishers, 1972.

Smith, Alexander Brent. *Schubert: The Symphonies.* London: Oxford University Press, 1926.

Smith, Julia. *Aaron Copland.* New York: E. P. Dutton, 1955.

Synder, Kerala J. *Dieterich Buxtehude.* New York: Schirmer Books, 1987.

Specht, Richard. *Johannes Brahms.* Translated by Eric Blom. London: J. M. Dent and Sons, 1930.

Spink, Ian. *English Songs: Dowland to Purcell.* London: B. T. Batsford, 1974.

Spitta, Philipp. *Johann Sebastian Bach.* Translated from the German by Clara Bell and J. J. Fuller-Maitland. 3 vols. London: Novello, 1899.

Stedman, Preston. *The Symphony.* Englewood Cliffs, NJ: Prentice-Hall, 1979.

Stehman, Dan. *Roy Harris: An American Musical Pioneer.* Boston: Twayne, 1984.

Stein, Deborah J. *Hugo Wolf's "Lieder" and Extensions of Tonality.* Ann Arbor: UMI Research Press, 1985.

Steinitz, Paul. *Bach's Passions.* London: Paul Elek, 1979.

Steptoe, Andrew. *The Mozart–Da Ponte Operas.* Oxford: Clarendon Press, 1988.

Sternfeld, Frederick W., et. al., eds. *Essays on Opera and English Music in Honour of Sir Jack Westrup.* Oxford: Blackwell, 1975.

Stevens, Denis. *Monteverdi: Sacred, Secular, and the Occasional Music.* Rutherford, NJ: Fairleigh Dickinson University Press, 1978.

———. *Thomas Tomkins, 1572–1656.* New York: St. Martin's Press, 1957.

Stevens, Halsey. *The Life and Music of Béla Bartók.* New York: Oxford University Press, 1953.

Strainchamps, Edmond, and Maria Rika Maniates, eds. *Music and Civilization: Essays in Honor of Paul Henry Lang.* New York: W. W. Norton, 1984.

Stuckenschmidt, H. H. *Maurice Ravel: Variations on His Life and Work.* Philadelphia: Chilton Book Co., 1968.

———. *Schoenberg: His Life, World and Work.* Translated by Humphrey Searle. London: John Calder, 1977

Suchoff, Benjamin, ed. *Béla Bartók Essays.* New York: St. Martin's Press, 1976.

Suckling, Norma. *Fauré.* London: J. M. Dent and Sons, 1946.

Sutherland, Edward H. *Rossini and His School.* London: Sampson, Low, Marston, n.d.

Swalin, Benjamin F. *The Violin Concerto: A Study in German Romanticism.* Chapel Hill: University of North Carolina Press, 1941.

Talbot, Michael. *Vivaldi.* London: J. M. Dent and Sons, 1978.

Tansman, Alexandre. *Igor Stravinsky: The Man and His Music.* Translated by Therese and Charles Bleefield. New York: G. P. Putnam's Sons, 1949.

Tawaststjerna, Erik. *The Pianoforte Compositions of Sibelius.* Helsinki: Kustannusosoakeyhtiö Otava, 1957.

———. *Sibelius: 1856–1905.* Vol. 1. Berkeley: University of California Press, 1976.

Templier, Pierre-Daniel. *Erik Satie.* Translated by Elena L. French and David S. French. Cambridge, MA: M.I.T. Press, 1969.

Terry, Charles Sanford. *Bach: An Introduction.* 1933. Reprint. New York: Dover Publications, 1963.

Thompson, Oscar. *Debussy: Man and Artist.* New York: Dover Publications, 1967.

Thomson, Katherine. *The Masonic Thread in Mozart.* London: Lawrence and Wishart, 1977.

Tierney, Neil. *William Walton: His Life and Music.* Dover, NH: Longwood, 1985.

Tischler, Hans. *The Perceptive Music Listener.* Englewood Cliffs, NJ: Prentice-Hall, 1955.

———. *A Structural Analysis of Mozart's Piano Concertos.* New York: Institute of Medieval Music, 1966.

Tobin, John. *Handel's "Messiah."* London: Cassel, 1969.

Tobin, Joseph Raymond. *Mozart and the Sonata Form.* 1916. Reprint. New York: Da Capo Press, 1971.

Tommasini, Anthony Carl. *Virgil Thomson's "Musical Portraits."* New York: Pendragon, 1986.

Tovey, Donald Francis. *A Companion to "The Art of the Fugue."* London: Oxford University Press, 1931.

———. *A Companion to Beethoven's Pianoforte Sonatas.* London: Associated Board of the Royal Schools of Music, 1931.

———. *Essays in Musical Analysis.* 6 vols. London: Oxford University Press, 1935–1939.

———. *Essays in Musical Analysis: Chamber Music.* London: Oxford University Press, 1944.

———. *The Main Stream of Music and Other Essays.* New York: Meridian, 1959.

Toye, Francis. *Giuseppe Verdi: His Life and Works.* New York: Alfred A. Knopf, 1931.

———. *Rossini: A Study in Tragi-Comedy.* New York: W. W. Norton, 1963.

Truscott, Harold. *Beethoven's Late String Quartets.* London: Dennis Dobson, 1968.

667

Tunley, David. *Couperin*. London: British Broadcasting Corporation, 1983.

Tusler, Robert L. *The Style of Bach's Choral Preludes*. 1956. Reprint. New York: Da Capo Press, 1968.

Tyrrell, John. *Leos Janáček: "Kát'a Kabanová."* Cambridge: Cambridge University Press, 1982.

Tyson, Alan, ed. *Beethoven Studies*. New York: W. W. Norton, 1973.

————, ed. *Beethoven Studies 2*. London: Oxford University Press, 1977.

————, ed. *Beethoven Studies 3*. Cambridge: Cambridge University Press, 1982.

Ulrich, Homer. *Chamber Music*. 2d ed. New York: Columbia University Press, 1966.

————. *Music: A Design for Listening*. New York: Harcourt, Brace, 1957.

Vallas, Léon. *César Franck*. Translated by Hubert Foss. London: Oxford University Press, 1951.

Van Solkema, Sherman, ed. *The New Worlds of Edgard Varèse: A Symposium*. New York: Institute for Studies in American Music, 1979.

Vaughan Williams, Ralph. *Some Thoughts on Beethoven's Choral Symphony*. London: Oxford University Press, 1959.

Veinus, Abraham. *The Concerto*. Rev. ed. New York: Dover Publications, 1964.

Veress, Sandor. *Béla Bartók: A Memorial Review*. New York: Boosey and Hawkes, 1950.

Vlad, Roman. *Stravinsky*. Translated from the Italian by Frederick Fuller and Ann Fuller. 2d ed. London: Oxford University Press, 1967.

Vogel, Jaroslav. *Leoš Janáček: His Life and Works*. Translated by G. Thomsen-Muchova. London: Hamlyn, 1962.

Vuillermoz, Émile. *Gabriel Fauré*. Translated by Kenneth Schapiro. Philadelphia: Chilton Book Co., 1969.

Walker, Alan, ed. *The Chopin Companion*. New York: W. W. Norton, 1966.

————, ed. *Franz Liszt: The Man and His Music*. New York: Taplinger, 1970.

————, ed. *Frederic Chopin: Profiles of the Man and the Musician*. New York: Taplinger, 1967.

————, ed. *Robert Schumann: The Man and His Music*. London: Barrie and Jenkins, 1972.

Walker, Frank. *Hugo Wolf.* New York: Alfred A. Knopf, 1968.

Walsh, Stephen. *The Lieder of Schumann.* London: Cassell, 1971.

Walton, Charles W. *Basic Forms in Music.* Port Washington, NY: Alfred Publishing Co., 1974.

Warburton, A. O. *Analyses of Musical Classics.* Book 4. London: Longman, 1974.

Warlock, Peter. *Frederick Delius.* New York: Oxford University Press, 1952.

Warrack, John. *Carl Maria von Weber.* London: Hamish Hamilton, 1968.

———. *Tchaikovsky: Symphonies and Concertos.* Seattle: University of Washington Press, 1969.

Watkins, Glenn. *Gesualdo: The Man and His Music.* Chapel Hill: University of North Carolina Press, 1973.

———. *Soundings: Music in the Twentieth Century.* New York: Schirmer Books, 1987.

Watson, Derek. *Bruckner.* London: J. M. Dent and Sons, 1975.

Weinstock, Herbert. *Chopin: The Man and His Music.* New York: Alfred A. Knopf, 1959.

———. *Tchaikovsky.* New York: Alfred A. Knopf, 1943.

———. *Vincenzo Bellini: His Life and His Operas.* New York: Alfred A. Knopf, 1971.

Weismann, John. *Béla Bartók: A Memorial Review.* New York: Boosey and Hawkes, 1950.

Wellesz, Egon. *Arnold Schoenberg.* Translated by W. H. Kerridge. 1925. Reprint. New York: Da Capo Press, 1969.

Wellesz, Egon, and F. W. Sternfeld, eds. *The New Oxford History of Music.* Vol. 7, *The Age of Enlightenment, 1745–1790.* London: Oxford University Press, 1973.

Wenk, Arthur. *Claude Debussy and the Poets.* Berkeley: University of California Press, 1976.

———. *Claude Debussy and Twentieth Century Music.* Boston: Twayne, 1983.

Werner, Eric. *Mendelssohn.* Translated from the German by Dika Newlin. New York: Free Press of Glencoe, 1963.

Werner, Jack. *Mendelssohn's "Elijah."* London: Chappell, 1965.

Westrup, Jack. *Bach Cantatas.* London: British Broadcasting Corporation, 1966.

———. *Purcell.* London: J. M. Dent and Sons, 1975.

———. *Schubert Chamber Music.* Seattle: University of Washington Press, 1969.

Whenham, John. *Claudio Monteverdi: "Orfeo."* New York: Cambridge University Press, 1986.

White, Eric Walter. *Benjamin Britten: His Life and Operas*. London: Faber and Faber, 1983.

———. *Stravinsky: The Composer and His Works*. Berkeley: University of California Press, 1966.

———. *Tippett and His Operas*. London: Barrie and Jenkins, 1979.

White, Pamela C. *Schoenberg and the God-Idea: The Opera "Moses und Aron."* Ann Arbor: UMI Research Press, 1985.

Whitesitt, Linda. *The Life and Music of George Antheil, 1900–1959*. Ann Arbor: UMI Research Press, 1983.

Whittall, Arnold. *The Music of Britten and Tippett: Studies in Themes and Techniques*. Cambridge: Cambridge University Press, 1982.

———. *Music Since the First World War*. London: J. M. Dent and Sons, 1977.

———. *Schoenberg Chamber Music*. Seattle: University of Washington Press, 1972.

Wilkins, Nigel. *Music in the Age of Chaucer*. Totowa, NJ: Rowman and Littlefield, 1979.

Williams, C. F. Abdy. *Bach*. London: J. M. Dent and Sons, 1934.

Williams, Peter. *Bach Organ Music*. Seattle: University of Washington Press, 1972.

———. *The Organ Music of J. S. Bach*. Cambridge Studies in Music. Cambridge: Cambridge University Press, 1980.

———, ed. *Bach, Handel, Scarlatti: Tercentenary Essays*. London: Cambridge University Press, 1985.

———. *Stockhausen: Life and Work*. Translated and edited by B. Hopkins. Berkeley: University of California Press, 1973.

Wolf, Eugene. *The Symphonies of Johann Stamitz*. Utrecht: Bohn, Scheltema, and Holkema, 1981.

Wolff, Konrad. *Masters of the Keyboard: Individual Style Elements in the Piano Music of Bach, Haydn, Mozart, Beethoven, and Schubert*. Bloomington: Indiana University Press, 1983.

Wolff, Werner. *Anton Bruckner: Rustic Genius*. New York: Cooper Square, 1973.

Wood, Vivian. *Poulenc's Songs: An Analysis of Style*. Jackson: University Press of Mississippi, 1979.

Wörner, Karl H. *Schoenberg's "Moses and Aaron."* Translated by Paul Hamburger. London: Faber and Faber, 1963.

Young, Percy M. *The Choral Tradition*. New York: W. W. Norton, 1971.

———. *Elgar, O. M.: A Study of a Musician*. London: Collins, 1955.

———. *Handel*. Rev. ed. London: J. M. Dent and Sons, 1975.

———. *The Oratorios of Handel*. London: Dennis Dobson, 1949.

JOURNALS

About the House
Acta Musicologica
American Choral Review
American Harp Journal
American Music Teacher
American Organist
American String Teacher
Bach
CAUSM Journal
Caecilia
Choir
Choral Journal
Chord and Discord
Clarinet
Clavier
College Music Symposium
Composer (London)
Consort
Contemporary Keyboard
Current Musicology
Delius Society Journal
Diapason
Early Music
Grainger Journal
Guitar Review
Haydn Yearbook
High Fidelity
In Theory Only
Indiana Theory Review
Instrumentalist
Interface
Journal of Aesthetics and Art
  Criticism
Journal of the American Liszt
  Society
Journal of the American Musi-
  cological Society
Journal of the Arnold Schoen-
  berg Institute
Journal of Band Research
Journal of the Graduate Music

Students at the Ohio State
  University
Journal of Music Theory
Journal of Musicology
Journal of Research in Music
  Education
Journal of the Royal Musical
  Association
Juilliard Review
Key Notes
Keyboard Magazine
Latin American Music Review
Miscellanea Musicologica
Modern Music
Monthly Musical Record
Music (AGO)
Music Analysis
Music and Dance
Music and Letters
Music and Musicians
Music Educators Journal
Music in Education
Music Journal
Music Perception
Music Review
Music Teacher
Music Teacher and Piano Stu-
  dent
Music Theory Spectrum
Musica Disciplina
Musical Analysis
Musical Newsletter
Musical Opinion
Musical Quarterly
Musical Times
Musicology
NACWPI
NATS Bulletin
NATS Journal
New Hungarian Quarterly
Nineteenth Century Music

Opera
Opera Journal
Opera News
Opera Quarterly
Orbis Musicae: Studies in Musicology
Organ Yearbook
Ovation
Percussionist
Perspectives of New Music
Piano Quarterly
Piano Teacher
Proceedings of the Royal Musical Association
Radford Review
Reihe
Revue Belge de Musicologie
Sacred Music
School Musician

Score
Sonus
Soundings
Source
Stereo Review
Strad
Studia Musicologica
Studia Musicologica Norvegica
Studies in Music (Australia)
Studies in Music (Canada)
Studies in Romanticism
Symposium
Tempo
Theory and Practice
Triangle
Woodwind World—Brass and Percussion
Yale Review

DISSERTATIONS AND THESES

Acord, Thomas Wadsworth. "An Examination of Leoš Janáček's Compositions for Solo Voice and Piano." D.M.A., University of Texas at Austin, 1981, 302 pp., DA 42-1042A.

Adams, Byron. ". . . Part 2: Frank Martin's *Petite Symphonie Concertante:* An Analysis." D.M.A., Cornell University, 1984, 64 pp., DA 45-1905A.

Ai, Chia-Huei. "Chopin's Concerto in E Minor, Op. 11: An Analysis for Performance." D.M.A., Ohio State University, 1986, 83 pp., DA 47-1523A.

Albers, Bradley Gene. "*Da Natura Sonoris* I and II by Krysztof Penderecki: A Comparative Analysis." D.M.A., University of Illinois at Urbana, 116 pp., DA 39-2605A.

Albert, Thomas Russell. "The Harmonic Language of Charles Ives' *Concord* Sonata." D.M.A., University of Illinois at Urbana, 1974, 109 pp., DA 35-4580A.

Alfred, Everett Maurice. "A Study of Selected Choral Works of Claude Debussy." Ph.D., Texas Technical University, 1980, 415 pp., DA 41-4878A.

Allman, Anne Williams. "The Songs of Frederick Delius: An Interpretive and Stylistic Analysis and Performance of Representative Compositions." Ed. D., Columbia University Teachers College, 1983, 265 pp., DA 44-3314A.

Almond, Frank W. "Melody and Texture in the Choral Works of Francis Poulenc." Ph.D., Florida State University, 1970, 85 pp., DA 31-4811A.

Altman, Ian Henry. "Liszt's Grand Etudes After Paganini: A Historical and Analytic Study." D.M.A., University of Cincinnati, 318 pp., DA 45-1565A.

Anagnost, Dean Z. "The Choral Music of Virgil Thomson." Ed.D., Columbia University Teachers College, 1977, 200 pp., DA 38-1962A–3A.

Anderson, Allen. "Recitative and Act II, Scene V, of Arnold Schoenberg's *Moses und Aron*" Ph.D., Brandeis University, 1984, 156 pp., DA 45-1565A.

Anderson, Charles Allen. "Some Aspects of Melodic Structure and Style in the Early and Middle-Period Keyboard Sonatas of Joseph Haydn." D.M.A., University of Illinois at Urbana, 1970, 183 pp., DA 31-4812A.

Anderson, William Woodrow. "The Stylistic Development of Henry Purcell As Revealed by His Sacred Verse Anthems." D.M.A., University of Kansas, 1980, 182 pp., DA 41-2818A.

Andre, Don Alan. "Leonard Bernstein's Mass As Social and Political Commentary on the Sixties." D.M.A., University of Washington, 1979, 186 pp., DA 41-841A.

Andreacchi, Peter. "Part 1: An Examination of the Relation of Text to Music in Claude Debussy's *Trois poémes de Mallarmé*" Ph.D., City University of New York, 1986, 360 pp., DA 47-703A.

Andrus, John Clarke. "Schubert and His Public: The Songs from 1817 to 1828." Ph.D., University of California at Santa Barbara, 1974, 224 pp., DA 42-4193A–4A.

Anthony, Jimmy Jess. "Charles-Marie Widor's Symphonies Pour Orgue: Their Artistic Context and Cultural Antecedents." D.M.A., University of Rochester, Eastman School of Music, 1986, 293 pp., DA 47-1102A–3A.

Arnsdorf, Mary Hunter. "Schumann's *Kreisleriana*, Op. 16: Analysis and Performance." Ed.D., Columbia University Teachers College, 1976, 193 pp., DA 37-1284A.

Asarnow, Elliot Bruce. "Arnold Schoenberg's Heimweh' from *Pierrot Lunaire:* Registral Partitioning of the Harmonic Structure." Ph.D., Brandeis University, 1979, 109 pp., DA 7042A.

Ashley, Douglas Daniels. "The Role of the Piano in Schumann's Songs." Ph.D., Northwestern University, 1973, 375 pp., DA 34-3449A.

Aster, Samuel Shea. "An Analytical Study of Selected Preludes from Shostakovich's Twenty-four Preludes for Piano, Op. 34." Ed.D., Columbia University, 1975, 304 pp., DA 36-1361A–2A.

Augenblick, John Walter. "J. S. Bach's Cantata No. 5: A Conductor's Analysis." D.M.A., University of Miami, 1978, 79 pp., DA 39-6385A.

Axsom, Richard Hayden. "*Parade:* Cubism As Theater." Ph.D., University of Michigan, 1974, 196 pp., DA 35-7803A.

Bach, Jan Morris. "An Analysis of Britten's *A Midsummer Night's Dream.*" D.M.A., University of Illinois at Urbana, 1971, 424 pp., DA 32-4647A.

Badolato, James Vincent. "The Four Symphonies of Charles Ives: A Critical, Analytical Study of the Musical Style of Charles Ives." Ph.D., Catholic University of America, 1978, 231 pp., DA 39-1912A.

Ballan, Harry Reuben. "Schoenberg's Expansion of Tonality, 1899–1908." Ph.D., Yale University, 1986, 230 pp., DA 47-2786A.

Bante-Knight, Mary Martha. "Tonal and Thematic Coherence in Schubert's Piano Sonata in B-Flat (D. 960)." Ph.D., Washington University, 1983, 125 pp., DA 44-3197A.

Bargmann, Theodore John. "The Solo and Instrumental Chamber Works for Piano by Roy Harris." D.M.A., American Conservatory of Music, 1986, 158 pp., DA 47-1524A.

Barkin, Elaine Radoff. "Pitch-Time Structure in Arnold Schoenberg's Op. 23, No. 1: A Contribution Toward a Theory of Non-Tonal Music." Ph.D., Brandeis University, 1971, 130 pp., DA 32-4041A.

Barnard, Jack Richard. "The Choral Music of Vincent Persichetti: A Descriptive Analysis." Ph.D., Florida State University, 1974, 300 pp., DA 35-7940A.

Barrington, Clyde. "The Organ Works of Olivier Messiaen and Their Importance in His Total Oeuvre." S.M.D., UnionTheological Seminary, 1974, 593 pp., DA 35-1686A–7A.

Bashour, Frederich Joseph. "A Model for the Analysis of Structural Levels and Tonal Movement in Compositions of the Fifteenth Century." Ph.D., Yale University, 1975, 295 pp., DA 36-2473A.

Bates, Karen Anne. "Harmonic Language in the First Symphony of Jean Sibelius." M.Mus., University of Arizona, 1984, 141 pp., DA 23-319A.

Bates, Karen Anne. "The Fifth String Quartet of Béla Bartók: An Analysis Based on the Theories of Erno Lendvai." Ph.D., University of Arizona, 1986, 261 pp., DA 47-1103A.

Bawel, Frederick Henry. "A Study of Developmental Techniques in Selected Haydn Symphonies." Ph.D., Ohio State University, 1972, 258 pp., DA 33-4450A–51A.

Beckstrom, Robert Allen. "Analysis of Elliott Carter's Variations for

Orchestra (1955)." Ph.D., University of California at Los Angeles, 1983, 170 pp., DA 45-1233A.

Beeks, Graydon Fisher. "The *Chandos* Anthems and *Te Deum* of Georg Frideric Handel (1685–1759)." Ph.D., University of California at Berkeley, 1981, 969 pp., DA 42-2921A.

Beeler, Charles Alan. *"Winter Music, Cartridge Music, Atlas Eclipticalis:* A Study of Three Seminal Works of John Cage." Ph.D., Washington University, 1973, 78 pp., DA 34-6016A.

Bein, Joseph H. "Debussy's Orchestral *Images:* Harmonic Analysis and Other Features of the Style." Ph.D., University of Rochester, 1970, 240 pp., DA 30-3965A–6A.

Bellamy, Kathrine Elizabeth. "Motivic Development in Two Larger Choral Works of Johannes Brahms." Ph.D., University of Wisconsin, 1973, 370 pp., DA 34-6680A.

Bellardo, Samarah J. "A Study, Analysis, and Performance of Selected One-Movement Piano Sonatas of the Nineteenth and Twentieth Centuries." Ed.D., Columbia University Teachers College, 1973, 126 pp., DA 34-1471A.

Bendell, Christine Jean. "Federico Mompou: An Analytical and Stylistic Study of the *Canciones y Danzas* for Piano." D.A., University of Northern Colorado, 1983, 223 pp., DA 44-2283A.

Benitez, Vincent Perez, Jr. "Musical-Rhetorical Figures in the *Orgelbüchlein* of J. S. Bach." D.M.A., Arizona State University, 143 pp., DA 46-2118A.

Bland, Stephen F. "Form in the Songs of Gabriel Fauré." Ph.D., Florida State University, 1976, 108 pp., DA 37-3251A–2A.

Blasch, Robert Edward. "A Structural and Interpretive Analysis of the Suite for Piano, Op. 25." Ed.D., Columbia University, 1971, 169 pp., DA 32-1180A.

Bloch, David Reed. "The Music of Edgard Varèse." Ph.D., University of Washington, 1973, 288 pp., DA 34-6018A–19A.

Bloomquist, Marvin Robert. "Songs of Ned Rorem: Aspects of the Musical Settings of Songs in English for Solo Voice and Piano." D.M.A., University of Missouri at Kansas City, 1970, 104 pp., DA 31-4194A.

Bobetsky, Victor V. "An Analysis of Selected Works for Piano (1959–1978) and the Sonata for Violin and Piano (1964)." D.M.A., University of Miami, 1982, 109 pp., DA 44-10A.

Boge, Claire Louise. "The Dyad As Voice in Schoenberg's Op. 19: Pitch and Interval Prolongations, Voice-Leading, and Relational Systems." Ph.D., University of Michigan, 1985, 354 pp., DA 46-3184A.

Bolitho, Albert George. "The Organ Sonatas of Paul Hindemith."

Ph.D., Michigan State University, 1968, 157 pp., DA 30-353A–4A.

Borders, Barbara Ann. "Formal Aspects in Selected Instrumental Works of Milton Babbitt." Ph.D., University of Michigan, 1987, 232 pp., DA 40-4290A.

Borton, Bruce. "The Sacred Choral Works of Domenico Scarlatti." D.M.A., University of Cincinnati, 1983, 377 pp., DA 44-1617A.

Boubel, Karen Brandser. "The Conflict of Good and Evil: A Musical and Dramatic Study of Britten's *Billy Budd*." Ph.D., University of Wisconsin at Madison, 1985, 236 pp., DA 46-2119A.

Boyer, Daniel Royce. "Gustav Holst's *The Hymn of Jesus*." D.M.A., University of Texas at Austin, 1968, 142 pp., DA 29-3629A.

Brantley, John Paul. "The Serial Choral Music of Igor Stravinsky." Ph.D., University of Iowa, 1978, 453 pp., DA 39-4577A–8A.

Breslauer, Peter Seth. "Motivic and Rhythmic Contrapuntal Structure in the Chamber Music of Johannes Brahms." Ph.D., Yale University, 1984, 188 pp., DA 46-548A.

Brewer, Tracey Adams. "Characterization in Dominick Argento's Opera, *The Boor*." D.M.A., University of Texas at Austin, 1981, 138 pp., DA 42-2921A.

Brooks, William Fordyce. "Sources and Errata List for Charles Ives' Symphony No. 4, Movement 2." D.M.A., University of Illinois at Urbana, 1976, 170 pp., DA 37/05-A.

Browne, Bruce Sparrow. "The Choral Music of Lukas Foss." D.M.A., University of Washington, 1976, 184 pp., DA 37-1287A.

Bruner, Ellen Carole. "The Relationship of Text and Music in the *Lieder* of Hugo Wolf and Gustav Mahler." Ph.D., Syracuse University, 1974, 389 pp., DA 35-7340A.

Buell, Timothy John. "Aspects of Stravinsky's *Abraham and Isaac*." Ph.D., University of Pittsburgh, 1986, 81 pp., DA 47-4225A.

Butcher, Norma Perkins. "A Comparative-Analytical Study of Sonata-Allegro Form in the First Movements of the *London* Symphonies of Franz Joseph Haydn." Ph.D., University of Southern California, 1971, 179 pp., DA 32-4647A.

Butler, Douglas Lamar. "The Organ Works of Felix Mendelssohn-Bartholdy." D.M.A., University of Oregon, 1973, 268 pp., DA 34-6020A.

Cable, Susan Lee. "The Piano Trios of Bohuslav Martinu (1890–1959)." D.A., University of Northern Colorado, 1984, 203 pp., DA 45-3022A.

Cadwallader, Allen Clayton. "Multileveled Motivic Repetition in Selected Intermezzi for Piano of Johannes Brahms." Ph.D., University of Rochester, Eastman School of Music, 1983, 238 pp., DA 43-3450A.

Cai, Camilla. "Brahms' Short, Late Piano Pieces-Opus Numbers 116–119: A Source Study, An Analysis, and Performance Practice." Ph.D., Boston University, 1986, 563 pp., DA 47-340A.

Caldwell, Donald Graham. "The Choral Music of Frederick Delius." D.M.A., University of Illinois at Urbana, 1975, 311 pp., DA 36-5622A.

Campana, Deborah Ann. "Form and Structure in the Music of John Cage." Ph.D., Northwestern University, 1985, 197 pp., DA 46-2119A.

Campbell, Bruce Benedict. "Beethoven's Quartets Op. 59: An Investigation into Compositional Process." Ph.D., Yale University, 1982, 359 pp., DA 47-1917A.

Campbell, Lawrence Bracey. "A Study of Selected Vocal Chamber Music of Robert Schumann." Ed.D., Columbia University, 1973, 334 pp., DA 34-3110A–11A.

Campfield, Donald John. "A Study of Interval Configuration and Related Parameters in Selected Chromatic Melodies of Béla Bartók." D.M.A., Cornell University, 1985, 74 pp., DA 46-830A.

Cantrick, Susan Birdsall. "Charles Ives's String Quartet No. 2: An Analysis and Evaluation." M.M., Peabody Conservatory of Music, 1983, 153 pp., DA 22-280A.

Carlsen, Philip Caldwell. "The Player Piano Music of Conlon Nancarrow: An Analysis of Selected Studies." Ph.D., City University of New York, 1986, 188 pp., DA 47-1525A.

Carr, Cassandra Irene. "Wit and Humor As a Dramatic Force in the Beethoven Sonatas." Ph.D., University of Washington, 1985, 309 pp., DA 47-1104A.

Carr, Maureen Ann. "Keys and Modes Functions and Progressions in Mussorgsky's *Boris Godounov*." Ph.D., University of Wisconsin, 1972, 410 pp., DA 33-5762A.

Case, Nelly Maude. "Stylistic Coherency in the Piano Works of Aaron Copland." Ph.D., Boston University, 1984, 1127 pp., DA 45-980A.

Chamblee, James Monroe. "The Cantatas and Oratorios of Carl Philipp Emanuel Bach. Vol. 1: A Style Analysis. Vol. 2: Musical Supplement." Ph.D., University of North Carolina at Chapel Hill, 1973, 543 pp., DA 34-2676A.

Cherlin, Michael. "The Formal and Dramatic Organization of Schoenberg's *Moses und Aron*." Ph.D., Yale University, 1983, 413 pp., DA 47-1917A.

Christensen, Jean Marie. "Arnold Schoenberg's Oratorio *Die Jakobsleiter*." Ph.D., University of California at Los Angeles, 1979, 797 pp., DA 40-3612A.

Churgin, Bathia Dina. "The Symphonies of G. B. Sammartini." Ph.D., Harvard University, 1963, 888 pp., DA 35-3790A–91A.

Cinnamon, Howard. "Third-Relations As Structural Elements in Book II of Liszt's *Années de Pèlerinage.*" Ph.D., University of Michigan, 1984, 302 pp., DA 45-3475A.

Citron, Marcia Judith. "Schubert's Seven Complete Operas: A Musico/Dramatic Study." Ph.D., University of North Carolina at Chapel Hill, 1971, 232 pp., DA 32-5262A.

Clark, Sondra Rae. "The Evolving *Concord* Sonata: A Study of Choices and Variants in the Music of Charles Ives." Ph.D., Stanford University, 1972, 382 pp., DA 32-7027A.

Cole, Vincent Lewis. "Analyses of *Symphony of Psalms* (1930, rev. 1948) and Requiem Canticles (1966) by Igor Stravinsky." Ph.D., University of California at Los Angeles, 1980, 143 pp., DA 41-4879A.

Colson, William Wilder. "*Four Last Songs* by Richard Strauss." D.M.A., University of Illinois at Urbana, 1975, 187 pp., DA 36-16A–17A.

Conely, James Hannon, Jr. "An Analysis of Form in *Arcana* of Edgard Varèse and *Trilogy* of Samuel Beckett." Ed.D., Columbia University, 1968, 157 pp., DA 29-3606A–7A.

Conrad, John Alan. "Style and Structure in Songs by George Gershwin, Published 1924–1938." Ph.D., Indiana University, 1985, 302 pp., DA 46-3528A.

Coulter, Beverly Norton. "The Affective Nature of the Harmonic Content in the Third Masque of Karol Szymanowski." D.M.A., University of Miami, 1985, 73 pp., DA 47-341A.

Cowen, Carol Vanrandwyk. "Analogical Observations: Gunther Schuller's Settings of *Artworks* by Paul Klee." M.M., Michigan State University, 1984, 81 pp., DA 23-9A.

Crabb, Richard Paul. "Wolfgang Amadeus Mozart's Grand Mass in C Minor K. 427/417a: A History and Comparative Analyses of Performance Editions." Ph.D., Florida State University, 1984, 174 pp., DA 45-1677A.

Crawford, John Charlton. "The Relationship of Text and Music in the Vocal Works of Schoenberg, 1908–1924." Ph.D., Harvard University, 1963, 376 pp., DA 29-4035A–6A.

Crawford, Robert Sheldon. "Dynamic Form and the Adagio of Alban Berg's Chamber Concerto, An Essay." Ph.D., Washington University, 1982, 121 pp., DA 44-316A.

Crotty, John Edward. "Design and Harmonic Organization in Beethoven's String Quartet, Op. 131." Ph.D., University of Rochester, Eastman School of Music, 1986, 215 pp., DA 47-1104A.

Cubbage, John Rex. "Directed Pitch Motion and Coherence in the First Movement of Arnold Schoenberg's Fourth String Quartet."

Ph.D., Washington University, 1979, 303 pp., DA 40-3613A.

D'Angelo, James P. "Tonality and Its Symbolic Associations in Paul Hindemith's Opera *Die Harmonie der Welt*." Ph.D., New York University, 1983, 599 pp., DA 44-1966A.

Danes, Robert Harold. "Stravinsky's *The Rake's Progress:* Paradigm of Neoclassic Opera." Ph.D., Washington University, 1972, 242 pp., DA 33-4452A.

Darter, Thomas Eugene. "The Futurist Piano Music of Leo Ornstein." D.M.A., Cornell University, 1979, 222 pp., DA 39-6386A.

Daugherty, Robert Michael. "An Analysis of Aaron Copland's *Twelve Poems of Emily Dickinson*." D.M.A., Ohio State University, 1980, 224 pp., DA 41-2819A.

Davidson, Audrey Jean Ekdahl. "Olivier Messiaen's *Tristan Trilogy:* Time and Transcendence." Ph.D., University of Minnesota, 1975, 433 pp., DA 36-3199A.

Davidson, Celia Elizabeth. "Operas by Afro-American Composers: A Critical Survey and Analysis of Selected Works." Ph.D., Catholic University of America, 1980, 526 pp., DA 41-452A.

Davis, Alycia Kathleann. "Samuel Barber's *Hermit Songs*, Op. 19: An Analytic Study." M.M., Webster University, 1983, 101 pp., DA 22-63A.

Davis, Deborah Louise Bodwin. "The Choral Works of Ned Rorem." Ph.D., Michigan State University, 1978, 243 pp., DA 40-730A.

Dean, Jerry Mac. "Schoenberg's *George* Songs, Op. 15." Ph.D., University of Michigan, 1971, 209 pp., DA 32-6474A–5A.

Deavel, R. Gary. "A Study of Two Operas of Benjamin Britten: *Peter Grimes* and *Turn of the Screw*." Ph.D., University of Rochester, Eastman School of Music, 1970, 344 pp., DA 31-1831A.

DeBaise, Joseph Ralph. "George Crumb's *Music for a Summer Evening:* A Comprehensive Analysis." Ph.D., University of Rochester, Eastman School of Music, 1983, 546 pp., DA 43-3748A.

DeBold, Conrad. "*Parade* and Le Spectacle Interieur: The Role of Jean Cocteau in an Avant-Garde Ballet." Ph.D., Emory University, 1982, 253 pp., DA 43-2139A.

DeKenessey, Stefania Maria. "The Quartet, the Finale, and the Fugue: A Study of Beethoven's Opus 130/133." Ph.D., Princeton University, 1984, 341 pp., DA 44-3198A.

Dellinger, Michael Eldon. "An Analysis of Frank Martin's Second Piano Concerto." D.M.A., Ohio State University, 1985, 143 pp., DA 46-549A.

Demaree, Robert William Jr. "The Structural Proportions of the Haydn Quartets." Ph.D., Indiana University, 1973, 264 pp., DA 34-6682-3A.

De Zeeuw, Anne Marie. "Tonality and the Concertos of William Walton." Ph.D., University of Texas at Austin, 1983, 432 pp., DA 45-677A.

Dieckow, Almarie. "A Stylistic Analysis of the Solo Keyboard Sonatas of Antonio Soler." Ph.D., Washington University, 1971, 281 pp., DA 33-346A.

Dobay, Thomas Raymond De. "Harmonic Materials and Usages in the Lorca Cycle of George Crumb." Ph.D., University of Southern California, 1982, DA 43-1739A.

Dorfman, Allen Arthur. "A Theory of Form and Proportion in Music." Ph.D., University of California at Los Angeles, 1986, 472 pp., DA 47-1105A.

Dougherty, William Patrick. "An Examination of Semiotics in Musical Analysis: The Neapolitan Complex in Beethoven's Op. 131." Ph.D., Ohio State University, 1985, 258 pp., DA 46-2479A.

Dundore, Mary Margaret. "The Choral Music of Benjamin Britten." D.M.A., University of Washington, 1969, 166 pp., DA 30-5012A–13A.

Dwelley, Robert R. "An Analysis of Luigi Dallapiccola's *Piccola Musica Notturna.*" Ph.D. University of Rochester, Eastman School of Music, 1985, 110 pp., DA 46-831A.

Earle, Diane Kay. "An Analytical Study of the Piano Concerto in A Minor, Op. 54 of Robert Schumann." D.M.A., Ohio State University , 1984, 189 pp., DA 45-1566A.

Ebensberger, Gary Lee. "The Motets of Francis Poulenc." D.M.A., University of Texas at Austin, 1970, 200 pp., DA 31-3579A.

Eiseman, David. "Charles Ives and the European Symphonic Tradition: A Historical Reappraisal." Ph.D., University of Illinois at Urbana, 1972, 279 pp., DA 33-347A.

Ellison, Ross Wesley. "Unity and Contrast in Mendelssohn's *Elijah.*" Ph.D., University of North Carolina at Chapel Hill, 1978, 381 pp., DA 40-16A–17A.

Enyart, John William. "The Symphonies of Heitor Villa-Lobos." Ph.D., University of Cincinnati, 1984, 501 pp., DA 45-1907A.

Epsey, Jule Adele (Sister). "Formal, Tonal, and Thematic Structure of the Hindemith String Quartets." Ph.D., Indiana University, 1973, 193 pp., DA 34-6683A–4A.

Faulkner, Quentin. "The *Symphoniae Sacrae* of Heinrich Schuetz: A Manual for Performance." S.M.D., Union Theological Seminary, 1975, 405 pp., DA 36-17A.

Fay, Auarel Elizabeth. "The Last Quartets of Dmitri Shostakovich: A

Stylistic Investigation." Ph.D., Cornell University, 1978, 158 pp., DA 39-3905A.

Feinstein, Bernice. "The Seven Capriccios of Johannes Brahms: Op. 76, Nos. 1, 2, 5, 8, and Op. 116, Nos. 1, 3, 7." Ed.D., Columbia University, 1972, 245 pp., DA 33-891A–2A.

Ferguson, Thomas Clarence. "An Analysis of Four American Symphonies for Band." Ph.D., University of Rochester, Eastman School of Music, 1971, 388 pp., DA 33-347A.

Filosa, Albert James. "The Early Symphonies and Chamber Music of Felix Mendelssohn Bartholdy." Ph.D., Yale University, 1970, 229 pp., DA 31-6646A.

Fleisher, Robert Jay. "Schoenberg, Dualism, and *Moses und Aron.*" D.M.A., University of Illinois at Urbana, 1980, 151 pp., DA 41-4534A.

Fletcher, Marylynn Louise. "Pitch Constructions in the Masques, Op. 34 of Karol Szymanowski." D.M.A., University of Texas at Austin, 1984, 85 pp., DA 45-1907A.

Francis, John Richard. "Structure in the Solo Piano Works of John Cage." Ph.D., Florida State University, 1976, 111 pp., DA 37-3255A.

Freund, Cecilia Kathryn Van de Ramp. "Alessandro Scarlatti's Duet Cantatas with Obbligato Instruments." Ph.D., Northwestern University, 1979, 740 pp., DA 40-2969A.

Friday, Raymond. "Analyses and Interpretations of Selected Songs of David Diamond." Ph.D., New York University, 1984, 200 pp., DA 45-2295A.

Garcia, David Manuel. "Tonality in Schoenberg's Theme and Variations for Band, Op. 43a, and Symphony for Band." D.M.A., Ohio State University, 1986, 113 pp., DA 47-2362A.

Gilliam, Bryan Randolph. "Richard Strauss's *Daphne:* Opera and Symphonic Continuity." Ph.D., Harvard University, 1984, 329 pp., DA 45-1908A.

Gilmer, Carl DuVall. "Messiaen's Musical Language in *Méditations sur le Mystère de la Sainte Trinité.*" D.M.A., Memphis State University, 1978, 68 pp., DA 39-3905A.

Gingerich, Lora Louise. "Processes of Motivic Transformation in the Keyboard and Chamber Music of Charles E. Ives." Ph.D., Yale University, 1983, 288 pp., DA 44-2617A.

Godes, Catherine Anne. "Stylistic Evolution in Szymanowski's Three Piano Sonatas." D.M.A., University of Cincinnati, 1984, 97 pp., DA 46-550A.

Goetz, Wilhelm A. "An Analytical Study of Milhaud's Neuf Preludes for Organ." Ed.D., Columbia University Teachers College, 1976, 110 pp., DA 37-1289A.

Goldwire, Bettsylynn Dunn. "Harmonic Evolution in the Piano Poems of Alexander Scriabin." D.M.A., University of Texas at Austin, 1984, 57 pp., DA 45-1908A.

Gorelick, Brian Lee. "Movement and Shape in the Choral Music of Roger Sessions." D.M.A., University of Illinois at Urbana-Champaign, 1985, 296 pp., DA 46-1772A.

Grace, Irwin. "An Analysis of the Dramatic Content of the Music of Verdi's *Otello*." Ed.D., Columbia University, 1969, 275 pp., DA 32-999A–100A.

Gras, Alfred H. "A Study of *Der Freischütz* by Carl Maria von Weber." Ph.D., Northwestern University, 1968, DA 31-1832A.

Griffiths, Richard Lyle. "Ned Rorem: Music for Chorus and Orchestra." D.M.A., University of Washington, 1979, 200 pp., DA 40-526A–7A.

Grim. William Edward. "Form, Process, and Morphology in the *Sturm und Drang* Symphonies of Franz Joseph Hydn." Ph.D., Kent State University, 1985, 354 pp., DA 47-13A.

Grossman, Orin Louis. "The Piano Sonatas of Jan Ludislaw Dussek (1760–1812)." Ph.D., Yale University, 1975, 258 pp., DA 36-2479.

Habermann, Michael R. "A Style Analysis of the Nocturnes for Solo Piano by Kaikhosru Shapurji Sorabji with Special Emphasis on *Le Jardin Parfumé*." D.M.A., Peabody Conservatory of Music, 1985, 292 pp., DA 46-550A.

Hadley, Richard Thomas. "The Published Choral Music of Ulysses Simpson Kay—1943 to 1968." Ph.D., University of Iowa, 1972, 358 pp., DA 33-3694A–5A.

Hallquist, Robert Nels, Jr."Stravinsky and the Transcriptional Process: An Analytical and Historical Study of *Petrouchka*." D.M.A., North Texas State, 1979, 74 pp., DA 40-1142A.

Hankla, Jesse R. "Mozart's Fourhand Piano Sonatas with a Theoretical and Performance Analysis of K. 358 in B-Flat Major and K. 497 in F. Major." D.M.A., University of Oklahoma, 1986, 156 pp., DA 47-3231A.

Hansard, Mary Ethyl Patricia. "The Vocal Polyphonic Style of the Latin Church Music by Thomas Tallis (c. 1505–1585)." D.M.A., University of Kentucky, 1974, 211 pp., DA 32-5266A–7A.

Harris, Jane Duff. "Compositional Process in the String Quartets of Elliott Carter." Ph.D., Case Western Reserve, 1983, 320 pp., DA 44-3200A.

Hawthorne, Walter William. "Inventions and Sinfonias: An Analysis." Ph.D., University of Cincinnati, 1980, 197 pp., DA 41-2821A–2A.

Hayes, Laurence Melton. "The Music of Ulysses Kay, 1939–1963." Ph.D., University of Wisconsin, 1971, 405 pp., DA 32-3351A.

Hiatt, James Smith. "Form and Tonal Organization in the Late Instrumental Works of Carl Nielsen." Ph.D., Indiana University, 1986, 131 pp., DA 47-2790A.

Hicken, Kenneth Lambert. "Structure and Prolongations: Tonal and Serial Organization in the Introduction of Schoenberg's Variations for Orchestra." Ph.D., Brigham Young University, 1970, 192 pp., DA 31-5446A.

Hiebert, Elfrieda Franz. "The Piano Trios of Beethoven: An Historical and Analytical Study." Ph.D., University of Wisconsin, 1970, 407 pp., DA 31-5447A.

Hilliard, John Stanley. ". . .Charles Ives' *Robert Browning* Overture: Style and Structure." D.M.A., Cornell University, 1983, 166 pp., DA 44-317A.

Hilliard, Quincy Charles. "A Theoretical Analysis of the Symphonies of Aaron Copland." Ph.D., University of Florida, 1984, 230 pp., DA 45-1910A.

Hodges, Janice Kay. "The Teaching Aspects of Bartók's *Mikrokosmos.*" D.M.A., University of Texas at Austin, 1974, 97 pp., DA 35-5444A–5A.

Holt, Marilyn Barnes. "Developmental Procedures in the Sonata Form Movements of the Symphonies of Beethoven, Schubert, Mendelssohn, and Schumann." Ph.D., Case Western Reserve, 1973, 359 pp., DA 34-7807A.

Hopkins, William Thomas. "The Short Piano Compositions of Max Reger (1873–1916)." Ph.D., Indiana University, 1972, 259 pp., DA 32-6477A–8A.

Hough, Bonny Ellen. "Schoenberg's *Herzgewächse,* Op. 20: An Integrated Approach to Atonality Through Complementary Analysis." Ph.D., Washington University, 1982, 303 pp., DA 43-1341A.

Hsu, Samuel. "Imagery and Diction in the Songs of Claude Debussy." Ph.D., University of California at Santa Barbara, 1972, 218 pp., DA 33-2413A.

Huband, Joseph Dance. "The First Five Symphonies of Dmitri Shostakovich." D.A., Ball State University, 1984, 172 pp., DA 2296A–7A.

Hunt, Mary Angela. "Franz Liszt: The *Mephisto* Waltzes." D.M.A., University of Wisconsin at Madison, 1979, 176 pp., DA 40-2971A.

Hurst, Rolland Wood. "A Study, Analysis, and Performance of Selected Songs by Charles Ives." Ed.D., Columbia University, 1971, 169 pp., DA 32-752A.

Hutchings, Edward Gilmore. "The Published Songs of Frederick Delius." D.M.A., University of Miami, 1980, 109 pp., DA 41-4881A.

Ide, Yumiko. "A Structural and Stylistic Analysis of Selected Inventions and Sinfonias of Johann Sebastian Bach." Ed.D., Columbia University, Teachers College, 1980, 271 pp., DA 41-1463A.

Jack, Dwight Christian. "Two Romantic Song Cycles: An Analytical Description of the Schumann-Eichendorff *Liederkreis II*, Op. 39 and the Brahms-Tieck *Romanzen aus Magalone.*" D.M.A., University of Miami, 1973, 131 pp., DA 35-500A.

Jacobson, Allan S. "A Study of . . . *Abegg* Variations, Op. 1, by Robert Schumann." D.M.A., University of Wisconsin at Madison, 1982, 84 pp., DA 43-3451A.

James, Roberta Aileen. "Johannes Brahms: Concerto No. 1 in D Minor, Op. 15." D.M.A., Stanford University, 1981, 60 pp., DA 42-2924A.

Jeffers, Grant Lyle. "Non-Narrative Music Drama: Settings by Virgil Thomson, Ned Rorem and Earl Kim of Plays by Gertrude Stein and Samuel Beckett." Ph.D., University of California at Los Anteles, 1983, 168 pp., DA 44-3201A.

Jessop, Craig Don. "An Analytical Survey of the Unaccompanied Choral Works for Mixed Voices by Felix Mendelssohn-Bartholdy." D.M.A., Stanford University, 1981, 111 pp., DA 41-4536A.

Johnson, Richard Oscar. "The Songs of Charles Tomlinson Griffes." D.M.A., University of Iowa, 1977, 192 pp., DA 38-1727A–8A.

Johnston, Stephen Keith. "The Clarinet Concertos of Louis Spohr." D.M.A., University of Maryland, 1972, 164 pp., DA 33-2413A–14A.

Jones, Robert Frederick. "Thematic Development and Form in the First and Fourth Movements of Mahler's First Symphony." Ph.D., Brandeis University, 1980, 123 pp., DA 41-1827A.

Jones, William Isaac, Jr. "A Study of Tonality in the Symphonies of Carl Nielsen." Ph.D., Florida State University, 1973, 80 pp., DA 34-21951A–2A.

Jordan, Alan T. "Harmonic Style in Selected Sibelius Symphonies." Ph.D., Indiana University, 1984, 229 pp., DA 46-14A.

Jordan, Roland Carroll, Jr.. "Schoenberg's String Trio, Op. 45: An Analytic Study." Ph.D., Washington University, 1973, 279 pp., DA 34-7808A.

Joyce, Sister Mary Ann. "Charles E. Ives: An Analysis and a Corrected Version." Ph.D., Washington University, 1970, 122 pp., DA 31-6099A.

Kabbash, Paul Andrew. "Form and Rhythm in Webern's Atonal Works." Ph.D., Yale University, 1983, 175 pp., DA 44-2618A.

Kaderavek, Milan Robert. "Stylistic Aspects of the Late Chamber Music of Leoš Janáček: An Analytic Study." D.M.A., University of Illinois at Urbana, 1070, 284 pp., DA 31-6649A.

Kang, Nakcheung Paik. "An Analytical Study of the Piano Sonatas of Carl Maria von Weber." Ph.D., New York University, 1978, 222 pp., DA 39-4582A.

Kaplan, Richard Andrew. "The Musical Language of *Elektra*: A Study in Chromatic Harmony." Ph.D., University of Michigan, 1985, 190 pp., DA 46-832A.

Kazakova, Tatyana. "Orchestral Style Development in the Symphonies of Dmitri Shostakovich." M.A., California State University at Fullerton, 1983, 268 pp., DA 21-237A.

Kazenas, Bruno. "The *Litaniens* of Wolfgang Amadeus Mozart: A Comparative Analysis." D.M.A., University of Cincinnati, 1985, 182 pp., DA 46-1773A.

Keating, Roderic Maurice. "The Songs of Frank Bridge." D.M.A., University of Texas at Austin, 115 pp., DA 31-3583A.

Kessler, Richard Carner. "Béla Bartók's Etudes Op. 18: An Analysis for Performers." Mus.A.D., Boston University, 1984, 177 pp., DA 45-982A.

Kielian-Gilbert, Marianne Catherine. "Pitch-Class Function, Centricity, and Symmetry As Transposition Relations in Two Works of Stravinsky." Ph.D., University of Michigan, 1981, 278 pp., DA 42-908A.

Kies, Christopher R. "A Discussion of the Harmonic Organization in the First Movement of Elliott Carter's Sonata for Violoncello and Piano." Ph.D., Brandeis University, 1984, 131 pp., DA 47-342A.

Kim, Kyoung-Im. "A Critical Analysis of the First Movements of Schumann's Piano Sonatas." D.M.A., University of Oklahoma, 1980, 204 pp., DA 40-6062A.

Kinderman, William Andrew. "Beethoven's Variations on a Waltz by Diabelli': Genesis and Structure." Ph.D., University of California at Berkeley, 1980, 281 pp., DA 42-908A.

Kirk, Elise Kuhl. "The Chamber Music of Charles Koechlin (1867–1950)." Ph.D., Catholic University of America, 403 pp., DA 38-1728A–9A.

Klimisch, Sister Mary Jane. "The Music of the Lamentations: Historical and Analytical Aspects." Ph.D., Washington University, 1971, 200 pp., DA 32-5268A.

Knapp, Calvin Horace. "A Study, Analysis and Performance of Representative Piano Works of Various Periods of Béla Bartók." ED.D., Columbia University, 1973, 209 pp., DA 34-4825A.

Koh, Bo Young Yum. "Ravel's *Le Tombeau de Couperin:* A Study of the Work and Its Historical Significance." D.M.A., University of Miami, 1986, 88 pp., DA 47-3903A.

Kolbuck, Edith Henry. "An Analytical Study of Selected Toccatas of Johann Jakob Froberger: Some Possible Insights into Problems of Performance Practice." D.M.A., University of Oregon, 1976, 144 pp., DA 37-7394A–5A.

Koon, Margery A. "Aspects of Harmonic Structure in Piano Works of Erik Satie." D.M.A., University of Wisconsin, 1974, 121 pp., DA 35-3038A.

Koper, Robert Peter. "A Stylistic and Performance Analysis of the Bassoon Music of Paul Hindemith." Ed.D., University of Illinois at Urbana, 1972, 364 pp., DA 33-349A.

Korf, William E. "The Orchestral Music of Louis Moreau Gottschalk." Ph.D., University of Iowa, 1974, 264 pp., DA 35-4589.

Kosakowski, Anne Louise. "Karol Szymanowski's Mazurkas: Cyclic Structure and Harmonic Language." Ph.D., Yale University, 1980, 329 pp., DA 43-2488A.

Koska, Linda Jean. "The Structure and Harmonic Language of the *Domestic* Symphony by Richard Strauss." M. M., University of Arizona, 1986, 77 pp., DA 24-319A.

Kosnik, James Walter. "The Toccatas of Johann Jakob Froberger: A Study of Style and Aspects of Organ Performance." D.M.A., University of Rochester, Eastman School of Music, 1979, 168 pp., DA 40-1143A.

Kovalenko, Susan Chaffins. "The Twentieth-Century Requiem: An Emerging Concept." Ph.D., Washington University, 1971, 336 pp., DA 34-6023A–4A.

Kranz, Kathleen Nee. "Structural Functions of Rests in Franz Schubert's Works for Piano." Ph.D., University of California at San Diego, 1985, 148 pp., DA 46-1774A.

Kreiling, Jean Louis. "The Songs of Samuel Barber: A Study in Literary Taste and Text-Setting." Ph.D., University of North Carolina at Chapel Hill, 1986, 379 pp., DA 47-1526A.

Krenek, Thomas B. "An Examination and Analysis of the Choral Music of Carl Nielsen (1865–1931)." D.M.A., University of Cincinnati, 1984, 96 pp., DA 45-2298A.

Kresky, Jeffrey Jay. *Requiem Canticles:* A Study in Analysis." Ph.D., Princeton University, 1974, 125 pp., DA 35-3038A.

Kuchera-Morin, Joann. "Structure in Charles Wuorinen's String Trio" Ph.D., University of Rochester, Eastman School of Music, 1984, 111 pp., DA 45-1568A.

Kumlien, Wendel Clark. "The Sacred Choral Music of Charles Ives: A

Study in Style Development." D.M.A., University of Illinois, 1969, 576 pp., DA 30-2061A.

Lam (Fang), Julia Tiev-Luong. "Chopin's Approach to Form in His Four Piano Scherzos." Ph.D., Michigan State University, 1979, 121 pp., DA 40-3617A.

Lamb, James Boyd. "A Graphic Analysis of Brahms, Op. 118, with an Introduction to Schenkerian Theory and the Reduction Process." Ph.D., Texas Technical University, 1979, 162 pp., DA 41-454A.

Laporta, Mark Stevens. "Patterns of Invariance and Repetition As Structural Functions in Schoenberg's Op. 36." D.M.A., Cornell University, 1983, 188 pp., DA 44-1620A.

Leckie, Thomas Conley. "A Comparison of Thematic and Episodic Analysis of the Bach Two-Part Invention." Ph.D., University of Oklahoma, 1980, 212 pp., DA 41-845A.

Lewis, Christopher. "Tonality and Structure in the Ninth Symphony of Gustav Mahler." Ph.D., University of Rochester, Eastman School of Music, 1983, 257 pp., DA 44-101A.

Lieberson, Peter Goddard. "Milton Babbitt's *Post-Partitions*." Ph.D., Brandeis University, 1985, 67 pp., DA 46-1550A.

Lipkis, Larry Allen. "Aspects of Temporality in Debussy's *Jeux* and Ives's Symphony No. 4, Fourth Movement." Ph.D., University of California at Santa Barbara, 1984 100 pp., DA 45-2689A.

Litten, Jack Dane. "Three Song Cycles of Benjamin Britten." Ed.D., Columbia University, 1969, 293 pp., DA 31-788A.

Little, Ricky Ricardo. "A Comparative Study of . . . the Original Play, and the Two Operas, *Il Barbiere di Siviglia* by Giovanni Paisiello and Gioachino Rossini." D.M.A., Ohio State University, 1985, 103 pp., DA 46-2480A.

Locke, Benjamin Ross. "Performance and Structural Levels: A Conductor's Analysis of Brahms's Op. 74, No. 2, 'O Heiland, Reiss Die Himmel Auf.' " D.M.A., University of Wisconsin at Madison, 1985, 240 pp., DA 47-15A.

Lockwood, Larry Paul. "Rhythmic Analysis: A Theory, A Methodology, and a Study of Stravinsky's Requiem Canticles." D.M.A., Cornell University, 1975, 113 pp., DA 36-1893A–4A.

Loewen, Wesley James. "The Relationship of Text and Vocal Aspects in the *Mörike* Songs of Hugo Wolf." D.M.A., University of Missouri at Kansas City, 1983, 377 pp., DA 44-607A.

Lohman, Peter Nathan. "Schoenberg's Atonal Procedures: A Non-Serial Analytic Approach to the Instrumental Works, 1908–1921." Ph.D., Ohio State University, 1981, 336 pp., DA 42-446A.

Mabry, Sharon Cody. *"Twelve Poems of Emily Dickinson* by Aaron Copland: A Stylistic Analysis." D.M.A., George Peabody College for Teachers, 1977, 234 pp., DA 38-2403A–4A.

Maes, Lloyd Rodney. "The Choral Style of Florent Schmitt: An Analysis." D.M.A., Stanford University, 1983, 143 pp., DA 44-1967A.

Magers, Roy Vernon. "Aspects of Form in the Symphonies of Charles E. Ives." Ph.D., Indiana University, 1975, 392 pp., DA 36-2482A.

Magrill, Samuel Morse. "The Principles of Variation: A Study in the Selection of Differences with Examples from Dallapiccola, J. S. Bach, and Brahms." D.M.A., University of Illinois at Urbana, 1983, 253 pp., DA 43-3749A.

Maki, Paul-Martin. "The Three Chorale-Fantasias, Op. 52 of Max Reger: Commentary and a Practical Edition." D.M.A., University of Rochester, Eastman School of Music, 1975, 179 pp., DA 36-2483A.

Malloy, Joseph Thomas. "Musico-Dramatic Irony in Mozart's *Magic Flute.*" Ph.D., University of Virginia, 1985, 224 pp., DA 47-539–40A.

Mancini, David Lee. "Form and Polarity in Late Works of Luigi Dallapiccola." Ph.D., Yale University, 1984, 278 pp., DA 46-1123A.

Mann, Richard Ensor. "Pitch Structure and Poetic Imagery in Luciano Berio's *Wasserklavier* and *Erdenklavier.*" Ph.D., University of Rochester, Eastman School of Music, 1986, 68 pp., DA 47-15A.

Marinaro, Stephen John. "The Four Piano Sonatas of Carl Maria von Weber." D.M.A., University of Texas at Austin, 1980, 54 pp., DA 41-2823A.

Marks, Frank William. "Form and the Mazurkas of Chopin." D.M.A., University of Washington, 1970, 168 pp., DA 31-5449A.

Marley, Marie Annette. "The Sacred Cantatas of Giovanni Battista Sammartini." Ph.D., University of Cincinnati, 1978, 360 pp., DA 39-2610A.

Martin, Rebecca Gena. "The Nine Piano Sonatas of Sergei Prokofiev." D.M.A., University of Kentucky, 1982, 118 pp., DA 43-3749A.

Mason, Charles Norman. "A Comprehensive Analysis of Roger Sessions' Opera *Montezuma.*" D.M.A., University of Illinois at Urbana, 1982, 179 pp., DA 43-3452A.

Mast, Paul Buck. "Style and Structure in *Iberia* by Isaac Albéniz." Ph.D., University of Rochester, Eastman School of Music, 1974, 419 pp., DA 35-2322A.

Mathes, James Robert. "Texture and Musical Structure: An Analysis of First Movements of Select Twentieth-Century Piano Sonatas." Ph.D., Florida State University, 1986, 271 pp., DA 47-2363A.

Mathews, Theodore Kenneth. "The Masses of Anton Bruckner." Ph.D., University of Michigan, 1974, 397 pp., DA 5449A.

Matthews, Nell Wright. "George Crumb's *Makrokosmos*, Vols. 1 and 2: Considerations for Performance, Including Observations by David Burge, Robert Miller, and Lambert Orkis." D.M.A., University of Oklahoma, 1981, 178 pp., DA 42-4641A.

Mayer, Karl Eby. "The Anthems of Thomas Tallis." D.M.A., University of Rochester, Eastman School of Music, 1980, 472 pp., DA 41-2347A.

Mayer, Mark. "A Structural and Stylistic Analysis of the Benjamin Britten *Curlew River*." Ed.D., Columbia University Teachers College, 1983, 89 pp., DA 44-1370A.

McCandless, William Edgar. "Cantus Firmus Techniques in Selected Instrumental Compositions, 1910–1960." Ph.D., Indiana University, 1974, 329 pp., DA 35-4593A.

McCrae, Elizabeth. "Ravel's *Valses nobles et sentimentales:* Analysis, Stylistic Considerations, Performance Problems." D.M.A., Boston University, 1974, 196 pp., DA 35-1688A.

McGreary, George L. "A Structural and Interpretive Analysis and Performance of Piano Trios by Haydn, Schubert, and Ravel." Ed.D., Columbia University, 1973, 247 pp., DA 34-3702A.

McGee, William James. "An Expanded Concept of Timbre and Its Structural Significance, with a Timbral Analysis of George Crumb's *Night of the Four Moons*." Ph.D., University of Arizona, 1982, 251 pp., DA 43-1741A.

McIntosh, Robert Dale. "The Dramatic Music of William Boyce." Ph.D., University of Washington, 1979, 357 pp., DA 40-530.

Meeks, John Samuel. "Aspects of Stylistic Evolution in Scriabin's Piano Preludes." D.M.A., Peabody Conservatory of Music, 1975, 344 pp., DA 37-1866A–7A.

Merryman, Marjorie Jane. "Aspects of Phrasing and Pitch Usage in Roger Sessions' Piano Sonata No. 3." Ph.D., Brandeis University, 1981, 53 pp., DA 42-3803A.

Miles, Marmaduke Sidney. "The Solo Piano Works of Mrs. H. H. A. Beach." D.M.A., Peabody Conservatory of Music, 1985, 175 pp., DA 46-1775A.

Miller, Lynus Patrick. "From Analysis to Performance: The Musical Landscape of Johannes Brahms' Op. 118, No. 6." Ph.D., University of Michigan, 1979, 161 pp., DA 40-530A–31A.

Miller, Mina Florence. "The Solo Piano Music of Carl Nielsen: An Analysis for Performance." Ph.D., New York University, 1978, 328 pp., DA 39-4585.

Miller, Roger L. *Pli Selon Pli:* Pierre Boulez and the 'New Lyricism.' " Ph.D., Case Western Reserve, 1978, 456 pp., DA 39-5794A.

Mitchell, Jon Ceander. "Gustav Holst: The Works for Military Band."

Ed.D., University of Illinois at Urbana, 1980, 314 pp., DA 41-5019A.

Mizell, John. "Trends, Analysis, and Style of Specific Compositions by Twentieth Century Composers." D.M.A., University of Missouri, 1972, 83 pp., DA 33-2414A.

Moore, William Howard. "The Cyclical Principle As Used in the Construction of Piano Sonatas." Ed.D., Columbia University, 1975, 189 pp., DA 36-1365A.

Morrongiello, Lydia A. "Music Symbolism in Selected Cantatas and Chorale Preludes." Ed.D., Columbia University, 1975, 184 pp., DA 36-1158A.

Nelson, Gary Lee. "Anton Webern's Five Canons, Op. 16: A Text Case for Computer-Aided Analysis and Synthesis of Musical Style." Ph.D., Washington University, 1974, 237 pp., DA 35-2324A–5A.

Nelson, Mark Allan. "The Brass *Parables* of Vincent Persichetti." D.M.A., Arizona State University, 1985, 120 pp., DA 46-1124A.

Newman, Joyce E. "Formal Structure and Recitative in the Tragedies Lyriques of Jean-Baptiste de Lully." Ph.D., University of Michigan, 1974, 389 pp., DA 35-5450A.

Ng-Quinn, David. "Improvisations on Hungarian Peasant Songs, Op. 20 for Solo Piano by Béla Bartók." D.M.A., Stanford University, 1984, 161 pp., DA 45-3023A.

Nygren, Dennis Quentin. "The Music for Accompanied Clarinet Solo of Claude Debussy: An Historical and Analytical Study of the *Première Rhapsodie* and *Petite Piece.*" D.M., Northwestern University, 1982, 183 pp., DA 44-2922A.

Oberacker, Betty. "The Preludes of the *Well-Tempered Clavier,* Vol. 1, of Johann Sebastian Bach: A Commentary and Analysis." D.M.A., Ohio State University, 1972, 63 pp., DA 33-1771A.

O'Leary, Jane Strong. "Aspects of Structure in Webern's Quartet, Op. 22." Ph.D., Princeton University, 1978, 98 pp., DA 39-3214A–15A.

Oosting, Stephen. "Text-Music Relationships in Benjamin Britten's Serenade for Tenor, Horn, and Strings." D.M.A., University of Rochester, Eastman School of Music, 1985, 203 pp., DA 46-1124A.

Ore, Charles William. "Numbers and Number Correspondences in Op. 40 by Arnold Schoenberg: Pythagoras and the Quadrivium Revisited." D.M.A., University of Nebraska at Lincoln, 1986, 263 pp., DA 47-1109A.

Ott, David Lee. "The Role of Texture and Timbre in the Music of George Crumb." D.M.A., University of Kentucky, 1982, 277 pp., DA 44-2704A.

Owens, Samuel Battie. ". . . Four Lenten Motets of Alessandro Scarlatti." D.M.A., George Peabody College for Teachers, 1974, 295 pp., DA 35-4597A–8A.

Owens, Samuel Battie. "The Organ Mass and Girolamo Frescobaldi's *Fiore Musicali* of 1635 . . ." D.M.A., George Peabody College for Teachers, 1974, 295 pp., DA 35-4597A–8A.

Packales, Joseph. "Benjamin Britten's *Peter Grimes:* An Analysis." Ph.D., Kent State University, 1984, 118 pp., DA 45-983A.

Palmer, Kenneth Robert. "A Performer's Guide to Charles Ives' Piano Sonata No. 2, *Concord*, Mass., 1840–1860." Ph.D., Washington University, 1986, 135 pp., DA 47-4228A.

Parish, George David. "Motivic and Cellular Structure in Alban Berg's *Lyric* Suite." Ph.D., University of Michigan, 1970, 328 pp., DA 31-6650A.

Parker-Hale, Mary Ann Elizabeth. "Handel's Latin Psalm Settings." Ph.D., University of Rochester, Eastman School of Music, 1981, 174 pp., DA 42-4036A.

Paul, Sharon June. "Robert Schumann's Choral Music for Women's Voices." D.M.A., Stanford University, 1984, 172 pp., DA 45-3023A.

Payne, Dorothy Katherine. "The Accompanied Wind Sonatas of Hindemith: Studies in Tonal Counterpoint." Ph.D., University of Rochester, Eastman School of Music, 1974, 227 pp., DA 35-2325A.

Peacock, Kenneth John. "Alexander Scriabin's *Prometheus:* Philosophy and Structure." Ph.D., University of Michigan, 1976, 269 pp., DA 37-1291A.

Pearlmutter, Alan Jay. "Leonard Bernstein's *Dybbuk:* An Analysis Including Historical, Religious, and Literary Perspectives of Hasidic Life and Lore." D.M.A., Peabody Conservatory of Music, 1985, 376 pp., DA 46-1776A.

Peckham, Mary Adelaide. "The Operas of George Philipp Telemann." Ph.D., Columbia University, 1972, 309 pp., DA 33-2415A.

Pellman, Samuel Frank. "An Examination of the Role of Timbre in a Musical Composition, As Exemplified by an Analysis of *Sequenza* V by Luciano Berio." D.M.A., Cornell University, 1979, 160 pp., DA 40-4794A.

Peterman, Timothy James. "An Examination of Two Sextets of Carlos Chávez: Toccata for Percussion Instruments and Tambuco for Six Percussion Players." D.M.A., North Texas State University, 1986, 85 pp., DA 47-2793A.

Peterson, William John. "Debussy's *Douze Etudes*." Ph.D., University of California at Berkeley, 1981, 271 pp., DA 42-2927A.

Petkus, Janetta. "The Songs of John Cage (1932–1970)." Ph.D., University of Connecticut, 1986, 266 pp., DA 47-2365A.

691

Pettyway, B. Keith. "The Solo and Chamber Compositions for Flute by Bohuslav Martinu." D.M.A., University of Southern Mississippi, 1980, 154 pp., DA 41-4537A.

Phipps, Graham Howard. "Schoenberg's 'Grundgestalt' Principle: A New Approach with Particular Application to the Variations for Orchestra, Op. 31." Ph.D., University of Cincinnati, 1976, 608 pp., DA 37-6133A.

Piscitelli, Felicia Ann. "The Chamber Music of Mrs. H. H. A. Beach (1867–1944)." M.M., University of New Mexico, 1983, 85 pp., DA 22-384A.

Plate, Stephen W. "A Study and Comparison . . . with Particular Attention to Instrumentation, Orchestration, and Variation Technique." D.M.A., University of Cincinnati, 1986, 200 pp., DA 47-2793A.

Pohl, Norma Doris. "*Gaspard de la nuit* by Maurice Ravel: A Theoretical and Performance Analysis." Ph.D., Washington University, 1978, 283 pp., DA 40-23A.

Polley, Jo Ann Marie. "An Analysis of John Corigliano's Concerto for Clarinet and Orchestra." Ph.D., Michigan State University, 1983, 124 pp., DA 44-2619A.

Prescott, Elliot Jordan. "A Study, Analysis, and Recital of the Last Two Piano Sonatas of Franz Schubert: A Major (D. 959); B-Flat Major (D. 960)." Ed.D., Columbia University Teachers College, 1976, 183 pp., DA 37-2046A.

Prussing, Stephan Henry. "Compositional Techniques in Rachmaninoff's Vespers, Op. 37." Ph.D., Catholic University of America, 1980, 237 pp., DA 40-5644A.

Quilling, Howard Lee. "An Analysis of Olivier Messiaen's *Couleurs de la Cité Céleste.*" Ph.D., University of California, Santa Barbara, 1984, 346 pp., DA 45-3477A.

Ráfols, Alberto Pedro. "Debussy and the Symbolist Movement: The Preludes." D.M.A., University of Washington, 1975, 195 pp., DA 37-683A.

Ralph, Bobbie Jeffers. "A Study of the Use of Contrapuntal Techniques in Selected Piano Sonatas of Ludwig van Beethoven." Ph.D., University of Oklahoma, 1970, 205 pp., DA 31-2960A–61A.

Ramsier, Paul. "An Analysis and Comparison of the Motivic Structure of *Octandre* and *Intégrales*, Two Instrumental Works by Edgard Varèse." Ph.D., New York University, 1972, 206 pp., DA 33-1772A.

Ray, Karen. "Alban Berg As *Liedkomponist:* An Analytical Study of His Two Settings of *Schliesse mir die Augen beide*, 1907 and 1925." M.M., North Texas State University, 1986, 178 pp., DA 24-320A.

Rea, John Rocco. "Franz Liszt's New Path of Composition: The Sonata in B Minor As Paradigm." Ph.D., Princeton University, 1978, 447 pp., DA 39-3217A.

Reade, Eugene Walter. "A Study of Rhythm in the Serial Works of Igor Stravinsky." Ph.D., Indiana University, 1979, 287 pp., DA 40-1743A.

Reible, John Joseph. "Tristan-Romanticism and the Expressionism of the Three Piano Pieces, Op. 11 of Arnold Schoenberg." Ph.D., Washington University, 1980, 381 pp., DA 41-846A.

Rice, Paul Francis. "The Fontainbleau Operas of Jean-Philippe Rameau: A Critical Study." Ph.D., University of Victoria (Canada), 1982, DA 43-249A.

Richards, James Edward, Jr. "Pitch Structure in the Opera *Don Rodrigo* of Alberto Ginastera." Ph.D., University of Rochester, Eastman School of Music, 1983, 156 pp., DA 46-3530A.

Richter, Leonard. "An Analytic Study of Selected Piano Concertos of Jan Ladislav Dussek." Ph.D., New York University, 1985, 179 pp., DA 46-642A.

Rindo, John Patrick. "A Structural Analysis of Giuseppe Verdi's Early Operas and Their Influence on the Italian Risorgimento." Ph.D., University of Oregon, 1984, 333 pp., DA 45-1922A.

Rinehart, Arthur Edward. "The Factors Present in the Transitional Musical Vocabulary of Alexander Nikolayevitch Scriabin Which Suggest Later Compositional Techniques." D.M.A., University of Missouri, 1975, 82 pp., DA 36-7037A.

Rinsinger, Dan Howard. "The Seven Song Collection of Gabriel Fauré." D.M.A., University of Illinois at Urbana, 1971, 211 pp., DA 32-5827A.

Rodda, Richard Earl. "The Symphonies of Michael Tippett." Ph.D., Case Western Reserve, 1979, 533 pp., DA 40-3621A.

Roennfeld, Peter John. "The Double Piano Concertos of Felix Mendelssohn." D.M.A., University of Cincinnati, 1985, 169 pp., DA 46-2851A.

Rolf, Marie. "Debussy's *La Mer:* A Critical Analysis in the Light of Early Sketches and Editions." Ph.D., University of Rochester, Eastman School of Music, 1976, 367 pp., DA 37-6833A–4A.

Romain, Edwin Philip. "A Study of Francis Poulenc's Fifteen Improvisations for Piano Solo." D.M.A., University of Southern Mississippi, 1978, 183 pp., DA 39-1920A.

Rose, Juanelva M. "The Harmonic Idiom of the Keyboard Works of Carl Philipp Emanuel Bach." Ph.D., University of California at Santa Barbara, 1970, 293 pp., DA 31-6102A.

Rose, Michael Paul. "Structural Integration in Selected Mixed A Cappella Choral Works of Brahms." Ph.D., University of Michigan, 1971, 280 pp., DA 32-4051A.

Rosner, Arnold. "An Analytical Survey of the Music of Alan Hovhaness." Ph.D., State University of New York at Buffalo, 1972, 377 pp., DA 33-779A.

Russom, Philip Wade. "A Theory of Pitch Organization for the Early Works of Maurice Ravel." Ph.D., Yale University, 1985, 216 pp., DA 46-3188A.

Sabbeth, Daniel Paul. "Principles of Tonal and Dramatic Organization in Verdi's *Falstaff*." Ph.D., City University of New York, 1976, 234 pp., DA 37-3980A.

Sandlin, Julkian Dan. "Romantic Elements in the Piano Sonatas of Jan Ladislav Dussek (1760–1812)." D.M.A., University of Miami, 1974, 53 pp., DA 35-3798A.

Scherperel, Loretta Fox. "The Solo Organ Works of Camille Saint-Saens." D.M.A., University of Rochester, Eastman School of Music, 1978, 179 pp., DA 40-23A.

Schindler, Christopher John. "A Stylistic Analysis of the Piano Music of Carl Nielsen." D.M.A., University of Oregon, 1984, 193 pp., DA 45-680A.

Schoffman, Nachum. "The Songs of Charles Ives." Ph.D., Hebrew University of Jeruselem, 1977, 456 pp., DA 39-5205A.

Schram, Albert-George. "Gustav Mahler: Symphony No. 2 (C Minor): A Historical Background and Analysis." D.M.A., University of Washington, 1985, 172 pp., DA 46-2852A.

Schultz, John A. "The Soli-Tutti Concept in the Choral Works of Johann Sebastian Bach." D.M.A., University of Illinois at Urbana, 1980, 161 pp., DA 41-456A.

Seidler, Richard David. "The Bassoon Concertos of Antonio Vivaldi." Ph.D., Catholic University of America, 1974, 787 pp., DA 34-7811A–12A.

Shanks, Marilyn E. "Sibelius Symphonies 3 Through 6: Degrees of Departure from Traditional Sonata-Allegro Structure." M.M., Duquesne University, 1984, 68 pp., DA 23-11A.

Sheeler, William Scott. "Movement 1. Harmonic Motion in the Music of Roger Sessions." Ph.D., Brandeis University, 1984, 93 pp., DA 45-15A.

Shelton, Gregory Allard. "An Analysis of Charles Ives's *Three-Page Sonata* for Piano." M.A., American University, 1985, 238 pp., DA 23-415A.

Shelton, Margaret Meier. "The ABC of *Phaedra:* Word Painting As Structure in Britten's *Phaedra*." Ph.D., University of California, 1983, 113 pp., DA 44-2289A.

Shinn, Randall Alan. "An Analysis of Elliott Carter"'s Sonata for Flute, Oboe, Cello, and Harpsichord (1952)." D.M.A., University of Illinois at Urbana, 1975, 183 pp., DA 36-5631A.

Shreffler, Theodore Wilson. "An Analysis of the Violin Concerto (1935) by Alban Berg." Ph.D., University of California at Los Angeles, 1979, 161 pp., DA 40-3622A.

Shuffett, Robert Vernon. "The Music, 1971–1975, of George Crumb: A Style Analysis." D.M.A., Peabody Conservatory of Music, 1979, 576 pp., DA 40-1744A–5A.

Sidoti, Raymond Benjamin. "The Violin Sonatas of Béla Bartók: An Epitome of the Composer's Development." D.M.A., Ohio State University, 1972, 55 pp., DA 33-17773A.

Sifferman, James Philip. "Samuel Barber's Works for Solo Piano." D.M.A., University of Texas at Austin, 1982, 140 pp., DA 43-2151A.

Silverton, Jann Jacobs. "A Grundgestalt Analysis of Op. 15, *Das Buch der Hängenden Gärten* by Arnold Schoenberg on Poems by Stefan George." Ph.D., Northwestern University, 1986, 233 pp., DA 47-707A.

Sine, Nadine. "The Evolution of Symphonic Worlds: Tonality in the Symphonies of Gustav Mahler with Emphasis on the First, Third and Fifth." Ph.D., New York University, 1983, 308 pp., DA 44-3538A.

Skoog, James Alfred. "Set Syntax in Béla Bartók's *Mikrokosmos*." Ph.D., Indiana University, 1985, 225 pp., DA 47-342A.

Smith, Arthur Dove. "Recurring Motives and Themes As a Means to Unity in Selected String Quartets of Dmitri Shostakovich." D. Mus. Ed., University of Oklahoma, 1976, 480 pp., DA 37-2487–8A.

Snyder, Linda June. "Leonard Bernstein's Work for the Musical Theatre: How the Music Functions Dramatically." D.M.A., University of Illinois at Urbana, 1982, 290 pp., DA 43-3751A.

Sommers, Paul Bartholin. "Fauré and His Songs: The Relationship of Text, Melody, and Accompaniment." D.M.A., University of Illinois, 1969, 175 pp., DA 31-791A.

Spacht, Thomas. "Sweelinck's Organ Music: A Study of Structure and Style." D.M.A., University of Rochester, Eastman School of Music, 1975, 82 pp., DA 38-1109A.

Spicknall, Joan Singer. "The Piano Music of Aaron Copland: A Performance-Tape and Study of His Original Work for Piano Solo." D.M.A., University of Maryland, 1974, 33 pp., DA 36-595A.

Stauffer, George Boyer. "The Free Organ Preludes of Johann Sebastian Bach." Ph.D., Columbia University, 1978, 322 pp., DA 39-1921A–2A.

695

Steen, Philip Lewis. "Zoltán Kodály's Choral Music for Children and Youth Choirs." Ph.D., University of Michigan, 1970, 225 pp., DA 31-6653A.

Stehman, Dan. "The Symphonies of Roy Harris: An Analytical Study of the Linear Materials and of Related Works." Ph.D., University of Southern California, 1973, 1598 pp., DA 34-7272A.

Stein, Alan. "The Musical Language of Charles Ives' *Three Places in New England*." D.M.A., University of Illinois at Urbana, 1975, 231 pp., DA 36-6362LA–3A.

Stein, Deborah Jane. "Extended Tonal Procedures in the *Lieder* of Hugo Wolf." Ph.D., Yale University, 1982, 421 pp., DA 45-2690A.

Stocker, Leonard L. "The Treatment of the Romantic Literary Hero in Verdi's *Ernani* and in Massenet's *Werther*." Ph.D., Florida State University, 1969, 188 pp., DA 32-3358A.

Stoner, Thomas Alan. "Mendelssohn's Published Songs." Ph.D., University of Maryland, 1972, 440 pp., DA 33-6956A.

Strickert, Jane Elizabeth Bernsten. "Richard Strauss' *Vier letzte Lieder:* An Analytical Study." Ph.D., Washington University, 1975, 240 pp., DA 36-5632A–3A.

Swickard, Ralph James. "The Symphonies of Darius Milhaud: An Historical Perspective and Critical Study of Their Musical Content, Style and Form." Ph.D., University of California at Los Angeles, 1973, 459 pp., DA 34-3458A.

Szabo, Edward Joseph. "The Violoncello-Piano Sonatas of Ludwig van Beethoven." Ed.D., Columbia University, 1966, 149 pp., DA 31-418.

Taggart, Mark Alan. "An Analysis of Suite for Cello, Op. 72, and Second Suite for Cello, Op. 80, by Benjamin Britten." D.M.A., Cornell University, 1983, 84 pp., DA 44-320A.

Tashjian, Beatrice Chapman. "Stravinsky's Symphony in Three Movements: An Analysis." D.M., Northwestern University, 1985, 63 pp., DA 46-838A.

Telesco, Paula Jean. "A Harmonic Analysis of Selected Piano Music of Emmanuel Chabrier." M.M., University of Arizona, 1985, 170 pp., DA 23-415A.

Thurston, Richard Elliott. "Musical Representation in the Symphonic Works of Richard Strauss." Ph.D., University of Texas at Austin, 1971, 384 pp., DA 32-5832A–3A.

Thurston, Viscount Francis. "Hindemith's Third Piano Sonata: A New Assessment." D.M.A., Ohio State University, 1984, 51 pp., DA 45-1570A.

Tibbetts, George Richard. "An Analysis of the Text-Music Relationship in Selected Songs of Benjamin Britten." Ed.D., Columbia University Teachers College, 1984, 166 pp., DA 46-17A.

Tommasini, Anthony Carl. "The *Portraits for Piano* by Virgil Thomson." D.M.A., Boston University School for the Arts, 1982, 219 pp., DA 43-970A.

Townsend, Alfred S. "Unity and Variety in *A Dylan Thomas Trilogy* by John Corigliano." Ph.D., New York University, 1986, 341 pp., DA 47-2941A.

Trembath, Shirley Elizabeth. "Text and Texture in the Solo Vocal Works, Opp. 14–15 of Anton Webern." Ph.D., University of Texas at Austin, 1985, 337 pp., DA 46-3532A.

Trenkamp, Wilma Anne. "A Throw of the Dice: An Analysis of Selected Works by Pierre Boulez." Ph.D., Case Western Reserve, 1973, 254 pp., DA 34-5237A.

Trimmer, Maud Alice. "Texture and Sonata Form in the Late String Chamber Music of Haydn and Mozart." Ph.D., City University of New York, 1981, 594 pp., DA 42-3805A–6A.

Truelove, Nathan M. "Karlheinz Stockhausen's *Klavierstück XI:* An Analysis of Its Composition . . . and the Translation of Rhythm into Pitch." D.M.A., University of Oklahoma, 1984, 200 pp., DA 45-2301A.

Tusa, Michael Charles. "Carl Maria von Weber's *Euryanthe:* A Study of Its Historical Context, Genesis, and Reception." Ph.D., Princeton University, 1983, 614 pp., DA 43-3453A.

Valicenti, Joseph Anthony. "The Thirteen Nocturnes of Gabriel Fauré." D.M.A., University of Miami, 1980, 108 pp., DA 41-1833A.

Van der Slice, John DeWitt. "An Analysis of György Ligeti's *Atomosphères.*" D.M.A., University of Illinois at Urbana, 1980, 51 pp., DA 41-457A.

Vancil, Gregory Kent. "A Study of Robert Schumann's 'Adventlied' and 'Neujahrslied,' with English Translations." D.M.A., University of Southern California, 1983, 44-1969A.

Vander Weg, John Dean. "Symmetrical Pitch and Equivalence Class Set Structure in Anton Webern's Op. 5." Ph.D., University of Michigan, 1983, 161 pp., DA 44-1969A.

Vantine, Bruce Lynn. "Four Twentieth-Century Masses: An Analytical Comparison of Style and Compositional Technique." D.M.A., University of Illinois at Urbana, 1982, 427 pp., DA 43-583A–4A.

Vitercik, Gregory John. "The Early Works of Felix Mendelssohn: A Study in the Romantic Sonata Style." Ph.D., State University of New York, 1985, 508 pp., DA 47-344A.

Vlahcevic, Sonia Klosek. "Thematic-Tonal Organization in the Late

Sonatas of Sergei Prokofiev." Ph.D., Catholic University of America, 1975, 251 pp., DA 36-1897A.

Wade, Rachel W. "The Keyboard Concertos of Carl Philipp Emanuel Bach: Sources and Style." Ph.D., New York University, 1980, 511 pp., DA 40-5645A.

Walker, Alvah John. "The A Capella Choral Music of Paul Hindemith." Ph.D., University of Rochester, Eastman School of Music, 1971, 416 pp., DA 32-7036A.

Ward, Kelly Mac. "An Analysis of the Relationship Between Text and Musical Shape and an Investigation of the Relationship Between Text and Surface Rhythmic Detail." Ph.D., University of Texas at Austin, 1978, 387 pp., DA 39-3912A–13A.

Watrous, John. "Harmonic and Transpositional Logic in the First Movment of the Schoenberg's Violin Concerto." Ph.D., Brandeis University, 1986, 157 pp., DA 47-1528A.

Waxman, Sheila. "Béla Bartók's Sonata for Piano: An Analytical Study." D.M.A., Boston University, 1985, 186 pp., DA 47-17A.

Wegren, Thomas Joseph. "The Solo Piano Music of Gabriel Fauré." Ph.D., Ohio State University, 1973, 301 pp., DA 34-7272A.

Westafer, Walter. "Over-All Unity and Contrast in Brahms' *German Requiem.*" Ph.D., University of North Carolina at Chapel Hill, 1973, 330 pp., DA 35-507A.

Westlund, John Otto. "The Mass Settings of Johann Nepomuk Hummel: A Conductor's Analysis of the Mass in B-Flat." D.M.A., University of Iowa, 1975, 264 pp., DA 36-7726A–7A.

Whang, Un-Yong. "An Analysis of Dello Joio's Chamber Music for Piano and Strings with Performance Suggestions." Ed.D., Columbia University Teachers College, 1986, 261 pp., DA 47-2072A.

Wheeler, William Scott. "Harmonic Motion in the Music of Roger Sessions." Ph.D., Brandeis University, 1984, 93 pp., DA 45-15A.

Wheelock, Gretchen Ann. "Wit, Humor, and the Instrumental Music of Joseph Haydn." Ph.D., Yale University, 1979, 322 pp., DA 43-2827A.

White, Charles Willis. "The Masses of Franz Liszt." Ph.D., Bryn Mawr College, 1973, 457 pp., DA 34-6694A.

White, Pamela Cynthia. "Idea and Representation: Source-Critical and Analytical Studies of Music, Text, and Religious Thought in Schoenberg's *Moses und Aron.*" Ph.D., Harvard University, 1983, 518 pp., DA 44-3538A.

Whitlock, Prentice Earle. "The Analysis, Development of Form, and Interpretation of the Epistle Sonatas of Wolfgang Amadeus Mozart (1756–1791)." Ph.D., New York University, 1985, 262 pp., DA 46-643A.

Wilde, Denis Gerard. "Melodic Process in the Tone Poems of Richard Strauss." Ph.D., Catholic University of America, 1984, 436 pp., DA 45-1571A.

Wilkins, Judith Ann. "Harmony and Tonality in Franck's Symphony in D Minor." M.Mus., University of Arizona, 1985., 194 pp., DA 23-421A.

Wilson, John Duane. "Ravel's *L'Enfant et les sortilèges:* Musical-Dramatic Analysis and Guide to Its Musical Preparation for College Opera Workshop Production." D.M.A., University of Rochester, Eastman School of Music, 1974, 304 pp., DA 35-3802A.

Wilson, Mark Edwards. "An Analysis of Igor Stravinsky's *Agon.*" Ph.D., University of California at Los Angeles, 1974, 89 pp., DA 35-5458A.

Winfield, George Alexander. "Ferruccio Busoni's Compositional Art: A Study of Selected Works for Piano Solo Composed Between 1907 and 1923." Ph.D., Indiana University, 1981, 218 pp., DA 42-4972A.

Winters, Thomas Dyer. "Additive and Repetitive Techniques in the Experimental Works of Charles Ives." Ph.D., University of Pennsylvania, 1986, 348 pp., DA 86-24038.

Wolterink, Charles Paul. "Harmonic Structure and Organization in the Early Works of Igor Stravinskii, 1952–1957." Ph.D., Stanford University, 1979, 373 pp., DA 39-7050A.

Wood, Darrell Elroy. "A Paradigm for the Study and Performance of *Intégrales* and *Hyperprism*, Two Instrumental Works by Edgard Varèse." D.A., Ball State University, 1974, 179 pp., DA 35-6188A–9A.

Wood, Vivian Lee Poates. "Francis Poulenc's Songs for Voice and Piano." Ph.D., Washington University, 1973, 164 pp., DA 34-6031A.

Woodward, Francis Lewis. "The Solo Songs of Felix Mendelssohn." D.M.A., University of Texas at Austin, 1972, 233 pp., DA 33-5229A.

Woodward, Gregory S. "Non-Pitch Aspects As Structural Determinants in the Atonal Works of Anton Webern." D.M.A., Cornell University, 1986, 123 pp., DA 47-2368A.

Woolsey, Timothy Dwight. "Organizational Principles in Piano Sonatas of Alexander Scriabin." D.M.A., University of Texas at Austin, 1977, 167 pp., DA 38-2408A.

Wyatt, Lucius Reynolds. "The Mid-Twentieth-Century Orchestral Variation, 1953–1963." Ph.D., University of Rochester, Eastman School of Music, 1974, 504 pp., DA 34-7273A.

Yannay, Yehuda. "Toward an Open-Ended Method of Analysis of Contemporary Music: A Study of Selected Works by Edgard Varèse and György Ligeti." D.M.A., University of Illinois at Urbana, 1974, 163 pp., DA 35-7952A–3A.

Yarrow, Anne. "An Analysis and Comparison of the Three Sonatas for Violin and Piano by Edvard Grieg." Ph.D., New York University, 1985, 404 pp., DA 46-1777A.

Zipay, Terry Lee. "Closure in the Motets of Machaut." Ph.D., State University of New York at Buffalo, 1983, 299 pp., DA 44-12A.

INDEX OF DISTINCTIVE TITLES

References are to Item Numbers

713